ISBN 978-1-330-07894-5
PIBN 10020413

1 MONTH OF
FREE
READING

at
www.ForgottenBooks.com

By purchasing this book you are eligible for one month membership to ForgottenBooks.com, giving you unlimited access to our entire collection of over 700,000 titles via our web site and mobile apps.

To claim your free month visit:

www.forgottenbooks.com/free20413

English
Français
Deutsche
Italiano
Español
Português

www.forgottenbooks.com

Mythology Photography **Fiction**
Fishing Christianity **Art** Cooking
Essays Buddhism Freemasonry
Medicine **Biology** Music **Ancient
Egypt** Evolution Carpentry Physics
Dance Geology **Mathematics** Fitness
Shakespeare **Folklore** Yoga Marketing
Confidence Immortality Biographies
Poetry **Psychology** Witchcraft
Electronics Chemistry History **Law**
Accounting **Philosophy** Anthropology
Alchemy Drama Quantum Mechanics
Atheism Sexual Health **Ancient History**
Entrepreneurship Languages Sport
Paleontology Needlework Islam
Metaphysics Investment Archaeology
Parenting Statistics Criminology
Motivational

545

UNITED STATES
TAX CASES

BRIEFS OF
FEDERAL AND STATE CASES ON
INCOME TAXES, EXCESS PROFITS TAXES,
AND INHERITANCE, STAMP
AND MISCELLANEOUS BUSINESS TAXES

RESEARCH, BRIEFS AND COMPILATION BY
KixMILLER AND BAAR
ATTORNEYS AT LAW

COMMERCE CLEARING HOUSE
SERVICE OFFICES IN
NEW YORK   **WASHINGTON**   **CHICAGO**

K6589Fi
1921

FOREWORD

This book does not contain briefs of selected cases only. It is intended as a reference guide and therefore the greatest effort has been made to find all cases on the tax laws named on the Title Page. The plan of this book suggested itself to us as a result of our need for a publication that would clear all tax cases in a convenient, authentic manner. Using as a nucleus our collection of cases gathered in the course of tax practice, we searched extensively, during the past summer, through the nation's largest law libraries for every possible case that might properly be briefed and included in the book. It would have been easier to have reprinted these cases in full but, having found that for our own use a permanent record of the essential facts, questions decided, and selected language was not only valuable but almost essential, we have ventured to attempt such an analysis and selection in this book. There is also included a selection of leading decisions by The Committee on Appeals and Review. We hope that our efforts will make easier the work of attorneys, accountants and others engaged in tax practice.

KIxMILLER & BAAR

WM. KIxMILLER	G. B. ERICKSON
ARNOLD R. BAAR	L. MALCOLM SCHWEERS
LEO H. HOFFMAN	H. T. REILING
CHARLES O. PARKER	W. C. MARTIN
PAUL W. KURZ	C. R. THARP
JAMES J. LEAHY	W. D. MCFARLANE

October 1, 1921

TABLE OF CONTENTS

Pages 7 to 66 have been omitted in this edition printed January, 1924, because they have been superseded by a revised *Synopsis* printed in the Supplement at pages 759 to 833.

545 UNITED STATES TAX CASES

ALLEN v. FRANCISCO SUGAR CO.
(Court of Chancery of New Jersey, April 6, 1920)
(110 Atl. 37)

Record: Bill of complaint filed by a stockholder against a corporation. Conclusions for complainant.

Facts: The directors of the defendant corporation adopted a resolution proposing to form a Cuban corporation (practically all of defendant's property consisting of land in Cuba) in which the defendant corporation would own all the capital stock, and then lease to the Cuban corporation the defendant company's land and personal property for a term of years at a fixed annual rental. When complainant received notice of the meeting of stockholders to which the resolution of the directors was to be submitted for approval, he filed this bill praying that the company and the stockholders be enjoined from acting, as proposed. The bill did not allege that the purpose of the plan was to avoid a large amount of Federal Income Tax, but the answering affidavits disclosed such purpose.

Question: Will a state court of equity enjoin the proceeding in question, for the reason that its purpose was to avoid the payment of a large amount of Federal Income Tax?

Decision: "To permit the stockholders of this company to go through the form of leasing their property while retaining its substance, and not only receive profits therefrom in a substantial amount, but also to add to those profits a large sum of money which the company is now required by law to pay as its pro rata share, with the rest of the public, for governmental war and other purposes, is a proceeding which equity will not sanction because it is against public policy." The company was, therefore, enjoined from carrying out the plan.

ALTHEIMER & RAWLINGS INV. CO. v. ALLEN, COLLECTOR
(U. S. Circuit Court of Appeals, Eighth Cir., February 28, 1918)
(248 Fed. 688)

Record: Act of August 5, 1909. Action at law to recover taxes paid under protest on net income under Sec. 38 of the Act.

Judgment for defendant (246 Fed. 270), and plaintiff brought error. Affirmed. Petition for writ of certiorari in U. S. Supreme Court dismissed, Nov. 11, 1918, 248 U. S. 578.

Facts. The Corporation Tax Act of August 5, 1909, provided that corporations pay an annual excise tax of 1% upon the entire net income of the corporation in excess of $5,000. The statute provided that net income shall be ascertained by deducting from the gross income from all sources, certain items including interest actually paid on indebtedness, not exceeding the amount of paid up capital outstanding at the close of the year. Plaintiff is a stock and bond broker and in that capacity purchased securities for its customers, paying but part of the price at the time of purchase, and paying interest on the balance it owed. In these transactions, the interest received by plaintiff from its customers exceeded the interest it paid. In making return of income, plaintiff returned as gross income only the excess received from its customers over the amount paid, contending that when it borrowed money to carry the securities for its customers, the indebtedness was theirs, and that the interest received from them on their own unpaid balances was, so far as required, paid for the customers on such indebtedness. The Commissioner contended that such interest paid by the company, was paid on the company's indebtedness and that all interest received should be included in gross income, allowing as a deduction therefrom only so much interest as was paid upon indebtedness which did not exceed the amount of paid-up capital outstanding at the close of the year.

Question: Must a brokerage corporation, receiving from its customers interest on account of margins, list all such interest as a part of its gross income and not deduct the interest on the indebtedness in excess of its paid-up capital which it incurred in purchasing securities for them?

Decision: "The suggestion upon which plaintiff's contention rests that it bought the stocks and bonds on time and that the sellers extended credit to plaintiff as agent for its customers and received interest from them directly, is quite inadmissable. In the usual course of the business, which it should be assumed the plaintiff followed, the seller of securities is paid in full by the broker, and is not thereafter interested in the relation between the latter and his customer. Doubtless, if the broker's capital is insufficient to carry his customers, he borrows money from time to time for the purpose, and in that sense he may be said to borrow 'on the purchases.' But the borrowing is from any available financial source, and is not for the customer personally, but is in the broker's own behalf. A recognized source of profit to the broker is in the difference between the interest rate he charges his customers and that which he pays on moneys to carry them. He deals in debits and credits for a profit. The borrowing by the broker supplements the capital employed in his business, and in the case of a corporation subject to the excise tax the deduction from gross income for interest paid on its indebtedness is limited to interest on an amount of indebtedness not exceeding its paid-up capital stock outstanding at the close of the year. In this particular the plaintiff's borrowing to carry its customers was not unlike that of a mercantile corporation, whose capital is insufficient for the volume of its business.'' Consequently, all of the interest received from customers was held taxable, while only a portion of the interest paid was held deductible.

AMBROSINI v. UNITED STATES

(U. S. Supreme Court, October, 1902)

(187 U. S. 1)

Record: War Revenue Act of 1898. Writ of error brought to reverse a judgment of the District Court (105 Fed. 239) finding defendant guilty of executing certain bonds without affixing revenue stamps thereto. Judgment reversed and cause remanded with direction to quash the indictment.

Facts: The ''dramshop act'' of Illinois and the Revised Code of Chicago provided for the giving of bonds by all applicants to whom licenses were granted to sell liquor in the city of Chicago. Defendant gave two such bonds but failed to affix thereto United States revenue stamps.

Question: Was the legislation in question and the ordinance of the city of Chicago requiring such bonds a strictly governmental function and a part of the transaction of obtaining the license so that a tax by the Federal government would impair the efficiency of state and municipal actions?

Decision: "The general principle is that as the means and instrumentalities employed by the General Government to carry into operation the powers granted to it are exempt from taxation, so are those of the States exempt from taxation by the General Government. * * * The question is whether the bonds were taken in the exercise of a function strictly belonging to the state and city in their ordinary governmental capacity, and we are of the opinion that they were, and that they were exempted as no more taxable than licenses."

AMERICAN PRINTING COMPANY v. COMMONWEALTH
(Supreme Judicial Court of Massachusetts, Oct. 29, 1918)
(231 Mass. 237; 120 N. E. 686)

Record: Revenue Acts of 1916, 1917, and Massachusetts statute. Petition for abatement of state income tax by American Printing Company. Decree of abatement of part of the tax.

Facts: A Massachusetts statute provided that "every corporation * * * shall pay a tax to the commonwealth computed upon the net income for its fiscal or calendar year * * * upon which income such corporation is required to pay a tax to the United States." The petitioner paid an excess profits tax under act of October 3, 1917. In computing the tax, the amount of the excess profits tax was not deducted by the commission.

Question: Under a state statute taxing a corporation upon the basis of the net income upon which it pays a tax to the United States, is a corporation to be taxed upon the amount which it pays as excess profits tax to the government?

Decision: "It is indubitable that a corporation which is liable for a war excess profits tax is not required to pay a tax to the United States upon the amount of that war excess profits tax, even though as a step toward reaching the final result that amount may be included in the 'net income' as shown on the return and as abstractly defined in the Acts of Congress. * * * The net income upon which the tax is required to be paid to the

United States is the amount designated as net income in the form of the corporation tax return and in the Acts of Congress minus the war excess profits tax. That subtraction must be made before the net income actually subject to the federal tax can be found. * * * The final sum of income upon which the United States income tax is computed is the essential amount to be found." Therefore, the excess profits tax was deductible in computing the state income tax.

AMES v. HOGAN
(U. S. Circuit Court, N. D. California, Sept. 17, 1898)
(36 Fed. 129)

Record. Clause 4, Sec. 629, Rev. Stat. Action to recover $375.75. Defendant demurs. Demurrer overruled.

Facts: The action in question arose under the revenue laws to recover draw-back on grain-bags claimed to be illegally withheld. The ground of the demurrer was that, the sum sought to be recovered being less than $2,000, the court had no jurisdiction under the Act of March 3, 1887.

Question: Was the fourth clause of Section 629 Rev. Stat. which gave to the circuit courts jurisdiction of all "suits at law or in equity arising under any act providing for revenue from imports or tonnage" repealed by the subsequent acts of 1875 and 1887, which limited such jurisdiction to cases where the matter in dispute exceeded $2,000?

Decision: "Although in some doubt on the point, I shall hold that only the first three clauses are covered and therefore repealed, by the acts of 1875 and 1887 and that, under the fourth clause, it is not necessary that the amount in dispute should exceed $2,000 in order to give the court jurisdiction. Although this clause speaks of 'suits at law or in equity, arising under any act providing for revenue from imports or tonnage,' the supreme court has held that a suit of this character is not a common-law suit on a promise, but a suit under a statute." Accordingly, the court held that a suit arising under the revenue laws was not a suit at law, and that the amount in dispute need not exceed $2,000 in order for the circuit court to have jurisdiction.

ANDERSON v. FARMERS' LOAN & TRUST CO.

(Circuit Court of Appeals, Second Cir., March 13, 1917)

(241 Fed. 322)

Record: Act of October 22, 1914. Action at law to recover taxes paid under protest. Judgment for plaintiff and defendant brought error. Reversed.

Facts: The act puts tax on bankers on the capital used or employed, "and in estimating capital, surplus and undivided profits shall be included." The plaintiff is chartered to do a banking business as well as a trust business. It is one of the principal companies in New York which acts as executor, trustee, guardian and depositary, and it also does a large banking business under the definition of "banker" given in the Act. The trust company held long time investments to an amount exceeding the capital, surplus, and undivided profits. It opened an account called "Capital Investment Account" to which bonds and mortgages were debited to an amount exceeding the capital, surplus, and undivided profits. This gave the appearance that no part of the capital, surplus, and undivided profits was used in the banking business. The Commissioner, having a letter from the company saying that it did a banking business, assessed it without requiring another return, although the one made by the company showed no capital, surplus, and undivided profits for the banking business.

Questions: (1) Can a trust company, which also does a banking business, carry certain items which it wishes, as bonds and mortgages from the securities account, to a so-called "Capital Investment Account," thus indicating that none of its capital is employed in banking, and avoid the tax on its banking business?

(2) May the Commissioner make an assessment without having required a return, after he has information that the company does a banking business, where the company did not disclose the amount of capital employed in the banking business?

(3) Can the company recover the taxes paid simply by showing that the Commissioner proceeded without proper evidence in making the assessment?

Decision: (1) "When a trust company is organized, obtains subscriptions for capital stock, and then opens its doors, begins business, and receives various deposits, its assets comprise all its property of every kind. Some of this property it will invest in mortgages, bonds, and stocks; other portions it will loan; still other portions, constituting its cash on hand, it will hold to be drawn against by its customers; other portions of its funds will be used to pay clerks who are engaged solely in the trust, and not in banking end of the business. We do not regard any specific assets as constituting capital of the company. The capital, and in the same way the surplus and undivided profits, are the residue left after paying the obligations of the bank to its depositors, and any other indebtedness it may have. These claims may be satisfied out of any property and the balance remaining, which is the capital, surplus and undivided profits, is to be imputed equally to all kinds of property which the trust company may possess. The proper way, therefore, to determine what part of capital, surplus and undivided profits is employed in banking, is to find out what part of the total assets is so employed; when that is done, the same proportion of the capital, surplus and undivided profits must be thus employed." This was not done. The method employed by the trust company can not be allowed, for that would mean that almost every trust company will escape the tax.

(2) "The evidence before the Commissioner, therefore, indicated that the capital, surplus, and undivided profits were employed both in the business of banking and trusts. In what relative proportions did not appear. The Commissioner might have required a further return, but we do not think that he was obliged to do this, and might make the assessment upon information derived from any source." Revised Statutes U. S., Section 3176.

(3) "In order to recover any part of the taxes, the Farmers' Loan and Trust Company should have shown just what portion of the tax was levied upon capital, surplus, and undivided profits which were not used or employed in banking. It was not sufficient to show that the Commissioner proceeded without proper

evidence, or otherwise erroneously, and then to rest; but the company had the burden of establishing by a preponderance of the evidence that the tax collected, or some part of it, was not due.''

ANDERSON, COLLECTOR, v. FORTY-TWO BROADWAY CO.
(U. S. Supreme Court, November 8, 1915)
(239 U. S. 69)

Record: Act of August 5, 1909. Suit in equity to recover amount of a tax paid under protest. Decree for complainant (209 Fed. 991), and defendant brought error. Affirmed (213 Fed. 777) and defendant brought a writ of certiorari. Reversed.

Facts: The respondent was a corporation commonly known as a realty corporation, and was organized for the purpose of constructing and renting a building, which is its only business. Its paid-up capital stock was only $600, while it had a bonded indebtedness of nearly five million dollars, secured by a mortgage upon its land purchased and its building constructed with borrowed money. The act provides that certain corporations shall pay annually a special excise tax with respect to the carrying on or doing business by such corporations, ''equivalent to one per cent upon the entire net income'' over and above a certain amount. It further provides for deductions from the gross income including all ordinary and necessary expenses, and interest paid on indebtedness not exceeding the paid-up capital. If the respondent is allowed to deduct all the interest paid on its indebtedness, thus regarding such as ordinary and necessary expenses, the result would leave no net income to be taxed. The Commissioner allowed a deduction of interest upon only $600, the amount of paid-up capital.

Questions: (1) Is the amount to be deducted, on account of interest paid by a realty corporation upon its mortgage indebtedness, in determining the excise tax imposed by the Act, to be governed by the clause allowing deductions for necessary expenses or by the clause allowing certain deductions for interest paid on bonded or other indebtedness?

(2) If the latter, is the Act discriminatory in that it limits the amount of deduction to interest on indebtedness not exceeding the paid-up capital stock?

Decision: (1) "The Act of 1909 was not in any proper sense an income tax law, nor intended as such, but was an excise tax upon the conduct of business in a corporate capacity, the tax being measured by reference to the income in a manner prescribed by the act itself. And it is clear, from a reading of section 38, that the phrase 'entire net income,' as used in its first paragraph, has no other meaning than that which is particularly set forth in the second paragraph, which declares, in terms, how 'such net income shall be ascertained.' It may well be that mortgage interest may, under special circumstances, be treated as among the 'ordinary and necessary expenses,' or as included among the charges 'required to be made as a condition to the continued use or possession of property.' But interest upon the 'bonded or other indebtedness' of the corporation, whether such indebtedness be secured by mortgage or not, comes within the specific provision of the third clause, whose effect, in our opinion, is not in this respect limited by anything contained in the first." The interest in excess of that allowed by the Commissioner was, therefore, not deductible.

(2) "Congress evidently had in view the fact that some corporations * * * carry a current indebtedness exceeding the amount of the paid-up capital stock, and with respect to such corporations intended to limit the interest deduction to so much of the indebtedness as did not exceed the capital. Nor can we see the least ground for the insistence that this results in an arbitrary classification."

ANDERSON, COLLECTOR, v. MORRIS & E. R. CO., ET AL
(Circuit Court of Appeals, Second Cir., July 9, 1914)
(216 Fed. 83)

Record: Act of August 5, 1909. Action to recover the amount of tax paid under protest. Judgment for plaintiff, and defendant brought error. Affirmed.

Facts: The plaintiff company was incorporated by a special Act of New Jersey, and by a lease, confirmed by the legislature, it leased its railroad and all its property and franchises to another company for the full term of its charter. The plaintiff company covenanted to maintain its corporate existence and to issue to the lessee stock or bonds to cover the expenses of the lessee in constructing new branch lines and equipping them. The lessee covenanted to pay all taxes, and to pay directly to the stockholders and bondholders of the plaintiff company a certain rental consisting of the interest on the stocks and bonds. The lessee company paid the rental to the stockholders and the bondholders, and the commissioner, after deducting an amount for expenses, assessed the plaintiff company upon the remainder paid to its stockholders and bondholders. During the year, the plaintiff company held an annual meeting of its stockholders, elected directors, and amended the by-laws, the board of directors held a special meeting electing officers, and the company issued bonds to the lessee company according to contract. The Act taxes every corporation "engaged in business" in any state.

Questions: (1) Is a company, which has leased all of its property for the full term of its charter to a company which has assumed all its obligations, "engaged in business" because of its issuance of bonds?

(2) Is the lessor company to be regarded as receiving no income where the rental is paid directly to the stockholder by the lessee?

(3) Does the fact that a corporation held an annual meeting, elected directors, amended the by-laws, and that its directors elected officers cause the company to be regarded as "doing business" within the state?

Decision: (1) "The lease for all practical purposes was a conveyance in fee. The lessor company, however, had retained the power to issue bonds and to execute deeds of the leased property, but such powers it could exercise only with the consent and at the request of the lessee company, which latter company guaranteed the payment of both the principal and interest and alone derived any advantage from their issuance, as the income of the lessor's stockholders was definitely fixed by the lease for all time. The act done was a purely formal act done by the lessor to enable the lessee to raise money on the security of the property for its development and operation in the conduct of the railroad business. In doing it the lessor was not 'carrying on or doing business' within the meaning of the Corporation Tax Act.''

(2) ''The notion that a corporation is an artificial entity distinct from the members who compose it is a fiction of the law which the courts recognize for some purposes and disregard for others. Without going into the matter at length, it suffices to say that the fact that the lessee paid the rent, not to the corporate entity but to the stockholders and bondholders, cannot prevent the Act from applying to the money so paid if the other conditions of the Act make its terms applicable.'' The payments constituted income of the lessor corporation.

(3) Maintaining the corporate existence and organization, holding annual and special meetings of stockholders and directors, and doing the other acts mentioned ''cannot be regarded as doing business within the purview of the Act * * * and surely no one can claim that the Act of 1909 imposes any excise tax upon the primary franchise or maintenance of the corporate organization.''

ARNSON v. MURPHY, COLLECTOR

(U. S. Supreme Court, November 18, 1883)

(109 U. S. 238)

Record: Act of June 30, 1864. Action to recover taxes illegally collected. Error to U. S. Circuit Court for the Southern District of New York, where a verdict was directed for the defendant. Judgment reversed and cause remanded.

Facts: The defendant pleaded, besides other defenses, that the cause of action was barred by the statute of limitations of New York, then in force. U. S. Rev. Stat. Sec. 3011 provided as follows:

''Any person who shall have made payment under protest and in order to obtain possession of merchandise imported for him, to any collector or person acting as a collector of any money as duties, when such amount or duties was not, or was not wholly, authorized by law, may maintain an action at law which shall be triable by jury, to ascertain the validity of such demand and payment of duties, and to recover back any excess so paid. But no recovery shall be allowed in such action unless a protest and appeal shall have been taken as prescribed in Section 2931.''

Section 2931 provided, among other things, that the decision of the Secretary of the Treasury on appeal should be final and conclusive, unless within 90 days after it was made suit was brought, and no suit should, in the meantime, pending the appeal, be brought unless the decision by the Secretary should be delayed more than 90 days from the date of the appeal. On the trial it appeared that appeal had been duly taken to the Secretary of the Treasury and that no decision by that officer had been rendered prior to the commencement of this action, and that this suit was not brought until after 90 days had elapsed from the date of the appeal and not until after the lapse of more than six years from the expiration of that period.

Questions: (1) What effect, if any, did the New York Statute of Limitations have upon the plaintiff's right of action?

(2) Was plaintiff's cause of action barred because suit was not commenced until more than 90 days after the appeal was taken?

Decision: (1) ''It follows that in such cases, of which the present is one, the limitation laws of the state in which the cause of action arose, or in which the suit was brought, do not, under Section 721, Rev. Stats., furnish the rule of decision, and that it was, therefore, an error in the Circuit Court to apply, as a bar to the action, the limitation prescribed by the statute of New York.''

(2) ''It appears to us quite plain, from the reading of the statute, that no action arises to the claimant, in such cases, until after a decision against him by the Secretary of the Treasury; and that his suit against the collector is barred unless brought within 90 days after an adverse decision upon his appeal; but with the proviso that if such decision is delayed more than 90 days after the date of his appeal, it is at the claimant's option

either to sue, pending the appeal, treating the delay as a denial, or to wait until a decision is in fact made, and then sue within 90 days thereafter.'' The present action was, therefore, not barred.

ASSOCIATED PIPE LINE CO. v. UNITED STATES
(U. S. Circuit Court of Appeals, May 18, 1919)
(258 Fed. 800)

Record: Act of August 5, 1909. Action by the United States to recover taxes assessed. Judgment for the United States, and the defendant brings error. Affirmed.

Facts: The Associated Oil Company and the Kern Trading & Oil Company agreed that a corporation, the Associated Pipe Line Co., should be created to own, lease, and operate pipe lines for the benefit of the two companies. Directors were to be selected by each of the parties to the agreement. The Associated Pipe Line Co. was to have vested in it, by purchase from the Kern Company, at actual cost, a certain line of pipe, and was to build another line. The expenses of constructing the line were to be advanced by the Kern Company, and Associated Oil Company agreed to pay interest on one-half of the entire cost, which it paid to the Pipe Line Co. One-half of the entire capital stock was to be issued to each of the two parties to the agreement. The Associated Pipe Line Company constructed the pipe lines and was, in the year in question, actually transporting oil. Its expenses were divided between the two holding companies. The company made its return for the year in question, including in gross income the interest charged against the Associated Oil Co. upon one-half of the cost of construction, and deducting a large amount for interest paid to the two companies, thus leaving no taxable income. The statute limited the amount of deductible interest to that paid upon an amount of indebtedness not exceeding the paid-up capital stock. Up to that time, according to the findings, the capital stock had not been paid. It is contended that the Associated Pipe Line Company books are used only as ''a clearing account,'' and the entry of interest as ''a mere matter of adjustment between the two owning companies to equalize the use of the capital investment,'' and that the Associated Pipe Line Company is merely a convenient agent of the two companies.

Questions: (1) Is a corporation organized to operate for the benefit of two holding companies "doing business" within the meaning of the Act?

(2) Where two companies advance money to another company, which money is not entered in the capital account and for which no stock is issued until after the income tax return has been made, is the interest charge on these moneys deductible if the company had no paid-up capital stock?

Decision: (1) "It may be that the stockholders in the Associated Pipe Line Company took the profit away from the corporation, but it is clear that the way in which the money was made was by a corporate organization; and the corporation, having achieved the object of its creation, became subject to the imposition of the tax with respect to doing business. * * * The Associated Pipe Line Company appears to have been active, and to be maintaining its organization for the purpose for which it was created; it has expended and received money, has borrowed money, has constructed pipe lines, has allowed itself to be charged interest, has had dealings with its stock and stockholders concerning moneys received, and in 1909 was actually transporting oil and performing its corporate functions."

(2) "According to the findings, none of the capital stock of the corporation was paid until December 31, 1911. If we accept this finding as true, clearly the plaintiff in error in 1909 had no paid-up capital stock and was therefore not in a position to include the interest charge in arriving at what its net income was. It is argued that, although the moneys were not entered in the capital stock account on the pipe line company books until December, 1911, the fact was there was no net income by way of interest on advances because such advances were not made by plaintiff in error and the interest was not earned or payable to the pipe line company, and that the pipe line company was merely a conduit through which the Associated Oil Company paid the Kern Company the interest on the advances by the Kern Company. * * * But this reasoning seems to lead to the conclu-

sion that the advances that were made were in payment of capital stock, and, if such is the correct view, there was a sale of stock and no indebtedness. The plainer view seems to be that there was an indebtedness on account of advances, but that there was no paid-up capital stock at the time of the return, therefore, that, as a matter of law no interest could be deducted.'' It was, therefore, held that the interest charged against the Associated Oil Company upon the cost of constructing the new line was taxable gross income of the Pipe Line Co., and that the interest credited to the two proprietor companies upon advances could not be deducted by the Pipe Line Co.

ATCHISON, T. & S. F. RY. CO. v. O'CONNOR
(U. S. Supreme Court, Feb. 19, 1912)
(223 U. S. 280)

Record: Session Laws of Colorado, 1907, c. 211. Action to recover taxes paid. Demurrer to declaration sustained by Circuit Court. Judgment reversed.

Facts: Plaintiff was a Kansas corporation. The greater part of its property and business was without the State of Colorado, and of the business done within that State, but a small proportion was local, the greater part being commerce among the States. The tax in question, which was paid by plaintiff, was two cents upon each one thousand dollars of plaintiff's capital stock. Defendant, who was the officer of the State, and who had collected the tax, did not argue that the tax could be maintained. By the law of the State, every corporation that fails to pay the tax shall forfeit its right to do business.

Questions: (1) Were the taxes in question paid under duress, so that an action would lie for their recovery?

(2) Was the defendant the proper person to be sued?

Decision: (1) "In this case, the law, besides giving an action of debt to the State, provides that every corporation that fails to pay the tax shall forfeit its right to do business within the State until the tax is paid, and shall pay a penalty. * * * As appears from the decision below, the plaintiff could have had

no certainty of ultimate success, and we are of the opinion that
it was not called upon to take the risk of having its contracts
disputed and its business injured and of finding the tax more
or less nearly doubled in case it finally had to pay. In other
words, we are of the opinion that the payment was made under
duress.''

(2) "The defendant collected the money and it is alleged
that he still has it. He was notified when he received it that the
plaintiff disputed his right. If he had no right, as he did not,
to collect the money, his doing so in the name of the State cannot
protect him.''

BAILEY, COLLECTOR, v. RAILROAD COMPANY
(U. S. Supreme Court, October Term, 1882)
(106 U. S. 109)

Record: Internal Revenue Act of June 30, 1864. Suit in
assumpsit to recover back sums as illegally exacted. Verdict for
plaintiff and defendant brought a writ of error. Reversed and
new trial awarded in 22 Wall. 604 (89 U. S. 604). Verdict for
plaintiff and defendant brought writ of error. Affirmed.

Facts: The board of directors of the railroad company
passed a resolution declaring each stockholder was entitled to
eighty per cent of his capital stock, since the company had expended this amount of its earnings for construction and equipment
purposes. Certificates were issued to the stockholders in accordance with this resolution, which certificates contained a clause
providing for dividends similar to the dividend clause in a stock
certificate. Under the so-called Income Tax Law, the basis of tax
was the amount paid in interest and dividends, expressly including
dividends in scrip.

Questions: (1) Are certificates issued under such a resolution, payable out of future earnings and calling for dividends as
upon shares of stock, dividends in scrip within the meaning of
Section 22 of the Act?

(2) If so, can the company show that the actual net income
is less for the years after the Act became effective than the **pro-**

portional amount for those years, where the accumulation had been going on for a number of years.

Decision: (1) "These certificates were considered to be a dividend declared, as of profits which had been, at some previous time, earned and converted into capital by an investment in permanent improvements of the railroad, and it was as representing such earnings that they were considered the subject of a tax." They were dividends in scrip.

(2) "It is entirely consistent with the declaration of dividends to show in point of fact what was the amount of earnings accrued during the period while the income tax was in force. * * * The declaration in the certificates could not be conclusive of anything not inconsistent with it for an estoppel only prohibits contrary allegations." It was quite legitimate for the assessor to treat the certificates as evidence of an amount of earnings which had never been taxed and make the assessment accordingly. The evidence tending to prove the exact amount of earnings accrued while the Income Tax Act was in force did not contradict the certificates, but served to rebut the presumption that all the dividend was of earnings accrued after the effective date of the Act. Therefore, it was proper for the company to show the actual amount of earnings accrued after the Act became effective, as it was subject to tax only upon such earnings.

BALDWIN LOCOMOTIVE WORKS v. McCOACH, COLLECTOR
McCOACH, COLLECTOR, v. BALDWIN LOCOMOTIVE WORKS
(U. S. Circuit Court of Appeals, Third Cir., March 24, 1915)
(221 Fed. 59, 136 C. C. A. 660)

Records: Act of August 5, 1909. Action at law to recover a tax which plaintiff has paid. Judgment for plaintiff (215 Fed. 967) for a part of amount sued for; both parties brought error. Affirmed.

Facts: A corporation sold bonds due in 30 years at a discount from their par value and it took over, at one valuation, certain property which was later appraised at a higher valuation. It claims the discount was an expense item for that year. The government contends that the increase in the valuation is income.

Questions: (1) Where bonds due in 30 years are sold at a discount, may the amount of the discount be deducted from the income in computing the tax on the corporation for the year in which the bonds were issued?

(2) Where the property of a corporation is appraised at a higher value than that at which it had been carried on the books, is the increase in valuation income under Section 38?

Decision: (1) The court allowed 1/31 of the discount as a proper charge for one year, and in regard to the money received for the bonds said: "The sum thus received was, of course, not income, either gross or net; in effect, the transaction transmuted a part of the corporation's assets from credit or property into liquid cash; but it added nothing to its income. If the cost of thus changing the form of its assets is an expense of the business, it has not yet been paid, and will not be paid until 1940."

(2) "The only thing done was to put upon the company's books an expression of expert opinion that certain property was worth a certain sum, and this can hardly be said to be income, or even gain in any proper sense."

BALTIMORE v. BALTIMORE RAILROAD
(U. S. Supreme Court, December Term, 1870)
(77 U. S. 543)

Record: Act of July 1, 1862. Action at law by city of Baltimore to recover interest. Judgment for defendant and plaintiff brought error. Affirmed.

Facts: In accordance with an agreement between the city of Baltimore and the Baltimore Railroad, the city issued bonds, the proceeds of which it loaned to the railroad, the railroad agreeing to pay all expenses incidental to the issue of the bonds. The railroad, after giving the city notice that the government was demanding the tax, paid the excise tax on the interest due the city and deducted the amount of it from the payments of interest to the city. The city brought suit to recover the amount withheld, claiming that the tax was one of the incidental expenses which the railroad was obligated to pay, and also that the railroad should not have paid the tax because it then knew that a tax on the securities of municipalities was invalid.

Questions: (1) Is an excise tax on all sums due for interest under the act an expense incidental to the issue of bonds, upon which a railroad company is paying interest, where the tax law is passed after an agreement to pay such expenses?

(2) Can a city recover of a company which has paid the excise tax due on interest which it owed the city even though the securities of a municipality are not taxable under the Act?

Decision: (1) "To carry out the arrangement between the parties required considerable expenditure of money for printing; clerk hire, stationery, advertising and similar matters. These expenses were incidental to the issue of the bonds, and it was right and proper that the railroad company—the party to be benefited by the transaction—should pay them, and it agreed to do so; but this agreement cannot be intended to cover the tax in question, for in no sense is it an expense incidental to the issue of the bonds. At the date of the mortgage there was no tax of the kind, nor any reasonable expectation of one." Therefore, the railroad was not obligated to pay the tax, and its payment of it was made on behalf of the city.

(2) The company "notified the city that the United States were enforcing the collection of the tax, and did not pay it until it was obliged to do so to avoid the consequences provided for in the act in case of refusal, and not then, without a written protest stating distinctly all the grounds of objection claimed by the city * * * ." The city "should have stepped in, and taken upon itself the burden of testing the legality of the assessment and collection of the tax." Having failed to do so, it could not rely upon the invalidity of the tax in denying that payment had been made on its behalf.

BARNES, COLLECTOR, v. THE RAILROADS
(U. S. Supreme Court, December Term, 1872)
(84 U. S. 294)

Record: Act of June 30, 1864, and Act of March 2, 1867.

Action of trespass against Barnes. Judgment for plaintiff (Fed. Cas. 11087) and defendant brought error. Reversed.

Facts: One railroad company on December 22, 1869, declared a dividend, payable January 17, 1870. Another on January 10, 1870, declared a dividend. Section 119 of the Act says "that the taxes on incomes herein imposed shall be levied on the first day of March, and be due and payable on or before the 30th day of April in each year, until and including the year 1870, and no longer." The companies refused to pay and the collector distrained.

Questions: (1) Is Section 122 of the Act, which declares a tax on all interest payable and dividends declared by a railroad company, meant to be a tax upon the company, so that the company must pay a tax on a dividend declared while the law was in effect, and payable after the termination of the Act?

(2) Is a company liable for a tax on a dividend declared after the tax law became inoperative.

Decision: (1) "Different regulations for the assessment and collection of the income taxes of every kind were prescribed in the prior laws imposing interest revenue duties, but they were not in all respects satisfactory, and many controversies had arisen calling in question the action of the revenue officers * * * ." "Congress, accordingly, in order to remove those difficulties, imposed the tax upon the railroad company, and enacted that the company should pay the same whenever and wherever the dividend should be payable."

(2) "Although the dividend was not declared until the 10th of January, 1870, yet it is true that the object taxed is the fund which accrued within the last six months of the preceding year," and the company is liable for the tax.

BAYFIELD COUNTY v. PISHON
(Supreme Court of Wisconsin, February 22, 1916)
(162 Wis. 503; 156 N. W. 463)

Record: Wisconsin Act of 1911. Action by Bayfield County to recover income tax assessed against the defendant. From a judgment for defendant, plaintiff appealed. Affirmed.

Facts: The defendant is a trustee under the will of a citizen of Wisconsin. By the terms of the will, the property was left in trust in favor of certain nonresident beneficiaries who still reside without the State. The defendant succeeded a trustee who moved out of the State, as soon as the assets of the estate were turned over to her, taking all the assets of the estate with her. The defendant has never resided in Wisconsin, and he has kept the assets of the estate in his possession. He was appointed trustee by the Wisconsin court, and renders his accounts to that court, as did the former trustee. The defendant has been assessed on the income of the estate for a number of years, including that part of the former trustee's term of office after the effective date of the Act. The Act levies a tax upon every nonresident on such income "as is derived from sources within the State or within its jurisdiction."

Question: Is income derived from trust property which is without the State taxable to a trustee who, as well as the beneficiaries, is living without the State, and renders his accounts to the Wisconsin court?

Decision: "This statute imposes a tax only upon such part of a nonresident's income as is derived from sources within the State or within its jurisdiction. It is quite obvious that the purpose of the statute to tax a nonresident upon his income derived from sources within the territorial jurisdiction of the State. Income Tax Cases, 148 Wis. 456, 134 N. W. 673; State ex rel. Manitowoc G. Co. v. Tax Commission et al., 152 N. W. 848. The income under consideration was not derived from property located or business transacted in the State of Wisconsin, and the owners of the property never resided in Wisconsin. But it is contended that the property was constructively in Wisconsin because the Bayfield county court in Wisconsin was administering the trust. We do not think the statute is capable of such construction. The language of the statute must be given its plain, ordinary meaning. The words of the statute are unambiguous, and this court must construe them according to their plain, ordinary meaning."

BEER et al. v. MOFFATT, COLLECTOR
(U. S. District Court, D. N. J., January 29, 1912)
(192 Fed. 984)

Record: War Revenue Act of 1898. Action to recover legacy taxes paid. Judgment for defendant.

Facts: Plaintiff, executor of an estate, was notified on February 17, 1904, by the collector to make a return of the tax on the estate under threats of penalties and punishments provided by the Act for failure to return and pay the tax. The plaintiff refused to make the return, and the collector made one and assessed the tax. The tax so assessed was paid by letter on March 7, 1904, the day after its assessment. This letter contained no word of protest or claim of illegality.

Question: Is a refusal to make a return a sufficient protest so that taxes, paid without protest at the time of payment, can be recovered by suit on the ground of illegality?

Decision: The fact that the plaintiff refused for a long time to make the return or pay the tax affords no warrant for a legal assumption that such refusal was based upon the illegality of the tax. Nothing in the case tends to show that the taxes were paid under protest or with notice that the plaintiff contended they were illegal, and that he intended to institute a suit for their repayment.

BEND v. HOYT, COLLECTOR
(U. S. Supreme Court, January Term, 1839)
(13 Peters 266)

Record: Tariff Acts of July 14, 1832, and March 2, 1833. Assumpsit to recover money paid as duties. Case came up on a certificate of division of opinion of the judges of circuit court.

Facts: On March 29, 1837, the plaintiff entered a case of goods at the custom house as cotton goods and made the usual oath. He then gave bond for payment of the duty, and the goods were delivered to him. In 1838, before the bond became due, the plaintiff discovered that the case actually contained not cotton goods, but silk hose, which were free from duty. Plaintiff asked to be relieved from payment of the duty, and when this request was refused, he paid under protest.

Question: Can plaintiff recover the amount of the duty paid under protest if at the custom house he entered as dutiable, goods which were free from duty, thinking they were another kind?

Decision: Plaintiff can not maintain his action because the mistake of fact arose under circumstances of culpableness on the part of the plaintiff and because the government could no longer be replaced in the same situation in which it stood at the time of the original transaction.

BERNHEIM DISTILLING CO. v. MAYES
(U. S. District Court, W. D., Kentucky, October 11, 1920)
(268 Fed. 629)

Record: Revenue Act of 1917. Action to recover taxes paid. Judgment for plaintiff.

Facts: Plaintiff paid, under protest, certain taxes specially assessed by the Commissioner on certain spirits plaintiff had rectified. Such assessment was based upon an investigation by internal revenue officers, the exact nature of whose findings were not disclosed when the Commissioner made the assessment. On the trial plaintiff offered testimony to prove that it was not in fact liable for the additional tax, and this testimony was not refuted by any offered by the defendant.

Question: The plaintiff having made out a prima facie case which was not overcome by any evidence introduced by the defendant, was it entitled to a judgment in its favor for the amount claimed, despite defendant's contention that the assessment was correct?

Decision: "The Commissioner of Internal Revenue having made the assessment, it was at the trial presumed, prima facie, to be accurate and proper. This presumption, however, was not conclusive, but was open to being overcome by adequate testimony. It this situation the burden, at the outset, was upon the plaintiff, and the testimony offered by it was clear and explicit. Unless refuted, it was sufficient to satisfy the court that this burden had been so far met as to make it prima facie certain that the assessment in question could not be sustained without further testimony in its support, so that the facts upon which the Commissioner had acted might be shown to be such as to justify what he did.   In such circumstances, cases like this demand an explicit showing of the real facts on both sides, so that the court can adequately understand the merits alike of the plaintiff's claim and the facts which tend to support the assessment.''

BETTMAN, COLLECTOR, v. WARWICK
(U. S. Circuit Court of Appeals, Sixth Cir., March 5, 1901)
(108 Fed. 46)

Record: War Revenue Act of 1898.   Action to recover alleged illegal tax paid.   Demurrer to petition overruled (102 Fed. 127) and defendant brought error.   Affirmed.

Facts: Plaintiff, having been appointed a notary public by the governor of Ohio, was compelled by the collector to pay fifty cents for a revenue stamp to affix to the qualifying bond required by Ohio law.

Question: Was the bond required by the State statute as a prerequisite to the exercise of plaintiff's official duties subject to the tax?

Decision: The United States and the States act separately of each other in the field within which each is sovereign, and neither has the power to impose a tax which will interfere with the exercise of the sovereignty of the other within its own sphere.   A power in the Federal government to exact a tax upon the right to qualify for the performance of the duties of a state office is inconsistent with any supreme governmental authority in the State.   The Federal stamp tax could not, therefore, be imposed upon the bond required of a notary public.

IN RE BIERSTADT'S ESTATE (HICKS et al. v. COMP-
TROLLER OF STATE OF NEW YORK)
(New York Supreme Court, App. Div., First Dep't, July 13, 1917)
(166 N. Y. Supp. 168)

Record: Revenue Act of 1916, and New York transfer tax

law. Appeal from Surrogate Court, New York County, from a final order of that court (163 N. Y. Supp. 1104), fixing the value of property transferred under decedent's will. Hicks and others, executors, appeal. Affirmed.

Facts: Mary S. Bierstadt died, leaving a will by which she disposed of an estate valued at upwards of $2,000,000. Of this estate she disposed of about $1,200,000 in specific legacies, and gave the residue to certain named relatives. The lower court refused to allow $97,309.58 paid as a Federal estate tax under the Revenue Act of 1916, as a deduction from the value of the estate fixed for assessment of the State of New York transfer tax.

Question: Is the Federal Estate Tax a proper deduction in determining the amount subject to State Transfer Tax on the theory that the tax provided for in the Federal Revenue Act is a tax upon the estate, as such, and not upon the transfer of the property under the will and the laws of the State of which the decedent was a resident?

Decision: The Federal Estate Tax is not deductible for State Transfer Tax assessment purposes. The court in the opinion refers to the fact that a similar claim for deduction of the succession tax levied under the Federal War Revenue Act of 1898 was decided adversely to the claimant in the matter of Gihon, 169 N. Y. 443, wherein it was held that the Federal tax was not a tax upon the property transferred, but upon the transfer itself, the amount of the tax being measured by the value of the property affected by the transfer. It follows, therefore, the court said, that if the tax imposed by the Act of 1916 is like that imposed by the Act of 1898, a tax on the transfer and not on the property, the claim of the executors was rightly denied. Without expressing an opinion on whether the 1916 Act imposes the tax distinctly and unequivocally upon the property transferred, and not on the transfer thereof, the court said, "if it must be construed as the executor's claim that it must be, it would be invalid on constitutional grounds, and no tax could be lawfully collected under it" (quoting Knowlton v. Moore, 178 U. S. 41). Under either construction, the court said the order appealed from is right, and concluded as follows: "All we are called upon to decide is that the executors are not entitled to deduct from the gross estate as an expense of administration the estimated tax provided for in the Federal Revenue Act of 1916, before the amount of the tax under the State law is fixed. The order appealed from is affirmed.''

BILLINGS v. UNITED STATES
UNITED STATES v. BILLINGS
(U. S. Supreme Court, Feb. 24, 1914)
(232 U. S. 261)

Record: Tariff Act of August 5, 1909. Action by United States for amount of tax with interest. Judgment for United States for sum claimed, but prayer for interest was rejected (190 Fed. 359). Both parties prosecuted error. Modified and affirmed.

Facts: Section 37 of the Tariff Act of August 5, 1909, provided for collection of an annual tax on September 1 upon the use of every foreign built pleasure boat. This Act went into effect on August 6, 1909, and the collector made demand thereafter upon the plaintiff in error for payment of tax on the foreign-built yacht Vanadis, owned by him.

Questions: (1) If the statute is construed so as to cause the first tax for the annual period to become due in September, 1909, is it unconstitutional because retroactive in effect?

(2) Should the statute be so construed as to cause the first tax to become due in September, 1910, thus preventing it from being retroactive?

(3) Can Congress constitutionally tax foreign-built yachts without also taxing domestic yachts?

(4) Was the government entitled to interest on the amount of tax due?

Decision: (1) The fact that a tax statute operates retroactively does not necessarily cause the Act to be beyond the power of Congress under the Constitution to adopt. Flint v. Stone-Tracy Company, 220 U. S. 107, cited.

(2) ''While the rule is that statutes should be so construed as to prevent them from operating retroactively, that principle is one of construction and not of reconstruction and, therefore, does not authorize a judicial re-enactment by interpretation of a statute to save it from producing a retroactive effect.'' The Act itself determined that the tax became effective for 1909.

(3) The difference between things domestic and foreign is recognized by the Constitution itself, hence the classification adopted in the Act in question was not a denial of due process of law. Nor is the tax unconstitutional because of lack of uniformity because the constitutional requirement of uniformity is not an intrinsic, but merely a geographical uniformity.

(4) The state rule as to interest on taxes differs from the United States rule. The former excludes interest unless the statute so provides; the latter allows interest unless forbidden by the statute.

BISCOE v. TAX COMMISSIONER
BLACKMAN v. SAME

(Supreme Court, Massachusetts, June 24, 1920)

(128 N. E. 16)

Record: Mass. Stat. 1916. Report from Superior Court without decision. Complaints for refusal to abate income taxes. Abatement of tax in each case ordered.

Facts: These are complaints under St. 1916, c. 269, Sec. 20, for refusal to abate income taxes assessed on the complainants and by report from the Superior Court they are before this court upon the pleadings and agreed facts. Sec. 12, c. 269, St. 1916, provides that: ''Every individual inhabitant of the commonwealth * * * whose annual income from all sources exceeds two thousand dollars shall annually make a return of his entire income, except income derived * * * (b) from wages or salaries received from the United States.'' Sec. 5 (b) of the same chapter provides that: ''the wages and salaries of employees and officers of the United States government shall not be taxed.'' On December 28, 1917, complainant Biscoe was vice-president of the New York Central R. R. Co. and complainant Blackman was

assistant counsel in Massachusetts of the N. Y., New Haven and
Hartford R. R. Co. By proclamation dated December 26, 1917,
the President of the United States took control of all transportation systems. The salaries of these officials were during 1918
paid out of funds earned by the railroads under federal control
and money received from the Treasury of the United States.

Questions: (1) Are the salaries of complainants, as officials
of railroads under Federal control, "wages and salaries of employees and officers of the United States Government"?

(2) Should the amount of exempt salaries be applied in reduction of the specific exemption allowed taxpayers?

Decision: Compensation of railroad officials from the United
States, while railroads were under federal control, are not subject
to the State Income Tax. The court explained that the property
of the railroads passed into the possession, control and operation
of the Government, and in 1918 each complainant received his
salary from moneys of the United States. They received all their
instructions with respect to the duties of their positions during
1918 solely from or through the Director General of Railroads.
The court, therefore, concluded: "It would seem to be plain that
any relation of employe that existed between these complainants
and the railroad on December 28, 1917, ceased to exist when the
control of the railroads passed to the United States Government,
and that a new relation began with the consent of the complainants and continued to exist during the year 1918 between the
complainants and the United States Government, represented by
the Director General."

(2) The specific exemption had no reference to exempt salaries. The court held that it could not agree with the contention
of the defendant that the exemption of a federal salary extends
only to the extent that, if it exceeds $2,000, no specific deduction
may be claimed in addition to the exemption of the salary, and if
the salary is less than $2,000, the taxpayer may claim as a deduction
only the difference between that sum and his federal salary. The
federal salary is exempt for distinct reasons and does not apply
against the amount of the specific personal exemption.

BLACK v. BOLEN, COLLECTOR

(U. S. District Court, W. D., Oklahoma, Sept. 14, 1920)

(268 Fed. 427)

Record: Act of Oct. 3, 1913. Action at law to recover sum paid as tax under protest. Judgment for plaintiff.

Facts: The plaintiff was engaged in buying and selling oil stocks through a broker. He made a profit which he intended to invest, but which was embezzled by the broker. The law permitted the deduction of losses "incurred in trade." Having filed a claim for abatement, which was rejected, the plaintiff filed no refund claim. Rev. St. Sec. 3226 provides that no suit for the recovery of any internal tax shall be maintained until "appeal shall have been duly made to the Commissioner," etc.

Questions: (1) Did the loss to the plaintiff from the embezzlement of the broker arise out of any trade or business in which he was engaged?

(2) Is a failure to file a refund claim a bar to recovery where claim for abatement has been rejected and where the Commissioner has said that the claim for refund need not be filed?

Decision: (1) "The fact that this profit made in the transaction was embezzled by a faithless broker constituted a loss to plaintiff in the income which he should and would have received, and on which, if by him received, he would have been compelled to pay the government tax. As this money was not received by plaintiff, under the agreed facts, but was embezzled by his broker, and thus lost to him, plaintiff did not profit, and the government should not do so, at his expense." The court therefore sustained the deduction.

(2) "The Honorable Commissioner should either have not given any advice to plaintiff on the subject, leaving him to work out his rights under the law, as he was advised by his counsel, or, the Commissioner having advised plaintiff as he did, should then have instructed his collector such defense is no longer open to be urged in this case."

BLALOCK, COLLECTOR, v. GEORGIA RY. & ELECTRIC CO
(U. S. District Court, N. D. Georgia, Nov. 7, 1917)
(246 Fed. 387)

Record: Act of Aug. 5, 1909. Action at law to recover taxes paid under protest on net income under Section 38 of the Act. Judgment for plaintiff (228 Fed. 296) and defendant brings error. Reversed.

Facts: The Georgia Ry. and Electric Co., a corporation, leased its property. By provision in the lease it was stipulated that the lessee pay to the stockholders of the lessor corporation, in lieu of and as rent, quarterly sums or dividends on dates stated, in each year during the term of the lease. A result of the lease was to make each stipulated installment of net rent, payable to those who were stockholders of the lessor corporation, in proportion to their respective holdings of stock, instead of to the lessor corporation itself. It was stipulated also, that this agreement be endorsed on each certificate of the capital stock of the company. In making returns of income as provided by the corporation Tax Act of 1909, which subjects the corporation to a tax of 1% on its net income from all sources, the Georgia company failed to include the amount of the net rent paid by the lessee corporation to the stockholders of the lessor corporation, contending that the lessor company had virtually assigned its interests in the leased property to its stockholders.

Question: Is the aggregate amount paid by the lessee corporation in lieu of rent, directly to the stockholders of the lessor corporation income to the lessor corporation?

Decision: The fact that the stockholder had no power to dispose of his share of the rent, without disposing of his share as a stockholder precludes the possibility of contending that what was done amounted to an assignment of the leased property to the stockholder. By the terms of the lease the installments of rent were made payable "to the persons registered as holders of said shares." The beneficial ownership of both continued in those who at any given time were the stockholders of the lessor corporation. "The difference between the way the rent under the lease was paid, and the way the same amounts would have been paid if the lease had made the installments payable to the corporation itself, is one of method and not of substance. It is a mere direction to the lessee corporation as to how it shall pay the obligation due the lessor corporation. The terms of the taxing statute are not such as to require that it be given a meaning that would invite and make easy evasions of its provisions." The rent payments were therefore income of the corporation.

BLUM v. WARDELL, COLLECTOR
(U. S. District Court, N. D. Calif., S. D., Dec. 30, 1920)
(270 Fed. 309)

Record: Revenue Act of 1916. Suit to recover estate tax paid. Demurrer to complaint overruled.

Facts: The executors of Moses Blum, who in his lifetime was a resident of San Francisco, paid under protest an estate tax based upon the value of the half interest of the surviving widow in the community personal property, under the laws of the state of California, in which her ownership became absolute upon the death of the husband.

Questions: (1) Was the Federal court bound by the construction of the California courts upon the community laws of that state?

(2) Under the California law, was there a transfer of any estate when one-half of the community property became vested in the widow upon death of the husband?

Decision: (1) The Federal tax is imposed on the transfer of the net estate, and whether there is a transfer upon the death of the husband depends upon the statutes and rule of decision in the state where the parties reside and the property is situated. Decisions of the California courts were therefore binding upon the Federal courts.

(2) The Community Property Act of 1917 recognizes in the wife a valid subsisting vested interest and estate during the life of the husband. She no longer takes her interest in the community property as heir, as she formerly did, and hence such interest is

not subject to the Federal inheritance tax imposed on the transfer of a decedent's estate. The taxable estate of the husband should therefore include only his one-half interest in the community property, and not the one-half belonging to the wife.

BOSKE v. COMINGORE, COLLECTOR
(U. S. Supreme Court, April 9, 1900)
(177 U. S. 459)

Record: U. S. Rev. Stats., Sec. 161. Action at law on writ of habeas corpus. Petitioner discharged in United States District Court. Appealed. Affirmed.

Facts: Appellee, a Collector of Internal Revenue, refused to file with his deposition copies of certain reports made to him by Block & Sons, distillers, concerning certain liquors deposited in bonded warehouses during a specified period. These reports were demanded by a court of limited jurisdiction of the State of Kentucky. Appellee could not file the copies called for without violating regulations formally promulgated by the Commissioner of Internal Revenue with the approval of the Secretary of the Treasury, which reads as follows: "All records in the offices of collectors of internal revenue or of any of their deputies are in their custody and control for purposes relating to the collection of the revenues of the United States only. They have no control of them and no discretion with regard to permitting the use of them for any other purpose."

Question. Is the regulation by the Treasury Department quoted above in violation of the Constitution of the United States?

Decision: The regulation adopted by the Secretary of the Treasury was authorized by Section 161 of the Revised Statutes, and that was consistent with the Constitution of the United States. To vest the Secretary with authority to prescribe regulations not inconsistent with law for the conduct of the business of his department and to provide for the custody, use and preservation of the records, papers, and property appertaining to it, was a means appropriate and plainly adopted to the successful administration of his department. "Reasons of public policy may well have suggested the necessity in the interest of the Government, of not allowing access to the records in the offices of collectors of internal revenue, except as might be directed by the Secretary of the Treasury. The interests of persons compelled, under the revenue laws to furnish information as to their private business affairs would often be seriously affected if the disclosures so made were not properly guarded. Besides, great confusion might arise in the business of the department if the Secretary allowed the use of records and papers in the custody of collectors to depend upon the discretion or judgment of subordinates.''

BOSTON & MAINE R. R. v. U. S.
(Circuit Court of Appeals, March 19, 1920)
(265 Fed. 578)

Record: Act of Aug. 5, 1909. Action at law to collect taxes due under Sec. 38 of this act. Judgment for the United States, and defendant brings error. Affirmed.

Facts: In fixing the basis upon which taxes shall be assessed upon corporations, Sec. 38 of the Corporation Excise Tax Law of 1909 provides for the deduction of: ''The amount of interest actually paid within the year on its bonded or other indebtedness to an amount of such bonded and other indebtedness not exceeding the paid-up capital stock of such corporation.'' The defendant railroad company, ''in its tax return for the year 1909, treated premiums * * * received from the sale of stock, when the stock was selling above par, as part of its paid-up capital stock'' for the purpose of calculating the amount of interest deductible under the above statute.

Question: Does the meaning of ''paid-up capital stock'' as used in Sec. 38 of the Act of August 5, 1909, include the premiums received from the sale of stock, when the stock is selling above par?

Decision: ''As commonly known, certificates of stock represent the shares. When the shares are at face value they are at par, and when worth more they are above par, or at a premium (Cent. Dict., Vol. 4, p. 4271), but by such fluctuations the shares of stock do not lose their identity or character as such, but remain shares of stock; and the sum total of the shares, at par, constitute the capital stock in the sense in which the term is ordinarily used in banking and commerce. It is quite manifest that Congress used the term 'paid-up capital stock' in the par value sense. This would be the common and ordinary understanding of the term; and it is perfectly plain that Congress did not intend a deduction, in this respect, beyond interest paid on indebtedness to the amount of outstanding capital stock, in the sense in which that expression is ordinarily accepted. And the term 'paid-up,' in the sense in which it was used in connection with the limitation of 'not exceeding,' obviously means paid-up to par value, but not exceeding that."

"Premiums received from the sale of stock are not outstanding capital stock; and they are no more the capital stock of a railroad than is undivided surplus in a bank the capital stock of a bank. The provisions describing the deductions to be made, in order to ascertain the taxable net income, are addressed to the business public, and to corporations generally, and define the manner in which tax returns shall be made; and in such circumstances, the rule would be that Congress used the term in the sense of its generally accepted meaning."

BOSTON TERMINAL CO. v. GILL, COLLECTOR
(U. S. Circuit Court of Appeals, First D., Oct. 25, 1917)
(246 Fed. 664)

Record: Act of Aug. 5, 1909. Action at law to recover taxes paid under protest. Judgment for defendant, and plaintiff brings error. Affirmed.

Facts: The Boston Terminal Railroad Co. was organized under a special statute of Massachusetts. The purpose of its organization was the building and maintaining of a union station. The capital stock to the amount of $500,000 was subscribed for by five railroad companies in equal shares. The railroad companies which used the station were required to pay therefor in proportion to the use made of it such amounts as should be necessary to pay the expenses of the corporate administration and of maintaining the station, the interest on the company's bonds, and dividends on its stock not exceeding 4%. The outstanding bonds amounted to $14,500,000. The railroad companies were also required in case of foreclosure to pay any deficiencies of the bonded debt. The ownership of the stock carried with it no voting power in the choice of the company's officers; the management being placed by the statute in the hands of five trustees, one to be appointed by each of said railroads. Each trustee was to be a director of the railroad appointing him. The terminal company received substantial income aside from payments by the railroad companies from facilities furnished to the traveling public and from leases and concessions. It had never paid any dividends on its stock. The plaintiff was compelled to pay the Corporation Excise Tax, and in computing the amount of the tax the plaintiff was not allowed to deduct the full amount of the interest paid on its indebtedness, because of the statutory limitation to an amount of indebtedness not exceeding capital stock.

Questions: (1) Was the plaintiff terminal corporation "organized for profit" within the meaning of the act of Aug. 5, 1909, Sec. 38, and, therefore, subject to pay Excise Tax with respect to the carrying on or doing business by it during the years here in question?

(2) Was the plaintiff corporation engaged in business within the meaning of the act during the years to which this case relates?

(3) Was the plaintiff corporation entitled to deduct the full amount of interest paid on its indebtedness, according to the Act, upon the theory that the receipts from the railroads used to pay the interest were not income?

Decision: (1) "The Massachusetts statute under which the plaintiff corporation was organized does not prohibit the sale of the shares of stock. That the owner of the stock, whether said railroad companies or other persons, might at some time and in some manner become entitled to dividends was a possibility for which express provision was made. The organization is, therefore, for profit, at least, upon contingencies which, however remote, are not wholly impossible of occurrence. The plaintiff says that the railroad shareholders would have to pay into the terminal railroad company the amount of any dividends declared only to receive back again as dividends the amounts so paid in, but this could be true only in case each railroad used the station in the same proportion as that which its holdings of stock bears to the entire capital. The facts of the case do not bear out this contention.

But apart from any question of dividends, the agreed facts show that the total operating expenses of the terminal railroad company are not wholly borne by the railroad companies, said railroad having an independent source of revenue. Since the railroads have been thereby relieved from having to meet out of their earnings a material part of the charges expressly ranked by the statute among their operating expenses, and their net earnings applicable by them to their dividends have been to that extent augmented, that the company organized is in no respect for profit, can hardly be reasonably said." In its enumeration of the classes of organizations to be exempted from the general liability to taxation under the act, the provision adds: "No part of the net income of which inures to the benefit of any private stockholder or individual." The court refused to regard the above provision as indicating that no organization is to be treated as one for profit, in the sense of the statute, unless it provides for or permits a net income inuring directly to the benefit of some private stockholder or individual. The court, therefore, considered the scheme of the plaintiff organization adapted to permit the acquisition of what may fairly be called "profit."

(2) The plaintiff contended that the operation of the terminal company was not "for profit" and that by "engaged in business" the act cannot mean business from which no profit is to result. This contention is in effect disposed of in the defendant's favor by what has been said above.

(3) "Plaintiff had deducted the full amount of interest paid on its bond indebtedness. Interest on bonded or other indebtedness paid within the year is to be deducted from gross income, according to the second clause of Section 38, but only the interest paid upon such indebtedness to an amount not exceeding the corporation's paid-up capital stock. The capital stock was only $500,000, while the bonded indebtedness amounts to $14,500,000.

The interest on the difference between these amounts were, therefore, properly disallowed as deductions from gross income. The plaintiff further contended that receipts devoted to the payment of interest on its bonds were not income at all within the meaning of the act. The railroads were not required by the state statute to make, nor did they in fact separate or specify, payments identified as payments to meet the interest semi-annually. To take this position is to say that no part of what the railroads paid in to it was gross income within the act."

BOUGHTON v. UNITED STATES

(Court of Claims, December, 1877)

(12 Ct. of Claims 284)

Record: 15 Stat. L., 166. Action at law to recover money deposited with collector of Internal Revenue for purposes of compromise only, after rejection of proposed compromise. Judgment for claimant.

Facts: Three indictments against Horace Boughton had been found for bribery, conspiracy and fraud in connection with internal revenue matters, and were pending in the United States Circuit Court in Texas when, on November 15, 1870, Boughton made a written application to the Commissioner of Internal Revenue for a compromise of these cases and other claims against him upon the payment by him of $1,250, and at the same time made a deposit of that amount of money with the Collector of Internal Revenue of the 4th District of Texas, subject to the order of the Secretary of the Treasury or Commissioner, to await the decision of the latter officer upon his proposition. On November 19, 1874, a tax on distilled spirits to the amount of $8,000, including penalty, assessed against said Boughton, was returned to said collector for collection. On January 9, 1871, the collector applied said $1,250 in part payment of said tax, reported the same in his account, and paid the money into the U. S. Treasury, where it was beyond the reach of anybody to refund without an appropriation by Congress or a judgment of this court. Thereafter the offer of compromise was rejected by the Commissioner in writing, and the district attorney was ordered to proceed with the trial of the indictments. Subsequently all the indictments were dismissed on motion of the district attorney, apparently without any direction from the Commissioner. On the second hearing of the case, the defendant filed a plea setting up said tax of $8,000, assessed against said Boughton, as a set-off and counter-claim, under the provisions of Revised Statutes, Sections 2059, 1061, and demanding judgment thereon in favor of the United States.

Questions: (1) Where plaintiff deposited money with a Collector of Internal Revenue for a special purpose, as related in the above facts, has the collector the right to apply such money to the payment of a tax, in disregard of the special instructions?

(2) In the event the claimant has the right to recover the money so deposited, can the government set up the tax due from said claimant as a counter claim?

Decisions: (1) Held, that the Collector of Internal Revenue had no authority to apply the money deposited in connection with the offer in compromise toward payment of the tax, an object wholly different from that for which it was specially entrusted to him, nor to retain the money after that proposition had been rejected.

(2) Held, government may set up the tax due from claimant as a counter-claim. (No reasons given or authorities cited.)

BOYD v. UNITED STATES
(U. S. Supreme Court, Decided Feb. 1, 1886)
(110 U. S. 616)

Record: Information against thirty-five cases of polished plate glass. Judgment in favor of the United States. Claimants sued out writ of error. Reversed.

Facts: The charge was that the goods in question were imported into the United States, subject to the payment of duties, and that by fraud the government was deprived of the lawful duties. On the trial it became important to show the quality and quantity of certain glass previously imported. For this purpose the district attorney secured a notice from the court directed to the claimants to produce the invoices for such glass. This notice was made under the 5th section of the act of June 22, 1874, which provided that in all suits other than criminal the attorney representing the government might make a written notice for the production of any books, papers, etc., which might tend to prove any allegations made by the United States, such motion to describe the bonds, papers, etc., and to set forth the allegations expected to be proved; and if, upon notice from the court, such books, papers, etc., were not produced the allegations stated in the motion were to be taken as confessed. Claimants produced the invoice which was introduced in evidence over their objections.

Question: Was the above mentioned provision of law requiring the production of books unconstitutional because repugnant to the Fourth and Fifth Amendments or either of them?

Decision: It it not necessary in order to constitute a violation of the Fourth Amendment that the Act should authorize the search and seizure of books. The Act in question provided that upon failure to produce the books the allegations which it affirmed they will prove shall be taken as confessed. This was tantamount to compelling their production. A compulsory production of a man's private papers to establish a criminal charge against him, or to forfeit his property for alleged fraud against the revenue laws is not a legitimate proceeding, but is an "unreasonable search and seizure," equivalent to compelling him to be a witness against himself, and thus is within the prohibition of the Fifth Amendment.

BRADY v. ANDERSON, COLLECTOR

(U. S. Circuit Court of Appeals, Second Cir., Feb. 8, 1917)

(240 Fed. 665)

Record: Act of Oct. 3, 1913. Action to recover tax paid. Judgment for defendant in district court, and plaintiffs bring error. Affirmed.

Facts: A. N. Brady died July 22, 1913, and his executors, in accordance with the requirements of the Commissioner of Internal Revenue, made a return of the income received by him between March 1, when the Act went into effect, and July 22, 1913, when he died. The Act was not passed until October 3.

Question: Is the tax, as the plaintiffs contended, against persons who are citizens or residents of the United States, and not upon property, and if so, does the language of the Act authorize collection of any tax upon income received by Brady, who was neither a citizen or resident of the United States, Oct. 3, 1913, at the time the Act was passed, because he died before that date?

Decision: "In our opinion the tax is against citizens and residents of the United States personally. * * * The effect of making it retroactive is, in our opinion, to apply it to Brady exactly as if it had been enacted March 1, 1913, and as, by reason of his death, he cannot make a return, his executors, into whose hands the estate has come, must do so."

IN RE C. BREWER & CO. LTD.
(Supreme Court of the Territory of Hawaii)
(23 Haw. 96)

Record: Hawaiian R. L. 1915, Sec. 3361. Appeal from a decision of the tax appeal court assessing an income tax on C. Brewer & Co. Affirmed.

Facts: Under the Act insurance companies pay a tax of 2% on gross premiums "in settlement of all demands of any taxes or licenses or fees of every character imposed by the laws of the Territory * * * for conducting said business of insurance in said Territory." The appellant was assessed an income tax on commissions received for acting as agent for certain foreign fire insurance companies which were subject to the tax on gross premiums.

Question: Is it double taxation to assess the agent of an insurance company an income tax on the commissions received, when the insurance company pays a tax on its gross profits for conducting the business within that territory?

Decision: "The tax imposed by Section 3361, R. L. 1915, is an excise tax imposed on insurance companies or corporations for the privilege of doing business within the territory. 'There is no levy by the statute on the receipts themselves either in form or fact; they constitute simply the means of ascertaining the value of the privilege conferred.' * * * In our opinion the fact that an income is derived from commissions paid out of gross premiums received by fire insurance companies and that such companies pay a privilege tax based on the amount of such gross premiums, does not render a tax on such income double.''

BRUSHABER v. U. P. RAILROAD COMPANY

(U. S. Supreme Court, Jan. 24, 1916)

(240 U. S. 1)

Record: Act of Oct. 3, 1913. Bill in equity to enjoin corporation from making returns and paying tax. Dismissed. Direct appeal to U. S. Supreme Court. Affirmed.

Facts: As a stockholder of the Union Pacific Railroad Company the appellant filed his bill to enjoin the corporation from complying with the income tax provisions of the Tariff Act of Oct. 3, 1913 (Section 11, Ch. 16, 38 Statutes 166). Because of constitutional questions duly arising the case is in the Supreme Court on direct appeal from a decree sustaining a motion to dismiss because no ground for relief was stated. The remaining facts are presented in the decision of the court.

Questions: (1) Has a stockholder a right to restrain a corporation from returning and paying a tax where claim of such right is "based upon many averments as to the repugnancy of the statute to the Constitution of the United States, of the peculiar relation of the corporation to the stockholders and their particular interests resulting from many of the administrative provisions of the assailed act, of the confusion, wrong and multiplicity of suits and the absence of all means of redress which would result if the corporation paid the tax and complied with the act in other respects without protest, as it was alleged it was its intention to do''?

(2) Are the twenty-one constitutional objections specified in the bill (which are summarized in the decision) well founded?

(3) Is there an unwarranted delegation of legislative authority to the Secretary of the Treasury?

Decision: (1) "To put out of the way a question of jurisdiction we at once say that in view of these averments and the
ruling in Pollock v. Farmers' Loan & Trust Co., 157 U. S. 429, sustaining the right of a stockholder to sue to restrain a corporation
under proper averments from voluntarily paying a tax charged
to be unconstitutional, on the ground that to permit such a suit
did not violate the prohibitions of Section 3224, Revised Statutes,
against enjoining the enforcement of taxes, we are of opinion that
the contention here made that there was no jurisdiction of the
cause, since to entertain it would violate the provisions of the Revised Statutes referred to, is without merit."

(2) "The various propositions are so intermingled as to
cause it to be difficult to classify them. We are of opinion, however, that the confusion is not inherent, but rather arises from
the conclusion that the Sixteenth Amendment provides for a
hitherto unknown power of taxation, that is, a power to levy an
income tax which, although direct, should not be subject to the
regulation of apportionment applicable to all other direct taxes.
And the far-reaching effect of this erroneous assumption will be
made clear by generalizing the many contentions advanced in
argument to support it, as follows: (a) The amendment authorizes only a particular character of direct tax without apportionment, and, therefore, if a tax is levied under its assumed authority which does not partake of the characteristics exacted by the
Amendment, it is outside of the Amendment and is void as a direct
tax in the general constitutional sense because not apportioned.
(b) As the Amendment authorizes a tax only upon incomes 'from
whatever source derived,' the exclusion from taxation of some
income of designated persons and classes is not authorized and,
hence, the constitutionality of the law must be tested by the general provisions of the Constitution as to taxation, and thus again
the tax is void for want of apportionment. (c) As the right to
tax 'incomes from whatever source derived' for which the Amendment provides must be considered as exacting intrinsic uniformity, therefore, no tax comes under the authority of the Amendment not conforming to such standard, and, hence, all the provisions of the assailed statute must once more be tested solely
under the general and pre-existing provisions of the Constitution,

causing the statute again to be void in the absence of apportionment. (d) As the power conferred by the Amendment is new and prospective, the attempt in the statute to make its provisions retroactively apply is void because so far as the retroactive period is concerned, it is governed by the pre-existing constitutional requirement as to apportionment.

"That the authority conferred upon Congress by Section 8 of Article 1 'to lay and collect taxes, duties, imposts and excises' is exhaustive and embraces every conceivable power of taxation has never been questioned, or, if it has, has been so often authoritatively declared as to render it necessary only to state the doctrine. And it has also never been questioned from the foundation, without stopping presently to determine under which of the separate headings the power was properly to be classed, that there was authority given as the part was included in the whole, to lay and collect income taxes. Again, it has never, moreover, been questioned that the conceded complete and all-embracing taxing power was subject, so far as they were respectively applicable, to limitations resulting from the requirements of Art I, sec. 8, cl. 1, that 'all duties, imposts and excises shall be uniform throughout the United States,' and to the limitations of Art I, sec. 2, cl. 3, that 'direct taxes shall be apportioned among the several states' and of Art. I, sec 9, cl. 4, that 'no capitation, or other direct tax shall be laid, unless in proportion to the census or enumeration hereinbefore directed to be taken.' * * *

"This is the text of the Amendment:

" 'That Congress shall have power to lay and collect taxes on incomes from whatever source derived, without apportionment among the several states, and without regard to any census or enumeration.'

"It is clear on the face of this text that it does not purport to confer power to levy income taxes in a generic sense—an authority already possessed and never questioned—or to limit and distinguish between one kind of income taxes and another, but that the whole purpose of the Amendment was to relieve all income taxes when imposed from apportionment from a consideration of the source whence the income was derived. Indeed, in the light of the history which we have given and of the decision in the Pollock case and the ground upon which the ruling in that case was based, there is no escape from the conclusion that the Amendment was drawn for the purpose of doing away for the future with the principle upon which the Pollock case was decided. * * * Second, that the contention that the Amendment treats a tax on income as a direct tax although it is relieved from apportionment and is necessarily therefore not subject to the rule of uniformity as such rule only applies to taxes which are not direct, thus destroying the two great classifications which have been recognized and enforced from the beginning, is also wholly without foundation since the command of the Amendment that all income taxes shall not be subject to apportionment by a consideration of the sources from which the taxed income may be derived, forbids the application to such taxes of the rule applied in the Pollock case by which alone such taxes were removed from the great class of excises, duties and imposts subject to the rule of uniformity and were placed under the other or direct class. * * *

"We come then to ascertain the merits of the many contentions made in the light of the Constitution as it now stands, that is to say, including within its terms the provisions of the Sixteenth Amendment as correctly interpreted. We first dispose of two propositions assailing the validity of the statute on the one hand because of its repugnancy to the Constitution in other respects, and especially because its enactment was not authorized by the Sixteenth Amendment.

"The statute was enacted October 3, 1913, and provided for a general yearly income tax from December to December of each year. Exceptionally, however, it fixed a first period embracing only the time from March 1, to December 31, 1913, and this limited retroactivity is assailed as repugnant to the due process clause of the Fifth Amendment and as inconsistent with the Sixteenth Amendment itself. But the date of the retroactivity did not extend beyond the time when the Amendment was operative, and there can be no dispute that there was power by virtue of the Amendment during that period to levy the tax, without apportionment, and so far as the limitations of the Constitution in other respects are concerned, the contention is not open. * * *

"Without expressly stating all the other contentions, we summarize them to a degree adequate to enable us to typify and dispose of all of them. (1) The statute levies one tax called a normal tax on all incomes of individuals up to $20,000 and from that amount up by gradations, a progressively increasing tax called an additional tax, is imposed. No tax, however, is levied upon incomes of unmarried individuals amounting to $3,000 or less nor upon incomes of married persons amounting to $4,000 or less. The progressive tax and the exempted amounts, it is said, are based on wealth alone and the tax is therefore repugnant to the due process clause of the Fifth Amendment. (2) The act provides for collecting the tax at the source, that is, makes it the duty of corporations, etc., to retain and pay the sum of the tax on interest due on bonds and mortgages unless the owner to whom the interest is payable gives a notice that he claims an exemption. This duty cast upon corporations, because of the cost to which they are subjected, is asserted to be repugnant to due process of law as a taking of their property without compensation, and we recapitulate various contentions as to discrimination against corporations and against individuals predicated on provisions of the Act dealing with the subject:

"(a) Corporations indebted upon coupon and registered bonds are discriminated against, since corporations not so indebted are relieved of any labor or expense involved in deducting and paying the taxes of individuals on the income derived from bonds.

"(b) Of the class of corporations indebted as above stated, the law further discriminates against those which have assumed the payment of taxes on their bonds, since, although some or all of their bondholders may be exempt from taxation, the corporations have no means of ascertaining such fact, and it would therefore result that taxes would often be paid by such corporations when no taxes were owing by the individuals to the Government.

"(c) The law discriminates against owners of corporate bonds in favor of individuals none of whose income is derived from such property, since bondholders are, during the interval between the deducting and the paying of the tax on their bonds, deprived of the use of the money so withheld.

"(d) Again corporate bondholders are discriminated against because the law does not release them from payment of taxes on their bonds even after the taxes have been deducted by the corporation, and therefore, if after deduction the corporation should fail, the bondholders would be compelled to pay the tax a second time.

"(e) Owners of bonds the taxes on which have been assumed by the corporations are discriminated against because the payment of the taxes by the corporation does not relieve the bondholders of their duty to include the income from such bonds in making a return of all income, the result being a double payment of the taxes, labor and expense in applying for a refund, and a deprivation of the use of the sum of the taxes during the interval which elapses before they are refunded.

"(3) The provision limiting the amount of interest paid which may be deducted from gross income of corporations for the purpose of fixing the taxable income to interest on indebtedness not exceeding one-half the sum of bonded indebtedness and paid-up capital stock, is also charged to be wanting in due process because discriminating between different classes of corporations and individuals.

"(4) It is urged that want of due process results from the provision allowing individuals to deduct from their gross income dividends paid them by corporations whose incomes are taxed and not giving such rights of deduction to corporations.

"(5) Want of due process is also asserted to result from the fact that the act allows a deduction of $3,000 or $4,000 to those who pay the normal tax, that is, whose incomes are $20,000 or less, and does allow the deduction to those whose incomes are greater than $20,000; that is, such persons are not allowed for the purpose of the additional or progressive tax a second right to deduct the $3,000 or $4,000, which they have already enjoyed. And a further violation of due process is based on the fact that for the purpose of the additional tax no second right to deduct dividends received from corporations is permitted.

"In various forms of statement, want of due process, it is moreover insisted, arises from the provisions of the act allowing a deduction for the purpose of ascertaining the taxable income of stated amounts on the ground that the provisions discriminate between married and single people and discriminate between husbands and wives who are living together and those who are not.

"(7) Discrimination and want of due process results, it is said, from the fact that the owners of houses in which they live are not compelled to estimate the rental value in making up their incomes, while those who are living in rented houses and pay rent are not allowed, in making up their taxable income, to deduct rent which they have paid, and that want of due process also results from the fact that although family expenses are not as a rule permitted to be deducted from gross, to arrive at taxable income, farmers are permitted to omit from their income return, certain products of the farm which are susceptible of use by them for sustaining their families during the year.

"So far as these numerous and minute, not to say in many respects hypercritical contentions, are based upon an assumed violation of the uniformity clause, their want of legal merit is at once apparent, since it is settled that that clause exacts only a geographical uniformity and there is not a semblance of ground in any of the propositions for assuming that a violation of such uniformity is complained of. * * *

"So far as the due process clause of the Fifth Amendment is relied upon, it suffices to say that there is no basis for such reliance since it is equally well settled that such clause is not a limitation upon the taxing power conferred upon Congress by the Constitution; in other words, that the Constitution does not conflict with itself by conferring upon the one hand a taxing power and taking the same power away on the other by the limitations of the due process clause. * * * And no change in the situation here would arise even if it be conceded, as we think it must be, that this doctrine would have no application in a case where, although there was a seeming exercise of the taxing power, the act complained of was so arbitrary as to constrain to the conclusion that it was not the exertion of taxation but a confiscation of property, that is, a taking of the same in violation of the Fifth Amendment, or, what is equivalent thereto, was so wanting in basis for classification as to produce such a gross and patent inequality as to inevitably lead to the same conclusion. We say this because none of the propositions relied upon in the remotest degree present such questions. * * * In fact, comprehensively surveying all the contentions relied upon, aside from the erroneous construction of the Amendment which we have previously disposed of, we cannot escape the conclusion that they all rest upon the mistaken theory that although there be differences between the subjects taxed, to differently tax them transcends the limit of taxation and amounts to a want of due process, and that where a tax levied is believed by one who resists its enforcement to be wanting in wisdom and to operate injustice, from that fact in the nature of things there arises a want of due process of law and a resulting authority in the judiciary to exceed its powers and correct what is assumed to be mistaken or unwise exertions by the legislative authority of its lawful powers, even although there be no semblance of warrant in the Constitution for so doing.''

(3) ''We have not referred to a contention that because certain administrative powers to enforce the act were conferred by the statute upon the Secretary of the Treasury, therefore it was void as unwarrantedly delegating legislative authority, because we think to state the proposition is to answer it. * * *''

BRYANT & MAY, LTD., v. SCOTT, COLLECTOR

(U. S. District Court, N. D. Calif., Sept. 14, 1914)

(226 Fed. 875)

Record: Act of August 5, 1909. Action to recover tax paid. Judgment for plaintiff.

Facts: Plaintiff, an English corporation, was at one time engaged in business in California and owned property there. In 1898 it sold all of said property under an executory contract which provided that legal title to the land should remain in the plaintiff until the final payment on the purchase price in 1912. Immediately after this contract was entered into, plaintiff surrendered possession of the property to the purchaser, and maintained no office in California and transacted no business there further than to hold the naked legal title to the property, and to maintain an agent in the state in compliance with the California statute.

Question: Was the plaintiff "doing business" within the meaning of the Act of 1909?

Decision: "The mere retention of the legal title to the property sold as security for the purchase price, and the continuance of the plaintiff's corporate capacity in the state for the protection of its rights under the contract and to receive the deferred payments of principal and interest, do not constitute 'doing business' in the sense of the statute."

BRYCE et al. v. KEITH, COLLECTOR

(U. S. District Court, E. D. New York, March 26, 1919)

(257 Fed. 133)

Record: Act of October 3, 1913. In equity to recover taxes paid. Judgment for defendant.

Facts: On various dates between October 6, 1908, and February 4, 1910, Edith C. Bryce had accepted 7,250 shares of stock, $100 per value, of the Peter Cooper's Glue Factory in exchange for various materials used in the manufacture of glue, and for rent, interest and insurance premiums, all of which had an agreed money value of $725,000. In 1914, all of the assets of the Peter Cooper's Glue Factory was sold for a sum insufficient to pay its debts and the stock thereupon became worthless. In 1915, decedent had filed her federal income tax return under the provisions of the federal income tax law of October 3, 1913, taking as a deduction from gross income $725,000 as a loss incurred in trade.

Question: Is the loss of the stock a loss "incurred in trade" which can be deducted from gross income under the Act of October 3, 1913?

Decision: "The stock transactions by which the decedent became the owner of the stock were carried on over a considerable period, were complicated in character, involved a large sum of money, and must have required much of her time and attention." In view of this, the court was of the opinion they were of the character contemplated by Congress as "incurred in trade." The court cites, to sustain its view, Treasury Decision 1989, dated January 2, 1914.

BULLEN v. WISCONSIN
(U. S. Supreme Court, April 10, 1916)
(240 U. S. 625)

Record: Proceeding to fix inheritance tax. Supreme Court of Wisconsin affirmed a judgment for a tax (143 Wis. 512) and plaintiff brought error. Affirmed.

Facts: Bullen conveyed certain property in trust, retaining income for life and reserving the power to repossess himself of all of the property at any time during his life and to use the principal and income for such beneficiaries and in such manner as he may from time to time appoint. The deed made certain appointments should he die before revoking the said trust.

Question: Is such an agreement sufficient to constitute a transfer of property so as to exempt it from the provisions of the Inheritance Tax statute of the state of Wisconsin?

Decision: The transaction does not amount to a transfer of the property, and the courts of Wisconsin did not err in sustaining the imposition of an inheritance tax under the law of that state on the whole fund as upon a transfer intended to take effect in enjoyment after the donor's death.

BUNDY v. NYGAARD
(Supreme Court of Wisconsin, January, 1916)
(158 N. W. 87)

Record: Statutes of Wisconsin, 1913. Relator sued out a writ of certiorari to review the proceedings of the income tax board of review of Eau Claire County and the State Tax Commission with respect to an income tax assessed against the relator for the year 1914. Assessment held void. Defendant appeals. Affirmed and motion for rehearing denied.

Facts: Relator purchased stock in 1907 at par; sold it in 1914 at an advance of $104,000; and was assessed as income for the year 1914 upon so much of the advance as was proportionate to the period between January 1, 1911, the date when the income tax became effective, and the date of sale with relation to the entire time from date of purchase to date of sale. This was the way the statute provided the tax was to be determined. In fact the stock in this case was worth as much on January 1, 1911, as it was on date of sale.

Question: Was it proper to tax this profit as income when all the profit involved had accrued before the income tax became effective on January 1, 1911?

Decision: The Constitution permitting the taxation of incomes and the statute purporting to tax incomes used the word income in its ordinary meaning, i. e., profit. At the time the statute was passed the stocks had a certain value which was property and as their value did not increase after the statute was passed there was no income that could be taxed. It was property on the date the statute was passed and no part of it could be made into income by legislature enactment. It was therefore not taxable.

BUTTERICK CO. v. UNITED STATES
FEDERAL PUBLISHING CO. v. UNITED STATES
(U. S. District Court, S. D. New York, March 5, 1917)
(240 Fed. 539)

Record: Act of August 5, 1909. Act of October 3, 1913. Actions to recover excise taxes paid under protest. Judgment for plaintiffs. Appealed to U. S. Supreme Court on writ of error. Appeal dismissed on motion of the Attorney General, October 8, 1918. 240 U. S. 587.

Facts: Plaintiff corporations were holding companies which did nothing more than receive and distribute income derived from dividends paid by subsidiary operating companies engaged in the publication of magazines. They necessarily held corporate meetings of the stockholders and directors and issued proxies to vote the stock of the operating companies. The Butterick Company also had indorsed notes of a subsidiary company to promote the successful operation of the latter. These actions were brought to recover excise taxes for the months of January and February, 1913, paid by the plaintiffs under protest.

Questions: (1) Were dividends received by the plaintiff corporations from stock of other corporations taxable for the period in question?

(2) If so, were plaintiffs exercising any franchise during the two months other than that of simply being corporations?

Decision: (1) The provisions of the Corporation Excise Tax of 1909, which embraced no tax upon dividends received by corporations from stock of other corporations, did not apply to taxes imposed for January and February, 1913, but the provisions of the Income Tax Act of 1913 applied, and the saving clause therein to the effect that it should not affect any right accruing under existing laws which were repealed thereby was not intended to cover excise taxes upon corporations under the 1913 Act for the two months in question. The dividends were therefore to be included in computing the tax.

(2) A corporation which merely held the stock of other corporations, received and distributed among its stockholders dividends received from the subsidiary corporations, directed such subsidiary corporations by issuance of proxies to vote at their meetings, and endorsed notes of the subsidiary companies, was not exercising any franchise under which excise taxes might be assessed under Income Tax Act of 1913 for the period in 1913 prior to the ratification of the income tax amendment to the Constitution.

BOSTON & P. R. CORPORATION et al. v. GILL, COLLECTOR

(U. S. District Court, D. Mass., September 13, 1916)

(257 Fed. 221)

Record: Act of August 5, 1909. Action at law to recover taxes paid under protest. Judgment for plaintiffs.

Facts: Plaintiffs were proceeding to recover from the Collector of Internal Revenue taxes illegally assessed. Plaintiffs, together with other claimants, had come to an understanding with defendants that their claims should await the decision of other pending cases. Subsequent to this understanding, it became apparent to the parties that the question of interest could not be adjusted by them and would have to be submitted to the court.

Questions: (1) Is the Collector of Internal Revenue liable for interest on taxes illegally assessed?

(2) Should plaintiffs forfeit the interest because of the lack of diligence in prosecuting their claims?

Decision: (1) The first question has been decided in favor of the plaintiffs in the case of Old Colonial Railroad Co. v. Gill, Collector, 252 Fed. 220.

(2) With reference to the second question, the court held that plaintiffs had exercised due diligence in presenting their claims, inasmuch as the delay was occasioned by the suggestion of defendants; that under such circumstances the plaintiffs' conduct had not been such as to bring them outside of the general rule.

CALKINS v. SMIETANKA, COLLECTOR

(U. S. District Court, N. D. Illinois, January 31, 1917)

(240 Fed. 138)

Record: Act of October 22, 1914. Suit in equity. Temporary restraining order granted. Application for injunction denied, and temporary restraining order vacated.

Facts: (1) A bill was filed by plaintiffs asking a decree against the Internal Revenue Collector declaring certain transfers on the Board of Trade not taxable and seeking an injunction. It appeared that members of the Board of Trade considered what they termed an "offer" was not subject to a stamp tax under the provisions of the Act of October 22, 1914, imposing on each sale, agreement of sale, or agreement to sell any products at any exchange or board of trade, either for present or future delivery, a tax of one cent for each $100 in value, etc. Where offers were made subject to deferred acceptance, only a small percentage developed into sales. The brokers received $10 for the execution of each offer of 10,000 bushels of grain.

(2) Plaintiffs further seek an injunction because the revenue officers are attempting to assess a tax upon certain transfers. The transfers in question are where A. offers to sell a large quantity of grain, which is accepted by B., and B. makes a resale to C., who in turn makes another sale to D., and so on, until at the close of the day the wheat belongs to Z. In the clearing house settlement that evening, the only transaction of interest to the members is the final transfer of grain to Z. The government contends that the stamp tax is imposed on each of these transactions.

Questions: (1) Are the "offers" to sell grain, which "offers" were made subject to deferred acceptances taxable only when the broker receives a sum in excess of $100, or when the price, for which the commodity therein named was to be sold, exceeded $100?

(2) Does the act put a tax on each sale or agreement to sell, though during the day several separate sales are made of the same lot of grain, and at the close of the day, the only memorandum made shows the transfer from the original seller to the last buyer?

Decisions: (1) "Plaintiffs' contention that the stamp tax is collectible on an offer only when the broker receives a sum in excess of $100 is, in the light of all the surrounding circumstances, not persuasive. It must be, and is, admitted that under existing circumstances, if plaintiffs' contention be adopted, practically all 'offers' would go untaxed, for the transaction must be large indeed, before the broker would exceed $100. If plaintiffs' contentions were adopted, all such 'offers' involving transactions of less than 100,000 bushels would be untaxed, while 'offers' involving the sale of 200,000 bushels would be taxed one cent, 'offers' to sell quantities aggregating 1,000,000 bushels (of wheat, of the value of $1,750,000) would be subject to a tax of only nine cents. Assuming Congress intended to impose a tax on 'offers,' then such a construction would lead to an absurdity."

(2) "The fact that the agreements made were not, in all cases, reduced to writing with the stamp attached, can not relieve the agreements from the tax. Congress imposed upon all members transacting business the duty of reducing their agreement to writing. Plaintiffs might as well contend that they were relieved of their taxes because they failed to pay them promptly, and when due, as to say that they were relieved from the stamp tax because they did not reduce their agreements to writing. They cannot plead their own neglect to relieve themselves of this tax."

CAMBRIA STEEL CO. v. McCOACH, COLLECTOR
(U. S. District Court, E. D. Penn., July 28, 1915)
(225 Fed. 278)

Record: Act of August 5, 1909. Action to recover special excise tax paid under protest. Upon rule for judgment for want of a sufficient affidavit of defense. Rule absolute.

Facts: In 1918, the Cambria Iron Company, a Pennsylvania corporation, leased all of its property to the Cambria Steel Company, plaintiff herein and a similar corporation, for a period of 999 years. The plaintiff agreed to pay as rental a sum equal to 4 per cent upon the outstanding capital stock of the Iron Company, and a further sum not exceeding $5,000 to cover cost of maintenance of the organization of the Iron Company, the rental, except the $5,000, to be paid direct to the stockholders of the Iron Company. Since the date of the lease, the Iron Company maintained its charter merely that it might exist as landlord and lessor, and received no income other than as above set forth, and did nothing else whatsoever, and had no quick assets, cash, or bank account. The defendant, as collector of internal revenue, made demand upon the Iron Company for a special excise tax of $3,337.20, assessed against it under the Act of 1909 as a corporation having a capital stock and engaged in business in Pennsylvania. The Steel Company, in order to avoid the penalties threatened by the collector, and because it knew that if it did not pay the tax, the defendant would collect by distraint upon and sale of the property.leased by the plaintiff from the Iron Company, paid the tax under protest and brought this action to recover the same.

Questions: (1) In view of the fact that the taxes paid by the Steel Company were due from the Iron Company, a different corporation, would the fact that there was no privity of contract between plaintiff and collector defeat the action?

(2) Was the Iron Company "doing business" within the meaning of the Act of 1909?

Decision: (1) Where demand for payment of tax is made upon a lessor corporation which has leased all of its property and cannot pay, and the corporation which is lessee of all of said property, being confronted with threatened distraint and sale thereof, pays the tax under protest, such circumstances are sufficient to constitute the payment one enforced by duress and compulsion and the lessor may maintain an action for the recovery of the amount paid, without regard to privity of contract between it and the collector. The Steel Company was therefore entitled to contest the tax of the Iron Company which it had paid and to recover the amount paid.

(2) A corporation which has leased its property, and the sole income of which consists of the rental, which is distributed to the lessor's stockholders, and which maintains its corporate existence merely for the purpose of carrying out the terms of the lease, is not doing business within the meaning of the Corporation Tax Act.

CAMPBELL v. SHAW

HONOLULU IRON WORKS CO. v. SHAW

(Supreme Court of the Hawaiian Islands, Aug. 26, 1897)

(11 Haw. 112)

Record: Act of June 12, 1896. Bills in equity to declare act unconstitutional and to enjoin assessor from assessing and collecting tax. Demurrer to the declaration overruled.

Facts: The Income Tax Act passed by Legislature of Hawaiian Islands provided for an exemption of two thousand dollars upon incomes under four thousand dollars, whereas no such exemption was allowed to incomes over four thousand dollars. Art. 11 of Constitution of Hawaii provides that each person "shall be obliged to contribute his proportion or share to the expense" of protecting his life, liberty and property.

Question: Is a tax allowing an exemption of two thousand dollars upon income under four thousand dollars, and no exemption where the income exceeds that amount, constitutional within the meaning of the Constitution of Hawaiian Islands?

Decision: "The effect of this section of the Act would be to place the burden of this tax upon those whose annual incomes are over four thousand dollars, and who constitute a minority of the community. It is argued that the exemption of incomes of two thousand dollars is reasonable and in furtherance of a public purpose, because the sum of two thousand dollars is the average annual cost of living of a family. But if it be once conceded that exemptions so large as this can be made as a public benefit then exemptions of a much larger amount can be made which might place the whole burden upon the rich and if pushed to an extreme be confiscation and not the proportional taxation authorized by the Constitution."

CAMP BIRD, LIMITED, v. HOWBERT, COLLECTOR

(U. S. Circuit Court of Appeals, Eighth Cir., Nov. 17. 1919)

(262 Fed. 114)

Record: Act of August 5, 1909. Action to recover taxes paid. Judgment for defendant rendered by U. S. District Court for the District of Colorado, was taken to Circuit Court of Appeals, Eighth Circuit, on writ of error and affirmed, 249 Fed. 27. Petition for writ of certiorari granted by U. S. Supreme Court, 247 U. S. 509. Judgment reversed by U. S. Supreme Court on confession of error by Assistant Attorney General, 248 U. S. 590, and a mandate of the Supreme Court issued to the Circuit Court of Appeals, Eighth Circuit, for further proceedings in conformity to the judgment of the Supreme Court. Judgment for defendant reversed and case remanded to District Court with directions to enter judgment in favor of the plaintiff (this decision). Petition for a writ of certiorari denied by U. S. Supreme Court, 252 U. S. 579.

Facts: Plaintiff corporation was the owner of mining property after the year 1902, and it made returns to the collector of

Internal Revenue for each of the years 1909, 1910, and 1911. The Commissioner of Internal Revenue found that the deductions claimed in each of these returns had been overstated and made additional assessments, including a penalty of one per cent per month, which assessments the plaintiff paid under protest, and an action was then begun to recover the amounts so paid. The District Court found that the plaintiff was entitled to more depreciation than that allowed by the Commissioner. It found, further, that, while plaintiff had understated its net income in the returns for the years in question, such understatement was made in good faith, and with the belief that the figures presented stated the facts, but recovery was denied on the ground that it was barred by Rev. Stat., Sec. 3225, which provided as follows:

"When a second assessment is made in case of any list, statement or return, which in the opinion of the collector or deputy collector was false or fraudulent, or contained any understatement or undervaluation, no taxes collected under such assessment shall be recovered by any suit unless it is proved that said list, statement or return was not false nor fraudulent, and did not contain any understatement or undervaluation."

Questions: (1) Was recovery in this case barred by Rev. Stat. Sec. 3225, because of the understatement, or does that section relate only to an understatement made with knowledge and intent?

(2) If not, did the facts show any taxes illegally collected, so as to entitle plaintiff to a recovery?

(3) If plaintiff was entitled to recover taxes illegally collected, could it also recover the penalty of one per cent per month which it had paid?

Decision: (1) "The only question decided by this court at the former hearing was that the action of the plaintiff was barred by section 3225, U. S. Rev. Stat., this being also the ground upon which the trial court denied recovery. There exists no record as to what the error was that the Attorney General confessed. We conclude, however, that as the bar of the statute was the only question decided by this court it is in regard to that question we erred in the opinion of the Assistant Attorney General, and we further conclude that as this case was remanded by the Supreme Court to this court for further proceedings instead of the District Court, it is our duty to proceed and render such judg·ment on its merits as this court shall deem proper, regardless of the bar of the statute."

(2) Plaintiff was entitled to recover excessive taxes paid because of the Commissioner's refusal to make proper allowance for depreciation of equipment.

(3) "We are of the opinion that where an illegal tax is paid, the fact that it was not paid within the time allowed by law will not prevent the taxpayer from recovering the penalty of one per cent per month paid by him for the nonpayment of the illegal tax, for, if such tax was illegal, it was never due, and therefore the penalty was as much unauthorized as the tax itself.'"

CARBON STEEL CO. v. LEWELLYN, COLLECTOR

(U. S. Supreme Court, March 1, 1920)

(251 U. S. 501)

Record: Munitions Tax, Revenue Act of 1916. Action to recover taxes paid. Judgment for defendant affirmed by Circuit Court of Appeals (258 Fed. 533), and plaintiff obtained certiorari. Affirmed.

Facts: Plaintiff had a contract with the British government for the delivery of shells. The making of the shells consisted of nine operations, of which the plaintiff only performed two; namely, it manufactured the steel in bar form and broke the bars into proper lengths. The rest of the work was done for plaintiff by independent contractors, plaintiff furnishing the materials, such as transit plugs, fixing screws, and copper tubing. Plaintiff was taxed on all the profits realized by it under the contracts mentioned above.

Questions: (1) Was it necessary for all the operations in the making of shells to be done by one person in order that he might be designated as "a person manufacturing" within the meaning of the law?

(2) Did the payment of a munition tax by subcontractors on their profits from making shells relieve the main contractor from the tax on his profits?

Decision: (1) The construction urged upon the court by the plaintiff must be rejected as it would reduce the Act to an empty declaration. The Act did not contemplate that the "person manufacturing" should use his own hands—it contemplated the use of instrumentalities, servants, machinery and general agents; it also contemplated the world's division of occupations, and in this comprehensive way, contemplated that all of the world's efficiency might be availed of, and when availed of for profits, the latter would not thereby escape being taxed. The plaintiff is therefore subject to tax.

(2) The question here is the tax on the profits of the contractor and not of the subcontractors. The question of the assessment against the subcontractors concerns them and not the plaintiff who is resisting a tax on the profits actually made by him. Therefore no deduction could be made from the contractors profits on account of profits of subcontractors.

CARTIER et al. v. DOYLE, COLLECTOR
(U. S. District Court, August 7, 1920)
(269 Fed. 647)

Record: Act of October 3, 1917. Action at law to recover excess profits taxes paid under protest under section 201. Judgment for defendant.

Facts: Plaintiff, a partnership consisting of two members, was engaged in the business of buying, selling and dealing in timber, lumber, and other forest products. A part of their net income for the year 1917 resulted from an isolated sale of timbered land, and the balance from the regular or customary lumber business of the partnership. It does not appear whether the income from this sale was a commission or a profit, except that the report states that the firm had never owned any lands, timber, plant, mill, or yard, and had never done any manufacturing or carried any stock of manufactured lumber. The business was conducted by the partners personally with the assistance of a small clerical office force. Plaintiff was a heavy borrower of money. At the beginning of the taxable year, 1917, liabilities exceeded assets. At the close of the same year, its assets exceeded its liabilities. The partnership agreement provided that one of the partners was to furnish all the capital and take the note of the partnership therefor. Before January 1, 1917, this agreement was modified so that working capital was obtained by borrowing money from banks upon firm notes endorsed by both members of the firm and secured by collateral furnished by one of the partners. The return of the partnership showed the excess profits tax computed under section 209 of the Act, applying to concerns having an invested capital not more than nominal. The Commissioner contended that the firm should be assessed under section 201, upon its invested capital, or under section 210, on the ground that the invested capital, although more than nominal, could not be satisfactorily determined. Additional tax was assessed accordingly and was paid.

Questions: (1) Is the income from a partnership dealing in lumber, derived from an isolated sale of timber land, attributable to the business of dealing in lumber and therefore taxable under section 201 of the Act of October 3, 1917?

(2) Under what section of the statute should plaintiffs' invested capital have been determined?

(3) Was the liability of the partnership to the tax based upon invested capital affected by the extent to which the income was produced by the personal services and efforts of the partners?

(4) What is the force of Departmental regulations in the interpretation of taxing statutes?

(5) What is the distinction between "invested capital" and "capital", as those terms are used in section 209 of the Act of 1917?

(6) Was the property pledged as security for money borrowed to be used in their business, a part of "invested capital"?

Decision: (1) The statute provided: "For the purpose of this title every corporation or partnership, not exempt under the provisions of this section, shall be deemed to be engaged in business, and all the trades and businesses in which it is engaged shall be treated as a single trade or business, and all its income from whatever source derived shall be deemed to be received from such trade or business." The court said: "Confessedly the company's principal business was dealing in lumber, and, under this statute, its entire income must be attributed to that business."

(2) "If, during the year 1917, Cartier-Holland Lumber Co. had invested capital, within the purview and meaning of that term as employed in the statute, more than nominal in amount, excess profits taxes upon its income could not be assessed under the provisions of section 209 of the statute, and, if the amount of such invested capital could not be satisfactorily determined, excess profits tax must have been assessed under sections 201 and 210 in accordance with proper regulations prescribed by the Commissioner of Internal Revenue. If the lumber company had invested capital more than nominal in amount, plaintiffs are not in position to complain of the regulations promulgated or of the method employed in determining the amount of the firm's invested capital, which forms the basis of computation of the taxes, because, under the undisputed evidence, the arbitrary or supposititious invested capital fixed upon was larger in amount than the invested capital actually possessed and employed, and the taxes imposed were correspondingly diminished."

(3) "Plaintiffs are not brokers within any accepted definition of the term. They are paid neither a salary nor commissions for their services. They buy and sell lumber, and undertake and assume all the risks and enjoy all the benefits of a merchandising business. They employ a large amount of capital; their income is dependent upon their personal services and efforts only in the same way and to the same extent that the farmer who works his own farm or the merchant who conducts his own store derives his income from his individual endeavors." The invested capital was therefore not improper as a basis of tax.

(4) "While, in doubtful cases, Departmental regulations may be an aid in construction and interpretation, they can neither add to nor subtract from plain congressional enactments."

(5) "In this instance, differences in the meaning of the terms 'invested capital' and 'capital' are wholly immaterial. If Cartier-Holland Lumber Co. had any invested capital, it was substantial and not merely nominal, and plaintiffs must fail. On the other hand, if the company had no invested capital, plaintiffs are entitled to recover, regardless of the amount of its borrowed or other noninvested capital."

(6) "That the partnership was doing business upon borrowed money is beyond dispute, and that invested capital does not include borrowed money is settled by the express terms of the statute. But the term 'invested capital' as here used, includes all working capital consisting of money or property employed in the business or for its benefit, and furnished or 'paid in' by one or more of the partners. Applying this test, it is clear this partnership had invested capital within the purview and meaning of the statute." · The property belonging to one of the partners which was pledged for loans of the partnership, "pledged by the partners became working capital and was used and employed in the business of the company to the same extent as if it had been paid directly into the firm treasury," and therefore constituted "invested capital."

CARY, COLLECTOR, v. THE SAVINGS UNION
(U. S. Supreme Court, October Term, 1874)
(22 Wallace 38)

Record: Act of 1864, as amended in 1866. Action to recover back taxes paid under protest. Judgment for plaintiff in the Circuit Court (Fed. Cas. 12,317) and defendant brought error. Judgment affirmed.

Facts: The Act provided for a tax on all dividends whenever payable to depositors as part of the earnings, income, or gains of any saving institution, but also provided that interest allowed to depositors should not be considered as dividends. The plaintiff bank operated under a plan by which every six months the profits of the business were ascertained and after certain deductions were made, the remainder was apportioned for a dividend upon the capital stock, reserve fund and deposits. The dividend apportioned to each account was in proportion to the time the several accounts represented in that account formed part of the funds of the corporation.

Question: Were the payments to depositors in accordance with the plan stated above made as interest or as dividends of profit?

Decision: Inasmuch as the depositors contracted not for a rate of interest to be paid upon their deposits, but for a share of the profits of the business in which their money was employed, the payments were dividends and not interest.

CASSODY v. ST. GERMAIN
(Supreme Court of Rhode Island, April 18, 1900)
(22 R. I. 53; 46 Atl. 35)

Record: War Revenue Act of 1898. Assumpsit on book account. Judgment for plaintiff, defendant brings exceptions. Overruled.

Facts: The personal estate of defendant was attached in the hands of a third party as garnishee. At the trial an assignee of the wages of the defendant intervened and claimed the fund under an assignment. The assignment had been recorded prior to the attachment, but no revenue stamp had been affixed. At the trial the plaintiff objected to the assignment being offered in evidence. The United States Internal Revenue Law of 1898 declared invalid and of no effect instruments from which stamps have been omitted with intent to evade the provisions of the Act.

Question: May an unstamped assignment be offered in evidence under the Act of 1898 which declares invalid instruments from which stamps have been omitted with intent to evade the provisions of the Act?

Decision: "There being nothing to show such intent in this case, the assignment in question was not shown to be invalid on that account. * * * The stamp was required only on the power of attorney which was embodied in this assignment; but, as the power of attorney was not necessary to the title of the complainant, it did not affect the validity of the assignment."

IN RE J. B. CASTLE
(Supreme Court of The Territory of Hawaii, Oct. 12, 1906)
(18 Haw. 129)

Record: Hawaiian R. L. Secs. 1278 and 1280. An appeal from a decision of the tax appeal court assessing an income tax against Castle. Appeal sustained.

Facts: The Income Tax Act provided that the first taxation period should be "the half year immediately preceding the first day of January, 1906." It also provides that the income, gains and profits be derived "during said taxation period" in order to be taxable. The appellant bought stock in 1898 and sold it between July 1 and December 31, 1905.

Question: Is the profit, made from the sale of stock shortly after an income tax law became effective, taxable where the law provides that the income be derived during the taxation period?

Decision: "The income in question was not derived during the six months preceding January 1, 1906, and therefore was not taxable as gains, profits and income derived during that period."

CATAWISSA R. CO. v. PHILADELPHIA & R. RY. CO.
(Supreme Court of Pennsylvania, Oct. 25, 1916)
(255 Pa. 269; 99 Atl. 807)

Record: Act of October 3, 1913. Assumpsit to recover money paid to defendant's use under the terms of a lease. Judgment for plaintiff, and defendant appealed. Reversed.

Facts: Before the income tax act was passed the plaintiff leased to the defendant its road and equipment, the lease containing the following clause: "The Railway company shall and will also punctually and faithfully pay all taxes, charges, and assessments which, during the continuance of the term hereby demised, shall be assessed or imposed under any existing or future law on the demised premises or any part thereof, or on the business there carried on, or on the receipts, gross or net, derived therefrom, or upon the said several issues of bonds or the interest thereon, or upon the capital stock of the Catawissa Company or the dividends thereon, or upon the franchises of the said company, for the payment or collection of any of which said taxes the Catawissa Company may otherwise be or become liable or accountable under any lawful authority whatever." The lessor paid an income tax upon the rental paid under the lease, the lessee having refused to pay it, and now claims the defendant is liable for it under the terms of the lease.

Question : Is a lessee, who covenants to pay all taxes upon the demised premises, the business, the receipts, gross or net, and the bonds issued by the lessor, liable for the income tax upon the rental, the income tax act having been passed after the date of the lease ?

Decision : "The lease provides specifically what taxes it is to pay, and expressio unius est exclusio alterius : The income tax was not imposed by the government upon 'the demised premises or any part thereof,' nor 'on the business there carried on', nor 'on the receipts, gross or net, derived therefrom,' nor 'upon the capital stock of the Catawissa Company, or the dividends thereon,' nor 'upon the franchises of the said company.' It was imposed upon rental received by the lessor from the lessee." Since the lessee did not covenant to pay the tax imposed upon the rental, he can not be held for it under the terms of the lease.

CENTRAL BLDG., LOAN & SAVINGS CO.
v. BOWLAND, COLLECTOR
BELLEFONTAINE BLDG. & LOAN CO.
v. McMAKEN, COLLECTOR
(U. S. District Court, S. D. Ohio, W. D., May 11, 1914)
(216 Fed. 526)

Record : Act of August 5, 1909. Action at law to recover taxes paid under protest on net income under Sec. 38 of the Act. Judgment for plaintiffs.

Facts : Plaintiffs were incorporated under the Ohio laws as building and loan associations and in addition to other powers granted, were authorized "to make loans to members and others on such terms, conditions and securities as may be provided by the association." Plaintiffs claim exemption from taxation as imposed by the Act of August 5, 1909, under the proviso in the Act which exempts "domestic building and loan associations, organized and operated exclusively for the mutual benefit of their members," which exemption the government denies on the grounds that (1) in addition to its mutual features it does a business akin to a general banking business and (2) that plaintiffs are qualified to receive deposits or borrow funds from other than members. The government therefore concludes that plaintiffs cannot be considered as organized and operated for the "exclusive benefit" of their respective members and the case is brought before the court for decision.

Question: Would the fact that the corporations made loans to and received deposits from other than members exclude them from the classification of "domestic building and loan associations, organized and operated exclusively for the benefit of their members," which associations were exempt from the taxation under the 1909 Act?

Decision: "A non-member borrowing or lending receives no benefit from the building association as such, but only the same benefit which he would receive by dealing generally with his money in the market. By this method of acquiring additional income for the association there is no disturbance of the mutuality of interest, which is the distinguishing feature of building associations; indeed by indulging in it the essential principle to that end underlying building associations is maintained. The conclusion is that building associations under the laws of Ohio, notwithstanding their power to borrow money from, or loan money to non-members are 'organized and operated exclusively for the mutual benefit of their members,' come strictly within the proviso giving them exemption from the tax in question, cannot be required to pay it, and the plaintiffs are entitled to recover the amounts paid by them under protest."

CHARTIERS & R. T. CO. v. McNAMARA
(Supreme Court of Pa., Jan. 6, 1873)
(72 Pa. St. 278)

Record: Act of July 13, 1866. Action of assumpsit by McNamara. Verdict for plaintiff, and defendants removed the record to the Supreme Court, and assigned for error the rejection of their offer of evidence. Judgment affirmed.

Facts: Defendants offered in evidence a special written contract for the performance of work done by the plaintiff. Objection to its reception in evidence was made "because the paper is not stamped as required by the Act of Congress." The paper being unstamped, the court rejected the evidence.

Question: Is a contract which is unstamped, admissible in evidence in a state court, under the Act of 1866?

Decision: "It seems to us very clear that the provisions of the Act of 1866, which excludes an unstamped writing or paper from record, and as evidence in any court until the tax is paid, is not a rule for the mere regulation of evidence, but is a disqualification attached to the document, making it incompetent to fulfill its purpose as an instrument of evidence, until the stamp duty is paid. It is a provision necessary and proper to carry the taxing power into execution, and is binding on all courts."

CHEATHAM v. UNITED STATES
(U. S. Supreme Court, October, 1875)
(92 U. S. 85)

Record: Act of July 13, 1866. Action at law to recover taxes paid under protest. Judgment for defendant, and plaintiff brings error. Affirmed.

Facts: For the year 1864 plaintiff was assessed an income tax amounting to $99,726. Upon appeal to the Commissioner of Internal Revenue this assessment was set aside and a new assessment amounting to $29,971.91 was made March 15, 1868. This sum, with interest and penalty was paid under protest, and suit for the recovery of the money so paid was commenced. Plaintiff made no appeal to the Commissioner of Internal Revenue from the second assessment.

Question: Has plaintiff a right of action to recover taxes paid under the above facts under the following statute:

"That no suit shall be maintained in any court for the recovery of any tax alleged to have been erroneously or illegally assessed or collected until appeal shall have been duly made to the Commissioner of Internal Revenue * * * and a decision of said Commissioner shall be had thereon, unless such suit shall be brought within six months from the time of said decision * * *"?

Decision: "The assessment on which this money was paid was a different assessment from the one upon which the appeal to the Commissioner was taken." The first assessment was set aside and a new assessment was made by the local collector materially different from the first and according to a different rule. From this assessment plaintiff had the right to appeal, and in failing to do so comes within the provision of the section forbidding suit unless appeal has been taken to the Commissioner. If the two assessments could be treated as one transaction, the suit cannot be maintained because it was not brought within the allotted time. "All governments, in all times, have found it necessary to adopt stringent measures for the collection of taxes, and to be rigid in the enforcement of them."

CHEMUNG IRON CO. v. LYNCH
(U. S. Circuit Court of Appeals, Eighth Circuit, December 6, 1920)
(269 Fed. 368)

Record: Act of August 5, 1909. Action to recover corporation tax paid under protest. Appeal from judgment for defendant. Affirmed.

Facts: Plaintiff, a corporation, was on January 1, 1913, the owner of certain mining leases and on that date it entered into a contract with another company, by which it subleased all the lands covered by the leases, the lessees to pay plaintiff a certain royalty per ton on all ore mined. Plaintiff was to have access to the lands in question for the purpose of exploration, and spent $59,898 for this purpose in the years 1909, 1910, and 1912, the years for which it paid the tax under protest. The plaintiff also employed a secretary, a bookkeeper, and a mining engineer during these years, and its income consisted of royalties received from the lessee.

Question: Was the plaintiff doing business within the meaning of the Corporation Excise Law of 1909?

Decision: A corporation lessee of iron ore lands, which subleases them for mining purposes, receiving a royalty on all ore mined and which employs an engineer for the purpose of supervising and inspecting the work of the sublessee and which expends money in the exploration of the ore land, is doing business within the meaning of the Act of August 5, 1909, and the net receipts from royalties are taxable as income thereunder.

CHESEBROUGH v. UNITED STATES
(U. S. Supreme Court, January 25, 1904)
(192 U. S. 253)

Record: Act of June 13, 1898. Action at law to recover taxes. Judgment for defendant and plaintiff brought error. Affirmed.

Facts: The Act of 1898 required the affixing of Revenue stamps to deeds of conveyance. Plaintiff was compelled to purchase and affix stamps to certain deeds before receiving the selling price for the property. He purchased the stamps voluntarily and affixed them to the deed, and in this suit sought to recover the amount paid for the stamps on the ground that the act was unconstitutional.

Question: May taxes voluntarily paid be recovered?

Decision: "* * * taxes voluntarily paid cannot be recovered back, and payments with knowledge and without compulsion are voluntary. At the same time, when taxes are paid under protest that they are being illegally exacted, or with notice that the payer contends they are illegal and intends to institute suit to compel their payment, a recovery in such suit may, on occasion, be had, although generally speaking, even a protest or notice will not avail if payment be made voluntarily with full knowledge of all the circumstances, and without any coercion by the actual or threatened exercise of power possessed, or supposed to be possessed, by the party exacting or receiving the payment over the person or property of the party making the payment, from which the latter has no means of immediate relief other than such payment."

CHICAGO TITLE & TRUST CO. v. SMIETANKA, COLLECTOR
(U. S. District Court, N. D. Ill., E. D., March 14, 1921)
(Not reported)

Record: Act of October 3, 1913. Suit to recover tax paid. Demurrer to declaration sustained.

Facts: Persons owning the capital stock of five street railways in Chicago executed an agreement by which the legal title of all the capital stock of those companies was conveyed to certain trustees, who were to do certain specified things. The trustees issued participating shares in lieu of the capital stock of the corporations, and the holders of these certificates elected a committee. The whole agreement was full of provisions for the control of the trustees by the committee, the latter even controlling the power of the trustees to vote the capital stock of the company.

Question: Did the agreement create a joint-stock company or association subject to income tax under the Revenue Act of 1913?

Decision: The words "no matter how created or organized" in the 1913 Act do not relate only to insurance companies but refer back to the words "every corporation, joint-stock company or association. * * * In Crocker v. Malley, the Supreme Court does not undertake to say whether there could be such a thing as an association not organized under some law, but I am of the opinion that there can be such an association and that the organization here shown is within the statute."

CHICAGO & ALTON R. R. CO. v. UNITED STATES
(U. S. Court of Claims, December 3, 1915)
(53 Ct. Cls. 41)

Record: Act of August 5, 1909. Action to recover taxes paid. Petition dismissed.

Facts: Claimant railroad company, in 1906, issued and sold at a discount $11,000,000 of refunding bonds and $1,960,000 of equipment notes. The transaction was fully consummated within the above year, and the books of the company disclosed the loss under the profit and loss account. In its returns under the Act of 1909, for the years 1911 and 1912, no reduction of taxes was claimed because of the bond and note transaction. Subsequently, however, it brought this action claiming a right to a refund of tax for the proportionate amount for the years in question of the full discount suffered by it in the sale of said notes. The claim was not predicated upon any express provisions of the statute, but upon a ruling of the Commissioner which held that the contention now put forward by claimant company was tenable.

Question: Would the bookkeeping entry made by the

company in 1906 charging off the entire loss prevent it from later making a yearly deduction of a proportionate amount of the loss when making its return of annual income?

Decision: Maryland Casualty Co. v. United States, 52 Ct. Cls. 201, is followed, and the deduction claimed held not allowable. The claimant, prior to the passage of the Act of 1909, had fully closed the transaction insisted upon. As affecting its income or deductions therefrom it was simply one of claimant's past fiscal transactions appearing upon its books to be treated by the Commissioner as a closed transaction.

CHIEF JUSTICE TANEY TO MR. CHASE
(U. S. Supreme Court, March 10, 1863)
(157 U. S. 701)

Record: Act of July 1, 1862. Letter to Secretary of the Treasury on order of court.

Facts: The Treasury Department had construed the act taxing officers in the employment of the United States to embrace judicial officers, and the amount of the tax was deducted from the salaries.

Question: Does Congress have the power to tax the salaries of the judges of the Supreme and Inferior Courts of the United States who are already holding office?

Decision: After citing Sec. 1, Art. 3, of the Constitution, Chief Justice Taney said "The Act in question, as you interpret it, diminishes the compensation of every judge three per cent, and if it can be diminished to that extent by the name of a tax, it may in the same way be reduced from time to time at the pleasure of the legislature." The conclusion was that the tax could not be imposed.

CHILE COPPER CO. ads. EDWARDS, COLLECTOR
(U. S. Circuit Court of Appeals, Second Cir., April 27, 1921)
(273 Fed. 452)

Record: Action at law in U. S. District Court for the Southern District of New York to recover $17,500 paid as a stamp tax on certain bonds. Demurrer overruled. Judgment for plaintiff. The defendant, the Collector, appealed by writ of error. Judgment of lower court affirmed.

Facts: Early in 1917, at which date there were no applicable stamp taxes, the Chile Copper Co. borrowed $35,000,000 to be evidenced by bonds. The borrowed money was receivable in two installments. A temporary $35,000,000 bond was issued and delivered on May 25, 1917, to the trustee under a trust agreement, and thereupon on May 29, 1917, the first installment of 50% on the purchase price of the bonds was paid by the stockholder subscribers and installment receipts were given binding the company to deliver permanent bonds on payment of the second installment on May 29, 1918. The Revenue Act of Oct. 3, 1917, imposed a stamp tax on bonds "issued after December 1, 1917." On May 29, 1918, the second installment of the loan was paid by the receipt holders and permanent bonds were delivered to them. The Commissioner of Internal Revenue held that the issue of bonds in question occurred when the permanent and engraved bonds were handed to the subscribers and underwriters on May 29, 1918, after the effective date of the stamp tax and that therefore the bonds in question were taxable.

Question: Where temporary bonds are issued and delivered before effective date of the Act and permanent bonds to take their place were issued after the date of incidence of the stamp tax, are the permanent bonds taxable?

Decision: "It was never intended by the statute to impose the tax on the exchange of the permanent bonds for temporary bonds or upon the exchange of registered or unregistered bonds or vice versa, or for the substitution of several small bonds for one large one, and vice versa. For us to hold as contended for by the defendant below, would be to reach such a conclusion. No additional tax is required upon the issuance of a permanent or definite bond in substitution for a temporary bond which has been delivered. The term 'issued,' as used in the statutes, implies not merely delivery, but delivery of an instrument creating or renewing an obligation and not merely furnishing a different expression of a pre-existing obligation. We think that the bonds were issued prior to the effective date of the Stamp Tax Act and that the demurrer was properly overruled."

CHRIST CHURCH v. COUNTY OF PHILADELPHIA
(U. S. Supreme Court, December Term, 1860)
(24 Howard 300)

Record: Pennsylvania Act of 1851. Writ of error from Supreme Court of Pennsylvania. Judgment affirmed.

Facts: In 1833, the legislature of Pennsylvania enacted that "the real property, including ground rents now belonging and payable to Christ Church Hospital, in the City of Philadelphia, so long as the same shall continue to belong to the said hospital, shall be and remain free from taxes." In 1851, they enacted "that all property, real or personal, belonging to any association or incorporated company, which is now by law exempt from taxation," shall hereafter be subject to taxation as other property is now by law taxable.

Question: Does a general act taxing the property of certain associations and incorporations repeal a special act exempting the property of a certain corporation "so long as the same shall continue to belong to" the corporation?

Decision: "The plaintiffs claim that the exemption conceded by the Act of 1833 is perpetual, and that the Act itself is in effect a contract. This concession of the Legislature was spontaneous, and no service or duty, or other remunerative condition, was imposed on the corporation. It belongs to the class of laws denominated privilegia favorabilia. It attached only to such property as belonged to the corporation, and while it remained as its property; but it is not a necessary implication from these facts that the concession is perpetual, or was designed to continue during the corporate existence. Such an interpretation is not to be favored, as the power of taxation is necessary to the existence of the state, and must be exerted according to the varying conditions of the commonwealth. The Act of 1833 belongs to a class of statutes in which the narrowest meaning is to be taken which will fairly carry out the intent of the Legislature."

CHRISTIE-STREET COM. CO. v. UNITED STATES
(Circuit Court of Appeals, Eighth Circuit, March 27, 1905)
(136 Fed. 327)

Record: Act of March 3, 1887, and Rev. Stat. Sec. 3227. Action at law to recover taxes paid under protest under this Act. Demurrer was sustained and action dismissed (129 Fed. 506) and plaintiff brought error. Affirmed.

Facts: Plaintiff in his petition sets forth that after payment of taxes under the war revenue Act of 1898 under protest, the Commissioner of Internal Revenue decided that the money thus collected had been erroneously taken; that he agreed to repay them; and thereupon the plaintiff presented his claim to him for the repayment of the moneys, but the Commissioner never either allowed or disallowed the claim. Plaintiff brought this suit to recover said taxes against the United States, the action being commenced more than two years after the cause of action accrued. Plaintiff brought suit under authority of the Act of March 3, 1887, which was a general Act conferring jurisdiction upon the federal courts in numerous classes of claims founded upon laws of Congress. It contained a provision that suit should be brought within six years after the right accrued. Sec. 3227 Rev. Stat., passed subsequently to the Act of 1887, placed a limitation of two years upon the bringing of suits for recovery of internal revenue taxes.

Questions: (1) May one whose claim for a repayment of internal revenue taxes illegally collected has been presented to, but has not been allowed by the Commissioner of Internal Revenue, maintain an action against the United States to recover those taxes under authority of the Act of March 3, 1887?

(2) If so, does the limitation of two years fixed by section 3227 Rev. Stat., or the limitation of six years provided by section 1 of the Act of 1887, fix the time within which the action may be successfully brought?

Decision: (1) A claim to recover internal taxes exacted under a misconstruction of the war revenue law of 1898 is a claim founded on a law of Congress, within the true meaning of the Act of March 3, 1887; and it may be enforced by an action directly against the United States under that Act after it has been presented to the Commissioner of Internal Revenue, whether it has received his approval or not, and whether it is an action on a contract or an action sounding in tort.

(2) "The limitation of two years prescribed by section 3227 of the Revised Statutes for the commencement of actions to recover back internal taxes illegally exacted is not inconsistent with and is not repealed by, the Act of March 3, 1887, which provides that no suits shall be allowed under that law unless they are brought within six years after the causes of action respectively accrue."

CINCINNATI G. & E. CO. v. GILLIGAN, COLLECTOR
(U. S. District Court, S. D. Ohio, W. D.)
(Not reported)

Record: Suit to recover taxes paid. Demurrer to petition sustained.

Facts: The taxes were paid to Mr. Gilligan's predecessor in office, Mr. Bettman.

Question: May a suit be maintained against a collector for recovery of taxes collected by his predecessor?

Decision: Suits against collecting officers to recover taxes ordinarily should be brought against the officer who collected them, and not against his successor. That is the reason for the rule requiring protest at the time the taxes are paid and notice that suit will be brought to recover the taxes paid, to enable the collecting officer to protect himself, as far as he may, upon making settlement with the government. Therefore, the present suit could not be maintained.

CITY OF SUPERIOR v. ALLOUEZ BAY DOCK CO.
(Supreme Court of Wisconsin, May 15, 1917)
(166 Wis. 76; 164 N. W. 362)

Record: Wisconsin Rev. Stats. Sec. 5102. Action of debt to recover income tax assessed against defendants. Judgment for defendant, and plaintiff appeals. Affirmed.

Facts: The defendant corporation operated ore docks at Superior, which formed the lake terminal of the Great Northern R. R. Co. All the ore handled was consigned to Eastern ports; the railroad cars carrying the ore were run out upon the elevated dock; and the ore was dumped immediately into lake vessels or deposited in pockets to be run into lake vessels a few days later by the defendant. The defendant was assessed upon its net income derived from handling the ore. There was a statute exempting railroad companies, and defining railroad company, as any corporation "owning or operating any station, depot, track terminal or bridge for railroad purposes."

Questions: (1) Is a tax upon a corporation engaged in unloading railroad cars carrying ore consigned to Eastern ports, and in the loading the same on vessels, a burden upon interstate commerce?

(2) Is a corporation so engaged a railroad company within the meaning of an act which defined a railroad company as any corporation owning a terminal for railroad purposes?

Decisions: (1) "Income taxation is not taxation of property, but is more nearly akin to taxes levied upon privileges or occupations. Its amount may be measured by the receipts of a business; but it is not in any true sense a tax upon the business itself, and so is not a burden on interstate commerce."

(2) "The State, perceiving that this business is, under such circumstances, simply a branch of the railroad business, directs that it be taxed in the same class with railroad companies." The language used by the statute covered and exempted the defendant corporation.

CLOPTON v. PHILADELPHIA & READING R. R. CO.

(Supreme Court of Pennsylvania, February 21, 1867)

(54 Penn. 356)

Record: Bill in equity to compel the payment of interest without deduction. Bill dismissed, and plaintiff appealed. Affirmed.

Facts: The plaintiff was a holder of bonds of defendants secured by a mortage which provided that the defendants would pay interest on the bonds "without any deduction, defalcation or abatement to be made of anything for or in respect of any taxes, charges or assessments whatsoever." The defendants paid the United States taxes chargeable upon the holders of the bonds secured by mortgages, and withheld that amount out of the interest due the plaintiff.

Question: Is the federal tax upon bonds a tax such that the one issuing the bonds is liable for the tax where he has covenanted to pay the holder interest without deductions for taxes?

Decision: "The taxes, charges and assessments referred to are those which may be charged upon the premises conveyed in the mortgage, * * * The tax levied by the United States Government is a tax upon the debt secured by the mortgage, and not a tax upon the debtor. The company is constituted the agent of the government to collect the tax, but the burden of collecting it is imposed upon the bondholder." The company was, therefore, entitled to withhold from the interest the amount of tax which it had paid.

COCHRAN et al. v. UNITED STATES
(U. S. Supreme Court, January 3, 1921)
(254 U. S. 387)

Record: Act of June 13, 1898, and repealing clause in Act of April 12, 1902. Suit by executors of estate of William F. Cochran, deceased, against the United States to recover taxes paid under the War Revenue Act of June 13, 1898, and amendments, upon certain legacies made in decedent's will. Judgment of Court of Claims against claimants denying right of recovery (54 Ct. Cls. 219). Appeal from Court of Claims. Judgment affirmed.

Facts: Cochran died on December 27, 1901, leaving a will and a personal estate. Letters testamentary were issued January 9, 1902. The time for presentation of claims expired August 4, 1902. Prior to September 30, 1902, debts and claims against the estate were presented, and for the most part paid. Litigation was in progress which might involve the payment of several hundred thousands of dollars. The tax law was repealed on July 1, 1902, upon which date the value of the residuary estate had not been ascertained. In compliance with Sec. 30 of the Act of June 13, 1898, the executors on February 17, 1903, made a return and filed it with the collector of internal revenue, giving a schedule of the legacies arising from the personal property of the estate and the amount of tax due thereon. The collector accepted this as correct. The schedule showed the taxes on each legacy, and the total which was paid. On July 16, 1904, a demand was made upon the Commissioner of Internal Revenue for the repayment to the executors of the sum paid, on the ground that no tax was ever payable because of the repeal of the law prior to any assessment of tax. On March 15, 1915, the Commissioner recommended the claim for allowance in part and for rejection in part, refusing to refund the tax upon the interests of eight different legatees, of which six were residuary legatees. The Government claims that if an assessment was necessary the right to make it was reserved by the repealing Act, and that the making by the appellees as executors of a report of the legacies and the taxes thereon, and its acceptance by the collector was to all intents and purposes an assessment.

Question: What construction is to be placed on the word "imposed" as used in the clause of the repealing act of April 12, 1902, which provides that "all taxes or duties imposed by Section 29 and amendments thereof prior to the taking effect" of the repealing Act should "be subject, as to lien, charge, collection and otherwise to the provisions of Section 30 and amendments thereof" and be "continued in force?"

Decision: The reasonable certainty of the amount of tax, where a return was rendered scheduling the legacies and the tax due thereon, and where no liability requiring repayment of the legacies has developed after 14 years, warrants the conclusion that the tax assessed was therefore "imposed" prior to the taking effect of the repealing act of April 12, 1902. "We cannot agree that there was uncertainty. We have seen the amount of taxes imposed by the statute was definite and the appellants had no trouble in estimating and returning the value of the legacies on which it was imposed. The basis of the claim of uncertainty is that the estate was and is not settled and that there is a possibility that the legatees may be called upon to pay debts. This contention is as strained and baseless as that rejected in Simpson v. United States, 252 U. S. 547. * * * It is to be remembered besides that the case does not present a case of resistance to the payment of the tax, but of the recovery of taxes voluntarily paid; and that, therefore, the legality of them should be shown not only by averment but by proof." Since the legacies that had been paid prior to July 1, 1902, were taxable, the tax had been imposed on them, and so it was not refundable because of the repealing statute of April 12, 1902.

CODMAN v. AMERICAN PIANO CO.
(Supreme Judicial Court of Massachusetts, January 14, 1918)
(229 Mass. 285; 118 N. E. 344)

Record: Act of Oct. 3, 1913. Action of contract against the company to recover amount of federal income taxes. Judgment for defendant.

Facts: The defendant company is a lessee holding under a lease from the plaintiff, in which it covenanted to pay "all taxes and assessments whatsoever which may be payable for or in respect of the leased premises." The lessor was assessed and paid an income tax on the rent received, and sues to collect that amount from the lessee.

Question: Is the federal income tax upon rent which the lessor receives a tax payable for or in respect of the leased premises?

Decision: "Such an assessment is upon an entirely distinct kind of property than is the assessment upon the real estate. While under the federal income tax law a tax on rent is a tax on land and so a direct tax, yet a tax on land is not a tax on rent; the defendant did not covenant to pay taxes for or in respect of the rent; his undertaking is to pay the taxes for or in respect of the premises." The tenant was, therefore, not liable for the income tax on the rent.

COHEN v. LOWE, COLLECTOR
(U. S. District Court, New York, July 18, 1916)
(234 Fed. 474)

Record: Act of October 3, 1913. Action at law to recover taxes paid under protest. Judgment for defendant.

Facts: The plaintiff contends that the amount of income tax paid to the Government for the year 1913 was excessive in three respects: First, the 3% allowed for depreciation on an apartment building owned by the plaintiff is not sufficient, the rental value of the building having decreased because of a change in the neighborhood, and the construction of more modern buildings; second, that a part of the profits upon which he has been assessed were earned by a partnership, composed of the plaintiff and others, before the act became effective; third, the surtaxes were assessed upon the plaintiff's net income in excess of $20,000 without deducting the exemptions that apply in computing the net income subject to the normal tax.

Questions: (1) Is an allowance of 3% for depreciation a reasonable allowance, and should the depreciation allowance reflect the diminished rental value due to the construction of more modern buildings or to a change in the neighborhood?

(2) Is the burden of proof upon the one suing to recover taxes to show that the taxes were excessive?

(3) In assessing the additional tax or surtax on the excess of the plaintiff's net income over $20,000, are the same exemptions to be made as in computing the net income subject to the normal tax?

Decision: (1) "This allowance is for the wear and tear suffered by the building during the tax year, which means the physical deterioration that the building suffered during that period. It does not take into account depreciation in value, due to a loss in rental value because of the construction of more modern buildings with improved facilities, or due to a change in the neighborhood. It is to be based upon the life of the building, in the sense of the number of years the building would remain in a condition to be habitable for the uses for which it was constructed

and used, and which was in the instant case for an apartment
house, and not merely the number of years it would stand without being condemned and torn down. The annual depreciation
would be an amount represented by a fraction having one, the
tax year, for the numerator and the number of years, representing
the ascertained life of the building, as the denominator. This as-
sumes that there would be an average deterioration suffered each
year during the life of the building, and that the plaintiff would
keep the building in good repair during the life of it. This the
law exacts of him. Upon these assumptions, and giving this meaning to the words of the statute, 'a reasonable allowance for the exhaustion, wear and tear of the property arising out of its use or
employment in the business,' the amount of the deduction allowed
by the government to the plaintiff on this account is deemed to be
reasonable.''

(2) ''The plaintiff suing to recover a tax claimed to be excessive, has the burden of showing its illegality, and in this
case must show that profits were earned by the partnership prior
to March 1, 1913, and in what sum. * * * It may well have
been that no profits accrued to the partnership till after March 1,
1913, and that none were taxed accordingly, except such as were
properly subject to the tax. In the absence of a showing to the
contrary, the court must assume that the tax was legally collected;
the burden being on the plaintiff to establish its illegality.''

(3) The law ''provides that the additional tax shall be
assessed on the excess of net income over and above $20,000. If
the exemptions that apply in favor of the normal tax, are extended also to the surtax, the result would follow that the excess
taxed would be that over and above a net income of $20,000, plus
the respective exemptions in favor of single or married persons,
as the case might be.'' These exemptions, the court said, are not
expressly or impliedly allowed.

COLE v. RALPH
(U. S. Supreme Court, March 15, 1920)
(252 U. S. 286)

Record: Act of October 22, 1914. Two writs of certiorari
to the United States Circuit Court of Appeals for the Ninth Cir-

cuit to review judgments which reversed judgments of the District Court in favor of plaintiffs, and ordered a new trial. Judgment of the Circuit Court of Appeals reversed and judgment of the District Court affirmed.

Facts: Certain deeds showing title in some of the plaintiffs, which were without the stamps required by the Act of October 22, 1914, were received in evidence over defendant's objection in the U. S. District Court of Nevada.

Question: Are deeds without the stamps required by the Act admissible as evidence in the U. S. District Court?

Decision: It is true that the deeds showing title in some of the plaintiffs—they were received in evidence over the defendant's objection—were without the stamps required by the Act of October 22, 1914, Chap. 331, Section 22, Schedule A., 38 Stat. at L. 762. But this neither invalidated the deeds nor made them inadmissible as evidence. The relevant provisions of that Act, though otherwise following the language of earlier acts, do not contain the words of those acts which made such an instrument invalid and inadmissible as evidence while not properly stamped. These words were carefully omitted, as will be seen by contrasting Sections 6, 11, 12 and 13 of the Act of 1914 with Sections 7, 13, 14 and 15 of the Act of June 13, 1898.''

COLLECTOR v. DAY

(U. S. Supreme Court, April 3, 1871)

(78 U. S. 113)

Record: Civil War Income Tax Law. Action at law to recover taxes paid. Judgment for plaintiff and defendant brought error. Reversed.

Facts: Plaintiff was required by the Federal Government to pay a tax on his salary received in 1866 and 1867 from the State of Massachusetts as a probate judge of that state.

Question: Can Congress, under the Constitution of the United States, impose a tax upon the salary of a judicial officer of a state?

Decision: "In the case of Dobbins v. Erie Co., 16 Peters 435, it was decided that it was not competent for the legislature of a state to levy a tax upon the salary or emoluments of an officer of the U. S. The decision was placed mainly upon the ground that the officer was a means or instrumentality employed for carrying into effect some of the legitimate powers of the government, which could not be interferred with by taxation or otherwise by the states, and that the salary or compensation was inseparably connected with the office * * * ." The same construction of the Constitution prohibits the Federal Government from taxing the salary of a state judicial officer. "It is a familiar rule of construction of the Constitution of the Union, that the sovereign powers vested in the state governments by their respective constitutions remained unaltered and unimpaired, except so far as they were granted to the government of the United States. The general government, and the states, although both exist within the same territorial limits, are separable and distinct sovereignties, acting separately and independently of each other, within their respective spheres. The former in its appropriate sphere is supreme; but the states within the limits of their powers not granted, or in the language of the Tenth Amendment, 'reserved,' are as independent of the general government as that government within its sphere is independent of the states."

In view of the separate and independent condition of the State and Federal Governments, and the existence of which is so indispensible, it follows "that the means and instrumentalities employed for carrying on the operations of their governments, for preserving their existence, and fulfilling the high and responsible duties assigned to them in the Constitution, should be left free and unimpaired; should not be liable to be crippled, much less defeated by the taxing power of another government, which power acknowledges no limits, but the will of the legislative body imposing the tax."

COLLECTOR v. HUBBARD
(U. S. Supreme Court, April 10, 1871)
(79 U. S. 1)

Record: Act of June 30, 1864. Action at law to recover taxes paid under protest. Judgment for plaintiff and defendant brought error. Reversed.

Facts: Plaintiff, the majority stockholder in two different manufacturing corporations, was assessed on his aliquot part of the annual earnings of such corporations, notwithstanding the fact that said earnings were used by the corporations to pay their debts incurred in previous years, and to purchase additional assets, and had never been received by plaintiff as a regularly declared dividend. Plaintiff made no appeal to the Commissioner of Internal Revenue, but paid the amount of tax due into the Treasury of the United States before bringing suit to recover taxes in the Connecticut State Court.

Questions: (1) Under the Act of June 30, 1864, is a stockholder in a corporation required to pay tax on that portion of the earnings used by the corporation to pay debts incurred previous to the taxable year and to purchase additional assets?

(2) Did the failure of plaintiff to make appeal to the Commissioner of Internal Revenue bar his suit to recover taxes in the State Court?

Decision: (1) "Section 117 of the Act of June 30, 1864, declares what shall be included in estimating the annual gains, profits, income of any person, and among other things, expressly provides that the gains and profits of all companies, whether incorporated or partnership, other than the companies specified in that section, shall be included in estimating the annual gains, profits or income of any person entitled to the same, whether divided or otherwise." 13 Stat. at L. 282. Manufacturing companies are not mentioned in Section 117, but the words "all companies" as used in this section include manufacturing companies. When Section 117 above is read with Sections 120, 121 and 122 it is clear "that the policy of Congress was to tax all gains and profits whether divided or undivided, and that the construction that the undivided gains and profits of manufacturing companies are properly included in that rule is just and reasonable."

(2) The 19th section of the Act of July 13, 1866, provides that no suit shall be maintained "in any court" to recover a tax illegally assessed until the taxpayer has made an appeal to the Commissioner of Internal Revenue, and such appeal has been decided by him. This provision operates on all suits brought in State courts as well as in Federal.

COMM'L TRAVELERS LIFE & ACCIDENT ASS'N v. RODWAY, COLLECTOR

(U. S. District Court, N. D. Ohio, E. D. Dec. 3, 1913)

(235 Fed. 370)

Record: Act of Aug. 5, 1909. Action at law to recover taxes paid under protest under Section 38 of this Act. Judgment for defendant.

Facts: The plaintiff insurance company was organized under the statutes of Ohio as a mutual protective association. It collects assessments from its members and disburses the same in the payment of benefits on the death or injury of members. Its only source of revenue was assessments paid by its members. After losses sustained during the year and expenses of administration were paid, the surplus, if any, was paid into a reserve fund, which fund is the sole and only resource for the payment of losses, should any occur in excess of the amount of net income during any year. The net income each year is paid into the reserve fund in order to have on hand sufficient reserves to meet the outstanding liabilities of the association. The plaintiff corporation does not pay dividends to any of its members.

Questions: (1) Is plaintiff an insurance company and not a fraternal benefit society, and, therefore, subject to the Act of Aug. 5, 1909, Section 38?

(2) Is the collection of assessments and payment of benefits by plaintiff a "doing business" within the provision of the Act?

Decision: (1) Plaintiff organization is an insurance company within the purview of the Act. It cannot be classed as one of the companies specifically exempted from the operation of the Statute, as it does not fall within the legal definition of a fraternal beneficiary association. Congress used this term according to its legal significance at the time the Act was passed. After an examination of a number of representative cases and state statutes, defining the term, the court concluded that no State has a definition of a fraternal beneficiary association, which would include an organization doing the business of the plaintiff and organized as it is. The facts in the case do not show that the plaintiff was engaged in a work, fraternal and beneficiary in character. The absence of a profit in the operation of the association is not a criterion, but rather the lack of a fraternal side and object, which it is in some measure organized to promote.

(2) "The transactions in which plaintiff deems itself engaged constitute doing business as the term is used in the Act, for that expression unquestionably means the substantial doing of some work or exercise of some functions for which the corporation was created."

COMMISSIONER v. BUCHNER
(U. S. Circuit Court, D. Ky., Dec. 1, 1891)
(48 Fed. 533)

Record: Special Act of June 16, 1890, entitled "An act for the relief of the board of the commissioners of the sinking fund of the City of Louisville, Kentucky." Action at law to recover taxes alleged to have been illegally collected. Judgment for defendants.

Facts: The City of Louisville, Kentucky, was during the taxable periods in question a large stockholder in the Louisville & Nashville Railroad Company. Under various acts of Congress said railroad voluntarily paid a tax upon its gross earnings, undivided surplus and dividends, including the share of the City of Louisville. No application for the refund had been made within the time or in the manner required by the Acts of Congress. Congress passed a Special Act on June 16, 1890, as follows:

"That the Secretary of the Treasury and the Commissioner of Internal Revenue be, and they are hereby, authorized and required to audit and adjust the claim of the board of the sinking fund commissioners of the City of Louisville, Kentucky, for internal revenue taxes on dividends on shares of stock owned by said board for said City of Louisville in the Louisville & Nashville Railroad Company, to the extent that such taxes were deducted from any dividends due and payable to said board, and to pass upon said claim, and render judgment thereon in the same manner, and with the same effect, as if said claim had been presented and prosecuted within the time limited and fixed by law.''

Plaintiffs presented their claim under the special act of June 16, 1890, quoted above, and was allowed $42,514.03. This sum was a refund of taxes collected on dividends which had been paid to the City of Louisville by the Louisville & Nashville Railroad.

Question: Can the plaintiff recover interest on the amount of taxes refunded under the above circumstances?

Decision: The taxes were originally paid without protest, no appeal was taken to the commissioner of internal revenue, and no demand made for repayment. In view of this no interest would have been allowed on the claim under the general law if it had been prosecuted before the statute had run to completion. The Special Act of June 16, 1890, authorized judgment to be rendered on the claim ''in the same manner and with the same effect as if said claim had been presented and prosecuted within the time fixed by law.'' Held, no right to interest given thereby.

COMMONWEALTH v. OCEAN OIL CO.
(Supreme Court of Pennsylvania, May 18, 1868)
(59 Penn. State 61)

Record: Income Tax Law of Pennsylvania. Appeal from settlement of the Auditor-General and State Treasurer. The Commonwealth appealed from a judgment for only a part of the tax claimed. Judgment reversed and venire de novo awarded.

Facts: An oil company, capitalized at $1,000,000, which had already paid dividends of over $600,000, claimed that it made no net earnings until the entire $1,000,000 had been returned to the stockholders. The trial court instructed the jury that if the company was dividing and consuming its capital, this fact might be taken into consideration in fixing the amount to be recovered by the Commonwealth.

Question: Did the entire net earnings of the corporation for the year involved constitute taxable income under the statute in question?

Decision: "The income * * * after deducting all expenses appear to have been paid to the shareholders as dividends, and were, no doubt, advertised as such, thus enhancing largely the value of the stock in the market. When capital is paid into a corporation * * * it is presumed to remain until its dissolution. The value of the stock into which it is divided may rise and fall, according to the success of the enterprise. Capital may be utterly lost, the theory of incorporated companies being that capital invested remains either really or nominally to their close. The plaintiff company pays dividends which are, of course, its net present earnings or income, and it is the net income, whether declared or not, the state intended to tax. This is the plain common sense use of the term made familiar to everyone since the formation of the internal revenue system." Lower court, therefore, was held to be in error in allowing a portion of the net earnings to be applied to the reduction of the capital stock instead of being taxed as income.

COMMONWEALTH v. PENN. GAS COAL CO.
(Supreme Court of Pennsylvania, July 6, 1869)
(62 Penn. 241)

Record: Act of April 30, 1864. Action at law to recover taxes paid. Judgment for plaintiff, and defendant brought error. Reversed.

Facts: Plaintiff is a corporation organized under the laws of Pennsylvania for the purpose of mining coal. In estimating net income for the purpose of taxation plaintiff had deducted the value of the amount of coal exhausted during the taxable years in question.

Question: Under the Act of April 30, 1864, may the value of coal exhausted in mining be deducted from receipts in estimating the net earnings of a corporation?

Decision: This case cannot be distinguished from Commonwealth v. The Ocean Oil Co. 59 Penn. 61. "All capitals of mining companies, whether of coal, iron, copper, tin or silver, and so of quarrying companies, whether of stone, marble or slate, are nominal like those of petroleum companies, and fixed by their promoters at such large figures, that, by applying the principle of returning capital before returning income, the whole annual income would have to be retained to supply the loss of capital, which would disappoint the stockholders of their dividends and the state of her taxes. The difficulties pointed out in our former opinion, of adopting and applying any such principle to these companies make it necessary to establish one general invariable rule that the net earnings or income are the product of the business after deducting the expenses only.''

COMMONWEALTH v. STANDARD OIL CO.
(Supreme Court of Pennsylvania, May, 1882)
(101 Penn. 119)

Record: Acts of May 1, 1868, April 24, 1874, March 20, 1877, June 7, 1879. Action at law to recover taxes and penalties. Judgment for plaintiff and defendant brought error. Reversed.

Facts: The defendant, an oil company, was chartered by the state of Ohio with authority to manufacture and deal in petroleum products. Defendant bought petroleum in Pennsylvania through brokers and others, but never made a permanent investment in that state. The petroleum was shipped out of Pennsylvania for the purpose of refining. Defendant corporation owned interests in individual partnerships, limited partnerships and shares of stock in corporations doing business in Pennsylvania as producers, refiners and transporters of oil. Defendant never received any special authority to transact business in Pennsylvania.

For additional facts see second question.

Questions: (1) Do the above facts constitute a doing of business in the state of Pennsylvania so as to subject the defendant to taxation under the acts of May 1, 1868, April 24, 1874, March 20, 1877, and June 7, 1879, requiring foreign corporations doing business in Pennsylvania to pay a certain tax upon their capital stock?

(2) Where a statute contained a section imposing a penalty upon any corporation that neglected or refused to make the report

therein required, is repealed and another is enacted, saving the right to collect any tax accrued or accruing under the prior act, can the state recover a tax and penalty assessed under the prior statute when suit was not commenced at the time of its repeal?

Decision: (1) The power of taxation is limited to subjects within the jurisdiction of the state, and it was not the intent of these acts to tax the whole capital stock of foreign corporations, irrespective of the plan of its investment, but to tax the property of such company, that is, its capital stock to the extent that it brings such property within the state in the transaction of its business. The defendant did not actually or constructively bring all of its capital stock into the state of Pennsylvania. The defendant is taxable only on so much of its capital stock as represents the proportion which its property and assets invested in the individual partnership, bore to its entire property and assets. The defendant oil company, being domiciled in Ohio, from which it cannot migrate, is not taxable upon such portion of its capital stock as represents the shares of stock in Pennsylvania corporations or the interests in the limited partnerships aforesaid. Defendant is not taxable upon that portion of its capital stock used in the purchase of oil in the state of Ohio through its agents.

(2) "The law upon this state of facts is well settled. The commonwealth reserved the right to collect this tax only. The right to the penalties was gone. No judgment can be rendered in any suit for a penalty after the repeal of the act by which it was imposed. The repeal of a statute puts an end to all suits founded upon it, even thought commenced before the date of the repeal. In reserving in the repealing acts all taxes accrued and accruing, the Commonwealth reserved the right to employ all the ordinary remedies for their collection. But the penalties are in no sense such remedy. They are merely a punishment for the omission to make the reports required by the law. * * * Penal statutes must be construed strictly, and never extended by implication."

COMMONWEALTH v. WERTH
(Superior Court of Appeals, Va., Sept. 7, 1914)

(82 S. E. 695, 116 Va. 604)

Record: Virginia Acts of 1902-04, C. 148, as amended by Act March 14, 1912, c. 279. Action by the State to recover income tax. Judgment for defendant, and plaintiff brought error. Reversed.

Facts: The defendant, a citizen and resident of Virginia, received an income from the practice of law in that state, for the year 1913, in excess of $2,000. By Schedule D of the Act in question, income included: (1) rents, salaries, interest; (2) premiums on gold, silver, or coupons; (3) amount of sales of live stock and meat; (4) amount of sales of wood, butter, cheese, etc.; and (5) "All other gains and profits derived from any source whatever."

Questions: (1) Must the fifth clause of Schedule D be limited to income derived from sources of the same character as the one enumerated in previous clauses in accordance with the doctrine of ejusdem generis, and if so, will such construction relieve the defendant from taxation on his professional income?

(2) Is taxing the income of a lawyer double taxation since he is required to pay a license tax?

Decision: (1) The doctrine of ejusdem generis does not apply because the language of the statute, read as a whole, leaves no escape from the conclusion that it was the intention of the legislature to impose a tax on incomes generally. But even if the doctrine were applicable, the result would be the same, for "all salaries" are included in Schedule D, and salaries of judges, lawyers, physicians, who receive compensation in that way, are similar in kind to earnings received in the form of fees.

(2) There is no double taxation in this case. A license tax is distinguishable from an income tax because it is exacted for the privilege of engaging in a particular vocation or business, and is not a tax on the income from such vocation or business.

CONANT v. KINNEY
(U. S. Circuit Court, D. R. I., June 24, 1908)
(162 Fed. 581)

Record: Revenue Statute Section 3220. (U. S. Comp. St. 1901, p. 2086.) Action at law, to recover a legacy tax paid under protest.

Facts: See Question.

Question: Should judgment against a collector of internal revenue for an amount of tax collected by him without legal authority include interest from the time of payment of such tax to the date of entry of judgment?

Decision: The following language of the statute is broad enough to cover interest. " * * * also to repay any collector or deputy collector the full amount of such sums of money as may be recovered against him in any court for any internal taxes collected by him with the costs and expenses of suit, also all damages and costs recovered against any assessor, assistant assessor, collector, deputy collector or inspector, in any suit brought against him by reason of anything done in the performance of his official duty." (Rev. St. Sec. 3220.) A suit against a collector of internal revenue to recover with interest taxes assessed without legal authority is not a suit against the United States, even where the collector is required by law to pay into the U. S. Treasury each day all sums collected by him.

CRAIG v. DIMOCK
(Supreme Court of Ill., January, 1868)
(47 Ill. 308)

Record: Act of June 30, 1864. Action at law to replevin personal property levied on in behalf of judgment creditor. Judgment for plaintiff and defendant appeals. Affirmed.

Facts: .A chattel mortgage filed for record prior to the levy in favor of a judgment creditor, did not contain a revenue stamp as required by the Act of June 30, 1864.

Question: Was the above described mortgage admissible in evidence in a state court, though containing no revenue stamp?

Decision: While Congress has the power to require instruments, created and valid under State laws, to be stamped, and has the consequent power to punish by fine, any intentional evasion of the law in that regard, yet it has not the power to require such instruments to be stamped as a prerequisite to their validity and binding force, or to their admissibility in evidence in the State court. Congress has power to prescribe rules of evidence, and specify what shall be instruments of evidence in the Federal courts, but it belongs to the States exclusively to declare what shall be received in evidence in their own courts.

CRAWFORD v. NEW SOUTH FARM & HOME CO.
(U. S. District Court, S. D. Florida, Oct. 7, 1915)
(231 Fed. 999)

Record: Act of October 22, 1914. In equity. Suit by William Crawford, as trustee, against the New South Farm & Home Co. On master's request for instructions. Master instructed in accordance with the opinion.

Facts: This matter comes before the court upon the report of the special master appointed by the court to make a sale of the property and execute a conveyance. The master asked instructions upon the questions stated below.

Questions: (1) Should documentary revenue stamps be attached to the master's deed made pursuant to decree of the court?

(2) If so, then what amount?

Decision: (1) "As I read the various cases deciding questions relating to the taxing acts by the Congress, the test seems to be whether the act involves the performance of a judicial duty, such as the certificate of the notary to the depositions, etc., or is a mere ministerial act. Now it does not appear that a special master appointed to make a sale of property and execute a conveyance to same is performing any judicial function under order of the court. But, it is said, it is the court making the sale and conveying the property through its master. Would Congress have a right to tax a proceeding by this court? Is this such taxation, or is it not a taxation on the litigants? The title sold and conveyed is the title of the defendant, in the action, not the title held by the court or its officer. By the master's deed only the title possessed by the defendant is conveyed. Instead of the defendants actually making the deed (in which case stamps would clearly have to be affixed), his title is conveyed through the master to the purchaser at the foreclosure sale. On principle I cannot see that this should make the stamps requirement of the act inapplicable to master's deeds."

(2) "The amount of such stamps is 50 cents for the first $500 of the consideration, and can be readily arrived at by a computation."

CROCKER et al., TRUSTEES, v. MALLEY, COLLECTOR
(U. S. Supreme Court, March 17, 1919)
(249 U. S. 223)

Record: Act of Oct. 3, 1913. Action at law to recover taxes paid under protest. Circuit Court of Appeals ordered judgment for the defendant (250 Fed. 817), reversing judgment of District Court. Judgment of Circuit Court of Appeals reversed.

Facts: A Maine paper manufacturing corporation conveyed and leased to a corporation formed in Massachusetts, its mills and lands, receiving the stock of the Massachusetts corporation in return. The Maine corporation then transferred to the plaintiffs as trustees the fee of the property subject to lease, left the Massachusetts stock in their hands, and was dissolved. By the declaration of trust the plaintiffs declared that they held the real estate and all other property at any time received by them thereunder, subject to the provisions thereof, "for the benefit of the cestui que trusts (who shall be trust beneficiaries only, without partnership, associate or other relation whatever inter sese)," upon trust to convert the same into money and distribute the net proceeds to the persons then holding the trustees' receipt certificates—the time of distribution being left to the discretion of the trustees, but not to be postponed beyond the end of twenty years after the death of specified persons then living. In the meantime the trustees were to have the powers of owners. They were to distribute what they determined to be fairly distributable net income, according to the interests of the cestui que trusts, but could apply any funds in their hands for the repair or development of the property held by them, or the acquisition of other property, pending conversion and distribution. The trust was declared to be for the benefit of the eight shareholders of the Maine company who were to receive certificates subject to transfer and subdivision. A written consent of a majority in interest of the cestui que trusts was required for the filling of a vacancy among the trustees, and for a modification of the terms of the trust. In no other matter had the beneficiaries any control. The title of the trust was fixed for convenience as the Massachusetts (sic; in fact—Wachusett) Realty Trust.

Questions: (1) Should plaintiffs be assessed as a joint stock association within the meaning of the Income Tax Act of Oct. 3, 1913, or were they simply trustees, and subject to the duties imposed upon fiduciaries by the Act?

(2) If the latter, may the government retain the amount of taxes that should have been paid by the plaintiffs as trustees?

Decision: (1) "There can be little doubt that in Massachusetts this arrangement would be held to create a trust and nothing more. 'The certificate holders * * * are in no way associated together nor is there any provision in the [instrument] for any meeting to be held by them. The only act which (under the [declaration of] trust) they can do is to consent to an alteration * * * of the trust' and to the other matters that we have mentioned. Williams v. Milton, 215 Mass. 1, 10, 11; ibid. 8. * * * The question is whether a different view is required by the terms of the present act. * * * The trustees by themselves cannot be a joint-stock association within the meaning of the act unless all trustees with discretionary powers are such, and the special provision for trustees in [section] D is to be made meaningless. We perceive no ground for grouping the two—beneficiaries and trustees —together, in order to turn them into an association, by uniting their contrasted functions and powers, although they are in no proper sense associated. It seems to be an unnatural perversion of a well known institution of the law.

"We do not see either that the result is affected by any technical analysis of the individual receipt holders' rights in the income received by the trustees. * * * But even if it were said that the receipt holders were not entitled to the income as such until they got it, we do not discern how that would turn them into a joint-stock company. Moreover, the receipt holders did get it, and the question is what portion it was the duty of the trustees to withhold."

(2) "The District Court, while it found for the plaintiffs, ruled that the defendant was entitled to retain out of the sum received by him the amount of the tax that they should have paid as trustees. To this the plaintiffs took a cross writ of error to the Circuit Court of Appeals. There can be no question that although the plaintiffs escape the larger liability, there was probable cause for the defendant's act. The Commissioner of Internal Revenue rejected the plaintiff's claim, and the statute does not leave the matter clear. The recovery, therefore, will be from the United States. Rev. Sts., Sec. 989. The plaintiffs, as they themselves alleged in their claim, were the persons taxed, whether they were called an association or trustees. They were taxed too much. If the United States retains from the amount received by it the amount that it should have received, it cannot recover that sum in a subsequent suit." It was, therefore, held that the collector should not be required to pay back more than the excess over the amount properly payable by the plaintiffs as trustees.

CRYAN v. WARDELL, COLLECTOR

(U. S. District Court, N. D. Calif. 2nd Div., Feb. 2, 1920)

(263 Fed. 248)

Record: Revenue Act of 1916. Action at law to recover taxes paid. Judgment for defendant.

Facts: Plaintiff was the owner of a lot upon which her tenant erected a building in 1910. The lease made by plaintiff in 1908 was for a term of 26 years, and provided that "in no event shall the lessee hereunder have any right to remove any building from said premises." In 1916 the tenant defaulting in accrued rent, the lease was terminated and possession of the premises surrendered to plaintiff.

Question: Is the lessor required to pay an income tax in 1916 on the value of a building surrendered to him in that year, under the Act of 1916, where the tenant erected the building several years prior to the Act?

Decision: The government contended that under the following provision of the act and regulation made thereunder plaintiff should pay tax on the value of the building as income.

"The net income of a taxable person shall include gains, profits, and income derived from * * * sales, or dealings in property, whether real or personal, growing out of the ownership or use of or interest in real or personal property, also from interest, rent, dividends, * * * or gains * * * from any source whatever." Sec. 2A, Revenue Act of 1916.

"Permanent improvements under lease or rental contracts, when improvements become a part of real estate, the difference between cost of the improvements and allowable depreciation during the lease term, is gain or profit to the lessor at the end of the lease term, and is to be accounted for as income at that time." Paragraph 50, Reg. No. 33, Treasury Department.

The moment the building was erected title passed to the plaintiff. The terms of the lease show that the building was "to become and remain an integral part of the land upon which it was constructed, and title thereto vested as completely in the plaintiff as though constructed by plaintiff herself." The erection of the building was a part of the consideration of the lease, and was taken into consideration when the rent was reserved. When completed in 1910, it became income bearing property, and was subject to taxation as of that date. "The regulation of the Treasury Department cannot be applied to such a state of facts, if so intended, it must give way, as the Department has no power to abrogate a substantive rule of law." Whatever accession of value resulting to plaintiff's property accrued and became vested in 1910 prior to the enactment under which the tax was levied and cannot, therefore, be taxed.

DALE ads. ADAMS
(Supreme Court of Indiana, 1868)
(29 Ind. 273)

Record: Action on written contract. Appeal from decision of the trial court overruling demurrers to the complaint. Judgment reversed.

Facts: Among the points raised by the defendant was the contention that he did not affix a revenue stamp to the contract, or authorize it done.

Question: Is the right to sue upon a contract affected by the question of who affixed the revenue stamps, or whether or not they were cancelled?

Decision: "It was wholly immaterial who affixed the stamps. The plaintiff could properly do it. Nor did the failure to cancel the stamps, if there was a failure, render the instrument void."

DARLINGTON v. MAGER, COLLECTOR
(U. S. Supreme Court, April 18, 1921)
(No. 716, October Term, 1920, — U. S. —)

Record: Revenue Act of 1918. Suit for refund of alleged erroneous assessment under said Act. Demurrer to declaration sustained (Feb. 1, 1921) by U. S. District Court, N. D. Ill. E. D. (no opinion). Writ of error issued Feb. 1, 1917. Affirmed.

Facts: Plaintiff purchased certain shares of stock as an investment prior to March 1, 1913, and held same continuously until time of sale in 1919. The sale price was in excess of the fair market value of the securities on March 1, 1913. Tax was assessed and collected under the Revenue Act of 1918 on the excess of the sales price over the March 1, 1913, value.

Question: Is appreciation in value since March 1, 1913, of the securities "income" within the purview of the 16th Amendment?

Decision: The U. S. Supreme Court on April 18, 1921, affirmed the decision of the lower court sustaining the government on the authority of cases decided March 28, 1921 (Merchants' Loan & Trust Co. v. Smietanka, etc.) In which cases it was held that the excess of the sale price over the value on the effective date of the act, of property acquired prior to that date, was income for the year in which it was received.

DARNELL v. INDIANA ·
(U. S. Supreme Court, Dec. 23, 1912)
(226 U. S. 390)

Record: Burns Indiana Stats., 1908, Secs. 10143, 10233, 10234. Action to recover taxes. Error to the Supreme Court of Indiana, which rendered judgment for the plaintiff, 174 Ind. 143. Judgment affirmed.

Facts: The State of Indiana brought this action for taxes on stock of a Tennessee corporation owned by the defendant. The Indiana statutes purported to tax all shares in foreign corporations, except that national banks, owned by inhabitants of the state. The declarations were demurred to on the ground that the statutes were contrary to the commerce clause, Art. 1, Sec. 8, and the Fourteenth Amendment of the Constitution of the United States.

Question: Were the statutes in question unconstitutional as contended by the defendant?

Decision: "The case is pretty nearly disposed of by Kidd v. Alabama, 188 U. S. 730, where the real matter of complaint, that the property of the corporation presumably is taxed in Tennessee is answered. * * * But it is said that the former decision does not deal with the objection that the statutes work a discrimination against stock in corporations of other States contrary to principles often recognized. * * * The most serious aspect of this objection is that the statutes of Indiana do not make allowance if a corporation has property taxed within the state. But as to this it is enough to say that, however the statutes may be construed in a case of that sort, the plaintiffs in error do not show that it is theirs and that as they do not belong to the class for whose sake the constitutional protection would be given, if it would, they cannot complain on that ground."

DAVIS v. EVANS
(Supreme Court of North Carolina, Nov. 10, 1903)
(45 S. E. 643)

Record: Act of June 13, 1898. Action of assessment by Davis against Evans, administratrix. From a judgment for defendant, plaintiff appealed. Reversed.

Facts: The plaintiff sued on a promissory note dated November 7, 1898. The court excluded the note when offered in evidence because it was not stamped as required by the United States Internal Revenue Act of 1898.

Question: Can a promissory note which is not stamped as required by the Act be offered in evidence in a suit in a state court?

Decision: "The stamp is a fiscal provision of the United States government for the purpose of raising revenue, which is to be enforced only in its own courts. Its nonobservance does not affect the validity of the instrument when offered in evidence in a state court. The provision that the unstamped paper shall not be admitted 'in any court' applies only to the United States courts. Congress cannot prescribe the rules of evidence for the state courts."

DAWE v. JACKSON
(Superior Judicial Court of Massachusetts, Jan. 7, 1921)
(129 N. E. 606)

Record: Income Tax Act of 1916, c. 269, State of Massachusetts, and Acts in amendment thereof. Petition for writ of mandamus. On report by a single justice of the Superior Judicial Court to the full court. Petition dismissed.

Facts: See question.

Question: Does the fact that the revenue derived from income tax is not commingled with and treated as part of the general fund of the commonwealth, established by St. 1917, c. 227, Sec. 1, but is kept separate and designated as an "agency account" by the treasurer and receiver general, affect in any respect the constitutionality of St. 1919, c. 314?

Decision: "The methods of bookkeeping and accounting of a state official have no bearing upon the conformity to the Constituton of the statute by which a state-wide tax is collected, and distributed. The principal of long-continued interpretation of a statute * * * as evidence of its meaning has no pertinency to the case at bar, where there has been only a single instance of action by the treasurer and receiver general."

DAYTON BRASS CASTINGS CO. v. GILLIGAN
(U. S. District Court, S. D. Ohio, W. D., Sept. 23, 1920)
(267 Fed. 872)

Record: War Munitions Act of Sept. 8, 1916. Action to recover tax paid under protest. Judgment for defendant.

Facts: Plaintiff made certain rough castings for use in fuses for shrapnel shells from ingots and patterns supplied by another company, herein referred to as the Recording Company, which had a contract for the delivery of these fuses. Each fuse when completed consisted of 45 parts. The work done by plaintiff concerned but 4 of the 45 parts. None of such 4 parts was at the time of delivery fitted for insertion into the fuse. The castings made by plaintiff, if not used in fuses, were serviceable only as scrap. At the request of the Commissioner a return was filed by plaintiff under protest, and tax and penalty were assessed and paid under protest on Dec. 8, 1917. A refund claim was filed, and the Commissioner ordered repayment of the penalty but rejected the rest of the claim.

Questions: (1) Was the plaintiff a "manufacturer" within the meaning of the Act?

(2) Were the articles made and delivered by plaintiff "relatively complete" within the regulations of the Commissioner?

(3) Since plaintiff never had any title to the articles, was there any sale or disposition of the same by the plaintiff as required by the Act?

(4) Where a penalty paid under protest was subsequently refunded, was the taxpayer entitled to interest on the amount thereof?

Decision: (1) If the application of labor to an article effects some transformation in the character of the article, and converts it into a new and different article, having a distinctive name, character, or use, such article is a manufactured article and the person producing it is a manufacturer. The conclusion here must be that plaintiff was a manufacturer and engaged in the making of parts of fuses.

(2) The articles produced by plaintiff lost their identity as a commercial commodity, and, without further treatment, could not be used for any purpose, other than that for which they were respectively intended. "Relatively" means in relation or respect to something else. Each of the parts was complete within itself in respect to the raw materials out of which it was made. The parts were relatively complete.

(3) Plaintiff's contention that the articles delivered must be the property of the person taxed is unsound. A meaning must if possible be given to the words "disposed of." They mean something more than the word "sell." They were intended to embrace every sort of transaction or device other than a sale. The plaintiff by delivering the parts made by it disposed of them.

(4) The recovery of interest on the penalty must be denied for the reason that the penalty, when repaid, was accepted without any agreement or reservation that its acceptance should not effect the question of the payment of interest or the right to demand the same.

DAYTON WESTERN TRACTION CO. v. GILLIGAN,
COLLECTOR

FORT WAYNE, VAN WERT & LIMA TRACTION CO. v. SAME

COLUMBUS, NEWARK & ZANESVILLE ELECTRIC RAILWAY CO. v. SAME

INDIANA, COLUMBUS & EASTERN TRACTION CO. v. SAME

CINCINNATI STREET RAILWAY CO. v. SAME

(U. S. District Court, Western Division Ohio, June 25, 1914)

(T. D. 2000)

Record: Act of Aug. 5, 1909. Action at law to recover tax paid under Section 38 of this Act. In questions (1) (2) and (3) below, judgment was for plaintiff, in question (4) for defendant.

Facts: (1) Plaintiff, a railroad corporation, leased its property for a term of years, but continued its corporate powers and issued bonds to pay for additions, improvements and betterments of its property, in accordance with the terms of its lease.

(2) In 1911 plaintiff corporation reduced its capital stock.

(3) Lessor covenanted that the lessee might use the name of the lessor in bringing, prosecuting or defending any suits or proceedings at law or in equity, necessary or proper in the opinion of the lessee for the protection, preservation and full enjoyment by the lessee of the property. Lessee's attorney was directed to bring suit in the lessee's name, under the Ohio statute, against the Baltimore and Ohio Ry., to establish its right to cross such company's tracks. The attorney, notwithstanding his instructions, brought the suit in the name of the lessor. The lessee is conducting the litigation, has control of it, and is required to bear all expenses of the suit.

(4) In each of the years 1911 and 1912 the lessor (plaintiff in this case) joined in the exchange of certain real estate theretofore owned by it for other real estate, conveying the former and taking deeds for the latter. Plaintiff's lease provides that when any of the real estate leased shall become unsuitable or unnecessary for the operation of the railroad, the lessee may sell and dispose of it with the concurrence of the lessor as to the advisability of the selling and the price to be paid, to be evidenced by its joining in the deed, and the proceeds of the sale in every case to be applied to the purchase of other property, to be mutually agreed upon by the lessor and lessee; title to the same to be taken in the name of the lessor and the property to be purchased to be returned and used as part of the leased property.

Questions: (1) Under the circumstances stated in division 1 of facts above, is plaintiff corporation doing business as defined by the Act of Aug. 5, 1909?

(2) Is reduction of capital stock engaging in business under the Act of Aug. 5, 1909, so as to require payment of tax?

(3) Do the circumstances stated in division 3 of facts above constitute engaging in business under Act of Aug. 5, 1909?

(4) Did the plaintiff's joining in the deed constitute a doing of business within the meaning of the Act?

Decision: (1) Plaintiff was held not to be engaging in business for the taxable year 1911, the year in which the bonds were issued. (The reasoning of the court is not stated in the T. D. 2000.)

(2) "The reduction of capital stock is the exercise of corporate powers. Reduction of or increase of capital stock is a transaction had between the corporation and its stockholders, and not between the corporation and the general public. What should be done in such a situation in the absence of prejudice to creditors is to be determined wholly by the stockholders and the corporation, and is, so to speak, so far a family arrangement as not to concern the public or to be engaging in business."

(3) Although the plaintiff, after learning that the suit was instituted in its name, did not forbid its continuance, it does not appear to have taken any part in it. However, the plaintiff should not be regarded as engaging in business as the intention to do business was wanting.

(4) "The doing of a single act of business, accompanied with the purpose to perform other corporate acts of the same kind or other corporate business, may very properly be held to constitute the doing of business." A much broader meaning than ordinary is given to the words 'doing business,' under a tax statute." Flint v. Stone Tracy Co., 220 U. S. 107. "A railroad system as extensive as that of the plaintiff must necessarily have various pieces of real estate. There is in this provision of the lease a purpose to transact business from time to time. The location of stations, power plants, car barns and other structures, used in and by the operation of the road, is frequently a matter not only of great convenience to the public, but wise business policy, and is of consequence in the transaction of a carrier's business. Under the provisions mentioned the plaintiff may seldom be called upon to act. On the other hand, the shifting of residential or business districts, growth of business in sections

sparsely populated, etc., may require frequent sale of properties, and the purchase of others to a considerable extent." The court held that the plaintiff's joining in the deed in the years 1911 and 1912 constituted the transaction of business.

Note: This case is reversed by Traction Companies v. Collectors, 223 Fed. 984, infra.

DE BARY v. CARTER
(U. S. Circuit Court of Appeals, Fifth Circuit, May 1, 1900)
(102 Fed. 130)

Record: Internal Revenue Law, Rev. Stat., Sec. 3220. Action at law to recover taxes paid. Judgment for defendant, and plaintiff brought error.

Facts: This suit was commenced in the state court to recover from the collector of internal revenue taxes alleged to have been illegally assessed and collected from the plaintiff as a wholesale liquor dealer. The case was removed by certiorari to the Circuit Court for the Eastern District of Louisiana, and there tried, resulting in verdict for defendant. On writ of error this court reversed the judgment of the Circuit Court, and remanded the cause for a new trial. If the case had been decided in the state court, in which it was originated, the prevailing party to the suit would have been allowed costs.

Question: Should plaintiff be denied costs under the above circumstances on the ground that the real party in interest is the United States, it being against the rules of the court to allow costs in the Circuit Court of Appeals for or against the United States?

Decision: It was held in "Field v. Schell, Fed. Cases No. 4,771, that plaintiff should recover costs under circumstances similar to the above. Section 3220, Revised Statute, reads, in part, as follows:

'The Commissioner of Internal Revenue, subject to regulations prescribed by the Secretary of the Treasury, is authorized * * * to repay to any collector or deputy collector the full amount of such sums of money as may be recovered against him in any court, for any internal taxes collected by him, with the costs and expenses of suit; also all damages and costs recovered against any assessor, assistant assessor, collector, deputy collector, or inspector, in any suit brought against him by reason of anything done in due performance of his official duty.'

"This statute seems to contemplate that in suits similar to the present one costs will be awarded against the government officers and that in due course they will be paid by the United States. In our opinion, it would be an injustice to require a party who is compelled to pay an illegal assessment to bear all the burden of the successful litigation necessary to recover the same."

DE BARY et al., v. DUNNE, COLLECTOR
(U. S. Circuit Court, D. Oregon, June 15, 1908)
(162 Fed. 961)

Record: Rev. Stat., Sec. 3226. Action to recover taxes paid the collector. Motion to dismiss overruled. Judgment for defendant in 172 Fed. 940, deciding the question as to where the sale was made.

Facts: The defendant moved to dismiss upon the ground that the action is barred because the plaintiffs have not made the appeal to the Commissioner, required by Sec. 3226. The plaintiffs at first relied upon the appearance of the defendant as a waiver. Later, the complaint was amended and showed that before the payment of the tax, the plaintiffs filed a claim for abatement, which claim was rejected by the Commissioner.

The plaintiffs are wholesale liquor dealers in the city of New York. They had no office or resident sales agent in Oregon, but kept a stock of imported wines on storage in the warehouse of the J. McCracken Company, at Portland. The plaintiffs purchased wines in France and shipped them to Portland in bond. The goods, when taken to the warehouse, were placed in storage as the property of the plaintiffs, and they paid the storage thereon. The plaintiffs furnished the McCracken Company a list of persons in Portland to whom that company was authorized to deliver wines, when requested to do so by such persons. The McCracken Company reported these deliveries to the plaintiffs, who sent an invoice to the purchaser, and the purchaser made payment by mail to the plaintiffs.

Questions: (1) Is the appearance of the defendant, the collector, a waiver of the provisions of Sec. 3226, where the plaintiff has not alleged that an appeal was made in accordance with that section?

(2) Is the filing of a claim for abatement before the payment of the tax a sufficient appeal as required by Sec. 3226?

(3) Are sales by the plaintiffs who are in New York, where a warehouse company in Portland delivered the goods to the purchasers, according to instructions from the plaintiffs, made in Portland and subject to the federal wholesale liquor dealers' tax in Oregon?

Decision: (1) " * * * the statute could not be likened to the ordinary statute of limitations. If the section had merely limited the time of bringing action to the period of two years, then there would be an entire analogy. But it goes further and positively prescribes that until an appeal shall have been duly made no suit shall be maintained in any court, for a recovery of the tax. Nothing could be more explicit than this. And it seems to me that there could be no waiver of such a statute by the appearance and answer to the merits."

(2) "Now, in this case it appears from the amended complaint that the plaintiffs were permitted to make a claim for abatement and the revenue officer was required to delay the collection until the claim was passed upon; that under the ruling of the Commissioner plaintiffs filed such claim, which was in due time brought to the attention of the Commissioner, and by him passed upon and rejected. This I construe to be tantamount to an appeal to the Commissioner of Internal Revenue under the statute, and, hence, that plaintiffs were entitled to sue at the time of filing their complaint. It is a rule, under the regulations of the revenue system, that no suit can be brought until the tax is paid; but it is not absolutely necessary that an appeal be taken after the payment of the tax. But if an appeal is had in regular course from the assessment, or by request for an abatement to the Commissioner, and he has acted thereon, then no further step need be taken in the way of perfecting the cause of suit."

(3) "In my opinion the transaction was clearly a sale and

delivery of the goods in Portland. A sale is briefly defined as a contract by which property is transferred from the seller to the buyer for a fixed price in money, paid or agreed to be paid by the buyer. All the essential requisites of such a transaction took place in Portland. The goods, which were the subject matter of the contract and which were to be transferred from the seller to the buyer, were in Portland, in the possession of a warehouseman holding them for the seller, but with authority to deliver them to the buyer. They were so delivered with the intent that title should pass. The buyer then and there became the owner of the goods, and liable to the seller for the market value thereof in money. The fact that the warehouseman reported the delivery to the seller at New York, and the bill or invoice was there made out and forwarded to the buyer, is unimportant. That was after the delivery of the goods and title had passed, and was nothing more than a presumably convenient method of advising the buyer of the price and the manner in which he would be expected to make payment.''

DE GANAY v. LEDERER, COLLECTOR

(U. S. Supreme Court, June 9, 1919)

(250 U. S. 376)

Record: Act of October 3, 1913. Action at law to recover taxes paid under protest on net income under this Act. Judgment for defendant, 239 Fed. 568. Questions certified by Circuit Court of Appeals answered in affirmative. Affirmed.

Facts: Plaintiff was a citizen of France and lived in that country. Her father was an American citizen and upon his death she inherited from him a large amount of personal property consisting of stock, bonds, mortgages, etc., in her own right, free from any trust. The P. Co. acted as her agent in this country under power of attorney and in that capacity invested and reinvested her property in American securities, in this country, and collected and remitted to her the net income therefrom. Her agent filed a return for her of the income collected for her in 1913 and paid the tax as provided by the Act of October 3, 1913, which levies a tax upon the net income from all property owned and every business carried on in the United States by persons residing elsewhere. The tax was paid under protest and recovery was sought by plaintiff by the proper action.

Questions: (1) Are stock and bonds, etc., property, within the meaning of the Act of 1913?

(2) Granting stock, bonds, etc., to be property, are they property within the United States, and in view of the maxim that the situs of personal property is at the domicile of the owner?

Decision: (1) Stocks, bonds, etc., are "property." "Unless the contrary appears, statutory words are presumed to be used in their ordinary and usual sense, and with the meaning commonly attributed to them. To the general understanding and with the common meaning usually attached to such descriptive terms, bonds, mortgages and certificates of stock are regarded as property. By State and Federal statutes they are often treated as property, not as mere evidences of the interest which they represent. The Congressional intent in using the term 'property' was as used in the ordinary and usual sense.'"

(2) "The Supreme Court of the United States has frequently declared the maxim that the situs of personal property is at the domicile of the owner, is a fiction. A fiction may yield to the facts and circumstances of cases which require it. In this case the stocks and bonds were those of corporations organized under the laws of the United States and authority over them was given to a local agent. Any income derived from such property was clearly within the meaning of Congress as expressed in the statute under consideration." The court refused to follow the maxim, and decided that stocks and bonds held by the plaintiff's agent in the United States are property within the United States and the income from them is taxable.

DEGGE v. HITCHCOCK, POSTMASTER GENERAL
(U. S. Supreme Court, May 26, 1913)
(229 U. S. 162)

Record: Rev. Stat., Secs. 3929 and 4041. Appeal from decisions of the Supreme Court of the District of Columbia and the Court of Appeals of the District, denying writs of certiorari. Judgment affirmed.

Facts: Defendant, after reviewing a report made as a result of an investigation of plaintiff's business by the postal authorities, decided that a fraud order should issue. Plaintiff, in his petition, alleged that the order was arbitrary, in excess of the power of the Postmaster General, and void.

Question: Will a Federal court issue a writ of certiorari to review a ruling by an executive officer of the United States Government, in this case, the Postmaster General?

Decision: "It is true that the Postmaster General gave notice and a hearing to the persons specially to be affected by the order and that in making his ruling he may be said to have acted in quasi-judicial capacity. But the statute was passed primarily for the benefit of the public at large and the order was given for them and their protection. That fact gave an administrative quality to the hearing and to the order and was sufficient to prevent it from being subject to review by a writ of certiorari. The Postmaster General could not exercise judicial functions, and in making the decision he was not an officer presiding over a tribunal where his ruling was final unless reversed. Not being a judgment, it was not subject to appeal, writ of error, or certiorari. Not being a judgment in the sense of a final adjudication, the appellants were not concluded by his decision, for had there been an arbitrary exercise of statutory power or a ruling in excess of the jurisdiction conferred, they had the right to apply for and obtain appropriate relief in a court of equity."

DE LASKI & THROOP C. W. TIRE CO. v. IREDELL, COLL.

(U. S. District Court, D. N. J., Nov. 9, 1920)

(268 Fed. 377)

Record: Revenue Act of 1917. Suit to recover excess profits tax paid for year 1917. On motion by defendant to strike out complaint. Motion dismissed.

Facts: Plaintiff, incorporated in 1903 with an authorized capital stock of $100,000, experimented unsuccessfully for a number of years at great expense in developing a pneumatic tire. During these experiments a new form of mold for vulcanizing tires was invented, a patent for which was secured, and assigned with certain other patents to the plaintiff for $1. In 1911, the plaintiff ceased to conduct any other business except that of granting licenses under its patents. Its capital was reduced to $10,000; and in 1917 its combined capital and surplus was $12,000, which was used as a fund from which to advance salaries, wages, etc., and to provide office equipment. The Government assessed the plaintiff under Section 210 of the Act at the comparative rate, as therein provided for in cases where the Secretary of the Treasury is unable satisfactorily to determine the invested capital, whereas the plaintiff contended it was entitled to be assessed under Section 209 at the eight per cent rate as a business "having no invested capital or not more than a nominal capital."

Questions: (1) Did Section 209 of the Revenue Act of 1917 apply only to persons rendering a personal service?

(2) Could treasury rulings indicating that the word "invested" was omitted in the Act by oversight in the phrase "not more than a nominal capital" be given any effect in construing the Act?

(3) Did the term "nominal capital" embrace patents?

(4) Was a corporation, which merely granted licenses for the use of its patents, engaged in rendering a personal service?

Decision: (1) If Congress had intended in Section 209 to provide only for persons rendering a personal service there seems to be no reason why it would not have used more exact language to convey such meaning. In the absence of such language the section should not be given the limited construction contended for by the Government.

(2) Treasury rulings can be given no force to modify or add to the clearly expressed language of Congress. The terms "invested capital" and "nominal capital" are distinctive and admit of exact definitions.

(3) Capital is wealth employed in or available for production, that is, those stored-up concrete things essential to afford shelter, tools, protection and materials which the work requires. Patents were never capital in an economic sense.

(4) The patents of the plaintiff were the concrete embodiment of skill possessed by it in its field of activity. This skill it bartered for a consideration. Hence it would seem that the plaintiff was employed in rendering a personal service, and was not employing "capital" and certainly no more than a "nominal capital."

DES MOINES U. RY. CO. v. CHICAGO G. W. RY. CO.
(Supreme Court of Iowa, April 13, 1920)
(177 N. W. 90)

Record: Act of October 3, 1913. Action at law on contract. Trial court overruled a demurrer to the petition and judgment was given for plaintiff. Defendant appealed. Reversed.

Facts: Plaintiff rendered certain services for defendant and defendant used a part of plaintiff's railroad property in Des Moines under an agreement by which defendant contracted to pay among other sums "one-third of all taxes or assessments, special or otherwise, and public charges of every kind and nature that shall or may be taxed or assessed against the Des Moines Company or its property during the aforesaid term of years." This suit was brought to recover one-third of all sums paid by the plaintiff to the United States from 1914 to 1918 as income and excise taxes.

Question: Did the clause of the contract above set forth include income and excise taxes paid to the United States?

Decision: Reading the clause in the light of the context and of all the circumstances under which it was made, including the fact that at the time the contract was made there was no law requiring payment of either an income or excise tax, the real intent of the contracting parties will be effectuated by including the tax then existing, that is, existing in 1871, but it is not broad enough to extend to an income tax levied under an act subsequently enacted. Furthermore, an income tax cannot be considered as a tax upon specific property or as a tax upon the business of the corporation. The defendant is, therefore, under no obligation under the lease to pay the tax.

DOBBINS v. THE COMMISSIONERS
(Supreme Court of the United States, January Term, 1842)
(14 U. S. 435)

Record: Pennsylvania Act of April 15, 1834. Action at law to recover taxes paid. Judgment for plaintiff, and defendant brought error. Reversed in 7 Watts 513. Plaintiff brought error. Reversed.

Facts: The plaintiff has been an officer of the United States, a captain in the revenue-cutter service for a number of years, and for three years was assessed with county taxes for his office as such. The act makes it the duty of the assessor "to rate all officers and posts of profit, professions, trades, and occupations, at their discretion, having a due regard to the profits arising therefrom."

Question: Can the State tax an officer of the United States revenue-cutter service for his office, or its emoluments?

Decision: "The execution of a national power by way of compensation to officers, can in no way be subordinate to the action of the state legislature upon the same subject. It would destroy also all uniformity of compensation for the same service, as the taxes by the states would be different. To allow such a right of taxation to be in the states would also in effect be to give the states a revenue out of the revenue of the United States, to which they are not constitutionally entitled, either directly or indirectly; neither by their own action, nor by that of Congress. * * * But the unconstitutionality of such taxation by a state as that now before us may be safely put—though it is not the only ground—upon its interference with the constitutional means which have been legislated by the government of the United States to carry into effect its powers, to lay and collect taxes, duties, imposts, etc., and to regulate Commerce."

DODGE v. BRADY, COLLECTOR
(U. S. Supreme Court, February 21, 1916)
(240 U. S. 122)

Record: Act of October 3, 1913, and Section 3224 Revised Statutes. Bill to restrain the collection of taxes, and supplemental bill to recover taxes paid under protest. Injunction denied, bill dismissed, direct appeal to Supreme Court because of constitutional questions. Affirmed.

Facts: Plaintiff by original bill sought to enjoin the collection of the surtaxes under Act of October 3, 1913, because of unconstitutionality of statute. Court below denied the injunction, whereupon a supplemental bill was filed alleging the payment of the tax under protest since the filing of the original bill and praying a recovery of the amount paid. The defendant moved to dismiss the bill for want of jurisdiction because the suit was brought to enjoin the collection of a tax contrary to the provisions of Section 3224 Revised Statutes and for want of equity because the Income Tax Law was constitutional and valid. The court sustained the motion on the latter ground and dismissed the bill on the merits.

Questions: (1) Was the court without jurisdiction to decide the constitutional question because the original bill was brought to enjoin the collection of the tax?

(2) Is the supplemental bill fatally defective since it fails to allege that an appeal was taken to the Commissioner after payment of the taxes and that he refused to refund them as required by Sections 3220 and 3224 of the Revised Statutes?

Decision: (1) "It is apparent if the original bill alone is taken into view that the suit was brought to enjoin the collection of a tax and the court was without jurisdiction by the reasons stated in the previous case" (Dodge v. Osborn, 240 U. S. 118, in this book, the case next following). However, in view of the supplemental bill and the considerations mentioned in the next paragraph, the objection to jurisdiction was not sustained.

(2) "* * * Broadly considering the whole situation and taking into view the peculiar facts of the case, the protest to the Commissioner and his exertion of authority over it and his adverse ruling upon the merits of the tax, thereby passing upon every question which he would be called upon to decide on an appeal for a refunding of the taxes paid, we think that this case is so exceptional in character as not to justify us in holding that a reversible error was committed by the court below in passing upon the case upon its merits, thus putting an end to further

absolutely useless and unnecessary controversy. We say useless and unnecessary because on the merits all the contentions urged by the appellants concerning the unconstitutionality of the law and of the surtaxes which it imposes have been considered and adversely disposed of in Brushaber v. Union Pacific Railroad Company.''

This court had previously declared the law constitutional. The plaintiff could not have recovered the taxes paid on the ground that the law was unconstitutional, even if the supplemental bill was not defective. Therefore, the court did not give any opinion as to the sufficiency of the supplemental bill.

DODGE v. OSBORN, COMMISSIONER
(U. S. Supreme Court)
(240 U. S. 118)

Record: Act of October 3, 1913. Bill in equity to enjoin payment of tax on net income under this Act. Bill dismissed. 43 App. S. C. 144. Affirmed.

Facts: Plaintiffs filed their returns showing their taxable income and were assessed the normal and surtax under the Act of Congress approved October 3, 1913. To the assessment and collection of the surtax, they filed a protest in which they alleged that the surtax levied upon individuals under the said income tax law is in conflict with the fifth amendment to the Constitution of the United States and that the provision providing for the assessment and collection of the surtax discriminates against individual taxpayers and in favor of corporations. The protest further alleged that the tax imposed is not uniform, and that no opportunity is afforded for a hearing before the assessment of the tax, hence the law is unconstitutional and void. Defendant moved to dismiss on the ground that no suit could be maintained, since its object was to restrain the assessment and collection of a tax, and that plaintiffs have an adequate and complete remedy at law. To the government's second contention, plaintiffs reply that they are properly in equity since to assess a tax under a law which is unconstitutional works a hardship on them, in that the tax creates a lien upon the property of the plaintiffs.

Question: Are plaintiffs properly in equity when their aim is to restrain the assessment and collection of a federal tax?

Decision: Congress has afforded a complete and adequate remedy at law, open to all persons aggrieved by the collection of an erroneous or illegal revenue tax. The taxpayer must pay the tax, and he may then bring an action to recover it back. Before a court of equity will in any way help a party to thwart the intent of Congress, it must affirmatively and clearly appear that there is an absolute necessity for its interference in order to prevent irreparable injury. No considerations of mere convenience are sufficient. The statute aims at assuring speedy collection of governmental revenues. In order that the revenues to meet the requirements of the government may be assessed, the courts persistently refuse an injunction to aid taxpayers in attempts to defeat the collecting agents of the government. To make absolute the restriction upon the Federal courts, Congress provided by Sec. 3224 R. S. that "no suit for the purpose of restraining the assessment or collection of any tax shall be maintained in any court."

DOERSCHUCK v. UNITED STATES OF AMERICA
THOMAS v. UNITED STATES OF AMERICA
(U. S. District Court, E. D. of New York, March 17, 1921)
(... Fed. ...)

Record: Revenue Act of 1916. Suit to recover taxes paid under protest for the year 1916. Complaint dismissed.

Facts: "The plaintiff, in each of the above actions, has paid income tax on one-quarter of an issue of debenture bonds of the North American Brewing Company, which came into the hands of the plaintiffs because of the ownership by each of 1,230 shares (or one-quarter) of the entire capital stock of said North American Brewing Company. The directors of said corporation had voted an issue of $738,000 of debenture bonds from a surplus or undivided profits amounting to $840,368.09, which had accrued between 1906 and July 1, 1916. The portion of the bonds representing surplus earned before March 1, 1913, was not taxed and hence is not involved in these actions. The balance, viz., $262,-

334.44, was assessed as income for the year 1916, during which year each of the plaintiffs had received his one-quarter part of said funds."

Question: Is the dividend paid in debenture bonds of a corporation income to the stockholders?

Decision: Eisner v. Macomber (252 U. S. 189) distinguished. "In Eisner v. Macomber, supra, at p. 208, the court says:

" 'The stockholder has the right to have the assets employed in the enterprise, with the incidental rights mentioned; but, as stockholder, he has no right to withdraw, only the right to persist, subject to the risk of the enterprise, and looking only to dividends for his return.'

"It is apparent, therefore, in the present case, that the plaintiffs received an actual payment (in the form of securities available for disposition in the market, and entirely severed or distinguished from their control of the property as stockholders) of profits which the company wished to distribute as earnings to its stockholders. It did this by distribution of obligations which, like a promissory note, called for the payment of cash, and did not invest the holder with merely a different form of holding of stock. As stated in Eisner v. Macomber, supra, at p. 212:

" 'It is said that a stockholder may sell the new shares acquired in the stock dividend; and so he may, if he can find a buyer. It is equally true that if he does sell, and in doing so realizes a profit, such profit, like any other, is income, and so far as it may have arisen since the Sixteenth Amendment is taxable by Congress without apportionment.'

"The debenture bonds in the suit at bar fall into the class of stock sold rather than stock held in a continued status of shareholder, and are taxable to the stockholders."

DOLLAR SAVINGS BANK v. UNITED STATES
(U. S. Supreme Court, October, 1873)
(87 U. S. 227)

Record: Act of July 13, 1866. Action at law to recover taxes paid. Judgment for defendant and plaintiff brought error. **Affirmed.**

Facts: "Plaintiff is a banking institution created by the state of Pennsylvania, without stockholders or capital stock, and doing the business of receiving deposits to be loaned or invested for the sole benefit of its depositors. The charter authorizes the retention of a contingent fund accumulated from the earnings to the extent of ten per centum of its deposits for the security of its depositors. The bank has earned and added to the said contingent fund or undistributed sum, from July 13, 1866, to December 31, 1870, $107,000, and such earnings were carried to and added to said contingent or undistributed fund semi-annually. * * *"

Questions: (1) Does the Act of July 13, 1866, authorize the collection of a tax upon the accumulated earnings carried to the contingent fund described in the statement of facts above?

(2) What effect does the construction of a statute by the Commissioner of Internal Revenue have where the statute on which construction has been placed has been re-enacted?

Decision: (1) The intent of the Act was to impose a tax upon the income of the institutions mentioned therein. "The tax is laid upon two subjects—the one dividends or sums due and payable and the other the undistributed surplus, gains or earnings carried to a surplus or contingent fund." These subjects, though together making up the entire net earnings, are distinct from each other. The plaintiff contended that a proviso excepting from the tax interest paid to depositors on savings banks includes also earnings carried to the contingent fund. The proviso makes no reference to the undistributed surplus which may be carried to a surplus fund. It leaves it as it was in the body of the section subject to the tax therein imposed. "If it had been the intention of Congress to exempt savings banks from liability to pay the tax on both the interest paid to its depositors and on all undistributed sums carried to the surplus fund, the plain mode of expressing such a purpose was to say in the proviso that such banks should be excepted from the operation of the section. Why take out one subject of taxation specifically and leave the other unmentioned, if such was the purpose?"

(2) The court held that the construction given to an Internal Revenue Act by the Commissioner of Internal Revenue, even though published in an Internal Revenue Record is not a construction of so much dignity that a re-enactment of the statute subsequent to such construction is to be regarded as a legislative adoption of that construction; especially not when the construction makes a proviso to an act repugnant to the body of the act.

DOWELL v. APPLEGATE, et al.
(U. S. Circuit Court, D. Oregon, July 8, 1881)
(7 Fed. 881)

Record: Act of June 30, 1864, and July 13, 1866. Bill in equity to set aside certain conveyances as fraudulent and void. Demurrer to bill sustained.

Facts: The defendant is a debtor of the plaintiff, and conveyed land to the other parties joined as defendants. The plaintiff claims that the deeds did not state the actual consideration, and, since they did not, they did not have the stamps affixed to them required by the federal act. The plaintiff also states in his complaint that the ones that were affixed were not cancelled, as required by law, and he seeks to have the conveyances set aside as illegal, and a fraud under the act.

Question: May a creditor maintain a bill to set aside conveyauces, made by the debtor, as fraudulent and void where they were not sufficiently stamped or the stamps not cancelled?

Decision: "It must be alleged and proven by the plaintiff not only that the conveyance to the Drains was insufficiently stamped or the stamps not cancelled, but that the omission in either case arose, not from accident or ignorance, but was the result of an 'intent to evade the provisions' of the law; that is, with intent to defraud the government of the stamp duty. * * * It appears from the bill that the conveyance in question is not sufficiently stamped—the true consideration being $2,000, while that expressed in the deed and for which it is stamped is only $500—and that the stamp actually used is not cancelled. But it does not appear that the omission to stamp the conveyance as for a consideration of $2,000 rather than $500, or the omission to cancel the one actually used, was the result of an intention to defraud the government; and this intent will not be presumed from the mere fact of the omission, which may have been caused by ignorance or accident * * *. An act done with a purpose to defraud or aid in defrauding the creditors of J. S. is not an act done, so far as appears, with intent to defraud the government." The consideration expressed in the deed must not only have been inadequate, but less than the actual amount paid, and the omission to stamp the conveyance, or to cancel the one actually used must have been done with an intent to defraud the government. Since the complaint did not state such a case, the action can not be maintained.

DUFFY v. HOBSON

(Supreme Court of California, October Term, 1870)

(40 Calif. 240)

Record: Act of June 30, 1864. Action to enforce performance of a written contract of sale of certain lots, and for damages for failure to perform the contract. Judgment for plaintiff, and defendant appealed. Reversed upon the ground that the verbal authority of agent to sell real estate is not sufficient.

Facts: The plaintiff offered in evidence a written contract, by the terms of which he claimed that the defendant had sold and agreed to convey to him certain lots. This contract was not stamped with the United States revenue stamps, and the defendant objected to its introduction, which objection was overruled.

Question: Is a contract admissible as evidence in a state court, though it is not stamped as required by the Act?

Decision: "The Act does not in terms extend to proceedings had under the laws of the state, and does not, on its face, import any interference with those laws. Upon the settled rules of interpretation, it must be construed to embrace only proceedings had, and acts done, in public offices and courts established under the Constitution of the United States, and by authority of Acts of Congress framed in pursuance thereof. Congress has no constitutional authority to legislate concerning the rules of evidence, administered in the courts of this state, nor to affix conditions or limitations upon which those rules are to be applied and enforced; nor can it rightfully convert those courts into tax gatherers for the benefit of the Federal Government, or charge them with the duty of inquiring whether or not the revenue laws of the United States have been observed, or of investigating into the motives of the parties in omitting to affix revenue stamps to the contracts they may have made." Thus the Supreme Court of California affirmed the ruling of the lower court which admitted the contract in evidence.

DUGAN v. UNITED STATES
(U. S. Court of Claims, Decided June 5, 1899)
(34 Ct. Cls. 458)

Record: The claims in this case, based on awards of certificates of allowances made by the Commissioner of Internal Revenue for the repayment of special tax, were transmitted to the court by the Secretary of the Treasury.

Facts: The claimant was an army officer in charge of the post exchange at Jefferson Barracks, Mo. For selling beer and wine at the exchange the collector required him to pay the special tax as a "retail liquor dealer." Subsequently, the Commissioner made allowances in his favor for the repayment to him of the special tax so paid. The Auditor for the Treasury Department certified the allowances for payment but the Acting Comptroller declined to approve his action and the claims were transmitted to this court for decision.

Questions: (1) Had the Commissioner authority and power to make the allowances?

(2) If so, what was the legal effect of such allowances?

Decision: (1) The statute gives to the Commissioner the power to pay back all taxes erroneously or illegally collected. Inasmuch as post exchanges are under the complete control of the Secretary of War as governmental agencies, they are exempt from the payment of the special tax. It therefore follows that the Commissioner had jurisdiction of the subject matter of the claims for repayment.

(2) Given a claim where the Commissioner has jurisdiction, his decision on the merits thereof, in the absence of fraud or mistakes in mathematical calculation, is final and therefore not subject to revision by the accounting officers.

EATON, COLLECTOR, v. CONNECTICUT GENERAL LIFE INS. CO.
SAME v. CONNECTICUT MUTUAL LIFE INS. CO.
(223 Fed. 1022)

Record: Act of August 5, 1909. Action at law to recover taxes paid under protest on net income, under Sec. 38 of this Act. Judgment for plaintiff (218 Fed. 188, 206) and defendant appealed. Affirmed.

Facts: (1) Defendant insurance companies are conducted on the mutual plan. Policies are issued providing for a definite yearly premium, whch is usually fixed somewhat above the amount required to insure safety. When a certain time has passed, and it is found that a less sum may safely be taken for a specific year, the premium for that year is reduced to the lower sum, and the insured is allowed to invest the difference, if he cares to do so, in additional paid-up insurance, without further medical examination. In company bookkeeping the premiums are frequently entered at their full amount and the amounts of rebate are entered as "dividends."

(2) Defendant expended a sum for alterations in its home office which it deducted from gross income. This amount was disallowed by the Commission, and court is asked to rule on the deductibility of such an item.

Questions: (1) Are such "dividends" income of the defendant insurance companies, subject to tax under the Corporation Excise Tax of August 5, 1909, which Act provides for a tax of 1% to be paid upon all net income of corporations over and above $5,000, received during the year?

(2) May an insurance company deduct from its gross income the amount expended for alterations in its home office?

Decisions: (1) "Such rebates or 'dividends' are in no sense dividends or income subject to tax but are in fact partial abatements of premium. Such 'dividends' or rebates allowed policy holders are really a return of prior excessive premium payments which have been accounted for, for tax purposes, in the year received and when credited to policy holders, furnish no basis for taxation within the meaning of the Act."

(2) "The changes made in the office do not appear to have been such as to be properly included under the head of 'permanent improvements'—tending to enhance the rental or market value of the building in case of sale. It should be remembered, also, that in these days of up-to-date business method requirements it often becomes necessary for business concerns to change the layout of the places wherein they carry on business—to the end that net running expenses will result. It seems to the court that business concerns, in matters of this kind, should be allowed a reasonable discretion, and the law so enforced as to help rather than to hinder them in making reasonable progress in the development of their business." Such expenditures are deductible.

EBERSOLE v. McGRATH, COLLECTOR
(U. S. District Court, S. D. Ohio, W. D., Oct. 5, 1920)
(271 Fed. 995)

Record: Revenue Act of 1916. Action at law by the executors of the will of Omer T. Glenn, deceased, to recover estate tax paid under protest. Defendant's demurrer to petition overruled and judgment entered for the plaintiff.

Facts: Omer T. Glenn by his last will and testament exercised a power of appointment given to him under the will of his father, William Glenn, who died prior to the enactment of the estate tax law of 1916, whereby Omer T. Glenn, the donee of the power, was granted a right of support and maintenance from the income of a trust estate for life without power of anticipation, but with power of disposing by will of the remainder of the property to vest upon the death of his surviving brother and sisters, which power was exercised after the passage of the said Act. The Act provides that the gross estate of a decedent shall include, among various kinds of property interests enumerated, all property "(a) to the extent of the interest therein of the decedent at the time of his death which after his death is subject to the payment of the charges against his estate and the expenses of his administration, and is subject to distribution as part of his estate," and "(b) to extent of any interest therein of which the decedent has at any time made a transfer, or with respect to which he has created a trust, in contemplation of or intended to take effect in possession or enjoyment at or after his death. * * * " The tax involved is a tax upon the value of the appointed estate.

Questions: (1) Is the appointed estate an interest in the property of the decedent at the time of his death, which after his death was subject to his debts, the costs of administration, and to distribution as part of his estate?

(2) Is the appointed estate an interest in property of which the decedent has made a transfer in contemplation of, or intended to take effect in possession or enjoyment at or after his death?

Decision: (1) It is true, as contended by the defendant, that in equity, property passing under will by exercise of a general power of appointment is subject to the debts of the donee's estate. This point, however, does not settle this case because such property to be subject to the estate tax involved here must also be property subject to distribution as a part of the decedent's estate. It is the general rule of the common law that the appointee takes from the donor and not the donee of the power. "Suppose, in the present case, that the donor, William Glenn, had died after the passage of the Act. There is no doubt that the transmission of the estate in question would have been subject to the tax notwithstanding the appointee remained yet to be named. Now, if the tax be also imposed upon the nomination of the appointee by the donor's son, Omer, it would be twice taxing what was, at common law, but one succession." That Congress might have rejected the common law rule is conceded, but the Act contains no language imparting such an intention.

(2) Question(2) was not discussed, the court apparently regarding it as settled inferentially in plaintiff's favor by its decision of Question (1). Therefore, the plaintiff was held to be entitled to recover the amount of the estate tax paid upon the value of the appointed estate.

EDISON ELEC., ETC., CO. v. UNITED STATES
(U. S. Court of Claims, January 19, 1903)

(38 Ct. Cls. 208)

Record: Act of June 13, 1898. Action to recover taxes illegally collected. Judgment for plaintiff.

Facts: Claimant executed a mortgage securing bonds to the value of $10,000,000. Bonds to the value of $2,000,000 only were issued and stamps on such amount affixed to the mortgage. Subsequently, it was held that claimant must pay a tax on the entire amount of bonds authorized and an additional tax of $4,000 was assessed and collected by distraint. Upon petition to the Commissioner a refund of this amount was allowed. This amount was certified to the Treasury Department where payment was refused.

Questions: (1) Was the suit properly brought against the United States?

(2) Was the award of the Commissioner binding upon the Government?

Decision: (1) If a claim for refund is disallowed by the Commissioner an action lies against the collector. When, however, the claim is allowed, and payment for any reason refused, suit may be brought directly against the United States in the Court of Claims.

(2) Under decisions of the Supreme Court in United States v. Kaufman (96 U. S. 567) and United States v. Savings Bank (104 U. S. 728) the functions of the Commissioner are not intermediate like those of a collector who may levy an unjust tax and refuse to remit its payment but his allowance of a claim is an award all sufficient for the foundation of a judgment. It puts upon the Government the burden of showing fraud or mistake by competent evidence.

EDWARDS, COLLECTOR, v. WABASH RY. CO.

(U. S. Circuit Court of Appeals, February 18, 1920)

(264 Fed. 610)

Record: Act of October 3, 1917. Suit at law by plaintiff railroad company to recover the amount of stamp taxes demanded by the Commissioner of Internal Revenue, which it paid under protest. Judgment for plaintiff in trial court. Defendant brought the case to this court by writ of error. Judgment affirmed.

Facts: Plaintiff, an Indiana corporation, was organized in 1915 with a capital stock fixed at $143,460,000 and 1,434,600 shares of $100 par value. Of such capital stock, 462,000 shares, it is provided in the certificate of incorporation, shall be issued as 5% profit-sharing preferred stock A, 499,700 as 5% convertible preferred stock B, and 472,900 as common stock. Capital stock was issued in accordance with this classification. In 1918, pursuant to resolution of the Board of Directors, the company executed and delivered certificates representing 115,889 shares of preferred stock A, and the same number of shares of common stock in exchange for and conversion of 231,778 shares of preferred stock B. The Commissioner of Internal Revenue ruled that the stock as issued was an original issue of stock and taxable as such under the provsions of Section 800, Schedule A of Title VIII, Act of October 3, 1917.

Question: Does an exchange and conversion of stock for stock of another class involve an issue of "original" stock taxable to the corporation so doing?

Decision: "In the case at bar when the plaintiff paid at the time of its organization the tax of 5 cents for each $100 of face value of its total capital stock, including the A stock, the B stock, and the common stock, such payment was made once for all, and constituted the payment of the tax on each original issue of the certificates of stock whenever and to whomsoever thereafter the plaintiff delivered. Whenever thereafter the plaintiff delivered the first certificate of the B stock it was not under obligation to pay again the tax on the B certificates. That had already been done, and when subsequently the plaintiff exchanged the certificates of the B stock for certificates of the A stock and of the common stock it was not bound to pay again the tax on the certificate. That tax too had already been paid. The exchange of stock was an exchange of original certificates of one kind of stock for original certificates of two other kinds of stock, the tax on all of which had been previously paid."

EHRET MAGNESIA MFG. CO. v. LEDERER, COLLECTOR
(U. S. District Court, E. D. Penn., June Sessions, 1920)
(273 Fed. 689)

Record: Revenue Act of 1917. Suit to recover excess profits tax paid under protest. Judgment for defendant.

Facts: The question in this case arose out of the method adopted in computing plaintiff's excess profits tax. The construction placed by the Commissioner of Internal Revenue upon the language of section 201, which imposes a tax of 20 per cent of the net income in excess of the deduction allowed and not in excess of 15 per cent of the invested capital, 25 per cent of the net income in excess of 15 per cent and not in excess of 20 per cent of such capital, and, thereafter, at other progressive percentages until the maximum of 60 per cent is reached, is that "the amount of the net income in excess of the deduction" means that the first of the graduated percentages of invested capital, namely, 15 per cent, is first to be ascertained, and the deduction is to be made from the amount thereof; and if the deduction is not in excess of 15 per cent of the invested capital, the difference between the amount of the deduction and the 15 per cent of invested capital is to be taxed at 20 per cent. The plaintiff contended that the deduction was to be made from the whole of the net income and out of the balance of net income remaining an amount not in excess of 15 per cent of the invested capital was to be taxed at 20 per cent.

Question: Is the Commissioner's construction of section 201, as given above, justifiable?

Decision: The Commissioner's construction of section 201 is a correct one. Apparently it was the intention of Congress to impose no tax upon the net income up to the amount of the deduction, the lowest rate upon the difference between the deduction and 15 per cent of the invested capital, and the net tax upon the difference between 15 and 20 per cent of the invested capital, and so on, until in the last percentage paragraph the highest rate of 60 per cent applies to all net income in excess of 33 per cent of invested capital. Such a construction does not render the law unconstitutional as preventing uniformity and equality in the application of the tax.

EHRLICH et al. v. BROGAN et al.
(Supreme Court of Pennsylvania, October 7, 1918)
(262 Pa. 362; 105 Atl. 511)

Record: Act of October 3, 1913. Suit in assumpsit to recover ground rent. From a judgment of the Superior Court (65 Pa. Superior Ct. 384), reversing a judgment in favor of defendants, defendants appealed. Affirmed.

Facts: Mary Pan Beil conveyed to Brogan a lot of ground, reserving a yearly ground rent. In the deed Brogan covenanted to pay the rent "without any deduction, defalcation or abatement for any taxes, charges or assessments * * * on the yearly rent" and to "pay all taxes whatsoever that shall hereafter be laid, levied or assessed by virtue of any law whatever * * * on the said yearly rent." The assignee of Brogan claims that by the provisions of the Federal Income Tax it is entitled to deduct the amount of the normal income tax and to pay the same to the government.

Question: Where the grantee has covenanted to pay ground rent to the grantor without deduction, defalcation, or abatement for any taxes, charges or assessments on the yearly rent, and to pay all taxes levied on the yearly rent, is the grantee entitled to deduct that amount of income tax which he is required by the Act to pay?

Decision: The court adopts the reasoning and judgment of the court in Van Beil v. Brogan, 65 Pa. Super. Ct. 384, and adds that "it may be said that if the accruing yearly rent reserved in the deed from Mary Van Beil to Daniel E. Brogan is not income, within the meaning of the Act of Congress of October 3, 1913, then no income tax was due thereon, and, appellant not having paid to or for plaintiff the whole of the annual ground rent 'due and payable June 1, 1914' either it or its land is liable for the balance thereof. On the other hand, if the accruing yearly rent is income within the meaning of the Act, as it was agreed in the deed that the reserved rent should be paid 'without deduction, defalcation or abatement for any taxes, charges or assessments * * * on the yearly rent hereby and thereout reserved,' and as the grantee covenanted for himself, his heirs and assigns to 'pay all taxes whatsoever that shall hereafter be laid, levied or assessed by virtue of any law whatever * * * on the said yearly rent,' when appellant, as his assignee, paid to the United States the normal tax thereon, it only paid that for which, in addition to the annual rent itself, it was liable; and hence it or its land is still liable to plaintiff for the balance of the ground rent claimed.''

EISNER, COLLECTOR, v. MACOMBER
(U. S. Supreme Court, March 8, 1920)
(252 U. S. 189)

Record: Revenue Act of 1916. Action to recover income tax paid. In Error to U. S. District Court for the Southern District of New York wherein judgment was rendered for the plaintiff. Judgment affirmed.

Facts: On January 1, 1916, the Standard Oil Company of California, a corporation of that State, out of an authorized capital stock of $100,000,000, had shares of stock outstanding, par value $100 each, amounting in round figures to $50,000,000. In addition, it had surplus and undivided profits amounting to about $45,000,000, of which about $20,000,000 had been earned prior to March 1, 1913, the balance thereafter. In January, 1916, the board of directors decided to issue additional shares sufficient to constitute a stock dividend of 50 per cent of the outstanding stock and to transfer from surplus account to capital stock account an amount equivalent to such issue. Appropriate resolutions were adopted, an amount equivalent to the par value of the proposed new stock was transferred accordingly, and the new stock issued and divided among the stockholders. Defendant in error, being the owner of 2,200 shares of the old stock, received a certificate for 1,100 additional shares, of which 18.07 per cent, or 198.77 shares, par value $19,877, were treated as representing surplus earned between March 1, 1913, and January 1, 1916. She was called upon to pay, and did pay under protest, a tax imposed under the Revenue Act of 1916, based upon a supposed income of $19,877, because of the new shares. This action was brought against the collector to recover the tax.

Questions: (1) Does the Revenue Act of 1916, which taxes a stock dividend as income of the stockholder, violate Art. 1, Sec. 2, Cl. 3 and Art. 1, Sec. 9, Cl. 4 of the Constitution of the United States, requiring direct taxes to be apportioned according to population?

(2) Can the provision of the Revenue Act of 1916 which taxes stock dividends as income of the stockholder be upheld under the Sixteenth Amendment to the Constitution on the ground that a stock dividend comes within the term "income" as used in said Amendment?

Decision: (1) The Revenue Act of 1916, in so far as it imposes a tax upon the stockholder because of his having received a stock dividend, is unconstitutional as taxing without apportionment. Following Towne v. Eisner, 245 U. S. 418.

(2) A stock dividend is a mere book transfer of accumulated profits from a surplus account and the issue of certificates representing such transfer. Therefore it is not "income" to a stockholder within the meaning of the Sixteenth Amendment. A characteristic and distinguishing attribute of income is that it is derived from or severed from capital, and does not include a growth or increment of capital. This attribute is lacking in a stock dividend.

ELDORADO COAL & MINING CO. v. MAGER, COLLECTOR

(U. S. Supreme Court, March 28, 1921)

(No. 609, October Term 1920, not reported)

Record: Revenue Acts of 1916 and 1917. Assumpsit to recover income and excess profits taxes for the year 1917 paid under protest. Demurrer to declaration sustained. In error to Dist. Ct. N. D. Ill. Affirmed.

Facts: "The Eldorado Coal and Mining Company is an Indiana corporation, which operated a bituminous coal mine and mining plant, which it sold in May, 1917, for cash. * * * It is averred in the declaration that, taking the fair market value as of March 1, 1913, of the capital assets of the company invested and employed in its business, and adding thereto the cost of additions and betterments, and subtracting depreciation and depletion to the date of sale, it appears that there was an appreciation in value of the property after March 1, 1913, of $5,986.02, and it was on this profit realized by the sale that the assessment of $3,073.16 was made, which the company paid and in this suit seeks to recover."

Question: Is appreciation of capital assets realized by sale, "income" within scope of the Sixteenth Amendment?

Decision: "It is obvious from this statement of the case that it presents in so nearly the same form precisely the same questions as were considered in No. 608, The Merchants' Loan & Trust Company, etc. v. Julius F. Smietanka, Collector, etc., this day decided, that further discussion of them is unnecessary, and, on the authority of that case, the judgment of the District Court is affirmed." The appreciation in value of the property after March 1, 1913, when realized by sale, is income.

ELLIOT v. FREEMAN
MAINE BAPTIST MISSIONARY CONVENTION
v. COTTING, COLLECTOR
(U. S. Supreme Court, March 13, 1911)
(220 U. S. 178)

Record: Act of Aug. 5, 1909. Action at law to recover taxes paid under protest under Sec. 48 of this Act. Judgment for defendant. Appeal. Reversed.

Facts: Certain trusts were created in Massachusetts for the purpose of purchasing, improving, holding and selling lands and buildings. The trusts had all of the characteristics of a corporation except that they were to terminate at the end of certain lives in being, or at the end of 20 years, or by an instrument in writing signed by the owners of three-fourths of the value of stock held by shareholders. The trusts were not the creation of any statute, nor were any of their powers derived from any legislative act. The contention of Government is that these trusts are such "joint stock companies" as come within the meaning of the Act.

Question: Are these trusts subject to tax under the Corporation Excise Tax Act of Aug. 5, 1909, which taxes "corporations, and joint stock companies, now or hereafter organized under the laws of the United States, etc."?

Decision: "It was the intention of Congress to embrace within the Corporation Tax statute only such corporation and joint stock companies as are organized under some statute. The language of the Act * * * 'now or hereafter organized under the laws of the United States,' imports an organization deriving power from statutory enactment. The statute does not say under the law of the United States, or a state, or lawful in the United States, or in any state, but is made applicable to such as are organized under the laws of the United States. To be taxable, the organizations must be the creation of statutory law, from which they derive their powers and are qualified to carry on their operations."

ELLIOTT NATIONAL BANK v. GILL
(U. S. Circuit Court of Appeals, First Circuit, Dec. 21, 1914)
(218 Fed. 600, 134 C. C. A. 358)

Record: Act of Aug. 5, 1909. Action at law to recover taxes paid. Judgment for the defendant and plaintiff brings error. Affirmed.

Facts: Plaintiff bank is required under a Massachusetts statute to pay tax assessed upon the shares of its stockholders, and in case of default is made liable in an action of contract for such tax. "Plaintiff bank, having paid the tax, is, under the statute, given a lien on all the shares in such bank and on all the rights and property of the shareholders in the corporate property for the payment of said tax."

Questions: (1) May plaintiff bank deduct from gross income, under Act of Aug. 5, 1909, the amount of tax paid, under the circumstances stated?

(2) May the word "false," as used in par. 5 of Sec. 38 of the Act of Aug. 5, 1909, authorizing assessment of additional tax, be construed so as to include erroneous or incorrect returns made with no intent to defraud?

Decision: (1) "The payment the Massachusetts statute requires a bank to make, as above, is plainly not assessed upon it or its property; and besides giving it a lien for the amount upon the shares in respect of which the taxes are assessed, the provision of the Massachusetts statute is such as to result in making the respective shareholders liable to the bank for the amount of taxes paid in respect of their shares. The lien and right of recovery distinguish such payments in their nature from other payments which the corporation tax law allows to be deducted in ascertaining taxable net income. Though payment of such taxes is a duty imposed upon the bank, it cannot be said that the taxes are imposed either upon it or its property. The taxes are imposed upon the shareholders and their property and the payment is by the bank only as their representative." The bank cannot deduct the amount of such payment from its gross income.

(2) The court held that the Commissioner was not without power to make additional assessment for the amount of the deductions, as contended by plaintiff, because of the provision authorizing the Commissioner, in case a return is false or fraudulent, to amend the same at any time within three years and assess and collect the correct amount of tax. The word "false," as so used, did not include only returns fraudulently made, or with intent to defraud, but should be construed as including all erroneous or incorrect returns, and to authorize the correction of an incorrect return within the three year period, though made under a mistake of law and though the tax under the return had been paid.

NOTE: The Act of October 3, 1913, contains a similar limitation, but the Revenue Act of 1916 in Sec. 9 (a), permits reassessment also in cases of "erroneous" returns, and the Revenue Act of 1918 provides in Sec. 250 (b) for assessment and collection of "the correct amount of tax," whether "greater or less than that shown in the return."

ELLIOTT v. SWARTWOUT
(U. S. Supreme Court, January Term, 1836)
(10 Pet. 137)

Record: Action to recover sum paid as duties to defendant as collector of port of New York. Upon the trial in the court below the judges were divided in opinion upon certain questions, among which were the following:

Questions: (1) Is the collector personally liable for an excess of duties paid to him when he has acted in good faith and no protest was made at the time of the payment?

(2) Is the collector liable where, although he has acted in good faith, the payment of the excess duties was made under protest?

Decision: (1) A payment of duties made without protest or declaration of intention to sue for recovery of the money is a voluntary payment under mutual mistake of law, and, in such case, no action will lie to recover back the money.

(2) A collector cannot, however, exonerate himself from personal responsibility by paying the duties over to his principal if he has had notice not to pay them over. The collector is personally responsible when such notice is given or protest is made at the time of payment, although he may subsequently pay over the money into the treasury.

EQUITABLE LIFE ASSURANCE SOCIETY v. HART
(Supreme Court of Montana, June 13, 1918)
(173 Pac. 1062)

Record: Montana Acts of March 1, 1911, March 4, 1915, and March 3, 1917. Action at law against the State Treasurer and the State Auditor for fees under the statutes. Judgment for defendants, and plaintiff appealed. Affirmed.

Facts: The Act of 1911, as amended by Act of 1915, required all insurance companies, associations and societies, before commencing to do business within the state, to pay a certain fee to the state auditor. The Act of 1917, which contains a general repealing clause, required every corporation engaged in business in the state to pay a license fee, for carrying on its business, of a certain per centum upon the total net income. In the case of a corporation engaged in interstate and intrastate commerce, the fee was based upon the net earnings derived from the intrastate business; whereas, in computing the net income, certain deductions were allowed only to a corporation doing business wholly within the state. The plaintiff is a foreign corporation doing business in this and other states, and has been held to pay the fees under both statutes.

Questions: (1) Is a license tax upon all insurance companies, associations and societies repealed by the general repealing clause in a later license tax act, which requires a fee of *all* corporations doing business within the state?

(2) If not, is it double taxation to require the insurance company to pay the second fee?

(3) Is an Act invalid which allows corporations doing business wholly within the state to make certain deductions from the gross income, and does not allow the same deductions for a corporation doing business within and without the state?

Decisions: (1) "The range of the former (Act of 1911) is over all insurance companies, whether corporate or not, and it is confined to them; the range of the latter (Act of 1917) is over all corporations save those excepted, without regard to the business pursued, and it does not apply to unincorporated concerns. One is unconditional, requiring no net income, imposing a license to carry on a particular business subject to control by a specific department of the state * * * ; the other is conditional, requires a net income, imposes an excise upon the valuable privilege of doing business as a corporation measured by that income, and its principal purpose is the raising of revenue for the exclusive use of the state. There is, therefore, no manifest conflict between the two enactments." The later Act, therefore, does not repeal the earlier one.

(2) "This is not a case of double taxation in any proper acceptance of the term * * *. They are not for the same thing."

(3) "A corporation whose business is wholly within this state presents a case where the basis of every public demand, state, national, or foreign is here; that business constitutes its only resource

available to answer such demands, and a balance struck between that business and those demands in connection with other deductions allowed is a true measure of its net income * * *. This arrangement leaves the two classes upon a substantial equality." The Act is not discriminating, and, therefore, is not invalid.

EQUITABLE TRUST CO. OF NEW YORK
v. W. PACIFIC RY. CO. et al.
(U. S. District Court, N. D. Calif., Second Div. Aug. 21, 1916)
(236 Fed. 813)

Record: Revenue Act of 1916. In equity on application by receivers for instructions whether to make a return under the Act. Directed to make no return.

Facts: See question below.

Question: Is a fund in the hands of receivers, which represents the net proceeds in conducting the operations of a railroad while in their hands, over and above the expense and authorized expenditures made by them, subject to tax under the Federal Income Tax Act as net earnings of the corporation, and as such required to be returned by them to the Collector of Internal Revenue?

Decision: Upon the authority of the Pennsylvania Steel Co. v. New York Ry. Co., 198 Fed. 775, 117 C. C. A. 556, it is held that such fund is not subject to the tax and no return need be made.

EVANS v. GORE, COLLECTOR
(U. S. Supreme Court, Decided June 1, 1920)
(253 U. S. 245)

Record: Revenue Act of 1918. Action to recover portion of income tax paid. Upon demurrer judgment was entered for defendant (262 Fed. 550). Plaintiff brought error.

Facts: The plaintiff, a United States district judge appointed in 1899, was assessed and paid under protest a tax on his salary as district judge. This was in accordance with the provision in Section 213 of the Act in question.

Question: Has Congress the power under the Constitution to levy a tax on the salary of a federal judge appointed to office before the enactment of the taxing statute?

Decision: The Constitution, in Art. I, Sec. 1, Cl. 6, expressly forbids diminution of a federal judge's compensation, by providing that the compensation of the judges "shall not be diminished during their continuance in office." This limitation being for the public weal and not for the private benefit of the judges, should be liberally construed. Any diminution which by its necessary operation and effect withholds or takes from the judge a part of that which has been promised by law for his services must be regarded as within the prohibition. The Sixteenth Amendment does extend the taxing power to new or excepted subjects but merely removes all occasion otherwise existing for an apportionment among the states. Diminution of the judge's salary by taxation thus remains prohibited by the Constitution.

IN RE INCOME TAXES, EWA PLANTATION CO.

(Supreme Court of Hawaii, January 3, 1918)

(18 Haw. 530)

Record: Hawaiian R. L. Secs. 1280 and 1281. Appeal from Tax Appeal Court which allowed the deduction claimed. Reversed.

Facts: The Ewa Plantation Company is engaged in the production of sugar upon a plantation which it has leased. In making its return, since its building and machinery will revert to the lessor, it made a deduction for depreciation, which was computed by dividing the book value of the property at the beginning of the year by the remaining years of the lease, and the quotient is the depreciation for the year. The Income Tax Act provides for the deduction of all losses actually sustained, and one section provides a tax on "the amount of sales of all movable property, less the amount expended in the purchase or production of the same."

Questions: (1) May a corporation, operating upon a leased plantation, apportion the cost of permanent improvements to each year of the term of the lease, and charge that to depreciation un der the section providing for the deduction of losses sustained, since the improvements will revert to the lessor?

(2) If it cannot be deducted as an expense or loss actually sustained, does it fall under "amount expended" in that section including as income the amount of sales of all movable property less the "amount expended" in the purchase or production of the same!

Decisions: (1) "In the present case it is claimed that one-thirty-fourth of the value of the mill buildings, roads and bridges, storm ditches and reservoirs was 'expended' in the production of the crop, not because their use had lessened their actual value by this amount, but because at the end of thirty-four years they would revert to the lessor. 'Depreciation' on this class of items is merely in the nature of a sinking fund to recoup their cost, a deduction eminently proper between the corporation and its stockholders, but not within the deductions allowed by the statute."

(2) "A corporation engaged in buying and selling movable property suffers the same depreciation as the corporation in this case, but it could hardly be urged that depreciation upon their buildings or office furniture was an amount expended in the purchase of the goods in which they dealt. It is sufficient to say that we do not consider that this language can be made to cover depreciation of plant."

EX PARTE IVES
(U. S. District Court, D. Conn., April 3, 1865)
(Fed. Case 7114)

Record: Act of June 30, 1864. Application by assessor for an attachment as for a contempt. Motion dismissed.

Facts: The defendant, Ives, was a stockholder in a corporation which earned a large amount of money in 1863, which was not divided among the stockholders, and no part thereof was returned as income by Ives. Ives declined to answer questions put to him by the assessor respecting his stock interest in the company and profits made by it.

Question: Are undivided earnings of a corporation gains and profits to which the stockholders are entitled and, hence, under Section 117 of the Act requiring the profits of all companies to be included in estimating the income of any person entitled to the same, whether divided or otherwise, to be returned by the stockholders as income?

Decision: "* * * the law commits the care of the corporate funds to the directors or trustees, or to the stockholders exercising their corporate functions, and not to the stockholders, in their individual capacity." The latter are not entitled to gains and profits, which the corporation itself has not set aside for division, and hence such earnings are not taxable as income to the stockholders.

FARMER'S LOAN & TRUST CO.
v. COUNCIL BLUFFS G. & E. L. CO.
(Circuit Court S. D. Ia. W. D., Dec. 22, 1898)
(90 Fed. 806)

Record: Chapter 448, Laws 55th Cong. 2d Sess. Rule on county recorder of Pottawattamie County, Iowa, to show cause why he should not file a certain master's deed without the same having revenue stamps affixed. Rule dismissed.

Facts: This court appointed a receiver in a foreclosure proceeding against the defendant. Subsequently the property of defendant was sold at public sale by the master's commissioner. The recorder refused to file the master's deed because no revenue stamps were affixed.

Question: Was a master's deed exempt from the requirements of the Act as to stamping conveyances?

Decision: The deed in question is not a conveyance by the government. It does not purport to, nor does it convey any title, interest, or right held by the government. The sale and conveyance are not for the benefit of the Government. The instrument would have to be stamped if executed by the owner of the property and no reason exists why the case should be otherwise where the master executes it in place of the owner.

FAULKNER et al. v. TREFRY
(Supreme Judicial Court of Massachusetts, January 3, 1918)
(118 N. E. 229)

Record: Massachusetts Act of May 26, 1916. Appeal from the determinations of the tax commission as provided in statute, an application for abatement having been denied. Taxes ordered repaid.

Facts: The petitioners, who are the executors of the will of Faulkner, filed a return for the period from January 1, 1916, to November 29, 1916, the date of the death of the testator, and a return for the remainder of the year. Both were filed under protest, and the Commissioner levied assessments. The Act provides for a tax on incomes to be levied "in the year nineteen hundred and seventeen and in each year thereafter." It also provides that income of certain classes of the inhabitants for the calendar year prior to the assessment of the tax are taxable, but all that it says about estates is that "the income received by persons since deceased shall be taxed to their estates."

Question: Do the words "since deceased" in the Act make the statute retroactive as to the estates of deceased persons, when the Act expressly provides that as to certain classes it shall be retroactive?

Decision: "The tax year began to run from January 1, 1917, and the words 'since deceased' refer only to the estates of those who died after the commencement of its operation * * *. The statute is not declared to be retroactive as to the estates of deceased persons; nor can it be extended by implication."

FIDELITY TRUST CO. OF BALTIMORE, MD.,
v. MILES, COLLECTOR
BALTIMORE TRUST CO. v. SAME
(U. S. District Court, D. Maryland, June 18, 1919)
(258 Federal 770)

Record: Act of October 22, 1914. Action to recover tax paid under protest. Judgment for defendant in each case.

Facts: Each of the plaintiffs is a banker, and in addition to its regular banking business acts as a fiduciary—that is, as a trustee, receiver, executor and administrator. It also engages in underwriting and promoting new enterprises, thereby making loans to its associates, or to the company which they are launching; and they also deal in stocks, bonds or other securities for its own account; that is to say, it buys them when it thinks they are cheap, in order that it may subsequently sell them at a profit. No showing was made that any special portion of the assets was devoted to the foregoing purposes.

Question: Was sufficient evidence introduced to show that part of the capital, surplus and undivided profits was not used in the banking business and therefore should not be included in determining the special tax on banks imposed by the Act?

Decision: "I find that the plaintiffs have not shown that any part of its capital, surplus and undivided profits were not used in banking, because it was used in its fiduciary business. No attempt was made to show that any special portion of its assets was devoted to this part of its business, nor indeed, except for the purpose of giving it such a standing as inspires confidence and attracts patronage, is any needed. In the syndicate operations they make loans, taking as security the pledge of the borrower's interest in the adventure, and much of this is banking, within the definition of the Act." In regard to dealing in stocks and bonds for profit: "Most banks, state and national, do the same thing, as a usual and useful incident to their banking business." Therefore, "to my mind, sitting as a jury, there is no preponderance of evidence that any determinable portion of the capital of either is not used in banking." The tax should be assessed upon the entire amount of capital, surplus and undivided profits.

FIDELITY TRUST CO. v. LEDERER, COLLECTOR
(U. S. District Court, E. D. Penn., December Term, 1920)
(Fed. Case 8118)

Record: Revenue Act of 1918. Sur rule for judgment. This case is in effect a case stated by the litigants in the determination of which this court is simply asked to decide a question of law. Rule for judgment discharged.

Facts: All the facts, the opinion states, which enter into the discussion are established and conceded to be in the record. The facts are therefore not set forth in the opinion. The certificates, so called, as to which the taxability thereof under the stamp tax provisions of the Revenue Act of 1918 is the sole question for determination, are described in the opinion substantially as follows: They are strictly neither evidences of debt nor of shares in corporate assets. This is because of their peculiar form and of the plan under which created. They have all the same general purpose and character and would doubtless be classified by a securities dealer as "Car Trust Certificates." They are called for because some railroad or other transportation company is in need of rolling stock or equipment and is without funds or credit with which to supply itself, and there is some legal or other difficulty in the way of a direct pledge of the property. They are issued under a number of different plans, but the one involved here is the Philadelphia plan. Those willing to share in the venture are invited to place their contributions in the hands of an acceptable trustee. The rolling stock, or other property, is then purchased in the name of this trustee, as owner. The trustee then enters into a form of bailment or conditional sale agreement with the carrier, the periodical and final payments upon which are sufficient to pay the interest on the investment and the principal at maturity. In the meantime the contributors hold the certificates or acknowledgment of the trustee of their respective shares in the venture.

Question: Are these so called trust certificates under the "Philadelphia plan" taxable under the provisions of the stamp tax portion of the Revenue Act of 1918?

Decision: Trust certificates issued under the "Philadelphia plan" are held taxable as certificates of indebtedness. In holding that these certificates are not within the literal verbiage of the Act of Congress in question, not being "certificates of indebtedness issued by any person" nor "instruments issued by any corporation," the court said: "The only obligation in the nature of a debt or promise to pay money is the obligation and agreement of the carrier to pay the agreed price for the hire and use of the property, or the rentals as they are commonly termed. The trustee is a mere purse, and only in a secondary sense can be said to owe anything to any one other than faithfulness to its trust obligations, and is not a debtor even in this secondary sense unless and until and as the moneys which belong to the contributors come into its

hands. * * * The Act of Congress, however, includes more
than the two kinds of securities mentioned above, because we think
it includes everything 'known generally as corporate securities'.
That these certificates are so known would not be denied. The
denial would be of the correctness of this construction of the Act
of Congress. There are two obstacles to be surmounted before
reaching this construction. One is that the rule of the nearest ante-
cedent makes the quoted phrase relate to and serve as a definition of
the described kinds of 'instruments issued by corporations', and
the other is that the finding of a meaning to tax all instruments
'commonly known as corporate securities' involves presence of a
grammatical error in the Act of Congress. Neither of these obstacles are, however, insurmountable, if this was the meaning of
Congress, and we so find. Nor do we see any conflict between a
ruling that these certificates are taxable and the doctrine of the
cases to which we have been referred that there is no such thing as
a doubtful tax. U. S. v. Isham, 84 U. S. 496. * * * The real
truth back of the whole discussion is that if these certificates are
not taxable, it is because of the accidental circumstances of a wholly
nominal separation of the security held by the taxpayer from the
obligation of the debt entered into by the carrier corporation. The
real security is the promise not of one corporation but of the two
to pay to the certificate holders the sums due them. The real transaction is the request of the carrier company made to the certificate
holders to advance the money required for equipment, in consideration of which the carrier agrees to pay back the sum advanced,
with interest. * * * judgment discharged.'' The trust certificates in question were therefore held taxable.

FINK, COLLECTOR,
v. NORTHWESTERN MUT. LIFE INS. CO.
(U. S. Circuit Court of Appeals, Seventh Circuit, June 24, 1920)
(267 Fed. 968)

Record: Act of Aug. 5, 1909. Action at law to recover taxes
paid on net income under Sec. 38 of the Act. Judgment for plaintiff (248 Fed. 568), and defendant brought error. Modified.

Facts: Plaintiff is a mutual insurance company, organized

under the laws of Wisconsin, and annually collects level premiums which are sufficiently large to pay the insurance cost, including reserves, and all the expenses of the business. Usually there is something left over for a surplus, which surplus is required by the laws of Wisconsin to be divided among the policyholders. The commissioner amended defendant in error's returns for the years 1909 and 1910 and included as net income for these years the surplus together with other items described in questions below.

Questions: (1) Are dividends applied at the option of the policyholders to purchase paid-up additions and annuities net income for the years in which so applied, within the meaning of the Act?

(2) Are dividends applied at the option of the policyholders in partial payment of renewal premiums, net income for the year in which so applied within the meaning of the Act?

(3) Are premiums due and deferred, and interest due and accerned but not actually collected in cash, net income within the meaning of the Act?

(4) Is interest on policy loans, which by the terms of the contract is added to the principal of the loan when it becomes due and remains unpaid, income within the meaning of the Act?

(5) Are decreases in value of assets because of amortization of premiums on bonds deductible from income as "depreciation" under the Act?

(6) Are additions to the reserve fund, because of liability on supplementary contracts not involving life contingencies, deductible from income within meaning of Act which permits insurance companies to deduct "the net addition, if any, required by law to be made within the year to reserve funds"?

Decision: (1 and 2) "The dividend of surplus is in no sense a dividend of profits. It is simply a fund made available to the policyholders which may be used for the payment of premiums, paid-up additions, annuities or for whatever use they may choose to make of it. The Excise Law did not take effect until Jan. 1, 1909, and inasmuch as the surplus converted into dividends in 1909 was received by the company before the law went into effect, that surplus, converted into dividends, was not income for 1909. The surplus from premiums out of which dividends for 1910 were declared, was a part of the income for 1909, and formed a basis for taxation under the Excise Law for that year, and could not, as dividends, form a basis for further taxation. In other words, the fair interpretation of the statute is that income forms a basis for taxation only for the year in which it was received."

(3) "The expression, 'income received during such years,' employed in the Act of 1909, looks to the time of realization, rather than to the period of accruement, except as the taking effect of the Act on a specified date (Jan. 1, 1909) excludes income that accrued before that date." Hays v. Gauley Mt. Coal Co., 247 U. S. 189.

(4) "This question is answered contrary to the government's contention by Board of Assessors, etc., v. N. Y. Life Ins. Co., 216 U. S. 517," in which the Court said it was not income within the meaning of the Act.

(5) "Amortization of bonds does not come within any definition of 'depreciation' under the Act of 1909. The item arose from mere book adjustments. Depreciation, as used in the Act, refers to wear and tear and obsolescence of structures, machinery, and personality in use in the business." It does not cover the items in this case which arose from mere book adjustments.

(6) "The reserve meant in the law is that fund which is built up to mature the policy. Of course, at the time when money is taken out of the reserve account and is not used for immediate payment, it must be held somehow. In other words, it is reserved for the purpose of future payment. The full amount is there at the beginning, and there is nothing that has to be built upon or matured. Nothing more can be reserved on that account." This being a reserve account created to replace one wiped out, the amount thereof cannot be deducted.

FIRST NATIONAL BANK OF GREENCASTLE
v. UNITED STATES

(U. S. Court of Claims, December, 1879)

(15 Court of Claims 225)

Record: Act of June 6, 1872. Action at law to recover taxes paid under protest. Judgment for claimant.

Facts: "On the 7th of August, 1879, the Commissioner of Internal Revenue allowed the refund of the tax erroneously taxed to and paid by the claimant and certified the same in writing to the acting officer for payment by warrant on the Treasury in the usual manner. The allowance thus made was rejected by the first comptroller, who refused to certify it for payment on the ground that the claim upon which it was founded was not presented to the Commissioner within two years next after the cause of action accrued."

Question: May the comptroller refuse to certify for payment or allowance a claim under Act of January 6, 1872, under the circumstances set out above?

Decision: "By Sections 3220 and 3228 of this Act Congress has conferred upon the Commissioner of Internal Revenue the power and duty of passing upon the merits and determining the validity of all claims for refund of taxes therein specified. His decisions thereon are in the nature of an award made by the arbitrator. There are several classes of cases in which jurisdiction over the adjustment of demands against the government are entrusted by law to certain executive officers. Until the designated officer has exercised his power and decided in favor of such a claim the United States is not liable to an action thereon. But when the officer who is clothed with that power has allowed the claim and made his certificate to that effect, a new cause of action arises by the implied contract or statute upon that section, into which the original demand is merged, and it may be prosecuted to judgment in this court if for want of an appropriation or other cause its payment is refused by the Treasury. If claimant has applied to the Commissioner for the refund of a tax alleged to have been illegally assessed and wrongfully paid, it is for him to lay before that officer all the evidence upon which he relies to prove the facts; and it then becomes the duty of the Commissioner to weigh the evidence, to exercise his best and impartial judgment upon it, and to decide whether or not the claim shall be allowed. From the Commissioner's decision there is no appeal to any other executive officer. If the decision is against the claimant his legal remedy in the Treasury Department is exhausted unless the claim be such that he can maintain an action upon it against the collector. The Commissioner's decision as to whether or not the claim reached his office in due time, in the absence of fraud or illegality, is conclusive and cannot be set aside in this court.''

FIRST NATIONAL BANK OF JACKSON v. McNEEL, COLL.
(U. S. Circuit Court of Appeals, Fifth Cir., Jan. 8, 1917)
(238 Fed. 559)

Record: Act of August 5, 1909. Action at law to recover taxes paid under protest under Section 38 of this Act. Judgment for defendant and plaintiff brought error. Affirmed.

Facts: See Question.

Question: May a bank, in computing the Corporation Excise Tax, deduct from its gross income the amount of State taxes assessed on its shares of stock under the following State statute:

"Banks; How Taxed (Laws 1890, page 6).—The president, cashier, or other officer having like duties of each bank or banking association in this State, * * * shall deliver to the assessor of taxes of the county in which it is located, a written statement on or before the first day of May in each year, under oath, of the number and amount of all the shares of its capital stock paid in, or if it be not a corporation or joint stock company, then the amount of its capital, and of the sum of all undivided profits or surplus or accumulation of any sort constituting part of the assets of the bank and not including its real estate; and the value of such shares estimated at par and increased by the proportion of the par value of all the shares of stock to the said surplus fund or accumulation, or of the amount of its capital so increased, shall be the basis of the taxation of such shares to the holder or of the capital to the owner thereof; but if the shares of such bank or association are of less value than par, they shall be valued accordingly''!

Decision: In construing the statute set out above, the Supreme Court of Mississippi, in the case of Bank v. Oxford, 70 Miss. 504, said:

"If a bank has added to its capital stock any sum, by whatever name, which augments the value of its stock and puts that in non-taxable securities, that does not entitle it to any deduction in taxation, but that capital stock, at its increased value, by reason of such accumulations, is the basis of taxation, the purpose of the law being to impose on holders of bank stock taxes according to value as on other forms of property. The owner of bank stock is not required to give it in to the assessor. Another mode of reaching it is provided, and that is through the bank, whose officers are required to report it, and the bank to pay it. In other words, the shareholder is to be taxed, and pay through the bank." The statute as so construed does not impose the tax on the bank or its capital, but upon the shareholders; the bank being required to pay for them. The absence of express provision in the statute giving the bank the right to recover from its several shareholders their proportionate part of the amount so paid for them does not show that there is no such right of recovery, or that the intention was for the tax to fall ultimately upon the bank and not upon its shareholders. That the tax fell upon the shareholders and not upon the bank is sufficiently shown by the language of the statute, given the meaning which the Supreme Court of Mississippi has found that it expresses. (Bank v. Oxford, 70 Miss. 504.) The conclusion is that the payment in question was not for taxes imposed within the meaning of those words, as used in the provision of the Corporation Tax Act as to deductions allowable in ascertaining the corporation's net income, as the tax in question was imposed, not on the corporation, but upon its shareholders. Therefore, the amount of such taxes was not deductible.

FIRST TRUST & SAVINGS BANK v. SMIETANKA, COLL.
(U. S. Circuit Court of Appeals, Seventh Circuit, October 5, 1920)
(268 Fed. 230)

Record: Act of October 3, 1913. Action to recover income taxes paid under protest. Judgment for defendant, and plaintiff brought error. Reversed and remanded.

Facts: Plaintiff was trustee under the will of Otto Young, deceased, which will disposed of portions of the annual income of the trust during the lives of the widow and four daughters, and provided for final distribution among the grandchildren, or their surviving issue when the last survivor of the daughters shall have deceased and the youngest of the grandchildren shall have attained the age of twenty-one years. The annual income exceeded the amount required by the trustee to pay the annuities to the widow and children. A tax was assessed upon all income received by the plaintiff as trustee.

Question: Is annual income in excess of the amount necessary to pay annuities to widow and children under will, and payable to persons not now determinable, taxable income for year in which earned, under Act of October 3, 1913?

Decision: "This ruling (T. D. 2231, requiring payment of tax on income of unascertained residuary legatees) was the cause of the present and similar suits. It illustrates the not unnatural tendency of tax officers to increase the revenues by implications and strained constructions." Such income is not taxable under Act of Oct. 3, 1913. It was, however, taxed by Revenue Act of 1916.

FISH v. IRWIN
(U. S. District Court, N. D. N. Y.)
(Not reported)

Record: Revenue Acts of 1913 and 1916. Suit to recover additional income taxes paid for the years 1914, 1915, 1916. The case was tried on stipulation but certain questions were sent to the jury.

Facts: (1) The plaintiff operated the Continental Village Farm, consisting of 1,300 acres, of which 900 were woodland, and 400 cultivated. There were cow barns on the farm, and there was evidence of its being a cattle farm. No profits had ever been realized from the farm but there was a reasonable probability of profits in the future.

(2) The Glennclyffe Farm, also operated by the plaintiff, consisted of 480 acres of which but 70 were cultivated. There never had been a profit from this farm and there was no reasonable expectation of one. The evidence further disclosed that expenses were greatly in excess of a legitimate farm enterprise, and that the raising of crops was more of a hobby than a business. The plaintiff claimed the right to deduct expenses incurred in the operation of these farms from his gross income.

Questions: (1) Was the plaintiff engaged in carrying on farming as a business at the Continental Village Farm?

(2) Was the plaintiff engaged in carrying on farming as a business at the Glenclyffe farm?

Decision: The instructions of the court to the jury were as follows:

"That if the plaintiff was a person cultivating and operating a farm for recreation or pleasure, other than on the recognized principles of farming, then he was not a farmer.

"That if the jury find that the plaintiff was the owner of a body of land devoted to agriculture, either to the raising of crops or pasture, for the purpose of selling the products as a business, then they are entitled to find a verdict in the favor of the plaintiff on this issue.

"Business is that which occupies the time, attention and labor of man for the purpose of a livelihood or profit. It is that which is his personal concern, interest or regular occupation."

The jury's findings, which were sustained by the court, were as follows:

(1) That the plaintiff was carrying on the business of a farmer at the Continental Village Farm.

(2) That the plaintiff was not carrying on the business of a farmer at the Glenclyffe Farm.

FLINT v. STONE TRACY CO.
(U. S. Supreme Court, March 13, 1911)
(220 U. S. 107)

Record: Act of August 5, 1909. Action at law to test the constitutionality of the Act. Judgment for United States.

Facts: The facts are necessarily stated by the court in rendering its opinion and are omitted here to avoid repetition.

Questions: (1) Is the Act of August 5, 1909, unconstitutional because it is a revenue measure originating in the Senate?

(2) Is the Act unconstitutional insofar as the tax is measured by the income from bonds, non-taxable under said statute, and from state and municipal bonds beyond the federal power of taxation?

(3) Is the Act void as taxing a function of a state because it levies a tax upon franchises which are the creation of the state in its sovereign right and authority?

(4) Is the Act so arbitrary as to place it beyond the authority conferred upon Congress in that it taxes a business when carried on as a corporation and exempts a similar business when carried on by a partnership or individual?

(5) Is the selection of the measure of income from all sources void because it includes some corporations, notably insurance companies having large investments in municipal bonds and other non-taxable securities, and in real estate and personal property not used in the business?

(6) Is the measurement of the tax by the net income of the corporation or company received by it from all sources so unequal, arbitrary, and baseless as to fall outside the authority of the taxing power?

(7) Is the power of taxing corporations so exercised by Congress as to practically destroy the right of states to create corporations?

(8) Were real estate companies doing business to such extent that the tax applies?

(9) Is the Act unconstitutional with special respect to public service companies inasmuch as it is imposed upon a public agency engaging in carrying on municipal or state enterprises?

(10) Did Congress exceed its power in permitting a deduction to be made of interest payments, only in case of interest paid by banks and trust companies on deposits and interest actually paid within the year on its bonded or other indebtedness, to an amount not exceeding the paid-up capital stock of the corporation or company?

(11) Is the tax so unequal that by definition it is not such an act as Congress has delegated power to impose?

(12) Is the Fourteenth Amendment protecting against unreasonable seizures and searches violated in that the law requires that returns be filed in the office of the Commissioner of Internal Revenue and constitute public records open to inspection as such?

Decision: (1) "* * * The bill originated in the House, and the Senate in substituting the corporation tax for another tax provided for in the original bill did no more than exercise its undoubted power of amendment."

(2) A direct tax may be void if it reaches non-taxable property, but the measure of an excise tax on a privilege may be the income from all property even though part of it may be from tax-exempt property. It follows that a corporation tax is not invalid because it is levied on total income including that derived from municipal bonds and other non-taxable property.

(3) "The cases unite in exempting from federal taxation the means and instrumentalities employed in carrying on the governmental operations of a state." But this limitation does not extend to state agencies and instrumentalities used for carrying on a business of a private character. South Carolina v. United States, 199 U. S. 437.

(4) "* * * The only limitation upon the authority of Congress is uniformity in laying the tax, and uniformity does not require the equal application of the tax to all persons or corporations who may come within its operation, but is limited to geographical uniformity throughout the United States. Knowlton v. Moore, 178 U. S. 41. In levying excise taxes the most ample authority has been recognized from the beginning to select from and omit other possible subjects of taxation, to select one calling and omit another, to tax one class of property and forbear to tax another." The exemption in this case was not beyond the authority which Congress has.

(5) " * * * This argument confuses the measure of the tax upon the privilege with the direct taxation of the estate or thing taxed. * * * Where a tax is lawfully imposed on the exercise of privileges, within the taxing power of the nation, the measure of such tax may be the income from the property of the corporation, although a part of such income is derived from property in itself non-taxable. The distinction lies between the attempt to tax the property as such and to measure a legitimate tax upon the privileges involved in the use of such property."

The latter is within the power of Congress, and that was what was done in this case.

(6) "The tax must be measured by some standard and none can be chosen which will operate with absolute justice and equality upon all corporations. The measurement of the corporation tax by net income is not beyond the power of Congress as arbitrary and baseless. Selections of the measure and objects of taxation devolve upon Congress and not on the courts." It is not the function of the courts, "to inquire into the reasonableness of the excise either as to the amount or property on which it is to be imposed."

(7) " * * * The judicial cannot prescribe to the legislative department of the government limitations upon the exercise of its acknowledged powers. The powers to tax may be exercised oppressively upon persons, but the responsibility of the legislature is not to the courts, but to the people by whom its members are elected. So, if a particular tax bears heavily upon a corporation or a class of corporations, it cannot for that reason only be pronounced contrary to the Constitution."

(8) "Business is a very comprehensive term and implies everything about which a person can be employed." It has been defined as "that which occupies the time, attention, and labor of men for the purpose of a livelihood or profit." " * * * It is clear that corporations organized for the purpose of doing business and engaged in such activities as leasing property, colleeting rents, managing office buildings, making investments of profits, or leasing ore lands and collecting royalties, managing wharves, dividing profits, and in some cases investing the surplus, are engaged in business within the meaning of this statute * * * ."

(9) "It is no part of the essential governmental functions of a state to provide means of transportation, supply artificial lights, water and the like. These objects are often accomplished through the medium of private corporations, and, though the public may derive a benefit from such operations, the companies carrying on such enterprises are, nevertheless, private companies, whose business is prosecuted for private emolument and advantage. For

the purpose of taxation they stand on the same footing as other private corporations, upon which special franchises have been conferred. The true distinction is between the attempted taxation of those operations of the states essential to the execution of its governmental functions, and which the state can only do itself, and those activities which are of a private character.''

(10) "This provision may have been inserted with a view of preventing corporations from issuing large amounts of bonds in excess of the paid-up capital stock, and thereby distributing profits so as to avoid the tax.'' In any event, this method of ascertaining the deductions allowed should not invalidate the Act. "Such details are not wholly arbitrary, and were deemed essential to practical operation. Courts cannot substitute their judgments for that of the legislature. In such matters a wide range of discretion is allowed.''

(11) " * * * The law operates uniformly, geographically considered, throughout the United States, and in the same way wherever the subject matter is found. A liquor tax is not rendered unlawful because it may yield nothing in those states which have prohibited the liquor traffic. No more is the present law unconstitutional because of inequality of operation, owing to different local conditions.'' Knowlton v. Moore 178 U. S. 41.

(12) "This amendment was adopted to protect against abuses in judicial procedure under the guise of law, which invade the privacy of persons in their homes, papers and effects, and applies to criminal prosecutions and suits for penalties and forfeitures under the revenue laws. * * * Certainly the amendment was not intended to prevent the ordinary procedure in use in many, perhaps most of the states, requiring tax returns to be made, often under oath. * * * Congress may have deemed the public inspection of tax returns a means of properly securing the fullness and accuracy thereof. Many of the state laws make the tax returns public documents and open to inspection, * * * '' while under the Act in question " * * * returns shall be open to inspection only upon the order of the President under the rules and regulations to be prescribed by the Secretary of the Treasury and approved by the President.''

FONTENOT, COLLECTOR, ads. ACCARDO
SAME ads. STRUVE
SAME ads. CARLISI

(U. S. District Court, E. D. La., New Orleans Div., Dec. 23, 1920)

(269 Fed. 447)

Record: National Prohibition Act and Rev. Stat. Sec. 3224. Bills to enjoin collection of taxes and penalties. Preliminary injunctions issued.

Facts: In each of the three cases here involved the plaintiffs were assessed taxes and penalties under section 35, tit. 2, of the National Prohibition Act. In one case the plaintiff had been tried on a criminal charge and acquitted; in the second the plaintiff had been arrested but never brought to trial, and in the third the plaintiff had never been arrested. In none of the cases was the plaintiff required to make, or given the opportunity of making, a return, nor was any notice of any kind given before the assessment was made. In all three cases collection by distraint was proceeding or was being threatened.

Questions: (1) Are the taxes (so called) and the penalties prescribed by section 35, tit. 2, of the Act, taxes within the meaning of section 3224, Rev. Stat., declaring that no suit for the purpose of restraining the assessment or collection of any tax shall be maintained in any court?

(2) Are the provisions of the Internal Revenue Laws (Rev. Stat., section 3172 et seq.) relative to the assessment and summary collection of internal revenue taxes applicable to the assessment and collection of the taxes and penalties prescribed by the National Prohibition Act?

Decision: (1) The taxes and penalties provided for by section 35, tit. 2 of the National Prohibition Act, lack every fundamental element of a tax. There is not the slightest pretense of raising revenue, and it should not be presumed that Congress intended to levy a tax for the purpose of prohibition on something already prohibited. It is evident these so-called taxes and penalties are simply additional penalties for the violation of a criminal statute, and section 3224, Rev. Stat., is no bar to relief in equity in a proper case.

(2) Under the material provisions of the Internal Revenue Law relative to assessment and summary collection, it is the duty of all persons liable to a tax to make a return to the collector. If any person refuses, he may be interrogated by the collector. Obviously these laws could not be applicable to the collection of penalties under section 35, tit. 2, of the National Prohibition Act, as this would be requiring the offender to testify against himself in violation of his constitutional privilege.

FORGED STEEL WHEEL CO. v. LEWELLYN, COLLECTOR
(U. S. Supreme Court, March 1, 1920)
(40 Sup. Ct. 285)

Record: Munitions Tax Act. Action to recover taxes paid under protest. Verdict and judgment for plaintiff in District Court. Reversed by Circuit Court of Appeals (256 Fed. 533). Judgment of latter court affirmed.

Fact: Plaintiff manufactured rough steel forgings for shells for parties who had war contracts with the British government. To make these rough shell forms suitable for use required some 27 different processes after they were delivered by the plaintiff. The collector exacted a tax based on the amount of profits realized by plaintiff from the manufacture of these forgings.

Question: Did the making of these rough shell forms bring plaintiff within Section 301 of the Act which imposes a tax on "every person manufacturing * * * shells * * * or any part" of them?

Decision: The phrase "any part" can not be limited, as contended by the plaintiff, to mean "a substantially finished part." The question is not the quantum of manufacture, but the fact of manufacture resulting in profits. The plaintiff is taxable within the meaning of the Act.

FORTY FORT COAL CO. v. KIRKENDALL, COLLECTOR
(U. S. District Court, M. D. Pennsylvania, December, 1915)
(233 Fed. 704)

Record: Act of Aug. 5, 1909. Action at law to recover taxes paid under protest under Section 38 of this Act. Judgment for plaintiff.

Facts: Plaintiff company's property suffered actual depletion by reason of the mining of coal from it to the extent of 15 cents per ton for each ton mined. The plaintiff is suing to recover the tax on the amount of actual depletion. Plaintiff admits carrying on its books a certain sum of money as surplus which it should have properly entered on the books as depletion reserve. The government's claim is based upon this book entry.

Question: Is plaintiff barred from recovery because of carrying depletion on its books as surplus instead of reserve for depletion?

Decision: The decisions under the Excise Tax law and under the Income Tax law are uniform to the effect that the government cannot base a claim for taxes on mere bookkeeping. Mere reappraisement of property by a corporation on its books cannot form the basis of assessment of taxes on net income, even though the books show that during the tax year the value of the property was increased by the amount on which the government claimed the regular rate of tax. The amount temporarily shown on the books as surplus was not properly surplus or net income, or profit, but was merely a return of capital assets. No argument is required to demonstrate that under a tax law which makes allowances for depletion or depreciation, if an owner has a ton of coal in the ground worth 15 cents and he digs it up and sells it for 15 cents, the amount so received is not income, but in fact, only a return of the value of coal as part of the capital asset. Where amounts which should have been charged to depletion of corporate assets were carried in a surplus account, income taxes can not be based on such amounts, for that would allow the basing of taxes on mere bookkeeping.

FOSTER v. HOLLEY'S ADMINISTRATORS
(Supreme Court of Alabama, 1873)
(49 Ala. 593)

Record: Act of July 13, 1866. Action of debt on promissory note. Judgment for plaintiff affirmed.

Facts: Plaintiff introduced in evidence, over the objection of defendant, a note stamped with revenue stamps, which had not been affixed when the note was signed and issued, but some time afterwards and shortly before the note was offered in evidence. These stamps were not cancelled until this was done in court at the trial, but the initials of the person cancelling same were not written on the stamps.

Question: Was the note admissible in evidence?

Decision: A note may be stamped after its issue so as to make it admissible in evidence unless the stamps were "omitted with intent to evade" the tax. The failure to write the person's initials who cancelled the stamps does not affect its admissibility.

FREEDMAN v. SIGEL, COLLECTOR
(U. S. Circuit Court, S. D. New York, Jan. 2, 1873)
(Fed. Case 5080)

Record: Act of June 30, 1864. Action at law to recover taxes exacted by collector. Judgment for plaintiff.

Facts: The plaintiff was a justice of the Superior Court of the City of New York, and paid under protest a tax upon his salary as judge, which salary was fixed by the board of supervisors and paid out of the city treasury.

Questions: (1) Is the salary of a justice of the Superior Court of the City of New York, which salary is fixed by the board of supervisors, taxable, since the salary of a state judge can not be taxed?

(2) If not, does the fact that the salary is payable out of the city treasury make it taxable?

Decision: (1) "The manner in which a state chooses to determine the salary of its judicial officers, neither changes the character of the tribunals over which they preside, nor the relation of these officers or offices to the state, or to the Federal government." The legislature "saw fit to leave the amount of the salaries of the judges to be determined by the board of supervisors, and conferred upon the latter authority to that end." This was within the power of the legislature, and as the justice is an officer of the state his salary can not be taxed.

(2) "To assert such a proposition would be to maintain that the sovereign power of a State depends upon the manner in which

it exercises its discretion, in the details of its administration, and the distribution of its public burdens.'' This clearly is not the basis of the sovereign power of the State. The manner in which the justice is paid does not determine whether he is not a State judge, and does not make his salary taxable under the Federal Act.

GAAR, SCOTT & CO. v. SHANNON
(U. S. Supreme Court, Decided Feb. 19, 1912)
(223 U. S. 468)

Record: Suit against Secretary of State of Texas for taxes paid under protest. Defendant's demurrer sustained in state courts and judgment entered accordingly. Plaintiff brought error. Affirmed.

Facts: Plaintiff, an Indiana corporation, in 1901 paid the Franchise Tax required of foreign corporations and secured a permit to do business in Texas for ten years. The Texas legislature in 1905 passed an Act requiring foreign corporations doing business in Texas to pay a still higher tax and providing for heavy penalties for failure to pay. The plaintiff paid the tax under protest. The plaintiff's petition alleged that it transacted only an interstate business in Texas.

Question: Could the constitutional question of impairment of contract raised by the plaintiff be considered by this court in view of the fact that the State Court found that the plaintiff was not entitled to recover because the taxes had been voluntarily paid?

Decision: If the records afford a basis for sustaining the proposition found by the State Court, this court will not consider the federal questions involved. An Act which declares that when the Franchise Tax is not paid by a given date a penalty of 25% shall be incurred, the license of the company shall be cancelled, and the right to sue shall be lost, operates as duress; and payment to avoid such consequences is compulsory and not voluntary. However, in this case, the plaintiff was not within the class to which the statute applied, because the Supreme Court of Texas has held that the Franchise Tax had no application to corporations doing an interstate business. While a payment of tax by one included in the class to which a statute applies in order to avoid penalties and forfeiture is compulsory, it is not so as to one not included in such class, and payment thereof by such person is voluntary and not under duress.

GAITHER v. MILES, COLLECTOR
(U. S. District Court of Maryland, Oct. 23, 1920)
(268 Fed. 692)

Record: Revenue Act of 1918. Suit by plaintiff executor against the collector of internal revenue to recover back an estate tax paid under protest. Judgment for plaintiff for part of amount sued for.

Facts: Plaintiff as executor of the estate of Thomas H. Gaither, deceased, sued to recover $3,469.63 paid under protest as an estate tax upon $34,695.25, the proceeds of five insurance policies upon the life of the testator, who, about two months before his death, had caused them to be made payable to his son and daughter. In the transfer of one of the policies he reserved to himself the right to again change the beneficiary. Another was an endowment policy which had about 19 months longer to run, and concerning which he provided that the proceeds therefrom should be paid to him at its maturity, should he then be living. In none of the other three policies did the testator reserve any interest either to himself or his personal representatives. The transfers were made without consideration and within much less than two years before his death. They aggregate $21,973.69. About the time he transferred the policies he transferred other property, reserving to himself a life estate. At the time the transfers were made the testator was 83 years of age. For a man of his age he was in a fair state of health.

Questions: (1) Is the policy transferred with reservation of the right to change the beneficiary, taxable as part of the estate, and is the endowment policy transferred with reservation of the right to receive payment of proceeds at maturity, if then living, also taxable as part of the estate?

(2) Are the policies assigned without reservations transferred within the meaning of the statutary phrase "transferred in contemplation of death," and so taxable?

Decision: (1) "In neither of the above instances was the transfer intended to take effect in possession or enjoyment until the death of the assignor, and the proceeds of these policies, amounting to $12,921.60, were accordingly subject to tax as part of his estate."

(2) "Under the circumstances I do not feel justified in holding that the three policies, which were absolutely assigned, were within the statutory meaning of the phrase 'transferred in contemplation of death.'" These three policies, therefore, did not remain a part of the decedent's estate, so as to be subject to the estate tax.

GALIN v. UNITED STATES

(U. S. Court of Claims, Sec. 7, 1903)

(39 Ct. Cls. 55)

Record: Act of July 1, 1862. Petition for travel pay. Demurrer to petition sustained.

Facts: The claimant, an officer during the Civil War, who, upon discharge, did not receive full travel pay, filed a claim under the provisions of the Act of March 3, 1901, which made an appropriation to pay arrears. In the meantime the Income Tax Law of July 1, 1862, had been repealed, but an income tax was deducted from his pay when received.

Questions: (1) How much of the travel pay of an officer of the United States army is taxable as income where the officer renders no account of the actual expense incurred?

(2) Is the sum received under an appropriation by Congress to pay officers arrears of pay, after an income tax law has been repealed, taxable under the Income Tax Act?

Decision: (1) "It does not follow that the amount of such transportation and subsistence thus commuted was necessarily consumed in defraying the claimant's expenses, and so, to ascertain that amount and secure the exemption of the same from taxes, the accounting officers held that it was incumbent upon the claimant to render an account thereof. This he does not appear to have done." Section 86 of the Act expressly imposes the tax on "all salaries of officers or payments to persons" in the military service. "Congress by the language used evidently intended that whatever sums of money were paid to such officer by the United States * * * should share the tax." The officer can not secure the exemption unless he renders an account.

(2) "The claimant did not at the time the Act of 1862 was in force make application for the payment of such travel pay and commutation of subsistence, and for that reason no formal deduction from the amount could be made of the tax, but in law, if the amount due the claimant was subject to the deduction, then the tax attached thereto the moment the claim accrued, and was not taken away by the repealing Act of July 14, 1870."

GERMANTOWN TRUST CO. v. LEDERER, COLLECTOR
(U. S. Circuit Court of Appeals, Third Cir., March 5, 1920)
(263 Fed. 672)

Record: Act of October 22, 1914. Action to recover tax paid. Judgment for defendant below, and plaintiff brought error. Affirmed.

Facts: The defendant collector assessed a tax against plaintiff trust company on its entire capital, surplus and undivided profits under authority of the Act of October 22, 1914, imposing a tax of $1 for each $1,000 of capital used in banking. The plaintiff was doing business in Pennsylvania, with general powers conferred upon trust companies by the laws of Pennsylvania which included, administering trusts, acting as surety, insuring titles, transacting a general real estate business, renting safe deposit boxes, receiving deposits of money and loaning money on collateral. Its assets consisted of capital, undivided profits, surplus, trust funds and money received on deposit. In the course of its business the plaintiff invested a large part of these moneys in permanent investments. Except trust funds, it did not separate or distinguish its capital from its other assets. The company sought to prove at the trial that no part of its capital was used in banking and, hence, that it was not taxable, by showing that none of its depositors' money was invested in permanent investments, the deduction, of course, from such proof being that the capital was permanently invested. This evidence was rejected by the court below.

Questions: (1) Was the trial court in error in rejecting plaintiff's evidence above set forth?

(2) Upon whom is the burden of proof in an attack upon a tax assessment?

Decision: (1) What constitutes capital and how and in what amount it is employed in different departments of a trust company, including that of banking, is a question of fact to be determined by the use to which its assets of different kinds are put and established by evidence of real transactions, not by evidence merely that its permanent investments equal or exceed its capital, or by inference arising from a claimed exclusive use of "depositors' money" in banking. The distinction to be valid cannot be fanciful, mental, or merely one of bookkeeping, or based upon artificial transactions; it must be actual and determined by real transactions. The plaintiff's evidence should not have been admitted.

(2) An assessment made by an official within his jurisdiction is prima facia valid. One attacking his assessment has the burden of showing that it is unlawful. Therefore, it was held that the plaintiff was not entitled to recover.

GLASGOW v. ROWSE

(Supreme Court of Missouri, March Term, 1869)

(43 Mo. 479)

Record: Missouri Act of Feb. 20, 1865. Action of trespass for seizing and detaining a package of paper money. Judgment for plaintiff, and the defendant appealed. Reversed.

Facts: The Act provided that there should be levied, and collected, for the year 1865, a tax of a certain per cent, on the salaries of all officers who were exempt from military duty, and a tax of a lower per cent on the salaries and incomes of all other persons, and "that the assessment upon all salaries, not fixed by law and upon all incomes, should be based upon the amount of such salary or income received by the person assessed in the year preceding." The auditor of public accounts was authorized to give instructions to assessors and collectors, and he instructed the assessors that the assessment must be made upon the year ending

March 31, 1865. The plaintiff was assessed according to these instructions, and the collector collected under a tax warrant.

Questions: (1) Where the act simply says that the tax shall be assessed on the income of a certain year, and gives the auditor authority to give instructions to assessors, does he exceed his authority by his arbitrarily fixing a certain period as the year?

(2) If so, can a collector, who has collected the tax, be held in trespass where he has collected the tax under a tax warrant?

(3) Is a Tax Act unconstitutional which taxes officers exempt from military duty differently than others?

Decisions: (1) "Unless otherwise expressed, the word 'year' will always be intended to mean a calendar year; but when applied to matters of revenue, the presumption is in favor of its referring, to a fiscal year. * * * The plain meaning and true intent was that the additional tax on incomes should be levied on an assessment for the preceding year, which would coincide with and be founded on the books, therefore, made out by the respective officers. The auditor, then, in designating the 31st day of March ensuing, after the passage of the law, overstepped his authority, and the action of the assessors in obeying and conforming to his instructions was irregular."

(2) "To have this effect it would be necessary that the writ, process, or warrant, should disclose the defect."

(3) "It seems plain that the constitutional requirement that 'taxation upon property shall be in proportion to its value' does not include every species of taxation. * * * A large proportion of revenue is derived from other sources than a direct levy on property, and the doctrine contended for would release the former and throw the whole burden upon the latter." The Act is not unconstitutional.

GOLDFIELD CONSOLIDATED MINES CO. v. SCOTT, COLL.

(U. S. Supreme Court, May 20, 1920)

(247 U. S. 126)

Record: Act of August 5, 1909. Action at law to recover taxes paid under protest. Judgment for plaintiff in District Court and plaintiff brings error. Certified from the Circuit Court of Appeals. Judgment affirmed.

Facts: The plaintiff made a return of annual net income for the year 1909 claiming deduction for the actual value of ore in the ground before it was mined upon the theory that such ore constituted a source of the capital value of the property owned by it. This deduction was denied and an additional assessment was made, which the plaintiff paid and then filed claim for refund. Thereafter plaintiff filed an amended return in which the value of the ore in the ground was computed at cost. Plaintiff was required by the Commissioner to make calculation for 1909 and previous years of operation to ascertain the total exhaustion of ore during such time, and enter the amount in its books. Plaintiff was also required to print the same in its annual report to its stockholders with appropriate explanations. The Commissioner disallowed plaintiff's application for refund.

Questions: (1) Under the provisions of the Act of August 5, 1909, is a mining corporation, for the purpose of determining its net income, entitled to deduct from its gross income, any amount whatever on account of exhaustion of ore bodies caused by its operations for the year for which it is taxed?

(2) Is plaintiff mining corporation under said Act entitled, in the ascertainment of its net income, to a deduction against gross profits from the mining and treatment of ores to the extent of the cost value of the ore in the ground before it was mined, ascertained in strict compliance with the rules and regulations of the Treasury Department of February 14, 1911, Treasury Decision 1675?

(3) Where the mining corporation claimed originally in its return of net income a deduction for depreciation from exhaustion of ore for the year equal to the actual value of the ore in the ground before it was mined, and having been denied any deduction whatever for exhaustion of ore, and having been assessed accordingly, and having paid the resulting tax, made application pursuant to sections 3220 and 3226 Revised Statutes for refund, during the pendency of which application said corporation was granted leave to amend and did amend its return of net income in strict accordance with the rules and regulations promulgated February 14, 1911,

sections 80-89, Treasury Decision 1675, resulting in an amended return based upon cost, as provided in said regulations and showing deductions therefrom less than the corporation's net realizations for the year for the ore actually mined, is such corporation entitled to an allowance of deductions and refund accordingly?

(4) In what, if any, is the right to such claimed deductions affected by the fact that such corporation in obedience to regulations imposed by the Commissioner at the time of filing its amended return showing the cost value as of January 1, 1909, of its ores mined during the year, caused to be entered in its official books of account and printed in its annual report of that current year to all the stockholders and to the public, a statement of the total amount of all exhaustions, multiplied by the unit cost per ton on its mining properties for that and all previous years?

Decision: The court adhered to the principles laid down in Stratton's Independence v. Howbert, 231 U. S. 399, and Von Baumback v. Sargent Land Co., 242 U. S. 503, holding that these cases are conclusive against the contentions of the plaintiff mining company, and that it is unnecessary to enter upon further distinction of the matters disposed of in them. It follows that the first and second questions must be answered in the negative and that it is unnecessary to answer the third and fourth questions.

GOLDMAN v. TREFRY

(Supreme Judicial Court of Massachusetts, June 25, 1918)

(120 N. E. 74)

Record: Massachusetts Act of May 26, 1916. Petition for the abatement of income tax against Trefry, Tax Commissioner. Petition dismissed.

Facts: Section 2 of the Act lays a tax on income received as "as interest from * * * money at interest." Section 5 put a lower tax upon income from a "profession, employment, trade, or business," and lastly, provides that interest and dividends taxable under the first mentioned section shall not be taxed under this section. The petitioner, who is a pawnbroker and dealer in second hand articles, received interest on loans made by him as pawnbroker, and was taxed on this as interest received from money at interest.

Question: Is the money received by a pawnbroker by way of interest on loans made by him in the course of his business taxable as interest received from money at interest or as income derived from a business?

Decision: "This clause at the end of Section 5 is a direct implication that interest and dividends received as part of an income 'derived from professions, employment, trade, or business,' can be taxed as income under Section 2. In other words, this clause at the end of Section 5 is a direct implication that the Tax Commissioner can analyze the income 'derived from professions, employments, trade, or business,' and tax at 6%, so much of it as is income within Section 2, and the balance of that income 'from professions, employments, trade, or business,' at 1½%. It follows that the interest * * * received by the petitioner in the course of his business as a pawnbroker was taxable under Section 2."

GOODRICH v. EDWARDS, COLLECTOR

(Supreme Court of the U. S. March 28, 1921)

(No. 633-October Term, 1920—U. S.—)

Record: Revenue Act of 1916. Suit to recover income taxes assessed in 1920 for the year 1916, and paid under protest to avoid penalties. Demurrer to complaint sustained. In error to Dist. Ct., S. D. of New York. Reversed in part, affirmed in part.

Facts: "Two transactions are involved.

"(1) In 1912 the plaintiff in error purchased 1,000 shares of the capital stock of a mining company, for which he paid $500. It is averred that the stock was worth $695 on March 1, 1913, and that it was sold in March, 1916, for $13,931.22. The tax which the plaintiff in error seeks to recover was assessed on the difference between the value of the stock on March 1, 1913, and the amount for which it was sold.

"(2) The plaintiff in error being the owner of shares of the capital stock of another corporation, in 1912 exchanged them for stock, in a reorganized company, of the then value of $291,-

600. It is averred and admitted that on March 1, 1913, the value of this stock was $148,635.50, and that it was sold in 1916 for $269,346.25. Although it is thus apparent that the stock involved was of less value on March 1, 1913, than when it was acquired, and that it was ultimately sold at a loss to the owner, nevertheless, the collector assessed the tax on the difference between the value on March 1, 1913, and the amount for which it was sold.

"The plaintiff in error seeks to recover the whole of these two assessments."

Questions: (1) Could the case properly be considered on writ of error, on contention that fund taxed was not "income" within the scope of the 16th Amendment?

(2) Are increments in the value of securities, while owned and held as an investment, "income" within the scope of the Sixteenth Amendment after having been realized by sale?

(3) Where selling price is greater than March 1, 1913, value, and March 1, 1913, value is greater than cost, what is the taxable gain?

(4) Where selling price is greater than March 1, 1913, value, but less than cost, is there any taxable gain?

Decision: (1) "The constitutional validity of a law of the United States is so involved that the case is properly here on writ of error. Towne v. Eisner, 245 U. S. 418."

(2) This question was decided in No. 608, Merchants' Loan & Trust Co. as Trustees v. Smietanka, Collector, where it was held that such increments are income.

(3) Where selling price is greater than March 1, 1913, value, and March 1, 1913, value is greater than cost price, the taxable gain is the excess of the selling price over the March 1, 1913, value.

(4) Where selling price is greater than March 1, 1913, value, but less than cost, no taxable gain arises.

"The Act under which the assessment was made provides that the net income of a taxable person shall include gains, profits and income derived from * * * sales or dealings in property whether real or personal * * * or gains or profits and income derived from any source whatever. (39 Stat. 757; 40 Stat. 300, 307.) Section 2(c) of this same Act provides that 'for the purpose of ascertaining the gain derived from a sale or other disposition of property, real, personal or mixed, acquired before March 1, 1913, the fair market price or value of such property as of March 1, 1913, shall be the basis of determining the amount of such gain derived.' * * * It is thus very plain that the statute imposes the income tax on the proceeds of the sale of personal property to the extent only that gains are derived therefrom by the vendor, and we, therefore, agree with the Solicitor General that since no gain was realized on this investment by the plaintiff in error no tax should have been assessed against him.''

GOUGE v. HART, COLLECTOR
(U. S. District Court, W. D. Virginia, Dec. 7, 1917)
(250 Fed. 802)

Record: Rev. Stat., Sec. 3224. Suit in equity to have the sale of complainant's property by collector declared void. On motion to dismiss. Motion granted.

Facts: The complainant did not pay an assessment made by the Commissioner, and the collector, having levied upon the complainant's property, sold it, but no transfer has been made. This is a suit to have the sale declared void. Section 3224, Rev. Stat., reads: "No suit for the purpose of restraining the assessment or collection cf any tax shall be maintained in any court.''

Questions: (1) Is Section 3224, Rev. Stat., to be construed in its technical sense so that the word "restraining" does not prohibit an action to nullify a sale of property by the collector under an assessment?

(2) If so, is the government an indispensable party, so that the suit is in effect against the United States?

Decision: (1) The court held that the section was not to be construed in its technical sense, as applicable only to suits praying for restraining orders and injunctions for the following reasons:

(a) "The necessity for freedom by the executive officers of the government from judicial interference in the matter of collecting taxes is so obvious * * *.''

(b) "It is a general rule that words used in statutes are to be construed as used in their popular signification * * * ."

(c) "If Section 3224 is construed as forbidding only injunction suits, we have, unless other reasons forbid it, the result * * * that a court which is forbidden to enjoin the doing of an illegal act, may, after such an act has been done, set it aside as a nullity."

(d) "The taxpayer's property will afford a sufficient basis of credit to enable him to borrow and pay the taxes as preliminary to action to recover the money," thus no hardship.

(2) "This is in reality, though not in form, a suit against the government. * * * If the relief here asked is granted, the government alone will suffer." The purpose of the suit is to have the court nullify a claim of ownership of land vested in the government.

GOULD v. GOULD
(United States Supreme Court, Nov. 19, 1917)
(245 U. S. 151)

Record: Act of Oct. 3, 1913. Petition for order of court to allow the petitioner the full amount of alimony with no deduction on account of income taxes payable by husband. Order affirmed in New York Supreme Court (152 N. Y. Sup. 1114; 168 App. Div. 900). Affirmed.

Facts: A decree of the Supreme Court for New York County entered in 1909 forever separated the parties to this proceeding, then and now citizens of the United States, from bed and board; and further ordered the plaintiff in error to pay to Katherine C. Gould during her life the sum of $3,000 every month for her support and maintenance.

Question: Did such monthly payments during the years 1913 and 1914 constitute parts of Mrs. Gould's income within the intendment of the Act of Congress approved Oct. 3, 1913, and were they subject as such to the tax prescribed therein?

Decision· "The net income of the divorced husband subject to taxation was not decreased by payment of alimony under the court's order; and, on the other hand, the sum received by the wife on account thereof cannot be regarded as income arising or accruing to her within the enactment.'' The payments of the alimony were made by the husband out of his net income, which was taxable, but they are not taxable to the divorced wife.

GRANBY MERCANTILE CO. v. WEBSTER
(U. S. Circuit Court D. S. C., Dec. 27, 1899)
(98 Fed. 604)

Record: Suit to recover taxes paid under protest.

Facts: The Granby Mercantile Co. had an understanding with the Granby Mills, under which the company sold merchandise to the mill employees on credit. The accounts for such sales were presented to the treasurer of the mills, who paid them out of the moneys due the employees as wages. To protect itself and as a voucher, the company took at each sale an order from the purchaser drawn on the mills, payable to the company, for the amount of the purchase. The collector forced the company to pay a stamp tax for each of these orders taken.

Questions: (1) Could the fact that the instruments in question were not intended for presentation and were never presented, but were kept simply as vouchers, affect their liability to a stamp?

(2) Who is liable for the stamp?

Decision: (1) The liability of an instrument to a stamp, as well as the amount of the duty, is determined by the form and face of the instrument, and can not be affected by proof of facts outside the instrument itself.

(2) The drawer is liable for the stamp and so also is the company, for the instruments were drawn for its benefit and under the Act payment must be made by the person who makes, signs or issues the order or by the party ''for whose use or benefit the order shall be made, signed or issued.''

GRAND RAPIDS & INDIANA RAILWAY CO. v. DOYLE, COLLECTOR
(U. S. District Court, W. D. Mich., S. D., March 16, 1915)
(245 Fed. 792)

Record: Act of Aug. 5, 1909. Action at law to recover taxes paid under protest. Judgment for defendant.

Facts: In ascertaining the amount which should be charged to the ordinary expense account of the railroad and the amount which should be charged to the account of additions and betterments, the plaintiff charged to the expense account the estimated value and cost of replacing the old equipment with equipment of the same kind, and there was charged to the additions and betterments accounts the excess over and above the sum charged to the expense account. Both amounts were deducted from the gross income by the railroad in making its return.

Question: Is the portion of the cost of equipment charged to the additions and betterment account a part of the "ordinary and necessary expenses * * * in the maintenance and operation" of the railroad company's business and property, and should it be allowed as a deduction from gross income?

Decision: The excess of the cost of the new equipment over that of the old and the cost of additional equipment represents an addition to the property, and an addition to the value of the property of the railroad company. Corporations in general often use a part of their net earnings and income in the extension and improvement of their plants. In many cases industrial corporations do not declare dividends for a number of years after their organization for the very reason that they are extending and improving and adding to their property. But amounts so expended in additions are no less income than they would be if paid to the stockholders as dividends, and no less income than if the amount had been carried to the surplus account and placed in the bank. By the operating expenses of a railroad company is meant the payment for labor and materials which go into the actual operating of the road and property. "Maintenance" as used in this statute, means the up-keep or preserving of the condition of the property to be operated. It follows that the deductions of the amounts charged to the additions and betterments account were improperly made.

GRANT, COLLECTOR, v. HARTFORD & N. H. R. R. CO.
(U. S. Supreme Court, October Term, 1876)
(93 U. S. 225)

Record: Act of June 30, 1864. Action at law against collector to recover the sum of income tax and penalty paid under protest. Judgment for plaintiff (Fed. Case 6159) and defendant brought error. Affirmed.

Facts: The controversy arose upon the question of the company's income for two fiscal years. During that period they expended from their earnings a large sum in constructing a new stone bridge, to be used in place of a wooden bridge which was deemed insecure. This amount was charged to current expenses. The assessor made an assessment on this amount, claiming it was "earnings used in construction" within the meaning of the Act. The Act put a tax on "profits used in construction."

Question: Is a company liable under the Act for an income tax upon the amount of earnings expended in constructing a new bridge simply because they were used in constructing a new bridge?

Decision: "The counsel for the government insists that this bridge was a betterment, because it was more valuable than the old wooden bridge. But the assessor did not include the excess merely: he assessed the whole expenditure bestowed upon the new bridge, without making any allowance for the old one. His idea seems to have been that all earnings used in new construction are made taxable by the Act, without reference to betterments, or to their being substituted for other constructions. Indeed, his assessment is not for 'profits used in construction,' but for 'earnings used in constructing new Windsor Bridge, $55,-712.60.' In this view he was decidedly wrong. Earnings expended on a new structure may or may not be profits. Whether they are or not depends on other things to be taken into the account besides the mere fact of such expenditure."

GRAY v. DARLINGTON
(U. S. Supreme Court, December Term, 1872)
(82 U. S. 63)

Record: Act of March 2, 1867. Action at law to recover income tax paid under protest. Demurrer to declaration overruled and defendant brought error.

Facts: Before the Income Tax law was passed the plaintiff was the owner of certain United States Treasury notes, which he later exchanged for United States five-twenty bonds. The first year after the Act became effective he sold the bonds at an advance over the cost of the treasury notes, but not at an advance over their value when the law became effective. Upon this advance he was assessed an income tax.

Question: Is the advance in the value of the bonds during the period of years before the Act became effective, realized by their sale, subject to taxation as income for the year in which the bonds are sold?

Decision: "The advance in the value of property during a series of years, can in no just sense, be considered the gains, profits or income of any one particular year of the series, although the entire amount of the advance be at one time turned into money by a sale of the property. The statute looks, with some exceptions, for subjects of taxation only to annual gains, profits and income. The actual advance in value of property over its costs may, in fact, reach its height years before its sale. * * * The mere fact that property has advanced in value between the date of its acquisition and sale does not authorize the imposition of the tax on the amount of the advance."

Note: The statute here under consideration levied the tax upon "the gains, profits and income for the year," etc., and for this reason, the decision is generally regarded, as held in Hays v. Gauley Mt. Coal Co., 247 U. S. 179, and in Merchants Loan and Trust Co. v. Smietanka (Not Rep.), to have little or no weight under the modern statutes. It was, however, followed to a considerable extent by the opinion in Lynch v. Turrish, 247 U. S. 221.

GREAT NORTHERN RY. CO. v. LYNCH, COLLECTOR

(U. S. District Court, D. Minn., Third D., Jan. 10, 1921)

(T. D. 3147)

Record: Act of August 5, 1909. A syllabus of the decision in this case was published by the Treasury Department for the information of revenue officers and others concerned.

Decision: (1) The amount of obligations of a railroad corporation carried on the books as liabilities, which became outlawed and were therefore written off during the taxable years 1910 and

1911, represented profit to the company which was properly included in its net income for the year in which so written off.

(2) The excess of the sale price over the value on January 1, 1909, of property acquired prior to that date, and sold during 1909 and 1910, was income for the year in which received, although the sale price was less than the purchase price of the property.

(3) The sale in 1910 and 1911 of property acquired prior to January 1, 1909, for an amount equivalent to its market value on that date, but in excess of its purchase price, did not result in income for the purposes of the Corporation Excise Tax of August 5, 1909.

GREENPORT BASIN & CON. CO. v. UNITED STATES

YOUNG v. UNITED STATES

(U. S. District Court, E. D. N. Y., Nov. 18, 1920)

(269 Fed. 58)

Record: Revenue Act of 1917. Actions to recover an amount of excess profits tax paid. On demurrer to complaints. Demurrer sustained.

Facts: See questions below.

Questions: (1) Was it necessary for the plaintiff to plead duress or protest?

(2) If so, was an allegation that plaintiff computed the tax under compulsion of the regulations and filed a claim for abatement of the taxes assessed before payment sufficient?

(3) What was the force of regulations issued by the Commissioner of Internal Revenue?

(4) Were Articles 16 and 17 of Regulations No. 41, in conformity with Section 201 of the Act in requiring a method of computing the excess profits tax by which the deductions authorized by that section were not made from the net income before computation of the tax, but as a part of the computation?

Decision: (1) Section 252, Revenue Act of 1918, authorizing a refund of income, war profits or excess profits taxes paid in excess of that properly due, notwithstanding the provision of Rev. St., Section 3228, has made a refund a matter of right, without proof of duress or protest.

(2) Even if it were necessary to plead duress or protest, the allegations in the petition complied with every requisite of a payment under protest. The objection of the taxpayer when the computation was made and by the filing of his claim notified the government of his attitude. To require a protest at time of actual payment would be a useless thing.

(3) Regulations of the Commissioner have no binding force if they alter, amend, or extend the statute.

(4) Under Section 201 of the Act imposing a tax on the net income in excess of the deductions and not in excess of 15% of the invested capital, and a tax at greater rates on income exceeding 15%, the deductions are to be made only in computing the amount of the tax, and not to be made from the net income before computation begins. The regulations were in conformity with the Act.

GULF OIL CORPORATION v. LEWELLYN, COLLECTOR

(U. S. Supreme Court, December 9, 1918)

(248 U. S. 71)

Record: Income Tax Act of Oct. 3, 1913. Action at law to recover taxes paid under protest. Judgment for plaintiff, 242 Fed. 709. Reversed by Circuit Court of Appeals, 245 Fed. 1 and 158 C. C. A. 1. On certiorari, judgment reversed.

Facts: Petitioner was a holding company, owning all the stock in the other corporations concerned, except the qualifying shares held by the directors. These companies, with others, constitute a single enterprise, carried on by the petitioner for producing, buying, transporting, refining and selling oil. The subsidiary companies had retained their earnings, although making some loans among themselves, and all their funds were invested in properties or actually required to carry on the business, so that debtor companies had no money available to pay their debts. In January, 1913, the petitioner decided to take over the previously accumulated earnings and surplus, and did so in that year by votes of the companies that it controlled. But, disregarding the forms gone through, the result was merely that the plaintiff became the holder of the debts previously due from one of its companies to another.   It was no richer than before, but its property now was represented by stock in and debts due from its subsidiaries, whereas it was formerly represented by stock alone, the change being effected by entries upon the respective companies' books.   The earnings thus transferred had been accumulated and had been used as capital before the taxing year.

Question: Were the earnings and surplus accumulated previous to the taxable year and taken over by the plaintiff holding company taxable as dividends received by said plaintiff holding company?

Decision: "It is true that the plaintiff and its subsidiaries were distinct beings in contemplation of law, but the fact that they were related as parts of one enterprise, all owned by the plaintiff, that the debts were all enterprise debts, due to members, and that the dividends represented earnings that had been made in former years, and that practically had been converted into capital, unite to convince us that the transaction should be regarded as bookkeeping rather than as 'dividends declared and paid in the ordinary course by a corporation.' " The case was held to be covered by the principle of Southern Pacific Co. v. Lowe, 247 U. S. 330.

IN RE HACKFELL & CO.
(Supreme Court of Hawaii, March 27, 1905)
(16 Haw. 559)

Record: Hawaiian R. L. Sec. 1281.   Appeal by the tax assessor from the tax appeal court sustaining the deduction made by the taxpayer.   Reversed.

Facts: The taxpayer owned stock of a certain company, and the books of the taxpayer showed a large indebtedness of this company.   The taxpayer wrote off on its books a large part of the indebtedness to profit and loss.

Question: Can a sum written off be regarded as a loss "actually sustained during the year," by the mere act of writing it off?

Decision: "The taxpayer's deduction from its income for the year 1903 of the sum of $150,000 by reason of its estimate of the loss in respect of the Hawaii Mill Company, which it owns, can not

be regarded as a loss 'actually sustained during the year.' This
estimate of the loss did not become an actual loss by the mere act of
writing it off to the account of profit and loss, and it can not be
allowed.''

HAIGHT v. RAILROAD COMPANY
(U. S. Supreme Court, December Term, 1867)
(73 U. S. 15)

Record: Act of June 30, 1864. Action at law to recover
arrears of interest. Judgment for defendant (Fed. Case 5903),
and plaintiff brought error. Affirmed.

Facts: The plaintiff was the holder of bonds, issued by the
defendant company and secured by a mortgage. The mortgage
contained, in the clause of defeasance, the stipulation, "without
any deduction, defalcation, or abatement to be made of anything
for or in respect of any taxes, charges, or assessments whatsoever." The defendant company paid the income tax on the interest on the bonds, and deducted from the interest due the plaintiff according to Section 122 of the Act.

Question: Does the stipulation in the mortgage oblige the
company to pay the interest on its bonds clear of the duty, which,
by Section 122 of the Act, such a company is authorized to deduct
from all payments of interest?

Decision: "The provision in the condition of defeasance of
the mortgage has reference only to covenants between mortgagor
and mortgagee, and is usual in every mortgage; being put there in
order to secure the mortgagee, who may not be in possession from
demand for taxes incurred while the mortgagor was in possession.
It can have no possible application to the income tax of bondholders." The defendant company is entitled to deduct from the interest due the holder of bonds the amount of income tax paid by it
on the interest on the bonds.

HAIKU SUGAR CO. ET AL v. JOHNSTONE
(Circuit Court of Appeals, April 1, 1918)
(249 Fed. 103)

Record: Income Tax Act of October 3, 1913. Action at law
to recover taxes paid under protest. Judgment for defendant and

plaintiff brought error. Reversed and remanded with instructions.

Facts: Under the laws of Hawaii permitting corporations to enter into a partnership with each other for the transaction of any lawful business, several corporations formed a general partnership. Under the provisions of the indenture of partnership the partners have definite shares in the capital of the partnership evidenced by certificates. These certificates were not transferable, and had no par value. A board of managers was provided for, with a representative selected by each partner. A tax was assessed and collected from the partnership.

Question: Is the plaintiff organization a partnership and excepted from the Income Tax Law of 1913, which besides applying to persons, applies, subject to certain enumerated exceptions, to "every corporation, joint stock company or association, and every insurance company, organized in the United States?"

Decision: Plaintiff company is not a regularly created corporation but a partnership formed of corporations. "The right given to a corporation to become a member of a partnership pertains to the power of the corporation to gain membership in a partnership, but does not make the aggregation of partners itself a corporation. There may yet be upon a corporation member the liability of a partner as to third persons. Plaintiff organization registered as a general partnership and the agreement between the partners has all the ear-marks of a co-partnership, which shows, so far as intent may serve to determine its character, that the theory of partnership is reasonable; but notwithstanding intent, if the legal effect of the language used by the parties was to create a joint stock company rather than a partnership, the court will hold it liable as such. The arrangement under examination lacks the element of changeability of membership or transferability of shares, an element often used as a determining criterion between ordinary partnerships and joint stock companies. The management of the company by a board of managers is not inconsistent with the right of partners to make their own arrangements for the management of the partnership affairs. A joint stock company often consists of a large number of persons, between whom there is no special relationship of confidence; the retirement or death of a member works no dissolution; while a partnership, although it may consist of several persons, generally is made up of a few, who are drawn to each other by feelings of mutual confidence, and no member is at liberty to retire and substitute another as a partner. In a joint stock company the business is generally managed by directors, and a shareholder as such is without power to contract for the corporation, whereas, in a partnership any member may bind the company. In the interpretation of statutes levying taxes, it is the established rule not to extend their provisions by implication beyond the clear import of the language used or to enlarge their operations so far as to embrace matters not specifically pointed out. In case of doubt they are construed most strictly against the government and in favor of the citizen." Following this general rule, although the court did not decide the question as to whether the plaintiff organization was a partnership, it did hold there was sufficient doubt for it to hold the plaintiff not subject to the tax under the Act of 1913.

HALSTEAD v. PRATT

(Supreme Court of Hawaii, February 15, 1902)

(14 Haw. 38)

Record: Hawaiian Act of 1901. Original submission on agreed facts. Judgment for defendant.

Facts: The plaintiff received his share of the estate of his father, and upon this he paid the federal succession tax. There was no territorial succession tax law, but the plaintiff was taxed under the territorial income tax law which contained a proviso "that in assessing the income of any person or corporation there shall not be included * * * any bequest or inheritance otherwise taxed as such." The father died before the tax year, but the bequest was received by the plaintiff during the year. The act says "all personal property acquired by gift or inheritance" shall be taxed.

Questions: (1) Is an inheritance which has been taxed under the federal inheritance act taxable under a territorial income tax act which exempts bequest and inheritances "otherwise taxed as such?"

(2) Was an inheritance from one who died before the year began but actually received during the year "acquired" during the year within the meaning of the statute?

Decisions: (1) "The general rule is that a statute should be construed with reference to the system of laws of which it is a part, unless a contrary intention clearly appears, * * *. The intention of the legislature in this instance was to provide revenue for the government of the territory irrespective of what taxes were paid to other governments. This intention would limit the reason for the exemption to inheritances otherwise taxed by the territorial government."

(2) "It would seem more natural and just to assess inheritances as income when actually received, or at least when payable, than when only the legal title passes and when it remains a matter of doubt whether any or how much, will ever be received."

IN RE HAMLIN
(New York Court of Appeals, May 20, 1919)
(226 N. Y. 407)

Record: Revenue Act of 1916. Appeal by the executors and residuary legatees of the estate of Mary E. Daniels, deceased, from an order of the Appellate Division of the Supreme Court, Fourth Department, reversing in part a decree of the Surrogate Court for Erie county, apportioning among legatees of the testatrix payment of the Federal Estate Tax in a proceeding for settlement of the accounts of the executors of her estate. Affirmed.

Facts: Mary E. Daniels died on January 3, 1917, a resident of Erie county, N. Y. By her will testatrix made certain specific bequests of money aggregating $160,000, and left the residue and remainder of the estate to trustees for Grace E. and Chauncey J. Hamlin, with remainder to the children of the latter. The executor paid to each of the legatees named in the will the amount of the legacies given them after deducting from each legacy the amount of the Federal Estate Tax. To the account of the executor filed in the Surrogate Court the three legatees in the $25,000 class filed objections to such deductions made against each of them, on the grounds that the inheritance taxes were not chargeable against them, but, if so, should not exceed $250 against each, and that under the Act of Congress no apportionment of the Federal tax could be made, the whole thereof being payable out of the estate. The objections were overruled and a decree confirming the account entered. The respondent legatees appealed to the Appellate Division of the State Supreme Court, which reversed the decree of the Surrogate Court (185 App. Divi. 153, 172 N. Y. Supp. 787), the court unanimously holding that the tax was payable from the estate and the legacies were not chargeable with any part of the same.

Question: Was any portion of the Federal Estate Tax chargeable against the legacies of the respondents?

Decision: Under the Statute of 1898 the tax was imposed upon legacies and distributive shares, and on any interest that may have been transferred, while under the Act of 1918 the tax was imposed on the net value of the estate of the decedent, without regard to the number of legatees. The 1916 Act taxes the estate and not the legacies. The plain intent and obvious meaning of the Act of Congress under consideration was to impose an estate tax as distinguished from an inheritance tax, and the tax is payable by the estate rather than by the legatees. Under this construction of the Act the residuary legatees bear the burden of the tax. "As to the equity of requiring payment of the tax by the residuary legatees and relieving the remaining legatees from any contribution to the same, the question is susceptible of conflict of opinion. The Congress has spoken and it is our function to interpret, not to legislate." Therefore, no portion of the Federal Estate Tax was chargeable against the legacies of the respondents.

HAMPTON v. HAMPTON

(Kentucky Court of Appeals, February 13, 1920)

(221 S. W. 496)

Record: Revenue Act of 1918. Appeal by plaintiff from a judgment of the Circuit Court of Clark County in favor of defendant, in an agreed case, filed to determine whether the whole of the Federal estate tax should be paid out of the estate of plaintiff's decedent. Finding of Circuit Court that the estate tax was payable before distribution, and that there should be deducted from the personal property going to the widow such proportion of the entire estate tax as the value of all the property allotted to her bore to the entire estate, and that her interest in the estate should be ascertained by adding the value of her dower, as fixed by life tables, to one-half of the surplus personalty after paying funeral expenses, costs of administration, and debts of decedent, including state and county taxes due upon assessments made. Administrators appeal. Affirmed. Petition for rehearing denied

Facts: A. B. Hampton, a resident of Clark County, Kentucky, died intestate and without issue in February, 1919. His estate passed to his widow and certain collateral kindred. Under the Kentucky statute, where the husband dies intestate, the widow, in addition to her dower, is entitled to one-half of the surplus personalty. The estate consisted of personalty worth about $30,000 and several hundred acres of land. In a proper proceeding the land, other than the widow's dower, was sold by the master, commissioner of the Clark Circuit Court, for $295,236.26. The ordinary indebtedness of the estate amounted to about $5,000. The estate tax of the Federal government was approximately $20,000.

Question: Is the Federal estate tax payable out of the personal property of decedent, and is the widow entitled to any portion of the personal property before all the estate tax is paid?

Decision: Every portion of an estate should bear its proportionate part of the tax. The court says that in view of the inequality that would result it could not subscribe to the theory that the estate tax is a charge on the personal estate, unless it was compelled to do so by the language of the Act itself. It is conceded that there is no express provision to that effect, but it is urged that the nature of the tax, method of collection, and other considerations make it clear that such was the purpose of Congress. The court did not regard as controlling the fact that the primary duty of paying the tax is imposed on the executor, as this is a mere administrative rule which does not affect the rights of the heirs and distributees as among themselves. The word "prior liability" in the statute was held not necessarily to refer to the liability of the personal estate of decedent. "Considering the Act as a whole and particularly the provisions with respect to reimbursement and contribution we cannot escape the conclusion that Congress did not intend to discriminate between the heirs and distributees, but intended that every portion of the estate should bear its proportionate part of the tax, subject, however, to the right of the decedent to provide by will out of what portion of his estate the tax should be paid. * * * Laying aside the Federal Act as not controlling on the question of descent and distribution, and coming to our own statutes, we find that the widow is entitled to one-half of her husband's surplus personalty (Kentucky Statutes, Sec. 2132), and that the surplus is obtained by deducting from the whole of the personalty the decedent's funeral expenses, charges of administration, and debts. Clearly the estate tax, which was never an obligation of the decedent, cannot be regarded as a debt within the meaning of our statute." It follows then that the widow is entitled to one-half of the surplus personalty after paying funeral expenses, costs of administration, and debts of decedent, and that the amount of estate tax paid by the administrator deductible from the personal property going to the widow is such proportion of the entire estate tax as the value of all the property alloted to her bore to the entire estate.

HAWAIIAN COMMERCIAL & SUGAR CO. v.
TAX ASSESSOR AND COLLECTOR
(Supreme Court of Hawaii, Feb. 19, 1903)
(14 Haw. 601)

Record: Hawaiian Act of 1901. An appeal by the Tax Assessor from the decision of the Tax Appeal Court, allowing certain deductions as losses. Reversed.

Facts: The Hawaiian Commercial and Sugar Company owned and operated a large plantation. The area of cultivated land having been extended, it was deemed necessary to build a new and larger mill at a more central location and to construct a new railroad capable of sustaining the increased traffic. This was done, and the old mill, with part of the old machinery, and the old railroad are no longer being used. The company, in making its return, deducted a large sum for losses on old mill buildings and railroad property. The statute provided for a deduction of "all losses actually sustained during the year incurred in trade or arising from losses by fire not covered by insurance, or losses otherwise actually incurred."

Question: Is the value of buildings and equipment, which a company no longer uses, deductible as losses under the statute, where the growth of the business demanded larger and other buildings and equipment?

Decision: "If the property is lost it has passed from the control and out of the possession of the loser. No one can lose property and still have it in his possession and be conscious of the fact that he has it. There is a difference between lost and abandoned property, still the actual loss to the owner may be the same in each case. * * * If the Hawaiian Commercial and Sugar Company had used the property or had needed its use and been able to make the same use of it as formerly, the property would have been of the same value after as before the substitution of the new appliances, but since the company no longer needed the use of the property, from its view point, there was depreciation in its value and great loss. This was not a loss, however, 'actually sustained during the year incurred in trade,' or by fire, or 'otherwise actually incurred' within the meaning and intent of the statute."

IN RE HAWLEY

(U. S. District Court S. D. New York, Feb. 5, 1915)

(220 Fed. 372)

Record: War Tax Law of 1914. A proceeding in bankruptcy to review a referee's order refusing to certify certain instruments unless internal revenue stamps were attached. Referee's order affirmed.

Facts: The referee in bankruptcy refused to accept a general letter of attorney in the usual official form authorizing the attorney in fact to attend meetings of creditors of the bankrupt and vote therein for trustee, or for any other proposal or resolution that may be submitted under the Act, to accept any composition proposed, by the bankrupt, and to receive payment of any dividends or money due under any composition, etc., unless there should be affixed to such letter of attorney a twenty-five cent internal revenue stamp. He has likewise refused to certify that an order approving the bond of the trustee is a correct copy, unless there is attached to such certificate a ten-cent internal revenue stamp.

Question: (1) Can a referee in bankruptcy under the War Tax Act of 1914 refuse to accept a general letter of attorney unless an internal revenue stamp is attached?

(2) Can a referee in bankruptcy proceedings refuse to certify that an order approving the trustee's bond is a correct copy of the one on file in his office, unless an internal revenue stamp is attached?

Decision: (1) A consideration of the War Tax Act of 1862 and amendments, and of the War Tax Act of 1898, from which the language of the present law is derived, indicates that it was the intention of Congress to require stamps in general upon powers of attorney. It was contended that when the Act of 1862 was passed letters of attorney in bankruptcy proceedings could not be presumed to have been in the mind of Congress because no bankruptcy law was then in force, but the court held that the clause was broad enough to cover all powers of attorney, and was, therefore, sufficient to cover any powers of attorney that might thereafter be executed.

(2) This certificate, if taxable, is rendered so by the following provision of Schedule A of the War Tax Act of 1914, which is identical with that of the Act of 1898: "Certificates of any description required by law not otherwise specified in this act, ten cents." After reviewing the cases decided under the Act of 1898 interpreting the above clause, the court concludes: "That the purpose of the clause was to impose stamp taxes on those instruments only which have their origin in the private transactions of individuals and corporations, or to such instruments or writings as are executed mainly for their benefit, rather than for the benefit of the public. While it may in some cases be difficult to draw the line as to what is and is not a governmental function, where a private individual applies to a judge, referee in bankruptcy, or a clerk for a certificate, that a certain instrument is a copy, and it does not appear that it is to be used for any governmental purpose, it is taxable under the provisions of the Act." It was, therefore, held that the certificate in question was taxable.

HAYS, COLLECTOR, v. GAULEY MOUNTAIN COAL CO.
(U. S. Supreme Court, May 20, 1918)
(247 U. S. 189)

Record: Act of Aug. 5, 1909. Action at law to recover taxes paid under protest on net income under Sec. 38 of this Act. Judgment for defendant in District Court, reversed by Circuit Court of Appeals (230 Fed. 110), whereupon writ of certiorari was allowed. Judgment of Circuit Court of Appeals reversed.

Facts: The coal company purchased certain shares of another mining company for $800,000 in 1902, and in 1911 sold them for $1,010,000. The Commissioner held that a proportion of the profit of $210,000, represented by the ratio of the 1,019 days that elapsed between Jan. 1, 1909, when the Corporation Excise Tax Act became effective, and Oct. 16, 1911, the date of the sale, to the 3,233 days that elapsed between the date of purchase and the date of sale, constituted income of the corporations for the year 1911 within the meaning of the Act. The apportioned sum was made the basis of an additional assessment, and this assessment having been collected by duress, formed the subject of the present suit.

Question: Is income realized by the sale of stock in one year, although accrued in a previous year, subject to tax in the year in which received?

Decision: "The expression 'income received during such year', employed in the Act of 1909, looks to the time of realization rather than to the time of accrument, except as the taking effect of the Act on a specified date (Jan. 1, 1909), excludes income that accrued before that date. It results that so much of the $210,-000 of profits as may be deemed to have accrued subsequent to Dec. 31, 1908, must be treated as part of the gross income of respondent."

In re HAYES
(Supreme Court of Hawaii, March 17, 1905)
(16 Haw. 796)

Record: Appeal by the assessor from Tax Appeal Court, sustaining the taxpayer's claim. Reversed.

Facts: The assessor added to the taxpayer's return of his income the sum allowed him by his employer for his expenses during the year, at a certain rate per month.

Question: Is the sum allowed a person by his employer for expenses income?

Decision: "The statute does not require the assessor to take the taxpayer's return of his income as true. The item in controversy was properly added by the assessor, forming an actual part of the taxpayer's income."

In re HELLER, HIRSH & CO.
(U. S. Circuit Court of Appeals, Second Cir., May 14, 1919)
(258 Fed. 208)

Record: Revenue Act of 1916. Petition by government for an order directing the trustee of bankrupt corporation to pay to the collector of internal revenue taxes said to be due. Order denied upon appeal, judgment affirmed.

Facts: Trustee of bankrupt corporation received in 1916 funds said to constitute net income, as the result of a compromise made by him with a foreign corporation of a claim for non-payment of salary and commissions by the foreign corporation to the bankrupt corporation as its agent between the years 1910-1914. The trustee was not engaged in business, but was engaged solely in the work of marshalling and distributing the assets of the bankrupt corporation among its creditors.

Question: Is income received by a trustee of a bankrupt corporation, which income is not the result of operating the business, subject to tax under Sec. 13(c) of the Act of Sept. 8, 1916, which provides that a receiver operating the business of a corporation shall make a return for the corporation in the same manner as the corporation is required to make the return?

Decision: "The language used in subdivision (c) shows that the subdivision was not intended by Congress to apply in the case of securities of trustees in bankruptcy or assignees who merely marshalled and distributed the assets of an insolvent corporation, among its creditors. In terms subdivision (c) applies only in cases where receivers or trustees in bankruptcy or assignees 'are operating the property or business of corporation,' and thus 'may be in receipt of 'net income' as defined in the prior sections of the Act.''

HENRY v. UNITED STATES
(U. S. Supreme Court, Feb. 2, 1920)
(251 U. S. 393)

Record: Act of June 13, 1898. Action at law brought by the executor in the U. S. Court of claims to recover back a legacy or Federal estate tax paid under protest. Claim disallowed. Plaintiff appealed to this court. Judgment of Court of Claims affirmed.

Facts: Suit was brought in the trial court to recover taxes paid under the Spanish War Revenue Act of June 13, 1898, repealed by the Act of April 12, 1902. By the Act of June 27, 1902, the Secretary of the Treasury was directed to refund taxes upon legacies collected upon contingent beneficial interests that should not have become vested before July 1, 1902, and the claim for refund herein is made pursuant thereto. Hendricks, the testator, died, domiciled in New York, on March 5, 1902. Claimant was executor and trustee under the will. ` By that instrument $50,-000 was left to claimant in trust for Florence Lester for life. The residue of the estate was left to the testator's five sisters. On July 1, 1902, the time for proving claims against the estate had not expired, but before that date the executor having correctly estimated that a large sum would be left after all debts were paid, paid over $135,870 to the five sisters in equal shares, and established the trust fund for Florence Lester, transferring the sum of $50,000 to his separate account as trustee. The taxes in question were levied on these two interests.

Questions: (1) Were the interests bequeathed by this will to be construed as having been vested in absolute possession or enjoyment prior to July 1, 1902, or were they simply contingent on that date?

(2) Where property is left in trust to a person for life, does the fact that the life tenant received no income from the trust estate before July 1, 1902, keep the life tenant from having a vested interest?

Decision: (1) The payments to legatees rendered their interests vested, although made in advance of their right to receive same. The court stated that had the claimant retained the funds in his hands, as he had a legal right to do, the interest of the legatees would not have been vested in possession within the meaning of the statute, whatever the probabilities and however solvent the estate (quoting United States v. Jones, 236 U. S. 106, and other cases). On the contention of claimant that the same is true if he saw fit to pay over legacies before the time came when they could be demanded as of right, the court said that, assuming that if the estate had proved insufficient the executor not only would have been responsible, but could have recovered such portion of his payments as needed to pay debts, still the consequences asserted does not follow. There was no question but that the interest of the sisters was held in possession as was that of the trustee, according to the opinion. The interest was vested also in each case. The mere fact that the funds in the hands of the legatees might have to be returned no more prevented their being vested in possession and taxable, than the possibility that a life estate might end at any moment, prevented one that began before July 1, 1902, being taxed at its full value as fixed by the mortuary tables (United States v. Fidelity Trust Co., 222 U. S. 158).

(2) The interest transferred to a trustee for ascertained persons is vested in possession, even though the life tenant received no income from it before July 1, 1902. The court stated that with regard to the trust for Florence Lester the case did not stand differently on account of the contention that the life tenant received no income from it before July 1, 1902. It was held that for the purpose of this Act the interest in a fund transferred from an estate to a trustee for ascertained persons is vested in possession no less than when it is conveyed directly to them (United States v. Fidelity Trust Co.).

HEROLD, COLLECTOR, v. KAHN, et al.
(U. S. Circuit Court of Appeals, Third Cir., Feb. 7, 1908)
(159 Fed. 608; 163 Fed. 947)

Record: War Revenue Act of 1898. Suit to recover legacy taxes paid under protest. Judgment for plaintiff in court below and defendant brought error. Affirmed (159 Fed. 608). On subsequent petition judgment modified by allowing interest (163 Fed. 947).

Facts: Plaintiffs were executors of Abraham Wolff, who died Oct. 1, 1909, leaving two daughters surviving. The bulk of the estate was left in trust to pay the income thereof in equal portions to these daughters for life, and then to be divided among stated beneficiaries. One of the daughters, Clara W. Wertheim by name, died on Aug. 15, 1903. On Oct. 26, 1903, the executors received notice of an assessment of $107,398.16 as a tax upon the legacies provided for in the will. This amount included a tax on the legacy to Clara Wertheim, the value of which was estimated by resorting to mortuary tables. The tax was paid Nov. 4, 1903, under written protest. This suit was instituted for recovery of tax assessed upon the interest of Mrs. Wertheim.

Question: (1) Must payment of tax be made under something like actual duress in order to be recoverable?

(2) If payment must be so made, what was sufficient to constitute such duress?

(3) Could the legacy tax on a life interest be assessed upon the basis of life tables when the life tenant had died prior to such assessment?

Decision: (1) The true doctrine is that, when taxes are paid under protest that they are being illegally exacted, or with notice that the payor contends that they are illegal and intends to institute suit to compel their repayment, a sufficient foundation for such a suit has been established.

(2) Payment of a tax under protest upon demand of the collector, coupled with a threat that unless promptly paid, the same would be collected with a penalty and interest at the rate of 1 percentum per month constituted such a duress as clearly made the payment involuntary.

(3) In the assessment of inheritance tax upon a life estate, the actual duration of the tenant's life, and not the fictitious duration derived from mortuary tables, should be used where the tenant died before the assessment, even though this fact was unknown when the assessment was made.

HEROLD, COLLECTOR, v. MUTUAL BENEFIT LIFE INS. CO.

(U. S. Circuit Court of Appeals, Third Circuit, Jan. 27, 1913)

(201 Fed. 918)

Record: Act of Aug. 5, 1909. Judgment for plaintiff. Collector brought error. Affirmed. Certiorari denied Dec. 15, 1913. (231 U. S. 755.)

Facts: See District Court case, Mutual Benefit Life Ins. Co. v. Herold (198 Fed. 199) infra.

Question: See District Court case, Mutual Benefit Life Ins. Co. v. Herold (198 Fed. 199) infra.

Decision: "Several questions were raised and decided below, but in this court only one question needs attention: Does the Act tax the so-called 'dividends' awarded annually to policyholders? The answer must be in the negative unless such 'dividends' are a part of company's 'net income * * * received by it * * * during such year * * * .' But we need not discuss the subject; that duty has been performed by Judge Cross with such fullness and ability that we cannot do better than adopt his opinion. The case in the District Court is reported in 198 Fed. at page 199, and the discussion we refer to extends from page 200 to 212, inclusive. But we do not adopt what is said on page 212 concerning dividends on fully paid participating policies, nor what is said on the same page concerning stock companies, not because we wish to suggest disapproval, but merely because no opinion about these matters is called for now, as they do not seem to be directly involved."

HEROLD, COLLECTOR, v. PARK VIEW BLDG. & LOAN ASS'N

(Circuit Court of Appeals, Third Circuit, Jan. 23, 1914)

(210 Fed. 577)

Record: Act of Aug. 5, 1909. Action at law to recover taxes paid under protest on net income under Sec. 38 of this Act. Judgment for plaintiff (203 Fed. 876), and defendant brought error. **Affirmed.**

Facts: The Park View Co. was organized as a building and loan association under the laws of New Jersey. The company is authorized by the laws of New Jersey to issue prepaid stock and installment stock. The latter class of stock shares in the general profits of the company, whereas the former class is allowed 5% yearly "out of the profits of the association" on the amount prepaid. The government insists that such issues of stock take the company from the class of building and loan associations exempted by the Act in question, in that the company is not organized for the "mutual benefit of its members."

Questions: (1) Is the foregoing arrangement for the mutual benefit of the parties?

(2) What effect should be given the clause, "no part of the net income of which inures to the benefit of any private stockholder or individual," which provision follows the list of corporations specifically exempted by Sec. 38 of the Act of 1909.

Decision: (1) "Congress intended the word 'mutual' to mean 'substantially equal,' and a building association is organized and operated for the mutual benefit of its members when they share in the profits on substantially the same footing. Exact equality is probably not possible, where part of the stock is prepaid, and part is installment, but an approximate equality, sufficiently close for all purposes, is certainly not beyond the reach of calculations. We have no doubt that such a calculation is always made before the terms are adopted upon which prepaid stock is allowed to share in the profits. * * * The Park View Bldg. and Loan Association was 'organized' exclusively for the mutual benefit of its members. The members would not agree to any arrangement that would disturb their substantially equal footing."

(2) The clause "no part of the net income of which inures to the benefit of any private stockholder or individual" applies only to that class of corporations immediately preceding the proviso, viz., "any corporation organized and operated exclusively for religious, charitable, or educational purposes." "The character of the first three groups is well known. In none of them (as nor-

mally conducted) does the net income inure to the benefit of private stockholders or individuals, and it would have been superfluous to add that feature to the description.''

HOLBROOK v. MOORE, COLLECTOR
(U. S. District Court, E. D. Missouri, Feb. 8, 1921)
(Not reported)

Record: Act of Oct. 3, 1913. Suit to recover income tax paid. Case submitted to court sitting as a jury on agreed statement of facts. Oral opinion rendered. Judgment for defendant.

Facts: Plaintiff was president, and active manager of a real estate company. He is also a director in the company. It was deemed by plaintiff and two of the directors that his services for the years 1909, 1910, 1911 and 1912 were such as to entitle him to additional compensation to that allowed him by the rules and by-laws of the board of directors. No agreement as to the amount of that compensation was ever arrived at until December, 1913. Before December, 1913, the plaintiff had become indebted to the company to the amount of $70,000. This indebtedness was carried on the books of the company as overdrafts. In December, 1913 (plaintiff and two other directors concurring), the plaintiff was allowed a credit upon the books of the company for $50,000. Two other directors have never affirmatively acquiesced in this allowance, but the company, in making its return for 1913, took credit for the $50,000. The plaintiff was assessed an income tax on the $50,000.

Question: Is the allowance of a credit against overdrafts of an officer as compensation on the books of the company, income to the officer for the year of the allowance of the credit?

Decision: ''It may be said, since only two members of the board (in addition to plaintiff himself) acquiesced in this, that, therefore, it was no order, and that since the other two directors and the stockholders have never to this good day acquiesced in it, that it was no order. I take it that the company is foreclosed by the fact that they took credit for it when they made their income tax return for the year following the year at which they passed this credit to plaintiff upon the corporation's books.'' The court found for the government on the authority of the case of Jackson v.

Smietanka, 267 Fed. 932, infra, and the plaintiff was not allowed
to recover the tax assessed on the $50,000 as income.

HOME TELEPHONE & TELEGRAPH CO. v. CITY OF LOS ANGELES, et al.

(District Court of Appeals, State of California, March 28, 1919)

(181 Pac. 100)

Record: Ordinance of the City of Los Angeles. Action at
law to recover license tax paid under protest. Judgment for plaintiff and defendants appeal. Affirmed.

Facts: Plaintiff was a telephone and telegraph company carrying on business in the city of Los Angeles. It was required
to pay a license tax under a city ordinance and was punishable by
fine and imprisonment upon failure to do so. Plaintiff protested
orally to the collector against the payment of the tax and was
thereupon threatened with the enforcement of the penalties. Fear-
ing the proceedings of arrest, it paid the tax accompanied by written protest.

Question: Was the payment of the tax by the plaintiff under
the above circumstances voluntary, or under duress?

Decision: " * * * It is not essential to a recovery of
such a tax that the person be threatened with actual imprisonment
or threatened with the penalty of having his right to do business
taken away. There may be penalties which fall perhaps short of
this mark, to avoid which the person paying may protect himself
by protest. If under the ordinance here considered, the tax collector had only recourse to a civil action to collect the license tax,
then there could be no payment under protest sufficient to divest
the payment of its voluntary character; for the protestant could
then contest the validity of the tax without suffering the risk of
incurring excessive penalties or arrest." The court held that in view
of fact that there was available to the collector the machinery of
the criminal courts by means of which plaintiff could be heavily
fined and imprisoned, the payment was not voluntary and plaintiff
was entitled to recover.

HOME TITLE INS. CO. v. KEITH

(U. S. District Court, E. D. New York, March 3, 1916)

(230 Fed. 905)

Record: Act of October 22, 1914. Action at law by plaintiff against collector of internal revenue to recover the amount paid under protest for certain revenue stamps. Defendant filed a demurrer to the complaint. Demurrer sustained and complaint dismissed.

Facts: The plaintiff brought action against the collector of internal revenue to recover the amount paid for certain revenue stamps affixed by the plaintiff to a deed given to it by a referee in foreclosure in an action in the Supreme Court of the state of New York. The plaintiff was not a party to that foreclosure action, but purchased the property on the sale. The referee did not affix the stamps required by the law (Act of Congress of October 22, 1914) nor did he deduct any amount as a part of the expenses of the sale for the purchase of these stamps. The plaintiff under protest procured the stamps and affixed them before recording the deed.

Questions: (1) Does the Act in question require the vendee or grantee in a deed to pay the stamp tax?

(2) Is the Act unconstitutional if it imposes a tax of any kind upon the deed given by a referee in pursuance to the order and as a part of the procedure by the state court?

Decision: (1) "Section 6 of the law imposes the penalty upon any one who makes, signs, or issues (that is, uses or delivers) the deed. But this does not mean that the stamp must be attached to the paper before the paper can be signed at all. It simply places upon each of these individuals the responsibility of being charged with a misdemeanor if the paper is not duly stamped before its actual issuance or use, and of course the lack of the stamp must be rectified before recording. The "or" is disjunctive as to persons but conjunctive as to complete act of making, signing, and using. Under Section 8, the initials of the person using or affixing the stamp and the date must be placed upon the stamp as a cancellation. It would not be held that a signature or partial execution of the paper, followed by a subsequent affixing of the stamp, was a failure to comply with section 6, if the stamp was properly affixed and cancelled before the paper was issued. But all persons sharing in the transaction, if the paper is not properly stamped in time, are liable. Hence, a grantee or vendee who participates in the making or issuing of a paper without the proper stamp could be charged in the criminal sense with acts equivalent to 'causing' it to be issued without a stamp and section 6 is not governed by the meaning of the words 'caused to be issued,' as viewed from the steps in the foreclosure suit, in order to determine upon whose motion or by whose application the deed was issued. Therefore, upon the failure of the one conveying the land to affix the stamps to the deed, the grantee is required to affix them.''

(2) The requirement of the Act that a stamp should be affixed to a deed as applied to a deed executed by referees appointed by state courts in foreclosure proceedings, is not invalid as imposing a tax upon the state's exercise of its governmental functions, as the tax imposed is an excise tax on the business transaction involved in the purchase of the land and its transfer to the purchaser and the transfer is in its nature the same as any transfer from one individual to another. It was, therefore, held that the deed was taxable and consequently that plaintiff could not recover.

HOOD & SONS v. COMMONWEALTH
(Supreme Judicial Court of Massachusetts, May 20, 1920)
(127 N. E. 497)

Record: Massachusetts Act of 1918. Petition for abatement of tax. Allowed.

Facts: Plaintiff is a corporation organized under the laws of Maine, and having its usual place of business in Boston. Its business is buying milk in the country, 90% of which originates in New York and the New England States, other than Massachusetts. At Boston the milk is pasteurized and distributed to its customers. Plaintiff's net income derived from sales outside of Massachusetts or by direct shipment to its customers inside Massachusetts from outside its limits are approximately 15% per cent of its total net income. The statute in question imposes an additional tax on foreign corporations doing business within the State, but expressly exempts from its scope interstate commerce and property outside of the State. Under this statute the plaintiff corporation was taxed upon its income derived from sales within Massachusetts.

Question: Is the portion of plaintiff's net income derived from sales in Massachusetts of milk shipped in from outside exempt from income taxation because such taxation would impose a direct burden on interstate commerce?

Decision: The court held that interstate commerce comes to an end when the milk bought outside the State is delivered in Boston, as a new and distinct method of dealing with the milk is undertaken which is utterly different from interstate commerce. Plaintiff corporation removes the milk from the cans in which it has been the subject of interstate commerce, and makes it a part of the common stock of merchandise within the State of Massachusetts. It then pasteurizes the milk, which is a subjection of it to heat for the purpose of inducing certain chemical changes. This process closely resembles "manufacture" as that word is applied to fabricated articles. The milk is then put in other cans and sold within the State of Massachusetts. Net income is derived from the sale of stock which became a part of the common stock within the State of Massachusetts. Interstate commerce has been utilized as a preliminary step. The part it played ended when the milk reached Boston. The sales within Massachusetts were not a part of interstate commerce, and, hence, a tax upon the income derived from such sales was valid and not a burden upon interstate commerce.

HOUSTON BELT & TERMINAL RY. CO. v. UNITED STATES
(U. S. Circuit Court of Appeals, Fifth Cir., April 10, 1918)
(250 Fed. 1)

Record: Act of Aug. 5, 1909. Action at law by United States to recover taxes claimed to be due. Judgment for United States and defendant brought error. Affirmed.

Facts: Defendant was organized under laws of Texas for the purpose of performing terminal services for four railroad companies, which were its stockholders. In order to finance the organization, it was necessary to borrow a large sum of money, and, the credit of the terminal company not being sufficient to obtain the needed loan, it was arranged that the several railroad companies should pay in equal parts the annual interest and sinking fund requirements of a loan from a trust company to the terminal company which was to be evidenced by bonds secured by a mortgage on the property of the terminal company. The terminal company paid a corporation tax during 1909, 1910 and 1911, but, in estimating it, did not take into account interest payments made by the four tenant companies to the trust company. The amount sued for represents the taxes due on the amounts paid by the four tenant companies, less the interest on the amount of the capital stock of the terminal company. Act of Aug. 5, 1909, permits a deduction of interest paid by the corporation, but not in excess of interest on the amount of its capital stock.

Question: Are the amounts paid by the tenant companies, upon the loan from the trust company to the terminal company, income to the latter company for the purpose of ascertaining the amount of the excise tax of the terminal company?

Decision: As the title to the property vested in the terminal company subject to the mortgage, and the interest payments were for its benefit, such interest payments should be treated as income for the purpose of ascertaining the amount of the Excise Tax, it being immaterial whether the railroad companies were primarily liable for the interest payment.

HUBBARD v. BRAINARD

(Supreme Court of Errors of Connecticut, February Term, 1869)
(35 Conn. 563)

Record: Acts of June 30, 1864, and July 13, 1866. Assumpsit to recover money paid as income tax to the defendant, a collector of internal revenue of the United States. Dismissed for want of jurisdiction. Plaintiff appeals. Judgment for plaintiff.

Facts: The plaintiff owned a majority of the stock in two manufacturing corporations, in each of which he was a director. During the year 1864 the companies made earnings greater than the amount declared as dividends. This excess was expended, so the court found, by the company in the purchase of articles necessary to carry on the business and in the payment of debts. It was not shown that the company made an annual balance sheet, as required by law, and that the dividends were declared after making such a balance sheet. The plaintiff returned the amount paid to him by the company in the form of dividends. The assessor investigated the records of the company and assessed the plaintiff upon a proportional part of the earnings which were expended in the purchase of articles for carrying on the business and in the payment of debts. The Act of 1864 required that the profits of all companies be included in estimating the income of any person entitled thereto, whether divided or otherwise. The plaintiff paid the tax to avoid a seizure and sale of his property. Subsequent to this payment the Act of 1866 was passed, providing for an appeal to the Commissioner for recovery of tax before a suit could be maintained. The plaintiff did not make such appeal before bringing this action.

Questions: (1) May the assessor go behind the balance sheet of a corporation and assess a stockholder upon the gross earnings?

(2) Where the corporation has declared a dividend, but it is not shown that it made an annual balance sheet before declaring the dividend, is there an implication of bad faith, or intent to defraud the government on the part of the directors of the company?

(3) Is the plaintiff barred from his right of action to recover taxes paid, because he made no application to the Commissioner for a refund where such a procedure is prescribed by a later Act?

Decision: (1) "In a general sense a stockholder is entitled to a share of all the earnings as earned from day to day, or month to month, although required for the purpose of carrying on the business, as he is owner of the stock on hand, and other property of the corporation; but not in any practical sense, as the basis of taxation of income; and it is as we think, absurd to claim that Congress intended to tax the share of the stockholder in the gross profits or earnings, without deducting the cost of stock, and expenses, or any special part of the items of the gross profit, or that they contemplated any other method of ascertaining the taxable share of the stockholder as income than by the ordinary ascertainment of the net gains or profits, by a balance sheet made up in good faith. It may be admitted that it was proper that the assessor should go behind the balance sheet to see if by fraudulent under-valuation of the assets, or fraudulent exaggeration of the liabilities, the actual net gains and profits were to any extent concealed. But he obviously could not go behind the sheet to tax the gross amount of the earnings or any special part of them, at his pleasure."

(2) "This law has been in existence more than thirty years, and the universal practice has been to make up the annual accounts before declaring dividends. Looking at the requirements of the law, the universal course and custom of business, and the fact found that a dividend was made, we feel bound to presume that this company made up their accounts and struck their balance in January, 1865, and that the several items purchased upon which the assessment in question was made, were embraced in those accounts as a part of the assets of the company, to offset so much of the earnings as were expended in making them, and that the debts paid would have appeared among the liabilities of the company to offset the earnings used in paying them, if they had not been paid, and that, therefore, the balance actually found was all to which the plaintiff was entitled within any possible meaning of the law." This was the amount returned by the plaintiff, and there is no clear evidence of an intent to defraud the government, unless it is shown that there was an omission to make up the annual accounts or to include in them the items which the assessor assessed.

(3) "In the first place we think that the Act was prospective and not retrospective, and that Congress did not intend that it should retroact to affect an existing vested right. In the second place, we are not satisfied that the law should be construed to operate any further than to exclude the plaintiff from maintaining a suit upon the claim in the courts of the United States." And in the third place, the court said he had a vested right to recover, and that it was not competent for Congress by subsequent legislation to exclude the plaintiff from his right.

INDUSTRIAL TRUST CO. v. WALSH, COLLECTOR
(U. S. District Court, District of Connecticut, March 6, 1915)
(222 Fed. 437)

Record: Act of August 5, 1909. Action at law to recover an additional tax paid under protest. Judgment for plaintiff.

Facts: The plaintiff, a Rhode Island corporation, was engaged in the business of a bank and trust company. In June, 1912, it caused an adjustment to be made on its books of the value of securities which it then owned with the result that a net increase in their value was shown to the amount of $180,307.90. None of these securities were sold in 1912 except $43,000 par value of the Bristol and Warren Water Co. bonds, of which $6,000 par value was sold prior to the book adjustment and $37,000 thereafter. By the book adjustment the value of the securities, representing $37,000 par value, was increased $2,804. Plantiff included in his return for 1912 the amount realized from the securities sold. Subsequently the Commissioner amended the return by adding an amount of net income which he termed a prorated increase in the value of certain securities owned by plaintiff after deducting a prorated decrease in the value of others, both of which were computed in consequence of the adjustment made of book values in June, 1912. Payment under protest was made, demand for refund denied by Commissioner, and suit was brought to recover the additional tax assessed on the net increase in the book value of the securities shown by the book adjustment.

Question: Was the Commissioner justified in assessing the additional tax on the net increase in value of the securities as shown by the book adjustment, and does such net increase represent "income received by plaintiff during the year?"

Decision: Enhancement in value of itself does not constitute taxable income. The court referred to the decision of the U. S. Supreme Court in the case of Gray v. Darlington, 15 Wall. 63, (21 L. ed. 45), wherein the same subject matter with respect to the Act of Congress of 1867 was involved. The following paragraphs from the opinion in that case were quoted by the court and held to control herein: "The mere fact that property has advanced in value between the date of its acquisition and sale does not authorize the imposition of the tax on the amount of the advance. Mere advance in value in no sense constitutes the gains, profits or income specified by the statute. It constitutes and can be treated merely as increase of capital. The advance in the value of property during a series of years can in no just sense be considered the gains, profits, or income of any one particular year of the series, although the entire amount of the advance be at one time turned into money by a sale of the property." The court then concluded that the same interpretation given to the statute of 1867 with reference to what was taxable income under that statute, as held in the case of Gray v. Darlington, supra, must be given to the Act of 1909. Therefore, it was held that plaintiff was entitled to recover the additional taxes paid by it.

IN RE INCOME TAX APPEAL CASES.
(Supreme Court of Hawaii, February 8, 1908)
(18 Haw. 596)

Record: Hawaiian Act of 1905. Appeals from tax appeal court. Decisions reversed and total deductions disallowed with one exception.

Facts: (1) The Koloa Sugar Co. made deductions for buildings, which were a better class of laborer's quarters, made necessary by the introduction of European immigrants in place of Asiatics.

(2) The Lihue Plantation Co. made a deduction which was the cost of a steel and concrete bridge built to replace a wooden bridge which had become insecure. The expenditure within the year was within the cost of replacement.

(3) On account of the deterioration in one kind of cane, it became necessary to use another kind, and, to extract the juices from this cane, it became necessary to add new machinery, a part of which replaced the old machinery. Deduction was made for all the machinery bought.

(4) In 1906 a large amount of money was expended in clearing new land on which a crop of sugar would be harvested in 1908. The company deducted the entire cost as an expense in 1906.

Questions: (1) Can the cost of new buildings, which were necessary to accommodate a different class of employees, be deducted as an expense for the year?

(2) Can the cost of steel and concrete bridge built to replace a wooden bridge which had become insecure be deducted as an expense?

(3) Is the cost of additional machinery deductible where the machinery is necessary to keep the plantation up to its former efficiency?

(4) Is the amount expended for clearing new land, on which a crop of sugar will be raised two years later an item deductible the year the money is expended as necessary expense?

Decision: (1) "It is claimed that the buildings were a better class of laborer's quarters, made necessary by the introduction of European immigrants in place of Asiatics, and it did not increase the value of the property, but new buildings cannot be deducted under the first proviso of R. L. Sec. 1281, irrespective of this fact."

(2) "We are of the opinion that the allowance should be the cost of replacing the old bridge by a new but substantially similar structure, and that the difference between this and the concrete bridge is a betterment."

(3) "The only machinery discarded as a result of these additions was some iron tanks replaced by the crystallizers, the replacement of which would have cost $2,000. This is the only deduction that can be allowed."

(4) "Before the latter decision (18 Haw. 206) the plantations generally returned all cash outlays as necessary expenses; while since that decision they have gone to the other extreme, and so far as their returns show are running their large enterprises without expense of any kind. In the complexity of accounts of a large sugar plantation, having three crops under cultivation at the same time, it would be difficult in many cases to draw the line between necessary expenses of the business and the amount expended in the production of its sugar, but the item under consideration is so plainly within the latter class that it cannot be allowed as a deduction at this time."

JACKSON v. SMIETANKA, COLLECTOR

(U. S. Circuit Court of Appeals, Seventh Cir., March 12, 1921.)

(272 Fed. 970)

Record: Revenue Act of 1918. Suit to recover income taxes paid under protest. Demurrer to plaintiff's declaration sustained; plaintiff declined to plead over; judgment for defendant (267 Fed. 932). Writ of error. Affirmed.

Facts: "From May, 1913, to April, 1918, plaintiff served as a railroad receiver under appointment of the District Court at Chicago. Plaintiff accepted the employment under an order providing that he 'be paid on account of his services at the rate of $2,000 per month' and that on termination of his trust he 'shall be at liberty to apply for such further compensation as to the court may then appear reasonable and just.' For the years 1913 to 1917 inclusive, plaintiff made returns on the basis of 'income received;' and, respecting this receivership, he had neither a business system nor books nor unpaid allowances for service from which he could have made returns of 'income accrued.' In 1918 plaintiff was allowed and paid 'as final payment for all services rendered by him during the receivership herein, the additional sum of $100,000.' On March 14, 1919, plaintiff filed his return for 1918, showing the receipt of said $100,000 and also filed amended returns for 1913 to 1917, inclusive, in which he claimed that pro rata parts of said $100,000 were 'accrued income' of those years. On April 16, 1919, the collector rejected the amended returns, and demanded normal taxes and surtaxes on the $100,000 so received in 1918. Plaintiff then prepared and on April 22, 1919, presented to the District Court a petition for a nunc pro tunc order showing that the additional compensation was earned and had accrued in equal monthly instalments throughout the receivership, and the order as tendered was entered. Thereupon plaintiff, on May 28, 1919, paid $26,826, under protest, and subsequently brought this action to recover the difference, $19,973. * * * *Plaintiff from time to time during the receivership had applied to the court for additional compensation, and the court had always refused."

Questions: (1) May a receiver, who at the end of his receivership has been awarded compensation in addition to his salary, return such an award on the accrual basis?

(2) Can a nunc pro tunc order showing that the additional compensation was earned and accrued in equal monthly instalments affect the method for returning such income?

Decision: (1) "Unless some effect is to be given to the nunc pro tunc order, the collector was right. Sec. 213 of the Revenue Act of 1918, requires a return of 'income derived from salaries or compensation for personal service' and provides that the amount thereof 'shall be included in the gross income for the taxable year in which received by the taxpayer unless under methods of account permitted under subdivision (b) of Sec. 212 any such amounts are to be properly accounted for as of a different period.' That subdivision permits a return 'upon the basis of the taxpayer's annual account period (fiscal year or calendar year, as the case may be) in accordance with the method of accounting regularly employed in keeping the books of such taxpayer; but if no such method of accounting has been so employed, or if the method employed does not clearly reflect the income, the computation shall be made upon such basis and in such manner as in the opinion of the Commissioner does clearly reflect the income.' Not only do the facts of this case demonstrate that there is no permission in that subdivision to save plaintiff from the direct mandate of Sec. 213, but article 32 of Regulations 45 (authorized by Sec. 1309 of the Act) explicitly requires that 'where no determination of compensation for personal services is had until the completion of the services, the amount received is income for the calendar year of its determination.' * * * *And whether the regulation means that the compensation is income of the year in which the determination of the amount is made or is income of the year in which payment is made, is immaterial in the present case, for both determination of amount and payment thereof occurred in 1918." The award was compensation for personal services which was income of the calendar year of its determination and payment.

(2) " * * * In regard to the present order it suffices to say: There was no misprision of a clerical officer; no new facts; no newly discovered evidence concerning former issues of fact; no failure in the court to enter the original order exactly as the court intended to enter it; even if the petition for the nunc pro tunc order had tendered an issue which interested the original parties (the railroad company and its creditors), no steps were taken by the aforetime receiver to have them join issue; the petition was heard ex parte; and as to the government all the matters in the District Court were res inter alios." Such order was ineffective to alter the conclusion that the award was income for the year in which determined and paid. Therefore, plaintiff is not entitled to recover the tax paid by him.

JACOBS & DAVIES, INC., v. ANDERSON, COLLECTOR

(U. S. Circuit Court of Appeals, Second Circuit, November 9, 1915)

(228 Fed. 505)

Record: Act of August 5, 1909. Action by the corporation above mentioned to recover back corporate taxes paid under protest for the years 1909 and 1910. Judgment for defendant was rendered in the trial court, U. S. District Court for Southern District of New York. Plaintiff brought the case up for review by writ of error. Affirmed.

Facts: Two civil engineers formed a corporation in April, 1909, to carry on the business of civil engineering which they had prior thereto conducted as a partnership. Prior to the enactment of the Corporation Tax Act of Aug. 5, 1909, the partners entered into a written agreement with the corporation to devote their services to the business for stated salaries of $6,000, to be paid to each. The corporation also agreed to pay them on a percentage basis the net surplus profits as defined in the agreement. The amounts thus paid as further compensation was $73,136, during 1909, $204,810, during 1910, and $114,986, during 1911.

Question: Should these payments based on the percentage of profits be allowed as salary deductions from the corporation profits, or be treated as dividends of corporate earnings?

Decision: Compensation whereby percentage of profits based on stockholdings is paid, is treated as a dividend. The reviewing court in the decision of the case says: "To enable the company to deduct these amounts it must appear that they were paid as salaries for services actually rendered. If the payments were based on the stockholdings of the parties, as we think they were, they cannot be considered as expenses of administration. They were not compensation because the salaries of both the parties are fully provided for in the agreement of April, 1909. It seems plain that they were profits of the business and as such were subject to the tax. Their payment did not depend upon the services rendered. Whether the stock was distributed among a large number of holders or only two, it can hardly be maintained that the amount paid out in dividends should be deducted in order to ascertain the amount of the net income of the corporation." Therefore, these payments are not to be allowed as salary deductions but are to be treated as dividends of corporate earnings.

IN RE JACOBSON: SMIETANKA, COLLECTOR, v. ZIBELL
(U. S. Circuit Court of Appeals for Seventh Cir., January Sess., 1920)
(263 Fed. 883)

Record: Rev. St. Sec. 3466 and Bankruptcy Act of 1898. Petition by collector to review and revise order of District Court. Decree affirmed.

Facts: Sec. 3466, Revised Statutes, provides that, if any person indebted to the United States is insolvent, the debts due the United States shall be satisfied first. Sections 64 (a) and 64 (b) of the Bankruptcy Act of 1898, which was passed later, provides that all taxes due the United States shall be paid "in advance of the payment of dividends to creditors." The collector contends that taxes should be paid before the costs and expenses of administering the insolvent estate, which is contra to the order of the court in settling the estate of Jacobson.

Question: Are the costs and expenses of administering the estate of a bankrupt payable from the estate in priority to income taxes due the United States?

Decision: "Creditors shall include anyone who owns a demand payable in bankruptcy; thus Congress by Sec. 1, subdivision 9, of the Act comprehensively designates the class known as creditors, the class whose claims are subject to the claims of the United States, county, district or municipality, for taxes. By no stretch of the definition of this term 'creditor' could it be construed to include clerk, trustee, referee, or any one whose relation with the bankrupt or the bankrupt's estate began subsequent to the filing of the petition in bankruptcy." It was therefore held that costs and expenses were payable before taxes.

JAMES, ADMINISTRATOR v. HICKS
(U. S. Supreme Court 1, June 28, 1884)
(110 U. S. 272)

Record: Suit to recover taxes alleged to have been illegally exacted. Judgment for plaintiff below. Defendant brought error. **Affirmed.**

Facts: Plaintiff filed his first appeal with the Commissioner for the recovery of the taxes on Feb. 8, 1866, and this was rejected by the Commissioner on May 7, 1866, because it was not duly made on proper forms. Afterwards, on Jan. 8, 1868, he made an appeal in proper form which was entertained by the Commissioner and rejected on January 22, 1879. The defense raised to this suit was the statute of limitations.

Question: (1) Should the first appeal be treated as the basis for determining the time within which plaintiff must bring his suit?

(2) Treating the second appeal as the one to be considered, was the action barred by plaintiff's failure to start suit within twelve months from the date of that appeal?

Decision: (1) The first appeal was rejected for mere informality by the Commissioner who entertained the subsequent appeal, made in proper form, as rightly prosecuted. The latter was the appeal contemplated by the statute.

(2) When the Commissioner delays his decision on appeal for recovery of tax alleged to have been illegally exacted more than six months from date of appeal, action may be brought within twelve months from that date, or the claimant may wait for the decision and bring his action at any time within six months thereafter. The suit having been commenced within six months from the date of decision by the commissioner, the plaintiff comes within the option allowed him, and the suit is not barred by the statute of limitations.

JASPER & E. RY. CO. v. WALKER, COLLECTOR

(U. S. Circuit Court of Appeals, Fifth Cir., January 2, 1917)

(228 Fed. 533)

Record: Act of August 5, 1909. Consolidation of four separate actions by the railway company and others, to recover a tax for 1912, levied under the Act of 1909 and paid under protest. Trial had in U. S. District Court for Western District of Texas, where judgment for defendant was rendered. Plaintiffs bring case for review by writ of error. Reversed and remanded with direction to enter judgment for each plaintiff.

Facts: Each plaintiff is the owner of a railroad in Texas, which prior to 1912, under authority conferred by the Texas statutes, it leased to another corporation, the Gulf, Colorado and Santa Fe Ry. Co., for a period of years extending beyond 1912. Lessee agreed to maintain and operate at its own expense during the lease, the railroad lines and appurtenances thereto and pay as rentals all interest on bonds or other obligations of lessor, taxes, rentals and other sums for which lessor might become liable during the term of the lease, all necessary expenses incurred by lessor for purpose of maintaining its organization, and annually a sum equal to 6% on the par value of the capital stock of the lessor, issued when the lease was made or thereafter issued with the written consent of lessee. Since the execution of the lease the properties remained in possession of the lessee who continued to operate the railroads pursuant to the terms of the lease. The lessor continued to maintain its corporate organization, kept an office and office force, and retained the corporate powers conferred by its charter. During the time the lease was in effect, including the year 1912, the lessor collected rentals from lessee, invested same for the benefit of its stockholders and distributed to them the profits from such investments. During 1912, each plaintiff made specified improvements to its railroad. Except as stated none of plaintiffs engaged in any activities during the year 1912.

Question: Was the tax illegally assessed on the ground that plaintiffs were not "engaged in business" in 1912, within the meaning of the Act of August, 1909, imposing an excise tax on corporations carrying on or doing business during the preceding year?

Decision: The court in the opinion stated that it is settled by controlling decisions that what each of the plaintiffs did in 1912 in the way of maintaining its corporate organization, receiving rentals and other income, and making distribution among its stockholders, did not constitute the "carrying on or doing business" by it in such wise as to make it subject to the tax imposed by the Act of 1909. (Zonne v. Minneapolis Syndicate 220 U. S. 187; McCoach v. Minehill Ry. Co. 228 U. S. 295). The effect of the lease was the total cessation of the exercise by lessor of the railroad business which was the specified business that the charter authorized. The lessor may act as a proprietor of property without engaging in a business contemplated by its charter. "We think this happens, when as a result of an authorized lease, it foregoes for the space of a tax year the transaction of the business for use in which all its property was acquired, and the lessee corporation, by an exclusive use of that property in carrying on that business within that year subjects itself to liability for the excise tax imposed upon such an exercise of corporate power. * * * * It has the same meaning whether applied to a corporation or to a natural person. It is not apt or appropriate to describe one who has retired from business in which he had engaged and confines his activities to maintaining property let to another and used exclusively by the lessee in carrying on that business." The plaintiff corporations were not doing business within the meaning of the Act, and the tax assessed against them was illegal.

JEWELERS SAFETY FUND SOCIETY v. LOWE, COLLECTOR
JEWELERS SAFETY FUND SOCIETY v. ANDERSON, COLLECTOR

(U. S. Circuit Court of Appeals, Second Cir., May 18, 1921)
(274 Fed. 93)

Record: Acts of August 5, 1909, and October 3, 1913. Action at law to recover taxes exacted by collector. Judgment for defendants in District Court. Plaintiff brings error. Reversed.

Facts: The plaintiff corporation was organized to insure manufacturers and dealers in jewelry against loss by fire, theft, barratry and embezzlement. Although they were not liable to assessment until after each loss had occurred, the members, for their own convenience, deposited with the company an amount estimated by it to cover losses and expenses, which amount was invested by the company so that it earned interest.

Questions: (1) Are the deposits by the members of a mutual insurance company to cover estimated losses a part of the gross income of the company?

(2) Is the interest from the premium deposits, not currently required for the payment of losses, profits which are subject to tax?

(3) Is a corporation organized to insure its members who are jewelers, against loss by fire, theft, barratry, and embezzlement, a mutual fire insurance company within the two Acts?

Decision: (1) "The company has no right in the fund at all until a loss is ascertained, and the amount of its gross income must be the sum which it collects from these deposits of the members for the purpose of paying operating expenses and losses."

(2) "This interest belongs, not to the company, but to the depositors."

(3) The court below was correct in holding that the plaintiff was an insurance company, but not in holding that it was a fire insurance company. "That the plaintiff is not an insurance company under the laws of the state of New York is perfectly plain. * * * If, as the defendant contends, the character of the plaintiff corporation is not to be determined by the laws of the state of New York, but under the federal statutes, then this plaintiff is as much a corporation for insurance against burglary as it is a fire insurance company. We think it is plainly a corporation for the protection of a certain specific class of the community, to wit, manufacturers of, importers of, and dealers in jewelry, etc."

JOHNSON v. WELLS FARGO & CO.
JOHNSON v. AMERICAN EXPRESS CO.
(U. S. Supreme Court, November 29, 1915)

(239 U. S. 234)

Record: Article XI, section 2, constitution of the state of South Dakota. Suits in equity to enjoin the treasurer of the state of South Dakota from assessing certain property taxes. Bills to enjoin assessment of taxes dismissed in the District Court (205 Fed. 60). Reversed by the Circuit Court of Appeals (215 Fed. 180). Affirmed.

Facts: The state of South Dakota required plaintiff express companies to make statements of their gross earnings in the state. Gross earnings among other things were to form the basis of value of plaintiffs' property for the purpose of state taxation. The state constitution provides that: "All taxes to be raised in this state shall be uniform on all real and personal property, according to its value in money to be ascertained by such rules of appraisement and assessment as may be prescribed by the legislature by general law.

so that every person and corporation shall pay a tax in proportion to the value of his, her or its property. And the legislature shall provide by general law for the assessing and levying of taxes on all corporative property as near as may be, by the same methods as are provided for assessing and levying of taxes on individual property.''

Question: May gross income be used as a basis of assessment of corporate property when not used as such basis for individual property?

Decision: To use the gross income of corporations as a basis for taxation of property without also using a similar basis for the property of individuals is in violation of the provision of the constitution of the state requiring property of corporations to be taxed as nearly as may be as property of individuals.

KAUSCH v. MOORE, COLLECTOR
(U. S. District Court E. D. Mo. E. D. Dec. 9, 1920)
(268 Fed. 668)

Record: National Prohibition Act, and Rev. Stat., Sec. 3224. Bill in equity for injunction. On motion to dismiss bill, motion sustained.

Facts: Plaintiff's bill set forth that the Commissioner of Internal Revenue, acting on reports of investigators that plaintiff had violated some of the provisions of the above named Act, assessed a tax against him in double the amount required of retail liquor dealers, to wit:—$20.48, with penalty of $500 and a further penalty of $2.60; that the collector was threatening to distrain on plaintiff's business for collection of these amounts; that plaintiff was unable to pay such amounts; and that, if defendant levied upon his property and business, it would ruin his business and deprive him and his family of their livelihood.

Questions: (1) Would an injunction lie to restrain the collection of the tax?

(2) Would an injunction lie against the enforcement of the penalty?

(3) Was a distraint proceeding for collection of a penalty valid where no opportunity to be heard has been given to the person penalized?

(4) Would failure to pay the lawful tax due defeat a bill for injunction against the collection of the lawful tax and an unlawful penalty?

Decision: (1) Injunction will not lie to prevent the collection of an internal revenue tax, even in a case where, as here, the amount is doubled upon the contingency of the violation of the law.

(2) But a statute which merely forbids the injunction as against a tax ought not to be so extended as to include injunction against the enforcement of a penalty. Certainly, this ought not to be done in a case wherein the manner of the collection, as here, is not warranted by law.

(3) To allow property to be taken and sold by distraint for collection of a penalty imposed by the Commissioner without any opportunity on the part of the person penalized to be heard would be to take it and sell it without due process of law.

(4) A party can not enjoin collection of a tax bill until he has paid or tendered all lawful taxes assessed against him. He can not enjoin the collection of an illegal penalty if he has not paid the lawful tax due.

KEMPER MILITARY SCHOOL v. CRÚTCHLEY
(U. S. District Court, W. D. Missouri, W. D., March 23, 1921)

(274 Fed. 125)

Record: Revenue Act of 1918. Suit to recover income taxes, interest, and penalty exacted for year 1918. Judgment for defendant.

Facts: The plaintiff was incorporated June 15, 1909, under the provisions of chapter 12, article 9 of the Revised Statutes of Missouri, which deals with corporations organized for pecuniary profit and gain. Plaintiff was not organized under the article of the same chapter, which deals with benevolent, religious, scientific, educational, and miscellaneous associations not intended for pecuniary gain or profit. For many years prior to its incorporation it was owned by Colonel T. A. Johnston, now its president and principal stockholder. For the calendar year 1918 its gross income amounted to $205,153.26, of which the sum of $5,083.11 was received from sources other than tuition. After making statutory deductions the net income remaining amounted to $79,788.01. When the

school was incorporated Colonel Johnston transferred the property
to the corporation, receiving stock therefor. The remaining shares
of stock were subscribed for by teachers, and the officers and board
of directors are made up of such. These teachers paid for their
stock out of their earnings. A dividend of 6 per cent has been paid
upon all stock since the date of the incorporation. The corporation
is operated exclusively for educational purposes. In 1918 the plaintiff spent $13,086.68 in necessary furniture and fixtures, and $81,188.35
for buildings and other necessary improvements for the up-keep and
expansion of its plant and for the comforts and necessities of the
school.

Questions: (1) Is the plaintiff exempt from taxation as a
"corporation organized and operated exclusively for * * * educational purposes, * * * no part of the net earnings of which
inures to the benefit of any private stockholder or individual?

(2) If not, may the deductions be made for amounts expended
for furniture, fixtures, buildings and other necessary improvements?

Decision: (1) "This corporation, while devoted to educational
purposes, was confessedly organized for private pecuniary profit
and gain. Its teachers all receive salaries. In addition thereto,
they have all, including Colonel Johnston, received an annual dividend of 6 per cent upon their stock since the date the corporation
was organized. * * * Upon ultimate dissolution the holders
of these shares of stock would receive the proceeds of the property,
including accumulated income. The chief insistence is that because
all the shareholders are directors, and teachers in the institution,
they are not 'private stockholders or individuals.' This involves a
narrowness of definition that can not be entertained in view of the
obvious purpose and spirit of the Act. The distinction is not between private and official, whether the latter be used in a military
or an institutional sense. The word 'private' as here used is the
antonym of 'public,'—a private stockholder as distinguished from
the general public—the supposed beneficiary of the benevolent
activities of an institution devoted exclusively to public betterment.
Private pecuniary profit and gain is the test to be applied. This
corporation was, and is, undeniably organized and operated for
that purpose." Therefore, the corporation is not exempt from
income tax as an educational institution.

(2) "The law provides for a reasonable allowance for exhaustion, wear and tear, etc., as conceded by defendant, and as claimed by plaintiff in its return and allowed by the collector and Commissioner. It further provides that in computing net income no deduction shall in any case be allowed in respect of any amount paid out for new buildings, or for permanent improvements or betterments made to increase the value of any property or estate. It follows that this claim for deduction, in the sum of $94,275.03, or any part thereof, can not be indulged."

KETTERER v. LEDERER, COLLECTOR
(U. S. District Court, E. D. Penn. Oct. 13, 1920)
(269 Fed. 153)

Record: National Prohibition Act. In equity. On motion for preliminary injunction. Denied.

Facts: Plaintiff, a liquor dealer, was assessed a special tax for violation of the above named Act, which tax the collector attempted to collect by distraint.

Question: Would the court grant an injunction to restrain collection of an internal revenue tax?

Decision: "Congress has clearly declared its purpose that the collection of excise taxes shall not be hampered or delayed by resort to injunction process, and has provided a different and not inadequate remedy." The court, therefore, refused to grant an injunction restraining the collection of the tax.

KIDD v. ALABAMA
(U. S. Supreme Court, October, 1902)
(188 U. S. 730)

Record: Section 453, Code of 1886 and Sec. 3911, Code of 1896, State of Alabama. Action by the State to recover taxes. Judgment for plaintiff (125 Ala. 413). Writ of error. Judgment affirmed.

Facts: Defendant was the executrix of the will of a citizen of Alabama, and the tax in question was upon stock of railroads incorporated in other states than Alabama.

Question: Was the tax in question unconstitutional under the Fourteenth Amendment because no similar tax was levied on the stock of domestic railroads or of foreign railroads doing business in that State?

Decision: Held, that the tax was not unconstitutional. "We see nothing to prevent a state from taxing stock in some domestic corporations and leaving stock in others untaxed on the ground that it taxes the property and franchises of the latter to an amount that imposes indirectly a proportional burden on the stock. When we come to corporations formed and having their property and business elsewhere, the state must tax the stock held within the state if it is to tax anything, and we are now assuming the right to tax stock in foreign corporations to be conceded."

KIMBALL et al v. COTTING et al
(Supreme Judicial Court of Massachusetts, Feb. 28, 1918)
(229 Mass. 541; 118 N. E. 866)

Record: Acts of October 3, 1913, and Revenue Acts of 1916 and 1917. Action upon contract. against Cotting and others to recover a balance of rent. Judgment for plaintiff.

Facts: The plaintiffs leased to the defendants certain premises with a covenent that the lessees would "pay and discharge any taxes or excises which during the term may on any assessment day be lawfully levied or assessed to either the lessors or the lessees upon or against the rent payable hereunder for or in respect of the period between such assessment day and the last prior assessment day, or for or in respect of the period between the first of such assessment days and the one calendar year prior thereto, whether levied or assessed upon the same as rental or income, but not for any other taxes or excises in respect thereof." The defendants, having paid the Federal income tax assessed on the rent, withheld that amount out of the rent paid.

Question: Do the words "assessment day" where the lessee covenants to pay taxes on rent "for or in respect of the period between such assessment day and the last prior assessment day" make it impossible to hold the lessee for income tax on the rent, on the ground that there is no "assessment day" for the Federal income tax?

Decision: "An income tax necessarily has reference to moneys received during a specified period of time. At any single moment one can hardly be said to have income. Duration of time is required for measurement. On the other hand, a property tax requires a definite moment for its assessment, in order that its items and their value may be measured by reference to a known or ascertainable standard. Since by express words of the covenant the lessee is liable for the tax, whether levied upon the rental or income; it follows that the words 'assessment day' were not intended to refer immutably to a single date, but were designed to include whatever period not exceeding that elapsing between two successive assessment days might be established by any tax law thereafter enacted as the measurement of the income. * * * The Federal income tax law, here in question, was approved October 3, 1913. It expressly provides in paragraph D that income tax shall be computed upon the net income 'during each preceding calendar year ending December thirty-first.' That fixes the last day of each calendar year as the 'assessment day' for that kind of a tax, as definitely as was the first day of May fixed for the year ending on that date by R. L. C. 12, Sec. 4, Cl. 4, for the state income tax in force when the lease was executed. The return to be made by the taxpayer under each law is filed at some later time, and the actual completion of the tax is made still later, but the 'assessment day' is as definite under one statute as under the other, so far as it concerns a tax on income." The court held that the defendants were liable to plaintiff for the amount of rent which they withheld.

KIMBALL v. COTTING et al.

(Sup. Judicial Court of Massachusetts, Nov. 26, 1919)

(125 N. E. 551)

Record: Acts of October 3, 1913, and Revenue Act of 1916. Action to recover Federal income taxes paid on certain rents. On report from Superior Court, judgment ordered for plaintiff.

Facts: Defendants were lessees of plaintiff under a lease which contained the following covenant: "The lessees covenant and agree as far as at any time permitted by law to pay and discharge any taxes or excises which during the term may be lawfully levied, laid or assessed upon or against the rent payable hereunder whether levied or assessed upon the same as rental or as income of any person or persons entitled hereto." Defendants conceded liability for the normal tax.

Question: Are defendants liable for the amount of the surtax called for under the Acts of 1913 and 1916 as amended?

Decision: The surtax is only an additional income tax, graduated and collected as prescribed, and it is immaterial that this mode of taxation came into existence after the date of the lease.

KINGS COUNTY SAVINGS INSTITUTION v. BLAIR, COLLECTOR
(U. S. Supreme Court, Jan. 4, 1886)
(116 U. S. 200)

Record: Rev. Stat. Sec. 3228. Action for money had and received. Judgment for defendant.

Facts: The plaintiff paid a tax under protest. The statute says that all claims for refunding must be made within two years. This the plaintiff did not do.

Question: Is the failure to make claim for refund within two years under the section a bar to recovery, even though payment was made under protest?

Decision: When the law says the claim must be presented within two years, the implication is that, unless so presented, the right to demand repayment of the tax is lost and the Commissioner has no authority to refund it, and, of course, the right of suit is gone. We regard the presentation of the claims to the Commissioner of Internal Revenue for the refunding of a tax alleged to have been illegally exacted as a condition on which alone the government consents to litigate the lawfulness of the original tax.

KING v. UNITED STATES
(U. S. Supreme Court, October, 1878)
(99 U. S. 229)

Record: Rev. Stat. Sec. 3142. Action against a collector of internal revenue and his sureties on his official bond. Writ of error to a judgment of the Circuit Court in favor of the plaintiff. Judgment affirmed.

Facts: On June 1st, 1868, the T. W. & W. R. R. Co. made and delivered to the collector tax returns for the years 1865, 1866 and 1867, and at the same time paid to the collector the amount of the tax due on said returns. The returns were signed by the treasurer of the company, but were not sworn to, and had never been filed with or delivered to the assessor as prescribed by law. The collector gave the company a receipt as collector, specifying the taxes which were paid. All of the returns were delivered by the collector to the assessor, except those for August, September and October, 1867, which were never delivered to the assessor, and the amount of the tax paid under them was never delivered or reported to the government, but was retained by the collector. The collector contended that because the money was not received on any return made by the assessor, or on any assessment made by him or by the Commissioner of Internal Revenue, for such taxes, and because the returns were not verified by oath, that the money paid was not received by him in his official character, and that his sureties were not liable because it was an unofficial act.

Question: Was the sum delivered to the collector a valid payment for that amount, and might the collector lawfully receive the money and be bound to pay it to the government?

Decision: The payment of a tax due is not invalidated by the fact that no assessment thereof was ever made. "To hold to the contrary is to decide that a debt long past due and acknowledged to be due by the debtor cannot be paid, when he is willing to pay, and the proper officer of the government ready to receive it, because the debtor has neglected to report the same facts to some other officer, or that officer has neglected to make report of the facts. Of the duty of the railroad company to pay the money as speedily as possible, there can be no doubt. When it admitted the obligation and offered to pay it, was there no one to whom it could pay it?" The court holds that the payment to the collector was a valid payment and that the collector was liable to the government for the money collected.

KLAR PIQUETT MINING CO. v. TOWN OF PLATTEVILLE
(Supreme Court of Wisconsin, May 2, 1911)
(163 Wis. 215; 157 N. W. 763)

Record: Wisconsin Act of October 3, 1913. Action at law to recover taxes paid under protest. Judgment for defendant and plaintiff appeals. Affirmed.

Facts: Plaintiff, a mining corporation holding under a perpetual lease, in making its income return for the year 1912, claimed a deduction from gross income for depreciation on ore body although it had been allowed a deduction for royalties paid.

Question: Is the holder of a perpetual lease of a mine, who has already been allowed a deduction for royalties paid on ore mined, also entitled to a deduction for depreciation for ore mined?

Decision: For the purposes of income tax plaintiff's lease is not equivalent to ownership. Plaintiff mining company operating under its lease pays a certain sum for every ton mined whether such sum is stipulated in the lease or not. When stipulated it amounts to a royalty of so much per ton. In this case a specific sum was paid as royalty for the year and such sum was deducted from the gross proceeds of the business. By such deduction plaintiff was allowed the cost of the ore mined in the same sense that a manufacturer is allowed a deduction for the cost of raw material used. He can not, in addition to this deduction, deduct an amount for depreciation on ore.

KLOCK PRODUCE CO. v. HARTSON, COLLECTOR
(U. S. District Court, W. D. Washington, S. D. April 2, 1914)
(212 Fed. 758)

Record: Act of July 13, 1866. Action at law against collector to recover taxes and penalties. Verdict for plaintiff. Motion for new trial denied.

Facts: The plaintiff paid taxes and penalties under protest, and brought this suit after appeal had been made to the Commissioner. Interest was included in the verdict.

Question: Can one who has paid taxes under protest, having made the proper appeal to the Commissioner, recover the excess tax with interest?

Decision: The court said that "a suit, such as the present one, is, in effect, one not against the United States; that it will not be considered such until after final judgment and a certificate from the trial court that there was probable cause for the collection of the tax; that, upon such certificate being given, it becomes a claim against the United States, stopping the right to interest, unless a review of the judgment by an appellate court is obtained, in which event the judgment upon the mandate of the appellate court will be treated as a final judgment, to the rendition of which interest will be allowed, unless the plaintiff unduly delays the presentation of this claim." The plaintiff, having filed his claim within a reasonable time, was allowed to recover the taxes with interest.

KNOWLTON v. MOORE
(U. S. Supreme Court, May 14, 1900)
(178 U. S. 41)

Record: Act of June 13, 1898. Action at law by executors of will of Edwin F. Knowlton, deceased, against collector, to recover tax exacted on certain legacies which was paid under protest. Demurrer to complaint sustained and suit dismissed. Plaintiff brought error. Reversed.

Facts: Mr. Knowlton died at Brooklyn, in October, 1898, and his will was duly probated. Under Secs. 29 and 30 of the Act of Congress of June 13, 1898 (War Revenue Act) which provide for taxes on legacies and distributive shares of personal property, a return was made under protest by the executor. The return showed that the personal estate amounted to over two and a half million dollars, and that there were several legacies ranging from $10,000 each to over $1,500,000. The collector levied the tax on the legacies and distributive shares, but for the purpose of fixing the rate of the tax considered the whole of the personal estate of the deceased as fixing the rate for each, and not the amount coming to each individual legatee under the will. As the rates under the statute were progressive this decision greatly increased the amount of the tax. The executors protested on the grounds (1) that the provisions of the Act were unconstitutional; (2) that legacies amounting to less than $10,000 were not subject to any tax or duty; (3)

that a legacy of $100,000, taxed at the rate of $2.25 per $100, was only subject to the rate of one dollar twelve and a half cents.

Questions: (1) Were the taxes direct taxes, and not being apportioned, hence repugnant to article 1, section 8 of the Constitution of the U. S.?

(2) If not direct taxes, were they not repugnant to the Constitution for the reason that they were levied on rights created solely by state law and depending for their continued existence on the consent of the several states?

(3) If the taxes were not direct and were not assessed upon objects or rights which were beyond the reach of Congress, nevertheless were not the taxes void because they were not uniform throughout the United States, as required by article 1, section 9, of the Constitution of the United States?

(4) Even though constitutional, were the taxes not illegal, since in their assessment the rate was determined by the aggregate amount of the personal estate of the deceased, and not by the sum of the legacies or distributive shares, or the right to take the same, which were the objects upon which by law the taxes were placed?

Decision: (1) The court after reviewing the law relating to death duties as found in the Roman and ancient law, in the law of modern France, Germany and other continental countries, in England and those of her colonies where such laws have been enacted, in the legislation of the United States and the several States of the Union, says: "Although different modes of assessing such duties prevail, and although they have different accidental names, such as probate duties, stamp duties, taxes on the transaction, or the act of passing an estate or a succession, legacy taxes, estate taxes or privilege taxes, nevertheless tax laws of this nature in all countries rest in their essence upon the principle that death is the generating source from which the particular taxing power takes its being and that it is the power to transmit, or the transmission from the dead to living, on which such taxes are more immediately rested." They are not taxes on property, but on succession. The tax in question is a duty or excise tax on the right to take property by descent or devise as distinguished from a tax on property. Being a duty or excise it is not direct within the meaning of the constitution.

(2) The court then took up the objection that Congress cannot levy a tax of this kind, since the transmission of property by death is exclusively subject to the regulating authority of the several states. The court says this proposition would deny Congress the right to tax a subject matter which was conceded to be within the scope of its power very early in the history of the Government. It must be borne in mind, the court states, "that fundamentally considered it is the power to transmit, or the transmission or receipt of property by death which is the subject levied upon by all death duties." Subject to a compliance with the limitations in the Consitution, the taxing power of Congress extends to all usual objects of taxation. The fallacy which underlies the proposition contended for, that the power to regulate successions is lodged solely in the several states, is the assumption, the court says, that the tax on the transmission or receipt of property occasioned by death, is imposed upon the exclusive power of the State to regulate the devolution of property upon death. In legal effect this would mean that wherever a right is subject to exclusive regulation by either the Government of the U. S. or the several states, the exercise of such rights as regulated can alone be taxed by the Government having the mission to regulate. The court points out that property of persons engaged in interstate commerce is often within the exclusive regulating power of Congress, and it may not be asserted that such property is not subject to tax by the several states because of Federal regulations. "Certainly a tax placed upon an inheritance or legacy diminishes, to the extent of the tax, the value of the right to inherit or receive, but this is a burden cast upon the recipient and not upon the power of the state to regulate." Reference is made to many decisions quoted, including the License Tax Cases, 5 Wall. 462 at page 470, which, according to the court, establish the error in the proposition relied on in this behalf to sustain the invalidity of the tax. The court, in accordance with the foregoing, held that the tax in question was constitutional.

(3) Estate tax was not invalid for lack of uniformity. The words "uniform throughout the United States," as used in the Constitution with respect to duties, imposts and excises, do not relate to the inherent character of the tax as respects its operation on individuals, but simply requires that whatever plan or method Congress

adopts for laying the tax in question, the same plan and same method must be made operative throughout the United States, or, in other words, the requirement is that such taxes shall be geographically uniform.

(4) The Act of June 13, 1898, imposes the duty on the particular legacies or shares and not on the whole personal estate. The construction of the lower court validating the levy of the tax on the aggregate amount of the personal estate of decedent, rather than by the sum of each legacy or distributive share considered separately was error. The opinion acknowledges that the purpose of Congress was to tax the legacies and distributive shares, and proceeds to examine the question whether the progressive rate imposed by the Act shall be measured, not separately by the amount of each particular legacy, but by the sum of the whole personal estate. The holding of the court is that the latter construction is unsound. The court says:

"In other words, the statute itself by the reference clause, establishes the whole amount referred to is the sum or value of each particular legacy, etc., separately considered passing from the deceased to the taker thereof, * * * . We are bound, therefore, to give heed to the rule that where a particular construction of a statute will occasion great inconvenience, or produce inequality or injustice, that view is to be avoided if another and more reasonable interpretation is present in the statute."

The tax is on the legacies and the rate is primarily determined by the classifications, being progressively increased according to the amount of the legacies. The court, therefore, held that, although the taxes involved were constitutional, the plaintiff was entitled to recover because in their assessment the progressive rate had been fixed by the value of the whole estate instead of by the amount of each legacy.

KNOX v. ROSSI

(Supreme Court of Nevada, May 23, 1899)

(57 Pac. 179)

Record: Act of June 13, 1898. Action at law. Judgment for defendant and plaintiff appeals. Reversed.

Facts: During a trial in a state court, plaintiff offered in evidence two depositions taken under a commission issued to a notary public of the city of San Francisco. One of the depositions was objected to on the ground that the stamps required by the Act of Congress were not cancelled upon the same date which the notary's certificate bears. The other deposition was objected to on the ground that the notary's certificate was not stamped as required by the provisions of the Revenue law. Each objection was sustained in the lower court and the evidence excluded.

Question: Did the Act of June 13, 1898, providing that no instruments not duly stamped as required shall be admitted or used as evidence in any court, apply to state courts?

Decision: "This provision can have full operation and effect if construed as intended to apply to those courts only which have been established under the constitution of the United States and by acts of Congress, over which the Federal legislature can legitimately exercise control, and to which they can properly prescribe rules regulating the course of justice and the mode of administering justice." It was not the intention of Congress to enact rules regulating the competency of evidence on the trial of cases in the state courts. The lower court erred in excluding the evidence.

KOHLHAMMER v. SMIETANKA, COLLECTOR
(U. S. District Court, N. D. Illinois. E. D. January 31, 1917)
(239 Fed. 408)

Record: Act of October 22, 1914. Action in equity to restrain defendant, collector of internal revenue at Chicago, Ill., from proceeding to collect from plaintiffs by distraint certain penalties imposed for failure to pay the stamp tax on sales, agreements to sell, and agreements of sale, imposed by Sec. 22 of the Act of October 22, 1914. Temporary restraining order denied.

Facts: Defendant by means of affidavits asserted that the plaintiffs and many other members of the Board of Trade collected large sums of money from customers for taxes and failed to pay them over to the Government. The collector served demand notice on plaintiffs notifying them that a tax of $4,313.65, plus a penalty of $8,313.30 had been assessed by the Commissioner on sales made

by them for the period ending 1916. Defendant contended that
Sec. 3224 Rev. Stat., which provides that no suit for the purpose
of restraining the assessment or collection of any tax shall be
maintained in any court, is a bar of plaintiff's suit. Plaintiffs
contended that a proceeding to collect a penalty is not a proceeding
to collect a tax and so this section is not applicable.

Question: May the collector be restrained from proceeding to collect penalties imposed in addition to the tax?

Decision: The court in the decision states that "an examination of the many cases bearing upon this question, the last being
Dodge v. Osborn, 240 U. S. 118, convinces the court that Congress
intended to deny all relief by injunction to taxpayers who felt aggrieved by the act of officers intrusted by the Government with the
duty of determining and collecting taxes, general, special or stamp
taxes." In construing Sec. 410 of the Act of September 8, 1916,
and Sec. 23 of the Act of 1914, with the general administrative Act,
a portion of which is quoted from Sec. 3176 R. S., the court concluded
that the penalty in the present case is a part of the tax, the assessment
and collection of which are governed by Sec. 3224. Plaintiff's
application for a temporary restraining order was denied and the
order theretofore entered was directed to be vacated.

LA BELLE IRON WORKS v. UNITED STATES.
(U. S. Supreme Court, October Term, 1920)
(256 U. S. 377)

Record: Revenue Act of 1917. Petition for refund of $1,081,-
184.61, assessed and exacted as an "excess profits tax" under Title
II of this Act. Demurrer to petition sustained by Court of Claims.
Appeal to Supreme Court. Affirmed.

Facts: "Appellant is a domestic corporation and, prior to
the year 1904, acquired ore lands for which it paid the sum of $190,-
000. Between that time and the year 1912, extensive explorations
and developments were carried on (the cost of which is not stated).
It was proved that the lands contained large bodies of ore and had
an actual cash value of not less than $10,105,400; and at all times
during the years 1912 to 1917, inclusive, their actual cash value
was not less than the sum last mentioned. In the year 1912 the

company increased the valuation of said lands upon its books by adding thereto the sum of $10,000,000, which it carried to surplus, and, thereupon, in the same year, declared a stock dividend in the sum of $9,915,400, representing the increase in value of the ore lands. Theretofore appellant's capital stock had consisted of shares issued, all of one class, having a par value of $9,915,400. The declaration of the stock dividend was carried out by the surrender to the company of all the outstanding stock, and its cancellation, and the exchange of one share of new common and one share of the new preferred stock for each share of the original stock. In returning its annual net income for the year 1917, the company stated its invested capital to be $26,322, 904.14, in which was included the sum of $10,105,400, as representing the value of its ore lands. The Commissioner of Internal Revenue caused a reassessment to be made, based upon a reduction of the invested capital to $16,404.14; the difference ($9,915,400) being the increase in the value of the ore lands already mentioned. The result was an additional tax of $1,081,184.61, which, having been paid, was made the subject of a claim for a refund; and this having been considered and rejected by the Commissioner, there followed a suit in the Court of Claims."

Questions: (1) Should the increased value of the ore lands, placed upon the company's books in 1912, be included in invested capital under Sec. 207 (A 3) of the Revenue Act of 1917 as "paid in or earned surplus and undivided profits?"

(2) Should the stock of the company issued in 1912, consisting of $9,915,400 of preferred stock and an equal amount of common, be included in invested capital under Sec. 207, clause (2) as "the actual cash value of tangible property paid in other than cash, for stock or shares in such corporation," either by (a) tangible assets, including the ore properties at their increased value, or (b) by the surrender of all the certificates representing the old common stock, which, it is said, had an actual cash value equal to double its par?

(3) Would the result reached by the court in Question 1 be different if the appellant's petition had stated the cost of the extensive explorations and developments alleged?

(4) Does the construction put upon the Act by the Treasury Department, based, as it is said, not upon value but upon the single feature of cost, disregarding the time of acquisition, render the Act unconstitutional as a deprivation of property without due process under the Fifth Amendment, because so arbitrary as to amount in effect to confiscation; and hence require this construction to be avoided?

(5) Can the results arrived at by the court in this case be taken as a decision upon the effect of the Act with respect to deductions from cost values of capital assets, because of depreciation or the like?

Decision: (1-2) "A scrutiny of the particular provisions of Sec. 207 shows that it was the dominant purpose of Congress to place the peculiar burden of this tax upon the income of trades and businesses exceeding what was deemed a normally reasonable return upon the capital actually embarked, * * * Sec. 207 shows that Congress adopted a term—"invested capital"—and a definition of it, that would measurably guard against inflated valuations. The word "invested" in itself imports a restricted qualification. * * * It is clear that clauses (1) and (2) refer to actual capital contributions of cash or of tangible property at its cash value contributed in exchange for stock or shares specifically issued for it; and that neither these clauses nor clause (3), which relates to surplus, can be construed as including within the definition of invested capital any marking up of the value of the assets upon the books to correspond with increase in market value, or any paper transaction by which new shares are issued in exchange for old ones in the same corporation, but which is not in substance and effect a new acquisition of capital property by the company. * * * In view of the special language employed in Sec. 207, obviously for the purpose of avoiding appreciated valuations of assets over and above cost, the argument that such value is as real as cost value, and that in the terminology of corporation and partnership accounting 'capital and surplus' mean merely the excess of all assets at actual values over outstanding liabilities, and 'surplus' means the intrinsic value of all assets over and above outstanding liabilities plus par of the stock, is beside the mark. Nor has the distinction between capital and income, discussed in Doyle v. Mitchell Bros. Co., 247 U. S. 179, 187; Hays v. Gauley Mountain Coal Co., 247

U. S. 189, 193; and Southern Pacific Co. v. Lowe, 247 U. S. 330, 334-335, any proper bearing upon the questions here presented. Upon the strength of an administrative interpretation contained in a Treasury Regulation pertaining to the Revenue Act of 1917, under which 'stocks' were to be regarded as tangible property when paid in for stock or share of a corporation, it is insisted that apellant's stock dividend distribution of 1912 ought to be treated as paid for in tangible property, the old stock surrendered being regarded as tangible for the purpose. But that distribution, in substance and effect, is an internal transaction, in which the company received nothing from the stockholders any more than they received anything from it (see Eisner v. Macomber, 252 U. S. 189, 210-211); and the old shares cannot be regarded as having been 'paid in for' the new ones within the meaning of the Regulation, which is doubtful."

(3) "It is said that the admitted increase in the value of the appellant's ore lands is properly to be characterized as earned surplus, because it was the result of extensive exploration and development work. We assume that the proper sum, not exceeding the cost of the work, might have been added to earned surplus on that account; but none such was stated in appellant's petition, nor, so far as appears, in its return of income. In the absence of such a showing it was not improper to attribute the entire $9,915,400, added to the book value of the ore property in the year 1912, to a mere appreciation in the value of the property, in short, to what is commonly known as the 'unearned increment,' not properly 'earned surplus' within the meaning of the statute."

(4) "It is urged that this construction, defining invested capital according to the original cost of the property instead of its present value, has the effect of rendering the Act 'glaringly unequal' and of doubtful constitutionality, the insistence being that, so construed, it operates to produce baseless and arbitrary discriminations, to the extent of rendering the tax invalid under the due process of law clause of the Fifth Amendment. Reference is made to cases decided under the equal protection clause of the Fourteenth Amendment (Southern Ry. Co. v. Greene, 216 U. S. 400, 418; Gast Realty Co. v. Schneider Granite Co., 240 U. S. 55); but clearly they are not in point. The Fifth Amendment has no equal protection clause; and the only rule

of uniformity prescribed with respect to duties, imposts and excises laid by Congress, is the territorial uniformity required by Art. 1, Sec. 8, Pollock v. Farmers' Loan & Trust Co., 157 U. S. 429, 557; Knowlton v. Moore, 178 U. S. 41, 98, 106; Flint v. Stone Tracey Co., 220 U. S. 107, 150; Billings v. United States, 232 U. S. 261, 282; Brushaber v. Union Pacific R. R., 240 U. S. 1, 24. That the statute under consideration operates with territorial uniformity is obvious and not questioned.

"Nor can we regard the Act in basing 'invested capital' upon actual costs to the exclusion of higher estimated values as productive of arbitrary discriminations raising a doubt about its constitutionality under the due process clause of the Fifth Amendment. The difficulty of adjusting any system of taxation so as to render it precisely equal in its bearing is proverbial, and such nicety is not even required of the States under the equal protection clause, much less of Congress under the more general requirement of due process of law in taxation. Of course, it will be understood that Congress had very ample authority to adjust its income taxes according to its discretion, within the bounds of geographical uniformity. Courts have no authority to pass upon the propriety of its measures, and we deal with the present criticism only for the purpose of refuting the contention, strongly urged, that the tax is so wholly arbitrary as to amount to confiscation.

" * * * * * * * * * * There is a logical incongruity in entering upon the books of a corporation as the capital value of property acquired for permanent employment in its business and still retained for that purpose a sum corresponding, not to its cost, but to what probably might be realized by sale in the market. It is not merely that the market value has not been realized or tested by sale made but that sale cannot be made without abandoning the very purpose for which the property is held, involving a withdrawal from business so far as that particular property is concerned. Whether in a given case property should be carried in the capital account at market value rather than at cost may be a matter of judgment, depending upon special circumstances and the local law. But certainly Congress, in seeking a general rule, reasonably might adopt the cost basis resting upon experience, rather than anticipation.

"In organizing corporations it is not unusual to issue different classes of securities with various priorities as between themselves to represent different kinds of contributions to capital. In exchange for cash, bonds may be issued, for fixed property like plant and equipment, preferred stock may be given, while more speculative values like good will or patent rights, may be represented by common stock. In the present case, for instance, when appellant took the estimated increase in value of its ore lands as a basis for increased capitalization, it issued preferred stock to the amount of the former total, carrying those lands at cost, and issued a like amount of common stock to represent the appreciation in their market value. It does not appear that in form the new issues were thus allocated, but at least there was the recognition of a higher claim in favor of one part of the book capital than of the other. Upon like ground it was not unreasonable for Congress, in adjusting the "excess profits tax," to accord preferential treatment to capital representing actual investments, as compared with capital representing high valuations based upon estimates however confident and reliable, of what probably could be realized were the property sold or retained."

(5) "We intimate no opinion upon the effect of the Act with respect to deductions from cost values of capital assets because of depreciation or the like; no question of that kind being here involved." It therefore was held that plaintiff was not entitled to recover the additional tax assessed against and paid by it.

LANDRAM v. UNITED STATES
(Court of Claims, December 1880)
(16 Court of Claims 74)

Record: Rev. Stat. Sec. 1765. Action at law to recover salary due from the government. Judgment for plaintiff.

Facts: Claimant, a collector of internal revenue, was authorized by the Secretary of the Treasury to employ a deputy. He appointed Herndon at a salary of $1,200 who was then acting as distillery surveyor on a stipulated salary. Herndon brought an action against the government to recover his salary, but the court decided that there was no privity between him and the government. (15 Court of Claims R. 446). The collector who appointed him then brought this action to recover the salary. The defendant conceded that the collector was authorized by the treasury to appoint a deputy, and that the service was rendered; but averred that the deputy was at the same time acting as a distillery surveyor and could not receive dual pay.

Question: May a deputy collector of internal revenue receive dual pay from the Federal Government when acting in two different capacities as stated in the above facts?

Decision: "The traditions and usages of the United States recognize the policy and propriety of employing, when necessary, the same person at the same time in two distinct capacities." The court here cites a number of prominent examples of this practice. "On the other hand, it is the undoubted aim of general legislation respecting salaries to gauge the work so as to give full employment to the capacities of the man likely to be appointed to do it, and to measure the pay according to the work. In construing statutes restraining the executive from giving dual or extra compensation, courts have aimed to carry out the legislative intent by giving them sufficient flexibility not to injure the public service and sufficient rigidity to prevent executive abuse." The court, accordingly, held that the collector could recover the amount of the salary of the deputy.

LATHERS et al. v. HAMLIN et al.

(Supreme Court, New York County, February, 1918)

(170 N. Y. Supp. 98; 102 Misc. Rep. 563)

Record: Act of October 3, 1917. Action to foreclose a mortgage. Receiver's petition for instructions answered.

Facts: The receiver, appointed by the Court, had possession of the property, managed it, and received the rents of the premises. He is now ready to file his report and to render an account. He petitioned the court for instructions as to whether he will be obliged to file a return showing the net income received and to pay the tax thereon.

Question: Is a receiver, appointed by the court to take over and manage property, required to file an income tax return and pay the tax?

Decision: "The receiver in such a case as the present is a mere custodian and manager of the property under the direction of the court. He is not a trustee for creditors; he has no title; he has no powers, save such as are conferred by the order of appointment, * * * * * * . The moneys coming into the hands of the receiver are not the avails of trade, commerce, investments, employment, occupation, or service. They are not in any sense 'income,' within the meaning of the statute—at least so far as the receiver shall have accounted, and the moneys remaining in his hands shall have been paid to the parties entitled thereto,—doubtless these moneys will be taken into consideration by the recipients when making their tax returns." The receiver is under no duty to render a return or to pay the tax.

In re LAUPAHOEHOE SUGAR CO., UNION MILL CO., WAI-AKEA MILL CO., AND HAMAKUA MILL CO.

(Supreme Court of Hawaii. October 12, 1906)

(18 Haw. 206)

Record: Hawaiian Act of 1905. Appeals by the tax assessor from decisions of tax appeal court refusing to sustain his assessments. Affirmed.

Facts: One of the taxation periods provided for in the Act was a period of six months during a certain year. The assessor assessed the taxpayers upon their income, computing it by deducting the actual operating and business expenses paid during the period of six months from the gross amount of sales of movable property. The Act provides that "In estimating the gains, profits and income * * * * * * there shall be included * * * * * * the amount of sales of all movable property less the amount expended in the purchase or production of the same," and that "in computing income the necessary expenses actually incurred in carrying on any business * * * * * * shall be deducted."

Question: Under the Act is the income for a period of six months to be computed by deducting the operating and business expenses actually paid during the period from the gross amount of all sales of movable property, as contended by the assessor?

Decision: "The method contended for by the assessor was the one followed by these taxpayers in making their returns prior to the amendment of the statute in 1905. The actual operating and business expenses of one year were taken as approximating the actual cost of producing the sugars sold during that year. This approximation method was one of convenience which was recognized by all parties to be a fair one and reasonably accurate when applied to a period of one year, but when applied to a period of six months, during which the returns were large and the expenses small, it became inaccurate and unfair."

LAURENTIDE CO. v. DUREY, COLLECTOR
LAURENTIDE CO. v. IRWIN, COLLECTOR
(U. S. District Court, Northern District, New York, March 13, 1916)
(231 Fed. 223)

Record: Acts of August 5, 1909 and October 3, 1913. Actions at law by complainant, Laurentide Co., Ltd., a Canadian corporation against collectors of internal revenue above named to recover a special excise tax assessed for the year 1911 under the Act of August 5, 1909, paid under protest, and a tax assessed against it for 1912 and 1913 under said Act and the Act of October 3, 1913, also paid under protest. Judgment in each case directed, dismissing the complaint on the merits.

Facts: This Canadian corporation made newspaper paper, sent agents into the United States to solicit purchases of its products, paid their expenses, hired desk room in this country, empowered the salesmen to make contracts in the United States subject to approval in Canada, and paid rent and storage charges on paper shipped into the United States by checks drawn on banks in this country. It also shipped paper as consignee in this country, stored it in its own name at its own risk, pending delivery.

Question: Was the complainant exempt from assessment and payment of the taxes imposed by the aforementioned Acts on the ground it was a foreign corporation and was not "doing business" within the meaning of the acts?

Decision: Foreign corporations "transacting business" in and "receiving income from sources in the United States" are taxable thereon. The court quoted Sec. 38 of the Act of 1909, which provides that every foreign corporation engaged in business in any ate or territory of the United States shall be subject to the special excise tax with respect to the carrying on or doing business by such corporation, on the net income above the prescribed exemption, from business transacted and capital invested within the United States. The provision of the Act of October 3, 1913, was also quoted, in effect substantially similar. The court stated that in view of the character of the transactions of the company it would be difficult for it, or its attorney, to describe what it was doing in the United States, if it was not doing, carrying on, and transacting business therein. The opinion concludes as follows: "It seems to me clear that on the returns made the taxes were legally assessed, or imposed, and paid, and that plaintiff is not entitled to recover in either case. * * * * * * There will be judgment in each case dismissing the complaint on the merits with costs."

LAURER v. UNITED STATES
(Court of Claims, December, 1869)
(5 Ct. Cls. 447)

Record: Act of July 13, 1866. Action at law to recover taxes alleged to have been illegally assessed. Judgment for defendant and plaintiff appeals. Affirmed.

Facts: A brewer appealed to the Commissioner of Internal Revenue from an assessment. The proofs showed his appeal to be endorsed "examined and rejected" with the signature of a person unknown to the court. It does not appear what office this person held, nor that the Commissioner adopted or sanctioned his decision. No other decision is shown within six months from the time of taking the appeal.

Question: Did plaintiff show sufficient proof of a decision by the Commissioner of Internal Revenue as required by the following statute: "No suit shall be maintained in any court for the recovery of any tax alleged to have been erroneously or illegally assessed or collected until appeal shall have been duly made to the Commissioner of Internal Revenue * * * and a decision of said Commissioner shall be had thereon * * *." Act of July 13, 1866. (14 Stat. L. P. 152, Sec. 19)?

Decision: In an action in the court of claims due proof must be made of the Commissioner's decision. The court held that the above stated evidence was not sufficient.

LAWRENCE v. WARDELL, COLLECTOR
(U. S. Circuit Court of Appeals, 9th Cir. May 2, 1921)
(273 Fed. 405)

Record: Revenue Act of 1918. Action by plaintiff to recover sums paid under protest after claim for refund denied. Demurrer to complaint sustained. Writ of error by plaintiff. Affirmed.

Facts: Plaintiff, a citizen of the United States, was a resident of the Philippine Islands in 1918, and until March, 1919. In January, 1919, in the Philippines, plaintiff paid an income tax representing the full amount of tax upon his 1918 income computed in accordance with the Revenue Act of 1916, as amended by the Revenue Act of 1917. In March, 1919, plaintiff became a resident of California, and in July, 1919, was required by the defendant collector to pay income tax upon his 1918 income computed in accordance with the Revenue Act of 1918, with credit for the amount paid in the Philippines.

Questions: (1) Does the Revenue Act of 1918, passed in lieu of Acts of 1916 and 1917, tax only the income of individuals who were subject to the two prior acts, thus not taxing the income of a citizen of the United States who resided in the Philippine Islands during the year 1918?

(2) Does Sec. 8, Art. 1, of the Constitution require uniformity and apportionment when Congress is legislating for imposition of taxes for the Philippines?

(3) Is a citizen of the United States, residing in the Philippines, entitled to credits for income taxes paid there under Sec. 222 of the Revenue Act of 1918?

(4) Do Articles 1131 and 1132 of Regulations 45, present the correct construction of the Revenue Act of 1918?

Decision: (1) "Congress acting doubtless under the after-war needs, by the Revenue Act of 1918, changed the situation and made the net income of every individual citizen of the United States taxable no matter where he resides. * * * The comprehensiveness of the 1918 Act is as great as language could make it, for it applied to the income of every individual, changing the rates and obviously imposing taxes at the new rates where no tax could have been imposed prior to the 1918 Act." The Revenue Act of 1918 taxes the income of every individual, a citizen or resident of the United States, without respect to whether such individual had been subject to taxation under the Revenue Acts of 1916 and 1917; Congress did not, by using the words "in lieu of," mean to tax only those incomes of individuals who had been subject to taxation under the two prior acts. Therefore, the income of one who resided in the Philippines in 1918, is taxable.

(2) "The power of Congress in the imposition of taxes and providing for the collection thereof in the possessions of the United States is not restricted by Constitutional provision, Sec. 8, Art. 1, which may limit its general power of taxation as to uniformity and apportionment when legislating for the mainland or United States proper, for its acts in the premises under the authority of paragraph 2, Sec. 3, Art. IV, of the Constitution, which clothes Congress with power to make all needful rules and regulations respecting the territory or other property belonging to the United States. Binns v. United States, 194, U. S. 498; Downes v. Bidwell, 182 U. S. 244."

(3) "* * * Sec. 222 allows to one residing in the Philippines a credit upon the tax computed under Part II of the 1918 Act, but there is nothing to indicate that there is exemption to the citizen residing in the islands. He may have paid to the Island treasury such amounts as are due, but still be liable to the United States for a sum in excess of that paid in the Islands." In accordance with the foregoing, the court held that a citizen of the United States resident in the Philippines, is entitled to credit for the amount of taxes paid in the Philippines.

(4) "The regulations of the Treasury Department (Reg. 45, Arts. 1131, 1132) have been framed upon the Constitution which we have adopted; * * * * * *."

LEDERER, COLLECTOR v. PEARCE
(U. S. Circuit Court of Appeals, Third Cir., June 14, 1920)
(266 Fed. 497)

Record: Revenue Act of 1916. Action at law by executor of estate of Alfred Pearce, deceased, to recover an amount exacted as an inheritance tax. Judgment for plaintiff (262 Fed. 993), and defendant brings error. Affirmed.

Facts: Elizabeth Pearce, dying before the passage of the Act, by her will created a spendthrift trust for the benefit of her children, under which will the children were each given the income from a certain part of her property for life and the power of testamentary disposition of the principal. Alfred Pearce, son of Elizabeth Pearce, died after the passage of the Act, seised of an estate of his own and possessed of the power of appointment. He left a will whereby he provided for the payment of his debts, and also for the payment of certain legacies in excess of his own estate, and exercised the power of appointment by including in the dispositions the share of the principal of the mother's estate to which the power related. The executor of Alfred Pearce was assessed and paid under protest a Federal estate tax upon the property which passed under the power.

Question: Does the fact that the donee, in exercising the power of appointment, included the property of the power in his will and made it liable for the payment of his debts, "blend" the property passing under the power with property of his own and make it part of his estate, and, thus, liable for the Federal estate tax?

Decision: The law of Pennsylvania is the law which determines whose property passed on the exercise of the power of appointment. The law in that state is that the donee of a power is vested with no interest in its subject matter and therefore conveys none by the exercise of the power; that on the exercise of a power by the donee, property passes by the will of the donor as part of his estate, not as a part of the estate of the donee; and that the appointees of the donee of the power derive title immediately from the donor. This would seem to prevail even against the doctrine of blending, for, where the donee of the power in the exercise of it makes provision for the payment of his debts out of the property of the power, the appointment is to creditors, not to the estate, and the creditors take not qua creditors but qua appointees. The property passes to the creditor appointees, not from the donee through his estate, but from the donor through his estate. However, in this case by a later and final adjudication, the Orphans' Court, on being presented with an account which did not include any portion of the property of the power and on being shown that Alfred Pearce's own estate was sufficient to pay his debts, amended a previous award by which the property of the power was given to the executor for distribution, and awarded it directly to his appointees. Therefore, the court held that the doctrine of blending did not apply where the donee's own estate was sufficient to pay his debts, that the property in this case passed from his mother's estate, and that it was not subject to the Federal estate tax as part of the estate of the donee.

LEDERER, COLLECTOR, v. STOCKTON
(U. S. Circuit Court of Appeals, Third Cir. July 8, 1920)
(266 Fed. 676)

Record: Act of October 3, 1913; Revenue Acts of 1916 and 1917. Action to recover income tax paid for 1913, 1914, 1915 and 1916, and income and excess profits tax for 1917. Judgment for plaintiff below (262 Fed. 173) and defendant brought error. Affirmed. Petition in Supreme Court for writ of certiorari granted October 25, 1920, (41 S. C. 15).

Facts: The plaintiff was trustee under a will by which the residuary estate was devised to a certain hospital, no part of the net income of which hospital accrued to the benefit of any private stockholder or individual. The devise was subject to payments to certain annuitants, all of whom, save one, had died. The Supreme Court of Pennsylvania had held that the devise could not be paid to the hospital until after the death of all the annuitants. The trustee then adopted the expedient of lending the funds of the estate to the hospital, upon which loan the hospital paid interest sufficient to take care of the administrative charges and payment of the annuities. The collector assessed and collected from the trustee under protest for each of the years from 1913 to 1917, a tax based on the income of the residuary estate for those years.

Question: Was a trust estate taxable on the income thereof, when the income was to be accumulated for payment to a corporation organized exclusively for charitable purposes, and when the corpus of the estate was actually in the possession of such corporation?

Decision: The residuary estate which produced the income in question being the property solely of the hospital, no one but the hospital owning the income thereof, and the temporary holding of the income being by a trustee, it is clear that when substance and spirit, and not mere form and words, are the interpreters of the statute, the receipt of this income by the hospital's agent and representative was in truth and in reality a receiving by the hospital; and hence that the income was not taxable.

LEVY v. UNITED STATES
(U. S. Circuit Court of Appeals, Third Cir., Feb. 19, 1921)
(271 Fed. 942)

Record: Revenue Act of 1917, and Criminal Code, section 125. Criminal prosecution. Judgment of conviction, and defendant brought error. Affirmed in part.

Facts: This was a criminal prosecution of Jacob S. Levy, treasurer of the Pioneer Overall Company, on two counts—for perjury, and for wilfully and unlawfully attempting to evade the income and excess profits tax. The case arose over an amended corporation return filed by the above named company, and purporting to be sworn to by Levy, as treasurer, before the Commissioner of Deeds of New Jersey, in which return the value of the company's inventory was fraudulently understated.

Questions: (1) Can an amended return, not being prescribed by the statute, be the basis for a criminal prosecution?

(2) In a prosecution for perjury, what proof by the Government of the administering of an oath and of the authority of the official administering it, is necessary?

(3) Was proof of perjury necessary for conviction under the second count, i e., of unlawfully attempting to evade the tax?

Decision: (1) While amended or corrected income tax returns may not be prescribed by the statute, they are nevertheless allowed and received by the Treasury Department, and on such returns taxes are assessed by the Commissioner of Internal Revenue. When so assessed, these are the taxes which under the law are charged against and collected from the taxable. A person making a false return, although called an amended return, with intent to evade the tax, is subject to criminal prosecution.

(2) In a prosecution for perjury, proof, both that an oath was administered, and that the officer was authorized to administer it, is essential to conviction. Where the Government simply intro-

duced in evidence the tax return, purporting to show that the defendant had taken an oath before a Commissioner of Deeds for the state of New Jersey, a conviction for perjury cannot be sustained.

(3) While falsity in the amended return was an element of the offense, perjury was not involved; the essence of the offense was an act with intent, together amounting to an attempt to defeat and evade a tax assessment by a false and fraudulent return. Conviction on the first count, for perjury, set aside; and on the second count, for unlawfully attempting to evade the tax, sustained.

LEWELLYN, COLLECTOR, v. PITTSBURGH, B. & L. E. R. CO.,
SAME v. PITTSBURGH, M. & Y. R. R. CO.

(U. S. Circuit Court of Appeals, Third Cir. April 15, 1915)

(222 Fed. 177)

Record: Act of August 5, 1909. Actions to recover excise tax paid. Judgment for plaintiffs. Defendant brings error. Affirmed.

Facts: Plaintiffs were corporations organized under the laws of the State of Pennsylvania and prior to the Act of August 5th, 1909, they leased all of their property to the Pittsburgh & Lake Erie Railroad Company for a period of 999 years. As rentals for the properties demised, the lessee company promised to pay the taxes, dividends at a certain rate upon the capital stock, and interest upon the bonded indebtedness of the lessor companies. The lessor companies, on the other hand, undertook to maintain their corporate existence in order to hold title to the properties leased, and to exercise their reserved power of eminent domain in acquiring additional property, when the lessee company might request, for which it would furnish the money. Pursuant to this agreement, the lessor corporations did only such acts as were necessary to maintain their corporate existence and maintained no offices, kept no books, and received or disbursed no funds, inasmuch as the lessor paid interest and dividends direct to the trustee and stockholders. Subsequently, however, the lessee directed the lessors to acquire certain properties by condemnation proceedings, and this was done, the lessee furnishing the money, and the lessors acquiring title to the properties which were immediately delivered into the possession of the lessee and used by it under the term of its leases. Special excise taxes were assessed against the lessor companies for the years 1910,

1911 and 1912, under Section 38 of the Act of August 5th, 1909, and having paid under protest they brought this action to recover said taxes.

Question: Did the bare acts of the plaintiffs in acquiring property by purchase and condemnation in the manner and for the purposes stated, constitute "carrying on or doing business" within the meaning of the statute?

Decision: "Carrying on business" means conducting, prosecuting and continuing business by performing progressively all the acts normally incident thereto, and likewise the expression 'doing business' conveys the idea of business being done, not from time to time, but all the time. * * * * Net income as used in the Act of 1909 imports a gross income and the difference between the two implies the expenditure of income for some corporate purpose such as carrying on or doing business for which the corporation was organized." The corporations were not engaged in any business within their corporate purpose, and were not carrying on or doing business within the meaning of the Act.

LINCOLN CHEMICAL CO. v. EDWARDS, COLLECTOR
(U. S. District Court, S. D. New York, April 19, 1921)
(272 Fed. 142)

Record: Revenue Act of 1917. Action at law for refund of part of excess profits tax for 1917. Verdict directed for defendant.

Facts: The plaintiff was organized with a capital stock of $10,000. There were but two persons financially interested in it, Loeb and Riddle. Riddle agreed to work for the corporation for five years at a salary of $1,800, and to convey his process, still unperfected, for $2,400, par value, of the plaintiff's stock. Loeb agreed to convey the machinery and supplies for par in stock, $7,400, and $200 in cash. During the year 1910, the company borrowed nearly $20,000, which it spent in Riddle's further experiments upon the process, which was then complete. During that year it got one Schaefer, a manufacturing chemist, to make a contract for the exploitation of the process on a royalty basis. The business became very profitable, so that by January 1, 1917, all its debts were paid and it had a surplus of $13,000 after writing off a depreciation of

$7,700 upon the process. During the year 1917, the assets of the plaintiff, therefore, consisted only of its cash on hand, the contract with Schaefer, and the secret process finally perfected by Riddle. Its stock was $10,000, and its surplus, as stated, $13,000, of which over $7,000 was in cash. It necessarily followed that its other assets were valued at $16,000. The plaintiff claimed classification under Sec. 209 as a business having no invested capital or not more than a nominal capital.

Questions: (1) Can money used to develop a secret process be regarded as "paid in or earned surplus and undivided profits used or employed in the business" under Sec. 207 (a) (3) of the Revenue Act of 1917?

(2) Is an earned surplus of $2,000 more than "nominal"?

(3) Has the taxpayer the burden of proving the invested capital to be nominal under Sec. 209?

Decision: (1) "The case at bar is, however, one where money has been spent in changing the property itself, so that, in place of a formula which prescribed one sequence of steps, there emerged another which prescribed a different sequence. Fair analogies appear to me, for example, cattle fed for market, or houses rebuilt or enlarged. * * * When such changes have resulted from the expenditure of new capital, I see no reason why the statute should be construed as peremptorily directing that they should be disregarded. It is quite true still, as the plaintiff argues, that the "earned surplus" must be found in some assets, and that the only asset in the case at bar still remains the process; but it is a different process. * * * When money has been earned and spent in improving a process such as this, its increased value due only to that expenditure may figure as an asset in estimating under Sec. 207 'earned surplus,' if any, as an element of 'invested capital.' "

(2) "On the plaintiff's own admission it had an 'earned surplus,' of $2,000, which in view of the size of the business I should not consider 'nominal'." The receipts of the business were approximately $3,000.

(3) "The defendant was not bound by the plaintiff's admission. It was for the plaintiff to prove that it had only a nominal capital. The process was clearly of very substantial value. * * * The

plaintiff has certainly failed to prove that its value in 1917, over $10,000, was 'not more than nominal'."

LITTLE MIAMI, ETC., R. R. CO. v. UNITED STATES
(U. S. Supreme Court, April 16, 1883)
(108 U. S. 277)

Record: Acts of June 30, 1864, and July 13, 1866. Action of debt by Government to recover tax. Judgment for plaintiff (1 Fed. 700) and defendant brings error. Reversed and remanded with instructions.

Facts: Between July 1, 1864, and November 30, 1869, the defendant company made earnings which it either carried to certain funds or used for construction. During the year 1869, the defendant carried to the debit of profit and loss, various items of loss and depreciation amounting to more than the earnings, thus showing no profit for the period. It is not stated with certainty at what dates the losses actually occurred, but the court settles the law as to the losses occurring after July 1, 1864, and instructs the lower court to find the dates of the losses. The defendant had been taxed upon the full amount of the earnings. The Act placed a tax on profits of companies carried to any account or used in construction.

Questions: (1) May the company deduct items of loss and depreciation from the earnings which are carried to the account of some fund or used in construction, if the losses were sustained during the same period?

(2) Is the burden of proof upon the government to show that the losses did not actually occur within the period?

Decision: (1) "The tax in question is not upon earnings carried to the account of any fund used for construction, but upon profits. Earnings used to pay interest or dividends are taxable, whether actual profits or not, but earnings used for construction, or carried to the account of a fund, are not to be taxed, unless they represent profits of the company in its business as a whole, that is to say, the excess of the aggregate of gains from all sources, over the aggregate of losses." To ascertain the excess of the aggregate of gains from all sources over the aggregate of losses, it was necessary and proper for the plaintiff to deduct the amount of the losses from the amount of earnings used in construction.

(2) "The burden of proof is upon the Government. No more can be recovered than is shown to be due."

LITTLE SCHUYLKILL NAVIGATION RAILROAD AND COAL CO. v. PHILADELPHIA & READING RAILWAY COMPANY

(Pennsylvania Superior Court, March 2, 1918)

(69 Penn. Superior Court 122)

Record: Act of October 3, 1913. Action at law to recover income tax paid by plaintiff to the United States Government. Judgment for defendant and plaintiff appeals. Affirmed.

Facts: Appellant railroad company leased to the appellee all its property and franchises and appellee among other things undertook to "pay all taxes, charges and assessments which during the continuance of the term * * * shall be assessed or imposed under any existing or future law on the demised premises or any part thereof, or on the business there carried on or on the receipts, gross or net, derived therefrom * * * or upon the capital stock of the" lessor "or the dividends thereon, or upon the franchises of the" lessor "for the payment or collection of any of which said taxes the" lessor "may otherwise be or become liable or accountable under any lawful authority whatever."

Question: Is the lessee liable for the payment of the income tax levied against the lessor under the Act of October 3, 1913?

Decision: The decision of this case is controlled by the same principles laid down in Catawissa Railroad Co. v. Philadelphia and Reading Railway Company 255 Pa. 269, supra, from which it follows that lessee is not liable for the payment of the income tax levied against the lessor.

LOOMIS, COLLECTOR, v. WATTLES

(Circuit Court of Appeals, Eighth Cir. July 28, 1920)

(266 Fed. 876)

Record: Act of Oct. 3, 1913, and Rev. Stat. Sec. 3226. Action to recover taxes paid under protest. Judgment for plaintiff, and defendant brought error. Affirmed.

Facts: On January 13, 1917, the stockholders of the U. S. National Bank of Omaha, Neb., voted an increase of capital stock of $300,000. On the same day the board of directors declared a dividend of $300,000. Plaintiff, as a stockholder, received a check for $24,985.74. He endorsed this check back to the association and received therefor his proportion of the newly issued stock at par, which he entered in his books at a total valuation of $56,219. Defendant made an additional assessment on this transaction, treating it as a stock dividend and accepted the value placed by plaintiff on the stock. The plaintiff also claimed it was a stock dividend, but not taxable as income. Plaintiff made an application to have the tax remitted, which was rejected. He, then, took an appeal to the Commissioner, which was disallowed. The tax was thereupon paid under protest.

Questions: (1) Did the failure of plaintiff to appeal to the Commissioner after the tax was paid defeat his suit for recovery of the same?

(2) Were stock dividends taxable?

(3) Could the collector, after having levied a tax on the theory of a stock dividend, now claim that the transaction amounted to a cash dividend and therefore taxable as income?

Decision: (1) The object of the statute requiring an appeal to the Commissioner before institution of a suit for recovery of tax was to prevent litigation by giving the department an opportunity to pass upon the legality of the tax. Where an appeal was taken before the tax is paid no reason exists for requiring another appeal after payment and hence, notwithstanding Sec. 3226, U. S. Rev. St., such an appeal was not necessary.

(2) The stock dividend was not taxable as income. Eisner v. Macomber (252 U. S. 189) cited.

(3) The department, having levied the tax as a stock dividend tax, the court would not permit the defendant to say that it ought to have levied a tax upon the theory of a cash dividend, and then ask the court to do what the defendant failed to do. Assuming the transaction to have been a cash dividend, the tax levied was double what it ought to have been. Furthermore, the court has no power or authority to assess property and levy a tax thereon. It was, therefore, held that plaintiff was entitled to recover the taxes paid.

In re LORD'S ESTATE
(New York Supreme Court, June 18, 1920)
(183 N. Y. Supp. 131)

Record: Federal estate tax. Executors of the estate of Frances T. Lord, deceased, filed their account in the Surrogate's Court, New York County. Objections were filed thereto by interested legatees. Objections were sustained. Appeal to this court by executors. Decree of lower court sustained in part and in part overruled.

Facts: Testatrix died a resident of New York County. By a paragraph in her will it was directed that all inheritance, legacy or transfer taxes on certain legacies described by paragraph numbers should be paid by the executors out of the residuary estate. The account, as filed by the executors, charges to and deducts from the legacies given in paragraphs of the will other than those mentioned in the above paragraphs referred to, a proportionate amount of the sum paid by the executors for the Federal estate tax. To these deductions the objections are made.

Question: Should the Federal estate tax be charged to decedent's estate, or be apportioned to the legacies?

Decision: Federal estate tax is a charge against the estate of decedent and not apportionable to legacies. The court stated that the will does not indicate any intention on the part of testatrix to apportion the Federal estate tax, and it should be charged to the estate, (quoting Matter of Hamlin, 226 N. Y. 407, 124 N. E. 4; Matter of Whitmann Estate. 182 N. Y. Supp. 535; N. Y. Trust Co. v. Eisner, 263 Fed. 620).

LORING v. CITY OF BEVERLY
(Supreme Judicial Court of Massachusetts, January 7, 1916)
(222 Mass. 331; 110 N. E. 974)

Record: Massachusetts Act of 1909. Contract against the City of Beverly to recover the amount of tax paid under protest. Judgment for defendant, and plaintiff appealed. Affirmed.

Facts: The plaintiff as trustee under a will holds a part of the capital in trust, namely, shares of stock in a corporation. He deposited a sum of money in a bank, which sum was derived from dividends from these shares. This income was not added to the principal, but was later distributed to the beneficiaries. The plaintiff was assessed a tax on these dividends under the general law, which has a clause which provides that "incomes derived from property subject to taxation shall not be taxed," and a clause putting a tax on annuities, and on income from a profession, trade or employment. The corporations, from whose dividends this income came, paid taxes on their corporate franchises.

Questions: (1) Is money held in a bank by a trustee under a will, and made up of dividends from shares of stock of a corporation which has paid franchise taxes, exempt from taxation under a general law by which incomes derived from property subject to taxation are not taxable?

(2) If not exempt for the above reason, is money received as dividends taxable under an Act which taxes annuities and income from business?

Decisions: (1) "The words 'property subject to taxation' in this connection do not mean property in its inherent nature susceptible to taxation. Nor do they refer to property made subject to taxation by the broad phrase of some provision of the tax law if exempted by another provision. The words mean property which actually is rendered liable to taxation under the law, * * * . No tax was assessable or paid upon the shares of stock owned by the trustee according to the express terms of St. 1909." Therefore, the money was not exempt from taxation on the ground claimed.

(2) "The tax law does not purport to levy a tax upon income such as that derived from dividends on corporate stocks. The only kind of income which is made subject to taxation is that derived from 'an annuity' and the excess above $2,000 of the income from a profession, trade or employment, * * * . The present tax is upon money in bank on a tax day. It is a property, not an income tax."

LOTT v. HUBBARD

(Supreme Court of Alabama, June, 1870)

(44 Ala. 593)

Record: Revised code of Alabama, Sec. 435. Action at law to recover taxes paid under protest. Judgment for plaintiff, and defendant appeals. Reversed.

Facts: Plaintiff bought certain real estate in September, 1865, and paid thereon the state and the county property taxes for the year 1866. Plaintiff was also required to pay a tax on his income from October 1, 1865, to December 31, 1866, none of which was derived from said real estate. All of this income he had paid out as the purchase money on the said real estate.

Question: Can the plaintiff be relieved of paying a tax on his income because he has paid a tax on the real estate in which he has invested his income, on the ground that such a tax is double taxation?

Decision: "* * * *. The payment of an income tax, almost necessarily, involves in some indirect and limited sense, the payment of a double tax; for income oftener than otherwise either directly or indirectly is derived from or grows out of property subject to taxation. The planter pays a tax on his plantation as property, he also pays a tax derived from the cultivation of the same." This is in a limited and secondary sense a case of double taxation but it has never been held to be a reasonable or legal objection.

LUDLOW-SAYLOR WIRE CO. v. WOLLBRINCK
(Superior Court of Missouri, June 28, 1918)
(205 S. W. 196)

Record: Missouri Act of April 12, 1917. Bill in equity to enjoin enforcement of Act. Judgment for defendant and plaintiff appeals. Affirmed.

Facts: Plaintiff, a business corporation, during the last half of the calendar year 1917 earned a net income subject to taxation under an Act approved April 12, 1917. Being cited to make a return of its income, it refused, and brought this suit to enjoin the enforcement of said Act.

Questions: (1) Does the Act in taxing incomes thereby impose a tax on property in contravention of Sec. 4, Art. 10 of the Missouri constitution, which requires taxes on property to be laid in proportion to value?

(2) Is the exemption of certain incomes a violation of Art. 10, Secs. 6 and 7 of the State Constitution, which provides that laws shall be void if exempting any property other than property, real

and personal, of the State, counties, other municipal corporations, cemeteries, agricultural or horticultural societies and property used for religious, educational and charitable purposes?

(3) Does Art. 10, Sec. 8 of the State Constitution, limiting the rate of taxation of property not to exceed 20 cents on the hundred dollars valuation, apply to the tax on incomes laid by the income tax law in question, thus making the law unconstitutional?

(4) Does the Income Tax Act by classifying persons, corporations and entities with respect to the portion of net income of each class taxable, violate the State Constitution?

Decision: (1) "In law and in the broadest sense, 'property' means 'a thing owned,' and is, therefore, applicable to whatever is the subject of legal ownership." But it is the opinion of the court that the construction of the word "property" which has appeared as definitive of the subject of ad valorem taxation in all of the three constitutions of the State when originally made, is not in full accord with the broadest possible meaning of that term, in that literally it might include every species of property. The restricted construction (which excludes from its purview personal earnings and incomes) had been affixed to this term six years prior to the present constitution, and the principle of that construction has ever since been applied in sustaining taxes of a similar nature, although levied without apportioning the taxation to the value of the thing taxed. "It is apparent, therefore, that when the Constitution of 1875 was adopted the word 'property' as the basis of taxation, proportioned to value, had acquired a fixed and definite meaning preclusive of personal incomes occupations, privileges, and similar sources of revenue." Therefore, the Act was held not to be a violation of Sec. 4, Art. 10 of the Missouri constitution.

(2) From what has been said as to the construction of the word "property," it follows that the excluded classes of property embracing incomes in this Act are not within the regulative provisions of the Constitution (Secs. 6, 7, Art. 10) specifying what "property" shall be exempt from taxation.

(3) "Neither are the revenues proposed by the present Act measured by Section 8 of Article 10, since that provision also related to the limitation of the tax on property; which term, as has been

shown, whenever used in the clauses of the Constitution, does not embrace incomes."

(4) "By the necessary implication this constitutional provision recognizes the power of the Legislature to classify the subjects falling within its restriction, and only requires that the tax shall be uniform upon the classified persons, or the classified subjects of taxation. In the Missouri Act under review, persons, corporations, and entities are distinguished and classified. The Act also provides a classification as to the amount of the portion of the net income of each class of persons, corporations, or entities which is subject to taxation therein. The Act further provides for the payment of an identical rate of taxation upon each of the classifications of incomes subject to its burden, and that each person, corporation, or entity shall pay the same tax which is paid by every other person, corporation, or entity belonging to the same class. That the Legislature had the power to create such classification is implied by the very terms of the provision of the constitution (Section 3, Art. 10) that taxes thereunder shall be uniform upon the same class of subjects; necessarily this language would be meaningless unless interpreted to empower the Legislature to create distinct classes of subjects."

LUMBER MUTUAL FIRE INSURANCE CO. v. MALLEY, COLLECTOR

(U. S. District Court, D. Massachusetts, Dec. 29, 1916)

(256 Fed. 383)

Record: Act of August 5, 1909. Action to recover tax paid. Judgment for plaintiff.

Facts: Plaintiff, a Massachusetts Corporation, had a system of bookkeeping whereby securities bought for more or less than par were "amortized," and the books for the year 1909 showed a net increase in the value of bonds to the amount of $14,294.61. This amount was taxed as a part of net income under the Act of 1909, and plaintiff paid the tax under protest and brought this action to recover the same.

Question: Since the amount involved was not realized by sale or other disposal of the bonds, did it constitute income within the meaning of the Act?

Decision: Increase or decrease in the value of bonds held by a mutual insurance company as investment does not affect income received within the year within Excise Tax Act par. 38, cl. 2. The net increase in the value of the bonds is not taxable, since it is mere bookkeeping profit.

LUMBER MUTUAL FIRE INSURANCE CO. v. MALLEY, COLLECTOR

(U. S. District Court, D. Massachusetts, Dec. 29, 1916)

(256 Fed. 380)

Record: Act of August 5, 1909. Action to recover tax paid. Judgment for plaintiff.

Facts: Plaintiff, a mutual insurance company incorporated under the Massachusetts laws, sought to recover back part of the excise tax for the year 1909, paid by it under protest to defendant's predecessor in the office of collector. The tax, which it was claimed was illegally assessed, was the result of the action of the Commissioner of Internal Revenue in amending the return for the year in question by adding to the net income the amount of all premiums written in poicies or renewals issued during 1909 whether collected during thlat year or not.

Questions: (1) Should only premiums actually received in cash during the year properly be regarded as income for the purpose of the second clause of the Act of 1909?

(2) Would the fact that the plaintiff had also claimed, as a part of this action that a further amount of taxes had been illegally collected, but abandoned this claim at the hearing prevent the recovery thereon?

Decision: (1) The Act of 1909 required not a "revenue" but a "cash" basis of accounting, and consequently, premiums accrued or becoming due, but not paid, within the year, and money previously received in payment of a premium but applied within the year to pay a different premium was not required by the second clause of the Act of 1909 to be included as "income received within the year."

(2) When the plaintiff in an action to recover back part of excise tax assessed against it and paid under protest, abandons, at the hear-

ing, its claim as to a certain part of the item, the Court will rule that as to such item there was no illegal exaction.

LYNCH, COLLECTOR v. HORNBY
(U. S. Supreme Court, June 3, 1918)
(247 U. S. 399)

Record: Act of October 3, 1913. Action to recover income tax paid. Judgment for plaintiff in U. S. District Court affirmed by Circuit Court of Appeals for the Eighth Circuit (236 Fed. 661) Appealed on writ of certiorari. Judgment reversed and cause remanded to the District Court for further proceedings in conformity with this opinion.

Facts: Respondent from 1906 to 1915 was the owner of 434 (out of 10,000) shares of the Cloquet Lumber Company, an Iowa corporation, which had for more than twenty-five years been engaged in purchasing timber lands, manufacturing the timber into lumber and selling it. On and prior to March 1, 1913, the value of the company's timber lands increased so that respondent's stock, the par value of which was $43,400, had become worth at least $150,000. In 1914 the company distributed dividends aggregating $650,000, of which $240,000 were derived from current earnings, and $410,000 from conversion into money of the property that it owned or had an interest in on March 1, 1913. Respondent's share of the latter amount was $17,794, and this not having been included in his income tax return, the Commissioner of Internal Revenue levied an additional tax of $171 on account of it. Respondent, having paid this amount under protest, brought this action to recover the same.

Questions: Was the entire amount of $17,794 free from tax on the ground that it represented the conversion into money of an increase in value of lands which took place prior to March 1, 1913, the date when the Income Tax Act took effect?

Decision: Under the 1913 Act, dividends declared and paid in the ordinary course by a corporation to its stockholders after March 1, 1913, whether from current earnings or from a surplus acquired prior to that date, are taxable as income to the stockholder. This case was held to be distinguishable from Lynch v. Turrish, 247 U. S. 221, where the distribution in question was a single and final dividend in liquidation of the entire assets and business of the corporation and a return to the stockholder of the value of his stock upon the surrender of his entire interest in the company at a price that represented its intrinsic value at and before March 1, 1913, when the Income Tax Act took effect. The entire amount of $17,794 was taxable, though it was a dividend derived from an increase in the value of lands prior to the effective date of the Act, and realized by a sale after the passage of the Act.

LYNCH, COLLECTOR v. TURRISH
(U. S. Supreme Court, June 3, 1918)
(247 U. S. 221)

Record: Act of October 3, 1913. Suit to recover income tax paid under protest. On writ of certiorari to the United States Circuit Court of Appeals for the Eighth Circuit. Judgment for plaintiff affirmed.

Facts: Plaintiff acquired, prior to March 1, 1913, stock in the Payette Lumber & Manufacturing Company, with a par value of $79,975. The timber lands owned by the corporation increased in value so that on March 1, 1913, respondent's stock was worth twice its par value, or $159,950.00. In December, 1913, the Payette Company sold all of its assets, receiving a price which made available for distribution to its stockholders as a liquidating dividend, twice the par value of their stock. Respondent therefore, upon the surrender of his shares, received the sum of $159,950. The Commissioner of Internal Revenue considered that of this sum one-half was not taxable, being the liquidation of the par value of Turrish's stock, but that the other half was income for the year 1914, and taxable under the Act of 1913. A tax, based upon such income, was assessed and collected, and Turrish commenced this action to recover such tax, paid under protest.

Question: Since the increase in value of the stock took place prior to March 1, 1913, the effective date of the Income Tax Law, should any portion of the amount received upon liquidation constitute taxable income?

Decision: "The lands were the property, capital and capital assets, of their legal and equitable owner and the enhancement of their value during a series of years prior to the effective date of the income tax law, although divided or distributed by dividend or otherwise, subsequent to that date, does not become income, gains or profits taxable under the Act of 1913." The plaintiff was, therefore, allowed to recover the amount of taxes paid.

LYNCH v. UNION TRUST CO.
(U. S. Circuit Court of Appeals, October 5, 1908)
. (164 Fed. 161)

Record: Acts of June 13, 1898 and June 27, 1902. Action at law to recover legacy taxes alleged to have been illegally assessed. Judgment for plaintiff and defendant brings error. Affirmed.

Decision: The right given to a beneficiary by a will to receive a stated share of the net income from the entire residue of the estate, left in trust until the time fixed for its distribution, is not a "legacy" or "distributive share" within the meaning of such terms as used in the War Revenue Act of June 13, 1898, and the Act of June 27, 1902. The latter Act provides that no tax shall be assessed under Section 29 in respect of any contingent beneficial interest which shall not become absolutely vested in possession or enjoyment prior to July 1, 1902. The only interest of the legatee in such income which was subject to taxation was the amount thereof actually received by him prior to said July 1, 1902, provided such amount was $10,000.00 or more.

LUTTON v. BAKER
(Supreme Court of Iowa, Nov. 11, 1919)
(174 N. W. 599)

Record: Revenue Act of 1917. Appeal by defendant Baker from a judgment of the State District Court of Johnson County, Iowa, in favor of plaintiff in action on a note and for the establishment of a lien to secure its payment. Reversed.

Facts: Plaintiff asserted that he was an innocent purchaser of a note made by defendant Baker to one LeGrand. The trial court gave him judgment and defendant appealed. Defendant tendered evidence which would have been in bar of right of recovery of the payee, but the trial court held that these defenses were not permissible because the plaintiff was an innocent purchaser of the note in due course as defined in the negotiable instrument statute. The note did not have the revenue stamps thereon required by the Act of Congress of October 3, 1917.

Question: Is one who buys an unstamped note a holder in due course?

Decision: The court deciding this issue said: "We now hold that a note which lacks the stamping required by law is not 'complete and regular on its face,' and that, therefore, the plaintiff is not a holder in due course and must meet any defense that is good against the payee who transferred to plaintiff."

MACTAVISH v. MILES, COLLECTOR
(U. S. District Court of Maryland, January 17, 1920)
(263 Fed. 457)

Record: Revenue Act of 1916. Petition of Emily C. Mactavish, administratrix of estate of Mario M. Mactavish, requesting the court to investigate the facts set out in the petition and report them to the Secretary of the Treasury in the manner and form required by Sec. 5292, of the Revised Statutes (Comp. St. Sec. 10130). Petition dismissed.

Facts: The decedent died on April 17, 1917, in Brussels, Belgium. On account of delays of communication in war time, and other circumstances set forth in the petition, letters of administration were not granted until May 14, 1919. The administratrix was not able to make a return for the Federal Estate Tax purposes until September 30, 1919. In consequence, the Collector of Internal Revenue required her to pay in addition to the tax the sum of $1,025.- 51 as interest thereon at the rate of 10 per cent per annum from the time of decedent's death until February 25, 1919, and thereafter at 6 per cent per annum until the return was made. Sec. 204 of the Act of September 8, 1916, provides that the tax shall be due one year after decedent's death and if the tax is not paid within ninety days after it is due, interest at the rate of ten per cent per annum from the time of decedent's death shall be added as part of the tax. Petitioner alleged that this exaction, though called interest, is in fact a penalty, and asked that the Court summarily investigate the facts set forth in the petition and report them to the Secretary of the

Treasury in the manner and form required by Sec. 5292 of the Revised Statute.

Question: Is the court obligated to act on such a petition and what disposition should be made thereof?

Decision: Investigation of circumstances of alleged penalty for delinquency in payment of estate tax was refused. The court held that anything a judge does under a petition of this nature is in the capacity of special commissioner in an administrative and not a judicial position; that whether he will or will not act as such commissioner is optional with him; that it is not part of the judicial duties which Congress may require of him. The court concluded as follows:

"It is an anomalous proceeding. The Secretary of the Treasury cannot remit without findings of fact by the judge, but he may refuse to remit, no matter what those findings may be. It would appear a judge should not act unless there is some probability that his so doing will be of some use to somebody. In this case the United States says that which the petitioner says is a penalty is not, and therefore the statute has no application. Whether it is or not involves both a construction of the original statute and of the Act of 1916. It is clear that the judge in this proceeding has no power to pass on anything but the questions of fact. Under all the circumstances I must decline the office of special commissioner in this matter."

MAGEE v. DENTON, et al.
(U. S. Circuit Court, N. D. New York, Jan. 7, 1863)
(Fed. Case 8943)

Record: Act of July 1, 1862. In equity. Application for provisional injunction to restrain the defendant, collector, from collecting income tax. Injunction denied.

Facts: The corporation of which plaintiff was the principal stockholder had earned profits for the taxable year. The plaintiff objected to a part of the tax on the ground that he had received no profits or dividends from the company, and that the company had expended all its profits for the year in the improvement of its property.

Question: Is the plaintiff entitled to an injunction restraining the collector from collecting the taxes imposed on him as a stockholder in a company which had made a profit where he only alleges that he has received no dividends?

Decision: If the profits of an incorporated company, "* * * itself an artificial person, are not, in the contemplation of the Act of Congress, a portion of the gains, profits or income, of the stockholders, until they are distributed as dividends, or embraced in a dividend declared by the managers of the corporation, it is clear that when a dividend has been declared and has become payable, the mere omission of the stockholder to obtain or receive the dividend subject to his call, would not excuse him from embracing the amount of such dividend in his statement of his taxable income for the year." The bill for an injunction was defective in that it failed to show that no dividend had been declared, and in that there existed a complete remedy at law. Injunction denied.

MAGUIRE v. TREFRY
(U. S. Supreme Court, April 26, 1920)
(253 U. S. 12)

Record: Massachusetts Income Tax Act of 1916. Petition for abatement of taxes allowed in part (230 Mass. 503). Plaintiff brings error. Affirmed.

Facts: Plaintiff, a resident of Massachusetts, was taxed upon income from a trust created by will of a decedent who, in his lifetime, was a resident of Philadelphia, Pennsylvania. The plaintiff, under the will of the decedent, was the beneficiary of the trust thereby created. The securities, the income from which was held taxable in Massachusetts, consisted of the bonds of three corporations and certain certificates of the Southern Ry. Equipment Trust. These securities were held in the possession of the trustee in Philadelphia. The trust was being administered under the laws of Pennsylvania.

Question: May the State of Massachusetts tax the income of a beneficiary of a trust, residing in the state, although the trust itself is created and administered under the laws of another state?

Decision: "* * * The state of the owner's domicile may tax the credits of a resident although evidenced by debts due from residents of another state. This is the general rule recognized in the maximum 'mobilia sequuntur personam,' and it justifies, except under exceptional circumstances, the taxation of credits and beneficial interests in property at the domicile of the owner." The general rule as stated above is applicable in this case. Although the legal title to the property is held by a trustee in Pennsylvania, it is so held for the benefit of the beneficiary of the trust, and such beneficiary has an equitable right, title and interest distinct from its legal ownership. "The legal owner holds the direct and absolute dominion over the property in view of the law; but the income, profits, or benefits thereof in his hands, belong wholly, or in part, to others. It is this property right belonging to the beneficiary, realized in the shape of income, which is the subject matter of the tax under the Statute of Massachusetts." The beneficiary is domiciled in Massachusetts, has the protection of her laws, and there receives and holds income from the trust property. This income is taxable to the beneficiary by the State of Massachusetts.

MALLEY, COLLECTOR, v. BOWDITCH et al.

(U. S. Circuit Court of Appeals, First Cir., July 29, 1919)

(259 Fed. 809)

Record: Act of October 22, 1914. Action at law to recover taxes paid under protest under Section 5, Schedule A, of this Act. Judgment for plaintiff and defendant brought error. Reversed.

Facts: The Pepperell Manufacturing Company was organized as a common-law trust in the state of Massachusetts, and as such derived none of its rights, benefits or qualities from any statute. Under the trust agreement there was provided a share capital as a basis for the issue of transferable certificates evidencing a proportional interest therein and carrying with them certain rights while the company is a going concern and in winding up. The Act of October 22, 1914, imposed a stamp tax of 5c on each $100 of face value or fraction thereof, of certificates of stock issued by any "association, company, or corporation."

Questions: (1) Is this tax applicable to certificates of interest issued by common law trust companies not deriving any rights, benefits or qualities from any statute?

(2) Is the Act unconstitutional, in that it unlawfully discriminates between companies issuing certificates and those not
issuing certificates?

Decision: (1) Whether the share capital is fixed by agreement or under statutory authority seems immaterial, for the tax
is not a franchise tax or a corporation tax, but a stamp tax or document tax. If the word "association" be not broad enough to include a common law trust, it is included in the word "company,"
while the phrase "certificates of stock" discloses no intent to exclude common-law associations or companies, but evidences a legislative purpose to impose a stamp tax on certificates of stock as
muniments of title.

(2) A stamp tax on documents discriminates between those
who do, and those who do not issue documents; and a distinction
between unincorporated companies and associations which do and
those which do not issue certificates of shares of stock is not unreasonable, nor founded upon an immaterial difference between
two kinds of partnerships. Therefore, the plaintiff can not recover
the taxes paid.

MANDELL v. PIERCE, COLLECTOR

(U. S. Circuit Court, D. Massachusetts, May Term, 1868)
(Fed. Case 9008)

Record: Acts of June 30, 1864, and March 3, 1865. Assumpsit to recover tax paid under protest. Judgment for defendant.

Facts: The plaintiff's testatrix died about the middle of the
tax year and the plaintiff was required to make return of the income
received from the beginning of the year up to the time of her death.

Questions: (1) Is the income of a decedent, who died before
the time for making a return, taxable under the Act?

(2) If so, is the executor of one who has not made a return for
the year required to make the return?

Decision: (1) Holding that such income is taxable, the court
said, "in ascertaining the aggregate amount of the gains, profits
or income liable to such taxation, the same deductions were required
to be made, as would have been if the testatrix, instead of having

deceased, had ceased on that day to be the owner of any property, and for the residue, or income within the meaning of those laws."

(2) The decedent "can not make any return, and the duty of making it in that event devolves on the executor or administrator, as the legal representative of the deceased."

MANITOWOC GAS CO. v. TAX COMMISSION
(Superior Court of Wis., June 1, 1915)
(161 Wis., 111; 152 N. W. 848)

Record: Wisconsin Income Tax Act of 1911. Action at law to recover taxes paid. Judgment for plaintiff, and defendant appeals. Affirmed.

Facts: Plaintiff, a corporation under the laws of Wisconsin, issued and sold its bonds to investors domiciled in other states.

Question: Is the interest on the bonds of a Wisconsin corporation, paid to non-residents, subject to taxation under the Wisconsin Income Tax Act of 1911, which provides that an income tax shall be paid by every non-resident of the state upon such income as is derived from sources within the state or within its jurisdiction?

Decision: "The situs of the property out of which * * * income issues is that of the domicile of the creditor. The purchase of a bond is the making of a loan of money to the obligor. The bond represents so much money due from the debtor. The purchase of it does not constitute any business carried on within a state. The situs of a bond remains at the domicile of the bondholder. So the interest in question did not, as to non-resident bondholders, constitute an income derived from sources within the state within the meaning of Subsection 3 of Sec. 1087 m of the Act of 1911." It follows, then, that it is not subject to taxation under the Wisconsin Act.

MANSFIELD v. EXCELSIOR REFINING CO.
(U. S. Supreme Court, May 5, 1890)
(135 U. S. 326)

Record: Rev. Stat. Sec. 3196. Action in ejectment to recover possession of distillery premises. Judgment for defendant and plaintiff brings error. Reversed.

Decision: "Where distillery premises, in the occupancy of a distiller, who is operating the same under a lease to expire at a specified time, are seized and sold by a collector of internal revenue for taxes due from the distiller to the government, a sale of such premises, by the collector, by the summary mode of notice and publication provided in Sec. 3196 of the Revised Statutes, for the taxes so due, will pass to the purchaser only the interest of the delinquent distiller, and will not affect the interest in the premises, either of the owner of the fee or of a third person having a lien thereon, even where the government holds a waiver, executed by the owner of the fee or by such third person having a lien, consenting that the distillery premises may be used by the distiller for distilling spirits subject to the provisions of law, and expressly stipulating that the lien of the United States for taxes shall have priority of any and all interests and claims which the waiver may have to the distillery and premises."

MARCONI WIRELESS TELEGRAPH CO. v. DUFFY,
COLLECTOR
(U. S. District Court, D. N. J., May 31, 1921)
(273 Fed. 197)

Record: Revenue Act of 1918. Suit to recover stamp tax paid under protest. On motion to strike the petition. Sustained.

Facts: The plaintiff, for the purpose of effecting a consolidation, agreed to transfer its assets to the Radio Corporation for 2,000,000 shares each of Radio's preferred and common stock. Before the stock was issued, it was agreed between plaintiff and Radio that Radio should issue the stock direct to such stockholders of plaintiff as desired to receive it, Radio to be credited as though the stock had been issued direct to plaintiff. In accordance with this plan 238,095 shares were issued to plaintiff's stockholders, and the revenue stamps required by law were attached thereto. Subsequently, defendant required the plaintiff to pay an additional tax upon the shares so issued direct to plaintiff's stockholders, the stamps for which were affixed to plaintiff's minute book.

Question: Was the resolution of plaintiff's board of directors authorizing the issuance of shares of stock of another corporation direct to plaintiff's stockholders in consideration of the transfer of plaintiff's assets to said corporation, a transfer requiring payment of a stamp tax?

Decision: The substantial difference between a corporation and its stockholders cannot be ignored. The property sold was plaintiff's property and could be sold only by it. Had the plaintiff received the stock, as seemingly was originally contemplated, and disposed of it, whether to its stockholders or to other parties, a tax such as was here imposed would have had to be paid. Undoubtedly it was within the power of plaintiff, upon obtaining the necessary authority, to direct Radio to issue the stock to its stockholders. But this authority—resolution of the plaintiff's board of directors— was nothing less than a transfer of plaintiff's rights to such shares of stock, and is covered by one of the methods of transferring shares or certificates taxable under the Act, namely, a transfer of "rights to subscribe for or to receive such shares."

MARKLE v. KIRKENDALL, COLLECTOR
(U. S. District Court, M. D. Penn., September 27, 1920)
(267 Fed. 498)

Record: Rev. Stat. Sec. 3224. Suit to enjoin collector from distraining and selling certain property for payment of taxes. On motion to dismiss the bill. Motion granted, and bill dismissed.

Facts: The bill alleged that plaintiffs were doing business as a partnership known as Hazelton Manufacturing Company; that they owned certain property as such partnership; that the collector, under a claim that the company was a corporation, was about to distrain upon this property for the collection of income and excess profits taxes alleged to be due from the company as a corporation. The bill also set forth that the company had been incorporated in 1883, but that its charter expired in 1903 and was never renewed.

Question: Did the prohibition of a suit for an injunction against the assessment or collection of any tax, as provided in Sec. 3224, R. S. U. S., apply to parties whose property was being seized for taxes not assessed against them?

Decision: Unless it clearly appears that a proceeding on the part of the commissioner is an absolute nullity or that the property about to be seized is not liable for the assessment, a court of equity will not interfere. All that need be said is that the matter is in dispute and it is therefore not clear that the proceeding on the part of the Commissioner is an absolute nullity. Since it is not clear that the proceeding is an absolute nullity the court will not enjoin the collector from distraining and selling the property of the plaintiffs.

MARYLAND CASUALTY CO. v. UNITED STATES

(U. S. Supreme Court, Jan. 12, 1920)

(251 U. S. 342)

Record: Acts of August 5, 1909, and October 3, 1913. Suit in Court of Claims for a refund of certain excise and income taxes. Judgment allowing a recovery in part (52 Ct. Cl. 201; 53 Ct. Cl. 81) and claimant appealed. Modified and, as modified, affirmed.

Facts: (1) The claimant was engaged in casualty, liability, fidelity, guaranty and surety insurance. It did business in many states, through many agents, with whom it had uniform written contracts which allowed them to extend the time for payment of the premiums on policies, not to exceed thirty days from the date of policy, and required that on the fifth day of each calendar month, they should pay or remit, in cash or its equivalent, the balance due claimant as shown by the last preceding monthly statement, rendered to it. Under the provisions of such contracts, the agents were not required to remit premiums on policies written in November until the fifth of January of the next year and on policies written in December not until the following February. Claimant was required to return the full amount of premiums on policies written each year, which amount included premiums paid to its agents but not remitted to its treasurer.

(2) Claimant, in its return for 1909, included in its deductions for net increase to reserve funds required by law but three items, viz., unearned premiums, loss claims, and unpaid liability claims. In 1910 it added to these items a claimed deduction for unpaid taxes and unpaid salaries. In 1911 it added brokerage, etc., and reinsurance due other companies, and in 1912 claimed a total amount of $670,791.89, made up by including a claim for each item specified above. The state requirements relied upon are those of the insurance departments of New York, Penn-

sylvania, and Wisconsin, which require that "assets as reserved" must be maintained to cover "all claims," "all indebtedness," and "all outstanding liabilities."

(3) The year 1913 was the only one of those under consideration in which the aggregate amount of reserves which the claimant was required by law to keep fell below the amount so required for the preceding year. The Government allowed only "unearned premiums" and "unpaid liability loss," reserves to be considered in determining deductions. In 1913, the "unpaid liability loss reserve" decrease exceeded the "unearned premium reserve" increase, by over $270,000, and this amount the Government added to the gross income of the claimant for the year, calling it "released reserve," on the theory that the difference in the amount of the reserves for the two years released the decrease to the claimant so that it could use it for its general purposes, and therefore constituted free income for the year 1913.

(4) The claimant made its original returns without protest except for the year 1909, and, without appeal to the Commissioner of Internal Revenue, voluntarily paid the taxes computed on them, for each of the years. Payment was made for 1909 in June, 1910; for 1910 in June, 1911; for 1911 in June, 1912; for 1912 in June, 1913. No claim for a refund of any of these payments was made until April 30, 1915, and then the claim was in general terms. This claim was rejected and suit was commenced in February 8, 1916. The Commissioner had required various amendments to these prior returns, and in consequence thereof had assessed additional taxes. The claimant paid these taxes and filed claim for refund covering both the taxes originally paid and the new assessments. This claim was filed within the proper time from the date of the amended returns, but not from the date of the original returns for 1909, 1910 and 1911.

Questions: (1) Should claimant be charged, as a part of its gross income, each year with premiums collected by agents, but not transmitted by them to its treasurer within the year?

(2) May the amount of gross income of claimant be reduced by the aggregate amount of unearned premiums, loss claims, unpaid liability claims, taxes, salaries, brokerage and reinsurance unpaid

at the end of each year, under provisions in both the excise and
income tax laws allowing deductions of "net addition required by
law to be made within the year to reserve funds"?

(3) Should the decrease in amount of reserve funds required
by law for the year 1913 from the amount required for 1912 be
treated as "released reserve" and charged to the company as income for 1913?

(4) Does the filing of amended returns constitute the beginning of new proceedings which so superseded the original return
as to release the claimant from its entire failure to observe the
statutory requirement for the review of the latter?

Decision: (1) With respect to domestic corporations no
change was intended by the use in the Income Tax Act of 1913,
of the expression "income arising or accruing instead of income
received," as used in Excise Tax Act of 1909. Under both Acts
the tax should be levied upon income "received" during the year.
Premiums collected by agents, even though not remitted to the
company within the calendar year, are part of its gross income received for such year, for receipt by the agent is receipt by the
principal.

(2) "The term 'reserve' or 'reserves' has a special meaning
in the law of insurance. While its scope varies under different laws,
in general it means a sum of money, variously computed or estimated, which, with accretions from interest, is set aside, 'reserved'
as a fund with which to mature or liquidate, either by payment or
reinsurance with other companies, future unaccrued and contingent
claims, and claims accrued, but contingent and indefinite as to
amount or time of payment. In this case, as we have seen, the
term includes 'unearned premium reserve' to meet future liabilities
on policies, 'liability reserve' to satisfy claims, indefinite in amount
and as to time of payment, but accrued on liability and workmen's
compensation policies, and 'reserve for loss claims' accrued on
policies other than those provided for in the 'liability reserve,' but
it has nowhere been held that 'reserve' in this technical sense, must
be maintained for the ordinary running expenses of a business,
definite in amount and which must be currently paid, by every
company from its income if its business is to continue, such as
taxes, salaries, reinsurance and unpaid brokerage."

(3) "Since the findings of fact before us do not make the clear showing, which must be required, that the statutory deduction of net reserves in prior years was restored to the free use of the claimant in 1913, it should not have been charged as income with the decrease in that year, and, on the record before us, the holding of the court of claims must be reversed."

(4) "They are denominated 'amended returns' and while in dealing with the same items, the basis of computation was in some cases varied, in each case the purpose and effect of them was to increase the payment which the claimant was required to make under the law, and the payments made on the original returns were credited on the amounts computed as due on the returns as amended. The inapplicability of Cheatham v. United States, 92 U. S. 85, is obvious. * * * ." Amended returns filed by government for additional assessment do not constitute new assessments for anything over the additional tax levied. Consequently, so much of the claim as relates to original payments for 1909, 1910 and 1911 is barred. (Government conceded case in time with respect to additional assessment made on amended returns and assessment on original return for 1913.)

MAXWELL, COLLECTOR, v. ABRAST REALTY CO.

(U. S. Circuit Court of Appeals, Second D., Nov. 10, 1914)

(218 Fed. 457)

Record: Act of August 5, 1909. Action to recover amount of corporation tax paid under Sec. 38 of the Act, for the year 1911. Judgment for plaintiff, (206 Fed. 333), and defendant brought error. Dismissed.

Facts: Plaintiff, incorporated January 19, 1911, with general business powers, amended its articles December 31, 1911, so as to limit its activities to the mere ownership and rental of certain property occupied and used by its stockholders as a department store under leases of January 31 and December 7, 1911. Plaintiff applied the entire rent first to the payment of interest on mortgage liens, and then to payment of dividends to stockholders.

Question: Was the plaintiff doing business during the year 1911, within the meaning of the Act of August 5, 1909?

Decision: The plaintiff was not doing business during 1911 within the meaning of the Act, and, therefore, was not liable to pay an excise tax for 1911.

MAYOR, ETC., SAVANNAH v. HARTRIDGE
(Supreme Court of Georgia, January Term, 1850)
(8 Ga. 23)

Record: City Ordinance of Savannah, of November 11, 1842. Affidavit of illegality having been overruled by the city council, the case was carried to Superior Court by certiorari. Decision of Council was reversed, and the city brought error. Affirmed.

Facts: The city ordinance of Savannah provided that a tax be paid upon the gross income derived from commissions charged in various businesses. Hartridge returned a certain amount as "Commissions on purchases," and having failed to pay the tax, execution issued. He filed an affidavit of illegality on the ground that the ordinance was unauthorized by any of the State Acts. These Acts granted power to the city to assess a tax on every person who inhabited or used any place or building within the city, to lay an annual tax on all persons and property, to raise money by poll tax or assessments upon real and personal property, and to tax all persons peddling goods within the city.

Question: Has the city the power to impose a tax upon the gross income derived from commissions, under State Acts granting power to assess persons by a poll tax or a tax upon real and personal property?

Decision: "The subject of taxation has been, very properly, divided into three classes—capitation, property and income; and this distinction is recognized, not only by all writers on political economy, but in the general laws of all Governments; and when one or more is mentioned or treated of, the other is never intended, * * * . When we scrutinize other portions of this Act we are fully persuaded, that the legislature did not intend to include income, under the grant to tax 'real and personal estate.' By subsequent sections of the Act of 1825, the regulation of taverns and granting licenses, taxing vendue masters and peddlers, and persons vending goods, wares, and merchandize in the city, are powers specifically conferred. But this would have been unnecessary, if, under the general grant to tax all real and personal estate in the previous section, the corporation had the power to tax all private business." The power to impose a tax upon the gross income derived from commissions was not within the powers granted to the city by the state.

McCOACH v. CONTINENTAL PASSENGER RY. CO.
(U. S. Circuit Court of Appeals, Third Cir. May 19, 1916)
(233 Fed. 976)

Record: Act of August 5, 1909. Action to recover tax paid. Judgment for plaintiffs. Defendant brings error. Affirmed.

Facts: The plaintiff companies were all corporations organized under the laws of Pennsylvania for the purpose of owning and operating street railway lines. In 1902, one of the plaintiffs held and operated, under a series of leases and operating agreements all the lines previously owned or leased by the other plaintiffs, and it, in turn, leased all of said lines to another corporation which agreed to pay certain rentals and assume the obligations of the other corporations in the line of succession. One of the plaintiffs in the line of succession had no authority by its character to hold property by lease, and in that instance an operating agreement was entered into by which the preceding corporations turned over to it their lines and surrendered their operations as completely as by lease. In 1909, taxes were assessed against the plaintiffs under the Corporation Tax Law of August 5, 1909. These taxes were alleged by the plaintiffs to have been illegally collected and this action was brought for their recovery.

Questions: (1) Were the plaintiffs, during the year for which the tax in question was levied, "doing business" within the meaning of the Act of 1909?

(2) Did the operating agreement entered into by one of the plaintiffs amount to operating property by an agent, and so constitute "doing business."

Decision: (1) "A corporation which has ceased to pursue the occupation for which it was organized by reason of leasing its property, may continue to exist and to receive and disburse rentals, and pay or renew its debts, or create new indebtedness without being subject to the excise tax for 'doing business.'"

(2) "The fact that an operating agreement is entered into rather than a lease, but having the same effect, and achieving the same results as a lease will not make the lessor subject to the tax on the theory that it is 'doing business' through the operating company as its agent. The plaintiffs were therefore allowed to recover the taxes illegally imposed upon them under the Act."

McCOACH, COLLECTOR v. INSURANCE COMPANY OF NORTH AMERICA
(U. S. Supreme Court, October Term, 1916)
(244 U. S. 585)

Record: Act of August 5, 1909. Action at law by respondent, a fire and marine insurance company of Pennsylvania to recover a part of the excise taxes exacted of it for the years 1910 and 1911. The District Court rendered a judgment in plaintiff's favor, excluding however two disputed items, one for each of the years mentioned, representing the tax upon amounts added in each of those years to that part of what are called its reserve funds that is held against accrued but unpaid losses (218 Fed. 905). On plaintiff's writ of error the Circuit Court of Appeals reversed this judgment with instructions to allow the claim in full (224 Fed. 657). The case was brought here by writ of certiorari. Judgment of Circuit Court of Appeals reversed and that of District Court affirmed.

Facts: Plaintiff was chartered by a special act but is subject to the state insurance law. Under the laws of the State of Pennsylvania the insurance commissioner of that state required plaintiff and similar insurance companies to return each year as an item among their liabilities the net amount of unpaid losses and claims, whether actually adjusted, in process of adjustment, or resisted.

Question: Are the amounts so required to be held against unpaid losses in the case of fire and marine insurance companies deductible reserves under Par. 2 of Sec. 38 of the Act of August 5, 1909, which provides that net income of insurance companies shall be ascertained by deducting from gross income losses, depreciation, etc. "and the net addition, if any, required by law to be made within the year to reserve funds?"

Decision: Reserves against unpaid losses are not deductible from gross income of insurance companies when such reserves are not required by law. The Pennsylvania Act, the opinion states, specifically requires that debts and claims of all kinds be included in the statement of liabilities and treats them as something distinct from reserves. The Act of Congress, on the other hand, deals with reserves as they aid in determining what part of the gross income ought to be treated as net income for purpose of taxation. "There is a specific provision for deducting 'all losses actually sustained within the year and not compensated by insurance or otherwise.' And this is a sufficient indication that losses in immediate contemplation but not yet actually sustained, were not intended to be treated as part of the reserve funds, that term rather having reference to the funds ordinarily held as against the contingent liability on outstanding policies. In our opinion, the reserve against unpaid losses is not 'required by law' in Pennsylvania within the meaning of the Act of Congress." Therefore, the amount of this reserve is not deductible.

McCOACH, COLLECTOR, v. MINEHILL & S. H. R. R. CO.
(U. S. Supreme Court, April 7, 1913)
(228 U. S. 295)

Record: Act of August 5, 1909. Action to recover taxes paid under protest. Judgment for petitioner in U. S. Circuit Court (192 Fed. 670) affirmed in Circuit Court of Appeals for the Third Circuit. On certiorari. Judgment affirmed.

Facts: Respondent was incorporated in 1828 for the purpose of constructing and operating a railroad, and had the power of eminent domain. Under its charter, a railroad was built and for many years operated. In 1896, under authority granted by the legislature, respondent leased its entire property to the Philadelphia and Reading Railroad Company for a term of 999 years, at a yearly rental of $252,612. Pursuant to the lease, the entire railroad and all property connected therewith was turned over to the Reading Company. Respondent, however, maintained its corporate existence and organizations by the annual election of a president and board of directors, and this board annually elected a secretary and treasurer. It received annually the fixed rental called for by the lease, and also sums of money as interest on its bank deposits, and also maintained a "contingent fund," from which it received annual sums as interest or dividends. It paid annually the ordinary and necessary expenses of maintaining its office and keeping up the activities of its corporate existence, including the payment of salaries to its officers and clerks. It also kept and maintained at its offices, stock books for the transfer of its capital stock, and its stock was bought and sold upon the market. Respondent paid under protest taxes for the years 1909 and 1910, assessed against it under the Corporation Tax Act of 1909, and this action was brought to recover said taxes.

Question: Did the activities carried on by respondent constitute "doing business" within the meaning of the Act of 1909?

Decision: The receipt of income from property or investments by a company that is not engaged in business except the business of owning the property, maintaining the investments, collecting an income and dividing it among the stockholders, was not a "doing business" so as to be taxable within the meaning of the Act of 1909. Therefore, respondent was entitled to recover the taxes paid by it.

McELLIGOTT, ACTING COLLECTOR, v. KISSAM et al.

(U. S. Circuit Court of Appeals, Second Cir., Decision of
June 30, 1921)

(Not reported)

Record: Revenue Act of 1916. Action at law by Cornelia B. Kissam and John C. Knox, executrix and executor, respectively, of the will of Jonas B. Kissam, deceased, to recover an additional Federal estate tax paid under protest. On defendant's demurrer. Demurrer overruled and judgment entered for plaintiff. Defendant brings error. Reversed.

Facts: On July 15, 1912, Jonas B. Kissam assigned certain bonds and mortgages of individuals and certain bonds of corporations owned by him to John C. Knox, and subsequently Knox assigned them back to Jonas B. Kissam and his wife, Cornelia. In the instrument of assignment Knox assigned the bonds and mortgages "to the party of the second part, their survivor, such survivor's executors, administrators and assigns," and to hold "to the party of the second part, the survivor of them and to the successors, personal representatives and assigns of the said second party forever." It was further stated that "it is the intention of this assignment that the survivor of the said Jonas B. Kissam and Cornelia B. Kissam shall become the absolute owner of said bonds and mortgages and that neither the said Jonas B. Kissam nor the said Cornelia B. Kissam shall have power to affect the right of the survivor thereto." All parties, it is said, concede that the ownership was at least joint and that it could have been severed and turned into a tenancy in common by either party notwithstanding the reservation that neither party could affect the right of the survivor. Kissam died on June 2, 1917, leaving all his estate to his wife, Cornelia.

The Act of September 8, 1916, known as the Estate Tax Law, as amended by the Act of March 3, 1917, provides that the value of the gross estate shall include property "to the extent of the interest therein held jointly or as tenants in the entirety by the decedent and any other person, or deposited in banks or other institutions in their joint names and payable to either or the survivor, except such part thereof as may be shown to have originally belonged to such other person and never to have belonged to the decedent, * * * ."

The executors included in their return one-half of said joint property in the decedent's gross estate as being his property and paid the transfer tax on the net estate so ascertained, but the Commissioner upon review of the return included the whole of the joint property in the gross estate and assessed the net estate returned in this way. The executors claimed that the assessment was void as to the half of the joint property which vested in Cornelia before the passage of the Act of September 8, 1916, as amended, and also that the Act itself was unconstitutional as a direct tax upon property without apportionment among the several states, as required by Article 1, Section 9, subdivision 4 of the Constitution.

Questions: (1) Is the Act unconstitutional as a direct tax on property without apportionment?

(2) Is the surviving joint-tenant's original half interest in a joint-tenancy, created prior to the enactment of the statute, in property which formerly belonged solely to decedent, a part of decedent tenant's gross estate?

Decision: (1) Act of September 8, 1916, imposes an excise and not a direct tax on property and is constitutional. Held that "the joint property" mentioned in Section 202, subdivision (c) is included as a measure of the tax payable by the estate for the decedent's privilege of disposing of his property by will or intestacy. It is an excise tax and not a direct tax upon property (New York Trust Co. v. Eisner, 263 Fed. Rep. 620; Prentiss v. Eisner, 260 Fed. Rep. 587; 267 Fed. Rep. 16).

(2) Surviving tenant's original half interest in a joint tenancy created prior to the enactment of the statute is a part of the decedent tenant's gross estate. "The language of subdivision (c) of Section 202 of the Act plainly applies to property in which the decedent was interested jointly with any other person, and all of which was originally his, i. e., any part of the property which originally belonged to such other person and never at any time belonged to decedent is not to be included. The expression 'originally' refers not to the time of death, but to the time the joint interest was created. So the words 'never to have belonged to the decedent' mean at any time before the creation of the joint estate. The Act takes effect upon the death; it does not become retroactive because it measures a transfer tax payable by the estate in part by property which the decedent has given away in his lifetime. This seems to us perfectly fair, and an answer to the constitutional objection. Judgment reversed."

MELCHER v. CITY OF BOSTON
(Supreme Court of Massachusetts, 1845)
(50 Mass. 73)

Record: Action to recover taxes paid. Judgment for plaintiff. Judgment reversed.

Facts: Plaintiff was a clerk in the postoffice at Boston, having been appointed by the postmaster, and his appointment approved by the postmaster general. The postmaster general set apart for the postmaster at Boston, for clerk hire, a certain part of the sum annually appropriated by Congress for this purpose. A part of this was assigned to the plaintiff, and constituted his only income.

Question: Was the income received by the plaintiff taxable by the State of Massachusetts?

Decision: The court held that the plaintiff was not an officer of the United States within the meaning of the rule stated in Dobbins v. Commissioners 16 Pet. 435, and that the income in question was taxable.

MENTE v. EISNER, COLLECTOR

(U. S. Circuit Court of Appeals, Second Cir., April 14, 1920)

(266 Fed. 161)

Record: Act of Oct. 3, 1913. Action to recover taxes paid. Judgment for defendant below, and plaintiff brought error. Affirmed. Petition for writ of certiorari denied by Supreme Court Oct. 11, 1920 (41 S. C. 8).

Facts: Mente was a member of the firm of Mente & Co., engaged in the business of manufacturing bags and bagging. He had for three years been buying and selling cotton on the exchange for his own account, in no way connected with the business of Mente & Co.; and he deducted from his gross income in each year losses sustained in the year resulting from these transactions as "losses incurred in trade." The collector assessed an additional tax upon these deductions.

Question: Were losses suffered by a taxpayer in isolated transactions entered into for profit, but not connected with his business "incurred in trade" within the meaning of the Act?

Decision: The language "losses incurred in trade" was correctly construed by the Treasury Department as meaning in the actual business of the taxpayer, as distinguished from isolated transactions. If it had been intended to permit all losses to be deducted, it would have been easy to say so. Some effect must be given to the words "in trade." The losses suffered by the taxpayer in these isolated transactions can not be deducted from his gross income.

MERCHANTS INSURANCE CO. v. McCARTNEY, COLLECTOR

(U. S. Circuit Court D. Massachusetts, May Term, 1870)

(Fed. Case 9443)

Record: Act of June 30, 1864. Suit by plaintiff to recover tax paid by it under protest on dividends received. Case submitted to court on agreed facts. Judgment for plaintiff.

Facts: The plaintiff company owned stock in the Suffolk Bank and, as such stockholder, received $115,200 as their share of an extra dividend declared by the bank Jan. 3, 1865; of which they carried the odd $15,000 to their surplus fund and declared a dividend among their stockholders of the remainder. Of the dividend declared by the bank, about three-tenths consisted of profits laid aside before the passage of the first internal revenue law, and of profits of sales of real estate bought before that time. On the remaining seven-tenths the bank paid a tax of 5% to the Government, but denies their liability for the three-tenths, and it had never been exacted from them. The defendant collected from plaintiff against their protest a tax of 5% upon the whole sum so received by them. Sec. 120 of the Act of 1864 levies the duty on all dividends thereafter declared due as part of the earnings, income or gains of any insurance company, and on all undistributed sums made or added during the year to their surplus or contingent funds. In other words, it assesses the annual net income of such corporations whether they choose to divide them or add them to their funds. In Sec. 117 of the Act it is provided that in estimating the annual gains of any person there shall be deducted the income derived from dividends on shares in banks, etc., which shall have been assessed to and paid by the corporation. Sec. 121 provides that when any dividend is made which includes any part of the surplus or contingent fund of any bank, insurance company, etc., on which a duty has been paid, the amount of duty on the fund, so paid, may be deducted from the duty on the dividends.

Question: What part, if any, of the dividends paid by the bank to plaintiff is liable to assessment of the tax in their hands, upon the claim urged by plaintiff that the three-tenths did not represent income and the tax had already been paid by it on the seven-tenths?

Decision: With regard to the assessment on the three-tenths portion the court held that it was a division of capital, a return to plaintiff in money of a part of the property which was already in their ownership as capital stock when the first tax Act was passed. "If the Suffolk Bank had been wholly wound up and had returned to its stockholders the exact value of their shares in money, having made no profits since the passage of the original Act, this sum of money could not be taxed as income, gains or profits; and so of a part. If the plaintiff on receiving the money choose to divide it among their own stockholders, still it is not a dividend out of gains and profits, nor out of the surplus funds, because the surplus funds that are taxable are those which are or have been made out of profits since the passage of the Act. * * * And if this money was capital in the hands of the bank, it was still capital when it reached the stockholders. * * * The intent of Congress was to tax the income of the shareholders of the Suffolk Bank by a tax levied directly upon the bank. The income of these plaintiffs has been so taxed. I am not ready to believe that it was intended that the same income should be again returned to the Government for a new taxation merely because it passed through another corporation before reaching the individual owners."

The Court ordered that judgment be entered for plaintiff for the full amount of $5,760 and interest and costs.

MERCHANTS LOAN & TRUST CO., AS TRUSTEES, v. SMIETANKA, FORMERLY COLLECTOR

(Supreme Court of the U. S., March 28, 1921)

(No. 608, October Term, 1920, — U. S. —)

Record: Revenue Acts of 1916 and 1917. Assumpsit to recover taxes for the year 1917 paid under protest. Demurrer to declaration sustained. Plaintiff brings writ of error. Affirmed.

Facts: "Arthur Ryerson died in 1912, and the plaintiff in error is trustee under his will, of property the net income of which was directed to be paid to his widow during her life and after her death to be used for the benefit of his children, or their representatives, until each child should arrive at twenty-five years of age, when each should receive his or her share of the trust fund. The trustee was given the fullest possible dominion over the trust estate. It was made the final judge as to what 'net income' of the estate should be, and its determination in this respect was made binding upon all parties interested therein, 'except that it is my will that stock dividends and accretions of selling values shall be considered principal and not income.' The widow and four children were living in 1917. Among the assets which came to the custody of the trustee were 9,522 shares of the capital stock of Joseph T. Ryerson & Son, a corporation. It is averred that the cash value of these shares, on March 1, 1913, was $561,798, and that they were sold for $1,280,996.64, on Feb. 2, 1917. The Commissioner of Internal Revenue treated the difference between the value of the stock on March 1, 1913, and the amount for which it was sold on Feb. 2, 1917, as income for the year 1917, and upon that amount assessed the tax which was paid. No question is made as to the amount of the tax if the collection of it was lawful."

Questions: (1) Can the provisions of a will render the fund nontaxable?

(2) Do terms of the Revenue Act of 1916 include the income in question?

(3) Is the trustee a "taxable person" under the Revenue Acts of 1916 and 1917?

(4) Is appreciation of capital investment over a period of years realized by sale within the taxable year, by one not a dealer in such property, "income" within scope of Sixteenth Amendment?

Decision: (1) "The provision of the will may be disregarded. It is not within the power of the testator to render the fund non-taxable."

(2) "Section 2 (a) of the Act of Sept. 8, 1916 * * * applicable to the case, defines the income of 'a taxable person' as including 'gains, profits and income derived from * * * sales, or dealings in property, whether real or personal, growing out of the ownership or use of or interest in real or personal property * * * or gains or profits and income derived from any source whatever.' Plainly the gain we are considering was derived from the sale of personal property, and, very certainly the comprehen-

sive last clause 'gains or profits and income derived from any source whatever,' must also include it, if the trustee was a 'taxable person' within the meaning of the Act when the assessment was made.''

(3) ''That the trustee was such a single 'taxable person' is clear from Section 1204 (1) (c) of Act of Oct. 3, 1917 * * * .'' After quoting from Sections 2 (b) and (c) the court says: ''Thus, it is the plainly expressed purpose of the Act of Congress to treat such a trustee as we have here as a 'taxable person' and for the purpose of the Act to deal with the income received for others precisely as if the beneficiaries had received it in person.''

(4) ''There remains the question, strenuously argued, whether this gain in four years of over $700,000 on an investment of about $500,000 is 'income' within the meaning of the Sixteenth Amendment to the Constitution of the United States. The question is one of definition and the answer to it may be found in recent decisions of this Court. The Corporation Excise Tax Act of Aug. 5, 1909 (36 Stat. 11, 112), was not an income tax law, but a definition of the word 'income' was so necessary in its administration that in an early case it was formulated as 'a gain derived from capital, from labor, or from both combined.' (Stratton's Independence v. Howbert, 231 U. S. 399, 415.) This definition, frequently approved by this Court, received an addition, in its latest income tax decision, which is especially significant in its application to such a case as we have here, so that it now reads: 'Income may be defined as a gain derived from capital, from labor, or from both combined, provided it be understood to include profit gained through sale or conversion of capital assets.' Eisner v. Macomber, 252 U. S. 189, 207. The use made of this definition of 'income' in the decision of cases arising under the Corporation Excise Tax Act of Aug. 5, 1909, and under the Income Tax Acts is, we think, decisive of the case before us.''

''It is elaborately argued in this case, in No. 609, Eldorado Coal and Mining Company v. Harry W. Mager, Collector, etc., submitted with it, and in other cases since argued, that the word 'income' as used in the Sixteenth Amendment and in the Income Tax Act we are considering does not include the gain from capital realized by a single isolated sale of property, but that only the profits realized from sales by one engaged in buying and selling as a business—a merchant, a real estate agent, or broker—constitute income which may be taxed. It is sufficient to say of this contention, that no such distinction was recognized in the Civil War Income Tax Act of 1867 (14 Stat. 471, 478), or in the Act of 1894 (28 Stat. 509, 553), declared unconstitutional on an unrelated ground; that it was not recognized in determining income under the Excise Tax Act of 1909; * * * that it is not to be found, in terms, in any of the income tax provisions of the Internal Revenue Acts of 1913, 1916, 1917 or 1919; that the definition of the word 'income' as used in the Sixteenth Amendment, which has been developed by this Court, does not recognize any such distinction; that in departmental practice, for now seven years, such a rule has not been applied, and that there is no essential difference in the nature of the transaction or in the relation of the profit to the capital involved, whether the sale or conversion be a single, isolated transaction or one of many. The interesting and ingenious argument, which is earnestly pressed upon us, that this distinction is so fundamental and obvious that it must be assumed to be a part of the 'general understanding' of the meaning of the word 'income' fails to convince us that a construction should be adopted which would, in a large measure, defeat the purpose of the Amendment.

"The opinions of the courts in dealing with the rights of life tenants and remaindermen in gains derived from invested capital, especially in dividends paid by corporation, are of little value in determining such a question as we have here. * * * "

The following cases are cited and quoted from with approval: Hays v. Gauley Mountain Coal Co., 247 U. S. 189; United States v. C. C. C. & St. L. Ry. Co., 247 U. S. 195; S. P. Co. v. Lowe, 247 U. S. 330, 335; Doyle v. Mitchell Bros. Co., 247 U. S. 179, 185. (The following cases were distinguished: Gray v. Darlington, 15 Wall. 63; Lynch v. Turrish, 247 U. S. 221; and British Income Tax Decisions.) It was, therefore, held that plaintiff was not entitled to recover the tax paid on the profit realized from the sale of securities.

MERK v. TREAT, COLLECTOR
(U. S. Circuit Court of Appeals, Jan. 13, 1913)
(202 Fed. 133)

Record: Act of June 13, 1898. Action at law to recover taxes paid. Judgment for defendant and plaintiff brings error. Reversed.

Facts: (1) Plaintiff manufactured and sold a medical preparation known as "Ichthyol," on which prior to Dec. 1, 1898, he had paid a stamp tax under War Revenue Act June 13, 1898; but on that date, ascertaining that it had been determined that the substance was an uncompounded chemical and not taxable, he omitted to affix stamps to containers of the preparation sold between that date and Dec. 13. 1899. This being discovered, revenue officers insisted that the material was taxable, and that plaintiff should pay a sum equivalent to the face value of stamps, which the Government claimed should have been affixed. Plaintiff paid the tax under written protest.

(2) Plaintiff put out a chemical substance, known as "Ichthyol," on which the Government insisted on the payment of a war revenue stamp tax, notwithstanding it had been determined that the substance was uncompounded and not taxable. Plaintiff purchased stamps, which were later affixed to containers, and, being compelled to pay the tax on sales of the chemical sent out without stamps, did so after filing a protest against the imposition of the tax, past and future, on the ground that it was exempt from taxation as an uncompounded chemical, and notified the Government that plaintiff at different times had affixed stamps, and was still affixing the same, to the articles under duress.

Questions: (1) Was the payment of the stamp tax upon the goods which already had been marketed, voluntary and, therefore, not recoverable?

(2) Did the notice given by plaintiff under the above circumstances constitute a sufficient protest to entitle the plaintiff to recover the value of stamps affixed to goods sold after the giving of such notice?

Decision: (1) "The defendant concedes that this payment was made under a sufficient written protest; but the record does

not show any duress of goods. The claim thus paid was concerned
only with goods, which had been marketed, which were no longer
in plaintiff's possession, and which the Government, therefore,
could not take from him. For this part of the claim there can be
no recovery. The payment, although made under protest, seems
to have been voluntary.''

(2) Held that such notice was a sufficient protest to entitle
plaintiff to recover the value of stamps affixed subsequent to the
same, the tax not having been actually paid until the stamps were
actually affixed to the containers.

MIDDLESEX BANKING CO. v. EATON, COLLECTOR

(U. S. Circuit Court of Appeals, Second Cir., April 11, 1916)

(233 Fed. 87)

Record: Act of Aug. 5, 1909. Action at law to recover taxes
paid under protest on net income under Section 38 of this Act.
Judgment for defendant (221 Fed. 86), and plaintiff brought
error. Affirmed.

Facts: Charter of plaintiff gave it "the powers of a safe
deposit company, of a bank of deposit, and of a company to sell
securities." Practically the whole of the business done by the
plaintiff during the years in question was the sale of its own obligations, called debenture bonds, secured by mortgages on property
in the South and West, deposited with the Columbia Trust Company as trustee for the bondholders, and of the obligations of
borrowers to the plaintiff secured by mortgages which accompanied its own interest coupons for a less rate of interest than it
receives from its borrowers, it guarantees as to both principal and
interest and sells to purchasers. These latter are called "guaranteed real estate securities." Its profit in each case is represented
by the difference between the rate of interest which it receives from
its borrowers and the interest which it pays to its purchasers of
obligations.

Questions: (1) Is the interest paid to purchasers deductible
under subdivision 3 of par. 2 of Section 38 of the Act of Aug. 5,
1909, on the theory that the plaintiff is a bank or banking association, and that the interest in question is paid upon money deposited with it as such?

(2) If not, is this interest deductible as an "ordinary and necessary expense actually paid out of the income in the maintenance of the business provided for under the first subdivision of par. 2 * * * "?

Decision: (1) " ҂ * * * We think it perfectly clear that the interest in question is not interest on money deposited with it, but is interest paid on its own obligations or on the obligations of others guaranteed by it, which it has sold to the investing public. The purchase price is no more money deposited with the plaintiff at interest than is money paid in to a railroad company for the purchase of its bonds. The transaction is not a banking transaction at all, like the giving of a pass book or a certificate of deposit to a purchaser, but is a business of selling securities to investors." It was held, therefore, that the interest paid was not deductible upon the theory contended by the plaintiff.

(2) Interest is not deductible as expense, "because the whole subject of the deduction of interest is specifically regulated in subdivision 3."

MILLER, COLLECTOR, v. GEARIN
(U. S. Circuit Court of Appeals, Ninth Cir., May 5, 1919)
(258 Fed. 225)

Record: Revenue Act of 1916. Suit to recover income tax paid under protest. Demurrer to complain overruled. Judgment for plaintiff. Defendant brings error. Affirmed. Petition for a writ of certiorari denied Oct. 20, 1919 (250 U. S. 667).

Facts: Under the terms of a lease the lessee placed a building costing $140,000 on the property of the plaintiff, paid rent and all taxes and expenses. Some years later the lessee defaulted in payment of rent, whereupon, by an action of forcible entry and detainer, plaintiff acquired possession on Dec. 2, 1916. Since that time rentals have been insufficient to pay the expenses of maintenance, management and taxes. The defendant collector assessed the plaintiff for the value of this building as income for the year 1916.

Questions: (1) Is the building income of the plaintiff lessor, received in the year 1916 under the Income Tax Law of 1916?

(2) Is the question involved a doubtful one?

(3) If so, should the doubt be resolved in favor of the tax-payer?

Decision: (1) "The lessor acquired nothing in 1916 save the possession of that which for many years had been her own. The possession so acquired was not income. It was not a gain, but a loss. Assuming the building was income derived from the use of the property, we think it is clear that the time when it was 'derived' was the time when the completed building was added to the real estate and enhanced its value. At that time it represented a prepayment to the lessor of a portion of the rental, distributable over a period of 23 years. The lease provided that ownership of all buildings or improvements put upon the premises was to vest in the lessor immediately upon construction of the same, subject to the provisions of the lease." (Edwards v. Keith, 231 Fed. 111 distinguished). The ownership of the buildings vested in the plaintiff upon their construction and were not income received in 1916.

(2, 3) "We do not consider the question here involved a doubtful one; but if there is a doubt, it should be resolved in favor of the taxpayer." (Gould v. Gould, 245 U. S. 151 quoted from.)

MILLER, COLLECTOR, v. SNAKE RIVER VALLEY R. CO.

(U. S. Circuit Court of Appeals, Ninth Cir., May 26, 1915)

(223 Fed. 946)

Record: Act of Aug. 5, 1909. Action at law for tax paid under protest, under provisions of Sec. 38 of that Act. Judgment for plaintiff, and collector brings error. Affirmed.

Facts: On June 29, 1907, plaintiff, a railroad company, being the owner of a railroad line, with its rolling stock and equipment, leased same for a period of 5 years to be operated as a railroad. The lease obligated the lessee to pay all expenses of maintenance and renewal, taxes on the property, and other incidental expenses, but entitled the lessee to retain from the rental the cost of certain permanent improvements made. The lease was terminated by mutual consent Dec. 23, 1910. The lessor immediately sold and transferred all the property, and from the proceeds, paid its bonded and other indebtedness. During the continuance of the lease the lessor maintained its offices, transferred stock, collected and deposited the rental, and expended such sums as were necessary in maintaining its corporate existence, including the state corporation tax.

Question: "Was the Snake River Company engaged in business during the year 1910 within the meaning of the Act of Aug. 5, 1909?"

Decision: This case cannot be distinguished from McCoach v. Minehill Railway Company (228 U. S. 295). The difference in the length of the leases in the two cases (999 years and 5 years) "is a distinction without a difference." The sale of the property by the lessor, "as an incident of ownership," is not doing business within the statute, though the proceeds were used in payment of its indebtedness during the taxable year. "Had the lessor been organized for the purpose of buying, selling and leasing railroads, this sale would no doubt constitute engaging in business within the meaning of the law. * * * The business of operating the railroad during the entire year 1910 was conducted by the lessee or grantee. They were taxable because of that business, and to impose a like tax on the lessor would be double taxation, which the law does not contemplate." The Snake River Company was, therefore, not "engaged in business" during 1910 within meaning of Act and was not liable for the tax imposed upon it.

MITCHELL BROS. CO. v. DOYLE, COLLECTOR
(U. S. Supreme Court, May 20, 1919)
(247 U. S. 179)

Record: Act of Aug. 5, 1909. Action at law to recover taxes paid under protest on net income under Section 30 of. this Act. Judgment for plaintiff (235 Fed. 686), and defendant appeals. Affirmed.

Facts:- Plaintiff is a lumber manufacturing corporation which operates its own mills, manufactures lumber therein from its own stumpage, sells the lumber in the market, and from these sales makes its profit. In 1903 it purchased timber lands and paid for them at a valuation of approximately $20 per acre. After the passage of the Corporation Excise Tax Act of Aug. 5, 1909, the company revalued this timber land as of Dec. 31, 1908, at approximately $40 per acre. Under the Act the company made a return of income for each of the years 1909, 1910, 1911, 1912, and in each instance deducted from its gross income the market value, as of Dec. 31, 1908, of the stumpage cut and converted during the year covered by the tax. The Government contended that 1903 values should have been deducted from gross income to arrive at taxable income, and assessed the company an additional tax equal to 1% of the difference between 1903 and 1908 values of stumpage cut. The plaintiff paid this additional tax under protest and brought this suit to recover same.

Question: Was the difference between cost in 1903 and fair market value as of Dec. 31, 1908 (effective date of Act of 1909) income for the years in which it was converted into money, within the meaning of the Act?

Decision: The amount by which the timber so used had increased in value between the date of purchase and the effective date of the Act was not an element of income to be considered in computing the tax. The purpose of the Act of 1909 was not to tax property as such, on the mere conversion of property, but to tax the conduct of the business of corporations organized for profit by a measure based upon the gainful returns from their business operations and property from the time the Act took effect. A conversion of capital assets does not always produce income. In order to determine whether there has been gain or loss, and the amount of the gain, if any, it is necessary to withdraw from the gross proceeds an amount sufficient to restore the capital value that existed at the commencement of the period under consideration. When the Act took effect, plaintiff's timber lands, with whatever value they then possessed, were a part of its capital assets, and subsequent change of form by conversion into money did not change the essence. The increased value since the purchase, as that value stood on Dec. 31, 1908, was not in the proper sense the result of the operation and management of the business or property of the corporation while the Act was in force, and was not income for the year in which it was converted into money after the effective date of the Act. The plaintiff, therefore, was entitled to recover the additional tax paid by it.

MORRILL v. JONES
(U. S. Supreme Court, October, 1882)
(106 U. S. 466)

Record: Rev. Stat., Sec 2505. Action at law to recover duties paid under protest. Judgment for plaintiff and defendant appeals. Affirmed.

Facts: Plaintiff imported animals for breeding purposes. Section 2505 of the Revised Statutes provides that "Animals, alive, specially imported for breeding purposes from beyond the seas, shall be admitted free (of duty), upon proof thereof satisfactory to the Secretary of the Treasury, and under such regulations as he may prescribe." Article 303 of the Treasury Customs Regulations provides that before a collector admits such animals free he must, among other things, "be satisfied that the animals are of superior stock, adapted to improving the breed in the United States.'"

Question: Did the Secretary of the Treasury exceed his power in making the above regulation?

Decision: "The Secretary of the Treasury cannot by his regulations alter or amend a revenue law. All he can do is to regulate the mode of proceedings to carry into effect what Congress has enacted. * * * The statute clearly includes animals of all classes. The regulation seeks to confine its operation to animals of 'superior stock.' This is manifestly an attempt to put into the body of the statute a limitation which Congress did not think it necessary to prescribe." It was, therefore, held that the regulation was void.

MUTUAL BENEFIT LIFE INS. CO. v. HEROLD, COLLECTOR
(U. S. District Court, D. New Jersey, July 29, 1912)
(198 Fed. 199)

Record: Act of Aug. 5, 1909. Action at law to recover taxes paid under protest on net income under Section 38 of this Act. Judgment for plaintiff on all items. Subsequently defendant brought error and the case was affirmed with qualifications Jan. 27, 1913, by Circuit Court of Appeals, see 201 Fed. 918.

Facts: (1) Plaintiff was incorporated by charter granted by State of New Jersey in 1845 for insurance of life risks. It is a mutual company, without capital stock or stockholders. Its policy-holders are its only members, and they select its directors from their own number. Its business is conducted on the mutual level premium plan. This plan provides "that stipulated premium may not be increased, but may be lessened annually by so much as the experience of the preceding year has determined it to have been greater than cost of carrying insurance, and the difference between the amount of the stipulated premium and the cost of carrying the risk constitutes the so-called dividend." "Each policyholder may, at his option, withdraw his dividend in cash, or have it applied in reduction of subsequent year's premium, or to purchase additional insurance, or to accelerate the payment period." Where the policyholder exercised the option of withdrawal in cash the amount was reported as income and tax paid thereon. The department treated all dividends no matter which option was exercised as "income received" and imposed a tax.

(2) The plaintiff's policies contain an option to have the proceeds paid in annual installments for a given term of years, or during the lifetime of the beneficiary, instead of in one sum. If the option is exercised, such policies upon which payments have fallen due are styled "supplementary policy contracts." In life insurance, the word "reserve" means the sum which the company must have on hand in order to meet its policy obligations. The company's reserve is also defined as the value of all its outstanding policies. The insurance commissioners of New Jersey and of the other states of the United States require the plaintiff to cover its obligations on supplementary policy claims by reserve for that purpose.

(3) State Insurance Commissions require insurance companies to report each year the amount of uncollected and deferred premiums as of end of that year, but do not allow them to enter them upon their books as assets. The company did not include these items in its returns for 1909 and 1910. Interest due, but unpaid, and interest accrued on the plaintiff's investments, are not entered in plaintiff's books of account; nor did the plaintiff include those items in the returns.

(4) The plaintiff made deductions for ordinary renewals of office furniture, and for ordinary renewals of attendants' uniforms,

doormats, window shades, small hardware, oils and of electrical equipment, consisting of lamps, alterations of fixtures, shades, meters, fans, plugs, wiring, etc.

Questions: (1) Whether so-called dividends are or are not income received and so taxable?

(2) Whether so-called "supplementary policy contracts" should be represented in reserve funds, as being required by law?

(3) Whether for purposes of taxation the corporation's statement should be made on a "cash" or on a "revenue" basis?

(4) Whether expenditures for replacing furniture, etc., should be considered an investment or an expense?

Decision: (1) "This excess payment (the amount of the so-called dividends) represents, not profit or receipts, but an overpayment—an overpayment because, being entitled to his insurance at cost and having paid more than it cost, he is equitably entitled to have such excess applied for his benefit * * * Where any option but the withdrawal one is exercised, the dividends are not sums paid to the policyholder and by him returned in cash. They are not 'income * * * received.' The tax is 'on what comes in, on actual receipts, * * * not on what saves his pocket, but on what goes into his pocket.'" Therefore, the difference between the amount of the stipulated premium and the cost of carrying the risk, which the plaintiff allowed the policyholders to apply towards additional insurance, was not income, and not a taxable dividend.

(2) As to the 'supplementary policy contracts' the Court said that they "are required by law to be represented in the reserve fund, and that so much of that fund as is annually set apart for that purpose is not subject to the tax in question."

(3) The statute says "income received" and since its language is explicit in permitting only "such deductions from the gross income as were actually paid during the current year, it would be strange, indeed, if on the opposite side of the account the company were charged with what it had not received during the current year." "It seems almost to border upon absurdity to speak of including that which has not been received, and which in

the ordinary uncertainties of business may never be received. * * * The Act contemplates that the return shall be made on a cash basis; that is, upon a basis of money actually received and expenditures actually paid during the current year. Such a method, and such only, is fair to both parties. * * * "

(4) "The items being ordinary renewals, which may fairly be taken to mean annual renewals, " none being permanent benefits, but simply replacements on account of wear and tear, and, again the expenditures were no greater than the average of similar expenditures for other years. "The items are small, and should properly be charged to maintenance; they apparently did no more than maintain in proper condition and repair the ordinary equipment of office furniture and supplies."

NASHVILLE, CHAT. & ST. LOUIS RAILWAY CO. v. U. S.

(U. S. Circuit Court of Appeals, Sixth Cir., Dec. 7, 1920)

(Not reported)

Record: Act of Aug. 5, 1909. Suit by Commissioner to recover excise tax claimed due under said Act on ground of excessive depreciation charged. Case originally before Circuit Court of Appeals on pleadings was reversed and remanded (249 Fed. 678). Trial on the evidence. Judgment for Government and defendant brought error. Affirmed. Certiorari denied Mar. 7, 1921. — U. S. —.

Facts: Defendant arrived at the depreciation charges by estimating the value of the perishable structures as one-third the cost of the road (less equipment and real estate), and then taking 3% of this one-third value, on the theory that the average life of the various perishable elements was $33\frac{1}{3}$ years. It appeared that there was expended in round numbers for maintenance of way and structures, that is to say, for repairs, renewals, and replacements for the year 1909, $1,600,000, and for the year 1910, $1,554,000, and that no substantial part of these sums was carried in defendant's accounting as additions and betterments. It was admitted by defendant's chief engineer that the expenditures for 1909 kept the road in a normal condition to carry on its business, that its normal condition was a good condition, and that the expenditures had made good the normal amount of depreciation. There was testimony by competent witnesses of railway experience that there may be depreciation in the units comprising the roadway, track, and structures of the railroad, while there is no depreciation in the machinery as a whole; also that it is possible to maintain the roadway, track, and structures so that there will be no depreciation if we consider the roadway, track, and structures as a composite whole; also that the service life of any normally operated and normally well maintained railroad is perpetual, and it is maintained in the condition of properly serving its purpose by annual renewals and replacements.

The jury was specifically instructed to consider, first, the depreciation, either physical or functional, in the value of those parts of the roadway which have not been repaired or renewed or replaced, and second, what has been the effect of the repairs, renewals, and replacements that have been made to other parts, and determine whether, after you strike a final balance at the end of the year, the roadway is of greater or less value, or of equal value, than or to that which it was at the beginning of the year; and that if it should be found that the value of the roadway, its actual value, is as great at the end of the year, after these repairs and replacements have been made for which credit has been given as an expense deduction, then there is no depreciation in value of the roadway, within the meaning of the statute; but that if after making such repairs, replacements, and renewals in the different units of the roadway it should be found that some parts have been made more valuable by the putting in of new parts in place of worn-out parts, yet the depreciation in the rest of the roadway, in the deterioration, obsolescence, etc., of other units which have not been changed, and so little done in repairing and replacing that at the end of the year, taking it as a whole, the depreciation in value has exceeded the repairs, replacements and renewals, so that it is worth less than it was, to that extent the railway is entitled to a deduction of 1%.

Question: Did the instruction of the Court present the correct basis for determining depreciation?

Decision: "The contention on which defendant seems to rest its chief criticism seems to be that, notwithstanding the roadway as a whole was intrinsically just as valuable at the end of the year as at the beginning of the year, that is to say, although depreciation in given units had been fully overcome by appreciation in others, the railway company would still be entitled to credit for depreciation in such individual units as had depreciated. We think this contention of defendant not sustained by reason or authority, and that the Court correctly charged the true criterion. If, as is not entirely clear, it is meant to further suggest that the consideration of functional (as distinguished from physical) depreciation was not allowed by the charge to be taken into account, the suggestion is plainly without merit. * * * The testimony considered as a whole, tended to support the conclusion that the amounts expended by defendant during the years in question for repairs, renewals, and replacements should and would have fully offset the depreciation in the various units, and that the defendant's railway and structures were, as a whole, maintained throughout the years in question in fully as good condition, and were of fully as great intrinsic value as at the beginning of the respective years. The jury would have been clearly justified in inferring from the testimony of defendant's chief engineer, taken as a whole, that the value of the roadway had not depreciated during the two years in question; in other words, that the repairs and renewals that had been made were of such a character as to leave the road at the end of each year of value equal to that at the beginning of the year. * * * '' Therefore, the Court held that the defendant was not entitled to the deduction for depreciation claimed.

NATIONAL BANK OF COMMERCE IN ST. LOUIS v. ALLEN, COLLECTOR
(223 Fed. 472)

Record: Act of Aug. 5, 1909. Action to recover taxes paid under protest. Judgment for defendant (211 Fed. 743) and plaintiff brings error. Affirmed.

Facts: The bank is a national bank doing business at St. Louis, Mo. In making up the returns of gross and net income it deducted the sums it had paid as taxes imposed by the State of Missouri upon the shares of its capital stock, relying on Sec. 38 of the Act which says: "That every corporation shall be subject to pay annually a special Excise Tax * * * upon the entire net income over and above $5,000 received by it from all sources during such year. * * * Second. Such net income shall be ascertained by deducting from the gross amount of the income. * * * (4) All sums paid by it within the year for taxes imposed under the authority of the United States or of any State." The Commissioner made an assessment on the amount deducted.

Questions: Were the taxes paid to the State by the bank on the shares of its capital stock such taxes as the Act authorized it to deduct from its gross income?

(2) Was the Commissioner authorized by law to make the additional assessment on the amounts so deducted?

Decision: (1) The deduction was not proper because the State tax was levied upon the shares of the capital stock, and although paid by the bank, it had the right to recover back from the stockholder the amount so paid. The Court said: "The law is not a tax upon income, but a tax upon the right to do business as a corporation; the amount of tax being measured according to the income. Therefore, for the purpose of ascertaining the amount of the tax which the corporation shall pay, it is necessary to arrive at its own net income for any particular year. The bank, therefore, would have no right to deduct from its gross income taxes imposed by the State upon a third party, but which the bank itself had paid."

(2) The Commissioner has power to amend and reassess a return at any time within three years, where he finds the return to be "not true" or "incorrect."

NATIONAL LIFE AND ACCIDENT INSURANCE CO. v. CRAIG, COLLECTOR

(U. S. Circuit Court of Appeals, Sixth Cir., June 4, 1918)

(251 Fed. 524)

Record: Act of Aug. 5, 1909. Action to recover taxes paid under protest. Judgment for defendant, and plaintiff brings error. Affirmed.

Facts: The plaintiff is a Tennessee corporation, and as such was compelled by the insurance commissioner of that state to reserve sums sufficient to meet the following accrued and unpaid liabilities—death losses in process of adjustment, or adjusted and not due; weekly losses; death losses and other policy claims resisted by the company; premiums paid in advance or unearned premiums; due or accrued salaries, rents, commissions, and legal and medical fees: In making its return as required under the Act, plaintiff did not include the sums set apart to meet whatever liability it might have on the above mentioned items. Subsequently the Commissioner assessed an additional tax against plaintiff, based on these sums, which plaintiff paid under protest.

Question: Was the insurance company authorized to deduct this "reserve fund" for prospective liabilities from its gross income?

Decision: There is no provision in the state law which requires the reserving of other additional sums to meet unpaid losses and liabilities, accrued or prospective, and "our conclusion is that the reserves, held against liabilities and losses, incurred and contingent, shown in plaintiff's annual statements, are not "required by law of Tennessee" and, therefore, was not a proper deduction in the computation of the company's gross income.

NEW YORK CENTRAL & H. R. R. Co. et al. v. GILL, COLLECTOR

(U. S. Circuit Court of Appeals, First Cir., Jan. 13, 1915)

(219 Fed. 184)

Record: Act of Aug. 5, 1909. Action to recover taxes paid under protest. Judgment for defendant, and plaintiffs bring error. Reversed.

Facts: The Federal excise tax was assessed against the Boston & Albany Railroad Company, which had leased its railroad and property to the New York Central & Hudson Railroad Company. The lessor company retained its right to be a corporation and at the request of lessee made an issue of bonds, and on another occasion exercised its right of eminent domain.

Question: Is a railroad company, having leased its property to another railroad corporation which is operating the same, the lessor continuing its corporate existence, and at the lessee's request making an issue of bonds and exercising the power of eminent domain, "doing business" so as to render it liable to taxation under Corporation Excise Tax Act of 1909?

Decision: Even though the lessor company made an issue of bonds at the lessee's request, and also on certain occasion took steps in exercise of its right of eminent domain, the steps so taken were at lessee's request and benefit, and at the lessee's sole expense and under its direction and in accordance with provisions in the lease, and even though the bonds were issued to pay for the land thus acquired, the Court finds no reason for regarding these takings of lands as "doing business" and also holds that the issuance of bonds is not to be so regarded. The lessor corporation had practically gone out of business, and was disqualified from any activity respecting the operation and management of the railroad and, therefore, was not "doing business" so as to render it liable to taxation under Act of 1909.

NEW YORK LIFE INSURANCE CO. v. ANDERSON
(U. S. Circuit Court of Appeals, Second Cir., Jan. 14, 1920)
(263 Fed. 527)

Record: Act of Aug. 5, 1909. Action to recover taxes paid under protest. Verdict directed for plaintiff (262 Fed. 215, see also 257 Fed. 576), and both parties bring error. Reversed. Certiorari denied (— U. S. —, May 2, 1921).

Facts: The tax in question is not "in any proper sense an income tax," but is an excise on plaintiff's conduct of business in a corporate capacity. The plaintiff is an insurance company, and the business of such requires the maintenance of relatively enormous amounts of "securities" as the basis of its operations, and an asset sufficiently stable to answer the legal requirements of numerous states and countries, yet sufficiently liquid to respond to the needs of the holders of maturing policies. The securities of plaintiff were worth at the end of 1910 several million dollars less than they were at the beginning of that year, and not only was the busi-

ness custom of plaintiff to revalue its securities in accordance with
the market annually, but such procedure was and is a reasonable
business conservatism.   The plaintiff made a deduction of the depreciation which was disallowed by the Commissioner.

Question: Is depreciation in market value of securities a deductible loss within the meaning of this Act?

Decision: Depreciation was allowed as a deduction.   Court
said: "We have no doubt that this loss in market value is depreciation.   The word means, by derivation and common usage, a
'fall in value, reduction of worth,' and it seems to us to require
mention only to prove that the average citizen, for whom statutes
are assumed to be made, would judge depreciation of his own
bonds by the opinion of the public, however thoroughly convinced
of the .ultimate wisdom of holding on to what had depreciated.
The plain inference is that the phrase is used in the statute in a
sense that would be generally understood in business circles, and
we hold that the depreciation claimed by plaintiff in its return is
used in that sense, and should have been allowed as a deduction."

NEW YORK MAIL & NEWSPAPER TRANS. CO. v. ANDERSON
NEW YORK PNEUMATIC SERVICE CO. v. ANDERSON
(U. S. Circuit Court of Appeals, Second Cir. 1916)
(234 Fed. 590)

Record: Act of Aug. 5, 1909.   Action to recover taxes paid
under protest.   From the judgment both parties bring error.
Affirmed.

Facts: Two corporations, the Mail Co., and the Pneumatic
Co., chartered by special act of the New York Legislature to construct and operate pneumatic tubes between places in the state
for the conveyance of mails, newspapers and parcels, each owned
and operated tubes connecting the general postoffice in Manhattan
with branch offices at different places, which tubes were used exclusively for transportation of mails.   By the action of the postoffice
department, bids were invited for the carrying of mails by pneumatic tubes, but subject to the requirement that but one bid should
be made for the service of the tubes owned by such two corpora-

tions, whereupon one company leased all of its property for a term of years to the other which secured the contract and performed the entire service.

Questions: (1) Is a corporation, having leased its property to another corporation which is operating the same, "doing business" within the provisions of the Act?

(2) When does the Federal Statute of Limitations run?

Decision: (1) The Court held that a corporation, unless prohibited by explicit terms in its grant of power, may lease its property for a limited term of years, that such lease was valid, and that on its execution the lessor corporation ceased "doing business," within the meaning of the Act, and was not subject to the special excise tax thereby imposed. The Court also held that on recovery of a judgment against the collector of internal revenue for the amount of an internal revenue tax illegally collected, the plaintiff is entitled to have the judgment state that it is with interest.

(2) A suit for recovery of a tax alleged to have been erroneously or illegally assessed or collected, cannot be maintained unless claim is presented within two years after its payment.

N. Y., NEW HAVEN & HARTFORD R. R. CO. v. U. S.
(U. S. Circuit Court of Appeals, Second Cir.)
(Not reported)

Record: Act of Aug. 5, 1909. Suit by U. S. to collect excise taxes for the taxable years ending Dec. 31, 1909, 1910, 1911 and 1912. Judgment for plaintiff. Defendant appeals. Affirmed.

Facts: The plaintiff in error is a railroad corporation. Its capital stock was issued at the par value of one hundred dollars per share, but a very considerable number of shares were issued to stockholders for sums in excess of one hundred dollars per share. The prices varied from one hundred and forty-four dollars to two hundred and fifty-eight dollars per share. Before 1909 the plaintiff in error in its books treated the surplus above one hundred dollars as a premium paid for the stock, and it was accounted for in its profit and loss account. After that, it was treated in its "premium account."

Questions: (1) Do the words "paid-up capital stock of such corporation, * * * outstanding at the close of the year" in the Act of Aug. 5, 1909, used in reference to the limitation upon the amount of interest deductible include amounts paid for stock in excess of its par value?

(2) If not, is this interpretation in violation of the Constitution of the United States in that it denies to the plaintiff in error equal protection of the law?

Decision: (1) "The excess paid in price is, in fact, a premium paid for the stock. For when such shares of stock are at face value, they are at par, and when more is paid, they are above par or at premium. The total of the par value has always been considered capital stock. The term 'capital stock' has thus been used, not only in banking and commerce, but in the corporation acts in the several States. Full force and effect must be given to the term 'paid-up' as used in the statute, and its use in connection with 'not exceeding.' We think the employment of these words made the intention of Congress clear as obviously meaning paid-up to par value and not exceeding that." Therefore, the paid-up capital stock does not include the amount paid for stock by the purchaser, in excess of the par value.

(2) "Congress may impose different specific taxes upon different trades and professions and vary the rates of excises upon various products. It may tax real estate and personal property in a different manner. It may tax divisible (sic) property only and not tax securities for payment of money. It may allow deductions for indebtedness or not allow them. Such regulations of this character, so long as they proceed within reasonable limits and general usage, are within the discretion of Congress. There is no precise application of the rule of reasonableness of classification and the rule of equality permits of many practical inequalities. The rule of equality under the Constitution only requires that the law imposing it shall operate on all alike under the same circumstances. The differences here permitting deductions are not arbitrary because it is determined by an established value, namely, the par value of the capital stock." Such an interpretation is not in violation of the Constitution of the United States.

NEW YORK TRUST CO., EXECUTORS OF HARKNESS v
EDWARDS, COLLECTOR
UNITED STATES v. ROCKEFELLER
(U. S. District Court, S. District New York, Aug. 3, 1921)
(Not reported)

Record: Act of Oct. 3, 1913. Action to recover taxes paid on behalf of the decedent Harkness. Action by the United States to recover similar taxes from the defendant, Rockefeller. Judgment sustaining a demurrer and dismissing the complaint in the Harkness case and awarding recovery against the defendant in the Rockefeller case.

Facts: The Prairie Oil & Gas Co., a corporation, caused a new corporation to be organized in the winter of 1914-1915, to be known as the Prairie Pipe Line Co., and made a contract with the latter company by which it was to convey all its pipe line property to said new corporation which, in turn, agreed to distribute all of its own stock to the stockholders of the oil company in the same proportion as their existing holdings. In the case of the Ohio Oil Company there was a similar transaction, except that the agreements between it and the Illinois Pipe Line Company, which it organized, required the shares to be transferred direct to the oil company. However, the directors of the oil company, in the same resolution which accepted the contract declared these shares as a dividend to its stockholders. The agreements of both oil companies were carried out, and the shares so declared were taxed as income against Harkness and Rockefeller who received a portion thereof, as stockholders of the two oil companies. In both cases the properties conveyed represented a surplus above the par value of the oil companies' stock, and the conveyances, therefore, left the oil companies' capital unimpaired and required no reduction of their authorized issues.

Questions: (1) Was the distribution here a stock dividend under the rule of Eisner v. Macomber?

(2) If not, what was the effect of this distribution, and did it result in taxable income to the recipients?

Decision: (1) "In Eisner v. Macomber, 252 U. S. 189, the case was of a mere stock dividend, which was held to be no more than new evidence of the stockholder's original ownership. Had the shares been without par value, that would have been literally the case, but they were not. The stock dividend did change the relation of the corporation and the stockholder to the surplus, by permanently impounding it, as it were, in the business, and giving the stockholder a right to insist upon it as an investment, should his fellows later wish to realize it as profit. Yet, though, he thus got, and the corporation lost, this element of control over the surplus so declared, it was not regarded as a severance of the property. So far, therefore, Eisner v. Macomber, supra, helps the taxpayers here; it shows that there may be some changes in the relation of the stockholders to the surplus which do not amount to the severance of income. Nevertheless, the cases at bar go further than that case because in them the surplus was transferred to a new corporation altogether, and the question is whether that distinction changes the result. The taxpayers insist that if one looks at the very truth of the matter, disregarding corporate forms, this is no difference at all. Although the argument is plausible, it still seems to me, that, even when viewed with the completest disregard of forms, the pipe line properties were completely severed from the oil companies and that the resulting shares were new property derived from the oil shares.''

(2) ''The result of the conveyance of the pipe line property was to put it under the control of an association committed exclusively to its operation as a separate enterprise from that of the oil company. Indeed, this severance in management was the sole motive of the transaction, unless there were a surreptitious agreement between the two groups which nullified the dissolution, which is not suggested. Accepting, therefore, the taxpayers' argument that forms should be disregarded, the question is whether a group mutually agreeing to manage the pipe line property independently of the oil property, is a different group from one agreeing to manage the pipe line and the oil property jointly. If the association does not depend upon the number or make-up of its membership, but upon its character, there can be no question that the difference between the two is substantial, because to conduct two businesses as a unity has practical results very different from conducting them

in complete independence. For illustration let me assume that the pipe line property had been conveyed in specie to the stockholders as co-workers and that they had incorporated for convenience. The original conveyance to them would have fallen directly within Peabody v. Eisner, supra, and Lynch v. Hornby, supra. It would have made no difference that they had later incorporated. Yet, judged by results, this is exactly what happened; the pipe line was broken from an association committed to its joint management with the oil properties and consigned to an association which must manage it alone. Or suppose that the Prairie Pipe Line Company, for example, had been a going concern with property of its own. Upon its acquisition of the pipe line and the issue of its new shares to the oil company stockholders, they would have an interest in an association operating two properties. These new shares would certainly be income in their hands to some extent. Would they be altogether income or only in the proportion to which by taking the new shares they gave up their rights in the old pipe line and got in exchange an interest in the original property of the Prairie Pipe Line Company? I scarcely think that anyone would urge that the new shares were not altogether income. Yet, if so, they would become such only because the pipe line was being conducted in a new joint enterprise by the Prairie Pipe Line Company. Unquestionably the oil company stockholders would to some extent be still holding their old pipe lines and in the same relative proportions. Or consider again the analogy of many of the dissolutions under the Sherman Act. These consisted in no greater separation than was accomplished here, yet it was thought enough to sever the enterprises and create new rights in the new corporations. Nor was it thought to be an answer that the stockholders started out the same. Because the members might join or leave the new group which conducted only a part of the old business, it was considered that the old group was effectively broken up. Disregarding, therefore, all formalities, it appears to me, that the pipe line properties were as effectually severed from the old corporations as though they had been distributed in kind. Indeed, the form adopted was the only practicable way in which they could be so distributed. It is only when one fastens one's attention upon the momentary identity of the two resulting groups that there can be any question of the result. But, as I have perhaps too often said, that identity is nothing unless its continuance is insured for the future by some common agreement between the two. I think that the new shares were income under the law and that the tax was legal."

NEW YORK TRUST CO. v. EISNER
(U. S. Supreme Court, October Term, 1920)
(65 L. ed. 620)

Record: Revenue Act of 1916. Suit to recover Federal estate tax paid. On demurrer the district court dismissed the bill (263 Fed. 620). Plaintiff brought error. Affirmed.

Facts: The executors of the estate of one Purdy had been required to pay state inheritance and succession taxes, amounting in all to $37,769.88, which, under the term of the will, they paid out of the residuary estate. In the assessment of the Federal estate tax no deduction was allowed in computing the gross estate for any part of the above mentioned $37,769.88.

Questions: (1) Was the Estate Tax Act unconstitutional as interfering with the rights of the states to regulate descent or as imposing a direct tax?

(2) Was the Act properly construed as not allowing a deduction of state inheritance and succession taxes as charges within the meaning of Section 203, which authorized the deduction of "such other charges against the estate as are allowed by the laws of the jurisdictions * * * under which the estate is being administered"?

Decision: (1) The Act did not unconstitutionally interfere with the rights of the state to regulate descent and distribution. Knowlton v. Moore, 178 U. S. 41 cited.

The contention that this was a direct tax was disposed of "on an interpretation of language by its traditional use—on the practical and historical ground that this kind of tax always has been regarded as the antithesis of a direct tax." Knowlton v. Moore, supra, cited.

(2) State inheritance and succession taxes on the rights of individual beneficiaries are not deductible from the gross estate of

the decedent as charges against the estate that are allowed by the laws of the jurisdiction under which the estate is administered. Such charges are only those which affect the estate as a whole.

NICHOLS v. UNITED STATES
(U. S. Supreme Court, December, 1868)
(7 Wall. 122)

Record: Act of Feb. 26, 1845. Action at law to recover duties paid. Judgment for defendant and plaintiff appeals. Affirmed.

Decision: ''Under the Act of Congress of Feb. 26, 1845, relative to the recovery of duties paid under protest, a written protest, signed by the party, with a statement of the definite grounds of objection to the duties demanded and paid, is a condition precedent to a right to sue in any court for their recovery.''

NICOL v. AMES
(U. S. Supreme Court, April 3, 1899)
(173 U. S. 509)

Record: Act of June 13, 1898. Plaintiffs in error were convicted of violating a penal statute, and appealed. Affirmed.

Facts: The Act required a stamp for every sale or agreement of sale at any exchange or board of trade, and provided that on every sale or agreement for sale the seller should deliver to the buyer a bill, agreement, or memoranda thereof, with the stamp affixed thereto. Members of the Chicago Board of Trade sold for immediate delivery products or merchandise: (a) without making a memorandum, (b) making a memorandum but omitting to put stamps on it; and also for future delivery without putting stamps on the memorandum. The sales were made at the Union Stock Yards of Chicago and the vendor neglected and refused to affix revenue stamps to the memoranda.

Questions: (1) Is the Act of June 13, 1898, unconstitutional because (a) it is a direct tax and not apportioned as required by the Constitution?

(b) Not uniform throughout the United States as required by the Constitution?

(c) Congress does not have the power to require a party selling personal property, within the state, to make a written note or memorandum of the contract, and to punish him by fine and imprisonment for a failure to do so?

(2) Did the statute cover sales made at the Union Stock Yards?

Decision: (a) "The tax is not on the property or on the sale thereof. * * * The tax is in effect a duty or excise laid upon the privilege, opportunity or facility offered at boards of trade or exchange for the transaction of the business mentioned in the Act. It is not a tax upon business itself which is so transacted, but it is a duty upon the facilities made use of and actually employed in the transaction of the business, and separate from the business itself." And it is a constitutional exercise of the powers of taxation granted to Congress.

(b) "In this case there is that uniformity which the constitution requires. The tax or duty is uniform throughout the United States, and is uniform, or in other words, equal, upon all who avail themselves of the privileges or facilities offered at the exchanges, and it is not necessary in order to be uniform that the tax should be levied upon all who make sales of the same kind of things, whether at an exchange or elsewhere."

(c) "In holding that the tax under consideration is a tax on the privilege used in making sales at an exchange, we thereby hold that it is not a tax upon the memorandum required by the statute upon which the stamp is to be placed. The Act does not assume in any manner to interfere with the laws of the state in relation to the contract of sale. The memorandum required does not contain all the essentials of a contract to sell. It need not be signed and it need not contain the name of the vendee or the terms of payment. The statute does not render a sale void without the memorandum or stamp, which by the laws of the state would otherwise be valid. * * * It provides for a written memorandum containing the matters mentioned, simpy as a means of identifying the sale and for collecting the tax by means of the required stamp, and for that purpose it secures by proper penalties the making of the memorandum."

(2) "We cannot see any real distinction sufficient in substance to call for a different decision between the Union Stock Yards and an exchange or board of trade. We think it is a 'similar place' within the meaning of the statute under consideration." Therefore, the plaintiffs in error were properly convicted of violating the statute.

NILES, COLLECTOR, v. CENTRAL, ETC., INSURANCE CO.
NILES, COLLECTOR, v. OHIO UNDERWRITERS MUTUAL FIRE INS. CO.

(U. S. Circuit Court of Appeals, Sixth Cir., 1918)

(252 Fed. 564)

Record: Act of October 22, 1914. Action to recover taxes paid. Judgment for plaintiffs, and defendant brings error, affirmed.

Facts: The two insurance companies were incorporated under the laws of Ohio, without capital stock or stockholders, doing only a mutual fire insurance business, and that only with their members all of whom and who alone are their policyholders. The section of the act applicable provides: "That purely Co-operative or Mutual fire insurance companies or associations carried on by the members thereof for the protection of their own property and not for profit, shall be exempted from the tax herein provided."

Question: Must policies issued by these companies be stamped for one-half of one per cent on each dollar premium as provided under the Act, or do the companies come within the exemption clause?

Decision: These insurance companies, organized under the laws of Ohio, without capital stock and insuring property only of their members, are within the exemption of the Act, and not subject to the stamp tax on their policies imposed thereby, although under the state statute they may and do charge a cash premium in advance, and maintain a reserve on which they incidentally earn interest.

NORTH PENNSYLVANIA R. CO. v. PHILADELPHIA & R. RY. CO.

(Supreme Court of Pennsylvania, May 3, 1915)

(249 Pa. 326; 95 Atl. 100)

Record: Act of October 3, 1913. Assumpsit to recover amount of income tax paid by the plaintiff. Judgment for plaintiff on demurrer, and defendant appeals. Affirmed.

Facts: Before the passage of the Act of 1913, the plaintiff leased its road and equipment to the defendant, and, in the lease, the lessee covenanted to pay all taxes and assessments "upon the yearly payments herein agreed to be made by the party of the second part to the first party of the first part * * * for the payment and collection of which * * * the said party of the first part would otherwise be liable and accountable under any lawful authority whatever." The plaintiff paid to the government under the Federal Act an income tax upon the rent received from the defendant, and the defendant refused to reimburse the plaintiff.

Question: Is the lessee liable to the lessor for the income tax on the rent paid to the lessor under a lease in which the lessee covenanted to pay all taxes and assessments upon the yearly payments which were to be paid to the lessor?

Decision: "This clause is certainly broad enough to cover the income tax, payable out of and assessed upon the 'yearly payments agreed to be made.' The same paragraph provides that the defendant shall also pay the taxes and assessments upon the capital stock of the plaintiff. It was the apparent intention of the parties, that plaintiff should receive the amounts stipulated without deduction by reason of any tax, charge, or assessment of any kind. At the time the lease was made, there was no such thing as a Federal income tax, but the words 'taxes and assessments' are sufficiently broad to cover such tax." Therefore, the plaintiff, who has paid the income tax on the rent, is entitled to reimbursement from the defendant, the lessee.

NORTHERN CENTRAL RY. CO. v. JACKSON
(U. S. Supreme Court, Feb. 1, 1869)
(74 U. S. 268)

Record: Pennsylvania Tax Act, and Federal Act of 1864. Action to recover on interest coupons. Judgment for plaintiff (Fed. Case 7,142), and defendant brings error. Affirmed.

Facts: Defendant company refused to pay the plaintiff, Jackson, the full amount of certain matured coupons, but offered to pay the amount less the tax of five per centum per annum to the United States, and a further tax of three mills per dollar of principal claimed to be due to the state of Pennsylvania; which offer was refused. The defendant was incorporated and had a line of road in both Pennsylvania and Maryland. The bonds to which the coupons involved here were attached were a lien on all its property in both states.

Questions: (1) Was the defendant entitled to deduct from the amount of the coupons the Pennsylvania tax?

(2) Was the defendant entitled to deduct the Federal tax?

Decision: (1) The deducting of the Pennsylvania tax was not permissible because, since the bonds were secured by property in two states, this would be giving effect to Acts of the Pennsylvania Legislature upon property beyond its jurisdiction.

(2) The Federal tax deduction could not be permitted for the reason that it was believed to be not the intent of Congress under the Act of June 30, 1864, to impose an income tax on nonresident aliens.

NORTHERN PACIFIC RAILWAY CO. v. LYNCH, COLL.
(U. S. District Court, D. of Minn, March 22, 1920)
(Not reported)

Record: Act of August 5, 1909. Suit to recover tax paid under protest with interest. Judgment for plaintiff.

Facts: "The item, interest on advances * * * $1,603,-707.50, was interest accrued before January 1, 1909, on advances which the plaintiff made for construction of the railway of the Spokane, Portland & Seattle Railway Co. * * * The interest accruing on the advances was not entered up either on plaintiff's books or of those of the Spokane, Portland & Seattle Railway Co. until the construction work was completed in 1911, when the advances made by the Northern Pacific Railway Co. with interest were repaid.''

Question: Was interest, which accrued prior to 1909, but was paid in 1911, income within the provisions of the Act of August 5, 1909?

Decision: ''The item was definitely ascertained and vested in the plaintiff before the first day of January, 1909, and was on that day the property of the plaintiff. The court directs judgment in favor of the plaintiff against the defendant in the sum of $16,040.98, together with interest at the rate of 6 per cent from the 12th day of September, 1917, the date of plaintiff's payment to defendant under protest.'' The interest accrued before the effective date of the Act, and paid after that date, was not income subject to the tax under the Act.

NORTHERN RAILWAY CO. OF NEW JERSEY v. LOWE, COLLECTOR
(U. S. Circuit Court of Appeals, Second Cir., Feb. 13, 1918)
(250 Fed. 856)

Record: Act of October 3, 1913. Action to recover taxes paid under protest. Judgment for defendant, and plaintiff brought error. Affirmed. Judgment was affirmed on decision in Rensselaer & Saratoga R. R. Co. v. Irwin (249 Fed. 726, 161 C. C. A. 636).

Decision: A railroad company, although not engaged in business, but which has leased all of its property for a long term or for the life of its franchise, the rental to be paid by the lessee as interest on its bonds and a fixed dividend on its stock, direct to the bondholders and stockholders, is subject to tax on such amounts, because considered ''corporate income'' of the lessor corporation.

NORTHERN TRUST CO. v. LEDERER, COLLECTOR
(U. S. Circuit Court of Appeals, Third Cir., January 7, 1920)
(262 Fed. 52)

Record: Revenue Act of 1916. Action by Northern Trust Co. and Henry R. Zesinger, executors under the will of Lewis W.

Klahr, deceased, against Lederer, collector of internal revenue, to recover Federal estate taxes paid under protest upon assessment by the Commissioner. Judgment for plaintiffs (257 Fed. 812). Defendant brings error. Judgment affirmed. Petition for writ of certiorari by defendant denied May 3, 1920, by U. S. Supreme Court without comment.

Facts: The tax was assessed on decedent's estate under the provisions of the estate tax law in the Act of September 8, 1916. The statute in question provides for the determination of net estate subject to tax by stating the various items that are deductible from gross estate among which are, Sec. 203 a (1), "Such amounts for funeral expenses, administration expenses, claims against the estate, * * *, and such other charges against the estate as are allowed by the laws of the jurisdiction * * * under which the estate is being administered." Section 5 of the Collateral Inheritance Tax of the General Assembly of Pennsylvania, of May 6, 1887, provides that "before the executor or administrator shall pay any legacy or share in the distribution of an estate subject to the collateral inheritance tax, he shall deduct therefrom the tax prescribed," etc. The executors claimed that in ascertaining the net estate of decedent for purposes of the Federal estate tax there should have been deducted from gross estate the collateral inheritance tax of $39,450.92 due and subsequently paid the Commonwealth of Pennsylvania. If this had been allowed the Federal estate tax would have been reduced by $2,331.56.

Questions: Is the collateral inheritance tax paid the State of Pennsylvania, an administration expense, a claim against the estate, or one of such other charges against the estate as are allowed by said State, so as to be deductible from gross estate for purposes of determining net taxable estate on which to base the Federal estate tax, as provided for in Sec. 203 (a) (1) of the Act of September 8, 1916?

Decision: State collateral inheritance tax is deductible from gross estate for assessment of Federal Estate Tax imposed by Act of September 8, 1916. The court in the opinion in substance states that it is conceded that the Federal tax involved is a tax that relates not to an interest to which some person has succeeded by inheritance, bequest or devise, but an interest which has ceased by reason of death; and it is imposed not upon the interest of the recent owner or upon his privilege to dispose of it, but upon the transfer of the interest in its devolution. In analyzing the character of the Pennsylvania Collateral Inheritance Tax the court states that, if it is an estate tax similar to the Federal law and therefore a "charge" against the estate "allowed" in its settlement by the laws of Pennsylvania, then the refusal of the collector to deduct the amount from gross estate was unwarranted. If, on the other hand, it is a tax charged not against the estate but against the legatee as a condition imposed upon the transfer of the legacy, then the net estate, determined without deducting the State Tax, was properly computed. In determining the nature of the Pennsylvania Collateral Inheritance Tax, the court in the opinion said, that it was not necessary to go beyond a consideration of the Act itself and the interpretations thereof made by the Pennsylvania courts, that the decision of the Supreme Court of the State construing a statute of its own state are binding on this court in a case of this kind. After quoting the case of Knight's Estate, 261 Pa. 537 (104 Atl. 765); Jackson v. Myers, 257 Pa. 104 (101 Atl. 341) and other cases, the court said: "From these decisions it appears to be settled in Pennsylvania that the collateral inheritance tax of that state is an estate tax, not a legacy tax, and that as such it is levied upon and made a charge against the estate." For this reason the court held that the State Inheritance Tax should have been allowed as a deduction from gross estate before the imposition of the Federal estate tax.

NORTHERN TRUST CO. v. McCOACH, COLLECTOR
(U. S. District Court, E. D. Penn., July 14, 1914)
(215 Fed. 991)

Record: Act of August 5, 1909. Action at law to recover taxes paid under protest on net income under Sec. 38 of this Act. Judgment for defendant.

Facts: Corporation Tax Act of August 5, 1909, provided for a tax on the net income of corporations and authorized the deduction of all sums paid by corporations within the year for taxes imposed under the authority of the United States or any state. Plaintiff corporation made return of income under the Act and included as a deduction a tax imposed by the State of Pennsylvania upon its shares of stock under an Act levying a tax upon the shares of stock of certain specified classes of corporations, which included the plaintiff. The Pennsylvania statute provided that after the tax rate on each share is determined by the State Auditor, it shall be the duty of the executive officers of the corporation to post the tax settlements in the corporation's place of business, and within a specified time, the corporation, at its option, shall either pay the total amount of the tax out of its general funds or collect the same from its stockholders and pay the amount into the state treasury. The Act further declared that, if the corporation's officers fail to comply with the Act, they shall be adjudged in default, and as a penalty the corporation shall be responsible to the state for the tax assessed against the stockholders.

Question: Are these taxes paid by the corporation deductible from gross income in making return of income under the Corporation Tax Act of 1909?

Decision: "The criterion or test, or at least one criterion or test in cases such as this, is payment by the corporation, and the payment must have been for a 'tax imposed' upon the corporation. Plaintiff is a national banking institution. The State of Pennsylvania is without power to levy a tax upon the capital of national banks. It has, however, the power to levy a tax on the property of its own citizens, and can do so, notwithstanding that this property may exist in the form of shares of stock in national banks. This it did. Payment by the corporation was merely the exercise of an option and was not an obligation." The taxes paid by the corporation were assessed against the property of the individual stockholders, and not against the corporation or its property, and hence were not deductible from gross income in its return of income under the Act.

NYE JENKS CO. v. TOWN OF WASHBURN et al.
(U. S. Circuit Court, Nov. 11, 1903)
(125 Fed. 817)

Record: Rev. Stat., Sec. 3224. (U. S. Comp. St. 1901, p. 2088.) Suit in equity to enjoin the collection of a tax. Bill dismissed.

Decision: "This is a suit in equity to enjoin the collection of a tax upon personal property, and is in violation of the positive provision of the law of Congress (Section 3224, Rev. St. [U. S. Comp. St. 1901, p. 2088]) which provides that no suit for the purpose of restraining the assessment or collection of any tax shall be maintained in any court, and also is contrary to many decisions of the Supreme Court of the United States on the same subject. * * * The plaintiff has an adequate remedy in the law, by paying the tax, and bringing a suit at law to recover back the money. It is contrary to every principle of equity jurisprudence that the collection of taxes on personal property should be stayed by injunction."

OAHU R. & L. Co. v. PRATT
(Supreme Court of Hawaii, March 25, 1902)
(14 Haw. 126)

Record: Hawaiian Act of 1901. Original submission under the statute. Defendant claims right to collect income tax of the plaintiff. Judgment for plaintiff.

Facts: The Minister of the Interior had entered into a contract with the plaintiff's assignor that no taxes should be levied by the Hawaiian Government for twenty years upon the property of the plaintiff's assignor, "which shall be fairly necessary to the reasonable construction, maintenance and operation of the said railroad or railroads." This exemption was authorized by the legislature. The plaintiff has been assessed on income derived from property which defendant admits is fairly necessary to the reasonable construction, maintenance and operation of the railroad. It has also been assessed on income derived from wharfage collected from vessels using the plaintiff's wharves, from storage collected from persons using plaintiff's warehouse, from the use of plaintiff's scales by others, and from a subsidy received from the government. The wharves, warehouses and scales were used in connection with the railroad.

Questions: (1) Is the plaintiff exempt from taxation on its income derived from property which is exempt?

(2) Is the plaintiff exempt from taxation on its income derived from wharfage, storage, scales or subsidy where the wharves and

warehouses were built to facilitate the operation of its railroad which is exempt?

Decision: (1) "The real question is whether or not a tax on the income is a tax on the property from which the income is derived * * * . 'An annual tax upon the annual value or annual user of real estate appears to us the same in substance as an annual tax on the real estate, which would be paid out of the rent or income, * * *.' Pollock v. Farmers' Loan & Trust Co., 157 U. S. 429. It is clear that a tax on the income derived from exempt property would be in 'substance and effect' a tax on the property producing the income and a violation of the terms of the contract, existing between the plaintiff and the Government of Hawaii, exempting such property for twenty years." Therefore, the income from the exempt property is not taxable.

(2) "The fact that an additional and incidental use is made of the wharves and warehouses in excess of that for railroad purposes cannot operate to take these appliances out of the exemption so long as the principal use thereof is for railroad purposes."

OLD COLONY R. CO. v. GILL
SAME v. MALLEY
(U. S. District Court, Mass., June 28, 1916)
(257 Fed. 220)

Record: Act of August 5, 1909. Action at law to recover taxes paid under protest on net income under Sec. 38 of this Act. Judgment for plaintiffs.

Facts: Old Colony R. Co. leased its roads to the N. Y., N. H. & H. R. R. Co. The latter Company operated the demised roads during 1909 to 1912, as lessee, and not as agent. Corporation taxes imposed by the Act of August 5, 1909, were assessed against the lessor company which it paid under protest and now seeks to recover.

Question: Was plaintiff corporation "doing business" within meaning of Act of 1909 so as to make it subject to tax?

Decision: A company is not "doing business" within the meaning of the provisions of the Corporation Tax Act of August 5, 1909, when such company acts merely as a lessor and not as principal.

The plaintiff corporation was allowed to recover the amount of taxes which it had paid.

In re OPINION OF THE JUSTICES
(Supreme Court of New Hampshire, March 1, 1915)
(93 Atl. 311)

Record: Opinion of the Justices of the Supreme Court of New Hampshire, with respect to the constitutionality of a proposed bill. Held, nothing in proposed law that would violate any provision of the Constitution.

Facts: Sections 1 and 2 of a proposed bill in the Legislature of New Hampshire, read as follows: "Sec. 1. Personal estate liable to be taxed shall include money received during the year preceding the first day of April by each person as interest or dividends upon bonds, notes, interest bearing credits, certificates of shares, or interest on ownership in corporations, associations, joint-stock companies, trusts, and other organizations, and stocks not taxed to him, except dividends received from money deposited in New Hampshire savings banks."

Question: Would the above statute be unconstitutional if enacted by the Legislature upon any of the following grounds: (1) that it exempts certain dividends, (2) that it is double taxation, or (3) that to measure the tax by the amount of money received is not a reasonable measure?

Decision: In the opinion of the Justices, 76 N. H. 609, it was held that the Legislature may exempt from taxation certain classes of property.

A tax on money received as interest or dividends on specified securities and corporate stock at a "uniform rate" is valid if imposed at the same rate in proportion to value as is imposed on other property in the taxing district, for the tax is then proportional and reasonable, and within the power of the Legislature to impose. A statute that imposes a tax on dividends declared by corporations, in which the property represented by the stock is taxed to the corporation, does not present any question of direct double taxation to the same individual. So far as money at interest is concerned, the element of double taxation involved in the taxation of the debt to the creditor and the property in which the loan is invested by the debtor does not render the taxation of either illegal, and taxation of interest paid over to and in the hands of the creditor is not illegal. "It is a fundamental principle that the same property shall not be subject to a double tax, payable by the same party, either directly or indirectly." A tax upon dividends declared by a corporation and also upon the property represented by the stock is not a tax objectionable as double taxation, for where a corporation pays out the profit to its stock holders as dividends, it pays no tax thereon.

Whether money on hand or money received during the year shall be taken as the measure of the property to be taxed, is a legislative and not a judicial question. The power to establish rules by which each individual's just and equal proportion of a tax shall be determined is largely left to the Legislature in its sound discretion. As to the selection of proper subjects for taxation, the power of the Legislature is supreme.

"It may be said that the proposed tax is, in effect, an income tax. An income tax is generally understood to be a tax at an arbitrary rate—an excise tax. But the fact that this tax in certain of its features resembles an income tax does not place it beyond the legislative power of classification. The failure to tax all incomes would not be a constitutional objection. It is unnecessary now to express an opinion as to the validity of the taxation of incomes, for the proposed tax merely follows and taxes in the hands of the stockholder property which would have been taxed to the corporation if it were not distributed as a dividend." The court, therefore, held that such an Act would not be unconstitutional, that it was within the power of the legislature to exempt certain classes of property, that to tax the dividends declared by a corporation, where the corporation is taxed, was not double taxation, and that to measure the tax by the amount of money received rather than the amount on hand was a reasonable method of measure and within the power of the Legislature.

In re OPINION OF THE JUSTICES
(Supreme Judicial Court of Massachusetts, April 12, 1915)

(220 Mass. 613; 108 N. E. 570)

Record: Opinion of the Justices of the Supreme Judicial Court of Massachusetts ordered by the Senate and House of Representatives. Questions asked in pursuance of this order were answered in the negative.

Facts: "* * * The present system having failed to result in proportional and reasonable taxation upon the residents of, and estates lying within, the Commonwealth; and having effected extremely unequal and disproportionate distribution of the burden of taxation, * * * some change is imperatively demanded." In order to facilitate the changes sought (see questions below) the Supreme Judicial Court was requested to place its interpretation upon c. 1, Sec. 1, Art. 4 of the Constitution of Massachusetts which contains the entire grant to tax.

Questions: (1) Can the General Court enact a law providing "that certain forms of property shall be assessed upon their market value and other forms of property upon a certain number of times their annual value, the total assessments thus reached to be taxed at a rate uniform for each town or city; provided that the figure or multipliers used be fixed by some state authority, or by the General Court itself, with a view to securing a stricter parity of contribution, having regard to either the capital or the annual value of property and the taxes levied upon it, between the different classes of property and their owners in this commonwealth, than is possible under the present system?

(2) Can the General Court, under the provision of the Constitution authorizing it to impose and levy reasonable duties and excises, impose and levy a reasonable duty or excise upon incomes derived from intangible personal property, such as money, on deposit or at interest, debts due the taxpayer, public stock and securities and stocks, bonds, notes or other evidences of indebtedness of corporations, domestic and foreign?

(3) If so, can the General Court grant to the holders thereof the privilege (subject to the payment of a reasonable excise or duty thereon): (a), of establishing the existence of such facts by filing with the tax commissioner evidence thereof satisfactory to him; and having established such facts, (b), of procuring the registration of such securities by the tax commissioner to indicate that they are exempt from taxation?

(4) Can the General Court under the Constitution provide that moneys due an inhabitant of this Commonwealth from any foreign

corporation or any person or persons not residing within the Commonwealth, and all stock, bonds, notes or other evidences of indebtedness issued by foreign corporations and held by inhabitants of this commonwealth shall have no situs within the commonwealth for purposes of taxation and shall not be taxed under the provisions of Parts I and II of Chapter 490 of the Acts of the year 1909? And can the General Court then levy a reasonable duty or excise upon the income derived by inhabitants of the Commonwealth from the foregoing classes of property?

Decision: "The answer to all these questions depends upon the interpretation of C. 1, Sec. 1, Art. 4 of the Constitution of Massachusetts, whereby the General Court is empowered 'to impose and levy proportional and reasonable assessments, rates, and taxes, upon all the inhabitants of, and persons, resident, and estates lying within the said commonwealth; and also to impose and levy reasonable duties and excises upon any produce, goods, wares, merchandise, and commodities, whatsoever, brought into, produced, manufactured, or being within the same.' These words contain the entire grant to tax."

(1) A tax on property must be "proportional and reasonable" while an excise on a commodity need only be reasonable. A general property tax, in order to be proportional must be distributed so that the amount to be raised shall be contributed by the taxpayers according to the taxable real and personal estate of each; each taxpayer being obliged to bear only such part of the general burden as the property owned by him bears to the whole sum to be raised. The proposed bill does not rest the assessment of taxes upon any uniform method. "It enables the legislature or a public officer to readjust the multipliers according to a fluctuating judgment of what may be desirable even to the extent of accomplishing in practice great disproportion. The theory behind the bill would permit manifold classifications of diverse kinds of real as well as personal estate. If extended to its logical conclusions, it would be difficult to trace any remaining constitutional protection to the taxpayers." Therefore, the court answered this question in the negative.

(2) "These provisions of the proposed bill constitute a selection of specific articles of property to be assessed by themselves at an unvarying rate, differing from the rate which is assessed upon

other property. It is the arbitrary designation of a certain class of property without reference to any rule of proportion and without regard to the relative share of public charges, which it should bear as compared with that borne by other property and without regard to any special benefit accruing to the selected property. Such an imposition cannot be sustained under the clause of the constitution relating to excises. A tax upon the income of property is in reality a tax upon the property itself. Income derived from property is also property. Property by income produces its kind. The character of the tax cannot be changed by calling it an excise tax and not a property tax." The General Court can not impose an excise tax upon incomes derived from intangible property.

(3) (a) This question was expressly left open in the opinion of the Justices, 195 Mass. 607, and was not considered here because such consideration was not considered necessary.

(b) This part of the question is answered in 195 Mass. 607. "Briefly stated, the ground is that, even if there is a right to exempt this class of property wholly from taxation, a partial exemption conditional upon the property exempted contributing an arbitrary and disproportional percentage of its value, is not authorized. The mere right to hold and own such property cannot be made the subject of an excise."

(4) "As has been pointed out in answer to the second question, a tax upon the income of property is a tax upon the property itself. It is obvious, from the tenor of the question and from the phraseology of the bill, that the tax proposed is levied as an excise and not as a property tax. It does not purport to be in any sense proportional." Therefore, this question as well as the foregoing questions, was answered in the negative.

OSGOOD v. TAX COMMISSIONER
(Supreme Judicial Court of Massachusetts, Feb. 28, 1920)
(126 N. E. 371)

Record: Massachusetts Income Tax Act (St. 1916, C. 269, par. 20). On report on the petition, answer, and agreed statement of facts without decision to the Supreme Judicial Court. Judgment for complainant.

Facts: On January 1, 1916, complainant was the owner of 2,300 shares of stock of the Draper Company. In June, 1916, the directors of that corporation caused a new corporation to be organized, to be called the Draper Corporation, which voted to issue its stock for that of the Draper Company. Complainant accepted this offer, and received 4,125 shares of stock in the new corporation for the 2,300 shares of stock of the old corporation. The tax commissioner assessed a tax upon the gain, which he ascertained by subtracting the aggregate par value of the shares in the old company on January 1, 1916, from the aggregate par value of the shares of the new company at the time of the exchange in July of that year.

Question: Was the complainant subject to tax as a result of this transaction under the statute which provided that "the excess of the gains over the losses received by the taxpayer from purchases or sales of intangible personal property, whether or not said taxpayer is engaged in the business of dealing in such property, shall be taxed at the rate of three per cent per annum?"

Decision: "Whether the disposal of the stock in the old company be treated as a strict sale or not, there seems to be no escape from holding that the procurement of the stock in the new corporation was a purchase. * * * The gain had materialized by procuring title to a wholly different kind of stock in a new corporation, whose market value was definite and ascertained. The complainant had wholly parted with the old and become the legal owner of the new property. It follows that the tax on this gain was lawful."

OVERLAND SIOUX CITY CO. INC., v. CLEMENS
CLARK v. CLEMENS
(Superior Court of Iowa, November 16, 1920)
(179 N. W. 954)

Record: Revenue Act of 1917. Two actions at law, one for the recovery of part of purchase price paid for stock, and the other for recovery of part of dividends paid. Judgment for defendant. and plaintiffs appeal. Affirmed.

Facts: One of the plaintiffs is a corporation organized under the laws of Iowa, July 1, 1914, and the other a purchaser of stock of this corporation. Prior to July, 1917, all the stock of the plaintiff corporation was owned by the four directors, two of whom are the defendants in this case. Plaintiff's fiscal year ended July 1, 1917, and it made its tax return to the Federal Government on that date. On July 1, 1917, the plaintiff company had on hand a large surplus, out of which a substantial dividend was declared, leaving on hand a part of the surplus. On July 27 following, one of the directors, a plaintiff in the case, bought the shares of two others, defendants in the case, paying therefor to each one-fifth of the earnings and surplus on hand, and in addition thereto $150 per share for the stock held by each. All Federal taxes under then existing Acts had been provided for when the dividend mentioned above was declared. On October 3, 1917, following, the War Profits Tax Act was approved, which provided for the taxation of every corporation during the year of 1917—that is from December 31, 1916. Under this Act plaintiff corporation was compelled to pay a war profits tax covering the period from December 31, 1916, to July 1, 1917. None of the parties to these actions had any knowledge or intimation in July of 1917, that the Act of Congress approved October 3, 1917, was contemplated.

Questions: (1) May the plaintiff director, who purchased the stock of the defendants, recover part of the purchase price on the ground that because of a mutual mistake he paid too much?

(2) May plaintiff corporation recover from defendants any portion of the war profit taxes paid under the above circumstances, on the ground that the Act of October 3, 1917, was retroactive in effect, and by mutual mistake of law and fact, a dividend was declared on the stock for a sum larger than should have been declared, and owing to such mutual mistake, there was paid to each defendant an amount in excess of that which might have been legally paid as a dividend on said stock?

Decision: (1) In the sale of the stock by defendants there was no mistake of fact or law. "Each was aware of everything then known concerning the company's business and its property. None of the parties appear to have been possessed of prophetic powers. If, in negotiating for the sale of stock, the earning and surplus were taken into account, this does not appear to have been on the theory that defendants, as shareholders, had any legal claim or interest therein." Title to earnings or surplus does not pass to shareholders, except through the declaration of a dividend or the distribution of the company's assets. Earnings and surplus on hand enhance the value of shares of stock. Plaintiffs considered these facts when buying the stock, but what might happen in the future was not a matter of negotiation. The purchaser of the stock took chances on the change of laws as much as on the corporation's continued prosperity. The parties acted in good faith, and, as there existed no restrictions on the transfer of the stock, the defendants parted with and the purchasers acquired absolute title to the stock.

(2) Inasmuch as the Act does not pretend to undo anything that has been done before by any corporation nor charge the tax on any particular fund or income of any particular year it was merely a future charge on the corporation. No part of the tax was retroactive except that the unit for determining the tax was the income of 1917. The exaction of the tax was prospective and cannot be construed to have affected in any manner the legality of dividends paid. It was, therefore, held that neither the individual nor the corporation plaintiff was entitled to recover anything from the defendants.

PACIFIC BLDG. & LOAN ASSN. v. HARTSON, COLLECTOR
(U. S. District Court, W. D. Washington, S. D., Jan. 15, 1913)
(201 Fed. 1011)

Record: Act of August 5, 1909. Suit in equity asking refund of taxes paid under protest on net income under Sec. 38 of this Act. Demurrer to complaint sustained.

Facts: Plaintiff is a building and loan association organized under the laws of Washington. Its by-laws and charter provide for the loaning of funds of the corporation to nonmembers, for issuing preferred or guaranteed interest paying stock; and allow the directors, upon finding that the income of the association cannot be loaned profitably, to "cancel any outstanding certificates of general stock not borrowed upon," paying the holder the book value of the stock so cancelled, thereby authorizing them to retire any and all stock in their discretion.

Question: Is the corporation exempt from the payment of taxes under the Act as a corporation organized for the mutual benefit of its members?

Decision: Complainant cannot be said to be a corporation "organized * * * exclusively for the mutual benefit of the members, no part of the net income of which inures to the benefit of any private stockholders or individuals." If this corporation were dissolved the assets of the corporation would, unquestionably, be distributed pro rata among the then shareholders. Therefore, as to its present members it is a corporation having a capital stock represented by shares, although by the maturing of its stock and the retirement of shareholders, its shareholding membership is constantly changing. It is not exempt from taxation under the Act of August 5, 1909.

In re PACIFIC GUANO & F. CO.
(Supreme Court of Hawaii, March 27, 1905)
(16 Haw. 552)

Record: Hawaiian Act of 1901. Appeals by the assessor from action of tax appeal court in refusing to sustain his assessments. Reversed.

Facts: The taxpayer is a corporation organized for "exploiting the guano beds on Laysan Island." It obtained from an expert an estimate of the probable available guano there, and bought the beds upon that estimate. It discovered this year that the guano bed was almost exhausted and that there was only one-half what the expert had estimated. In making out its income tax return, the company wrote off a large sum to the account of profit and loss, because of this discovery. The assessor refused to allow the deduction.

Question: Is a loss resulting from an over-estimation of the value of a guano bed at the time it was bought, a loss occurring at the time the actual value is discovered years later?

Decision: "We are unable to regard this loss as one which occurred during the year 1903, when it was written off on the books of the taxpayer. The guano had not depreciated in value; none of it had been lost. It did not exist to the extent supposed at the time of the purchase. The income from the collecting and selling ceased when the deposits were removed. The loss which was finally ascertained upon the termination of that business did not occur at the time when it was learned that the guano supply had failed. but it occurred when the purchase money was paid." The action of the assessor in refusing to allow the deductions, therefore, was approved.

PACIFIC INSURANCE CO. v. SOULE
(U. S. Supreme Court, December Term, 1868)
(74 U. S. 433; 7 Wall. 433)

Record: Act of June 30, 1864, and amendment of July 13, 1866. Suit to recover excise tax paid under compulsion. Upon argument on defendant's demurrer to the complaint, the opinions of the Circuit Court were opposed upon seven questions. Review asked on certificate of division from this court. On the view taken by the Supreme Court the determination of two of said questions held sufficient for disposing of the case. Held that the tax involved is not a direct tax; that it was obligatory on plaintiff to pay it.

Facts: The plaintiff, a corporation engaged in the business of insurance in California, made returns upon the amounts insured, renewed, etc., by it, upon its premiums and assessments, and upon its dividends, undistributed sums, and income; all as required by statute. The different kinds of income returned had been received by the company in coined money (the currency of California) and the amounts as returned were the amounts in that form of currency. The aggregate tax under the statute upon this sum of coin was $53.76. The assessor, under protest of the insurance company, added to the amounts so returned, the difference in value between legal tender currency and coined money during the time covered by the returns. Sec. 9 of the Act required that if the return was in coined money the assessor should reduce the amount to legal tender currency. The tax thus increased by the assessor aggregated the sum of $7,365. Upon seizure by the Collector to enforce payment, payment was made under protest. Suit below was to recover the amount alleged to have been wrongfully exacted.

Questions: (1) Does Sec. 9 of the Revenue Act of July, 1866, deny to a person who has received in coined money income or moneys subject to tax, the right to return the amount thereof in the currency in which it was actually received and to pay the tax thereon in legal tender currency, and thus require the difference between coined money and legal tender currency to be added to his return when made in coined money and payment by him of the tax on the amount thus increased?

(2) Are the taxes paid by plaintiff direct taxes within the meaning of the Constitution?

Decision: (1) Difference between income returned on basis of coined money and amount thereof as computed in legal tender currency was held taxable. When any person, whose income or other moneys subject to tax or duty has been received in coined money, makes his return to the assessor, Sec. 9 of the Internal Revenue Act of July 13, 1866, is to be construed as denying him the right to return the amount thereof in the currency in which it was actually received, and to pay the tax or duty thereon in legal tender currency, and is to be construed to require that the difference between coined money and legal tender currency shall be added to his return when made in coined money; and that he shall pay the tax or duty upon the amount thus increased. Therefore, the plaintiff can not recover the tax paid on the difference between coined money and legal tender currency.

(2) The tax imposed on insurance companies by Act of June 30, 1864, and amendment of July 13, 1866, is not a direct tax. The court calls attention to the several provisions of the Constitution relating to taxation by Congress, namely, that representatives shall be apportioned among the several states according to their respective numbers; that Congress shall have the power to lay and collect taxes, duties, imposts and excises, but all of these shall be uniform throughout the United States; that no capitation or other direct tax shall be laid unless in proportion to the census of enumeration hereinbefore directed to be taken; that no tax or duty shall be laid on articles exported from any state. The national Government is of limited jurisdiction and has no faculties but such as the Constitution gives it, and "whenever any act done under its authority is challenged, the proper sanction must be found in its charter, or the act is ultra vires and void," the court said. What are direct taxes, it is said, were elaborately argued by this court in Hylton v. United States, 3 Dallas, 171. In that case Justice Chase said that direct taxes contemplated by the Constitution are only two, "a capitation or poll tax, simply, without regard to property, profession, or any other circumstance, and a tax on land." The same views expressed in this case are adopted by Chancellor Kent and Justice Story in their examination of the subject. The opinion then proceeds to define "duties, imposts and excises" respectively. "If a tax on carriages kept for his own use by the owner

is not a direct tax," as was held in the case of Hylton v. United States, supra, "we can see no ground upon which a tax upon the business of an insurance company can be held to belong to that class of revenue charges. * * * To the question under consideration it must be answered that the tax to which it relates is not a direct tax, but a duty or excise, and that it was obligatory on the plaintiff to pay it."

PARK v. GILLIGAN, COLLECTOR
(U. S. District Court, S. D. Ohio, W. D.)
(Not reported)

Record: Revenue Act of 1916. Suit to recover taxes paid. Submitted upon agreed statement of facts.

Facts: Plaintiffs were stockholders in John D. Park & Sons Co.

(1) During 1916 this company received $85,000 in settlement of a claim for damages, under the anti-trust law, by way of loss of profit suffered from 1891 to 1904, which was in litigation long prior to March 1, 1913. This amount was apportioned among the stockholders, including the plaintiffs, and credited to them upon the books of the company. The evidence showed that practically all of the profits accruing to the company from March 1, 1913, to January 1, 1917, were paid out in other dividends, so that the $85,000 could not have been paid out of earnings. Also there was no evidence that the chose in action was of any greater value in 1916 than on March 1, 1913.

(2) In the year 1916, the earnings of the company were distributed by crediting them to the stockholders upon the company's books. The dividend was not segregated from the general assets. Plaintiffs drew against their credits and obtained money thereon.

Questions: (1) Was a dividend paid by a corporation in 1916 from money received in settlement of a chose of action arising before March 1, 1913, taxable to the stockholders as income of 1916?

(2) Were stockholders taxable upon dividends credited to them on the books of a corporation but not segregated from its general assets?

(3) Was plaintiff entitled to interest on the amount of taxes illegally exacted?

Decision: (1) Since the distribution of the sum realized from the compromise of the chose in action was not out of profits accrued since March 1, 1913, it was not taxable to the distributees as income. Such sum could not have been profits because all earnings of the company were paid out in other dividends.

(2) The crediting of the pro rata shares of the amount of the dividend declared from earnings to the respective accounts of the plaintiffs merely evidenced the indebtedness of the company to them and did not constitute income. "Income means actual cash or its equivalent received, as opposed to contemplated revenue due or unpaid." But since plaintiffs have waived their objection to these items, they will be charged with the tax upon the credits so received upon the company's books.

(3) The general rule that claimants are not entitled to interest against the United States does not apply to actions like the present, and plaintiffs are entitled to interest upon the amount erroneously exacted.

PEABODY v. EISNER, COLLECTOR
(U. S. Supreme Court, June 3, 1918)
(247 U. S. 347)

Record: Act of October 3, 1913. Action at law to recover taxes paid under protest on net income. Judgment for defendant. Plaintiff brought error. Affirmed.

Facts: Plaintiff owned 1,100 shares of the common stock of the Union Pacific Ry. Co., which company had large holdings of the common and preferred stock of the B. & O. Ry. Co. On March 2, 1914, the Union Pacific declared and paid an extra dividend upon each share of its common stock, amounting to $3 in cash, $12 in par value of preferred stock of the B. & O., and $22.50 in par value of the common stock of the same company. In his income tax return for 1914, plaintiff included as taxable income, $4.12 per share of this dividend and paid his tax on the basis of this return. Afterwards he was subjected to an additional assessment upon a valuation of the balance of his dividend, and this, having been paid under protest, is the subject of the present suit. Plaintiff contends that the entire earnings, income, gains and profits from all sources realized by the U. P. Ry. Co. from March 1, 1913, to March 2, 1914, remaining after the payment of prior charges, did not exceed $4.12 per share of the U. P. Common stock, and that the cash and B. & O. stock disposed of in the extra dividend (so far as they exceeded the value of $4.12 per share of Union Pacific) did not constitute a gain, profit or income of the Union Pacific, and, therefore, did not constitute a gain, profit or income of the plaintiff arising or accruing either in or for the year 1914 or for any period subsequent to March 1, 1913, the date when the Income Tax Law took effect.

Question: Are dividends from corporate earnings accrued prior to March 1, 1913, paid in stock of a corporation other than the paying corporation taxable to the stockholders receiving the same?

Decision: "In this case the plaintiff stands in the position of the ordinary stockholder, whose interest in the accumulated earnings and surplus of the company are not the same before as after the declaration of a dividend; his right being merely to have the assets devoted to the proper business of the corporation and to receive from the current earnings or accumulated surplus such dividends as the directors in their discretion may declare; and without power or right on his part to control that discretion. The dividend of B. & O. shares was not a stock dividend but a distribution in specie of a portion of the assets of the U. P., and is governed for all present purposes by the sale rule applicable to the distribution of a like value of money." The dividends paid in stock of another corporation being subject to tax, the plaintiff can not recover.

Note: Under the 1913 Act dividends declared and paid in the ordinary course by a corporation to its stockholders after March 1, 1913, whether from current earnings or from a surplus accumulated prior to that date, were taxable as income to the stockholder.

PEACOCK & CO. LTD. et al. v. PRATT, COLLECTOR

(U. S. Circuit Court of Appeals, Ninth Cir., Feb. 9, 1903)

(121 Fed. 772)

Record: Act No. 20 Session Laws, 1901, of Hawaiian Territory. Bill in equity to enjoin the collection of an income tax. Demurrer by defendant which was sustained and bill dismissed. Appeal to this court. Decree dismissing bill affirmed.

Facts: The statute provided for the taxation of all individual incomes over $1,000. Corporations were also required to pay an income tax, except "insurance companies taxed under authority of another Act."

Questions: (1) Does the tax violate the organic act of the territory?

(2) Is the Act unconstitutional under the Constitution of the United States?

Decision: (1) By the organic Act of the territory it was expressly provided that the "legislative power of the territory shall extend to all rightful subjects of legislation not inconsistent with the Constitution of the United States." Therefore, since taxation is the rightful subject of legislation, it does not violate the organic Act unless such taxation is repugnant to the Constitution of the United States.

(2) It is not unconstitutional. First, it does not come within the clause requiring taxes to be uniform throughout the United States for that restriction was applicable only to the taxing power of the United States. Second, it did not make any illegal discriminations in violation of the Fourteenth Amendment. The exception of the insurance companies was merely a classification and by the terms of the Act they paid their tax in another way. The $1,000 personal exemption provided for is valid on the grounds of public policy. Such personal exemptions from taxation are valid as long as they are reasonable and the amount is largely within the discretion of the legislature. The fact that judges' salaries were not expressly exempted by the Act would not make the whole Act unconstitutional, but the Act would be read as if such an exemption were written in the Act.

PECK & CO. v. LOWE, COLLECTOR
(U. S. Supreme Court, May 20, 1918)
(247 U. S. 165)

Record: Act of October 3, 1913. Action at law to recover taxes on net income paid under protest. Judgment for defendant (234 Fed. 125) and plaintiff brought error. Affirmed.

Facts: Plaintiff is a domestic corporation chiefly engaged in buying goods in the several states, shipping them to foreign states, and there selling them. In 1914 an income tax, computed on the aggregate net income from domestic and foreign business, was assessed against the plaintiff and paid under compulsion. The tax was levied under the Act of October 3, 1913, which provided for annually subjecting every domestic corporation to the payment of a tax of a specified per centum of its "entire net income arising or accruing from all sources during the preceding calendar year."

Question: Is an act which taxes a domestic corporation upon its net income derived from selling goods in foreign states, unconstitutional in that it seeks to levy a tax on exports contrary to the constitutional provision (Art. 1, Sec. 9, Cl. 5) that "no tax or duty shall be paid on articles exported from any State"?

Decision: The tax in question is not laid on articles in course of exportation or on anything which inherently or by the usages of commerce is embraced in exportation or any of its processes. On the contrary it is an income tax laid generally on net income. While it cannot be applied to any income which Congress has no power to tax, it is both nominally and actually a general tax. It is not laid on income from exportation because of its source, or in a discriminating way, but just as it is laid on other income. At most exportation is affected only indirectly and remotely. The tax is levied after exportation is completed, after all expenses are paid and losses adjusted, and after the recipient of the income is free to use it as he chooses. The plaintiff can not recover the tax which it paid on the income derived from selling goods in foreign states.

PENN MUTUAL LIFE INSURANCE CO. v. LEDERER, COLLECTOR

(Supreme Court of the U. S., April 19, 1920)
(252 U. S. 523)

Record: Act of October 3, 1913. Action to recover income tax for period from March 1st to December 31, 1913. District Court allowed recovery for the full amount with interest (247 Fed. 559). Circuit Court of Appeals for Third Circuit, holding that nothing was recoverable except a small item, reversed the judgment and awarded a new trial (258 Fed. 81). Writ of certiorari from Supreme Court allowed (250 U. S. 656). Decision of Circuit Court of Appeals affirmed.

Facts: The Penn Mutual Life Insurance Co., a purely mutual legal reserve company which issues level-premium insurance, was assessed upon the sum of $686,503, alleged to have been wrongly included as a part of its gross income, for the period from March 1 1913, to December 31, 1913. This sum equals the aggregate of the amounts paid during that period by the company to its policyholders in cash dividends which were *not* used by them during that period in payment of premiums. The several amounts making up this aggregate represent mainly a part of the so-called redundancy in premiums paid by the respective policyholders in some previous year or years. They are, in a sense, a repayment of that part of the premium previously paid which experience has proved was in excess of the amount which had been assumed would be required to meet the policy obligations (ordinarily termed losses) or the legal reserve and the expense of conducting the business.

Question: Does Sec. II G (b) of Act of October 3, 1913, exclude from gross income only those premium receipts which are actually or in effect paid by applying dividends or does it also permit the deduction of dividends paid by the petitioner to policyholders, and not applied to the payment of premiums?

Decision: "(c) Life Insurance companies—that is, both stock and strictly mutual—'shall not include as income in any year such portion of any actual premium received from any individual policyholders as shall have been paid back or credited to such individual policyholder, or treated as an abatement of premium of such individual policyholder, within such year.' (II G (b) Revenue Act of October 3, 1913). The Government contends, in substance, for the rule that in figuring the gross income of life insurance companies there shall be taken the aggregate of the year's net premium receipts made up separately for each policyholder. The Penn Mutual Co. contends for the rule that in figuring the gross income there shall be taken the aggregate full premiums received by the company less the aggregate of all dividends paid by it to any policyholder by credit upon a premium or by abatement of a premium, and also of all dividends whatsoever paid to any policyholder in cash whether applied in payment of a premium or not. The noninclusion clause

(c) above excludes from gross income those premium receipts which were actually or in effect paid by applying dividends. The company seeks to graft upon the clause so restricted a provision for what it calls nonincluding, but which in fact is deducting, all cash dividends not so applied."

The Government's position was sustained. "The noninclusion clause in the Act of October 3, 1913, was doubtless framed to define what amounts involved in dividends should be 'non-included' or deducted, and thus to prevent any controversy arising over the questions which had been raised under the Act of 1909." (Mutual Benefit Life Insurance Co. v. Herold, 198 Fed. 199, approved). The plaintiff can not exclude from its gross income the dividends paid in cash and not applied by the policy-holder to the payment of premiums. The clause excludes from gross income those premium receipts which were actually or in effect paid by applying dividends. This is the exclusion that was allowed the plaintiff by the government, and the plaintiff is not entitled to recover.

PENNSYLVANIA STEEL CO. et al, v. N. Y. C. RY. CO. et al

CENTRAL TRUST CO. OF N. Y. v. THIRD AVE. R. CO. et al

(U. S. Circuit Court of Appeals, Second Cir., July 18, 1912)

(198 Fed. 774)

Record: Act of August 5, 1909. Receivership proceedings. Application by the United States for orders requiring the receivers to make and file returns under the above act. Denied (193 Fed. 286.) Upon appeal, affirmed.

Facts: Question of law only.

Question: Are the receivers of an insolvent corporation, duly appointed by a court of equity, which corporation was not engaged in business when the taxing act was passed and has done no business since, required to make returns and pay taxes upon the income realized by them while acting as officers of the court and under its direction?

Decision: The court is of the opinion that the Act of August 5, 1909, is inapplicable to receivers. "The Act in all its provisions, clearly contemplates that the tax is to be paid by a corporation which is actually engaged in business as an actively operating concern.

It nowhere intimates that the tax can be collected unless the corporation is carrying on the business. In this case 'the officers of the corporation could not make the return required by the Act for the obvious reason that the corporation had carried on no business during the years 1909 and 1910, and, therefore, had received no income from any source. The receivers could not make the return for the reason that they were neither the corporation nor the representatives thereof. During their administration the company had not been carrying on corporation business and had received no income in that capacity. They were in possession as officers of the court and were subject to its orders'." The court refused to order the receiver to make and file returns.

PEOPLE ex rel. BARCALO MFG. CO. v. KNAPP et al.

(Court of Appeals of New York, July 15, 1919)

(227 N. Y. 64; 124 N. E. 107)

Record: Revenue Act of 1917, and New York Acts of June 4, 1917, and April 19, 1918. Proceedings in certiorari to review the action of Knapp et al. v State Tax Commissioner, in the assessment of taxes. Determinations of the Commission affirmed (175 N. Y. Supp. 337) and relator appealed. Affirmed. People ex rel. American Broom and Brush Co. v. Knapp et al. (175 N. Y. Supp. 337) was affirmed on the opinion in this case (227 N. Y. 574; 124 N. E. 900).

Facts: Under the New York Franchise Act, the relator was obligated to pay an annual franchise tax, to be computed by the tax commission upon the basis of "its net income" for the year, "which income is presumably the same as the income upon which such corporation is required to pay a tax to the United States." Sec. 209. The state tax commission, in assessing the relator, did not credit upon the amount of income the amount of excess profits tax assessed by the United States.

Question: Does "net income," as defined in the Act of October 3, 1917, include the amount of excess profits tax imposed by Congress?

Decision: Section 29 of the Act of 1917 does not affect the definition of the words "net income" as established by the statute. "It provides that in the case of the corporation, partnership or individual liable for the excess profits tax, the net income returned to the United States, shall in assessing the income tax upon that net income, be credited with the amount of the excess profits tax. The net income is not changed. A part of it equal to the sum of the excess profits tax is not, in such case, taxed." There is nothing in this Act allowing the net income to be credited with the amount of the excess profits tax. The decision of the Tax Commission refusing to allow a deduction of the amount of the Federal excess profits tax, in computing net income, is affirmed.

PEOPLE OF STATE OF ILLINOIS v. NORTHERN TRUST CO.

(Supreme Court of Illinois; October 27, 1919)

(289 Ill. 475; 124 N. E. 662)

Record: State Act of September 8, 1916, involved. Appeal by defendant from a judgment of Cook County Court in favor of plaintiff in a suit to subject property of decedent to an inheritance tax. Reversed.

Facts: Testator died November 17, 1917, leaving an estate valued by the inheritance tax appraiser at $2,871,151.71 which he disposed of by will. The County Court in assessing the state inheritance tax, refused to deduct the Federal estate tax paid by the executor, amounting to $316,432.40.

Question: In computing the state inheritance tax on the value of property passing by will of a testator is appellant entitled to have first deducted therefrom the Federal estate tax?

Decision: The court, in holding that the Federal estate tax should be deducted before assessing the state inheritance tax, said: The Federal estate tax is a charge or an expense against the estate of the decedent, rather than against the shares of the legatees or the distributees and as part of the expense of administration this tax should be deducted before computing the state inheritance tax, (quoting People v. Pasfield, 284 Ill. 450).

Comment: An opinion to the contrary is contained in the case of In re Bierstadt's Estate, (Hicks et al v. Comptroller of State), reported in 166, N. Y. Supp. 168.

PERRY v. NEWSOME

(U. S. District Court, District of North Carolina, June 12, 1869)
(Fed. Case No. 11009)

Record: Act of July 20, 1868. Motion by Perry, supervisor, for a rule against defendant, Newsome, who was a clerk of a North Carolina railroad, having custody of the books of the company for failing and refusing to produce certain books and papers of the railroad for examination by the supervisor, as provided in Sec. 49 of the Act of July 20, 1868. Rule granted by District Judge.

Facts: A copy of the summons served on defendant by the supervisor of internal revenue pursuant to the above mentioned section of said Act, was read in evidence and the affidavit of the supervisor that service was duly made and that defendant neglected and refused to comply therewith. The District Attorney asked that a rule be entered on defendant to show cause why an attachment should not issue as for contempt as provided in Sec. 14 of the Act of March 3, 1865, amended July 3, 1866. Question was raised by counsel for defendant as to the constitutionality of the law authorizing the examination of private books and papers.

Question: Is the provision of the Act in question authorizing the supervisor of internal revenue to examine private books and papers constitutional?

Decision: Acts of Congress and of our own State Legislature conferring this high power not only upon committees, but upon officers, to send for persons and papers to be examined in furtherance of a stated purpose, has been for so long a time acquiesced in, and so frequently indulged without the right having been seriously questioned in the courts, that it was now scarcely worth while seriously to debate the question. The rule requested was therefore granted.

PFISTER LAND CO. v. CITY OF MILWAUKEE

(Supreme Court of Wisconsin, Nov. 13, 1917)
(165 N. W. 23)

Record: Wisconsin Act of 1911. Action against the City of Milwaukee to recover taxes paid under protest. Judgment for plaintiff and defendant appealed. Reversed and remanded.

Facts: The plaintiff is a domestic corporation and owns mines in Michigan. Prior to the Act of 1911, it leased the mines for a term of years, the lessee agreeing to pay certain specified royalties annually on the ore taken out. The income taxes in question were levied on account of the moneys received as royalties. The Income Tax Act provided that the term "income" should include "all rent of real estate," and that the tax should be levied upon "rentals" received by any resident from sources within or without the state, and it allowed deductions for necessary expenses, and for depreciation of the property from which the income was derived.

Questions: (1) Are royalties paid by the lessees of mines to the owner income within the meaning of the Act, or are they converted capital?

(2) If income, do they constitute rent within the meaning of the Act?

(3) If so, can there be a deduction for depreciation in the value of the mine by reason of the taking out of the ore?

Decision: (1) It seems that the most important questions involved here have been practically decided in favor of the city by the Supreme Court of the United States in the case of Von Baumbach v. Sargent Land Co., 242 U. S. 503. "In that case * * * it was held, citing former decisions of the same court, that royalties paid by the lessees to the corporation owner by virtue of leases substantially involved in the present case were not to be viewed as the proceeds of property sold, but as rents, and hence fairly within the term "income" under the terms of the Corporation Tax Act. We are content to follow this high authority * * * ." The plaintiff can not recover the taxes paid on the royalties.

(2) "The fundamental principle on which these holdings are based is that by the contract between the parties the legal relation of landlord and tenant is created, and when that relation is created whatever is paid for the occupation, whether it be money or kind, is equally in substance, rent. It seems clear to us that the Legislature intended to include such revenues as these under the term 'rent' and 'rentals'."

(3) "The word 'depreciation' was here used in its ordinary and usual sense as understood by business men, namely, as those amounts which business concerns usually charge off in the depreciation account for wear and tear, and obsolescence of structures, machinery,

and personalty in the business * * * . It would be a strained
use of the term to say that where ore is taken from a mine depreciation as generally understood in business circles follows."

<h1 style="text-align:center">PHELLIS v. UNITED STATES</h1>

(U. S. Court of Claims, March 14, 1921)

(Not reported)

Record: Act of October 3, 1913. Action to recover taxes
paid. Judgment for plaintiff for the sum of $5,657.97.

Facts: On and prior to September 1, 1915, plaintiff was the
owner of 250 shares of the common stock of the E. I. du Pont de
Nemours Powder Co., a New Jersey corporation. Under an agreement entered into on September 16, 1915, all of this company's
assets were transferred to, and its liabilities assumed by E. I. du
Pont de Nemours and Company, a corporation organized for the
purpose under the laws of the state of Delaware, the consideration
being cash, debenture stock and common stock. It was further
provided that all the common stock of the Delaware corporation
was to be distributed to the common stockholders of the New Jersey
corporation as a dividend, at the rate of two shares of the new stock
for each share · of the old stock held. The stockholders were to
continue to hold their stock in the old corporation. The personnel
of stockholders and officers of the two corporations was idèntical
on October 1, 1915. On September 30, 1915, the plaintiff's 250
shares in the New Jersey corporation were worth on the market,
$795 each, or the total sum of $198,750. On October 1st, 1915, the
day he received his 500 shares additional in the new corporation,
his 250 shares in the New Jersey corporation decreased in value,
$695 a share, and were then marketable at $100 per share, while
the 500 new shares he received were worth in the open market,
$347.50 each or a total value of $173,750.

Question: Did the dividend consisting of stock in the new
corporation constitute taxable income to the plaintiff?

Decision: "The figures indisputably demonstrate that by
the transaction the plaintiff did not gain or lose a penny, as will,
with more precision, appear from the following tabulation:

Sept. 30, 1915, 250 shares of stock of the New Jersey Corporation, at $795 each.............................$198,750
Total value Oct. 1, 1915............................. 198,750

Oct. 1, 1915, 500 shares of stock of the Delaware Corporation, at $347.50................................. 173,750
Oct. 1, 1915, 250 shares of stock of the New Jersey Corporation, at $100.................................... 25,000

      Total value of the 750 shares in both............$198,750
As a matter of fact, if the position of the defendant is to be sustained
the plaintiff herein, instead of receiving an income from the transaction, loses $5,657.97, which he must pay from gains derived from
a source other than the one in controversy, or out of his original
investment. The defendant contends that the New Jersey and
Delaware corporations must be regarded as separate and distinct
legal entities and that the case is within the rule of Peabody v.
Eisner, 247 U. S., 347. We think the whole transaction is to be
regarded as merely a financial reorganization of the business of
the company and that this view is justified by the power and duty of
the court to look through the form of the transaction to its substance.
In Eisner v. McComber, 252 U. S., 189 at 213, it is said: We have
no doubt of the power or duty of a court to look through the form
of the corporation and determine the question of the stockholder's
right, in order to ascertain whether he has received income taxable
without apportionment. It seems incredible that Congress intended
to tax as income a business transaction which admittedly produced
no gain, no profit, and hence no income. If any income had accrued to the plaintiff by reason of the sale and exchange made, it
would doubtless be taxable. Therefore, judgment was entered for
the plaintiff for the amount of taxes paid by him.

PHILADELPHIA H. & P. R. CO. v. LEDERER, COLLECTOR
(U. S. Circuit Court of Appeals, Third Cir. May 26, 1917)
(242 Fed. 492)

Record: Act of August 5, 1909. Action at law to recover
taxes paid under protest on net income under Section 38 of said

Act. Judgment for defendant (239 Fed. 184), and plaintiff brings error. Affirmed.

Facts: Plaintiff brought this action to recover from Lederer, collector of internal revenue, taxes paid for the years 1909, 1910, 1911 and 1912. These taxes for 1909, 1910 and 1911 were paid under protest to one McCoach, Lederer's predecessor, who remained in office until October 7, 1913. During McCoach's term, the plaintiff claimed the refund of these three taxes. Disposition of these claims was not made until 1914, when they were all denied. After Mc-Coach had retired from office, plaintiff filed petition to abate the tax of 1912 and at the same time asked the Commissioner to re-open and reconsider his refusal to refund the tax for 1909. In 1914 Lederer notified plaintiff that the petition for abatement was refused and that further action on the claims previously filed was denied. After claim for refund of tax for 1912 had been filed and refused, plaintiff commenced this suit against Lederer to recover the taxes for the four years, 1909-1912.

Question: Does the Act of February 8, 1899, c. 121, 30 Stat. 822 (Comp. St. 1916, Sec. 1594) providing that "no suit, action or other proceeding by or against any officer of the U. S. shall abate by reason of his death or expiration of his term of office," authorize an action against a collector to recover back taxes paid to his predecessor in office, since no suit, action or proceeding was pending against such predecessor, there being only a claim for refund of the taxes against the collector?

Decision: "Without statutory permission no suit to recover a Federal tax can be maintained. Moreover the statutes on this subject must be strictly obeyed; they lay down the conditions and limitations under which the sovereign consents to be sued, and this consent should not be enlarged by construction. * * * "The only 'suit or other proceeding' that could have been begun against McCoach while he was in office would have been a suit for the taxes of 1909 and 1910; but no such suit was brought and it cannot be successfully contended that a mere claim for refund, which is a matter wholly for the Commissioner is a suit or proceeding against the collector. The basis of an action against the collector is his receipt of the tax, and if he has not received it, he cannot be called on to pay it back." The Act of Congress does not apply to this case in that no suit was commenced against the collector's predecessor and the plaintiff was held not entitled to recover.

POLK v. MILES, COLLECTOR
(U. S. District Court of Maryland, May 10, 1920)
(268 Fed. 175)

Record: Revenue Act of 1916. Action at law by executors against collector of internal revenue to recover back a Federal estate tax paid under protest. Judgment directed for plaintiff.

Facts: Plaintiff sought to recover an inheritance tax paid under protest. In the spring of 1915, Lucius C. Polk, upon whose estate the tax was levied, was well advanced in years but was still vigorous. He died rather suddenly not long after the estate tax provisions in the Revenue Act of 1916 became effective. About May, 1915, Polk entered into a written agreement with his son, in order to settle family quarrels, whereby he transferred to the son all his stock in a brewery and all that it owed him, amounting to $105,-000. The son promised that during the lifetime of his mother, the wife of the transferrer, the brewery should pay the husband and father, monthly interest at the rate of 4 per cent per annum on this sum, and that after the death of the wife, as long as the father lived the son would guarantee that such payments would be made.

Question: Is the item of $105,000 taxable, as a transfer by the husband (1) in contemplation of death, or (2) intended to take effect in possession or enjoyment at or after his death?

Decision: The facts in this case did not bring it within any well considered definition ever given to the phrase "in contemplation of death." The court held also that the tax was not applicable on the ground that it was a transfer intended to take effect in possession or enjoyment at or after death. The court stated that there was no question but that the son at once entered into possession of the brewery's stock with whatever enjoyment there was possible to get out of it, that the transaction amounted to nothing more than the purchase by the father from the son of an annuity of $4,200 a year, payable in monthly installments, the buyer paying for it by assigning to the seller his claim against the brewery. The plaintiff, therefore, was not liable for an estate tax on the property re-

received from the father and he was allowed to recover the taxes paid.

POLLOCK v. FARMERS LOAN & TRUST CO.
(United States Supreme Court, May 20, 1895)
(157 U. S. 439; 158 U. S. 601)

Record: Act of August 15, 1894. Bill in equity to test constitutionality of Act. Demurrer to bill sustained in Circuit Court, S. D. of New York, whereupon the record recited that the constitutionailty of a law was drawn in question, and an appeal was allowed directly to this court. Demurrer overruled and decree entered for plaintiff.

Facts: Defendant corporation invested its assets in stocks of public corporations and bonds of the United States. Its net income was derived in part from real estate and interest from investments in municipal bonds. It was holding and executing a number of trusts committed to it, and held many parcels of land situated in the various states, and received from said real estate income and rents in its fiduciary capacity.

Question: Is a tax, under the Act of August 15, 1894, upon a person's entire income whether derived from personal property, real estate, products, stocks, bonds or other forms of personal property, a direct tax as this term is used in the Constitution of the United States?

Decision: "The words of the Constitution are to be taken in their obvious sense and to have a reasonable construction. As men whose intentions require no concealment, generally employ words which most directly and aptly express the ideas they intend to convey, the enlightened patriots who framed our Constitution, and the people who adopted it must be understood to have employed words in their natural sense and to have intended what they have said." The solution of this question depends on the meaning and intention of those who framed and proposed the Constitution, together with a reference to such sources of judicial information as are resorted to by all courts in construing statutes. In distributing the power of taxation, the states retained the general power of direct taxation by granting to the Federal Government such power upon condition that in its exercise such taxes should be apportioned among the several states according to numbers. This was done in order to protect the states who were surrendering to the Federal Government so many sources of income, that the power of direct taxation was their principal remaining resource. In order to determine what was in the mind of the convention with regard to direct taxation, the court considered historical evidence. Among the cases considered was that of Hylton v. United States, 3 Dall. 171. In this case, however, it was found that a tax on carriages was considered as excise tax, and was, therefore, not a direct tax. The court also found a definition of a direct tax given by Mr. Hamilton in his report on the public credit. In referring to contracts with citizens of a foreign country, Mr. Hamilton said: "This principle, which seems critically correct, would exempt, as well the income, as the capital of the property. It protects the use as effectually as the thing. What, in fact, is property, but a fiction without the beneficial use of it? In many cases, indeed, the income or annuity is the property itself." 3 Hamilton's Works 34. In the first hearing of the case, 157 U. S. 429, it was held that receipts from municipal bonds cannot be taxed by the Federal Government because this is a tax on the states and their instruments for borrowing money and consequently repugnant to the Constitution. If this be true, it follows "that if revenue derived from municipal bonds cannot be taxed; because the source cannot be, the same rule applies to revenue derived from any other source not subject to the tax; and the lack of power to levy any but an apportioned tax on real and personal property equally exists as to the revenue therefrom." Accordingly, the court held that the Act taxing income derived from personal property, real estate, products, stocks, bonds, or other forms of personal property, was unconstitutional in that it was a direct tax without apportionment by the Federal Government.

PORTER et al. v. LEDERER, COLLECTOR
(U. S. District Court E. D. Penn., July 27, 1920)
(267 Fed. 739)

Record: Revenue Act of 1917. Suit for recovery of excess profits tax paid. Judgment for plaintiffs.

Facts: The business of plaintiffs was that of a commission house. Incidentally and wholly because of exigencies arising out of war conditions, they engaged in more or less isolated transactions in which they bought and sold. Part of the profits of the business from prior years had been permitted to accumulate until there was a fund of $36,000, which was not used in the business but kept intact as money of the partners. Plaintiffs contended they were entitled to be assessed under Sec. 209 of the Act as a business "having no invested capital or not more than nominal capital."

Questions: (1) What was the meaning of the word "capital" as used in Sec. 209 of the Act?

(2) Did the isolated transactions of buying and selling mentioned above, prevent plaintiff's classification under Sec. 209?

(3) Did the accumulation of profits above mentioned prevent such classification?

Decision: (1) The word "capital" as used in the phrase "having no invested capita' or not more than nominal capital," means money or property, as distinguished from labor or personal service. The tax is to be measured by the return if the element of money or other property is part of the source from which the return comes, and the lesser rate of assessment (Sec. 209) is to be followed only in cases in which money or property plays no part in the source of the income, or such small part as to be practically negligible.

(2) The isolated transactions of buying and selling were not conducted by the plaintiffs as part of any trade or business, although the aggregate of the values involved was by no means an inconsiderable sum. They did not, therefore, affect plaintiff's claim in this case.

(3) The mere fact that the profits of a business having no capital are not wholly withdrawn, does not make of such undrawn profits a capital fund. Such profits must be used in the business to constitute capital. Plaintiffs were, therefore, entitled to be assessed under Sec. 209 rather than under Sec. 201.

PORTO RICO COAL CO., INC., v. EDWARDS, COLLECTOR
(U. S. District Court, S. D. N. Y., August 4, 1921)
(275 Fed. 104)

Record: Revenue Acts of 1917 and 1918. Action to recover taxes paid under duress. Demurrers to complaints sustained. Judgment dismissing the complaints upon the merits.

Facts: Plaintiff is a corporation organized under the laws of New York, but deriving all its income, with an insignificant exception, from Porto Rico, and doing all its business, owning all its property and keeping its books of account in that island. The taxes for the years 1917 and 1918, which the plaintiff now seeks to recover, were paid in the city of New York.

Questions: (1) Is the plaintiff, under the Revenue Act of 1917, subject to the excess profits tax in New York at the same general rates as though the income were derived from the continental United States, or is it liable to be taxed only in Porto Rico?

(2) Is the plaintiff likewise subject to income and excess profits tax for 1918 under the Revenue Act of 1918?

(3) Would taxation of the Porto Rican income of a New York corporation under the Revenue Act of 1917 or 1918 violate Section nine of the Organic Act of Porto Rico of 1917, by which it was provided that all laws should apply to Porto Rico except internal revenue laws?

(4) Does the fact that the plaintiff is taxed on its income in New York and its income is taxed under Section 261 of the Revenue Act of 1918 result in double taxation?

(5) If the Revenue Acts of 1917 and 1918 tax the plaintiff in New York, are they constitutional?

Decision: (1) The Revenue Act of 1917 provides that "the total net income received from all sources by every corporation organized within the United States" shall be subject to excess profits tax, and this includes an income derived from Porto Rico.

(2) The plaintiff is subject to income and excess profits taxes under the Revenue Act of 1918 on its income derived from Porto Rico.

(3) "The important thing is that the excess profits tax of 1917 has nothing to do with Porto Rico or with its tax system. While it does levy a tax on incomes there arising, it levies them against persons living in the United States. * * * If the Revenue Act of 1917 or 1918 endeavored to follow the incomes to Porto Rico and collect them out of the property there, the plaintiff's argument would begin to be relevant, but not till then. * * * The Porto

Rican taxes remain as 'intact' as ever, however little the plaintiff's income be 'intact'. By computing the tax on the basis of that income, Porto Rico can be affected only because the plaintiff may withdraw some part of the income which might otherwise remain. It could do that anyway, and the internal revenue laws do not 'apply' in Porto Rico because they make that result possible or even probable.''

(4) ''There is no final objection to a set of statutes that they involve double taxation, although the implication is against it, but in the case at bar, in spite of what I have said, there is no such duplication. The taxes levied under Section 23 of the Revenue Act of 1916 and Section 261 of the Revenue Act of 1918 are for the exclusive benefit of Porto Rico and for the matter of that Congress probably was acting merely as local sovereign when it passed them. The excess profits taxes of 1917 and 1918 and the income tax proper was for the support of the general government. The situation is not different from the case of the plaintiff if it had drawn its income from New York or Massachusetts or any other state of the Union having an income tax. It would have been subject to two taxes on the same property, one for local and one for general purposes. There is nothing illegal in such a local tax when the taxpayer is a nonresident.''

(5) There is no authority to support the argument that the construction of the statutes so as to tax the plaintiff's income violates the Porto Rico Bill of Rights which when once granted forever limits the legislative action of Congress. ''It might more plausibly be stated that the Organic Act extended to Porto Rico the Constitution of the United States, that such an extension could not be revoked, and that the legislation in question was within some of the limitations of that document. Assuming all of the premises, I cannot see that the plaintiff can complain. It has no standing as a Porto Rican to invoke the Porto Rican Bill of Rights. * * * The only ground for complaint that I can see is that Porto Rico has been exempted from these taxes while the plaintiff who draws its income from Porto Rico, has not. * * * But in the case at bar the exemption is of a territory having no share in the Government of the United States; it is granted by Congress acting for all the

states at their common expense. Obviously, there can be no taking without due process of law in such legislation. That phrase implies some oppression, and the joint action of all the states relieving a territory which has no share in the decision cannot result in oppression.''

PRENTISS v. EISNER
(U. S. Circuit Court of Appeals, Second Cir., June 16, 1920)
(267 Fed. 16)

Record: Act of October 3, 1913. Action to recover taxes paid. Judgment for defendant (260 Fed. 589) and plaintiff brought error. Affirmed. Petition for writ of certiorari denied by United States Supreme Court, October 25, 1920.

Facts: Plaintiff filed return of her net income for the year 1913, pursuant to the Act of Congress, approved October 3, 1913. Paragraph B of Act provided, "That subject only to such exemptions and deductions as are hereinafter allowed, the net income of a taxable person shall include gains, profits, and income * * * but not the value of property acquired by gift, bequest, devise, or descent * * *. That in computing net income for the purpose of the normal tax there shall be allowed as deductions; * * * third, all National, State, County, School and Municipal tax paid within the year, * * * ", and in par. D. " * * *, for the year ending December 31, 1913, said tax shall be computed on the net income accruing from March 1, to December 31, 1913, both dates inclusive, after deducting five-sixths only of the specific exemption and deductions herein provided for."

It appeared that in the year 1913, the plaintiff inherited a portion of her father's estate and upon the inheritance thus received by her the State of New York assessed against her an inheritance tax which she paid. The plaintiff in making her income return, included therein as a deduction, five-sixths of the inheritance tax which she had paid to the State of New York, contending that the inheritance tax so paid was a tax paid to a state, and therefore under the Act was deductible. This deduction was not allowed by the Commissioner who levied and assessed against her additional tax.

Question: Was the amount paid by the plaintiff as an inheritance tax to the State of New York a proper deduction in her income tax return for the year 1913?

Decision: The New York transfer act does not impose a tax on a legatee's right of succession which is deductible in the income tax return of such legatee. The legacy which the plaintiff herein received under the will of her father did not become her property until after it had suffered a diminution by the amount of the tax, and the tax that was paid thereon was not a tax paid out of the plaintiff's individual estate but was a payment out of the estate of her deceased father of that part of his estate which the State of New York had appropriated to itself, which payment was the condition precedent to the allowance by the state of the vesting of the remainder in the legatee. Therefore, the plaintiff was not entitled to the deduction claimed.

PRUDENTIAL INS. CO. v. HEROLD, COLLECTER

(U. S. District Court, D. New Jersey, February 8, 1918)

(247 Fed. 681)

Record: Act of August 5, 1909. Action at law to recover excess taxes exacted. Judgment for plaintiff.

Facts: (1) The plaintiff is a joint stock company engaged in writing industrial and life insurance, and has always conducted its business on the "level premium plan." Having discontinued issuing participation policies, it later, though under no obligation to do so, began awarding "dividends" to holders of non-participation policies, out of funds accumulated in prior years because the premiums then collected were in excess of the cost of insurance, which dividends could be used to reduce the amount of future premiums or to secure additional paid-up insurance. The company was assessed an additional tax resulting from adding to the gross income the amount of premiums and other payments represented by credits for the dividends, which amounts the company had not reported.

(2) The Act of 1909 permits a deduction from gross income of "the net addition, if any, required by law to be made within the year to reserve funds." By the law of New Jersey, the plaintiff company is required to maintain a reserve fund, the amount of which is fixed by a commissioner on the "all business written" basis, as distinguished from the "all paid for" basis. The plaintiff included

in the "reserve" the value of the policies upon which the premiums were due and uncollected, and deferred.

Questions: (1) Should the amounts allowed by a joint-stock insurance company to non-participating policy holders, and used to reduce renewal premiums and to purchase additional paid-up insurance, be treated as income received by the company and taxable under the Act?

(2) May a company, in figuring its net addition to the reserve funds which it was required by law to make, and which net addition is deductible from gross income under the Federal law, include the value of policies upon which premiums were due and uncollected?

Decision: (1) The "dividends" in question were mere excess premiums—overpayments which had been collected, and to which the participating policy holders were entitled as a matter of right, and the nonparticipating policy holders, both industrial and ordinary, as a matter of equity, and fair dealing. They arose "from income received during previous years (201 Fed. 918) as in the Mutual Benefit Case." Therefore they did not constitute income of the taxable year, although credited in that year as payment of premiums and for paid up insurance.

(2) The question is what sum "did the state law require the plaintiff to maintain as a 'reserve fund,' not the character of the assets making up the actual 'reserve funds'." "* * * it is of no materiality what the 'reserve funds' actually consisted of, whether cash, securities, real estate, or due and uncollected premiums." Since the company was clearly required by the law of New Jersey to maintain a reserve based upon "its outstanding policies, as the commissioner might value them, it follows that * * * the plaintiff was justified in making the deduction which it did. * * *."

PUBLIC SERVICE CORPORATION v. HEROLD
(Ten cases)

SAME v. MOFFET (three cases)
(U. S. District Court, D. New Jersey, June 14, 1921)
(273 Fed. 282)

Record: Act of Aug. 5, 1909, and Revenue Act of 1916. Suit to recover taxes paid under protest. On motion for judgment on the pleadings. Judgment for defendants.

Facts: In previous litigations between the parties, the taxes here involved were declared illegal, but the plaintiffs were held to be barred from recovering those assessed for the years 1909 and 1910, for failure to claim a refund within two years, as specified by Rev. Stat., Section 3228. (See Public Service Ry. Co. Cases, 227 Fed. 491 and 229 Fed. 902.) Subsequently to the rendition of the last of these decisions and the passage of the Act of Sept. 8, 1916, the plaintiffs, in accordance with Section 14a, which permits the filing of a claim for refund of taxes paid under the Act of Aug. 5, 1909, notwithstanding Rev. Stat., Section 3228, presented to the Commissioner their claims for refund of such taxes. The Commissioner rejected the claims, whereupon these suits were started. Later, the Commissioner, without knowledge of these suits, reconsidered his decision and allowed the claims. Upon learning of the pending suits, however, he cancelled the allowance.

Question: Did Section 14a of the Act of Sept. 8, 1916, remove the bar of Sections 3227 and 3228 Rev. Stat., so as to give the plaintiff a right of action against the collectors for taxes illegally exacted which otherwise would have been barred by said sections?

Decision: The liability of the collectors was denied in the previous suits. There is nothing in the Act of 1916 which points to a revival of their liability. The taxes illegally collected, having been paid into the United States Treasury, as required by the statute, the moral obligation to return them rested on the government and not on the collectors. The 1916 Act removed the legal disability (the bar of Rev. Stat., Section 3228), which prevented the government from discharging its moral obligations. This is all this Act expressly did. If it may be said that by so doing there arose an implied promise to pay, it was that of the government, and not that of the collectors, through whom the taxes reached its treasury. The defendants are entitled to judgments of no cause of action.

Note: Reversed in 279 Fed. 352.

PUBLIC SERVICE RY. CO. v. HEROLD, COLLECTOR
(and sixteen other cases)
(Circuit Court of Appeals, 3d Circuit, Jan. 21, 1916)
(229 Fed. 902)

Record: Act of August 5, 1909. Actions are to recover taxes paid under protest. From the judgments in all cases but two plaintiffs bring error, and in two cases defendants bring error. Certain of the judgments affirmed and others reversed.

Facts: The plaintiffs in these cases are public utility corporations organized under the laws of the State of New Jersey. They were lessors and lessees of certain property. This litigation, including seventeen cases grew out of the collection of taxes for the years 1909, 1910, 1911 and 1912, assessed against the lessor plaintiffs under Act of August 5, 1909. The tax under this law is imposed upon the privilege of carrying on or "doing business" in a corporate capacity. The taxes were paid under protest, and after claims for their refund had been made and rejected, these suits were brought to recover the amounts paid. The lessees were joined with their respective lessors as parties plaintiff, because the money paid was advanced by the lessees under terms of the leases which imposed upon them the payment of taxes. Under the terms of the leases, the lessor corporations surrendered their properties and franchises for a long term, reserving to themselves only their non-delegable powers or franchises, which under covenants, they undertook to exercise for the benefit of the lessees.

The jury found in special verdicts that under their reserved powers the plaintiffs had performed during the years in question such acts as authorizing the voting of stock owned in other corporations, selling stocks and bonds owned by them, receiving and distributing rents, etc. These acts were done in pursuance of the terms of the leases, and at the direction of the lessee corporations.

Questions: (1) Were the lessor plaintiffs engaged in business within the meaning of the Act, and therefore subject to the tax?

(2) Is the recovery of the amounts paid for the years 1909 and 1910 barred by the Federal statute of limitations?

Decision: (1) The statute imposes an excise, not because of every act performed by a corporation under its incidental powers, but upon the privilege of doing and carrying on the business for which the corporation is organized, and when the corporation ceases the conduct of such business by turning it over to be carried on by another, it ceases to be subject to the tax so long as it commits no act by which the resumption of its business is to be inferred. "The acts found by the special verdicts in the cases under review to have been done and performed by the lessor corporations were not done or performed by them in the conduct of the body or substance of the business for which they were organized and from which they had retired when they turned over their property to their lessees, but were corporate acts performed under the incidental powers of the corporations pursuant to the terms of contracts into which they had entered." The court held that the plaintiffs were not taxable as corporations "doing business."

(2) "No suit can be maintained for taxes illegally collected unless a claim therefor has been made within the time prescribed by the law. The law says the claim must be presented within two years, therefore, unless so presented, the right to demand repayment of the tax is lost and the right of suit is gone." No claim having been presented within two years for the amounts for the years 1909 and 1910, the present suit is barred as to those amounts.

PULLMAN'S PALACE CAR CO. ads. ALLEN
(U. S. Supreme Court, April 13, 1891)
(139 U. S. 658)

Record: Law of the State of Tennessee assessing privilege taxes for the years 1887, 1888 and 1889. Bill for an injunction restraining the defendant as controller of the State from collecting such taxes. Upon hearing, the relief sought was decreed and the taxes in question perpetually enjoined. Decrees reversed and causes remanded.

Facts: Plaintiff refused to pay the tax in question and brought this bill for an injunction alleging that the defendant was about to levy upon its sleeping cars.

Question: Was the plaintiff entitled to the relief asked because, as it alleged, distraint and seizure of its cars would involve an interference with interstate commerce?

Decision: "We have already decided in Sheldon v. Platt that purely injunction bills cannot be sustained to restrain the collection of taxes upon the sole ground of their unconstitutionality."

PURNELL v. PAGE, SHERIFF
(Supreme Court of North Carolina, Oct. 15, 1903)
(45 S. E. 534)

Record: State Income Tax Act. Suit for an injunction to restrain defendant from selling complainant's property for non-payment of a tax alleged to be illegal. Decree for complainant. Defendant appeals. Affirmed.

Facts: Complainant was a United States judge. A state income tax was assessed against him, upon his salary, and upon his refusal to pay the same, his personal property was levied upon. In order to prevent a sale of said property, this suit was commenced.

Questions: (1) Can a state impose an income tax upon the salary of a Federal judge, received by him from the United States?

(2) May a taxpayer maintain an injunction against the sale of his property under an illegal tax?

Decision: (1) The salary received by a Federal judge from the United States is not subject to the income tax of any state.

(2) A taxpayer may maintain an injunction against the sale of his property under an illegal tax, or he may pay the tax under protest and sue to recover it back.

RAILROAD CO. v. COLLECTOR
(United States Supreme Court, Oct. 1879)
(100 U. S. 595)

Record: Act of July 13, 1866. Action at law to recover taxes paid under protest under Sec. 122 of this Act. Judgment for defendant.

Facts: Plaintiff company had issued coupon bonds which were held by non-resident aliens, and to whom the interest was paid.

Question: May plaintiff corporation be taxed on the amount of interest coupons paid to non-resident alien bond holders under the Act of July 13, 1886?

Decision: The tax is essentially an excise on the income of the class of corporations mentioned in the statute. It was the manifest purpose of the law to levy the tax on the net earnings of com-panics engaged in furnishing road-ways and water-ways for the transportation of persons and property. In every well conducted corporation of this character, profits were disposed of in one of four ways; namely, distributed to its stockholders as dividends, paid out as an interest on its funded debts, used in construction of its roads and canals, or carried to a reserve or other fund remaining in its hands. "Looking to these modes of distribution as the surest evidence of the earnings which Congress intended to tax, and as less liable to evasion than any others, the tax is imposed upon all of them. The books and records of the company are thus made evidence of the profits they have made, and the corporation itself is made responsible for the payment of the tax." The tax was not laid on the bond holders who received the interest, but on the earnings of the corporation which paid the interest. "The tax is laid by Congress on the net earnings, which are the results of the business of the corporation, on which Congress had clearly a right to lay it; and being lawfully assessed and paid by it, it cannot be recovered back by reason of any insufficiency or ethical objection to the remedy over against the bond holders." Accordingly, the court held that the plaintiff corporation could be taxed on the amount of interest coupons paid to non-resident alien bondholders.

RANDOLPH v. CRAIG, COLLECTOR

(U. S. District Court M. D. Tennessee, Nashville Div.; February 23, 1920)

(267 Fed. 993)

Record: Revenue Act of 1916. Action at law against the collector of internal revenue by the executor and trustees under the will of Wm. M. Randolph, deceased, and by his widow to recover a portion of the tax assessed on the estate of decedent under the Act of September 8, 1916, which had been paid under protest; namely that portion of the tax based upon the value of the gross estate of the decedent without deduction, for the value of widow's homestead in Tennessee, her dower interest in lands in Tennessee and Arkansas, and her year's support out of Tennessee personalty. Issues involved raised by demurrer of defendant to plaintiff's declaration. Demurrer overruled.

Facts: The fourth, fifth and sixth grounds of the demurrer are special. The fourth raises the defense that the widow's dower and homestead interest is to be included in determining the estate of the decedent which is subject to the estate tax. The sixth ground raises this defense in another form, both as to the dower and homestead, and to the year's support.

Questions: (1) Is the estate tax involved in the Act of September 8, 1916, a property or succession tax?

(2) Do State or Federal laws control as to taxability of widow's interest in husband's estate under the Federal estate tax provisions of said Act?

(3) Are widow's dower, homestead and year's support taxable as part of the estate involved in the succession?

(4) Are these items deductible as "charges against the estate" under Sec. 203, cl. a (1) of said Act?

Decision: (1) Estate Tax of September 8, 1916, is imposed on the transfer. The estate tax is clearly not a tax on the property of the decedent, but upon its transfer or transmission by will or descent from the decedent, being in effect a tax on the succession from decedent.

(2) The laws of the state where decedent's property is located control the question of its taxability under the transfer provisions of the Act. Whether upon the husband's death the widow is entitled to homestead, dower and a year's support by the transfer from her husband's estate and in succession to him, or whether her right to these interests is vested in her by operation of law independently of her husband and not transmitted to her through him, is a question which the statutes and rules of decision in Tennessee and Arkansas, where the decedent's property is located, are controlling, (quoting Vaughn v. Hutchinson, 165 U. S. 566). The court said it is settled in Tennessee that a widow's right to dower is not a succession to the title of her husband on his death, but she derives it by the marriage and her right as wife, to be consummated in severalty to her upon her husband's death, and that she takes it adversely to the inheritance from the husband. A fortiori, the court said, this is true as to the widow's homestead in Tennessee. It is not a purchase from her husband, but an incumbrance upon

the title to the heir at law originating with the marriage and consummated by the husband's death. In Tennessee the widow does not succeed to the title of her husband of that part of the estate set apart as a year's support, but she acquires it adversely to his administrator by virtue of the statute conferring the right to her.

(3) The dower, homestead and year's support item are not part of the taxable estate. Since the widow does not receive such property or rights therein in succession to her husband, or by transfer from him, but takes them under statutory provisions vesting these rights in her independently of her husband and adversely to his estate, such property is not part of his estate upon which the tax is imposed by the Federal estate tax of the Act involved.

(4) Dower, homestead and widow's award or support item are "charges against the estate" and so deductible from gross estate. If her dower, homestead and year's support be deemed part of the decedent's gross estate, within the meaning of the estate tax, it seems that they would be in any event charges against the estate allowed by the laws of the jurisdiction under which the estate is being administered, and hence in any event to be deducted from the value of the gross estate under the express provisions of clause a (1) of Sec. 203 of the Act of September 8, 1916.

RAU v. UNITED STATES
(Circuit Court of Appeals, Second Cir., May 14, 1919)
(260 Fed. 131)

Record: Revenue Act of 1917. Rau was convicted of violating the provision of the Act, making it a criminal offense to fail to file an income tax return as prescribed by law, and he brings error. Reversed.

Facts: Rau was a broker, or salesman on commission, and was also engaged in selling stocks and securities. Rau admitted he had not filed an income tax return as required by the Act, and thereupon paid the tax and penalty to the collector, who informed the defendant that such payment would end the matter. After the acceptance of the check, this indictment was found.

Question: Was such payment, acceptance and statement by the collector a "compromise" and a bar to prosecution?

Decision: Where collector, after defendant admitted he had not filed a return as required, accepted not only the tax, but the penalty, informing defendant that such payment would end the matter, such acceptance and statement was a "compromise" within the Act and was a bar to prosecution. (Case on same point, Willingham v. U. S. 208 Fed. 137.)

REAL ESTATE TITLE INSURANCE & TRUST CO. v. LEDERER, COLLECTOR

(U. S. Circuit Court of Appeals, Third Cir., Feb. 9, 1920)

(263 Fed. 667)

Record: Act of October 22, 1914. Action at law to recover taxes alleged to have been unlawfully collected. Judgment for defendant (229 Fed. 779), and plaintiff brought error. Reversed.

Facts: Plaintiff was a corporation of the State of Pennsylvania, formed in 1876 for the purpose of insuring titles to real estate. In 1881 it embarked in the trust business. "The company subsequently added two other departments—a safe deposit, in which it rented safes, and received valuables on deposit, and also a real estate department, which buys, sells, rents, and collects the rents of real estate." The business of all these four departments was kept separate and distinct, and from these businesses it had from time to time made earnings, which were carried to surplus and undivided profits, and purchases of bonds, stocks and permanent investments were made. "Later on the company added a banking department, and business was done with the funds deposited with it in banking accounts. The permanent investments formed part of the assets of the company as a whole, and in case the company's banking operations proved unsuccessful, those assets would have to contribute toward making up the losses of depositors." The corporation was assessed and paid a tax upon its entire capital under the above named Act imposing an excise tax of $1 on each $1,000 of capital used by bankers.

Question: Whether any part, and if so, how much, of the trust company's capital, surplus and undivided profits was really used or employed in those specified business operations which the Act defines as constituting banking?

Decision: The company is not liable for tax under Act of October 22, 1914, on its entire capital, surplus, and undivided profits, but only on such capital, if any, as was used or employed in its banking department, and the fact that all of its capital would be liable for losses in that department was not determinative of that question. "The money used by the plaintiff company in its banking operations was the money deposited with it by its customers; and it would seem clear from anything that now appears that no banking use was made of the capital, surplus and undivided profits, which were located and segregated in its title, trust, safe deposit and real estate departments." The plaintiff was allowed to recover the amount of tax which the government required it to pay on the capital, surplus and undivided profits used in its title, trust, safe deposit and real estate departments.

RECH-MARBAKER CO. v. LEDERER, COLLECTOR

(U. S. District Court, E. D. Pennsylvania, Dec. 31, 1919)

(263 Fed. 593)

Record: Revenue Act of 1917. Action at law by plaintiff to recover tax exacted from it under Sec. 600, title VI of the Act. Judgment for plaintiff.

Facts: The tax imposed is an excise tax, measured at 3 per cent of the sales price, "upon all automobiles, automobile trucks, automobile wagons, and motorcycles sold by the manufacturer, producer or importer."

Question: Is the excise tax on the sale of automobile trucks sold by the manufacturer, producer or importer, imposed by Sec. 600 of the Act of October 3, 1917, collectible only on sales of automobile trucks as units?

Decision: The court says that when applied to the sales of automobiles or motorcycles the meaning of the Act is entirely clear. The thought is not clear, however, in respect to automobile trucks, because there are none which are "sold by manufacturers, producers and importers," and in consequence no transactions to which the taxing clauses or measuring clauses of the law can apply. This, it is pointed out, is because automobile trucks are never dealt in or sold by any manufacturer or importer as units, nor are the parts ever assembled or dealt in as units. The court says that there is no such a thing as a standard type of truck with which this case concerns itself. When the prospective user wants one he buys a chassis and sends it with the kind of body he wants to some one to have the body put on. It is then returned to him as an automobile truck, but there has been no truck sold. There has been the sale of a chassis or the sale of a body or separate sales of each, unless one or the other can be said to be a truck. The executive department, the court says, has done the best which could be done with such a difficult situation by dealing with the subject of each sale as a taxable unit, crediting the last with the tax paid on the previous sales of the parts. Congress has dealt with it by changing the law so as to make it apply to such sale transactions as take place. The executive action taken necessarily involved a construction of the law, and the court is asked to give it the same construction. This executive construction, however, although informative and helpful, is controlling only to the extent that it is persuasive. A judicial construction must be given to the law. The court then concludes as follows: "The words, 'producer, manufacturer or importer' necessarily imply one transaction. How then can we have several, as we do have under this executive construction? It is true that by the allowances made the sum of the taxes collected is limited to the one; but the fact is there are a number of taxes levied; so graded that in their aggregate they equal the tax measured by the sale of one automobile truck. The question for decision is one of such character, as that it must be disposed of in a more or less summary way, or it leads into an almost endless discussion. We dispose of it by the ruling that the Act of 1917 imposes no tax except the one measured by a sale of an automobile truck. Counsel will have leave to enter judgment in favor of plaintiff for the tax with costs."

REDPATH LYCEUM BUREAU v. PICKERING, COLLECTOR
(U. S. Circuit Court of Appeals, Seventh Cir., March 6, 1918)
(251 Fed. 49)

Record: Act of October 22, 1914. Action to recover taxes paid under protest. Judgment for defendant and plaintiff brings error. Affirmed. Certiorari denied (246 U. S. 677.)

Facts: Plaintiff is a corporation engaged in the business of supplying chautauquas and lyceum courses throughout the United States. As part of this business it makes contracts whereby certain lecturers, dramatic readers, musicians, and other entertainers, agree to appear for a fixed compensation, the plaintiff usually dividing the receipts with the local organizations. The collector assessed the excise tax under Sec. 3, clause 8 of the Act, which provides: "Eight. Proprietors or agents of all other public exhibitions or shows for money, not enumerated in this section, shall pay $10.00: * * * * Provided further that this paragraph shall not apply to chautauquas, lecture lyceums, agricultural or industrial fairs: * * * * * * * * * *".

Question: Is the plaintiff corporation within the terms of the exception of the statute, and therefore, not subject to the special tax?

Decision: This corporation does not come within the exemptions and is subject to the tax imposed. The court said,"we see no reason why a performance, which in one case might be a vaudeville performance and subject to the tax, should, when hired and produced by a so-called lyceum company, be exempt therefrom." The exemption does not apply to professional show features in and of themselves being complete entertainments. The plaintiff was, therefore, not allowed to recover the tax paid.

REGAL DRUG CORPORATION v. WARDELL, COLLECTOR

(U. S. Circuit Court of Appeals, Ninth Cir., May 2, 1921)

(273 Fed. 182)

Record: National Prohibition Act, Revenue Act of 1918, and Rev. Stat., Secs. 3220, 3224 and 3226. Suit to enjoin collection of taxes and penalties. From a decree dismissing the bill, plaintiff appealed. Affirmed.

Facts: The plaintiff, engaged in the drug business, under a permit authorizing it to sell liquors, spirits, etc., for non-beverage purposes withdrew from bonded warehouses and sold large quantities of the same. At the time of withdrawal it paid the tax thereon. In June, 1920, the plaintiff's permit was revoked, and the Commissioner levied a large assessment against it upon distilled spirits and wines previously withdrawn by it from bonded warehouses, and also penalties for retailing liquors, etc., for conducting the business of a rectifier, and for having manufactured intoxicating liquor in violation of law. Plaintiff alleged that these assessments and penalties were levied without any hearing or any notice to it; and that defendant had taken possession of plaintiff's drug store and was about to sell the same.

Question: Was plaintiff entitled to an injunction to prevent collection of the tax and penalties levied as above stated?

Decision: Conceding that the tax is in the nature of a penalty, it does not follow that its collection can be restrained by a suit in equity, if there is a speedy and adequate remedy at law. Such remedy is afforded by Sections 3220 and 3226 of the Revised Statutes, authorizing the Commissioner to refund taxes and penalties illegally collected. It does not appear from the amended bill of complaint, nor is it otherwise claimed that the plaintiff has appealed to the Commissioner for the abatement of the tax assessed against it in this case. That this suit cannot be maintained has been conclusively determined by the Supreme Court in Cheatham v. U. S., 92 U. S. 85, State Railroad Tax Cases, 92 U. S. 576, and Dodge v. Osborn, 240 U. S., 118.

RENSSELAER & S. R. CO. v. DELAWARE & H. CO.
(Supreme Court, Appellate Division, New York, July 1, 1915)
(168 App. Div. 699; 154 N. Y. Supp. 739)

Record: Act of October 3, 1913. Action at law against Delaware & H. Co. to recover the amount paid by plaintiff as an income tax. From an interlocutory judgment overruling demurrer (88 Misc. Rep. 639; 152 N. Y. Supp. 376) the defendant appealed. Reversed. Affirmed in 217 N. Y. 692, 112 N. E. 1072, without opinion.

Facts: The plaintiff leased its railroads to the defendant, the defendant covenanting to pay all taxes and assessments of every description upon the demised premises and the business done. "And if by any change of the law the present tax or duty required of the said party of the first part (lessor) shall be required of the said stockholders, the said party of the second part shall pay the same," (Subdivision 18). Subdivision 19 of the lease said that the lessee should not be required to pay the present income tax. The income tax law then existing was repealed and later the present one was passed. The plaintiff had to pay the tax under this Act as the result of litigation with the government, and now claims that the defendant is liable for it under the lease.

Question: Where the lessee has covenanted to pay all taxes against the property demised or the business done, but with the express exception of the then existing income tax, can it be held liable for the income tax paid by the lessor under a later Act?

Decision: "There is a broad distinction between a tax upon leased property and an income tax upon the rental. An income tax is not a tax upon specific property, but is a tax upon the annual net gain of the individual or corporation received from its business, the use of its property, or otherwise. The obligation of a tenant to pay taxes upon demised property rests solely upon the terms of the lease. By the eighteenth subdivision of the lease the tenant agrees to pay the taxes levied and imposed upon the demised premises. This income tax is clearly not a tax upon that property, *
* *. It is a tax of like nature, taking the place of the former tax, and the exemption of subdivision 18 makes it clear that the intention of the parties was that it must come from the plaintiff." The defendant, therefore, is not liable to the plaintiff, the lessor, for the income tax paid by it.

RENSSELAER & S. R. CO. v. IRWIN, COLLECTOR
(U. S. Circuit Court of Appeals, Second Cir., Jan. 16, 1918)
(249 Fed. 726)

Record: Act of October 3, 1913. Action at law to recover taxes paid under protest on net income under Sec. 2G (a) of this Act. On demurrer to the complaint. Demurrer sustained (239 Fed. 739) and plaintiff brought error. Affirmed. Petition for a writ of certiorari to the United States Circuit Court of Appeals for the 2nd Circuit denied (246 U. S. 671).

Facts: The plaintiff corporation leased its railroad, equipment and franchises for the term of its charter. The lessee was to operate the same, pay all expenses of operating and keeping in repair, and also pay the interest on its bonded indebtedness and

8 per cent dividend on its outstanding capital stock, but such dividends were to be paid not to the plaintiff company, the owner of the leased property, but directly to the stockholders, the lessee keeping books showing the owners of such stock and all transfers thereof.

Question: Does a lessor corporation, having leased and turned over all of its property with a provision that dividends of 8 per cent on the stock were to be paid directly to the stockholders by the lessee and not to the lessor, receive, within the meaning of the Income Tax Law, any taxable net income?

Decision: The interest and dividends paid directly to the stockholders as rent must be treated as "corporate income" subject to taxation. The court said "that it was true that the rent of its road did not go into the plaintiff's treasury, but nevertheless, the rent is the property of the plaintiff. While the rent is a debt of the lessee to the lessor, it is, as between the lessor and its stockholders, the lessor's income. The application of the rent under the lease is a mere labor saving device, the effect being exactly the same as if it be paid to the lessor and by it paid out as far as necessary to its bondholders for interest, and the surplus in dividends to its stockholders. The description of the fixed sum to be paid by the lessee to the lessor's stockholders as a dividend shows that the payment was made as agent of the lessor." The rent paid to the stockholders of the lessor corporation was income of the lessor, and it can not recover the tax imposed upon it upon such income.

REYNOLDS v. WILLIAMS
(U. S. Circuit Court, D. Indiana, September, 1867)
(Fed. Case 11734)

Record: Internal Revenue Law of 1866. Action of assumpsit to recover tax paid under protest. Demurrer. Demurrer overruled.

Facts: The Lafayette and Indiana R. R. Co. in 1863 had acquired $100,000 of U. S. bonds from their net earnings. In 1867 the railroad ceased to exist by consolidation with another company and the bonds came into the hands of the plaintiff, who held them as trustee for the stockholders of the old company. To avoid an action of distress the plaintiff paid a tax assessed against these bonds as income for the year 1867.

Question: Was the amount of these bonds income for the
year 1867 so as to be taxable under an income tax for that year?

Decision: The mere passage of this trust fund from the hands
of the old trustee, the railroad company, to the new trustee, the
plaintiff, did not give the beneficiaries any more than what they had
under the old trustee. The formation of the fund was in 1863 and,
therefore, there was nothing to tax as income in 1867.

RIDGWAY v. UNITED STATES
(U. S. Court of Claims; June 4, 1883)
(18 Ct. Cls. 707)

Record: Rev. Stat. Sec. 3220. Action brought by plaintiff
against United States upon a certified allowance made by Commissioner of Internal Revenue for a refund of a tax alleged to have been
wrongfully collected. Petition of plaintiff dismissed and judgment
entered accordingly.

Facts: Suit was brought under the provisions of Sec. 3220 of
Revised Statutes of the United States which provides for the remis-
sion, refund and payment back of all taxes erroneously or illegally
assessed or collected. The Commissioner certified to an allowance
to be paid to the claimant and transmitted the same to the fifth
auditor who, after examination and certification, transmitted it
to the first comptroller. Thereafter the papers having been returned by the first comptroller unpaid, the Commissioner decided
to reconsider the matter and he entered of record in his office that it
was reconsidered. Subsequently he rejected the claim. Claimant
brought this action after the Commissioner had entered of record
his order that the allowance was reconsidered and before his final
rejection of the claim.

Questions: (1) Did the Commissioner, under the circumstances
stated, have authority to revoke the allowance certified to by him?

(2) What was the effect of the action of the fifth auditor upon
such allowance?

Decisions: (1) "The statute under which the Commissioner
first certified to an allowance in this case provides that the Commissioner * * * *may refund and pay back* all taxes erroneously
or illegally assessed or collected, etc. Until, therefore, the taxes

were paid back the action of the Commissioner authorized by the statute was not consummated * * *. The processes of the Treasury Department are all ex parte and not finally consummated beyond recall until a check has been issued upon a warrant duly signed by the Secretary of the Treasury, as we have pointed out in former cases." The plaintiff can not recover the amount of the allowance on the theory that the Commissioner had no authority to revoke the allowance after it was once made.

(2) "The action of the fifth auditor in passing the allowance in this case is immaterial, since it is no part of the duty of the auditors (except the sixth auditor), to make decisions binding in any way upon anybody; and their opinions and decisions upon controverted questions, if they choose to give them, have no official determining force."

RIO GRANDE JUNCTION RY. CO. v. UNITED STATES

(U. S. Court of Claims, May 29, 1916)

(51 Ct. Cls. 274)

Record: Act of August 5, 1909. Action at law to recover taxes paid under protest on net income under section 38 of the Act. Judgment for defendant.

Facts: Plaintiff corporation was organized in 1899 to build and operate a railroad. Its articles of incorporation authorized it to "mortgage or lease the whole or any part of such railroad at pleasure." Six months after completion of the road, contract for a lease was executed, and since then the only business transacted by the plaintiff has been the collection of its rental under said contract, the payment of interest on its bonds and the distribution of dividends among its stockholders. For the year 1912 the income of the plaintiff was assessed at $2,279.39, which it paid under protest contending that the Corporation Tax Act of 1909, which provided for a tax of 1% upon the net income of "every corporation organized for profit," etc., did not apply to the plaintiff in that it was not engaged in doing business as contemplated by the Act.

Question: Is a corporation organized to build and operate a railroad, with authority to lease it, "doing business" within the meaning of the Act after it has leased the road immediately upon the completion of the same?

Decision: The true doctrine as to the taxability of corporations under the Act of 1909 is that if it is doing the business for which it was organized the income from such business is taxable. If the purpose for which it was organized was to build and lease property, then the rents derived from such lease are taxable, even though the corporation leases all the property and of necessity goes out of all corporate business except the collection of rents. A corporation should not be allowed to organize for the ostensible purpose of building and operating a railroad and then lease the road before it is built under such circumstances as to show that that was the original and only purpose, and thereby evade the payment of the corporation tax. The plaintiff cannot recover the tax imposed upon it as a corporation "doing business."

ROBERTS v. ANDERSON, COLLECTOR
(U. S. Circuit Court of Appeals, Second Cir., July 21, 1915)
(226 Fed. 7)

Record: Act of August 5, 1909. Action at law to recover taxes paid under protest on net income under Sec. 38 of this Act. Judgment for defendant, and plaintiff brought error. Affirmed.

Facts: This action was brought by the U. S. Express Company, to recover corporation excise taxes paid for the years 1909 and 1910, under protest. The tax was assessed under the Act of Congress approved August 5, 1909, known as the Corporation Tax Law which provides for a tax of 1% upon the net income over and above $5,000 of every "corporation, joint stock company or association, organized for profit and having a capital represented by shares, * * * now or hereafter organized under the laws of the United States or of any state or territory of the United States." The company contends that it is an unincorporated association or partnership formed by agreement in 1885 in the state of New York and that, ever since that time, it has existed solely by virtue of that agreement and extensions thereof. The company admits that it is organized for profit, and has a capital stock represented by shares; that the property and management of the company is vested in a board of directors and that the company has most of the attributes of a corporation. It denies, however, that it is organized, or has ever existed under any law of the United States or of any state or territory of the United States, or that it has ever contemplated that the association should derive a statutory privilege of doing business in a capacity other than that of a partnership or of individuals voluntarily associated for the purpose of carrying on the business provided for in the partnership agreement. Its articles provide for the assessment of its shares for losses, damages, or expenses and also that the company shall sue and be sued in the name of its president.

Question: Was the United States Express Company subject to the tax imposed as a "corporation, joint-stock company or association" because it has a capital stock represented by shares, a management vested in a board of directors, and the right to sue and be sued in the name of its president?

Decision: The company for all practical purposes is a corporation and subject to the tax. While the United States Express Company is without special charter and was not organized under any statute, but is a joint stock company created under articles of association or agreement, it nevertheless is in the enjoyment of valuable privileges which such a company did not possess at common law, but obtains by virtue of the statutes of New York. The company belongs to the class of joint stock companies which it was the intention of Congress to tax. The fact that its members do not possess the important corporate attribute of limited liability is not material. Corporations exist even under charter or statutory provisions where the members do not enjoy a restricted liability. The United States Express Company was in the enjoyment of certain rights or privileges which no unincorporated association enjoys at common law. The company derives from a statutory source a "quality or benefit not existing at common law" in being permitted to sue and be sued in the name of its president. The rule at common law is that an unincorporated association must sue or be sued in the name of all of the members composing it. Thus the statutes of New York have endowed the company with capacities and attributes not possessed by a partnership at common law. They have legalized attributes assumed by the company and made valid and effective its asserted rights. The company belongs to one of those classes of artificial beings described as a "corporation, joint stock company or association." It cannot recover the tax imposed upon it under this Act.

ROBERTS v. LOWE, COLLECTOR
(U. S. District Court, S. D. New York, March 18, 1916)
(238 Fed. 804)

Record: Act of Aug. 5, 1909, and Act of Feb. 8, 1899. Action at law to recover corporation excise taxes paid by plaintiff. Demurrer to the complaint sustained, and complaint dismissed.

Facts: Corporation excise taxes were collected from the U. S. Express Company by one C. W. Anderson, who was at the time collector of internal revenue. Subsequent to collection, the defendant succeeded Anderson in office.

Question: Can a succeeding collector of internal revenue be held liable for taxes illegally exacted from plaintiff by a predecessor collector?

Decision: The Act of February 8, 1899 (30 St. L. 822 c. 121) which provides that no action or other proceeding lawfully commenced against any officer of the United States in his official capacity, shall abate by reason of the expiration of his term, does not permit the plaintiff to sue a succeeding collector for his predecessor's act. This remedial act was to enable pending proceedings against public officials in their official capacity to be continued when necessary to obtain settlement of the questions involved. In this case there was no pending action against the former collector. No subsequent collector can be subjected to the liability of his predecessor. Therefore, the express company cannot recover the taxes from the defendant.

ROBERTSON v. PRATT, COLLECTOR
WAIMEA SUGAR MILL CO. v. PRATT, COLLECTOR
(Supreme Court of Hawaii, August 26, 1901)
(13 Haw. 590)

Record: Hawaiian Act of 1901. Original submission on agreed facts to test the validity of the Act. Judgment for defendant.

Facts: The plaintiffs paid the income tax assessed under the Act under protest. The Act provides for only one deduction of one thousand dollars from the aggregate annual income from all members of one family, and only one deduction in the case of a guardian of two or more minors in one family; there is a provision exempting all incomes of individuals under one thousand dollars; all servants and officers of the territory are taxed; all income derived from interest upon notes and bonds, is taxed.

Questions: (1) Is an income tax act discriminatory, which exempts incomes of individuals up to one thousand dollars, and allows only one deduction of a thousand dollars to be made from the aggregate annual income of all the members of one family?

(2) Is such an Act discriminatory which taxes all the income of all corporations, and exempts incomes of individuals up to one thousand dollars?

(3) Is an Act repugnant to the Constitution of the United States which contains a general clause taxing the incomes of officers of the territory, incomes derived from interest on notes and bonds, salaries of the Justices of the Supreme Court, and interest on United States bonds?

(4) Is a clause discriminatory which, in estimating the income from sales of personal property, permits the taxpayer to omit products produced and consumed by himself?

(5) Is an Act unlawful which taxes corporations and exempts insurance companies which are taxed under another Act?

Decision: (1) "Approximate equality and uniformity is all that is required. The legislature may classify objects and provide different methods of estimating amounts or values. So long as it acts in good faith and on general lines and makes distinctions on some reasonable basis, the courts cannot interfere. The provisions in question seem to be in harmony with the general theory of the Act. The Act seems to deal with units whether corporate or private. It treats as a unit all, whether few or many, large or small, whose income or incomes on the one hand and expenses on the other hand are combined * * *. If the thousand dollar exemption were made to apply to each individual, there would doubtless be much greater inequality in actual results than is the case under the law as it stands." The Act is not discriminatory in this respect.

(2) "Mr. Justice Brown said (158 U. S. 676): 'The exemption of $4,000 is designed, undoubtedly, to cover the actual living expenses of the large majority of families, and the fact that it is not applied to corporations is explained by the fact that corporations have no corresponding expenses'." This Act is valid for the same reason.

(3) "If the tax on such salaries and interest was provided for in a separate clause it is obvious that that clause would be separable and could be held invalid without affecting the remainder of the Act. But cannot one clause be held valid as to the bulk of the subjects to which it applies, and invalid or at least inoperative as to some subjects to which it would apply if taken literally? We think it can." The Act was, therefore, held to be valid but not to apply to Justices of the Supreme Court, and to interest on United States bonds.

(4) "It would be next to impossible for every one to keep an account and estimate the value of everything he produced and consumed. Accordingly, the law makes sales and expenditures the basis of estimating income in the case of movable property * * *." Such a basis is a reasonable one, and not discriminatory.

(5) "The two classes are taxed, as they properly might be, by different methods. One is taxed one per cent on property value and two per cent on net income; the other, one per cent on gross income. The court cannot say that this produces inequality in results." The court, therefore, held the Act constitutional.

ROCK ISLAND, ARK. & LA. RAILROAD CO. v. U. S.

(U. S. Supreme Court, Nov. 22, 1920)

(254 U. S. 141)

Record: Act of August 5, 1909, and Rev. Stat. Secs. 3220, 3226 and 3228. Suit to recover taxes paid. Dismissed because claimant had not complied with conditions imposed by the statute. Appealed. Affirmed.

Facts: After the tax was assessed a claim for an abatement was sent to the Commissioner of Internal Revenue in July, 1913. On December 18 of the same year the Commissioner rejected the application, whereupon on December 26 the claimant paid the tax with interest and a penalty. So far as appears there was no protest at the time of payment, and it is found that after payment nothing was done to secure repayment of the tax.

Question: Must plaintiff comply with the provisions of the revised statutes and regulations of the Treasury Department, requiring appeal to Commissioner for refund, before the court will consider the claim on its merits?

Decision: "Men must turn square corners when they deal with the Government. If it attaches even purely formal conditions to its consent to be sued, these conditions must be complied with. Lex non praecipit inutilia (Co. Lit. 127b) expresses rather an ideal than an accomplished fact. But in this case we cannot pronounce the second appeal a mere form. On appeal a judge sometimes concurs in a reversal of his decision below. It is possible, as suggested by the Court of Claims, that the second appeal may be heard by a different person. At all events the words are there in the statute and the regulations, and the court is of opinion that they mark the conditions of the claimant's right." The plaintiff, not having complied with the provisions of the statute and regulations of the Treasury Department, was not allowed to recover.

ROSTER GUANO CO. v. COMMONWEALTH OF VIRGINIA
(U. S. Supreme Court, January 1, 1920)
(253 U. S. 412)

Record: Virginia Act of April 16, 1903, and Amendments of March 22, 1916. Action at law to recover taxes paid. Judgment for defendant in the Virginia Corporation Court, and plaintiff applies to the Supreme Court of Appeals of Virginia for writ of error and supersedeas to review the judgment. Denied and judgment affirmed, and plaintiff brings error. Reversed.

Facts: Plaintiff is a corporation created under the laws of Virginia. It operates a manufacturing plant in the state of Virginia and several plants in other states. Plaintiff corporation was taxed under the laws of Virginia on net income earned within the state and without the state.

Question: Does a state law violate the equal protection clause of the Fourteenth Amendment of the United States Constitution, which taxes all the income of local corporations derived from business done both outside and within the state, while exempting entirely the income derived from outside the state by local corporations which do no local business?

Decision: "Equal protection of the laws required by the Fourteenth Amendment does not prevent the states from resorting to classification for the purposes of legislation. Numerous and familiar decisions of this court establish that they have a wide discretion in that regard. But the classification must be reasonable, not arbitrary, and must rest upon some ground of difference and a fair and substantial relation to the object of the legislation so that all persons similarly circumstanced shall be treated alike. The scope of discretion is notably wide in the classification of property for the purposes of taxation and in the granting of partial or total exemptions upon the grounds of policy." Virginia corporations deriving part of their income from without the state derive no more protection from the state of their origin with respect to their outside business and are no less subject to taxation by the state in which such business is conducted than the corporations which derive all of their income from without the state, and which are subject to the same laws as to the payment of organization taxes and annual registration fees and franchise taxes to the state of origin. Their business done within the state presumably is of some general benefit to the state, certainly it enriches its treasury by the amount of the taxes they pay upon the income derived therefrom; and the imposition upon them of taxes not only upon this income but also upon income that they derive from business conducted outside of the state has the effect of discriminating against them for that which ought to operate if at all in their favor. The Act violates the equal protection clause of the Fourteenth Amendment of the United States Constitution, and the plaintiff was allowed to recover the amount of taxes paid under the same.

SAFE DEPOSIT & TRUST CO. OF BALTIMORE, ETC., v. MILES, COLLECTOR

(U. S. District Court, Dist. of Md., May 26, 1921)
(Not reported)

Record: Revenue Act of 1918. Suit to recover taxes paid under protest after appeal to the Commissioner. Verdict for plaintiff.

Facts: The plaintiff, as guardian of one Frank R. Brown, an infant, sold for $12,546.80 the right to subscribe for thirty-five shares of the Hartford Fire Insurance Company. The shares of the Hartford Fire Insurance Company were worth, on March 1, 1913, $760 apiece. At the time of the death of the ward's father, intestate, the Government held that for the purpose of the Estate Tax, these shares were each of the value of $710 and that amount might be taken as their cost to the plaintiff. The insurance company determined to double the number of its shares and to give each of its stockholders the right, upon payment of $150 a share, to obtain as many new shares as he held old. The plaintiff, in the right of every share it held and which had cost it $710, could, by paying $150 a share more, get another, so that it would have two, which in the aggregate would have cost it $860, or $430 apiece.

Questions: (1) Is plaintiff's contention that what it received was capital, and not taxable as "income," well founded?

(2) Is the contention that as plaintiff paid nothing directly for the rights as such, all that it got from their sale was clear profit to it, well founded?

(3) If (2) above is not tenable, how shall the gain, if any, be determined on the rights sold and the stock retained when sold?

(4) May the value fixed by the government for the purpose of the Estate Tax at the time of the death intestate of the ward's father be taken as the cost to the plaintiff?

(5) May a profit be taxed before realized?

Decision: (1) This "contention * * * has * * * been negatived by the Supreme Court. The Merchants' Loan & Trust Co. v. Smietanka, decided March 28, 1921."

(2) "The issue thus joined is whether the law will look to the transaction as whole, or will close its eyes to everything that pre-

ceded the issue of the rights, and to all that came after their sale.
* * * What is taxable is the gain, profit or income derived
from the sale or dealing in property, whether real or personal.
* * * Congress, it is true, has very ample authority to adjust
its income taxes according to its discretion, and the rules it prescribes for the ascertainment of taxable income are binding upon
the courts unless they are palpably arbitrary and unjust. LaBelle
Iron Works v. The United States, decided May 16, 1921. The net
revenue from some peculiar kind of property, such as mines, may
include not only profit from operation, but a portion of the capital
as well. The problems of apportionment may be too difficult and
some of their factors too uncertain for adjustment by the courts,
and the tax may have to be assessed upon the entire net proceeds
with such deductions only, if any, as Congress may have authorized.
Von Baumbach v. Sargent Land Co., 242 U. S. 503. Nevertheless,
by and large, the statute means what it says, and that is that the
tax is to be levied on nothing else except gains, profits and income,
and upon them only when actually realized in money or in money's
worth, and in determining what is included therein, the courts will
look through form to substance. Doyle v. Mitchell Bros. Co., 247
U. S. 179; Eisner v. Macomber (Supra)." Looking through the
form, it is not true that the plaintiff paid nothing for the right and
he is not taxable upon all he received from the sale of the right.

(3) The plaintiff in the right of every share it held and which
had cost it as just mentioned, $710, could, by paying $150 a share
more, get another, so that it would have two, which in the aggregate would have cost it $860 or $430 apiece. "There
would be no way of distinguishing between the old (stock)
and the new. If the latter was something which had not
before existed, almost the same might truthfully be said of the
former. Its characteristics had undergone a great change. Before
the issue of the new stock, it represented one twenty-thousandth
of the capital of the company; afterwards it stood for but one
forty-thousandth. Moreover, if the plaintiff had in person taken
the new stock, and had had its old and new consolidated into one
certificate, and had subsequently sold a part of its holdings, it
could not say that that with which it parted was out of the old or

out of the new, or partly out of both. In determining its cost for the calculations of the profit or loss upon resale, it would be necessary to assume that they had one and all cost the holder an equal amount, which in the case of the plaintiff here was $430 a share. It certainly could make no difference that without waiting until the stock was issued, and then selling, it sold the right to the new stock, and made it a part of the consideration that the buyer should assume for it the payment of the $150 per share exacted by the company. All that would have to be borne in mind in comparing the two ways of reaching the same end, is that if the right was sold, the price really received for the new share was $150 more than the sum paid to the seller, which in the case at bar was $358.48. That was equivalent to $508.48 for a fully-paid-for share, and the $78.48 by which it exceeded the $430 which the share cost the plaintiff was the gain or profit it made out of the transaction. * * * If $78.48 be multiplied by 35, the number or shares of rights sold by the plaintiff, the product will be $2,746.80, and upon that it was properly taxable and upon nothing more.

(4) "It still retains thirty-five shares. When, if ever, they, or any of them are sold, there must be returned as profit in the year in which the price is received for them, the amount, if any, by which that price exceeds $430.'" In determining their cost for the calculation of the profit or loss, it is necessary to assume that they each cost the plaintiff $430 a share.

(5) "It is of course immaterial that if the plaintiff had chosen at the time it parted with the rights to the other thirty-five, to sell any of those it still held, it would have made a taxable profit of nearly $80 a share upon those so disposed of. There is no tax upon a profit until that profit is realized."

SAN FRANCISCO & P. S. S. CO. v. SCOTT, COLLECTOR
(U. S. District Court, N. D. Calif., Sept. 3, 1918)

(253 Fed. 854)

Record: Act of August 5, 1909. Action at law to recover taxes paid under protest on net income, under Sec. 38 of this Act. Judgment for plaintiff.

Facts: In its return for the years 1910 and 1912, plaintiff included in its deductions for ordinary and necessary expenses certain amounts for making repairs to the deck department, engine department and commissary department of its steamers, and also certain amounts for depreciation of such steamers, being 5% of the book value thereof. It was admitted that deductions for depreciation were reasonable and should be allowed, but the Commissioner ruled that the cost of making ordinary and necessary repairs was not a proper item to be included in the operation and maintenance expenses, but was covered by the deduction for depreciation, and required plaintiff to pay taxes thereon, which it did under protest, and hence this suit.

Question: Does the allowance of a deduction for depreciation of property include the cost of making ordinary and necessary repairs to it?

Decision: Under the law the tax is to be laid on net income and such net income is to be ascertained by deducting from gross income (1) all the ordinary and necessary expenses actually paid within the year out of income in the "maintenance and operation" of the business and property and (2) a reasonable allowance for depreciations, etc. It will thus be seen that the deductions allowed are to include not only ordinary and necessary expenses, but also the amounts paid out in the maintenance thereof, and in addition a reasonable sum for depreciation, if any. The operation of a business or property includes payments for labor and materials which go into the actual operation thereof, while maintenance means the upkeep or preserving the condition of the property to be operated and, therefore, includes the cost of ordinary repairs necessary and proper from time to time for that purpose. "Depreciation," as used in the statute, is not to be confused with ordinary repairs. It is intended to cover the estimated lessening in value of the original property, if any, due to wear and tear, decay or gradual decline from natural causes, which at some time in the future will require the abandonment or replacement of the property, in spite of current ordinary repairs. It does not include the cost of making repairs, which cost is a deductible item, and the plaintiff is entitled to recover the amount of tax paid because of the refusal of the Commissioner to allow the deduction.

SAVINGS INSTITUTION v. BLAIR
(U. S. Supreme Court, Jan. 4, 1886)
(116 U. S. 200)

Record: Sec. 3228 of Revised Statutes of the United States in regard to claims for refund. Action against Blair, as administrator for the estate of deceased collector of internal revenue to recover taxes alleged to have been illegally exacted. Judgment for defendant and plaintiff brought error. Affirmed.

Facts: Plaintiff made its amended return for internal revenue for the six months ending May 31, 1878. This return had written on it a statement that it was made in a certain way under protest and to prevent assessment of a penalty. Accompanying it was another return with a statement of what the plaintiff conceived to be the correct method of assessment. On June 18, 1878, the Commissioner assessed the tax at $1,796.25, which was paid by check stating on the face thereof that the payment was made under protest and to prevent distraint and penalty. Plaintiff contended the proper tax should have been $428.75. Defendant on the trial showed that for two years subsequent to the payments of the amounts assessed against plaintiff no appeal had been taken from such payments or claim made for refund to the Commissioner. Treasury Department regulations prescribing the forms and procedure for refunding of taxes in force from Jan. 1, 1871, to Dec. 31, 1878, were received in evidence.

Question: Were the facts of payment under protest endorsed on the checks and the making of prescribed and amended returns with protest and claim written thereon, adequate presentation of a claim for refund under Sec. 3228 of the Revised Statutes requiring that all claims for refund be presented within two years next after the cause of action accrued?

Decision: Failure to make claims for refund with Commissioner within two years after cause of action accrues bars suit. The court held that since it did not appear from the record that the protest upon the checks was ever brought in any way to the notice of the Commissioner, contention of the plaintiff in error that the protest, coupled with its amended return, is such a claim to the Commissioner as is required by law and regulations, was untenable. No claim for refunding of taxes can be made, the court said, until after the taxes have been paid and no claim whatever has been made since that time. "In our opinion," the court said, "no suit can be maintained for taxes illegally collected unless a claim therefore has been made within the time prescribed by the law." Judgment for defendant was affirmed.

SAYRE ET AL. v. BREWSTER, COLLECTOR
(U. S. District Court, N. D. N. Y., Oct. 30, 1920)
(268 Fed. 553)

Record: Revenue Act of 1916. Action to recover estate tax paid. On demurrer to the complaint. Demurrer overruled.

Facts: Plaintiffs, executors of the last will of Theodore S. Sayre, paid a transfer tax to the State of New York, which was approved in the Surrogate's Court as an administration expense. Plaintiffs were directed by the will to pay all taxes imposed upon the legacies and devises therein made.

Question: Was the transfer tax paid to the State of New York an allowable deduction in computing the net estate subject to the Federal Inheritance Tax?

Decision: The tax paid the State of New York, imposed by the laws of that State and approved and allowed by the Surrogate's Court, was one of "such other charges against the estate as are allowed by the laws of the jurisdiction whether within or without the United States, under which the estate is administered" (tit. 2, section 203 of the Act); and, therefore, the proper deduction for such payment must be made in computing the tax due the United States.

SHAFFER v. HOWARD
(U. S. District Court, E. D. Oklahoma, Feb. 4, 1918)
(250 Fed. 873)

Record: Oklahoma Income Tax Act. Bill in equity. Motion for a temporary injunction denied. Appeal to U. S. Supreme Court reached for hearing after the terms of office of the defendant officials had expired. Decree below reversed and cause remanded with directions to dismiss the bill for want of proper parties. 249 U. S. 200. See Shaffer v. Carter, 252 U. S. 37, passing upon the same points in a subsequent suit.

Facts: Plaintiff, a resident of Chicago, Ill., owned oil wells in Oklahoma. The Income Tax Law of the latter state, in addition to taxing the net income of residents thereof, imposed a tax upon that portion of the income of non-residents which was derived from sources within the state. Plaintiff, by this bill, sought to enjoin as invalid, the enforcement of said law to tax the income which he received from the oil wells in Oklahoma.

Question: Was the tax in question invalid, because, as the plaintiff contended, the income, or at least a material inseparable component part thereof (the directing or managing intelligence), was without the jurisdiction of the State of Oklahoma?

Decision: A state has jurisdiction to levy an income tax against a non-resident upon that portion of his income derived from property within the state.

SCHUYLKILL NAVIGATION CO. v. ELLIOTT, COLLECTOR
(U. S. Circuit Court, W. D. Pennsylvania, Oct. 4, 1875)
(Fed. Case 12497)

Record: Act of July 14, 1870. Action at law to recover taxes paid under protest. Judgment for defendant.

Facts: Plaintiff returned to the collector of internal revenue the amount of interest upon its bonded indebtedness payable on and between the first days of January and July, 1870, upon which the tax was assessed and paid.

Question: Has Congress the power to impose a tax under a statute when the measure of the tax is governed by the income of the past year, including income accrued before the passage of the Act?

Decision: The Supreme Court holds in the case of Stockdale v. Atlantic Insurance Company, 20 Wall. 323 (87 U. S.) that the 17th section of the Act of July 14, 1870, re-enacts Sections 122 and 123 of the Act of June 30, 1864, as modified by subsequent statutes, and subjects to the tax imposed by them the earnings of corporations which accrued before its passage. Although the contested assessment in the Atlantic Insurance Company case was upon corporate earnings, the principle of the decision is equally applicable to a tax levied upon the interest payable on corporate bonds because the tax upon the bonds is imposed by the same sections of the Acts of 1864, 1866 and 1867, which the court declares are continued in force by the Act of 1870. The court holds the tax in this case valid upon the authority of Stockdale v. Atlantic Insurance Company.

SCOTT, COLLECTOR. v. SCHWAB
(U. S. Circuit Court of Appeals, Ninth Cir., Jan. 6, 1919)
(255 Fed. 57)

Record: Act of Aug. 5, 1909. Action at law to recover taxes paid on net income under protest under Sec. 38 of this Act. Judgment for plaintiff and defendant brought error. Reversed and remanded, with instructions to sustain the demurrer.

Facts: The National Ice and Cold Storage Company was organized in 1911 to carry on the business of manufacturing, purchasing and selling of ice. In February, 1913, it sold all of its property and assets. The selling price exceeded by $190,000 the cost price in 1911. The tax on this gain, which was treated as income received during the year 1913, was paid under protest. This action was brought by plaintiff, as assignee of the company, to recover the amount of tax levied and paid under the Corporation Tax Act of 1909.

Question: Is gain realized on the sale of capital assets, which has accrued during a period of two years, income subject to tax the year received?

Decision: "Where property is sold by a corporation at an advance over the original purchase price, the amount of the advance must be deemed a gain or profit for the purpose of computing income for taxation" under the Corporation Tax Act of 1909. It was income subject to tax the year realized by sale, and the plaintiff is not entitled to recover the tax imposed upon it.

SHAEFER v. KETCHUM, COLLECTOR
(U. S. Circuit Court, S. D. New York, 1867)
(Fed. Case 12,693)

Record: Act of July 1, 1862. Action at law to recover tax paid. Verdict directed for the plaintiff.

Facts: Under Section 50 of the Act a tax was imposed on liquors "manufactured and sold, or removed for consumption and sale" after the 1st of September. The plaintiffs brewed beer during the month of April, and placed it in cool vaults during that month. It was removed for consumption and sale during the month of September. A tax was paid by the plaintiffs on this beer under a verbal protest noted by the collector on the receipt, the parties understanding that, if not paid, the law would be enforced.

Questions: (1) Are the words "removed for consumption and sale" to be construed as standing alone so that the plaintiff is liable for a tax on beer manufactured before Sept. 1, 1862, and removed for consumption and sale after that date?

(2) Is a verbal protest a sufficient protest where both parties are fully aware of the reason for the plaintiff's reason for paying, and of the action that will be taken if payment is not made?

Decision: (1) "The words 'removed for consumption or sale' are separated by the disjunctive 'or' from the 'manufactured and sold' as they must have been in order to make the provision intelligible. But it can not for a moment be supposed that Congress intended to allow beer made before the 1st of September to be sold after that date free of tax, while the same article made before, and removed for consumption or sale after the same date should be subject to tax. The obvious intent of the law was to subject all of this class of beverages in the hands of the manufacturer, made after the 1st of September, to a uniform tax, and the time when such tax should become payable was fixed at the date when the same should be sold or removed for consumption and sale." The beer having been manufactured before the 1st of September, the court held that it was not taxable.

(2) "The plaintiffs paid under this view of the matter and this must be deemed a constrained and not a voluntary payment. * * * If any protest at all was necessary, this was sufficient."

SHAFFER v. CARTER

(U. S. Supreme Court, March 1, 1920)

(252 U. S. 37)

Record: Oklahoma Income Tax law of 1915. In equity to en-join the collection of taxes. Judgment for defendant and plaintiff appeals. Affirmed.

Facts: Plaintiff, a nonresident of Oklahoma, was the owner in fee of certain oil producing land, and operated a number of oil and gas mining leases in Oklahoma. From properties thus owned and operated during the year 1916, he received a net income of $1,500,000. He made tax return under protest, but the state audi-tor overruled the protest and assessed the tax.

Question: Is the Income Tax Law of Oklahoma unconstitu-tional because (a) the state is without jurisdiction to levy a tax upon the income of nonresidents; (b) payment of the tax was en-forced by imposing a lien upon all of the taxpayer's property, real and personal without regard to its relation to the production of the income taxed; (c) the law subjects nonresidents to a tax more onerous than that imposed upon the citizens of Oklahoma?

Decision: (a) "In our system of government the States have general dominion, and, saving as restricted by particular pro-vision of the Federal Constitution, complete dominion over all per-sons, property and business transactions within their borders; they assume and perform the duty of preserving and protecting all such persons, property, and business, and, in consequence, have the power normally pertaining to governments to resort to all reason-able forms of taxation in order to defray the governmental ex-penses. Certainly, they are not restricted to property taxation, nor to any particular form of excises. In well ordered society, property has value chiefly for what it is capable of producing, and the activi-ties of mankind are devoted largely to making recurrent gains from the use and development of property, from tillage, mining, and manufacture, from the employment of human skill and labor, or from a combination of some of these; gains capable of being de-voted to their own support, and the surplus accumulated as an in-crease of capital. That the State, from whose laws property and business and industry derive the protection and security without which production and gainful occupation would be impossible, is debarred from exacting a share of those gains in the form of income taxes for the support of the government, is a proposition so wholly inconsistent with fundamental principles as to be refuted by its mere statement. That it may tax the land, but not the crop, the tree, but not the fruit, the mine or well, but not the products, the business, but not the profit derived from it, is wholly inadmissable. Income taxes are a recognized method of distributing the burdens of government, favored because requiring contributions from those who realize current pecuniary benefits under the protection of the government, and because the tax may be readily proportioned to their ability to pay. And we deem it clear, upon principle as well as authority, that just as a state may impose general income taxes upon its own citizens and residents whose persons are subject to its control, it may as a necessary consequence, levy a duty of like character, and not more onerous in its effect, upon incomes accruing to nonresidents from their property or business within the State, or their occupations carried on therein; enforcing payment, so far as it can, by the exercise of a just control over persons and property within its borders. This is consonant with numerous decisions of this court sustaining state taxation of credits.'' The Oklahoma Act confines the tax upon nonresidents to their net income from property and business carried on within the State. A similar distinction has been observed in all our Federal Income Tax laws. ''And so far as the question of jurisdiction is concerned, the due process clause of the Fourteenth Amendment imposes no greater restriction in this regard upon the several states than the corresponding clause of the Fifth Amendment imposes upon the United States.'' The appellant contended that an income tax is in the nature of a personal tax, ''or a 'subjective tax imposing personal liability upon the recipient of the income' and that as to a nonresident the state has no jurisdiction to impose such liability.'' This argument, upon analysis, resolves itself into a mere question of definitions and has no legitimate bearing upon any question raised under the Federal Constitution. For where the question is whether a state taxing law contravenes rights secured by that instrument, the decision must depend not upon any mere question of form, construction or definition, but upon the practical operation and effect of the tax imposed.'' The court, therefore, concluded that the state could tax nonresidents upon their income derived from within the state.

(b) Appellant ''was engaged in the business of developing and operating these properties for the production of oil, his entire business in that and other states was managed as one business, and his entire net income in the state for the year 1916 was derived from that business. Laying aside the probability that from time to time there may have been changes arising from purchases, new leases, sales, and expirations * * * it is evident that the lien will rest upon the same property interests which were the source of income upon which the tax was imposed. The entire jurisdiction of the state over appellant's property and business and the income derived from them * * * is a jurisdiction in rem; and we are clear that the state acted within its lawful power in treating his property interests and business as having both unity and continuity.'' Thus, the question, raised by the plaintiff, whether a state may create a lien upon any property of a nonresident for income taxes except the very property from which the income proceeded was not passed upon.

(c) Appellant contended ''that since the tax is as to citizens of Oklahoma a purely personal tax measured by their incomes, while as applied to a nonresident it is essentially a tax upon his property and business within the state, to which the property and business of a citizen are not 'subjected,' there was a discrimination against the nonresident.'' This reasoning was held incorrect ''in paying too much regard to theoretical distinctions and too little to the practical effect and operation of the respective taxes as levied; in failing to observe that in effect citizens and residents of the state are subjected at least to the same burden as nonresidents, and perhaps to a greater, since the tax imposed upon the former includes all income derived from their property and business within the state, and in addition, any income they may derive from outside sources. Appellant contends that there is a denial to noncitizens of the privileges and immunities to which they are entitled, and also a denial of the equal protection of the laws, in that the Act permits residents to deduct from their gross income not only losses incurred within the State of Oklahoma, but also those sustained outside of that state, while nonresidents may deduct only those incurred within the state. The difference, however, is only such as arises naturally from the extent of the jurisdiction of the state in its two classes of cases, and cannot be regarded as an unfriendly or unreasonable discrimination." The Act was, therefore, held to be constitutional, and the plaintiff was not entitled to an injunction restraining the collection of taxes upon his income taxed under the Act.

SHWAB v. DOYLE, COLLECTOR

(U. S. Circuit Court of Appeals, Sixth Cir., Dec. 10, 1920)

(269 Fed. 321)

Record: Act of Sept. 8, 1916. Suit at law by executor, plaintiff in error herein, against the collector of internal revenue to recover an estate tax paid under protest. Judgment for defendant. Writ of error to this court. Affirmed.

Facts: On April 22, 1915, decedent made to Detroit Trust Co. a deed absolute in form conveying about $1,000,000 of personal property in trust for payment of both interest and principal to certain beneficiaries with no reservations in favor of the grantor. The conveyance took effect immediately and was accompanied by delivery. It was voluntary and without monetary consideration. Decedent died Sept. 16, 1916. The tax here in question was assessed under Sec. 202 of this Act, as upon a transfer made in contemplation of death.

Questions: (1) Is the Act intended to reach absolute conveyances in contemplation of death made before the passage of the Act?

(2) If so intended, is it not unconstitutional?

(3) Is there any substantial evidence that the transfer was "in contemplation of death" within the meaning of the statute?

Decision: (1) "In our opinion the statute evidences an intent on the part of Congress that the tax should apply to all transfers in contemplation of death whether made before or after the passage of the Act, provided the transferrer's death occur after the

Act took effect." The opinion then discusses the considerations which the court stated evidence this intent of Congress.

(2) The Court held that the Act is not void as denying due process of law or as violating the Fifth Amendment to the Constitution; that the tax is not to be classified as a direct tax, thus void as within the constitutional requirement of apportionment, but is clearly an Excise or Duty Tax; that it is not invalid because applying to transfers made before its passage.

(3) The trial court correctly instructed the jury that "by the term in contemplation of death is not meant on the one hand the general expectancy of death which is entertained by all persons, for every person knows that he must die; that the meaning of the term is not necessarily limited to an expectancy of immediate death or a dying condition, but involves something between these two extremes; that it is not necessary in order to constitute a transfer in contemplation of death that the conveyance or transfer be made while death is imminent, while it is immediately impending by reason of bodily condition, ill-health, disease, or injury, or something of that kind; but a transfer may be said to be made in contemplation of death if the expectation or anticipation of death in either the immediate or reasonably distant future is the moving cause of the transfer." The transfer in trust was made April 22, 1915. Death occurred September 16, 1918, of apoplexy primarily resulting from hardening of the arteries. Deceased was a childless widow about 77 years of age and had lived for many years in the family of a sister whose children were the beneficiaries of the deed of trust. On May 26, 1915, deceased made her will and in it referred to the disposition of her estate. The court held that these were facts that were properly allowed to go to the jury, from which facts the jury found that the transfer was in contemplation of death.

SIMPSON ET AL. v. UNITED STATES
(U. S. Supreme Court, April 19, 1920)
(252 U. S. 547)

Record: Act of June 13, 1898. Action at law by plaintiffs to recover the Federal succession or estate tax assessed under the

Spanish War Revenue Act of June 13, 1898, and paid by executors. Plaintiffs filed a petition with U. S. Court of Claims for refund of these taxes. The Court of Claims dismissed the petition. Plaintiffs appeal to this court. Judgment affirmed.

Facts: John G. Moore died testate, while a citizen of New York, in June, 1899. On June 30, 1899, letters testamentary were issued to the executors. The decedent in his will directed his executors to convert a large residuary estate into money, to divide same into three equal shares, and to transfer two of such shares to a trustee to be selected by them, in trust to invest and reinvest, and to pay to each of his two daughters the whole of the net income of one share so long as she should live. Under the New York law the executors might have made payments on these legacies after Nov. 1, 1900, but because of pending litigation, the exact nature of which was not disclosed, no payments were made until after July 1, 1902. Pursuant to the authority derived from the Act the Commissioner of Internal Revenue, in order to provide for the determination of the amount of taxes to be assessed on legacies such as are here involved, issued instructions to collectors of internal revenue which contained tables showing the present worth of life interests in personal property with directions for computing the tax upon the same. These tables were based on "Actuaries" or "Combined Experience Tables," and were used in arriving at the amounts paid in this case. On April 1, 1901, the Commissioner levied a tax of about $12,000 on the share of each daughter, which was paid on April 15, 1901. The Act of Congress, approved June 27, 1902, provides for refunding to executors so much of any tax as may have been collected under warrant of that Act "on contingent beneficial interests which shall not have been vested prior to July 1, 1902." On October 29, 1907, plaintiffs presented their claim for the refund of the taxes paid.

Questions: (1) Did the Court of Claims err in refusing to hold that it was illegal to use mortuary tables, and to assume 4% as the value of money in computing the tax that was to be paid?

(2) Were the shares of the daughters in the residuary estate contingent beneficial interests not vested prior to July 1, 1902?

Decision: (1) Use of mortuary tables to determine value of life interests for purpose of estate tax is valid. The court stated that such tables, in fact the particular one used, had been resorted to for many years prior to 1899 by courts, legislatures and insurance companies for the purpose of determining the present value of future contingent interests in property, and that the court would take judicial notice of the fact that at the time this tax was collected 4% was very generally assumed to be the fair value or earning power of money safely invested. Both the method and the rate adopted in this case have been assumed by this court without discussion as proper in computing the amount of taxes to be collected under this War Revenue Act in prior cases, and "it is much too late to successfully assail a method so generally applied, and as to this claim of error the judgment of the court of claims is affirmed." Therefore, the use of the mortuary tables was not illegal, and the plaintiffs were not entitled to a refund.

(2) Under the laws of the state of New York in force when the estate was in process of administration the executors were obliged to discharge the specific legacies bequeathed by the will and pay the general legacies where there were sufficient assets after the expiration of one year from the date of letters. Amply sufficient assets were on hand in custody of the executors prior to July 1, 1920, to have increased the trust fund legacies of the daughters beyond the amount at which they were assessed for taxation. It was therefore the duty of the executors under the laws of New York to have made such payments prior to that date unless cause was shown for not doing so. The court held that no adequate cause for the delay in payment of the legacies was shown; that for many months prior to July 1, 1902, there was abundant assets with which to make payments upon the two legacies of the daughters; that for many months before that date it was the legal duty of the executors to make such payment; and that for a like time the legatees had a statutory right to institute suit to compel paymen. In conclusion on this question the court said: "It is obvious that legacies which it was thus the legal duty of the executors to pay before July 1, 1902, and for compelling payment of which a statutory remedy was given to the legatees before that date, were

vested in possession and enjoyment, within the meaning of the Act of June 27, 1902, as it was interpreted in United States v. Fidelity Trust Co., 222 U. S. 158, 56 L. Ed. 137, 32 Sup. Ct. Rep. 59; McCoach v. Pratt, 236 U. S. 562, 567, 59 L. Ed. 720, 721, 35 Sup. Ct. Rep.; 421 and Henry v. United States, 251 U. S. 393, 40 Sup. Ct. Rep. 185.'' Judgment of the court of claims dismissing the petition was affirmed.

IN RE SMITH
(Supreme Court of Hawaii, March 17, 1905)
(16 Haw. 796)

Record: Hawaiian Act of 1901. Appeal by the assessor from tax appeal court, sustaining the claim of the taxpayer. Reversed.

Facts: The taxpayer was a surveyor and made a deduction of a certain amount from his income for necessary expenses in carrying on his business, being the cost of instruments, books, etc.

Question: Is the amount that a surveyor expends in buying instruments and books a necessary expense in carrying on his business?

Decision: Without opinion, the court held that it was not.

SMITH v. DIRCKX, COUNTY CLERK
(Supreme Court of Missouri, May 31, 1920)
(223 S. W. 104)

Record: Missouri Income Tax Act of 1917, as amended by Act of 1919. Petition for an injunction. From judgment sustaining demurrer to plaintiff's petition, plaintiff appeals. Reversed and remanded with directions. Rehearing denied June 19, 1920.

Facts: The Act of 1917 provided a rate for the last half of calendar year of 1917, and for each calendar year thereafter of one-half of one percentum of the net income. The Act of 1919 provided that the rate for the calendar year 1919 and each year thereafter should be 1½ percentum. This Act was approved May 6, 1919, and effective Aug. 7, 1919.

Questions: (1) Did the General Assembly by the amendment of 1919 undertake to apply the increased rate to the net income received during the calendar year of 1919?

(2) If the amendment did so provide, does that portion of the amended rate which was an increase over the old rate operate retrospectively, in violation of Article 2, par 15, of the Wisconsin Constitution, as to that portion of the net income received by appellant during the year 1919 prior to Aug. 7, 1919, the effective date of the amendment?

Decision: (1) "We are of the opinion that the General Assembly intended that the amendment of 1919 should apply to the net incomes for the entire year of 1919."

(2) So much of the amendment of 1919 as undertook to assess an additional tax of 1% upon that portion of the net income for the year 1919, which was received prior to the going into effect of said amendment, operates retrospectively, and is in violation of Section 15 of Article 2 of our Constitution which provides, "That no ex post facto law, nor law impairing the obligation of contracts, *or retrospective in its operation* * * * can be passed by the General Assembly." "However, this should not operate to prevent the collection of a tax not exceeding one-half of 1% for the period above mentioned."

SOUTHERN PACIFIC CO. v. LOWE
(U. S. Supreme Court, June 3, 1918)
(247 U. S. 330)

Record: Act of Oct. 3, 1913. Action at law to recover taxes paid under protest on net income under this Act. Judgment for the defendant (238 Fed. 847), and plaintiff brought error. Reversed.

Facts: Each of two corporations, the Central Pacific and the Southern Pacific, had a nominal independent existence as a separate and distinct legal entity. Prior to Jan. 1, 1913, and at all times material to this case, the Southern Pacific, plaintiff herein, owned all the capital stock of the Central Pacific, and was in possession of and operated all the railroads and other assets of that company under a lease by which the Southern Pacific agreed to operate the property and make certain stipulated payments to the Central Pacific. The provisions of this lease were observed by both companies for bookkeeping purposes. A set of books was kept by each company, and transactions were entered as if each company was independent and separate, except for the contractual relation between them. As a result of these operations the Central Pacific Company showed upon its books a large surplus accumulated prior to Jan. 1, 1913, principally in the form of a debit to the Southern Pacific, which, as the sole stockholder, was entitled to all dividends that might be declared. During the first six months of the year 1914 this surplus was distributed in the form of dividends, which took the further form of payments to the Southern Pacific. The payments were only constructive, being carried into effect by book-keeping entries which simply reduced the apparent surplus of the Central Pacific and reduced the apparent indebtedness of the Central Pacific to the Southern Pacific by precisely the amount of the dividends.

Question: Are dividends received under these circumstances and in this manner by the Southern Pacific taxable as income of that company under the Income Tax Act of 1913?

Decision: While the two companies were separate legal entities, yet in fact and for all practical purposes they were merged, the Central Pacific being but a part of the Southern Pacific, acting merely as its agent and subject in all things to its proper direction and control. And besides, the funds represented by the dividends were in the actual possession and control of the Southern Pacific as well before as after the declaration of the dividends. The fact that books were kept in accordance with the provisions of the lease so that these funds appeared upon the account as an indebtedness of the lessee to the lessor, cannot be controlling, in view of the practical identity between lessor and lessee. Therefore, the court allowed the plaintiff to recover the amount of taxes paid upon the dividends.

SOUTHERN PAC. R. CO. v. MUENTER et al.

(U. S. Circuit Court of Appeals, Ninth Cir., Oct. 6, 1919)

(260 Fed. 837)

Record: Act of Aug. 5, 1909. Action at law to recover taxes paid under protest on net income under Sec. 38 of the Act. Judgment for defendants and plaintiff brought error. Affirmed.

Facts: During the years 1906, 1907 and 1908 plaintiff borrowed various sums of money and as security issued and sold interest bearing bonds, which bonds it was necessary to sell at a discount. Plaintiff reserved and set aside certain sums of money each year as the pro rata amount of the discount for the years 1909, 1910 and 1911, distributed over the entire period until the maturity of the bonds, and for the years 1909, 1910 and 1911 deducted such amounts from gross income, regarding the same as interest which it paid upon the loans.

Question: May money so reserved and set aside by book entries to meet the final payment of the discount be deducted from net income of the corporation under the Act of 1909?

Decision: The money set apart upon the books each year until the maturity of the bonds to meet the loss which came from selling the bonds below par was the application of a prudent and proper system of business, and was a wise provision for the future; but it was not the payment of interest, nor did it represent a loss actually sustained within the year. The money was in fact not paid out. Notwithstanding the books of the plaintiff in error, the money is still in its possession and subject to its control. A system of bookkeeping will not justify the government in claiming taxes, nor will it justify the taxpayer in claiming exemption from taxation. The plaintiff can not recover the tax assessed upon the amount set aside by the plaintiff each year to pay the bonds at maturity.

SPRINGER v. UNITED STATES

(U. S. Supreme Court, October, 1880)

(102 U. S. 586)

Record: Act of June 30, 1864, as amended by the Act of March 3, 1865. Action of ejectment to obtain possession of property levied upon by, and sold to the United States for non-payment of taxes. Judgment for plaintiff. Defendant appealed. Judgment affirmed.

Facts. Certain lands of plaintiff in error were distrained and sold because of his refusal to pay the income tax assessed against him under the Act of June 30, 1864, as amended by the Act of March 3, 1865, he having no goods or chattels known to the proper officers out of which the tax and penalty could have been satisfied. The United States became the purchaser of the lands, received a deed therefor, and brought ejectment against him.

Questions: (1) The plaintiff in error, not having objected at the trial to the admissibility of the deed on the ground that it referred to the Act of March 30, instead of that of June 30, could he raise this question in appeal?

(2) Was it improper for the collector to sell as an entirety lands which were separately assessed under the law of the state?

(3) Was the plaintiff in error deprived of his property without due process of law by reason of the fact that it was sold pursuant to distraint proceedings, without a judgment having been first obtained?

(4) Was the Act under which the taxes in question were assessed unconstitutional on the theory that it levied a direct tax without apportionment?

Decision: (1) The question of the misrecital in the deed, not having been brought to the attention of the court below, cannot be raised here.

(2) The state statute has no application to the question whether the premises should be sold by the collector en masse or in two or more parcels; and where the collector has acted in good faith, the sale cannot be questioned on this ground.

(3) Congress may, to enforce the payment of taxes, authorize the distraint and sale of either real or personal property. The owner of property so distrained and sold is not thereby deprived of it without due process of law.

(4) "Direct taxes, within the meaning of the Constitution, are only capitation taxes, as expressed in that instrument, and taxes on real estate." The tax in question was an excise or duty, and, therefore, not a direct tax within the meaning of the Constitution.

STANTON v. BALTIC MINING CO.
(U. S. Supreme Court, Feb. 21, 1916)
(240 U. S. 103)

Record: Act of Oct. 3, 1913. Suit in equity to enjoin the voluntary payment by the corporation and its officers of a tax assessed under this Act. Injunction denied.

Facts: Plaintiff, a stockholder of the Baltic Mining Co., alleged that the company would, if not restrained, "make a return for taxation conformably to the statute, and would pay the tax upon the basis of the statute without protest, and that to do so would result in depriving the complainant as a stockholder of rights secured by the Constitution of the United States, as the tax which it was proposed to pay without protest was void for repugnancy to that Constitution."

Question: (1) Is the Act of Oct. 3, 1913, unconstitutional and void under the Fifth Amendment, in that it denies to mining companies and their stockholders equal protection of the laws and deprives them of their property without due process of law for any or all of the following alleged reasons:

(a) Because all other persons were given a right to deduct a fair and reasonable percentage for losses and depreciation of their capital and they were, therefore, not confined to the arbitrary 5% fixed as the limit of deductions by mining corporations?

(b) Because by reason of the differences in the allowances which the statute permitted the tax levied was virtually a net income tax on other corporations and individuals, and a gross income tax on mining corporations?

(c) Because the statute established a discriminating rule as to individuals and other corporations as against mining corporations, in limiting the latter to a maximum allowance of five per cent of annual gross receipts or output for depletion?

(d) Because corporations were compelled to pay tax on dividends and individuals were not?

(e) Because of the discrimination resulting from the provision of the statute providing for a progressive increase of taxation or surtax as to individuals and not as to corporations?

(f) Because of the exemptions which the statute made of individual incomes below $4,000, and of incomes of labor organizations, and various other exemptions which were set forth?

(2) Is the Act of Oct. 3, 1913, void and unconstitutional in that:

(a) It is not within the authority of the Sixteenth Amendment, because that amendment authorizes an income tax without apportionment only when such tax is general and uniform?

(b) Its failure to provide for an adequate allowance for exhaustion of ore body makes the tax imposed a direct tax on property because of its ownership and, therefore, void because not apportioned?

Decision: (1) (a to f) It is apparent from the mere statement of these contentions that each and all of them were adversely disposed of by the decision in Brushaber v. Union Pacific Railway Company, 240 U. S. 1, and they all, therefore, may be put out of view.

(2) (a) This proposition is plainly in conflict with the meaning of the Sixteenth Amendment, as interpreted in the Brushaber Case, and may also be put out of view.

(b) "This contention merely asserts a right to take the taxation of mining corporations out of the rule established by the Sixteenth Amendment when there is no authority for doing so. It moreover rests upon the wholly fallacious assumption that, looked at from the point of view of substance, a tax on the product of a mine is necessarily in its essence and nature in every case a direct tax on property because of its ownership unless adequate allowance be made for exhaustion of the ore body to result from working the mine. We say wholly fallacious assumption because independently of the effect of the Sixteenth Amendment it was settled in Stratton's Independence v. Howbert, 231 U. S. 399, that such a tax is not a tax upon property as such because of its ownership, but a true excise levied upon the results of the business of carrying on mining operations." The Act of Oct. 3, 1913, therefore, is not unconstitutional for any of the reasons alleged.

STATE ex rel. OTTO EISENLOHR & BROS. v. DICKINSON
(Supreme Court of Wisconsin, Jan. 5, 1918)
(166 Wis. 501; 165 N. W. 1084)

Record: Mandamus proceeding to compel the defendant, the city treasurer, to accept personal property tax receipts as an off-set against income tax. From an order denying a motion to quash, and directing the peremptory writ to issue, the defendant appealed. Reversed.

Facts: During the year 1916 the tax commission assessed and levied an income tax for four omitted years, and placed it upon the 1916 tax roll. During the omitted years the relator paid taxes on personal property, and he tendered the personal property tax receipts as an offest against the income taxes. The Act provides that any person who shall have paid a tax assessment upon his personal property during any year shall be permitted to have the same applied in payment of income taxes assessed during that year.

Question: Where the income tax is assessed in a certain year for a number of omitted years, may personal property tax receipts for the omitted years be set off against the assessment, under an Act which permits such receipts to be received as payment "during any year?"

Decision: "The terms of the Statute do not provide for an offset of a personal property tax assessed during any other year than the year in which the income tax is assessed. Obviously plaintiff's personal property tax receipts for taxes assessed in 1912 to 1915, inclusive, are not applicable in payment of the income tax assessed against the plaintiff in 1916, which included an income tax for the omitted years of 1912 to 1915, inclusive." The court, therefore, refused to issue a mandamus to compel the treasurer to accept the relator's personal property tax receipts as an offset against the income tax assessed the relator.

STATE ex rel. ARPIN v. EBERHARDT
(Supreme Court of Wisconsin, June 17, 1914)
(158 Wis. 20; 147 N. W. 1016)

Record: Wisconsin Income Tax Act, Sec. 1087m. Petition against Eberhardt, County Clerk, to reverse and set aside a ruling of the County Board of Review. From a judgment for petitioner, defendant appeals. Affirmed.

Facts: The Wisconsin Income Tax Law passed in 1911, provided that: "The tax shall be assessed * * * upon all income not hereinafter exempted received by every person residing within the state, and by every nonresident of the state upon such income as is derived from sources within the state or within its jurisdiction. So much of the income of any person residing in the state as is derived from rentals, stocks, bonds, securities or evidences of indebtedness shall be assessed and taxed whether * * * derived from sources within or without the state," etc. The petitioner resided in Wisconsin and, in making his report, included an item of dividends on stocks. The income was, in fact, derived from a dredging business in Texas, carried on by a partnership, composed of the petitioner and others. The petitioner appealed to the board to correct his report, and it ruled to assess him on this item.

Question: Is the income of a person residing in Wisconsin taxable under the Act, where such income is derived from a business carried on in another state?

Decision: The first sentence "might well mean that *all* income of a resident of the state derived from any source whatever is taxable, and that all income of a nonresident derived from sources within the state is taxable. The sentence might also mean simply that all income of residents and nonresidents of the state, derived from sources within the state, is taxable. * * * To hold to the construction first suggested would make the first clause of the second sentence tautology pure and simple. * * * By adopting the second construction of the first sentence, the entire section is given force and effect, and this is as it should be. The profits received by Mr. Arpin were not rents, stocks, bonds, securities, or evidences of indebtedness, and, being derived from a source without the state, were not taxable."

STATE ex rel. BOLENS v. FREAR et al.

WINDING et al. v. FREAR et al.

(Supreme Court of Wisconsin, January 9, 1912)

(148 Wis. 456; 134 N. W. 673)

Record: Wisconsin Act of 1911. Actions in equity to enjoin the secretary of state and other state officers, including tax commission, from paying out any state moneys or enforcing the Act. Injunctions refused.

Facts: The Winding case was brought into this court on appeal, and is an action by various persons and corporations who claim that the Act is unconstitutional. The Bolens action attacks the constitutionality of the Act, and is an action sought to be brought within the original jurisdiction of the Supreme Court. The constitution of Wisconsin provided that the rule of taxation should be uniform, and that taxes might be levied on such property as the legislature might provide. This was amended by providing for a graduated income tax. The Income Tax Act provided that the taxpayer who had paid a personal property tax for the year should be entitled to have the amount so paid credited on his income tax, that the estimated rental of residence property occupied by the owner should be considered as income, that the income of a wife living with her husband should be added to the income of the husband, and that there should be a different rate on the incomes of corporations than on individuals.

Questions: (1) Is a tax upon the income derived from real property double taxation where there is a tax on the property?

(2) Is an Income Tax Act unconstitutional in that it is discriminatory if it allows one who has paid a property tax to have the amount credited on his income tax?

(3) Can the estimated rental value of a residence occupied by the owner be made income by an Act of the legislature?

(4) Is an Act, which provides that the income of the wife living with the husband be added to the income of the husband, discriminatory?

(5) Is an Act discriminatory which provides a different rate of income tax for corporations than for individuals?

Decision: (1) "There can be no doubt that income taxation is directly authorized by the constitution of Wisconsin as amended in 1908. Words could hardly be plainer to express that idea than the words used. From them it clearly appears that taxation of property and taxation of income are recognized as two separate and distinct things in the state constitution. Both may be levied, and lawfully levied, because the constitution says so. However philosophical the argument may be that taxation of rents received from property is in effect taxation of the property itself, the people of Wisconsin have said that 'property' means one thing, and 'income' means another; in other words, that income taxation is not property taxation, as the words are used in the constitution of Wisconsin." Since income taxation is not property taxation, to tax the income where there is a tax on the property is not double taxation.

(2) "It was evidently done with the idea of accomplishing, without too violent a shock to the taxing machinery, the substantial elimination of personal property taxation, and the substitution thereof of 'ability' taxation." It is a reasonable means of equalizing the burden of the new form of taxation, and is not discriminatory.

(3) "The clause was doubtless inserted in an effort to equalize the situation of two men each possessed of a house of equal rental value, one of whom rents his house to a tenant, while the other occupies his house himself. Under the clause in question, the two men with like property are placed on an equal footing, and in no other way apparently can that be done." The court, accordingly, answered this question in the affirmative.

(4) "The temptation to make colorable shifts and transfers of property in order to secure double or even triple exemptions, if there were not some provision of this kind in the law, would unquestionably be very great. There is no such temptation or opportunity in the case of the single man, or the man and woman who are living separately." This provision is not discriminatory, and is therefore valid.

(5) "It might be said with truth that the clause could be justified on the ground that it is an amendment to every corporate charter, which the legislature has the right to make, but it is not

necessary to rely on that proposition. The corporate privileges, which are exclusively held by corporations, and the real difference between the situation of a corporation and an individual * * * plainly justifies a difference of treatment in the levying of the income tax." The Act is not discriminatory and an injunction was refused.

STATE ex rel. MARINER v. HAMPEL
(Supreme Court of Wisconsin, June 23, 1920)
(178 N. W. 244)

Record: Wisconsin Income Tax Act of 1919. Petition to review proceedings of tax commission and to set aside assessments made by the tax commission. Determination of tax commission reversed and assessments set aside. Defendants appealed. Affirmed.

Facts: A corporation organized in Wisconsin owned land and mines in Michigan. By an agreement, it transferred the title to this property to trustees to hold in trust for the petitioners. The petitioners have been paid money, which the trustees received as rent from the mines, and have been assessed an income tax upon it as income received by them from business transacted within the state. The beneficiaries, the petitioners, are the stockholders of the corporation.

Question: Do the proceeds from the mines without the state belong to the trustees as such so that the disbursement of the fund is a business located within the state, and the money received by the beneficiaries is income from sources within the state?

Decision: "The provisions of section 1087 M 10 (5) make the fiduciaries specified therein the representatives of their beneficiaries for the purpose of income taxation, and their activities in Wisconsin in conducting the trust affairs concerning property and business located without the state can not be held as operating to transform the business of such trustees to a business conducted within the state * * * . It is considered that the income paid the beneficiaries as the net proceeds of rental of the Michigan mines under the trust agreement is received by them as income derived from sources without the state, and is therefore not taxable under the state income tax law."

STATE ex rel. ATWOOD v. JOHNSON et al.

(Supreme Court of Wisconsin, Nov. 17, 1919)

(170 Wis. 218; 175 N. W. 589)

Record: Soldiers' Bonus Act of Wisconsin, July 30, 1919. Action against state treasurer and others to test the constitutionality of the Act. Demurrer to complaint sustained, and action dismissed.

Facts: The Soldiers' Bonus Act was passed for the purpose of raising a sum sufficient to assure each soldier, sailor, marine and nurse who served in the armed forces of the United States during the war against Germany a certain sum, "as a token of appreciation of the character and spirit of their patriotic service, and to perpetuate such appreciation as a part of the history of Wisconsin." The amount necessary was to be raised by a surtax upon taxable incomes of individuals and of corporations in addition to the normal income tax. The surtax rate for individuals was not the same as for corporations.

Questions: (1) Is an act providing for the raising of money to give to soldiers who served in the army of the United States for a public purpose within the meaning of the constitution of the state?

(2) Does the power of Congress under the Federal Constitution to raise and support armies and to provide and maintain a navy exclude such state legislation as is involved in this Act?

(3) Is the Act unconstitutional because the state constitution has provided that taxes shall be uniform?

Decision: (1) "The benefit which flows to the United States from the services performed is also a benefit to the state. The United States is composed of a family of states which in the aggregate constitute the United States. The common defense by the nation can only be successfully maintained by co-operation of the states; hence, when a war is waged by a nation, those supporting it are performing service as well for their respective states as for the nation." Therefore, the money paid them in recognition of that service is for a public purpose within the meaning of the state constitution.

(2) "Powers not expressly or by necessary implication granted by the Constitution to the Federal government nor prohibited by it to the states are reserved to the states respectively, or to the people, * * * .It is clear under the Federal Constitution (Art. 2) as well as under our state constitution (Art. 1, Sec. 20) that a certain military power is reserved to the state * * * ." The Soldiers' Bonus Law under consideration does not interfere with the exercise of the power to raise and support an army by the United States, and since it does not interfere with the power of the United States it comes within the power reserved to the state, and not prohibited the state by the Federal Constitution.

(3) "The surtax provision is in effect an amendment to the Income Tax Law by increasing the tax upon incomes * * * . The only uniformity required under the Income Tax Law is uniformity within the class." This Act has uniformity within the class, and is not unconstitutional.

STATE ex rel. AMERICAN MFG. CO. v. KOELN, COLL.
(Supreme Court of Missouri, April 7, 1919)
(278 Mo. 28; 211 S. W. 31)

Record: Missouri Income Tax Act of 1917. The relator corporation seeks by mandamus to compel the collector to allow certain credits. Peremptory writ of mandamus was awarded, and collector appealed. Judgment reversed.

Facts: Sec. 32 of the Act provided that "Any person, corporation * * * who shall have paid a tax assessed upon his real or personal property to the state * * * shall be permitted to exhibit the receipt or receipts thereof to the *assessor* to the full amount in the payment of income taxes." The assessor was required to make assessments by March 1, and after that he had nothing to do with the income tax. Payment of the tax was required to be made to the *collector*. The corporation exhibited its receipts to the collector, who refused to allow credits. Some of the receipts were for school taxes.

Questions: (1) Should the word "assessor" in the Act, where it renders the Act absurd, be construed to read "collector," which is in harmony with the legislative intent?

(2) Does the phrase, "who shall have paid the tax assessed upon his real or personal property to the state" as used in the Act include taxes which the corporation paid for school purposes?

Decision: (1) "The Act says that the receipts shall be exhibited to the full amount not for the purpose of affecting the assessment of the income tax, but in the payment of income taxes. The payment of the income tax is required to be made to the collector and not to the assessor. Mere verbal inaccuracies * * * will be corrected by the court whenever necessary to carry out the intent of the legislature as gathered from the entire Act." Therefore, the collector is the person to whom the receipts should be exhibited.

(2) Under the law the only taxes on real and personal property which the state itself is permitted to levy and collect are taxes at a certain rate for each of the following purposes: To pay interest on the certificates of indebtedness of the state to the public school funds; for state revenue; for payment of interest and to create a sinking fund for payment of state capitol building bonds. "The school taxes * * * were not taxes paid to the state under levies made by the state for any of the above purposes, but evidently were taxes levied by and collected for the benefit of the local school district." For this reason credit is not to be allowed "for school taxes."

STATE ex rel. MEYER BROS. DRUG CO. v. KOELN, COLL.

(Supreme Court of Missouri, May 21, 1920)

(222 S. W. 389)

Record: Missouri Income Tax Act of 1917. Judgment for plaintiff and defendant appeals. Reversed.

Facts: Prior to March 1, 1919, plaintiff duly made a return of its income for the year 1918. By the Act of May 26, 1919, effective on that date, the legislature repealed Sec. 32 (section quoted in case of State v. Koeln, above) of the Income Tax Law of 1917. Thereafter during 1919 plaintiff paid its property taxes and received receipts therefor. On December 17, 1919, plaintiff exhibited these receipts to the state and demanded that the amount of the property tax receipts be credited on its income tax bill.

Question: Had plaintiff's right to credit for property tax paid vested prior to the repeal of Sec. 32 of the Act of 1917?

Decision: The property taxes deductible under Sec. 32 of the Act of 1917 were those which became due and payable in the same year in which the income tax from which they were deductible became due and payable. The plaintiff's income tax for 1918 was assessed prior to March 1, 1919. At the time plaintiff's income tax was assessed on income for 1918 (March, 1919) plaintiff had paid no property taxes which were deductible under Sec. 32. The same thing was true at the time Sec. 32 was repealed, May 26, 1919. No right or privilege had accrued to plaintiff on May 26, 1919. This right could never have accrued until after (1) payment of property taxes and (2) presentation of receipts therefor. All that plaintiff had when Sec. 32 was repealed was an "expectation based upon the continuance of" Sec. 32, and this was not an invested right. The result was that the plaintiff was not entitled to have the property tax receipts credited on its income tax bill.

STATE ex rel. MOON et al. v. NYGAARD

(Supreme Court of Wisconsin, January 13, 1920)

(175 N. W. 810)

Record: Wisconsin Act of May 21, 1917. Writ of certiorari to review the determinations of the tax commission. Judgment for relators, and defendant appealed. Affirmed.

Facts: The relators in this action were stockholders of the Sally F. Moon Company, which company is merely a holding company. The company of which the Moon Company owns all the stock, declared a dividend in 1917 to be paid out of a surplus which existed before January 1, 1911. The Moon Company in turn paid a dividend to its stockholders, the relators in this case. The Act of 1917 provided for the levying of a tax upon annual incomes; defined income to include dividends derived from stocks; and further provided "that the term 'dividends' as used in this section should be held to mean any distribution made by a corporation, joint stock company, or association, out of its earnings or profits accrued since January 1, 1911, and paid to its shareholders whether in cash or in stock of the corporation, joint stock company or association.''

Question: Are the dividends received from a holding corporation, which dividends were paid by the operating corporation to the holding corporation out of a fund which accrued before Jan. 1, 1911, taxable under an Income Tax Act defining "income" to include distribution of dividends out of earnings accrued since January 1, 1911?

Decision: "We construe the legislative definition now applicable to the 'term' dividend as it stands in the amended section 1087 m 2, as intended to permit the opening of the door of inquiry as to the source from which came the money paid by a corporation to its stockholders, although designated by it as dividends, the door which was in effect declared in the prior cases completely closed. The result now is that a stockholder in any corporation to whom, as stockholder, there has been paid a sum of money under the designation of dividends has the right to show that such payment or dividend was made out of capital or surplus, and therefore not taxable, instead of out of earnings or profits accrued since January 1, 1911, which would be taxable. That the fund in question passes through the treasury of the Sally F. Moon Company, after leaving that of the Northwestern Lumber Company, and before reaching the hands of the relators, does not change the nature of the transaction. At no time on its passage from the first company to the relators does it meet the present definition of the dividend, which is to be considered as part of the taxable income of an individual * * *. Giving the words 'earnings' and 'profits' their plain, every-day meaning, the payments in question here are not profits or earnings accrued since January 1, 1911, to the Sally F. Moon Company, and therefore do not meet the present statutory definition of taxable income." The court therefore set aside the assessment made by the tax commission upon the dividends received by the relators.

STATE ex rel. WICKHAM v. NYGAARD
(Supreme Court of Wisconsin, January 12, 1915)
(159 Wis. 396; 150 N. W. 513)

Record: Wisconsin Act of 1913. Certiorari proceedings to set aside an income tax assessment levied by the taxing officers. Judgment for defendant, and relator appeals. Affirmed.

Facts: The relator was a circuit judge of the state of Wisconsin, and was assessed an income tax on his salary. He appeared before the board of review, and objected to the assessment. The objection was sustained, and the income tax assessor appealed to the state commission. The commission reversed the decision of the board of review. The constitution provides that the compensation of any public officer shall not be increased or diminished during his term of office; and, by way of amendment, that a tax may be imposed on incomes, which tax may be progressive and graduated. Any person dissatisfied with any determination of the county board of review may appeal to the commission. The code contains the additional provisions set out in Question 2.

Questions: (1) Is the taxation of the salary of a circuit judge forbidden by the constitution which provides that the salary of a public officer shall not be diminished during his term, but later by amendment permits taxes on all incomes?

(2) Has the tax assessor the power to appeal from the decision of the board of review to the commission, as being a party to the proceedings, having an interest in the controversy, and being prejudiced by it, where the Income Tax Act provides that any person dissatisfied with any determination of the county board of review may appeal?

Decision: (1) "The real question is one of construction involving the comprehensiveness of the 1908 amendment. The language is broad and sweeping, making and containing no exception. Both constitutional provisions are somewhat general in their nature. As applied to the right to tax incomes of state officers, section 26 of article 4 is no more specific than is the amendment of 1908. Hardly as much so. The latter says taxes may be 'imposed on incomes.' We are not at liberty to rewrite this clause so as to read that taxes may be 'imposed on incomes' except where the income consists of a salary received by a public officer.' We perceive very little room for construction, and, if a doubtful question were involved, it should not be resolved against the exercise of the taxing power by the state." Accordingly, it was held that the constitution did not prohibit the tax upon the salaries of state judges.

(2) "It may be fairly said that taxpayers generally are interested in seeing that no property escapes taxation. A full disclosure tends to equalize the burden of taxation, and, theoretically at least, to lessen it as to those who comply with the law. An income tax assessor is charged with very important duties in reference to the administration of the Income Tax Law. He assessed this income in the first instance. He was a person dissatisfied with the action of the board of review and it seems clear that the statute conferred on him the right to appeal."

STATE ex rel. WISCONSIN TRUST CO. et al. v. PHELPS

(Supreme Court of Wisconsin, March 9, 1920)
(176 N. W. 863)

Record: Wisconsin Income Tax Act of 1917. Certiorari to review the validity of an assessment. From a judgment confirming the assessment the relators appeal. Affirmed. Motion for rehearing denied July 3, 1920, 178 N. W. 471.

Facts: Relators were trustees under a will and, as such, received income from various sources. In the year 1917 a Pennsylvania corporation from which the trust estate was entitled to receive dividends paid the amount thereof direct to one of the beneficiaries who was a resident of Pennsylvania. The beneficiary gave the Wisconsin Trust Company a receipt for this payment which was entered on the books of the trust estate and accounted for by the Wisconsin Trust Company, which was at all times in possession of the physical assets of the estate and kept all the accounts thereof.

Question: Did this transaction constitute a payment of income to the Wisconsin Trust Company with reference to which it was obliged to render a return and pay the tax?

Decision: The transaction constituted in law a payment to the Wisconsin Trust Company, and such income was "received" within the meaning of the statute in question and was properly assessed for income taxation.

STATE ex rel. HOUGHTON et al. v. PHELPS, COUNTY CLERK

(Supreme Court of Wisconsin, February 10, 1920)

(176 N. W. 217)

Record: Wisconsin Income Tax Act of 1917. Certiorari to review a determination of the board of income tax review for Milwaukee County. From judgment setting aside the action of the board, defendant appeals. Affirmed.

Facts: The plaintiffs were associated as partners in a law practice in Milwaukee. In 1916 the firm received a fee of $21,000 and expenses, amounting to $3,100, for certain services rendered and expenses incurred in litigation lasting from 1909 to 1916. Of these amounts $4,300 represented the proportionate amount of services for 1909 and 1910, and $172.31 the expenses incurred in those years. In their partnership return the plaintiffs showed the gross receipts of the firm, including the $21,000. They then deducted $4,300 as earned prior to 1911, and $172.31, expenses of 1909 and 1910. After making certain other deductions, which are not in question, the entire balance, which was distributed among the partners, was deducted as the reasonable value of the services of the firm members. Section 1087m-4 of the Act refers to deductions for persons other than corporations and provides for a reasonable allowance for services of co-partners or members of a firm actually rendered in producing the income of the firm.

Questions: (1) Does Section 1087 m 2, sub. 1, of the Wisconsin Act include a legal partnership, or is it confined to trade or mercantile partnerships?

(2) Should the items of $172.31 and $4,300 be treated as not income of 1916, because earned prior to 1911, the year of the first Wisconsin Income Tax Act?

(3) Does section 1087 m 4 entitle the plaintiffs to a deduction for the reasonable value of the services of the firm in producing the income, and if so, in what amount?

Decision: (1) The words "individual, firm, copartnerships" are used in the statute in their ordinary and usual meaning. The plaintiffs' firm was such a firm as is designated in the statute.

(2) The term "income" as used in the Act "covers and includes just such and all of such a fund as was the $21,000 fee received by the relators as part of their gross income of 1916. Cash thus received in that year is income of that year, and can not be separated for income tax purposes by any method of differentiation based upon questions as to when services may have been rendered for which such money was payment."

(3) The firm was entitled to a reasonable allowance for services rendered in producing the income irrespective of the time when the services were rendered. The testimony showed that "in such situations as we have here the money which a firm of lawyers distributes among its members out of its income as their earnings is the reasonable allowance to them for their services in producing such income." There was thus no taxable income to be assessed against the relators as a firm for the year 1916.

STATE v. PINDER
(Court of General Sessions of Delaware, October 18, 1919)
(108 Atl. 43)

Record: Income Tax Act of Delaware, Chapter 26, Vol. 29, Laws of Delaware. Action at law upon indictment of defendant for refusal to make return under provisions of this Act.

Facts: Defendant refused to make tax return in the form prescribed by the state treasurer for the calendar year, 1918.

Question: Is the Income Tax Law of Delaware unconstitutional for the following reasons:

(a) Because the legislature had, at the time of the enactment of said law, no authority under the constitution of the state to enact a statute providing for an income tax?

(b) Because said statute lacks the uniformity required of all tax laws by article 8, section 1, of the constitution?

(c) Because the statute by certain exemptions (see decision [b] below) denies to citizens of the state the equal protection of the law guaranteed by the Fourteenth Amendment to the Constitution of the United States?

Decision: (a) Section 1 of article 8 of the constitution of this state provides as follows: "All taxes shall be uniform upon the same class of subjects within the territorial limits of the authority levying the tax, and shall be levied and collected under general laws, but the general assembly may by general laws exempt from taxation such property as in the opinion of the general assembly will best promote the public welfare." The plaintiff contended that under section 1 article 8 quoted above, that nothing but "property" can be the subject of taxation, and income is not property. "The provision of the Delaware constitution respecting taxation is not a grant of power. The legislature is not restrained in the selection of the subjects of taxation." There is no provision "that taxes shall be 'uniform on all property or species of property taxes' or that 'taxation upon property shall be in proportion to its value or ad valorem'." The Delaware legislature has the power to tax the incomes of citizens, even though the power is not expressly given by the constitution, if there is no restriction against it. It is contended that there is an implied inhibition against taxation of incomes from the use of the word "property" in the exemption clause. The legislature having the inherent power to tax everything to which the legislative power extends, which necessarily includes income, the word "property" in the exemption clause is employed in its broadest sense, and comprehends everything, or class of subjects to which the legislative power extends. "All the constitution makers had in mind respecting taxation was uniformity and the public welfare. Everything else was left to the discretion of the legislature." The court "prefers to take the natural, logical, and reasonable position that income is property, within the meaning of the word as used in the exemption clause of section 1 article 8 of the Delaware constitution" and is inclined to believe that no court in this country today, in construing a constitutional provision similar to the one in question, would maintain the contrary position. The conclusion of the court is that the legislature did have authority to tax income.

(b) "The plaintiff contended that the statute is not uniform upon the same class of subjects, because salaries of state officials, rentals from real estate, income derived from agricultural operations, and incomes that do not exceed $1,000 are exempt from its operation. The question is whether the legislature can exempt certain incomes received by persons, and not whether it can exempt certain citizens, as was contended by the plaintiff. It was not a question whether such exemptions best promote the public welfare, but whether they do so in the opinion of the general assembly. The reason for exempting the rentals of real estate was found in the belief of the general assembly that the burden of taxation had not been fair, and that real estate had borne too great a proportion of such burden. In order to equalize the load, rentals were exempted and sources of income not previously reached were taxed. The reason for exempting gains or profits derived from agricultural operations was found in the fact that, if the tenant had to pay a tax upon his profits, he would be entitled to a lower rental, and to the extent the rental was decreased, the return of the landlord would be diminished." In other words, the owner would indirectly have to pay the tax levied against the profits of his tenant. On the other hand, if the owner of the land is operating the farm, he would be directly liable for the tax. In either case the exemption of gains or profits derived from agricultural operations is closely related to the one just considered and the same reasoning applies. "In the exemption of incomes that do not exceed $1,000, the general assembly believed that it would best promote the general welfare by exempting the incomes of persons with such limited means, and the classification is reasonable and proper. The only qualification the law affixes to the opinion of the general assembly is that it must be reasonable and not arbitrary. * * * The legislature is given much latitude in determining what kinds of property should be exempt from taxation as best promoting, in their opinion, the public welfare. The general assembly believed that the taxation of the salaries of state officers would render the Act unconstitutional, and the belief which influenced the legislature was a reasonable one in view of the fact that the Delaware constitution prevents the diminishing of the salary of a state officer, and that Congress made the same exemption in the Federal Income Tax Law because of the belief that otherwise the Act would be declared unconstitutional." Therefore, the statute was not in violation of the uniformity clause of the state constitution.

(c) "All the law requires is that the classification of persons who are to be exempt from the operation of the statute shall not be arbitrary and unreasonable, under the conditions which the legislature believed to exist; that it shall be possible for the court to say there was a fair reason for the exemption, and that the classification rests upon some difference which bears a reasonable and just relation to the Act in respect to which the classification was proposed." The statute was not unconstitutional in this respect, and the defendant was under a duty to make a tax return.

STATE ex rel. COLUMBIA CONST. CO. v. TAX COMMISSION
(Supreme Court of Wisconsin, December 4, 1917)
(165 N. W. 382)

Record: Wisconsin Act of 1915. Certiorari to review the proceedings of the tax commission of Wisconsin assessing an income tax against the relator. Judgment reversing the tax commission's determination, and commission appealed. Reversed, and action remanded, with directions to affirm commission's determinations.

Facts: The relator corporation owns stock in the Fidelty Gas Company, which, in turn, owns stock in Wisconsin Securities Company. The securities company paid an income tax on its entire income. The sole income of the gas company consisted of dividends on its stocks in the securities company, and it was exempted from the payment of any tax. The statute exempts dividends received from stocks in any corporation upon the income of which there has already been assessed an income tax. The relator, therefore, claims that dividends which it received from the gas company should be exempted.

Question: Does a statute, which exempts dividends received from stocks in any corporation, the income of which has already been assessed, exempt dividends received by a company from another company whose sole income was derived from dividends from a third company?

Decision: "The crucial question in this case is whether the word 'assess' means simply to list the income and decide whether it is subject to taxation or not, or whether it means to impose the charge or burden of income taxation thereon. The tax commission held the latter view, and this court adopted that view. * * * Under our construction of the word 'assessed' the income of the Fidelity Gas Company was not assessed, but exempted from assessment. * * * The relator had no stock in the securities company, and hence received no dividends from stock in a corporation whose income had already been assessed." The court therefore directed that the determination of the tax commission be affirmed.

STATE ex rel. BRENK v. WIDULE
(Supreme Court of Wisconsin, October 26, 1915)
(161 Wis. 396; 154 N. W. 696)

Record: Wisconsin Act of 1913. Certiorari against Widule, clerk of the county board of review, to revise the action of the income tax board of review. Judgment for relator, and defendant appealed. Affirmed.

Facts: The relator, a resident of Wisconsin, inherited real estate from his mother, which real estate was located in Michigan. Relator's mother was a resident of the state of Michigan at the time of her death. The relator, in making return of his income listed the inheritance under the head of "Gross Income," but claimed the right to deduct the inheritance under the head of "deductions and exemptions." Subdivision 3 of section 1087m-2, statutes 1911, assessed a tax upon every resident or nonresident upon such income as was derived from sources within the state or its jurisdiction. The Act of 1913 assessed a tax upon every resident or nonresident upon such income as was derived from property located or business transacted within the state.

Question: Is an inheritance of real estate located in another state taxable under the income tax Act, to a resident of Wisconsin who inherits it?

Decision: "The provisions of subdivision 3 of section 1087 m-2, statutes 1911, were fully considered and construed in the case of State ex rel. Arpin v. Eberhart, 158 Wis. 20, 147 N. W. 1016.

Upon full discussion and consideration of the different parts of
this statute, it was determined that: 'All income received by residents of the state from sources within it is taxable, and all income
of such residents from sources without the state on account of
rentals, stocks, bonds, securities or evidences of indebtedness is not
taxable. No other income is made taxable by the law and therefore
cannot be taxed.' Nothing is suggested nor do we perceive any
reasons why this was not the correct interpretation of the statute.
The provisions of this section as amended in 1913 do not change
the law in this respect. Assuming for the purpose of this case
that this inheritance is 'income' within the meaning of the income
tax law, it is within the class of incomes derived from sources
wholly without the state, and therefore is not taxable.''

STATE ex rel. HICKOX v. WIDULE

(Supreme Court of Wisconsin, April 4, 1917)
(166 Wis. 113; 163 N. W. 648)

Record: Wisconsin Income Tax Act of 1915. Appeal from
a judgment annulling an assessment of tax. Judgment reversed
and cause remanded with instruction to affirm the levy of the tax.

Facts: An executor, in making a return of income of the
estate, included, among other deductions, taxes paid upon unpro-
ductive property, and also $5,000, the amount of an annuity paid
to the widow, pursuant to the terms of the will. The Circuit Court
reversed the action of the tax commission in refusing to allow
these deductions. The statute allowed deductions for taxes paid
during the year other than inheritance taxes upon the property or
business from which the income taxed was derived.

Questions: (1) Are general taxes paid upon nonproductive
property a proper deduction under the income tax law?

(2) Was the amount of the $5,000 annuity a proper deduction
under the income tax law?

Decision: (1) Taxes paid on nonproductive property do not
come within the meaning of the statute allowing the deduction of
taxes paid upon property or business from which the income is
derived.

(2) When a testator wills property in trust to be invested and a specific amount per year paid out of the net income to a designated beneficiary for life, the fact that such beneficiary's interest in the estate was appraised and the statutory inheritance tax paid does not exempt from taxation the yearly income received by the executor as trustee for the beneficiary. The court affirmed the levy of the tax, thus not allowing a deduction of the $5,000 annuity.

STATE ex rel. PFISTER v. WIDULE
(Supreme Court of Wisconsin, June 12, 1917)
(166 Wis. 48; 163 N. W. 641)

Record: Wisconsin Act of 1911. Appeal by the county clerk from a judgment setting aside assessment of income tax. Judgment reversed and cause remanded with instructions to affirm the assessment of income.

Facts: Respondents were stockholders in the Prospect Hill Land Company, and dividends which said company paid in 1912, 1913, 1914 and 1915 were taxed to the stockholders as income. The company in 1893 acquired title to a tract of land which was purchased and held for resale in lots. The reasonable value of the property Jan. 1, 1911, the effective date of the Act, was fixed at $1,096,601, which exceeded the purchase price, improvements, and expenditures by $329,784.34. Apparently the amount of appreciation was written upon the books and thereafter the dividends were declared, inasmuch as it is not stated in the case that any profits were realized by the sale of property. Between Jan. 1, 1911, and Jan. 1, 1916, the value of the real estate held by the company decreased in value about thirty per cent. Error is assigned in holding that the dividends declared in 1912, 1913, 1914, and 1915, by the company were not subject to taxation as "income" under the Wisconsin Income Tax Law.

Question: Are sums of money paid by a corporation to its stockholders ostensibly as dividends, but actually from capital, taxable as ordinary dividends?

Decision: Dividends received upon stock of corporations are conclusively presumed to be earnings or profit and, therefore, taxable "income" under the Wisconsin Income Tax Law.

STATE ex rel. KEMPSMITH v. WIDULE
(Supreme Court of Wisconsin, Oct. 26, 1915)
(161 Wis. 389; 154 N. W. 695)

Record: Wisconsin Act of 1913. Certiorari action to test
the validity of an assessment of income tax. Appeal from a judgment reversing the determination of Tax Commission. Affirmed.

Facts: The relator was a beneficiary under a will by which
a considerable estate was left in trust, a part of the net income to be
paid annually to the relator for life. The bequest was valued
under the inheritance tax law of the state, and the inheritance
tax was paid by or on account of the beneficiary, the relator in
this case. An assessment was made under the income tax law
upon the annuity received according to the will. The Tax Commission overruled the relator's claim of exemption. The Income
Tax Act expressly exempted all inheritances, and devises which
were subject to and had complied with the inheritance tax laws of
the state. The inheritance tax laws imposed a tax upon any transfer of property or income therefrom in trust or otherwise, which
tax was due and payable at the time of the transfer. It also provided for an appraisal of the value in praesenti of the right to receive, as was done in this case.

Question: If a testator wills property in trust to be invested
and a specified sum per year paid out of the net income to a designated beneficiary for life, and such beneficiary's interest in the
estate is appraised and the statutory inheritance tax is paid thereon, do the yearly payments to the annuitant constitute income under the income tax law of the state?

Decision: "The right to receive being the subject of inheritance taxation, the amount is regulated, primarily, by the
value of the right. The right in the particular case has reference
to the privilege to receive, for life, the yearly payments. There
may be many payments, but the right is an entirety. That vested,
subject to the burden on the transfer, as soon as the will was allowed. * * * The annuity payment bequeathed to Mrs. Kempsmith, which was attempted to be taxed under the Income Tax
Law, was a part of the entire right to $3,600 per year for life, was
subject to the inheritance tax law and she complied therewith in

all respects. Therefore, it must follow that such payment was exempt as the circuit judge decided.''

STATE ex rel. WISCONSIN TRUST CO. v. WIDULE
(Supreme Court of Wisconsin, Oct. 3, 1916)
(164 Wis. 56; 159 N. W. 630)

Record: Wisconsin Act of 1915. Certiorari to review the action of assessor in levying the tax in question. Judgment rendered affirming the assessment, and relator appealed. Affirmed.

Facts: The relator is one of the three trustees under a will by which the trustees were given a number of shares of stock in a Pennsylvania corporation doing business in Wisconsin. The other two trustees reside in Pennsylvania, and one of them is the wife of the testator and the beneficiary of the trust of which she is entitled to the net income. The relator made a return, for and on behalf of all the trustees, of the dividends and interest received from the trust property. The assessor assessed the relator, the resident trustee, upon the dividends from the Pennsylvania company. The Income Tax Act provides for an assessment of a tax upon the income of all persons, derived from property or business transacted within the state, and provides that every trustee shall render a return of the amount of income received by him and shall be liable to assessment therefor. By the Act the trustee is entitled to reimbursement for taxes paid.

Question: (1) Is the resident trustee liable for the tax upon dividends derived from the stock of a foreign corporation doing business in the state, where the beneficiary and the co-trustees reside without the state?

(2) If so, is the provision in the Act allowing the trustee to reimburse himself by deducting the amount of the income tax from the amount to be paid the beneficiary invalid in that it impairs a contract obligation to pay the net income to the beneficiary?

Decision: (1) ''The Wisconsin Trust Company is a person as defined by the statutes, the fund for which it was assessed is dividends derived from stocks and interest derived from money loaned or invested in notes, credits, bonds, or other evidences of debt. The fund was received by the Wisconsin Trust Company as trustee at its office within the State of Wisconsin. Restatement and argument can not make plainer the fact that the Legislature intended that funds of this character should be taxed as income in the hands of trustees residing within this state. * * * The fact that in the present case the fund in question must be paid to the person entitled to enjoy it, that that person resides without the state and is a co-trustee, and that two of the trustees reside without the state of Wisconsin does not work a change in the character of the fund itself in the hands of the Wisconsin trustee, and it is a gain or profit derived from the securities constituting the trust fund, and hence income, and is subject to taxation as income.''

(2) ''No contract obligation is in any way impaired. The trust company will pay the net income in accordance with the terms of the will, which will be the amount remaining after the payment of the tax and other necessary administrative expenses.''

STATE ex rel. SALLIE F. MOON CO. v. WISCONSIN TAX COMMISSION

(Supreme Court of Wisconsin, June 22, 1917)

(166 Wis. 287; 163 N. W. 639)

Record: Wisconsin Act of 1911. Writ of certiorari to review the proceedings of the Wisconsin Tax Commissioner assessing against the relator an income tax. Judgment from Circuit Court reversed, and cause remanded with directions to enter judgment affirming action of the Commission. Motion for rehearing denied, 165 N. W. 470.

Facts: The Sallie F. Moon Company received dividends since Jan. 1, 1911, as a stockholder in a lumber company. The dividends were declared out of surplus on hand Jan. 1, 1911, when the Act became effective. The lumber company reported the surplus to the Tax Commission, which held that the surplus was not taxable as to the lumber company, but that the dividends distributed from such surplus after Jan. 1, 1911, to the relator were taxable. The Act provides that there shall be a tax on ''incomes received during the year ending Dec. 31, 1911,'' that ''income'' shall include all dividends from stock, and that incomes received from stocks in any company, the income of which shall have been assessed, may be deducted from the gross income.

Questions: (1) Are the dividends received from a fund, which accumulated before but which are distributed after the Act became effective, taxable as income received during the year of distribution?

(2) Where the Commission has determined that the funds in the hands of an operating company are not taxable, is that an assessment within the meaning of the Act so as to exempt from taxation the dividends received from that fund by the stockholders?

Decisions: (1) "Unlike the Federal Act there is no need to ascertain when the income arose or accrued in order to determine whether it is taxable. The fact that it was received during 1911 makes it taxable, irrespective of when it arose or accrued. * * * It is the relation that exists between the person sought to be taxed and specific property claimed as income to him that determines whether there shall be a tax. If the person sought to be taxed is the recipient during the tax year of such specific property as income in its ordinary significance, then the person is taxed. But the tax is upon the right or ability to produce, create, receive and enjoy, and not upon the specific property. Hence, the amount of the tax is measured by the amount of the income, irrespective of the amount of specific property or ability necessary to produce or create it." The dividends received by the relator from the lumber company are taxable for the year in which they are received.

(2) "To constitute an assessment within the meaning of the statute there must be the assessment or levy of a tax because of the existence of the fund as income. The surplus was not income to the Northwestern Lumber Company, but it was to its stockholders when distributed." The proceedings of the Commissioner assessing the relator an income tax are affirmed.

STATE LINE & S. R. CO. v. DAVIS

(U. S. District Court, M. D. Penn., December, 1915)
(228 Fed. 246)

Record: Act of Aug. 5, 1909. Action at law to recover taxes paid under protest on net income under Sec. 38 of this Act. Judgment for plaintiff.

Facts: This suit was brought to obtain the repayment of a special Excise Tax collected by the defendant from the plaintiff. The tax was assessed under the Federal Corporation Tax Act of 1909, and was paid under protest. Plaintiff had leased its properties prior to the enactment of the Act. Affidavit shows that plaintiff maintains an office and has an active president; annually elects officers; exercises some of its corporate functions; collects and distributes rents; has assumed certain mortgage indebtedness, the interest on which it pays; has reserved to itself the right to develop forests upon its lands; and is ready, whenever the terms of the lease shall be violated by the lessee, to resume the act of operation of its properties. The plaintiff filed a claim for refund, which was refused, and this suit is brought within two years from the date of the rejection of the plaintiff's claim.

Questions: (1) Is plaintiff "doing business" within the meaning of the Act of 1909?

(2) Is one, who begins suit for recovery of taxes within two years from date of the rejection of his claim for refund, barred by the Statute of Limitations?

(3) Is the plaintiff entitled to an allowance for interest where the taxes were paid under protest?

Decisions: (1) "Nearly all of the alleged activities of the plaintiff corporation were present in the controlling case of McCoach v. Minehill R. R. Co., where it was held that any and all of them were insufficient to constitute a 'doing of business,' within the meaning of the Corporation Tax Act. * * * It is not the power to act, but the actual activities in certain directions, which may constitute a 'doing of business'. * * * The tax provided for by the Act is not imposed on the franchises of the corporation, nor on its property, only on the 'doing of business' in a corporate capacity as authorized. The business of serving the public as a common carrier, which was the prime object of its incorporation, was turned over to its lessees. For this purpose the plaintiff must be regarded as out of business, and the taxes, therefore, were unlawfully imposed."

(2) "No suit can be maintained under the law until an appeal has been taken to the Commissioner. If on the appeal the

claim is rejected, an action may be maintained against the collector, and through him, on establishing the error or illegality, a recovery can be had. When the Commissioner rendered his decision, rejecting plaintiff's claim, the right of action was complete. It was then that plaintiff had a right to bring this suit, which was not barred when actually entered.''

(3) ''In suits against collectors to recover moneys illegally exacted as taxes and paid under protest, the settled rule is that interest is recoverable without any statute to that effect, and this although the judgment is not to be paid by the collector, but directly from the treasury.'' Redfield v. Bartels, 139 U. S. 694.

STATE TAX ON FOREIGN-HELD BONDS
(U. S. Supreme Court, December, 1872)
(15 Wallace 300)

Record: Pennsylvania Act of May 1, 1868. Action on behalf of the state of Pennsylvania for the collection of taxes. Judgment in favor of the state affirmed by the Supreme Court of Pennsylvania. Case brought to U. S. Supreme Court for review under the second section of the amended Judiciary Act of 1867. Judgment reversed and cause remanded for further proceedings.

Facts: The Cleveland, P. & A. R. R. Co. owned and operated a railroad, part of which was situated in Pennsylvania, and part in Ohio. The company, so far as it acted in Pennsylvania, was a corporation of that state, but there was only one board of directors which managed the affairs of the entire road. The company issued bonds secured by mortgage upon the entire road. The principal and interest of some of the bonds was payable in the city of Philadelphia, and that of others was payable in the city of New York. All of the bonds were executed and delivered in Cleveland, Ohio, and nearly all of them were issued to and ever since owned by non-residents of Pennsylvania. The state of Pennsylvania attempted to collect a tax from the company under an Act of its legislature which provided that the president, treasurer or cashier of every Pennsylvania corporation which paid interest to bondholders or other creditors should, before payment of the same, retain from said bondholders or creditors a tax of 5 per centum on every dollar of interest paid.

Questions: (1) Was the statute under which an attempt was made to collect the tax, in so far as it applied to the interest on bonds made and payable out of the state, issued to and held by non-residents of the state, citizens of other states, a valid and constitutional exercise of the taxing power of the state?

(2) Was the Act in question an interference, under the name of a tax, with the obligation of the contracts between the non-resident bondholders and the corporation?

Decision: (1) " * * * The bonds, being held by non-residents of the state, are only property in their hands, and * * * they are thus beyond the jurisdiction of the taxing power of the state. Even where bonds are held by residents of the state, the retention by the company of a portion of the stipulated interest can only be sustained as a mode of collecting a tax upon that species of property in the state. When the property is out of the state there can be no tax upon it for which the interest can be retained."

(2) The law in question impairs the obligation of the contract between the parties, and is, therefore, unconstitutional. "The obligation of a contract depends upon its terms and the means which the law in existence at the time affords for its enforcement. A law which alters the terms of a contract by imposing new conditions, or dispensing with those expressed, is a law which impairs its obligation, for * * * such a law relieves the parties from the moral duty of performing the original stipulations of the contract, and it prevents their legal enforcement. The Act of Pennsylvania of May 1, 1868, falls within this description." It was, therefore, held that the state could not collect the tax in question.

STEGALL v. THURMAN, SHERIFF

(U. S. District Court, N. D. Georgia, Jan. 27, 1910)

(175 Fed. 812)

Record: Rev. Stat., Sec. 161, 251, 3215, 3167. Proceeding for writ of habeas corpus. Petitioner discharged.

Facts: In a proceeding in a state court against parties alleged to have been operating a distillery, contrary to the laws of the state, petitioner, a storekeeper and gauger of the Internal Revenue Department, formerly assigned to duty at said distillery, was called as a witness. He declined to answer certain questions propounded to him on the ground that his knowledge of the operation of the distillery came to him solely in his official capacity. Thereupon, he was committed for contempt, and was in jail when the writ was issued. The regulations issued by the Secretary of the Treasury for the government of officers of the department provided that officers will "decline to testify as to facts contained in the records, or coming to their knowledge in their official capacity."

Questions: (1) What effect is to be given regulations issued by the Secretary of the Treasury with reference to the question of internal revenue?

(2) Could petitioner be required to testify to what he saw as an individual, notwithstanding his presence at the distillery as an official?

Decision: (1) Regulations issued by the Secretary of the Treasury with reference to internal revenue, and for the government of officers of the Revenue Department have the force and effect of law, and are as binding as if incorporated in the statute law of the United States.

(2) Under the regulations of the Internal Revenue Department promulgated with the approval of the Secretary of the Treasury, providing that officers of the department "will decline to testify as to facts contained in the records, or coming to their knowledge in their official capacity; and this prohibition is hereby extended to include also internal revenue storekeepers and gaugers and agents"—a storekeeper and gauger stationed at a distillery has no right to divulge information in regard to the business of the distiller obtained by him solely in his official capacity as an internal revenue officer, even when called as a witness in a state court. The petitioner was, therefore, discharged.

STEWART v. BARNES, COLLECTOR
(U. S. Supreme Court, May 14, 1894)
(153 U. S. 456)

Record: Act of July 15, 1866, and Act of June 6, 1872. Action in assumpsit by Stewart to recover tax paid and interest. Judgment for defendant, and plaintiff brought error. Affirmed.

Facts: The plaintiff drew out distilled spirits which had been placed in a United States bonded warehouse and was required to pay taxes which he did not owe. He made appeal to the Commissioner as required by the Act. Later the government paid him the sum illegally exacted.

Question: Does the acceptance from the government, without objection, of a sum which the government illegally exacted bar a recovery of interest?

Decision: "Where money is retained by one man against the declared will of another who is entitled to receive it, and who is thus deprived of its use, the rule of courts in ordinary cases is, in suits for the recovery of the money, to allow interest. Interest in such cases is considered as damages and does not form the basis of the action, but is an incident to the recovery of the principal debt. If the principal sum has been paid, so that as to it, an action brought can not be maintained, the opportunity to acquire a right to damages is lost." Therefore, no action will lie for the recovery of interest alone.

STOCKDALE, COLLECTOR, v. ATLANTIC INS. CO.
(U. S. Supreme Court, May 4, 1874)
(87 U. S. 323)

Record: Acts of June 30, 1864, and July 14, 1870. Action at law against collector to recover taxes paid under protest. Judgment for plaintiff below (Fed. Case 6662), and defendant brought error. Reversed.

Facts: The taxes complained of were assessed upon dividends declared by the Insurance Company from earnings which had accrued to the company between July 5, 1869, and June 30, 1870. The dividends were declared July 5, 1870, and were at once credited to the stockholders. The Act of June 30, 1864, was a tax on incomes, containing a provision for a tax of five per centum upon the dividends and undivided earnings of insurance companies. This Act was amended to expire Dec. 31, 1869. The Act of July 14, 1870, declared that laws of 1864 as subsequently amended "shall be construed to impose the taxes therein mentioned to the first day of August, 1870." It was argued that the entire income tax expired with the year 1869; that as the taxes were imposed upon the stockholders and were assessed on dividends declared in the year 1870, they were, therefore, assessed without authority of law. It was also argued that, if the tax was held to be one upon the corporation and not the stockholders as contended above, then with respect to the taxes on dividends represented by income accrued from Dec. 31, 1869, to July 5, 1870, the Act of 1870 was retroactive and, therefore, such taxes were invalid. The case raises the two questions stated below.

Questions: (1) Was the tax valid as to so much of the dividends as arose from the earnings of the year 1869?

(2) Was it valid as to that which arose from the earnings of the year 1870?

Decision: (1) In Barnes v. R. Co., 17 Wall. 294, in which the same question was considered, the argument turned mainly on the question whether the law intended to impose the tax on the income of the corporation, in which case it was obviously the income of 1869 which was taxed, and properly taxed; or on the income of the stockholder, "without reopening that subject for any inquiry into those differences, it may be said that the question whether the tax was a tax on the shareholder or on the corporation, was, and is, one of form rather than substance. The tax is imposed by statute alike on all dividends declared, and on all undistributed earnings of the corporation, and it is made the duty of the corporation to pay it. It is also made the duty of the corporation to make returns of these dividends and undivided earnings to the proper internal revenue officer, under a heavy penalty. In the case of dividends declared, the corporation is authorized to deduct the amount of the tax from the dividend due to the shareholder before paying it to him. * * * The effect of such a tax on the shareholder is the same whether it be considered a tax on his share for the dividend earned by his share or on the corporation on account of said earnings and it is the same whether the tax is imposed on the undivided earnings, or on those earnings after they have been divided. He in any and all these cases, in point of fact, ultimately suffers to that extent, or loses the amount of the tax. We are of the opinion that the statute intended to tax those earnings for the year 1869, whether divided or undivided, and that the tax now in question is to that extent valid.''

(2) ''But for the unfortunate and unnecessary use of the word 'construe' in this sentence (Act of July 14, 1870), we apprehend that none of the resistance to the class of taxes now under consideration would have been thought of. The right of Congress to have imposed this tax by a new statute, although the measure of it was governed by the income of the past year, can not be doubted; much less can it be doubted that it could impose such a tax on the income of the current year, though a part of that year had elapsed when the statute was passed.'' The Act of 1870 was a legitimate exercise of the taxing power by which a tax, which might be supposed to have expired, was revived and continued in existence for a longer period. ''It was, therefore, valid for that purpose and the tax must be upheld.''

STOFFREGEN v. MOORE
(U. S. District Court, E. D. Mo., E. D., March 26, 1920)
(264 Fed. 232)

Record: Act of Oct. 3, 1913. Suit to recover taxes paid. Judgment for defendant.

Facts: In December, 1913, the plaintiff and his son owned all the shares of stock in a certain corporation, which had a surplus of $631,826, of which amount only $62,715 represented earnings for 1913. In that month a dividend was declared of all the existing surplus, and the total amount was passed to the credit of the plaintiff on the books of the company. Against this credit there was made a charge of $350,000, being the aggregate of amounts loaned to employes by the plaintiff in order to enable them to acquire shares of newly issued stock of the company. The balance of the dividend was subsequently, and at some time prior to June, 1915, paid to the plaintiff in cash.

Question: Did the dividend declared to the plaintiff, and transferred to his credit in the mode stated, constitute taxable income under the Act of Oct. 3, 1913, notwithstanding that it was paid almost entirely out of earnings accrued prior to March 1, 1913?

Decision: This case is controlled by Lynch v. Hornby (247 U. S. 344), which holds that net income, under the Act of Oct. 3, 1913, includes all dividends declared and paid in the ordinary course of business by a corporation to its stockholders after the taking effect of the Act, whether from current earnings, or from the accumulated surplus made up of part earnings or increase in value of corporate assets, notwithstanding it accrued to the corporation in whole or in part prior to March 1, 1913. Such net income is taxable, and the plaintiff can not recover the tax paid.

STRATTON'S INDEPENDENCE LTD. v. HOWBERT, COLLECTOR

(U. S. Supreme Court, Dec. 1, 1913)

(231 U. S. 399)

Record: Act of Aug. 5, 1909. Action at law to recover taxes paid under protest on net income under Sec. 38 of this Act. Judgment for defendant.

Facts: This case was tried on an agreed statement of facts from which it appeared, as to the year 1909, that the company extracted from its lands during the year certain ores bearing gold and other precious metal, which were sold by it for sums largely in excess of the cost of mining, extracting and marketing the same; that the gross sales amounted to $284,682.85, the cost of extracting, mining and marketing amounted to $199,939.42; and, therefore, the company contended that the value of said ores so extracted in 1909, when in place in said mine and before extraction thereof, was $93,743.43, being the difference between the two amounts above stated. With respect to the operations of the company for 1910, the agreed facts were practically the same. It did not appear that the so-called "value of ore in place," or any other sum was actually charged off the books of the company as depreciation. Upon this state of facts each party moved the court for a directed verdict, at the same time presenting for consideration certain questions of law, and among them the following:

(1) Is the value of the ore in place that was extracted from the mining property of the plaintiff during the year in question properly allowable as depreciation in estimating the net income of the plaintiff subject to taxation under the Act of 1909?

(2) Is the right to such credit affected by the fact that plaintiff does not carry such item on its books in a depreciation account?

To the ruling of the trial court plaintiff took exceptions. The resulting judgment was removed by writ of error to the Circuit Court of Appeals, which court certified that the following questions were presented to it, the decision of which were indispensible to a determination of the cause.

Questions: (1) Does Sec. 38 of the Act of 1909 apply to mining corporations?

(2) Are the proceeds of ores mined by a corporation from its own premises income within the meaning of the Act of 1909?

(3) If the proceeds of ore sales are to be treated as income, is such a corporation entitled to deduct the value of such ore in place and before it is mined, as determined by deducting the cost of mining, extracting and marketing from gross sales, as depreciation within the meaning of Sec. 38 of the Act of 1919.

Decision: (1) "A mining corporation is (1) a 'corporation * * * organized for profit and having a capital stock represented by shares * * * and engaged in business' and (2) is not among that class of corporations specified to be exempt from taxation under Sec. 38 of the Act of 1909." "The very process of mining is in a sense, equivalent in its results to a manufacturing process. And, however the operation shall be described the transaction is indubitably business within the fair meaning of the Act of 1909." The Act therefor applies to mining corporations.

(2) "And the gains derived from it are properly and strictly the income from that business, for income may be defined as the gain derived from capital, from labor, or both combined, and here we have combined operations of capital and labor." "Income"

within the meaning of Sec. 38 need not be such an income as would have been taxable as such. Congress adopted income as the measure of the tax to be imposed with respect to the doing of business in corporate form because it desired that the excise should be imposed with regard to the amount of benefit derived by such corporations from the current operations of the government. Congress fixed upon income, without distinction as to source, as a convenient and sufficiently accurate index of the importance of the business transacted. And from this point of view it makes little difference that the income may arise from a business that theoretically or practically involves a wasting of capital. The proceeds of ores mined are income within the meaning of the Act.

(3) In the agreed statement of facts, there was a statement that the gross proceeds of the sale of the ores during the year were diminished by the moneys expended in extracting, mining, and marketing the ores, and the precise difference was taken to be the value of the ores when in place in the mine. The contention is then that if a part of the capital assets are removed and sold, the property, as it originally stood, is actually depreciated in value to the extent of such removal. ''In short, the depreciation of a mining property attributable to the extraction of ores according to principles that would be applicable if the ores had been removed by a trespasser. * * * In the first place, it is fallacious to say that, whatever may have been the original cost of a mining property or the cost of developing it, if in fact it afterwards yield ores aggregating many times its original cost or market value, this result merely proves and at the same time measures the intrinsic value that existed from the beginning. * * * And, secondly, assuming the depletion of the mineral stock is an element to be considered in determining the reasonable depreciation that is to be treated as a loss in the ascertainment of the net income of a mining company under the Act, we deem it quite inadmissible to estimate such depletion as if it had been done by a trespasser, to whom all profit is denied. * * * It would, therefore, be improper for us at this time to enter into the question whether the clause, 'a reasonable allowance for depreciation of property, if any' calls for an allowance on that account in making up the tax, where no depreciation is charged in practical bookkeeping; or the question

whether depreciation, when allowable, may properly be based upon the depletion of the ore supply estimated otherwise than in the mode shown by the agreed statement of facts herein; for to do this would be to attribute a different meaning to the term 'value of the ore in place' than the parties have put upon it, and to instruct the Circuit Court of Appeals respecting a question about which instruction has not been requested, and concerning which it does not even appear that any issue is depending before that court.'' Accordingly all the court held was that depreciation could not be allowed as computed by the parties.

STRAUS v. ABRAST REALTY CO.
(U. S. District Court, E. D. New York, July 22, 1912)
(200 Fed. 327)

Record: Act of Aug. 5, 1909. Action in equity to restrain payment of tax on net income under Sec. 38 of this Act. The court joined the collector of internal revenue as a party defendant by issuing an order to show cause. Injunction denied.

Facts: A stockholder of defendant company brought this action in equity to restrain that company from paying a tax levied under the Corporation Tax Act of 1909. Plaintiff's contention is that defendant company is not engaged in business in that the sole object of the corporation is to hold title to realty and, for the convenience of its stockholders, to receive and distribute rents for them. The statutes of the United States forbid the maintenance of any suit for the purpose of restraining the assessment or collection of taxes.

Question: Is plaintiff entitled to injunctive relief to restrain payment of a Federal Tax?

Decision: The complainant seeks to do the very thing that the law prohibits. If the stockholder cannot have the collector of the tax enjoined, it seems obvious that he cannot have the corporation enjoined from paying it, and thus do by indirection what he cannot do directly. To restrain a corporation or its officers from paying a tax, the collection of which cannot be restrained in any court, would be a palpable evasion of the statute. Upon this ground the court refused to enjoin the defendant company from paying the tax.

SUTER et al. v. JORDAN MARSH CO.

(Sup. Judicial Court of Mass., Sept. 21, 1916)

(113 N. E. 580)

Record: Act of Oct. 3, 1913. Action at law to recover taxes withheld under Sections 38 of this Act. Judgment for defendant, and plaintiff excepted. Reversed.

Facts: Defendant was the lessee of certain property. The lease provided that defendant (lessee) was to pay all taxes and assessments, except betterment taxes, which might be levied for or in respect of the premises or upon or in respect of the rent payable, however assessed. Defendant, in accordance with the requirements of the Act of Oct. 3, 1913, withheld at its source and paid to the United States the normal income tax on the rent due under the lease, and deducted the amount from the rent reserved in the lease.

Question: Is the money withheld by the defendant and paid to the United States under the Act of Oct. 3, 1913, a tax or assessment upon the rent payable under the terms of the above lease?

Decision: The Act of Oct. 3, 1913, paragraph E, imposes the duty upon all persons in the position of defendant as lessees "to deduct and withhold" from the rent "such sum as will be sufficient, and pay the normal tax imposed thereon by this section, and they shall pay to the officers of the United States government authorized to receive the same; and they are each hereby made personally liable for 'such tax.'" "The words 'imposed thereon' must refer to the rental. There is no other source of income of the lessors subjected to a tax to which these words can allude, the concluding phrase renders the lessee personally liable for the payment of what is described as 'such tax'; that also can relate only to the rental." Applying the phraseology of the Act to the covenant of the lease, it follows that the sum of money which the lessee has been compelled by that law to withhold from the plaintiffs belongs to the class of imposts correctly described as "taxes and assessments," and that it has been levied upon the rent payable under the lease. The defendant covenanted to pay the taxes levied upon the rent payable under the lease, and is liable to the plaintiff for the full amount of the rent reserved in the lease.

SYBRANDT et al. v. UNITED STATES

(U. S. Court of Claims, April 21, 1884)

(19 Ct. Cls. 461)

Record: Rev. Stat., Sec. 3220. Action to recover tax paid. Judgment for claimant.

Facts: Claimants had filed a claim for refund, the allowance of which had been successively recommended by three Commissioners of Internal Revenue, and disapproved by two Secretaries of the Treasury. The third Secretary did not approve in terms and said he had no objection to the claim being sent to the accounting officers. The latter rejected it and this action was then commenced.

Questions: (1) Does the recommendation of the Secretary control the final decision of the Commissioner?

(2) Do the accounting officers or the courts have authority to review the evidence upon which the Commissioner allowed a claim for refund and to reverse such allowance for insufficiency of evidence?

Decision: (1) The regulations prescribed by the Secretary of the Treasury under Rev. Stat., Sec. 3220, which requires the Commissioner, after examining a case "before it is finally decided, to transmit the case to the Secretary of the Treasury for his consideration and advisement" gives the Commissioner the benefit of the Secretary's suggestions, but does not control his final decision. Furthermore, it does not prevent a Commissioner from allowing a claim upon which there have been three adverse decisions by three successive Secretaries of the Treasury.

(2) The law imposes upon the Commissioner of Internal Revenue the duty of deciding whether a tax should be refunded, and, unless his decision is impeached for fraud or apparent mistake, neither the court nor any other officer of the government has the right to weigh the evidence upon which it is based. The claimant was, therefore, allowed to recover.

IN RE TAXATION OF SALARIES OF JUDGES
(Supreme Court of N. Carolina, Dec. 18, 1902)
(42 S. E. 970)

Record: Constitution of North Carolina. Art. 4, Sec. 23. Opinion of Attorney General adopted by Court.

Facts: See question.

Question: Are the salaries of the chief justice and associate justices of the supreme court of North Carolina exempt from taxation under Art. 4, Sec. 23 of the constitution of that State?

Decision: The constitution provides that "the salaries of judges shall not be diminished during their continuance in office." The power to tax judges' salaries is a power to diminish such salaries indirectly, and if the Legislature is unchecked by any other department in the exercise of this discretion it could violate at will this part of the constitution. If the General Assembly has the power to impose a tax of one per cent on the salary of a judge, upon the same principle it could lay a tax which would cripple, if not completely paralyze the state courts. The exercise of such destructive power is not likely to be invoked, but the improbability of the non-exercise of the power does not affect the principle. "There is no legislative power possessed by any legislature which it may not lawfully carry to an extreme, where extreme action is deemed expedient by a majority of the members." When the constitutional convention declared that the salaries of judges should not be diminished during their continuance in office, they meant to withdraw from taxation, either directly or indirectly, such salaries "because the power to tax is to diminish, or it may be to destroy." Therefore, the salaries of the chief justice and associate justices of the supreme court of North Carolina, who are holding office at the time of the passage of the Act, can not be taxed.

TITLE GUARANTEE & TRUST CO. v. MILES, COLLECTOR
(U. S. District Court D. Maryland, June 18, 1919)
(258 Fed. 771)

Record: Act of October 22, 1914. Action to recover tax paid under protest. Judgment for plaintiff.

Facts: The plaintiff was engaged solely in the business of examining and insuring real estate titles, and in other transactions closely associated therewith. This still constitutes the bulk of its business. A number of years ago it began to carry on a savings bank business in a small way, and this has gradually grown in volume and importance. The company has kept a perfectly distinct set of books for its banking business. Whatever profit it made out of banking has remained untouched, and it admits that this profit is capital employed by it in banking. The rest of its capital, surplus and undivided profits is not, and has never been, used in banking, except insofar as its possession of them gave and gives it a credit which facilitates the getting of customers for its bank.

Question: Should the total capital, surplus and undivided profits of the plaintiff be included as amounts used in "banking," when computing the special tax on banks imposed by the Act, or should only the amount used in the banking business as such be subject thereto?

Decision: "In this case it is only the capital which has been actually set apart and used in the banking business which is subject to the tax."

TOWNE v. EISNER, COLLECTOR
(U. S. Supreme Court, Jan. 7, 1918)
(245 U. S. 418)

Record: Act of October 3, 1913. Action at law to recover taxes paid under protest on net income under this Act. Judgment for defendant (242 Fed. 702) and plaintiff brought error. Reversed.

Facts: A corporation voted in 1913 to transfer $1,500,000 surplus, being profits earned before January 1, 1913, to its capital account and to issue 15,000 shares of stock representing the same to its stockholders. Plaintiff received as his proportion, 4,174½ shares. The defendant compelled him to pay an income tax under the Act of 1913, upon this stock as equivalent to $417,450 income in cash. The tax was paid under protest and this action was brought for its recovery.

Question: Are stock dividends income within the meaning of the Income Tax Act of 1913?

Decision: "A stock dividend really takes nothing from the property of the corporation, and adds nothing to the interest of its shareholders. Its property is not diminished, and their interests are not increased. The proportionate interest of each shareholder remains the same. The only change is in the evidence which represents that interest, the new shares and the original shares together representing the same proportional interest that the original shares represented before the issue of the new ones. In short, the corporation is no poorer and the stockholder is no richer than they were before." What has happened is that the plaintiff's old certificates have been split up in effect and diminished in value to the extent of the value of the new. The plaintiff was therefore, allowed to recover the amount of the tax which he had paid.

Note: Motion of government to dismiss on ground of question concerning jurisdiction was overruled.

TOWNE v. McELLIGOTT, COLLECTOR
(U. S. District Court, S. D. N. Y., Aug. 5, 1921)
(Not reported)

Record: Revenue Act of 1918. Suit to recover income taxes paid. On demurrer to complaint.

Facts: The plaintiff owned shares in a corporation before March 1, 1913, and bought other shares thereafter. Later he received a stock dividend of 50 per cent upon all his shares. In 1918 he sold some of his shares, including those certificates which he had held on March 1, 1913, those which he had bought later, and some of those which he had received as a stock dividend. The tax was collected on the following basis: the plaintiff was charged with the gross sale price and credited on each share sold with the average cost of all the shares. This average for each share was computed by dividing the gross cost of all such shares by the number of the shares, including the shares declared as a stock dividend. The plaintiff argued that he should be credited with the actual cost of each certificate, computing the cost of the shares declared as a stock dividend at nothing. The tax upon the profits realized amounted to seventy-two per cent of the amount of such profits.

Questions: (1) Was a tax of seventy-two per cent on the profits realized by the plaintiff confiscatory, and if so, void under the Fifth Amendment?

(2) Were the profits realized upon the sale of plaintiff's stock correctly computed?

Decision: (1) The case of Brushaber v. Union Pac. Ry., 240 U. S. 1, relied on by the plaintiff stands only for the proposition that there may be inequalities in the rates of levy great enough to become a confiscation of the income which suffered the highest rates. There is no suggestion in the books that when the inequalities are lawful the rates may be confiscatory as a whole. The Fifth Amendment must be interpreted in the light of practices which have become tolerated elsewhere among civilized nations, and the exigencies of the nation imposed by the Great War. Therefore, the tax of seventy-two per cent was not void as confiscatory.

(2) Under the doctrine of Eisner v. Macomber, 252 U. S. 159, a stock dividend is not regarded as new property at all. The old certificates represent precisely the same property as the old and new do thereafter. Each of the new shares, whether contained in the old or the new certificates, represents a part of the original property purchased, and in selling the first certificate the stockholder has not sold the whole of what he originally bought and should not be credited with the whole purchase price. The method employed by the government of averaging the cost of all purchases of stock before the declaration of the stock dividend was not strictly correct; each purchase should be treated separately and the portion of the stock dividend paid upon the number of shares involved in each purchase allocated to that particular purchase and not to the purchases as a whole. In a case where all the new shares received as a stock dividend are represented by one certificate and all are not sold at once, the first sales would be attributed to the first purchases still remaining unsold when the stock dividend was declared.

TRACTION COS. v. COLLECTORS OF INTERNAL REVENUE
(6 Cases)
(U. S. Circuit Court of Appeals, Sixth Circuit, June 8, 1915)
(223 Fed. 984)

Record: Act of August 5, 1909. Action at law to recover taxes paid under protest on net income under Sec. 38 of this Act. Judgment for defendant and plaintiff brought error. Reversed.

Facts: Under the above arbitrary title, six causes were heard as one. In each, the question involved was whether the plaintiff was carrying on business so as to be subject to pay the excise tax under the Corporation Tax Law of 1909. Each of the plaintiffs is a street railway company, organized under the laws of Ohio, which had built and operated a railroad, and then, before the accruing of the tax involved, had leased the railroad to an operating company and had ceased to carry on business, unless the maintenance of its corporate office and organization, receiving and distributing accrued rentals, investing its undistributed receipts and other acts, hereafter specified, constituted "carrying on" of business as required the imposition of the tax. Each case is analogous to McCoach v. Minehill. In these cases, as in that, it must follow that the lessor roads were exempt from the tax, unless the additional circumstances here presented are sufficiently distinguishing, which can be classified in three groups.

(a) Two of the leases provided for the sale of portions of the real estate and the substitution of other property. One lessee sold one, and the other sold two small parcels, and the lessors joined in the deeds. Another lessee made a traffic contract with another traction company, permitting the latter to run some of its cars over some of the railroad lines of the lessor company, which act was approved by the lessor company. The approval was not required by the lease or the traffic contract.

(b) Some of the lessors, during the year involved, had issued their treasury capital stock, or caused to be issued their reserve bonds in the hands of their mortgage trustees, for the purpose of financing the lessees in making extensions or betterments, pursuant to the lease.

(c) One of the lessees was the real party to a law suit, managed the same, and paid all expenses. The lessor had no connection therewith except to permit the use of its corporate name, pursuant to a provision in the lease.

Question: Do any or all of the above described activities constitute "doing business" within the meaning of the Corporation Tax Act of 1909?

Decision: "The true test of distinction must be, as applied to corporations of this class, whether they are continuing the body and substance of the business for which they were organized and in which they set out, or whether they have substantially retired from it and turned it over to another. If the latter appears, then their tax exempt status must be tested by the further query whether they have, during the critical period, done only such acts as are properly and normally incidental to the status of a mere lessor of such property, or whether they have exercised their peculiar corporate franchises outside of and beyond the fair scope of that status."

(a) Buying and selling real estate may be a carrying on of business, but such acts of that nature as were here done were merely incidental to the business carried on by the lessee companies. The lessors did not negotiate the sales of the original nor the purchase of the substituted properties.

(b) "Permitting the lessee to take and to sell reserved bonds and unissued stock presents a question of the same class. The case does not involve the sale of either bonds or stock by the lessor company. That might raise a different issue. Properties of the nature of those herein involved necessarily must be enlarged, extended and otherwise renewed at frequent intervals, and a long time lease must make suitable provisions on those points. It is a matter of contract whether the business of providing these improved facilities shall be carried on by the lessor or by the lessee. These leases provided that these things shall be done by the lessee; but the lessors had funds in the shape of unissued stock or reserve bonds, expressly devoted to the very purpose, and the lessors have merely permitted the lessee to take these funds and use them for the purpose for which the funds were created."

(c) "The permitted use of the lessor's name in a law suit brought and wholly carried on by the lessee has even less color of carrying on business than has either of the other classes of acts." It was, therefore, held that the plaintiffs were not carrying on business within the meaning of the Act, and they were given judgment for the amount of the taxes imposed upon them.

TRAVIS, COMPTROLLER, v. YALE & TOWNE MFG. CO.
(U. S. Supreme Court. Decided March 1, 1920)
(252 U. S. 60)

Record: New York Income Tax Act, c. 627, Laws 1919. Suit to restrain enforcement of the Act. Motion to dismiss bill denied and final decree awarded in favor of complainant below. Defendant appealed. Affirmed.

Facts: The complainant, Yale and Towne Manufacturing Company, was a Connecticut corporation doing business in New York where it had a number of employees who were residents of Connecticut and New Jersey. The Comptroller of the State of New York was threatening to enforce the provisions of the New York Income Tax Act against defendant, by requiring it to deduct and withhold from the salaries payable to its Connecticut and New Jersey employees, engaged in complainant's business in New York, the taxes provided for in the Act. Additional facts with respect to the Act appear below under "Questions."

Questions: (1) Has a state jurisdiction to impose a tax on incomes which within her borders accrue to non-residents?

(2) May a state income tax act confine deductions allowed non-residents to such as are connected with income arising within the state while allowing residents to make such deductions without regard to locality?

(3) Is a state income tax act unconstitutional because it provides for withholding the tax at the source only in the case of non-residents?

(4) Is a state income tax act unconstitutional which grants certain exemptions to residents without providing for similar exemptions to nonresidents?

(5) Is a discrimination as to exemption allowed residents and non-residents overcome by a provision excluding from taxable income of non-residents annuities and interest which are not a part of income from any business carried on in the state?

Decision: (1) That a state has jurisdiction to impose a tax upon incomes of non-residents arising from any business, trade or occupation carried on within its borders, enforcing payment so far as it can by the exercise of a just control over persons and property within the state, as by garnishment of credits (of which the withholding provision of the New York law is the practical equivalent), and that such a tax, so enforced, is constitutional is settled by the case of Shaffer v. Carter, 252 U. S. 37.

(2) Shaffer v. Carter, supra, also settled that there is no constitutional discrimination against citizens of other states in confining the deduction of expenses, losses, etc., in the case of non-resident taxpayers, to such as are connected with income arising from sources within the taxing state.

(3) The contention that an unconstitutional discrimination against non-citizens arises out of the provision confining the withholding at source to the income of non-residents is unsubstantial. The provision does not in any way increase the burden of the tax upon non-residents, but merely recognizes the fact that as to them the state imposes no personal liability, and hence adopts a convenient substitute for it.

(4) The court was unable to find any adequate ground for the discrimination between residents and non-residents with respect to the exemption allowed and hence was constrained to hold that it was an unwarranted denial to the citizens of Connecticut and New Jersey of the privileges and immunities enjoyed by citizens of New York, and so in violation of Sec. 2 of Art. IV of the Constitution.

(5) The discrimination referred to in Point (4) above cannot be deemed to be counterbalanced by the provision of the Act which excluded from the income of non-resident taxpayers annuities and interest which was not a part of income from a business, trade or occupation carried on in this state. This provision is not so conditioned as probably to benefit non-residents to a degree corresponding to the discrimination against them. The decree restraining the enforcement of the Act was therefore affirmed.

TRAYLOR ENGINEERING & MFG. CO. v. LEDERER, COLLECTOR

(U. S. District Court, E. D. Penn., June 29, 1920)

(266 Fed. 583)

Record: War Munitions Act of 1916. Action at law to recover taxes paid under protest as a munition manufacturer. Judgment for collector. Plaintiff brought error. Affirmed.

Facts: The plaintiff, a corporation munition manufacturer, entered into an agreement with two individuals by which, in conconsideration of their contributing to the expense of sending the president of the corporation to England to obtain a contract for furnishing munitions to the British Government and aiding by their influence and otherwise, not involving any expense, in procuring such a contract, they were to share in the profits made, in proportion to the amount advanced. The contract was secured and performed and the two individuals were paid from the profits an amount approximately 1,000 times the amount of their contributions. The plaintiff corporation in computing its profits deducted from the gross receipts the sums so paid to the individuals. The collector assessed the plaintiff upon this amount and required it to pay the tax.

Question: Are the sums paid as stated under "facts" deductions which may be made from the gross receipts?

Decision: "The plaintiff's contract with the Government of Great Britain was the only one of the two contracts that the Munitions Act was concerned with, for it was only under this contract that munitions were made and profits earned. Of the two parties to that contract the plaintiff was the only one that made and sold munitions—the other bought them. As profits thus made constitute the taxable subject of the Act, evidently the tax is directed against the 'person' producing them. If that person chose before creating profits to promise by a side contract to give or pay them to others when earned, then he could do so only after the Government had exacted the tax for the privilege of doing the particular business out of which he made profits of this kind. This we regard to be the true relation of the parties with its legal consequences, arising from two separate and distinct contracts made with reference to different subject matters and for different purposes. If profits distributed under the side-contract in no way entered into the cost of manufacturing munitions under the main contract, we are of opinion that they can not be regarded as an expense of manufacture deductible from the gross amount received from sales in ascertaining taxable net profits."

TREAT, COLLECTOR, v. FARMERS' LOAN & TRUST CO.
SAME v. CENTRAL TRUST CO. OF NEW YORK
(U. S. Circuit Court of Appeals, Second Cir., Feb. 14, 1911)
(185 Fed. 760)

Record: Act of June 13, 1898. Action to recover taxes paid. Judgments for plaintiffs below (171 Fed. 301, 302) and defendant brought error. Affirmed.

Facts: The plaintiffs, trust companies under the laws of New York, were compelled to make a return upon their capital and surplus and pay a tax as bankers. The case was submitted upon an agreed statement of facts to the court below, without a jury. This statement showed that the capital and surplus of both companies were permanently invested in stocks and bonds; that the only business the companies did as bankers within the meaning of the Act was the opening of credits by deposits or collections of money and paying out the same on check, draft or order and the loaning of money on stocks, bonds, or secured paper. This business was done entirely by means of the depositors' money.

Questions: (1) Upon the basis of the agreed statement of facts given above, were the plaintiffs using their capital or surplus in banking?

(2) Were interest and costs properly included in the judgment?

Decision: (1) The circuit judge was entirely right in holding as matter of law that the plaintiffs, not using their capital or surplus in banking, were not subject to the payment of any tax thereon.

(2) On judgment against a collector of internal revenue, for taxes paid under protest, costs and interest were properly awarded, although if the defendant had been the United States and not the collector, individually, they could not have been awarded without congressional warrant.

TREAT, COLLECTOR, v. WHITE
(U. S. Supreme Court. April 29, 1901)
(181 U. S. 264)

Record: Act of June 13, 1898. Action to recover tax paid. Judgment for plaintiff in District Court (100 Fed. 290). The case was taken to the Circuit Court of Appeals, which certified a question to the Supreme Court. Question answered in affirmative.

Facts: Defendant was a stock broker in New York. In the course of his business he sold "calls" which were in the following form:

"New York, May 18, 1899.

"For value received the bearer may call on me on one day's notice, except last day, when notice is not required. One Hundred shares of the common stock of the American Sugar Refining Company at one hundred and seventy-five per cent at any time in fifteen days from date. All dividends, for which transfer books close during said time, go with stock. Expires June 2, 1899, at 3 P. M."

(Signed) S. V. White."

The collector forced the plaintiff to affix a stamp to each "call" issued by him.

Question: Was a "call" in the form set out above an "agreement to sell" within the meaning of the Act and so taxable as therein provided?

Decision: "Calls" are not distributed as mere advertisements of what the owner of the property described therein is willing to do. They are sold, and in parting with them the vendor receives what to him is satisfactory consideration. Having parted, for value received, with that promise, it is a contract binding on him, and such a contract is neither more nor less than an agreement to sell and deliver at the time named, the property described in the instrument. A "call" is, therefore, taxable.

TREFRY v. PUTNAM
SAME v. GARFIELD
(Supreme Judicial Court of Mass.   June 28, 1917)
(116 N. E. 904)

Record: Income Tax Law of 1916 of the State of Mass. Petition for mandamus by Trefry, Tax Commissioner. Peremptory writs directed to issue.

Facts: See questions.

Questions: (1) Is an excess of gains over losses in the purchase and sales of intangible personal property by one not engaged in the business of dealing in such property "income" within the meaning of the 44th amendment to the constitution of Massachusetts, which authorizes a tax on incomes?

(2) Are gains derived from the sale of rights to subscribe for new shares of stock to be issued by an existing corporation, taxable as "income" as authorized by the constitution as amended?

(3) Is a stock dividend declared and issued by a corporation after the statute went into effect, out of an accumulation of profits earned and invested in its business before the statute was enacted taxable as "income" within the meaning of the constitution as amended?

(4) Is a cash dividend declared and paid after the statute went into effect out of profits earned before the statute took effect taxable as "income"?

Decision: (1) Sec. 5 of the Income Tax Law of 1916, provided:

"Income of the following classes received by any inhabitant of this commonwealth, during the calendar year prior to the assessment of the tax, shall be taxed as follows: "* * * (c) The excess of the gains over the losses received by the taxpayer from purchase or sales of intangible personal property, whether or not the said taxpayer is engaged in the business of dealing in such property, shall be taxed at the rate of three per cent per annum * * *."

The forty-fourth amendment to the Massachusetts constitution renders imperative the inference that the word "income" was therein used to set at rest any doubt about the full power of the Legislature to deal with income as a subject of taxation. The word must not be given a narrow meaning, but should be interpreted as including every item which by any reasonable understanding can fairly be regarded as income. In its ordinary and popular meaning "income" is the amount of actual wealth which comes to a person during a given period of time, and in most, if not all, connections the word involves time as an essential element in its measurement or definition. "Income may be derived from capital invested or in use, from labor, from the exercise of skill, ingenuity, or sound judgment, or from a combination of any or all of these factors." The word "income" has been discussed by legislators and in the press in connection with taxation, and in every day use, and the common meanings attached to the word by lexicographers have weight in determining what the people meant by the term as used in the forty-fourth amendment of the constitution. Before the adoption of the amendment, gains, derived from the business of buying and selling intangible property were subject to taxation. It is a matter of common knowledge that, under the Federal Income Tax Act, gains derived from the purchase and sale of intangible property by one not engaged in such dealings as a business, are subject to taxation; and that such right has been exercised by the authorities. The word "income" as used in the amendment has a generic meaning and includes the net proceeds realized by a private individual in dealing with intangible property, although his regular buisness is not that of a dealer in such property. The amendment provides that the tax shall be levied at a uniform rate on incomes derived from the same class of property. An individual who realizes profits from the sale of intangibles is taxed at the rate of 3% while dividends on stock and interest on bonds and notes are taxed at the rate of 6% but it is held there is a reasonable ground for such a classification, and that it is not arbitrary or unnatural. It was, therefore, held that gains in excess of losses from purchases and sales of intangible property are subject to an income tax.

(2) "The same reasons which already have been stated, as to the treatment of gains in excess of losses from purchases and sales of intangible property as subject to an income tax, lead to the conclusion that gains arising from the sale of rights to subscribe for new stock issued by corporations may also be treated as income for the purpose of taxation under the forty-fourth amendment. Such

rights are themselves a species of intangible property. They come
to the stockholder as a gratuity. They are a new thing of value
which he did not possess before. These rights commonly are represented by certificates and pass by endorsement. They are a species
of intangible property. They are not regarded ordinarily as a
profit from the prosecution of the business, but are an inherent and
constituent part of the shares. Their sale resulted from an exercise
of judgment to that effect on the part of the stockholder. They
are indistinguishable in principle from a sale of the stock itself, and
gains derived from sales of such rights fall within the same class of
income."

(3) "In essence the thing which has been done is to distribute
a symbol representing an accumulation of profits, which instead
of being paid out in cash is invested in the business, thus augmenting
its durable assets. * * * The substance of the transaction is
no different from what it would be if a cash dividend had been declared with the privilege of subscription to an equivalent amount
of new shares. That which the stockholder had before was a fractional interest in the property of the corporation. So far as concerned the accumulation of profits, there was a possibility that they
might be paid out in whole or in part, as a cash dividend by authority
of the corporation. By the issue of the stock dividend that possibility is gone, and the stockholder now has evidence of a permanent
interest in the corporate enterprise of which he cannot be deprived.
It is a thing different in kind from the thing which the stockholder
owned before. From the viewpoint of the stockholder, he has received in the form of dividend in stock a thing with which theretofore he could have no tangible dealings. The certificates for the
new shares of stock representing the stock dividend may have a
materially greater value than the less tactile right to a share in the
accumulated profits which he had before. The fact that the surplus had been accumulated before the Income Tax Law went into
effect is not of consequence in this particular. The thing of value
which is taxed as income, * * * did not come into his possession
or right to possession until the year for which he is taxed. It is
this thing of value which is taxable at the time when it comes into
his right of possession. The stock dividends, so far as regards the
source from which they come to the stockholder, and the impassive

nature of his receipt of them, are derived from the same class of property from which are derived ordinary dividends, and rightly may be classified with them under Sec. 2 of the Income Tax Act." The stock dividends were taxable as "income."

(4) "It is the general and long established rule in this commonwealth that cash dividends received on corporate stock are to be treated as income and not as capital. Talbot v. Milliken, 221 Mass. 367. The extra cash dividend was declared out of surplus earnings which had accumulated during 23 years previous to March 1, 1913. Although it was large and had been accumulating for a long time, it was not the less a cash dividend. It was not in substance or effect a distribution of capital." The cash dividends are "income" and, as such, are taxable.

TYEE REALTY CO. v. ANDERSON
(U. S. Supreme Court, Feb. 21, 1916)

(240 U. S. 115)

Record: Act of October 3, 1913. Action at law to recover taxes paid under protest on net income under this Act. Demurrer to complaint sustained. Plaintiff appealed by writ of error. Affirmed.

Facts: Plaintiffs paid under protest taxes assessed under the Income Tax Law of 1913. After an adverse ruling by the Commissioner of Internal Revenue on appeals which were prosecuted for a refunding of the taxes paid, these suits were commenced to recover the amounts paid on the ground of repugnancy to the Constitution of the section of the statute under which the taxes had been collected. Contentions of plaintiff are: "(a) that the tax imposed by the statute was not sanctioned by the Sixteenth Amendment because the statute exceeded the exceptional and limited power of direct income taxation for the first time conferred upon Congress by that amendment and, being outside of the amendment and governed solely therefore by the general taxing authority conferred upon Congress by the Constitution, the tax was void as an attempt to levy a direct tax without apportionment. * * * (b) That the statute is moreover repugnant to the Constitution because of the provision therein contained for its retroactive operation for a designated time and because of the illegal discrimination and inequalities which it creates, including the provision for a progressive tax on the income of individuals and the method provided in the statute for computing the taxable income of corporations."

Question: Is Act of October 3, 1913, unconstitutional in that it exceeded the power granted by the Sixteenth Amendment to levy direct income taxation, and because it was retroactive?

Decision: The Act is constitutional. No opinion was rendered, but the case of Brushaber v. Union Pacific Railroad Company (ante) was cited as controlling and decisive of the question involved.

UNION HOLLYWOOD WATER CO. v. CARTER, COLLECTOR
(U. S. Circuit Court of Appeals, Ninth Cir., Jan. 8, 1911)
(238 Fed. 329)

Record: Act of August 5, 1909. Action at law to recover taxes paid under protest under Sec. 38 of this Act. Judgment for defendant, and plaintiff brings error. Affirmed.

Facts: Plaintiff, a public water works company, had received from its customers amounts for service connections and extensions, the greater part of which it expended in making the connections and extensions. The total amount so received from customers was included in gross income, but the same had been claimed as a deduction.

Questions: (1) May money received by a public utility company for the purpose of making new service connections and extensions when so expended, be taken as a deduction from gross income in calculating net income under the Act of August 5, 1909, Sec. 38?

(2) Is a public utility corporation, organized under the laws of California, subject to the provisions of the statute?

Decision: (1) The court held that contributions by customers for service connections and pipe extensions are income within the meaning of the Act as the amounts received from these sources are properly included in statement of gross income "received within the year from all sources" and have come to the corporation in the ordinary course of business. Expenditures for connections and extensions were held to be a permanent investment in improvements of the company and therefore not coming within any of the permitted classes of deductions mentioned in the statute.

(2) The plaintiff contended that it should be distinguished from the ordinary corporation, in that it was a public utility corporation, and under the laws of California it was not the owner, in the sense of personal ownership, of its plant and property, but was merely entrusted with the use thereof which it must devote to the public. The court held that there is no ground for holding that public utility corporations in the State of California are not subject to the provisions of the statute. They are corporations "organized for profit and having a capital stock represented by shares." The statute makes no exception in favor of public utilities.

UNION PACIFIC COAL CO. v. SKINNER, COLLECTOR
(U. S. Circuit Court of Appeals, Eighth Cir., Feb. 23, 1918)
(249 Fed. 152)

Record: Act of October 3, 1913. Action at law to recover taxes paid under protest on net income under this Act. Judgment for plaintiff reversed and defendant brings error. Reversed. On subsequent appeal, judgment affirmed without opinion (252 U. S. 570).

Facts: Plaintiff owned all of the capital stock of the Superior Coal Company. The latter on June 18, 1913, declared, and on June 19 paid to plaintiff a dividend arising out of profits of its business for the fiscal year ending June 30, 1913, amounting to $500,000. In March, 1914, plaintiff made its return under the Income Tax Law for the calendar year 1913, but instead of including in its income the entire dividend, included only one half or $250,000, contending that the other half was not income of the calendar year 1913, for the reason that it was earned by the Superior Coal Co. during the latter half of the year 1912. The Commissioner amended plaintiff's return so as to include the other $250,000 and levied a tax of 1% thereon.

Question: Are the dividends declared and paid after the Act became effective taxable to the stockholder as income "arising or accruing" within the calendar year ending December 31, 1913, even though they were paid out of earnings accumulated before the effective date of the Act?

Decision: The Income Tax Law of 1913 did not deal with the period during which a corporation, which pays a dividend, accumulates the profits out of which the dividend is paid. It was concerned with the income of the corporation receiving the dividend. Viewed in that light, the dividend accrued to the Union Pacific Coal Co. in the year 1913 and all of it was taxable. "The Act provides that the tax shall be levied 'upon the entire net income arising or accruing from all sources during the preceding taxable year.' Also that 'net income shall be ascertained by deducting from gross income . . . received within the year from all sources' certain specified allowances. It follows that in the judgment of the framers of the Act the words 'arising and accruing' are equivalent to the word received'." It then follows that all of the dividend was taxable.

UNION PACIFIC RAILROAD CO. v. DODGE
(U. S. Supreme Court, Feb. 3, 1879)
(98 U. S. 541)

Record: General Statutes of Nebraska. Action at law to recover taxes paid under protest. Judgment for defendant and plaintiff brings error. Affirmed.

Facts: Plaintiff called at the county treasurer's office and paid taxes charged on the lists. No demand had been made for the payment of such taxes, but it was the duty of every person subject to taxation to attend at the treasurer's office and make payment. In case of default, the treasurer had authority to seize and sell the personal property of the persons defaulting. At the time of payment plaintiff filed with the treasurer a notice in writing protesting against the payment of said taxes "for the reason that they were illegally and wrongfully assessed and levied, and were wholly unauthorized by law, and that suit would be instituted to recover back the money paid."

Question: Was the payment of the taxes under the above circumstances compulsory in such sense as to give the plaintiff the right to recover back the amount thereof at common law, there being no statute giving or regulating the right of recovery in such cases?

Decision: "Where a party pays an illegal demand with a full knowledge of all the facts which render such demand illegal, without immediate and urgent necessity therefor, or unless to release his person or property from detention or to prevent an immediate seizure of his person or property, such payment must be deemed voluntary and cannot be recovered back. And the fact that the party at the time of making the payment files a written protest does not make the payment involuntary." It follows that the payment of taxes by the plaintiff was not compulsory and he cannot recover.

UNION TRUST CO. OF SAN FRANCISCO et al v. WARDELL, COLLECTOR

(U. S. District Court, N. D. Calif., S. D., Jan. 3, 1921)

(273 Fed. 733)

Record: Revenue Act of 1916. Suit at law by executors against collector of internal revenue to recover back a Federal estate tax paid under protest. Defendant interposed a demurrer to plaintiff's complaint. Demurrer sustained.

Facts: On May 31, 1901, decedent who died November 14, 1916, executed a declaration of trust by which she assigned 7,475 shares of stock of the Lachman estate to her sons as trustees, to pay the income therefrom to her during her lifetime and upon her death to deliver the stock to certain relatives named in the trust deed. The executors were required to pay a Federal estate tax of $9,545.50 assessed on this transfer under the provisions of Sec. 202 (b) of the 1918 Revenue Act. Plaintiffs paid under protest and sued to recover the sum.

Questions: Should the Act be construed as to include transfers made prior to its passage, and if so construed, is it not unconstitutional and void?

Decision: The Act is not unconstitutional because it includes transfers made prior to its passage. The court said that both of the above questions were determined adversely to the plaintiffs by the Circuit Court of Appeals (Eighth Circuit) in the case of Schwab v. Doyle, 269 Fed. 321. In that case, the court said, the transfer was made in contemplation of death, whereas in the present case it was made with intent to take effect in possession or enjoyment at or after death, but manifestly the same rule of construction will apply to both provisions and the same rule of constitutional validity. Accordingly the plaintiffs were not allowed to recover and judgment was given for defendant.

UNITED STATES v. ACORN ROOFING CO.
SAME v. BROADWAY BOWLING ACADEMY et al
(U. S. District Court E. D. New York, June 22, 1912)
(204 Fed. 157)

Record: Act of August 5, 1909. Action at law to recover penalties for failure to file return under Sec. 38 of this Act. Judgment for plaintiff and defendants move to set aside the same. Denied.

Facts: Defendants' net incomes were not taxable, each falling under the specific exemption of $5,000, but they had failed to file returns under the Act, which provides: "That every corporation, etc., organized for profit and having capital stock represented by shares, etc., shall be subject to pay annually an excise tax of 1% on its entire net income over $5,000, and that on or before the first day of March of each year a true and accurate return under oath or affirmation shall be made by each of the corporations, etc., subject to the tax imposed, etc., and declares that for willful neglect to make a return, 50% of the amount of the tax may be added and for a false return, 100% may be added, but in all cases the corporation is also liable to a penalty of not less than $1,000 nor more than $10,000" for not making the "return required by law."

Question: Under the Act of August 5, 1909, is every corporation not specifically exempted, and admittedly within the class defined in the above quoted statute, liable to the duty of making an annual return specified by the statute or only those that have a sufficient net income to make them liable to the payment of the tax?

Decision: The present statute has provided that from the amount of the net income of each of "such corporations," etc., "ascertained as provided in the foregoing paragraphs" of the law, $5,000 shall be subtracted and the remainder shall be taxed. The law then provides that on the 1st of March of each year "a true and accurate return under oath shall be made by each of the corporations "subject to the tax imposed by this section." It appears by the reading of the law itself that the statute makes every corporation of a certain kind subject to pay a tax upon income over and above a certain amount, and every such corporation, of the sort required to pay if their income be great enough, must make a return and must pay if taxable. There would be no difficulty in holding that the corporations which were taxable were the only corporations required to make return, "if it were not that the Congress did not specify a different penalty than is provided for a willful neglect to make a return or for a false or fraudulent return, if such be handed in." *In all cases* there is a penalty of not less than $1,000 nor more than $10,000 for not making the "return required by law." This means that in the case of willful neglect or false return the penalty is the same as that where the taxpayer conscientiously does not make return. In other words, the intent of Congress was that no discretion be left with the taxpayer as to whether the taxpayer's net income exceeded $5,000. This must mean that a return was required in all cases and the commissioner was to determine whether the corporation was subject to a tax.

UNITED STATES v. AETNA LIFE INSURANCE CO.
(U. S. District Court, D. Conn., August 13, 1919)
(260 Fed. 333)

Record: Act of August 5, 1909. Action by the United States against the Aetna Life Insurance company to recover additional taxes. Judgment for plaintiff.

Facts: Defendant, a corporation, owned shares of stock in other corporations. These corporations paid, on behalf of the defendant, the tax imposed by the State of Connecticut on such shares of stock. Although defendant never included in gross income the amount of the tax paid in its behalf by the issuing corporation, it seeks to take such amount as a deduction from gross income.

Question: Does the statute permitting the deduction of taxes by a corporation permit it to deduct from gross income the amount of taxes paid in its behalf by other corporations, although it has never included the amounts so paid in its gross income?

Decision: "While it is true that 'a statute providing for the imposition of taxes is to be strictly construed and all reasonable doubts in respect thereto resolved against the government and in favor of the citizen' (Mutual Benefit Life Ins. Co. v. Herold 198, Fed. 199 and cases therein cited), no doubtful meaning is here involved. The language is clear and explicit. * * * If it had been the intention to permit such a deduction as defendant urges, the Act would have provided that there be included 'all sums paid by it or in its behalf within the year. * * * ' " instead of "all sums paid by it within the year for taxes imposed under authority of the United States or any state or territory thereof, etc." The defendant also relied upon a decision by the Treasury Department rendered March 24, 1916. The court stated that this decision was not in point because it contains a requirement that the taxes paid in its behalf must also have been returned as income by a corporation in a case of this kind. This was not done here. Judgment was accordingly rendered in favor of the plaintiff.

UNITED STATES v. ALEXANDER et al
(U. S. Supreme Court, Feb. 4, 1884)
(110 U. S. 325)

Record: Action at law on a distillery warehouse bond. Judgment for defendants. Plaintiff brought error. Affirmed.

Facts: The defendants pleaded that the taxes, to recover which the suit was brought, had been abated by the Secretary of the Treasury, by an order dated August 5, 1875. The plaintiff replied that on October 13, 1875, the Secretary of the Treasury withdrew this order of abatement. The defendants showed that the notice of abatement of August 5, 1875, was given to the Commissioner of Internal Revenue, who gave notice of it to the collector, and that notice was also given to the principals and sureties on the bond sued upon. There was no proof that the order withdrawing the abatement ever came to the knowledge of the obligors upon the bond until it was produced at the trial.

Question: Could an abatement of taxes, of which notice has been given to the collector and the obligors on a bond given to secure payment of the tax, be revoked so as to restore the obligation on the bond?

Decision: The abatement of the tax with notice given was a virtual cancellation of the bond. The Secretary of the Treasury might reimpose the tax but he could not revive the bond and re-impose its liability upon the obligors after the taxes had once been abated and they had received notice thereof.

UNITED STATES ads. ALPHA PORTLAND CEMENT CO.

(U. S. Circuit Court of Appeals, Third Cir., Nov. 25, 1919)

(261 Fed. 339)

Record: Act of Aug. 5, 1909. Action at law against Alpha Portland Cement Company to recover taxes. Verdict for United States (242 Fed. 978); new trial denied (257 Fed. 432), and defendant brings error. Reversed, and new trial granted.

Facts: During the year 1909, the defendant purchased certain properties, the legal title to which was taken in the name of its president, as trustee. Later in the year, pursuant to a plan for increasing the capital stock of the defendant, these properties were conveyed by the trustee to the Cement Manufacturing Company, which had been formed for the purpose of acquiring the properties. The consideration of the conveyance was the issuance by the latter company to the trustee of its entire capital stock, except a few shares necessary to be held by the directors. The stock thus issued was immediately transferred by the trustee to the defendant, which in turn distributed it among its stockholders, share for share. A merger of the two corporations was effected and for the purposes of the merger the value of the properties conveyed was fixed as that at which the trustee had conveyed them, and the stock distributed by the defendant was valued at par. The par value of the stock greatly exceeded the price at which the property had originally been purchased by the defendant. The purchase and the sale having taken place within the tax year of 1909, the government brought this suit to recover a tax upon the alleged profit.

Questions: (1) Is the apparent profit shown by a sale of property by a certain corporation to another, where immediately after the sale there is a merger of the two, income and taxable to the first corporation?

(2) Was the question of whether there was a profit properly one for the jury in this case?

Decision: (1) "The ultimate and real result of the various transactions was that the defendant purchased some properties at one figure, and in working out a plan of recapitalization valued them at a higher figure. The intermediary corporation, to which the legal title of the properties was conveyed by the trustee, was brought into being by the defendant for the express purpose of working out the recapitalization plan, and ceased to exist as a separate entity after that plan had been carried out. The defendant was no richer after the alleged sale than it was before, notwithstanding the book entries, resolutions of directors, transfers of title, etc. Viewed in this light, we think that it needs no argument to demonstrate that the case falls within the principal of the decisions of the Supreme Court in Southern Pacific v. Lowe, 247 U. S. 330, and Gulf Oil Corp. v. Lewellyn, 248 U. S. 71. Indeed, it can not be distinguished on principle from the decision of this court in Baldwin Locomotive Works v. McCoach, 221 Fed. 59. Under the above stated facts, considered as a whole, the defendant was, therefore, not liable for the tax which the government sought to recover in this suit."

(2) "The evidence, which explained the transactions and placed them in the true light, was brought out during the presentation of the defendant's case, and, except for some resolutions in the defendant's minute book (which were fully explained), was given by the same witness from whom the facts upon which the Government relies were elicited. Moreover, his explanatory and supplementary version of the transactions is in no respect inherently unreasonable, improbable, or inconsistent with that given when called as a witness for the Government; nor is there anything to indicate that it is otherwise unreliable. In this situation, it was not permissible to consider only a part of the evidence, separate from that which supplemented and explained it, or to accept the former and discard the latter. It was necessary that it be taken as a whole. When thus considered, it was susceptible of only one inference, viz., that the defendant had in reality made no profit." Accordingly, there was no question for the jury to pass upon.

UNITED STATES v. AMERICAN CHICLE CO.
(U. S. Supreme Court. June 1, 1921)
(256 U. S. 446)

Record: Act of October 22, 1914, as extended. Action brought in U. S. District Court for the Southern District of New York, by plaintiff American Chicle Co., to recover the value of certain adhesive stamps attached to packages of chewing gum. Judgment for plaintiff in the District Court. Writ of error. Judgment reversed.

Facts: The American Chicle Co. manufactures chewing gum. The goods concerned had been removed from the factory at which they were manufactured and prepared for sale to other factories or warehouses of the company in other parts of the United States. They had upon them uncancelled revenue stamps, but were the property of the company and were subject to no contract of sale on September 9, 1916. The company sells only to wholesale dealers. It appears from the statements in its petition that it removed the goods for the purposes of sale to such places as deemed most likely to offer a market, although no sale had taken place. In its petition filed in the lower court the company made a claim for $6,318.56 paid by it for revenue stamps under the Act of October 22, 1914 (extended by resolution of December 17, 1915, through December 31, 1916), which it alleged were unused after January 1, 1916, and therefore were to be redeemed under Sec. 24 of the Act of October 22, 1914, and the Act of September 8, 1916, the stamps having been purchased within two years of the application for redemption, as required by the latter Act.

Question: Does the petition of the company disclose facts upon which it can be said that the goods were not "removed for sale" within the meaning of Sec. 5 which levies the tax mentioned in Sched. B, "manufactured, sold or removed for sale?"

Decision: The court concluded that notwithstanding the assumption that the tax is levied in respect of sale rather than of manufacture, nevertheless the statute contemplates a payment by the manufacturer. If the petitioner, the court said, should send a mass of chewing gum from its factory in New Jersey to a more promising market in another state, it does not appear that it could escape the tax obligation. Although the gum left the premises of the manufacturer it was destined to another warehouse that the petitioner also owned. The following is quoted from the opinion:

"The words 'sold or removed for sale' clearly mean that it falls due in some cases before a sale is complete. No one we presume would doubt that if the goods were removed for the purpose of satisfying an outstanding contract for a certain amount of chewing gum, the tax would be due at the moment of the removal although the goods were not yet appropriated to the contract in any binding way. It seems to us hardly more doubtful that the same would be true if goods were removed by a manufacturer to put into the window of a retail shop kept by it on the other side of the street. If we are right these examples show that removal for the purpose of forwarding a sale is a removal for sale within the meaning of the Act. But on the face of the petition that was the object of the transfer of these goods to other parts of the United States. * * * * It appears to us entirely natural that Congress should look to the original place of manufacture as the place for the identification of the taxable goods, and to the amount of leaving it, except in exceptional cases, as the time for the attaching of the tax." The judgment of the lower court was reversed, and the plaintiff can not recover the value of the stamps.

UNITED STATES ex rel. ANGARICA v. BAYARD
(U. S. Supreme Court, April 30, 1888)
(127 U. S. 251)

Record: Petition for a writ of mandamus. Writ denied and relator sued out writ of error. Sustained.

Facts: Pursuant to an agreement between the United States and Spain for the settlement of certain claims of citizens of the United States, the Commission authorized to settle such claims, made an award of $822,180 with interest at 6 per cent to Angarica. The whole amount was paid over by the Secretary of State, except 5 per cent of the amount, which sum was retained by the Secretary until the government of Spain should make provision for paying the expenses of the Commission. The amount retained was invested by the State Department until the expenses of the Commission were paid by Spain, and then the amount without interest was paid over to Angarcia. Angarcia sought to compel the Secretary to pay interest on the amount from the time of the withholding until the time of payment to him. Angarcia referred to a letter written to him by the Secretary of State, in which he alleged the Secretary had officially promised to pay the interest earned on the money.

Questions: (1) Are the United States liable to pay interest on the above stated claim?

(2) Was any obligation created by virtue of the alleged promise referred to?

Decision: (1) The United States are not liable to pay interest on claims against them, in the absence of express statutory provision to that effect, whether such claims originate in contract or in tort, and whether they arise in the ordinary business of administration or under private acts of relief, passed by Congress on special application. The only recognized exceptions are where the government stipulates to pay interest and where interest is given expressly by an Act of Congress, either by the name of interest or by that of damages.

(2) No claim for the allowance of interest can be predicated upon the language of any notification or circular or letter which issued from the Department of State. No binding contract was thereby created.

UNITED STATES v. BENOWITZ

(U. S. District Court, S. D. New York, Oct. 20, 1919)

(262 Fed. 223)

Record: Criminal prosecution by the United States for perjury under Criminal Code, Sec. 125 (comp. St. Sec. 10295). Demurrer to indictment overruled.

Facts: Benowitz was indicted for swearing falsely to his income tax return. The oath was taken before a Commissioner of Deeds, and his defense was that Article 406 of Regulations 45 did not authorize such an official to take oath to income tax returns, thus making the oath that he took, no oath at all. Article 406 opens with the statement that "all income tax returns must be verified under oath or affirmation", and concludes with provisions for returns of persons in the naval or military service and for returns executed abroad. Mention is not made of any officers in this country authorized to take oaths.

Question: What persons in the United States are authorized to take oaths to income tax returns?

Decision: The only possible interpretation of the article is that it meant to include all such persons as are authorized by the local law to take oaths in their several districts.

UNITED STATES v. BIWABIK MINING CO.
(U. S. Supreme Court. May 20, 1918)
(247 U. S. 116)

Record: Act of August 5, 1909. Action by the United States to recover tax on a sum omitted by the defendant from the income in making its return. Judgment for United States, and defendant brought error. Reversed (242 Fed. 9), and United States brought a writ of certiorari. Reversed.

Facts: The defendant, by assignment, acquired a lease by the terms of which lease it acquired the right for the term of fifty years to explore, mine out, and remove iron ore which might be found upon the lands described in the lease. The lessee contracted to remove a certain amount annually, and upon failure to do so the lessor might take possession of the premises. To the lessor, the defendant promised to pay a royalty of 30c per ton for each ton mined. To the prior lessee, the defendant paid the sum of $612,000. In making its return to the collector of internal revenue, the defendant deducted from its gross income a large sum "to recover realization of unearned increment." The amount of the deduction was arrived at by multiplying the number of tons of ore mined during the year by 48¾c, which was the market value of the ore at the beginning of the tax law. The defendant was requested to amend its return which it declined to do, and this suit was instituted.

Questions: (1) May the lessee, a mining company, which has the right to enter the lessor's land, explore for, mine out, and remove the ore, deduct the value of the ore mined during the year as a depreciation of capital assets, which value was the market value at the time the law began?

(2) Is the owner of such a lease the owner of the ore?

Decisions: (1) The court quoting from the opinion of the district judge said, "The defendant paid $612,000 for the lease under consideration and in addition assumed the payment of the royalties stipulated for therein. This may properly and justly be considered a payment in advance of an increased royalty on ore to be mined, and that is precisely the character which the defendant gave to the payment when dealing with it in its private accounts, in which the stipulation shows, Ex. H., that it carried one account entitled 'Rate of general ledger or capitalized value .03885 per ton,' and another entitled 'Rate of increment value, January 1, 1909, .44865 per ton.' These two values added make the 48¾c per ton which the defendant deducted in making its return. Thus in its own bookkeeping the defendant gives its private opinion as to the requisite reimbursement necessary to maintain its capital investment. * * *. And the court finds as conclusions of law from said facts that the defendant was entitled to deduct for and on account of the 544,353 tons of ore mined by it under its lease in the year 1910, the sum of .03885 cents per ton (which amount the parties agree hereby is the cost to defendant of said ore at the time it acquired the property in the year 1898, interest, taxes, surveys, and other carrying charges on the said ore up to the time of its removal from the said mine having been charged annually including the year 1910 into operating expenses) and defendant is not entitled to deduct the 48.75 cents per ton deducted by it in its return..* *..*."

(2) "The lessee takes from the property the ore mined, paying for the privilege so much per ton mined. He has this right or privilege under the form of lease involved so long as he sees fit to hold the same without exercising the privilege of cancellation therein contained. He is * * * in no legal sense a purchaser of ore in place."

UNITED STATES v. BLACKLOCK
(U. S. Supreme Court. January 13, 1908)

(208 U. S. 75)

Record: Acts of July 13, 1866, and July 20, 1868. Action at law to recover land sold by collector of internal revenue for delinquent revenue taxes. Judgment for defendant and plaintiff brings error. Affirmed.

Facts: A distillery owner conveyed a tract of land containing about 400 acres of land with improvements, including a distillery and all things appurtenant thereto, in trust to secure a certain loan made by plaintiff. Plaintiff later executed an instrument in writing consenting to the use of the distillery (occupying three acres of land) by the mortgagee, and to the priority of the lien of the United States for unpaid revenue taxes. Previous to the execution of the trust deed, taxes had accrued and were unpaid. The collector sold the distillery together with the 400 acre tract of land under distraint proceedings.

Question: Did plaintiff have a prior lien to that of the government under the above circumstances?

Decision: The lien of the Government for unpaid revenue taxes attached to the land when taxes became due and were unpaid, and attached to the entire tract owned by the distillery owner when he became delinquent. The plaintiff contended that the Act of July 20, 1868, providing for an action in equity by the collector of internal revenue (where he deemed it expedient) to enforce a lien of the United States for unpaid revenue taxes superseded the provisions of the Act of July 13, 1866, but the court held that such remedy was cumulative and did not supersede the remedy given by distraint. The plaintiff, having failed to take advantage of a right to redeem the land sold within a year by paying the amount of taxes due and costs, cannot recover.

UNITED STATES v. CAPITAL CITY DAIRY CO.

(U. S. District Court, S. D. Ohio., E. D.   April 13, 1915)

(252 Fed. 900)

Record: In Equity. Heard on application for a receiver. Receiver appointed.

Facts: The defendant corporation, engaged in the manufacture of oleomargarine, by fraudulent representation of its officers, defrauded the government of about $2,000,000 in taxes. When the fraud was discovered this sum was assessed, and the collector sold all the property of the corporation and applied the amount realized

$209,577.17, upon the tax. Defendant's officers and directors were its only stockholders, and during the time the government was being defrauded of these taxes, they paid to themselves sums amounting to more than $2,000,000 as dividends. The purpose of this bill was to recover from the stockholders such sums paid as dividends and to apply them to payment of the tax.

Questions: (1) Has equity jurisdiction over a suit by the government for the purpose of reaching assets wrongfully in the hands of stockholders and applying them to the payment of taxes due the government?

(2) Was a judgment by the government a prerequisite to such a suit?

Decision: (1) The plaintiff has no adequate remedy at law for the wrongs of which it complains. If the fraud charged was perpetrated, the money paid as dividends is still the defendant's money, and is held in trust by the several stockholders respectively. It is essentially an equitable proceeding for impounding the defendant's tangible (if any) and intangible assets, and applying them to the payment of the defendant's obligations to the plaintiff.

(2) On the facts presented, the plaintiff was not required first to obtain a judgment.

UNITED STATES v. CHAMBERLAIN
(U. S. Supreme Court, January 3, 1911)
(219 U. S. 250)

Record: Act of June 13, 1898. Action at law by the United States to recover stamp tax claimed to be payable. Judgment for defendant and plaintiff brings error. Reversed.

Facts: The plaintiff alleged that Straton had conveyed to a corporation certain lands by deed reciting a consideration of $4,850,000; that internal revenue stamps of the value of $4,850.00 were affixed to the deed, whereas the actual consideration of the conveyance was $9,733,000, and by reason thereof, there became due and payable to the United States from Straton a revenue tax amounting to $9,733, of which the sum of $4,883 remained unpaid, internal revenue stamps therefor not having been attached to the deed or cancelled.

Questions: Can the Government enforce the payment of a tax by any appropriate civil action, even though the taxing statute does not contain a specific grant of authority to proceed in that way?

Decision: The Act of June 13, 1898, created an obligation to pay the tax. "At common law, customs duties were recoverable by the crown by an information in debt or in exchequer information in the nature of a bill in equity for discovery and account. These informations rested upon the general principle that in the given case the common law or the statute creates a debt, charge, or duty in the party personally to pay the duties immediately upon the importation; and that therefore, the ordinary remedies lie for this, as for any other acknowledged debt, due to the crown." United States v. Lyman, 1 Mason, p. 499. It is a rule of the common law in England and in many of the states of this country "that where a statute creates a right and provides a particular remedy for its enforcement the remedy is generally exclusive of all common law remedies. But it is important to notice upon what the rule is founded. The reason of the rule is that the statute, by providing a particular remedy, manifests an intention to prohibit other remedies, and the rule, therefore, rests upon a presumed statutory prohibition. It applies and it is enforced when any one to whom the statute is a rule of conduct seeks redress for a civil wrong. He is confined to the remedy pointed out in the statute, for he is forbidden to make use of any other." But the United States is not prohibited from adopting any remedies for the recovery of a debt unless it be named in the prohibiting statute by special and particular words. This rule is "settled respecting the British Crown" and is equally applicable to this government. "The reason of the rule which denies to others the use of any other than the statutory remedy is wanting, therefore, in applicability to the government, and the rule itself must not be extended beyond its reason."

"A tax may or may not be a 'debt' under a particular statute, according to the sense in which the word is found to be used. But whether the Government may recover a personal judgment for a tax depends upon the existence of the duty to pay, for the enforcement of which another remedy has not been made exclusive. Whether an action of debt is maintainable depends not upon the question who is the plaintiff or in what manner the obligation was incurred, but it lies whenever there is due a sum either certain or readily reduced to certainty." Stockwell v. United States, 13 Wall. p. 542. It was contended "that the provision for penalties excludes the idea of a personal liability." But the court held that "these penalties were provided in order to induce the payment of the tax, and not as a substitute for payment. It cannot be supposed that Congress intended, by penalizing delinquency, to deprive the government of any suitable means of enforcing the collection of revenue."

UNITED STATES v. CHOUTEAU
(U. S. Supreme Court, October, 1880)
(102 U. S. 603)

Record: Rev. Stat., Sec. 3303. Actions at law to recover penalties for violation of Revenue Law. Judgment for defendant and plaintiff brings error. Affirmed.

Facts: The United States brought an action upon a bond executed by a distiller and his sureties. The breaches complained of were, first, that the distiller by omitting to make certain entries in a book which he, by Sec. 3303, Revised Statutes, was required to keep, was enabled to defraud, and did defraud, the United States of the tax imposed by law upon the spirits produced at his distillery; and, second, that in violation of Sec. 3296 he had removed spirits produced at his distillery to a place other than the distillery warehouse, without the tax thereon having been first paid. To the first ground of complaint the defendants answered by denying its allegations, and averring that whatever fraud was committed was effected through other means than those charged. For the second, they answered that before the suit was brought two bills for indictment, for the same removals of spirits now complained of, were found against the distiller, and that upon the recommendation of the Attorney General and the advice of the Secretary of the Treasury, the Commissioner of Internal Revenue accepted from him a specified sum, in compromise, satisfaction, and settlement of the indictments, which were thereupon dismissed and abandoned by the United States.

Question: Was the defendant's answer, the plaintiff having demurred to it, a bar to the action?

Decision: A party seeking damages for a specified breach of duty is not entitled to judgment in his favor, when admitting on the record that whatever damages he may have sustained resulted from other causes. This the plaintiff admitted by demurring to the defendant's answer. The compromise with the government "pleaded is a complete defense against a recovery of the penalty claimed." The amount paid in compromise was intended as a punishment for the violation of the statute and not as a substitute for the tax required. Even if the distiller had paid the tax after removal of the spirits in violation of the statute, the penalty has not been discharged. It could still be imposed upon him. The sureties on the distiller's bond cannot be subjected to the penalty attached to the commission of an offense, after the principal has affected a full and complete compromise with the government of prosecutions based upon the same offense and designed to secure the same penalty.

UNITED STATES v. CHRISTINE OIL AND GAS CO.

(U. S. District Court, W. D. La., Sept. 8, 1920)

(269 Fed. 458)

Record: Act of October 3, 1913. Suit by United States to recover a tax. Verdict directed for defendant.

Facts: The defendant sold certain oil leases, which cost it $115,000, to a solvent corporation, for $250,000. About $79,000 was paid in cash and $25,000 thereafter out of the proceeds of oil. The balance due was not represented by notes or secured in any way. Defendant paid income tax upon the amounts actually received and was additionally assessed $1,328.13 on the unpaid part of the selling price.

Question: Were the deferred payments of the selling price of property, not represented by notes or secured in any way, required to be treated as income of the year of sale of the property?

Decision: Where the effect of a transaction is a mere promise to pay, and not an actual payment, it cannot be said to be income, until it has been actually received, and is not subject to be taxed as such until its actual receipt. If the seller accepts the notes of third person in absolute payment, the rule would be different.

The ruling of the Treasury Department is to the contrary. However, the Regulations of the Department could not enlarge the net income made subject to the tax by the terms of the Act. Deferred payments of the selling price of property, not represented by notes or securities in any way, are not to be treated as income of the year of sale of the property.

UNITED STATES v. CLEVELAND, C. C. & ST. L. RY. CO.
(U. S. Supreme Court, May 20, 1918)
(247 U. S. 195)

Record: Act of August 5, 1909. Action by the Government for the collection of tax. Judgment for plaintiff in U. S. District Court reversed by Circuit Court of Appeals for the Sixth Circuit, 242 Fed. 18. Appealed on certiorari, and judgment of the Circuit Court of Appeals affirmed.

Facts: Respondent purchased 30,000 shares of stock in January, 1900, for $981,427.92, and sold them January 28, 1909, for $1,795,719 at a profit of over $814,000. It included no portion of this profit in its return for the year 1909 under the Corporation Excise Act of August 5, 1909, and the United States brought this action to recover a tax of one per cent thereon.

Question: Should the tax payable under the 1909 Act be limited to the difference between the sale price and the market value of the shares on December 31, 1908?

Decision: The judgment of the lower court was affirmed, and it was held that only so much of the profit as accrued after December 31, 1908, was "income" within the Corporation Tax Act of 1909.

UNITED STATES v. COULBY
(U. S. Circuit Court of Appeals, Sixth Cir., Jan. 7, 1919)
(258 Fed. 27)

Record: Act of October 3, 1913. Action at law to recover alleged unpaid income taxes. Judgment for defendant, (251 Fed. 982) and plaintiff brings error. Affirmed.

Facts: A portion of a dividend was paid to a partnership holding such shares of stock as an asset. The said portion was

ultimately paid to a member of the firm as his proportionate share
of the firm's profits.

Question: Was the dividend received by the partner, income
upon which the partner was bound to pay the normal tax?

Decision: "The Income Tax Law defines what shall constitute the net income of a taxable person and plainly includes such
gains and profits derived from and through a partnership. The
Act also states what deduction shall be made from the gross income
of a taxable person. Among these deductions is the amount received as dividends upon the stock of any corporation which is
taxable upon its net income. The law ignores for taxing purposes
the existence of a partnership. It is so framed as to deal with the
gains and profits of a partnership as if they were the gains and profits
of an individual partner." A member of a partnership is not required to include, as a part of his net income subject to the normal
tax, such part of his income derived from or through a partnership
which has been received by that partnership as dividends on stocks
owned by it in corporations taxable upon their net income under
the Act of 1913.

UNITED STATES v. CURRY
(U. S. District Court of the U. S., Dec. 27, 1912)

(201 Fed. 371)

Record: Oleomargarine Tax Rev. Stat. Sec. 3187-3196. Suit
in equity to recover taxes due the government. Judgment for
plaintiff.

Facts: Defendant, a manufacturer of oleomargarine, owed
stamp and special taxes to the amount of $7,044. She was notified
by the collector of the proper district of said assessment and formal
demand for the payment thereof was served on her. At the time
of aforesaid notice and demand, defendant was possessed of a lease-
hold interest in certain real estate and was seized in fee of other
real estate. Subsequent to demand and notice, defendant conveyed
all of the above interests in real estate to some of the other defendants, and these defendants had in turn conveyed their interests
to still other defendants. The manufacturer of oleomargarine,
and the subsequent transferees of the property were joined as

defendants in an action by the government to sell the land as an enforcement of its lien on the land for the taxes due.

Questions: (1) Was a demurrer sustainable to the Government's bill on the ground of multiplicity?

(2) Was it necessary, under Secs. 3187 and 3196, Revised Statute, to institute proceedings to recover taxes due the United States from the sale of chattels and personal effects of the delinquent before resorting to the sale of real estate?

(3) Can the United States enforce its lien against real estate in the hands of innocent purchasers for value?

Decisions: (1) Demurrer was not sustainable. "If the Government acquired a lien by the assessment of the tax and the demand for its payment, that lien attached to all of the property of * * * defendant, the original owner. It was not apportionable among the various tracts of land or terms of years then held by * * * defendant * * *. Justice could not be done to those who might have acquired interests in the property junior to the lien of the Government without making them all parties to one suit."

(2) This question is answered in the negative by the cases of Mansfield v. Excelsior Refining Co., 135 U. S. 326, and Blacklock v. United Stated, 208 U. S. 75.

(3) "It is admitted that the express language of the statute (Sec. 3186) is: 'That if any person liable to pay any tax neglects or refuses to pay the same after demand, the amount shall be a lien in favor of the United States from the time the assessment list was received by the collector * * *, until paid * * * upon all property and rights to property belonging to such person'." The court held "when the requirements of assessment and the demand have been complied with, the lien of the Government is superior to that of any one acquiring any interests in the property" after the date of demand. The government lien is unaffected by the fact that a subsequent incumbrancer or purchaser became such without knowledge that the government had any interest in the property or claim upon it." The law was criticised by the court and a remedy suggested.

UNITED STATES v. EMERY, BIRD, THAYER REALTY CO.
(U. S. Supreme Court, April 5, 1915)
(237 U. S. 28)

Record: Act of August 5, 1909. Action at law to recover taxes paid under protest under Sec. 38 of this Act. Judgment for plaintiff (198 Fed. 242), and defendant brings error. Affirmed.

Facts: Thayer Dry Goods Co., a business corporation of Kansas City, Missouri, occupied certain lands partly hired and partly owned by it for the purpose of its business. Eighteen months before the passage of the Corporation Tax Law, its members decided that the plaintiff should be organized, and it was, for the purpose of acquiring the Dry Goods Company's lands and of letting the same to the Dry Goods Co., the latter having the management of the property and assuming the responsibility in respect of it. The only business done by the plaintiff was to keep up the corporate organization and to collect and distribute the rent received from its single lessee; and the court found as a fact that it was not doing business within the statute, subject, of course, to the question whether the activities stated constituted such doing business as a matter of law. The chartered powers of the plaintiff included performing and enforcing the performance of the respective covenants in the lease taken over and the selling of the property or any part of it upon the vote of not less than two-thirds of the directors, who were very nearly the same as those of the Dry Goods Co. It was also covenanted to rebuild in case the buildings were destroyed. But there has been no occasion to perform any of these undertakings.

Question: Under the circumstances stated above, is the corporation doing business within the meaning of the Act of August 5, 1909?

Decision: The case is covered by the decisions in Zonne v. Minneapolis Syndicate, 220 U. S. 187 and McCoach v. Minehill Railway, 228 U. S. 295. "The question is rather on what the corporation is doing than what it could do, but looking even to its powers they are limited very nearly to the necessary incidents of holding a specific tract of land. The plaintiff's sale of the whole would be merely the winding up of the corporation. Such sale would signify that the Dry Goods Co. would not need it. The plaintiff's function and the only one it was carrying on was the bare receipt and distribution to its stockholders of the rent from a specified parcel of land." This was not a "doing business" within the meaning of the Act.

UNITED STATES v. ERIE RAILROAD COMPANY
(U. S. Supreme Court, November 27, 1882)
(106 U. S. 327)

Record: Act of June 30, 1864. Action at law to recover taxes and penalties under Sec. 122 of this Act. Judgment for defendant (Fed. Case 15056). Plaintiff brings error. Reversed.

Facts: Defendant had issued bonds, the principal and interest of which were payable in London, England. These bonds were sold directly to foreign bankers having their places of business in London and were by them sold to their customers in England and on the Continent. During the taxable years in question the bonds sold were held by non-resident aliens. The interest on the bonds was sent forward by the defendant to the foreign bank and as it fell due was paid by such bank to the bond holders.

Question: Was the defendant corporation liable for the payment of the tax on the amount of interest paid to non-resident aliens under the Act of June 30, 1864?

Decision: "The tax laid upon defendant corporation's bonds was intended to affect the owners of the bonds, and while the corporation was directed to pay it, it was authorized to retain the amount from the installment due to the bond holders whether citizens or aliens. The objection that Congress had no power to tax non-resident aliens is met by the fact that the tax was not assessed against them personally but against the rem, the claim, the debt due them. Congress has a right to lay a tax on property within the jurisdiction of the United States with certain exceptions not necessary to be noted. The money due to non-resident aliens in this case was in the United States * * * in the hands of the company * * * before it could be transferred to London or to the place where the bondholders resided. While here it was liable to taxation. Plausible grounds for levying such a tax are that the creditor is protected by our laws in the enjoyment of the

debt; that the whole machinery of our courts and the physical power
of the government are placed at the disposal of the bondholders
for the security of the interest and its collection." The defendant
corporation is, therefore, liable for the tax on the amount of interest
paid to non-resident alien bondholders.

UNITED STATES v. FIELD
(U. S. Supreme Court, February 28, 1921)
(Not yet reported)

Record: Revenue Act of 1916, as amended by Act of March 3,
1917. Suit brought by executors against the United States to recover an estate tax paid under protest. Judgment in the Court of
Claims for plaintiffs. Appeal made by the Government to this
court. Judgment affirmed.

Facts: Joseph N. Field, a resident of the State of Illinois,
died April 29, 1914, leaving a will by which he gave the residue
of his estate, after payment of certain legacies, to trustees, with
provision that one-third of it should be set apart and held as a
separate trust fund for the benefit of his wife Kate Field, the net
income to be paid to her during life, and from and after her death,
the net income of one-half of said share of the trust estate to be
paid to such persons and in such shares as she should appoint by
last will and testament. Kate Field died April 29, 1917, a resident
of Illinois, leaving a will by which she executed the power of appointment. The collector of internal revenue included as a part of her
gross estate the appointed estate passing under her execution of the
power, and assessed and collected an estate tax based on the net
value thereof and amounting to $121,059.60. Her executor, having
paid the tax under protest, made a claim for refund which the Commissioner of Internal Revenue rejected. This action was then commenced.

Question: Is the property, which passes by the exercise, in
a will, of a general power of appointment a part of the estate of
the testator, and subject to estate tax?

Decision: The Government sought to sustain the tax under
the provisions of Sec. 202 (a) and (b) of the 1916 Act which hold
that the value of the gross estate shall be determined by including
all property of decedents "to the extent of the interest therein of

decedent at the time of his death which after his death is subject to the payment of the charges against his estate and to distribution as part of his estate," and "to the extent of any interest therein of which the decedent has at any time made a transfer, or with respect to which he has created a trust in contemplation of, or intended to take effect at or after his death, except in the case of a bona fide sale for a fair consideration in money or money's worth." The chief reliance of the Government was upon the rule well established in England and followed generally in this country, that where one has a general power of appointment either by deed or will, and executes the power, equity will regard the property appointed as part of his assets for the payment of his creditors in preference to the claims of his voluntary appointees. After citing cases to show that the existence of the power does not of itself vest any estate in the donee, and after commenting to the effect that whether or not the power be or be not exercised, the property that was subject to appointment is not subject to distribution as part of the estate of the donee, the court makes the following statement:

"It follows that the interest in question, not having been property of Mrs. Field at the time of her death, nor subject to distribution as part of her estate, was not taxable under clause (a). We deem it equally clear that it was not within clause (b). That clause is the complement of (a), and is aptly descriptive of a transfer of an interest in decedent's own property in his lifetime, intended to take effect at or after his death. It cannot without undue laxity of construction, be made to cover a transfer resulting from a testamentary execution by decedent of a power of appointment over property not his own."

The judgment of the Court of Claims was affirmed, and the interest passing under the testamentary execution of a general power of appointment was held not to be taxable.

UNITED STATES v. FROST
(U. S. District Court, N. D. Illinois, Jan. Term, 1869)
(Fed. Case 15172)

Record: Act of July 1, 1862. Defendant was indicted for making a false return. Defendant acquitted.

Facts: The books of the defendant showed a greater profit than the return made by him. The profits entered in the books were made up by adding to the assets of the preceding year all debts and accounts whether good or bad. On his return, he included only the debts which he considered good.

Question: Where the law allows deductions to be made for "debts ascertained to be worthless," can one who has acted honestly in determining such deduction be convicted of an untrue return?

Decision: "The language is 'ascertained to be worthless,' by whom or how? The law is silent on this important point, and, therefore, there must be a discretion given to the person making his returns, and if that discretion is used fairly and honestly, there would seem to be no just ground of complaint. It certainly can scarcely be contended that every debt must be ascertained to be worthless by a suit at law, or in equity * * *." The Act must have intended that deductions be made for debts ascertained to be worthless by the person making his returns. The defendant acted honestly and, therefore, he can not be convicted of making an untrue return.

UNITED STATES v. GENERAL INSPECTION & LOADING CO.

(U. S. District Court D. New Jersey, November 9, 1911)

(192 Fed. 223, 204 Fed. 657)

Record: Act of August 5, 1909. Action at law by United States to recover taxes and penalties under Sec. 38 of this Act. Judgment for plaintiff.

Facts: The defendant corporation obtained a certificate of dissolution on February 14, 1910, from the State of New Jersey, pursuant to proceedings taken for that purpose. Defendant dissolved before March 1st, 1910, date on which return was due, and sought to avoid paying taxes for the taxable year ending December 31, 1909.

Question: Can a corporation, under the Act of August 5, 1909, be dissolved after the close of the taxable year and before March 1st, the date on which return is required, and thus avoid paying the tax for the taxable year ending December 31, 1909?

Decision: "Congress, by Sec. 38, in specific terms imposed the liability for an excise tax upon all corporations of the character of defendant doing business during the year 1909. It also imposed upon them the duty of making a return to the collector of internal revenue on or before March 1st of the following year as a basis or measure from which its liability could be determined. This is not a case of a liability to taxation accruing after dissolution, but rather of a liability incurred before dissolution and while the corporate scheme for the ascertainment of the extent of such liability and for its enforcement were in existence. The case does not differ greatly in principle from that in which a party, after having made and broken a contract, should die, in which case his death would not protect his estate from the liquidation and payment of any damages resulting from such breach. The defendant contended that although there was a liability to taxation existing against the defendant on December 31, 1909, as the extent thereof had not been ascertained at the time when the corporation dissolved, it was not a debt and that consequently the section of the New Jersey Act holding the directors liable as trustees for the debts of the corporation were not applicable. It may be that such a liability was not a debt, in the primary and strict sense of the word, but it is often given a broader meaning. 'Liability' is the state or condition of one who is under obligation at once, or at some future time, something which may be enforced by action. It may exist without the right of immediate action. The procedure to ascertain the amount of the tax in the manner provided by Congress in no wise affected the then existing liability of the corporation; indeed it assumed it, and was but an ordinary step looking to its ultimate enforcement. * * * As neither the tax nor any part of it has been paid, judgment will be entered in favor of the plaintiff, and against the defendant."

UNITED STATES v. GRAND RAPIDS & I. RY. CO.

(U. S. District Court, W. D. Michigan, Feb. 25, 1915)

(239 Fed. 153)

Record: Act of August 5, 1909. Action at law to collect excise tax. Demurrer to declaration overruled. Affirmed in 256 Fed. 989, without opinion.

Facts: The declaration showed that the suit was for additional tax due, the defendant's return having been false. Three years had elapsed and the Commissioner had made no assessment.

Questions: (1) Is the three year clause of the fifth subdivision of Sec. 38 of the 1909 Excise Law a limitation upon the right of the Government to sue for unpaid taxes, thus confining the government to the summary proceedings therein provided?

(2) Is an assessment necessary before an action will lie for the tax imposed by Excise Law, 1909, which is of a fixed percentage?

Decision: (1) The clause in question "is not a limitation upon the right of the government to sue for unpaid taxes, but, at most, is a limitation upon the right of the collecting officers to make assessment and to enforce payment by the summary statutory proceedings." In the collection of the taxes imposed by the statute, the government is not confined to the summary proceedings but may resort to a plenary suit.

(2) "Where a tax of a fixed percentage (like the one here sought to be recovered) is imposed by the statute on a subject or object which is so definitely described in the statute that its amount or value, on which the fixed per centum is to be calculated, can be ascertained by a court, a suit for the tax will lie without an assessment.

UNITED STATES v. GUARANTY TRUST & SAVINGS BANK

(U. S. District Court, S. D. Florida, Aug. 13, 1918)

(253 Fed. 291)

Record: Act of August 5, 1909. Action at law by the government to recover taxes. Judgment for defendant.

Facts: The defendant is a banking corporation, incorporated under the laws of Florida, and, in rendering its return of annual net income, made deductions for state, county, and municipal taxes paid under Sec. 8, Chap. 5596 of the laws of Florida which reads as follows: "The owner or holder of stock in any incorporated company doing business under the corporate name shall not be taxed for such stock: Provided that such stock is returned for taxation by such incorporated company and taxes are paid thereon by such company, or the property of said company is assessed for taxes where located and taxes are then paid on such property."

Question: Does the Florida statute place a tax upon the bank to be paid by the bank so that the amount thereof may be deducted from its gross income to ascertain net amount taxable under Act of August 5, 1909, Sec. 38, Cl. 2, Subdivision 4?

Decision: It is a tax upon the bank and not upon the stockholder. "It seems to me the primary obligation rests upon the bank to pay this tax, without provision to recover it from the stockholder, as is the case with national banks. Such being the case the tax so paid must be deducted from the gross income, to arrive at the net amount on which the 1 per cent of excise is to be calculated, under the fourth subdivision of the second clause of section 38 of the Act of August 5, 1909."

UNITED STATES v. GUEST
(U. S. Circuit Court of Appeals, Fourth Cir., Feb. 6, 1906)
(143 Fed. 456)

Record: Rev. Stat. Secs. 3184 and 1047. Action at law by the government on a distiller's bond to recover tax and interest of 1% a month. Judgment for plaintiff with only legal interest and plaintiff brings error. Affirmed.

Facts: The spirits upon which the tax was alleged to be due had been seized by the Collector of Internal Revenue, and were abstracted from the warehouse thereafter. The defendant, who was one of the sureties on the bond, alleged that the negligence of the Collector in guarding the goods resulted in such loss.

Questions: Is the loss of spirits while they were in the distillery warehouse in the possession of the Collector, a defense by a surety when sued on a distiller's bond for the tax on the spirits?

(2) Was the one per cent per month specified in the statute interest upon the debt due the government, the recovery of which is barred by the six year statute of limitations, or is the one per cent treated in the nature of a penalty and subject to the five year limitation prescribed by statute?

Decision: (1) "That the government is not liable for negligence of laches of its officers or agent is well recognized and settled, and such negligence constitutes no bar or defense to a recovery upon a bond taken up by the government. * * *. Sec. 3221 of the Revised Statutes * * * provides a method for the abatement of taxes on distilled spirits, where the same have been lost or destroyed, namely, by appeal to the Secretary of the Treasury, and it is only under this section that relief in such cases can be secured."

(2) "Sec. 3184 of the Revised Statutes * * * prescribes interest at the rate of 1 per cent per month upon taxes and assessments of the character involved here (stamp taxes) and our conclusion is that this is recoverable as interest, and is not a penalty; there being a 5 per cent penalty specifically prescribed on the amount of the tax. This is an ordinary suit, or, technically speaking, action of debt, upon a bond taken by the government to secure its revenue, and, on recovery under the same, interest runs at the rate of 1 per cent per month, or 12 per cent per annum, the rate prescribed by the Act of Congress; and the statute of limitations, as recognized by the court below, does not run against the government in the collection of its debts, while it does against the enforcement of the penalties, by reason of the Act of Congress in such case made and provided." Although the lower court allowed the government to recover only legal interest, the error of the lower court, so far as the government is interested in this case, is harmless in character, since the government was allowed to recover more than it was entitled to on the bond sued on. The surety was not liable in the first instance on a distiller's bond. Therefore the judgment of the lower court was affirmed.

UNITED STATES v. GUGGENHEIM EXPLORATION CO.

(U. S. District Court, S. D. New York, Jan. 4, 1917)

(238 Fed. 231)

Record: Act of August 5, 1909. Action at law by government to recover the excise tax. Judgment for defendant.

Facts: The defendant corporation had five years before transferred to another corporation mining property which the directors of the latter corporation appraised at $49,000,000 in return for $17,000,000 of preferred stock and $24,000,000 of common stock. A year before the sale of the stock by the defendant corporation, it received dividends of 7 per cent upon the common stock, which was reported by the president to be worth par, but it was carried on the books of the defendant company at the valuation of $1 per share. The common stock was sold for $60 per share, which was less than par.

Questions: (1) Is the net income of a corporation to be determined by the bookkeeping facts which show a profit, or by the real facts which do not show a profit for the year in question?

(2) Is the enhanced value of stock owned by a corporation which has accrued over a period of four years prior to the effective date of the law, income, gain, or profit?

(3) Does the government have the burden of proving that stock, which was carried on the books of a corporation at a valuation of $1, was worth but $1?

Decision: (1) "The net income of a corporation is not to be determined by bookkeeping facts, but by real facts. The bookkeeper creates nothing; his methods, figures and records must yield to proven and established facts."

(2) "The enhanced value of property which accrues from the gradual increase in its value during a series of years prior to the effective date of an income tax law * * * does not become income, gains or profits taxable under such an act."

(3) "The income of our capital is that which it does for us. Therefore, another essential inquiry, and, indeed, the basic one here, is the determination of a question of fact, as to what was the value of the common stock at the time it was acquired by the defendant. The burden of establishing its case is upon the government." The government has not sustained this burden and therefore can not recover.

UNITED STATES v. ISHAM
(U. S. Supreme Court, October Term, 1873)
(84 U. S. 496)

Record: Act of June 30, 1864. Criminal proceedings by the United States against defendant for issuing a certain instrument without a stamp. Judgment for defendant.

Facts: The defendant company issued the following instrument which was used in an isolated mining district as currency.

(V)   Iron Cliffs Company   (Five)

(1190)   Negaunee, Mich., June 3, 1870.

Pay to the order of E. B. Isham, Supt. or bearers,

Five Dollars,

Value received, and charge to account of

To C. J. Canda, Esq., New York   E. B. Isham

       Countersigned E. S. Green, Clerk.

C. J. Canda and E. B. Isham, named in the above instrument, were both agents of the Iron Cliffs Company.

Question: (1) Is a stamp required to be placed on the above instrument under a statute which provides that (a) "Every draft, or order for the payment of any sum of money at sight or on demand (except where the draft or order is so drawn on a person, company, or corporation, other than a bank, banker or trust company, and for a sum not exceeding $10), 2 cents." (b) "Every memorandum, check, receipt or other written or printed evidence of an amount of money to be paid on demand or at a time designated, for a sum not exceeding $100, 5 cents?"

(2) Was the defendant guilty of attempting to evade the stamp tax because a large debt was liquidated by several instruments in denominations smaller than taxable by the Act?

Decision: (1) The above instrument is in form a draft or order for the payment of money drawn upon a person other than a bank, banks, or trust company, and was for less than $10. It therefore falls within the exception in provision (a) above. "In settling whether an instrument should be stamped or not, regard is to be had to its form, rather than to its operation. Though it may be a device to avoid the revenue acts, and though its operation may have the effect of avoiding them, yet if the device be carried out by means of legal forms, it is subject to no legal censure." There was an error in punctuation in provision (b) above in that there should be a hyphen between the words "memorandum" and "check." It should read "memorandum-check." The stamp requirement for "check" was provided for in another part of the statute and it cannot be assumed that Congress intended to make two different provisions for the same subject. Provision (b) cannot apply to the above instrument when properly punctuated. Neither of the above provisions requires the defendant to place a stamp upon the instrument in question, and judgment was given for defendant.

(2) A case of the same nature as the one we are considering is where a careful individual having the amount of twenty dollars to pay, pays the same by handing to his creditor two checks of ten dollars each. He thus draws checks in payment of his debt to the amount of twenty dollars, and yet, under the Act of 1862, he pays no stamp duty. "He resorts to devices to avoid the payment of duties, but they are not illegal. He has the legal right to split up his evidences of payment, and thus avoid the tax." Another answer is that the adoption of a rule to disregard the form of the instrument and to investigate the real character for the purpose of determining the stamp duty would destroy the circulation capacity of bills, or drafts, or orders.

UNITED STATES v. KAUFMAN
(U. S. Supreme Court, October Term, 1877)
(96 U. S. 567)

Record: Rev. Stat. Sec. 3232. Action to recover taxes erroneously paid. Judgment for plaintiff in Court of Claims. Appeal by the United States. Judgment affirmed.

Facts: Plaintiff filed a claim for refund which was allowed by the Commissioner of Internal Revenue and by him certified to the Comptroller of the Treasury, but was never paid.

Questions: (1) Did the Court of Claims have jurisdiction of this suit?

(2) Was the allowance of the claim by the Commissioner conclusive?

Decision: (1) "Here the right has been given, and a liability founded upon a law of Congress created. Of such liabilities the Court of Claims has jurisdiction, and no other remedy has been provided."

(2) The allowance made by the Commissioner, unless it be impeached in some appropriate form by the United States, is conclusive. Judgment for plaintiff.

UNITED STATES v. MASTERS (MORAN, INTERVENER)

(U. S District Court, E. D. Missouri, March 25, 1920)

(264 Fed. 250)

Record: Act of February 24, 1919. Criminal prosecution. Application of intervener denied.

Facts: Masters was arrested on February 29, 1920, while transporting intoxicating liquor. The automobile he was using therefor was seized by the government and was ordered sold. Masters had theretofore pleaded guilty in this court and had been fined $500 and costs, which he paid. Moran intervened as the alleged holder of a chattel mortgage on the automobile to secure the note of Masters for $1,500. The note was dated February 3, 1920, and became due 30 days thereafter. The note had no documentary stamps affixed thereto as required by the Revenue Act of February 24, 1919. On this ground the government objected to its competency and admissibility as evidence.

Question: Was the unstamped promissory note competent in evidence?

Decision: The note was inadmissible as evidence for lack of documentary stamps thereon as required by the Revenue Act of 1919. Certain provisions of the 1919 Act provided for the retention in force of all laws relating to the assessment and collection of taxes, so far as applicable for the purpose of collecting stamp taxes omitted through mistake or fraud from any instrument. (Sec. 1105 c. 1840 Stat. 1134). The effect of this was by reference to read into the Revenue Act of 1919, the provisions of the Act of June 13, 1898, which has never been repealed, and which in effect holds that no instrument required to be stamped which has been signed or issued without being duly stamped, nor any copy thereof, shall be recorded, or admitted, or used as evidence in any court until a legal stamp or stamps denoting the amount of the tax shall have been affixed thereto. "It follows, therefore, that whatever may be the rule in the state courts as to the admissibility in evidence of documents which are not stamped, though required so to be, the Federal courts are bound by the statute quoted, and the note offered to establish the lien of intervener was not competent or admissible in evidence of such alleged lien."

Comment: A contrary and controlling decision on this issue has been rendered by the U. S. Supreme Court in the case of Cole v. Ralph, 252 U. S. 286.

UNITED STATES v. MAYER
(U. S. District Court, D. Oregon, November 10, 1865)
(Fed. Case 15753)

Record: Act of June 30, 1864. Indictment for perjury. The jury was unable to agree.

Facts: After having sworn to one income return, the defendant later swore to another return which showed the gross amount of profits to be much larger than was shown on the first return. The defendant also had entered in his books a list of what he deemed bad debts, some of which were afterwards collected.

Questions: (1) Is defendant guilty of perjury on account of a contradiction as to the amount of the gross profits in two affidavits made by him?

(2) Is it enough to prove the defendant guilty of perjury to show that he entered certain debts on his books as bad debts and that they were afterwards collected?

Decision: (1) The court, in its instruction to the jury, said: "The two affidavits standing alone, simply equalize each other—the proof afforded by them is in a state of equilibrium. There must be some other proof, besides the admission in the second affidavit that the first is false." The question is "whether the defendant committed perjury by willfully stating his gross gains and profits for the year 1864 to be only $8,000—knowing the same to be false." He is not guilty of perjury simply because there is a contradiction in the two affidavits.

(2) Further instructions to the jury were: "If you find from the testimony that any of these debts of which the witnesses have spoken, did become insolvent in the year 1864, or that the defendant as a reasonable man, had good reason to think so, then you will deduct these from the gains or profits, thus ascertained * * *. If a person is honestly mistaken in his sworn statement, this is not perjury." It must be shown that the oath was false, and "that

he knew that it was not true or that he took it rashly without knowing whether it was true or not."

UNITED STATES v. McHATTON et al.
(U. S. District Court, D. of Montana, May 6, 1920)
(266 Fed. 602)

Record: Revenue Act of 1916. Action by government to
recover tax from distributees without consideration of corporation
assets. Demurrer to complaint overruled.

Facts: The decision of the court discloses the facts.

Questions: (1) May an income tax be imposed by a retrospective law?

(2) What is the nature of the tax obligation?

(3) Are distributees without consideration of corporate assets,
as stockholders in case of dissolution, liable to the extent of the distribution for corporate tax under the trust fund doctrine?

Decision: (1, 2, 3) "When the corporation was in being and
at dissolution it owed the duty to pay all taxes lawfully imposed
upon it for income during its life at any time. Taxes could be lawfully imposed by retrospective law, and were. If material, the law
speaks of and from a time anterior to the dissolution, and takes
effect as though enacted prior to the dissolution. Taxes are not
debts nor government a creditor in strict sense. They are of higher
nature. But no reason is perceived why they are not within the
principle that those who gratuitously receive a debtor's property
to the extent thereof are liable for his debts and obligations then
inchoate or vested; within this principle otherwise known as the
'trust fund' doctrine in respect to corporations. Accordingly,
when this corporation without consideration distributed part of its
assets to these defendants, it was under obligation to plaintiff to pay
any taxes that might thereafter be imposed. Defendants received
the assets subject thereto and to the principles aforesaid. The
obligation was contingent, the plaintiff's right inchoate. The contingency happened, the right vested. And the corporation's assets
so distributed may be pursued in the hands of these defendants by
virtue of the principles aforesaid. In principle, the case is very
like the case of Brady v. Anderson, 240 Fed. 665; T. D. 2494."

UNITED STATES v. MELLON

(U. S. District Court, W. D. Penn., July 13, 1921)

(Not yet reported)

Record: Revenue Act of 1913. Suit by a collector for the recovery of additional income tax. Judgment for defendant.

Facts: The Gulf Oil Corporation declared a 100% dividend, payable in cash, but payment was to be accepted in stock, such payment being made possible by a concurrent increase in capital stock, which increase was affected by the capitalization of surplus. The principal stockholders undertook to accept the dividend in stock; and further, the majority stockholders (T. Mellon & Sons) agreed to purchase for cash, at par, so much of the 100% new issue as might be declined by minority stockholders. The plan was put through, and the holders of all but 1,740 shares accepted stock in payment of the dividend, and subscribed for their pro rata share of the new stock at par. Thus did the defendant, who owned 12,655 of the 112,082 shares originally outstanding. A 100% cash dividend was paid on account of the 1,740 declined shares and, in accordance with the agreement, the majority stockholders purchased 1,740 shares of the new issue at par in addition to their own pro rata allotment.

Question: Was the dividend received by defendant in fact a cash dividend, and taxable, as contended by the government, even though paid in stock?

Decision: The court, in holding that the distribution in question was a stock dividend said: "in the suit at bar, the learned counsel for the government urged upon the court the necessity of observing the form, not in so many words, but by their brief filed. They insist that the dividend was a cash dividend, because the resolution of the board so stated. By implication, therefore, they would place the defendant in the position of having the right to use the check of the corporation, which as a matter of fact never came into his hands, and which as a matter of fact must have been drawn against 'no funds,' notwithstanding his agreement with his associates and with T. Mellon & Sons, and notwithstanding the important fact that without such agreements the resolution of the board would never have been passed and that the board would never have passed such resolution if there had been no such agreement seems clear, not only from the testimony of witnesses to that effect, but from other facts which appear in evidence as, for instance, the absence of sufficient money and the limited credit possessed by the corporation, whose obligations to banks were given high standing by the endorsement of some of the very men who entered into said agreement. In every aspect of the case, the defendant was not in the position where he was merely entitled to carry out his agreement, but he was bound to do so."

UNITED STATES v. MINNEAPOLIS THRESHING MACH. CO.

(U. S. District Court, D. Minn., Fourth Division, December 28, 1915)

(229 Fed. 1019)

Record: Act of August 5, 1909. Action at law by government to recover excise tax. Judgment for plaintiff.

Facts: The defendant corporation's return incorrectly stated its net income; no correct or amended return was required or demanded within three years; and no additional excise tax had been assessed.

Questions: (1) Will an action of indebitatus assumpsit lie to recover the unpaid tax under Sec. 38 of the Act where there has been no assessment made?

(2) Does the three-year clause in Par. 5, Sec. 38, bar a recovery after three years has elapsed since the return was made?

Decision: (1) The court cited the case of United States v. Chamberlain, 219 U. S. 250, which construed Sec. 31 of War Revenue Act, June 13, 1898, as authorizing an action for debt under authority conferred by Sec. 3213, Rev. St. (Comp St. 1913, Sec. 5938) for the recovery of the amount of a stamp tax payable, but not paid, under said War Revenue Act. "The language contained in paragraph 8 of the Act under consideration in the present case is much clearer and broader than the language considered in the case of United States v. Chamberlain, supra, and clearly authorizes the present action."

(2) Without discussion the court held "that neither limitation of time upon the action of the Commissioner of Internal Revenue contained in paragraph 5 of said Sec. 38, nor any other statute of

limitation is binding upon the United States in bringing an action like the one at bar."

UNITED STATES v. MILITARY CONST. CO.
(U. S. District Court, W. D. Missouri, April 3, 1913)
(204 Fed. 153)

Record: Act of August 5, 1909. Suit by government to recover penalty for failure to make return. Judgment for plaintiff.

Facts: The defendant corporation is of the class that must pay an excise tax if its annual net profit is in excess of $5,000. Its profit was in fact less than $5,000.

Question: Must a corporation which is not in one of the excepted classes in Cl. 2, Sec. 38 of the Act make a return even though its net profits for the year does not exceed $5,000?

Decision: "The return required is a somewhat complicated one. It consists of eight sections, the proper interpretation of which controls the determination of what the net income may be. This is a matter for the exercise of the official judgment and discretion of the Revenue Department; in order that it may exercise judgment and discretion, it must have the facts before it. The officers of the corporation and those of the Revenue Department may differ as to the ultimate effect of such facts." In order for the Revenue Department to determine whether the defendant's net profit is less than $5,000, the defendant must file a return.

UNITED STATES v. NASHVILLE, C. & ST. L. RY.
(U. S. Circuit Court of Appeals, Sixth Cir., April 2, 1918)
(249 Fed. 678)

Record: Act of August 5, 1909. Action of debt to recover excise tax. A demurrer to the declaration was sustained, and the action dismissed, and plaintiff brings error. Reversed and remanded with directions. Judgment for plaintiff affirmed on subsequent appeal. See Nashville, C. & St. L. Ry. Co. v. U. S., supra.

Facts: The defendant, in its returns for 1909 and 1910, made deductions for expenses which, the government alleged, were not necessary expenses actually paid out of income; and made charges to depreciation of roadway, which were alleged to be incorrect in that they were not charged against the capital valuation of the roadway, and were not a reasonable allowance for depreciation. These items had been disallowed by the Commissioner, and an additional tax claimed, which the defendant had refused to pay. This action was then commenced.

Questions: (1) Is the remedy in Sec. 38 by way of another assessment on the part of the Commissioner exclusive of all other remedies so that debt will not lie?

(2) Will an action of debt lie for the recovery of taxes on the ground that they are owing to the United States by reason of untrue returns filed by the defendant?

(3) Does the failure of the Commissioner to make a reassessment within the three years bar a recovery in an action of debt for the tax due?

(4) Is a declaration which alleges that the charges to deprelation were not charged against the capital valuation on the corporation's books subject to attack on the ground that the Act does not require such items to be so charged.

Decision: (1) "The government may recover a personal judgment for a tax, either in a sum certain or when readily reducible to certainty." * * * the rule which denies the use of any but the statutory remedy has no application to the general government, unless clearly and specifically so declared."

(2) "The word 'false' when used in this connection in the statute means 'untrue' or 'incorrect,' and does not necessarily mean intentionally or fraudulently false. * * * It is the general rule, applicable, not only to customs duties, but to internal revenue taxes, that a common law action of debt lies in favor of the government whenever, by accident, mistake or fraud, no duties or short duties have been paid * * *."

(3) "* * * assuming that the administrative reassessment * * * cannot be made after the three year period, it by no means follows that the act intended to take from the government power to enforce the payment of a tax to which a corporation is subject, through judicial process and without addition of penalty, whereby the corporation is given full opportunity to be heard in its defense in advance of enforcement—merely because the untrue return was

not discovered within the three year period. * * * We think the adjudicated cases opposed to such construction.'

(4) "It is enough to say that the declaration expressly avers that the alleged deductions were not reasonable allowances for depreciation, within the meaning of the Act." The relief is by a bill of particulars. The defendant did not file a bill of particulars and the plaintiff is entitled to recover.

UNITED STATES v. N. Y. & CUBA MAIL S. S. CO.
(U. S. Supreme Court, February 19, 1916)
(200 U. S. 488)

Record: Act of June 13, 1898. Action at law to recover stamp tax alleged to have been illegally assessed. Judgment for plaintiff, and defendant brings error. Reversed.

Facts: Defendant in error purchased documentary revenue stamps from a dealer and affixed them to a manifest in accordance with the Act of June 13, 1898, in order to obtain a clearance for its vessel. Defendant in error bought the required stamps without presenting any claim or protest to the Collector of Internal Revenue or to the collector of the port from whom the clearance was obtained.

. Question: Was the payment for the revenue stamps made voluntarily under the above circumstances and therefore not recoverable?

Decision: Railroad Company v. Commissioner 98 U. S. 541, was cited as controlling in this case, and was quoted as follows: "Where a party pays an illegal demand, with full knowledge of all the facts which render such demand illegal, without an immediate and urgent necessity therefor, or unless to release his person or property from detention, or to prevent an immediate seizure of his person or property, such payment must be deemed voluntary and cannot be recovered back."

This court said "there was no such imminence in the duress charged by the defendant in error" as the above quoted law makes necessary. It was, therefore, held that the payment in this case was made voluntarily, and not recoverable.

UNITED STATES v. NEW YORK, N. H. & H. R. R. CO.
(U. S. District Court, D. Connecticut, May 17, 1919)
(265 Fed. 331)

Record: Act of August 5, 1909. Action by the government to recover additional excise taxes. Judgment for plaintiff. Affirmed on appeal. See N. Y., N. H. & H. R. R. Co. v. U. S., supra.

Facts: Capital stock of the defendant was issued to the public for sums in excess of $100, the par value. Some of the shares were offered for sale at $175, payable in installments. When the full subscription price for a share of this stock was received the corporation issued a full paid receipt, but when only an installment payment was made, a part payment receipt was given. Shortly after the entire subscription price of the stock had been fully paid, receipts for full paid subscriptions were issued, containing a statement that as soon as possible after January 2, 1904, the company would deliver to the legal holder in exchange therefor a certificate for shares of the new capital stock with interest from date to December 31, 1903, on $1\frac{99}{175}$ of said sum at the same rate as dividends paid on the capital stock of the company during said period. In keeping its books, the corporation entered all amounts received over the par value of the stock either in the "profit and loss account" or the "premium account," so that such excess was always shown separately.

Question: Should the "paid up capital stock of the corporation at the close of the year" referred to in Sec. 38 of the 1909 Act as a limitation upon the amount of interest deductible in computing the net income subject to tax, include, as the defendant contended, the aggregate amount received by the corporation for the outstanding full paid shares and the full paid and part-paid stock receipts, even though such sums were in excess of the par value of $100 per share, or should it be limited, as the plaintiff claimed, to an amount not exceeding the par value of the outstanding shares plus the amount received for any part paid stock?

Decision: "That no interpretation should be given other than the law intended, that the shares of the capital stock of the defendant should be figured as at par value, * * * seems fully supported by the interpretation which the bookkeeping department of the defendant must have considered the proper one. * * *

Therefore the conclusion is imperative, after a careful analysis of the law and a consideration of all the cases, cited by both sides, that the paid up capital stock of the corporation, as used in Sec. 38 of the Act means such an amount received by the corporation as does not exceed the par·value of the outstanding shares plus the amount received for any part-paid stock, and that it does not mean the aggregate amount received by the corporation for the shares, the full-paid stock receipts and part-paid stock receipts issued by it even though said sum be in excess of the par value." Judgment for the government.

UNITED STATES v. NIPISSING MINES CO.

(U. S. Circuit Court of Appeals, Second Cir., June 18, 1913)

(206 Fed. 431)

Record: Act of August 5, 1909. Action at law by the United States to recover taxes under Sec. 38 of this Act. Judgment for defendant, (202 Fed. 803), and plaintiff brings error. Affirmed.

Facts: Defendant is a corporation organized under the laws of Maine and is the owner also of all the shares of the capital stock of the Nipissing Mines Co., Ltd., a corporation under the laws of Canada. The defendant is called in the record the holding company and the Canadian Company is called the operating company. The stock of the operating company constitutes practically the sole assets of the defendant holding company, its only other assets being a small amount in the bank, its furniture, and trifling matters. There is nothing to show that it has ever done any other business than to receive dividends from the operating company and to distribute them as dividends among its stockholders. While the affairs of the defendant and the operating company are closely connected and they have officers in common, there is nothing in the record to warrant the ignoring of the distinct corporate existence or the treating of them as doing any other business than that which they are actually shown to do.

Question: Is the defendant corporation "carrying on or doing business" within the meaning of the Act of August 5 1909?

Decision: McCoach v. Minehill, etc., Railroad, 228 U. S. 295, is decisive of this case. "In that case it was held that a railroad company which had leased its road to another corporation was not 'doing business' as a railroad company notwithstanding that it received and distributed the rentals from its lease; maintaining its organization and held itself ready to exercise its power and franchise and resume its position when entitled thereto. Certainly the Minehill Company did as much corporate business in respect of its railroad interests as the defendant would in respect to its stockholding interests. But if there were nothing more to the Minehill case than that which has been outlined it might be possible to distinguish it upon the ground that the corporation tax law does not contemplate double taxation in regard to the same business; the lessee company there being really the one 'doing business' with respect to the leased road and subject to the tax—a situation analogous to that existing in the present case. But the Minehill decision goes further. In addition to its leased road it had a considerable amount of personal assets in the form of investments from which it derived an actual income. This was distributed as dividends. The substance of the decision was that receipt of the ordinary fruits incident to the ownership of property is not the doing of corporate business. That which the Minehill Company did with respect to its investments was what the defendant did. We are unable to say that it was engaged in any other business than that of owning property —shares in another corporation—collecting the dividends, and distributing its income among the stockholders." This is not a "doing business" within the meaning of the Act, and the United States can not recover the tax assessed.

UNITED STATES v. OREGON-WASHINGTON RAILROAD & NAVIGATION CO.

(U. S. Circuit Court of Appeals, Second Cir., April 24, 1918)

(251 Fed. 211)

Record: Act of August 5, 1909. Action at law by the United States to recover additional tax under Sec. 38 of this Act. Judgment overruling a demurrer to the answer, and dismissing the complaint and the United States brings error. Affirmed.

Facts: Defendant was organized in November, 1910, all its stock being held by the Oregon Short Line Railroad, itself a part of the Union Pacific Railroad System and controlled by that company. The Union Pacific caused certain property to be conveyed to the defendant by certain subsidiary corporations, which property was paid for by a draft in favor of the sellers, drawn by the defendant and accepted by the Short Line. This draft the Short Line paid, and received back its proceeds from the selling corporations as dividends upon their stock, substantially all of which the Short Line held. The amount of these dividends was somewhat larger than the value of the property conveyed as it stood on the books of the selling corporations or as the value of their stock stood on the books of the Short Line. The amount of this difference was the sum here in question, $6,190,769.57, which, therefore, showed as a profit on the books of the Short Line. The payment of the consideration by this acceptance the Short Line charged against the defendant, partly as payment for the stock of the defendant and partly as money loaned it; the total sum paid by the Short Line being $50,000,000 for the stock and $50,450,000 as money loaned. Early in 1911 the defendant delivered $40,000,000 of bonds to the Short Line for which it received a credit of $35,000,000 leaving it indebted to the Short Line for money loaned in the sum af about $14,450,000. To prevent an apparent profit to the Short Line from the transaction, it wished to reduce this indebtedness by the amount of that profit, and on January 30, 1911, released its debt against the defendant to the amount of $6,190,769.57. This relief the plaintiff seeks to treat as a part of the defendant's income.

Question: Where a debt in favor of a corporation is released by its sole stockholder which furnished all its capital, is such sum treated as capital or income of the corporation?

Decision: "We are not, therefore, disposed to say that a sole stockholder's release of a debt against the corporation is a mere matter of bookkeeping. As the stockholder views it, that is no doubt the case, at least while the corporation stays solvent; indeed it is no more than if a mortgage was changed into a debt. Viewed from the corporation's side, however, the increased value of the stockholder's share is not to be deemed a charge upon the corporation equivalent to the cancelled debt. * * * At least when we have, as here, a question turning upon the right to use the corporate form, the release must be treated as involving an actual addition to the corporate assets. * * * However, the tax, though it includes income 'from all sources,' nevertheless includes 'income' only, and the meaning of that word is not to be found in its bare etymological derivation, but is rather to be gathered from the implicit assumptions of its use in common speech. * * *. Yet the word unquestionably imports, at least so it seems to us, the current distinction between what is commonly treated as the increase or increment from the exercise of some economically productive power of one sort or another, and the power itself, and it should not include such wealth as it ordinarily appropriated to what would customarily be regarded as the capital of the corporation taxed. * * * The corporation had just commenced its business; the cancellation of the debt was a means of contribution to its capital account quite as though the money had been contributed by the stockholder only to enhance the value of his stock. The financial relief so given, will, it is true, eventually be reflected in the income, since the defendant will no longer be entitled under the Act to deduct the interest on the debt, but that only brings out more clearly its character as capital contribution." Hence, such sum should be treated as capital rather than income, and the judgment for the defendant is affirmed.

UNITED STATES v. PACIFIC RAILROAD AND OTHERS
(U. S. Circuit Court, E. D. Mo., March 13, 1880)
(1 Fed. 97)

Record: Act of July 13, 1866, and Rev. Stat., Sec. 3186. Bill in equity. Demurrer to bill sustained.

Facts: This was a bill to enforce a lien on property, formerly owned by the Pacific Railroad, for income taxes and penalties. The taxes accrued from 1864 to 1871. When the taxes accrued the Pacific Railroad was the owner of the property against which the lien was sought to be enforced, but since that time the property had been mortgaged and sold under a foreclosure deed, and conveyed by the foreclosure purchaser to the present owner, who was made a party to the suit. The tax was never assessed by any officer of the government but simply became due by operation of law. Demands were made for payment of the same but at dates subsequent to the purchase of the property by the present owner.

Questions: (1) Did the lien given in favor of the government for unpaid taxes attach to the property belonging to the delinquent if it attached at all, when the tax became due or not until demand made for payment?

(2) Was assessment of the tax essential for the creation of the lien?

Decision: (1) The lien for unpaid taxes does not attach until demand is made for payment; and while, once it attaches, it relates back to the time when the tax was due, it attaches of course only upon property belonging to the delinquent at the time of the demand and does not affect property transferred to innocent purchasers prior to demand. Therefore, the government had no lien which it could enforce.

(2) An assessment is one of the steps required by law in the establishment of a lien, although it is not necessary for the collection of the unpaid tax by action at law to recover judgment. A demand implies the previous ascertainment of the sum due, and this ascertainment is by means of the return or assessment.

UNITED STATES v. PHILADELPHIA, B. & W. R. CO.

(U. S. District Court, E. D. Penn., Jan. 2, 1920)

(262 Fed. 188)

Record: Act of August 5, 1909. Action by United States to recover amount of excise tax. On rule for judgment for want of sufficient affidavit of defense, leave to enter a special judgment for plaintiff.

Facts: The defendant corporation was an operating company, and operated the railroad of the Delaware Railroad through the part ownership of the stock of the latter company and an operating arrangement satisfactory to the two companies and their stockholders. The Delaware company had limited its activities to what was necessary to the continuance of its corporate existence, and so it was not liable for payment of an excise tax, and did not pay one. On February 28, 1910, the Delaware company paid dividends declared on the 21st of that month, of which the defendant received as follows:

Special cash dividend of 5 per cent..............$ 83,223.75

Extra cash dividend of 20 per cent 332,895.00

Stock dividend of 70 per cent................... 1,651,132.50

$1,581,251.25

The source of the cash dividends were earnings of the Delaware road as follows:

Before January 1, 1909.........................$334,819.29

Since January 1, 1909..........................   81,229.46

$416,118.75

Questions: (1) Was defendant liable for the tax measured by the stock dividend?

(2) Was defendant liable for the tax measured by the dividend represented by earnings before January 1, 1909?

(3) Could Congress constitutionally measure an excise tax by income which was not connected with the carrying on of the business of the taxpayer?

Decision: (1) No tax was payable because of the stock dividend under the rulings in Towne v. Eisner, 245 U. S. 418, and Peabody v. Eisner, 247 U. S. 349.

(2) There was nothing in the case to show that the Delaware Company was but another name for the defendant. The two companies were separate entities and defendant was simply a stockholder in the Delaware Company. As such, the dividends received in 1910 were part of the 1910 income of the defendant, notwithstanding that they were paid out of earnings made prior to January 1, 1909.

(3) The argument that an excise tax should be limited to the earnings of the occupation or business with respect to which the tax is imposed should be addressed to the Congress. Congress having adopted a large measure, the courts are powerless to make a correction. Defendant was, therefore, liable to a tax measured by both cash dividends.

U. S. v. PHILADELPHIA KNITTING MILLS CO.
(U. S. Circuit Court of Appeals, Third Cir., March Term, 1921)
(273 Fed. 657)

Record: Act of August 5, 1909. Suit by the government to recover taxes claimed due for the years 1909 to 1912. Judgment for taxpayer. Appealed. Reversed and remanded.

Facts: The Philadelphia Knitting Mills Company, in its returns for the years 1909 to 1912, inclusive, deducted from its gross income, as "ordinary and necessary expenses," salaries paid W. H. Bilyeu, its president, for the year 1909, $12,500, and for each succeeding year, $20,000. Regarding these salaries (in excess of $5,000 per annum) as unreasonable with reference to the services rendered, and therefore, not deductible, the Bureau of Internal Revenue demanded payment of the tax thereon and upon refusal the United States brought this suit. Philadelphia Knitting Mills Company was a close corporation with an outstanding capital of $330,000, of which William H. Bilyeu, its president, owned in stock approximately $240,000; his daughter, Mrs. Richards, $30,000; and Charles Moller, its vice-president, manager and superintendent, $60,000. The business of the corporation was started and its success established by Bilyeu at a time when Moller's connection with the company and his stock holdings were small. As Bilyeu advanced in years and his activities in the business decreased, Moller's duties and interests correspondingly increased until, at the time in question, Bilyeu did almost nothing and Moller did almost everything in the management of the corporation's affairs. In July, 1909—a month before the Corporation Excise Tax Act was approved—the Board of Directors increased the annual salary of Moller to $10,000, and in 1913 to $20,000. At the same meeting in 1909, the Board of Directors—the personnel of which was wholly controlled by Bilyeu's dominating stockownership—increased his salary from $7,500 to $20,000 a year, at which figure it has ever since remained. It was testified that Bilyeu, being greatly advanced in years, had nothing to do with the operation of the plant or with the conduct of the business. He would come to the office, open the mail, sign checks, and make deposits, and then would sit around an hour or two reading the newspaper until his chauffeur came to take him home. The only reason for the substantial increase in the salary of the president was given by Bilyeu himself. It was simply to the effect that as Moller's salary was $20,000, he thought his salary should be the same. In the corporation's tax returns both salaries were deducted from gross profits in ascertaining taxable net profits. The government raised no question about Moller's salary. There was evidence of the amount of salaries paid presidents of like concerns of relative output and earnings.

Questions: (1) Has the government the right, under the Act of August 5, 1909, to inquire and determine whether a salary paid by a corporation and deducted in its return as an "ordinary and necessary" expense, is reasonable and fair compensation for the services rendered, and thereupon to revise the return and limit the deduction to what it considers a reasonable salary; and, in the event of dispute to have a jury pass upon and decide the same?

(2) May the government inquire into the amount of salary fixed by a board of directors of a corporation to determine if same is salary or something else?

(3) If so, are the facts sufficient to make a prima facie case for the jury?

(4) Will the court approve a construction of the statute by the Bureau of Internal Revenue as though it were a part of it?

Decision: (1) "Such a power in the government, if it exists, must have been conferred by the statute. That statute provided for a tax at a named rate upon the net income of a corporation to be ascertained by deducting from its gross income 'all ordinary and necessary expenses.' * * * Confining our inquiry to the statute, it appears that the basis on which a salary may be allowed as a valid deduction is that it was in fact an 'ordinary and necessary expense (of the corporation) actually paid * * * in the maintenance and operation of its business.' To be a necessary expense it must have been paid for services actually rendered. Jacobs & Davies, Inc., v. Anderson, 228 Fed. 505, 506. Whether services were rendered and whether also they were commensurate with the salary paid are matters of judgment and discretion reposed by general law in the board of directors of the corporation. As the board of directors is charged with the duty and clothed with the discretion of fixing the salaries of the corporation's officers, the government has no right (until expressly granted by statute) to inquire into and determine whether the amounts thereof are proper, that is, whether they are too much or too little. * * *."

(2) "But while the amount of salary fixed by a board of directors is presumptively valid, it is not conclusively so, because the government may inquire whether the amount paid is salary or something else. Admittedly the government has a right to collect taxes on net income of a corporation based on profits after all ordinary and necessary expenses, including salaries, are paid. It has a right, therefore, to attack the action of a board of directors and show by evidence, not that a given salary is too much, but that, in the circumstances, the whole or some part of it is not salary at all, but is profits diverted to a stockholding officer under the guise of salary and as such is subject to taxation."

(3) On the facts "we think a jury could find that, as the increase of Bilyeu's salary as president was made without a corresponding increase of service or business responsibility, in fact, in the face of a progressive decrease of service and responsibility, the amount paid him was not all for services rendered. Just how much of the annual compensation paid Bilyeu was salary and how much was profits would not be left for the jury to conjecture, for there was evidence of the amount of salaries paid presidents of like concerns of relative output and earnings. This evidence was in no sense conclusive, but it was admissible and it had probative value. There was in addition evidence of the salary which the defendant corporation itself paid Bilyeu, its president, before it was increased without any reason except that Bilyeu thought his salary (for decreasing services) should keep apace with Moller's salary for steadily increasing services. This evidence was, to be sure, only prima facie, and might have been overturned by evidence produced by the defendant corporation showing that its president, because of his position in the trade, his connection with the banks, or otherwise, rendered services to the corporation on which the board of directors had exercised a bona fide discretion in voting him their substantial salary. But until some evidence of this character was produced by the defendant, we think the evidence for the government was sufficient to sustain a finding by fair-minded men that a part, and a definite part, of the compensation paid Bilyeu as salary was

profits distributed to him by reason of his stockholding." The part distributed to Bilyeu by reason of his stockholding was taxable to the corporation as profit.

(4) "The statute did not specifically make a salary an allowable deduction, though it was so construed by the Bureau of Internal Revenue when the salary is a 'reasonable and fair compensation for services rendered regardless of the amount of stock such officer may hold.' We are asked to approve this executive construction of the statute as though it were a part of it. In order not to beg the question, we must look to the statute alone to find the power which the government asserts."

UNITED STATES v. PITTARO
(U. S. District Court, Ohio, June 23, 1919)
(T. D. 2874)

Record: Revenue Act of 1918. Indictment for simulating receipt issued by the collector of internal revenue. Appended opinion of Judge Westenhaver in the District Court of the United States.

Facts: Defendant, who was not a collector of Internal Revenue, issued the following receipt:

"This is to advise that Mr. Michele Favole has met his entire liability for income tax as a non-resident alien under provision of Sec. 9, Par. C of the Act of October 3, 1917."

Stamped across the end thereof was the following: "Harry H. Weiss, collector of internal revenue, March 13, 1919, 18th District of Ohio, Cleveland, Ohio." Defendant was indicted for falsely and fraudulently simulating the receipt of a collector of internal revenue.

Questions: May the defendant establish his innocence by any of the following defenses:

(1) The receipt in question is not one required to be issued by the collector?

(2) Because the receipt was not made on the blanks regularly used by the collector?

(3) Because the party to whom the receipt was given was not subject to payment of the tax?

Decision: (1) "The fact that Sec. 251 of the Act of February 24, 1919, requires that full written or printed receipts be issued to taxpayers only on request therefor does not limit the collector's mandatory duty to issue them when requested and does not fail to make them documents required to be issued whenever requested, and the receipts are plainly documents required to be issued by such section.

(2) Such receipts are documents required by provisions of the internal revenue laws and by regulations made in pursuance thereof, within the meaning of Sec. 3451, R. S., making it an offense to simulate or falsely or fraudulently execute or sign any document required by the internal revenue laws, or any regulation made in pursuance thereof, or to procure the same to be falsely or fraudulently executed, or to advise, aid in, or connive at such execution thereof. The offense may be committed either where the receipt itself is a genuine receipt of the kind kept for that purpose in the office of the internal revenue collector but signed by the defendant without authority, or where, even if not a blank of the kind required to be kept, the blank is simulated or falsely or fraudulently executed and issued by a person who has no power or authority to do so.

(3) Where defendant was charged with violating Sec. 3451, R. S., in that he falsely, fraudulently, etc., simulated and executed and advised, aided in, and connived at the execution of certain income tax receipts required by Sec. 251 of the Act of February 24, 1919, to be given when requested, what defendant told the persons who paid the money is not material, nor is the question whether or not such persons were subject to the payment of an income tax, or to assessment and levy of such tax."

UNITED STATES v. RAILROAD COMPANY
(U. S. Supreme Court; December, 1872)
(84 U. S. 322; 17 Wall. 322)

Record: Act of June 30, 1864, as subsequently amended. Error to the Circuit Court for the District of Maryland. Suit in assumpsit was brought by the United States against the company in the court below to collect a tax levied under Sec. 122 of the above mentioned Act. Defendant pleaded the general issue. The court below gave judgment for the defendant company and the United States appealed by writ of error. Judgment affirmed. Justice Bradley concurred specially, and Justices Clifford and Miller joined in a dissenting opinion.

Facts: Sec. 122 referred to makes provision that railroads and other companies specified "indebted for money for which bonds shall have been issued * * * upon which interest is stipulated to be paid * * * shall be subject to and pay a tax of 5 per centum on the amount of all such interest." In 1854 the Legislature of Maryland gave to the City of Baltimore (then desirous of aiding the B. & O. Railroad Co. in the building of its road) authority to issue and sell its bonds to the extent of $5,000,000, payable in 1890; and to lend the proceeds to the company, less 10 per cent to be reserved as a sinking fund, to pay the principal of the loan at its maturity. This the city did, the railroad company giving to it a mortgage on all its road, revenue and franchises, to secure the payment of the bonds which the city had issued and the interest which it had bound itself to pay. The company refused to pay the tax levied on it on the ground that the tax was not a tax laid on it, but one laid on their creditor, the city, and the city being a municipal corporation could not have its revenues taxed by the Federal government.

Questions: (1) Does the section in question lay a tax upon the corporations named therein and by whom the tax is payable upon their own account, and use them merely as convenient means of collecting the tax from the creditor or stockholder upon whom the tax is really laid, or is the tax levied on the creditors themselves?

(2) Where the creditor is a municipal corporation may a Federal tax be levied against it?

Decision: (1) Sec. 122 of the Act of June 30, 1864, imposes the tax on the creditor and not on the corporation. The court said that on the first proposition the decisions in the cases of Railroad Co. v. Jackson, 7 Wall. 262, and Haight v. Railroad Co., 6 Wall. 17, were decisive. After quoting from those decisions the court says: "This is a clear, distinct, unqualified adjudication by the unanimous judgment of this court, that the tax imposed by the 122nd Section is a tax imposed upon the creditor or stockholder therein named; that the tax is not upon the corporation, and that the corporation is made use of as a convenient and effective instrument for collecting the same."

(2) The tax being against creditor and the city being the creditor it is not taxable. The court held that the city is a representative not only of the state, but is a portion of its governmental power; that as a portion of the state in the exercise of a limited portion of the powers of the state, its revenues like those of the state are not subject to taxation. The state conferred the power on the city to act in the manner it did and the act done by the city was in the course of its municipal business or duties. Accordingly, the court gave judgment for the defendant.

UNITED STATES v. RITCHIE
(U. S. District Court, D. Maryland, Jan. 13, 1872)
(Fed. Cas. 16168)

Record: Act applicable to incomes for year 1869. Decision of District Judge Giles on question submitted by defendant Ritchie and the government whether the compensation received by defendant as state's attorney was subject to tax. Judgment for defendant.

Facts: In 1869 John Ritchie was State's Attorney for Frederick County, State of Maryland. In assessing the internal revenue tax on his income for that year the assessor included as taxable the money received as compensation for his services as state's attorney. Mr. Ritchie took the ground that his compensation received as an officer of the state was exempt from the income tax and declined to pay the tax assessed on that part of his income. The $1,000 exemption under the law then in force was deducted from the aggregate amount returned.

Questions: (1) Is a state's attorney's compensation exempt from income tax?

(2) If so, may not the government then apply $1,000 of it to the exemption clause allowed persons from taxable income?

Decision: (1) Compensation of state employees is exempt from income tax. The court said that by virtue of the decision in the case of Collector v. Day, 11 Wall. (78 U. S. 113), the compensation received as state's attorney was not liable to the income tax, that "the office of state's attorney was established by the Constitution of the State, and was one of the means and instrumentalities for carrying on the state government, with respect to which the powers of the state are independent of the general government, and that the United States has no more right to tax these agencies than the state government has to tax the means and agencies of carrying on the Federal government."

(2) The compensation of the state officer cannot be applied to the satisfaction of the specific exemption from the income tax. The court held that by so doing the income which is exempt because compensation from a state would thereby in effect be liable to taxation; that to exhaust the exemption clause by taking the amount out of his official income would be to make it subject to the revenue law and deny to a state officer the advantage of the state's exemption. The defendant was found to be entitled to judgment.

UNITED STATES v. SAVINGS BANK
(U. S. Supreme Court, October Term, 1881)
(104 U. S. 728)

Record: Rev. Stat. Secs. 3220 and 3228, respecting Claims for Refund. Suit in Court of Claims to enforce refund, where judgment was given for claimant. Appeal by United States. Judgment affirmed.

Facts: On July 10, 1878, the Real Estate Savings Bank of Pittsburgh, Pa., paid to the collector of internal revenue for that district certain internal taxes which had before that time been assessed. On July 9, 1880, it presented to the same collector an appeal to the Commissioner of Internal Revenue made out on the blank form prescribed by the Secretary to refund $972.69 which it alleged had been illegally assessed and erroneously paid. This appeal was delivered to the collector in time to have reached Washington by due course of mail on July 10, if it had been promptly forwarded, but it was retained until July 15 when it was sent by the collector to the Commissioner with the collector's endorsement that it was warranted by the facts. The papers reached the Commissioner on July 17 and on October 13 he submitted them to the Secretary of the Treasury. On October 18 the Secretary of the Treasury signified to the Commissioner his approval of the payment and on

October 21 the Commissioner certified its allowance. Upon presentation through the accounting officers of the Treasury Department, payment was refused. It was urged that the claim is barred because not presented at the office of the Commissioner within two years. Sec. 3220 of the Revised Statutes is as follows:

"The Commissioner of Internal Revenue, subject to regulations prescribed by the Secretary of the Treasury, is authorized on appeal to him made, to remit, refund, and pay back all taxes erroneously or illegally assessed or collected, all penalties collected without authority, and all taxes that appear to be unjustly assessed or excessive in amount, or in any manner wrongfully collected. * * *."

Sec. 3228 of the Revised Statutes is as follows:

"All claims for the refunding of any internal tax illegally assessed or collected, or of any penalty alleged to have been collected without authority, or of any sum alleged to have been excessive or in any manner wrongfully collected, must be presented to the Commissioner of Internal Revenue within two years next after the cause of action accrued. * * *."

The material regulations in substance provided that claims for refund be presented through the collectors of the respective districts on Form 46; that the collector keep a record in a book prescribed therefor of all claims presented to the Commissioner and certify whether the particular claim has been before presented, or not; that where an appeal involves an amount exceeding $250, and before it is finally decided the Commissioner of Internal Revenue will transmit the case with the evidence to the Secretary of the Treasury for his consideration and advisement.

Questions: (1) Has the Court of Claims jurisdiction where a claim sued for was not founded on any laws of Congress, or upon contract?

(2) Was the appeal to the Commissioner taken within two years after the cause of action accrued?

Decision: (1) Court of Claims has jurisdiction in cases based on claims for refund of taxes. The court held that the case of United States v. Kaufman, 96 U. S. 567, disposed of the first question. That case arose under Sec. 3426 of Revised Statutes. The court, after stating that it could discover no material difference between the powers of the Commissioner under Sec. 3426 and those under Sec. 3220, said: "Until an appeal is taken to the Commissioner no suit whatever can be maintained to recover back taxes illegally assessed or erroneously paid. If on the appeal the claim is rejected, an action lies against the collector (Rev. Stat., Sec. 3226) and through him, on establishing the error or illegality, a recovery may be had. If the claim is allowed, and payment for any cause refused suit may be brought directly against the government in the Court of Claims. * * * A rejected claim may be prosecuted against the collector and an allowed claim, not paid, may be sued for in the Court of Claims."

(2) Lodging of appeal with collector was in effect legal presentation to the Commissioner within the prescribed time. The court said: "Upon the other branch of the case we are entirely satisfied with the conclusions reached by the court below, and that the lodging of the appeal made out in due form with the proper collector of internal revenue for the purpose of transmission to the Commissioner in the usual course of business, under the requirements of the regulations of the Secretary, was in legal effect a presentation of the appeal to the Commissioner. The effect of the Regulation was to designate the office of the collector of internal revenue as a proper place for the presentation of the appeal. * * *. Judgment affirmed."

UNITED STATES v. SCHILLINGER
(U. S. Circuit Court, S. D. New York, Dec. 21, 1876)
(Fed. Cas. 16228)

Record: Act of July 14, 1870. Action to recover income tax. Error to the U. S. District Court for the Southern District of New York, wherein judgment was rendered for the defendant. Judgment affirmed.

Facts: Defendant received notes in 1871, due in 1872, as part payment of the price for the sale of certain patent rights.

Question: Was defendant liable for an income tax for the year 1871 on the amount of the notes?

Decision: The Act of July 14, 1870, imposed a tax for the years 1870 and 1871, and no longer, upon the gains, profits and income of every person residing within the United States, and, under said Act, income must be taken to mean money, and not the expectation of receiving it, or the right to receive it at some future time. Therefore, until the notes were paid, they were not income.

UNITED STATES v. SMITH
(U. S. District Court, Oregon, Aug. 22, 1870)
(Fed. Cas. 16,341)

Record: Act of August 5, 1861; Act of July 1, 1862; Act of June 30, 1864; Act of March 3, 1865; Act of March 2, 1867. Defendant was found guilty of perjury. Motion for a new trial. Motion denied.

Facts: From 1862 to 1865, inclusive, defendant became the owner of eleven shares of stock which cost him, in the aggregate, $7,480. In 1868 he disposed of the stock for $10,000 in cash, 10 acres of land valued at $10,500, 960 acres of land valued at $6,000, and two notes, secured by a deposit of two shares of the stock, for $6,500. Later, in 1868, he sold the ten acres of land for $9,500 in coin, $1,000 being paid down and the balance in notes secured by mortgages. The affidavits of defendant, in connection with his return of income for the year 1868, with reference to the cost of the stock and of the ten acres of land, were the alleged acts of perjury.

Questions: (1) To what extent must profits made on a sale in the year 1868 be returned as taxable income for that year under the successive acts of Congress from August 5, 1861 to March 2, 1867?

(2) May an exchange of stocks for property result in taxable income under the Statutes in question?

(3) May taxable income result where stocks are sold and notes received in payment therefor?

Decision: (1) The successive acts of Congress from August 5, 1861 to March 2, 1867, were acts in *pari materia*, or upon the same matter, and are to be construed as one continuing and continuous act, and therefore the defendant was bound to state and return as income all gains and profits derived from the sale of stocks in 1868, whenever purchased, so that they were purchased since August 5, 1861, without reference to the year in which the increase in value of the stocks occurred.

(2) A bona fide exchange of stocks for other property is not a sale thereof from which profits are derived liable to taxation as income.

(3) A transfer of stocks for a promissory note, which is collectible, or an exchange thereof for land, followed by a sale of such land within the year for collectible promissory notes, is to be considered a sale of such stock for so much cash.

UNITED STATES v. SNYDER
(U. S. Supreme Court, May 1, 1893)
(149 U. S. 210)

Record: Act of March 1, 1879. Bill in equity to recover stamp taxes due the United States and to enforce lien upon real estate. Judgment for defendant and plaintiff brings error. Reversed.

Facts: Snyder was engaged in the business of manufacturing tobacco, and while so engaged, became indebted to the United States for internal revenue taxes. These taxes were duly assessed and certified to the collector of Internal Revenue, who made demand for payment in accordance with the law. Subsequently Snyder sold several lots to the International Cotton Press Company, named as co-defendant. The assessment on which the lien for taxes was claimed in behalf of the United States was never filed or inscribed in the mortgage office of the Parish of New Orleans, as required by the laws of the State of Louisiana; and the defendant purchased the property on which said tax lien was claimed to exist for full value, in good faith, and in ignorance of the said alleged assessment.

Question: Is a lien on real estate to secure the payment of internal revenue taxes subject to the laws of the State in which the real estate is situated with respect to the registering or recording of mortgages or liens?

Decision: The failure to record the lien with State of Louisiana does not bar the recovery of taxes by the United States. "If the United States, proceeding in one of their own courts, in the collection of a tax admitted to be legitimate, can be thwarted by the plea of a state statute prescribing that such a tax must be assessed and recorded under state regulation, and limiting the time within which such tax shall be a lien, it would follow that the potential existence of the government of the United States is at the mercy of state legislators." The lien attached to the real estate now held by the International Cotton Press Company, regardless of the laws of the State of Louisiana, and the plaintiff is entitled to enforce such a lien.

UNITED STATES v. THEURER
(U. S. Circuit Court of Appeals, May 18, 1914)
(213 Fed. 964)

Record: Act of July 13, 1866. Action at law to recover penalty for violation of revenue law. Judgment for defendant and plaintiff brings error. Affirmed.

Facts: In 1867 the government seized 50 barrels of whisky because the same had been removed from the place of manufacture to a place other than a bonded warehouse, as provided by law, before the duties thereon had been paid, contrary to the form of the statute. Upon this suit being instituted, a bond was given by Theurer and the whisky released to him. After that the case went to trial and resulted in a judgment against him in the district court, from which he took an appeal to the circuit court. And then he died. After his death various other proceedings were had, which eventually established the validity of the judgment of the district court. The present action is brought against "the heirs of his heirs and their heirs, even to the fourth generation."

Question: Can a judgment rendered by a Federal Court under a penal statute be enforced against the heirs of the party committing the criminal offense?

Decision: "It is true that a judgment is often in law regarded as creating a new and distinct liability. * * * But a judgment, after all, is nothing but a new form of an obligation. Its original essence remains unchanged. * * * The object of criminal punishment is to punish the criminal and not to punish his family. When A recovers a judgment against B for a tort, the recovery is undoubtedly based on defendant's misconduct; but the fundamental principle upon which the action is maintained is the idea of compensating the injured party; but when a court imposes a fine for the commission of a crime, there is no idea of compensation involved." It follows that the United States is not entitled to recover, as the forfeiture of the whisky was imposed as a punishment.

UNITED STATES v. TILDEN

(U. S. District Court, S. D. New York, March, 1878)

(Fed. Cas. 16, 519)

Record: Act of August 5, 1861; Act of July 1, 1862; Act of July 4, 1864; Act of June 30, 1864; Act of March 3, 1865; Act of July 13, 1866; Act of March 2, 1867; Act of July 14, 1870. Action by the United States to recover income taxes under the above Acts. Plaintiff demurs to the defense set up. Demurrer sustained.

Facts: Defendant made returns for the years 1862 and 1863 and was assessed and paid the tax. For other and subsequent years he made no returns, but was assessed in the manner prescribed by statute, and paid the tax assessed. This action was brought to recover additional taxes for the years in question.

Questions: (1) Can the Government recover, in an action of debt, income taxes which have never been assessed in the manner prescribed by statute?

(2) Would the fact that defendant had made a return and paid the tax for some of the years in question bar this action by the Government to collect further taxes for said years?

Decision: (1) Under the Acts of 1862 and 1864, the United States may sue for and collect a tax on income without prior assessment in the mode specified in the act creating the tax.

(2) Under the statutes in question the United States may maintain an action for the collection of income taxes in addition to those assessed and paid under a return if income is made. "The remedy by assessment and collection of taxes, through the machinery of assessors and collectors, is a remedy for the prompt, periodical ascertainment and collection of taxes, subject always to a concurrent right to bring suit for the tax; such latter right being one which exists both to collect a tax in the absence of the use of any statutory machinery, and to collect it where the statutory machinery has been used and has failed to collect the true amount of tax." Therefore, the plaintiff was allowed to recover the additional tax for the years in which the defendant had made a return and paid a tax.

UNITED STATES v. TURNER et al

(U. S. Circuit Court, S. D. Ohio, 1873)

(Fed. Case 16548)

Record: Act of July 13, 1866. Bill to subject a distillery to payment of tax upon whisky claimed to be a lien thereon. Decree in favor of the government.

Facts: The tax accrued in February, 1867, while the Turners, the then owners, were operating the distillery. The whiskey was, in the same month, removed upon transportation bonds, and was, without the payment of tax, sold in the markets. Suits were begun upon the bonds in September, 1867, and judgment recovered thereon in March and April, 1871. In June, 1867, the Turners sold their distillery, and in April, 1868, Stolz became the innocent owner for value.

Questions: Did the innocent purchaser for value take the premises discharged from the alleged lien of the government?

Decision: The Act of July 13, 1866, provided that the tax in question should be a lien on the interest of the distiller in the tract of land whereon the distillery was situated from the time the spirits were distilled until the tax should be paid, and secured to the government a lien upon the distilling premises as against innocent purchasers without notice. Decree in favor of the government to enforce the lien.

UNITED STATES v. VANDERBILT

SAME v. MERRIAM

SAME v. ANDERSON

(U. S. District Court, S. D. N. Y., Aug. 6, 1921)

(275 Fed. 109)

Record: Revenue Act of 1916. Actions by the United States to recover income tax. Demurrers to complaints overruled and judgment for plaintiff.

Facts: Alfred G. Vanderbilt died in 1915, leaving a will which contained bequests of $200,000 to each of the defendants, Merriam and Anderson, and $500,000 to the defendant, Vanderbilt, and which also appointed the defendants as executors and as trustees of the several trusts created by the will. The sixteenth clause of said will also contained the following provision: "The bequests herein made to my said executors are in lieu of all compensation or commissions to which they would otherwise be entitled as executors or trustees." The defendants qualified as executors and trustees, and administered the estate.

Questions: (1) Were the legacies so given exempt as "bequests" or liable to the income tax as compensation for personal services?

(2) Will the fact that the legacies are payable, though the executors do not complete their services, prevent the payments from being compensation?

(3) There being some question as to whether the bequests are entirely compensation, will the court attempt to divide the legacies and hold them in part non-taxable?

Decision: (1) "There seems to me no question whatever that these legacies in part anyway are compensation for personal services. Where the testator provided that they should be 'in lieu of all compensation or commissions to which they would otherwise be entitled as executors or trustees', he could only have meant to substitute the legacies in the place of their statutory compensation. If a substitute, these legacies must in themselves be compensation and since the commissions would certainly have been for 'personal services', the substitute itself was the same. It is true that the form of the compensation is a 'bequest' and a 'bequest' is exempt; hence there is a verbal contradiction between one part of the statute and the other. Yet I cannot doubt that all bequests are not exempt. Suppose, for instance, that a man agreed to leave another a legacy if he would take care of him while he lived. The legacy would be a 'bequest', but can anyone suppose that it would not be 'compensation' for personal services which would be taxable?"

(2) "It seems to me to make no difference whether such bequests be regarded as payable merely on condition of qualification, or only after the services are rendered. I assume the first to be the correct rule and certainly in the cases at bar the legacies were all payable long before the services could be completed * * *. I regard the point, however, as immaterial, because the bequests are in either case equally 'compensation for personal services.' * * *

Therefore, I attach no importance to the point of which so much is made, that the executor becomes entitled to his legacies on expressing his assent. More important is the opposite side of the same rule, that without such assent he does not become entitled. * * * If they were true legacies, he would get them whether he qualified or not.''

(3) ''But, the defendants say, such bequests as these are in any case not all compensation; in part, anyway, they are from the testator's bounty. As to the defendants, Merriam and Anderson, there is not the least reason to suppose they were not solely in compensation for their services. * * * As to the defendant, Vanderbilt, I confess it seems scarcely possible that the testator did not mean the legacy to do more than compensate him for his services. * * * But, if he has in fact bequeathed the same to him as compensation, how can I apportion it partly as such and partly as free bounty? Clearly not, if the language used be unambiguous. * * * I think the will means that all is to be compensation. * * * But, granting that it is ambiguous, there is no language through whose interpretation the legacies may be divided. That must be imputed into the will without any intimation from the testator at all, and the result will be not a will, but the creature of the court. I therefore conclude that the whole of the legacies must be treated as compensation and that the demurrers must be overruled.''

UNITED STATES v. WHITRIDGE, RECEIVER
UNITED STATES v. JOLINE & ROBINSON, RECEIVERS

(U. S. Circuit Court of Appeals, Second Cir.)

(231 U. S. 144)

Record: Act of August 5, 1909. Motion by government for orders directing the receivers to make returns of net income. Motion denied (193 Fed. 286: 198 Fed. 774), and government brings the cases here by writs of certiorari.

Facts: The officers and agents of the two corporations were ordered to turn over all property in their hands to the receivers, who, by order of court, were to run, manage and operate the railroads. This is a suit against the receivers for an order to direct them to make a return of the net income received by them.

Question: Does Section 38 of the Act impose a tax upon the income derived from the management of corporate property by receivers, where the management is by order of court?

Decision: "A reference to the language of the Act is sufficient to show that it does not in terms impose a tax upon corporate property or franchises as such, nor upon the income arising from the conduct of business unless it be carried on by the corporation. Nor does it in terms impose any duty upon the receivers * * * with respect to making any return of such income." Accordingly, the court refused to direct the receivers to make a return of the net income.

UNITED STATES v. WOODWARD
(Supreme Court of the U. S., June 6, 1921)
(256 U. S. 632)

Record: Revenue Act of 1918. Action to recover taxes paid under protest on net income under provisions of said Act. Judgment for plaintiff (Court of Claims, not reported). Government appealed. Affirmed.

Facts: "The testator died December 15, 1917. The Revenue Act of 1916 imposed upon the transfer of the net estate of every decedent dying thereafter a tax which it called an 'estate tax'. * * * Under that act these executors were required to pay an estate tax of $489,834.07. The tax became due December 15, 1918, and they paid it February 8, 1919. Shortly thereafter the executors made a return, under the Revenue Act of 1918 of the income of the testator's estate for the taxable year 1918 and claimed in the return that in ascertaining the net income for that year the estate tax of $489,034.07 should be deducted. The Commissioner of Internal Revenue refused to allow the deduction and assessed an income tax of $165,-075.78 against the estate."

Question: Was the estate tax paid by the executors an allowable deduction in ascertaining the net taxable income of the estate for 1918?

Decision: "The Act of 1918 * * * by Section 214 makes express provision for the deduction of 'taxes paid or accrued' within the taxable year imposed (a) by the authority of the United States, except income, war-profits and excess profits taxes. This last provision is the important one here. It is not ambiguous, but explicit, and leaves little room for construction. The words of this major clause are comprehensive and include every tax which is charged against the estate by the authority of the United States. The excepting clause specifically enumerates what is to be excepted. The implication from the latter is that the taxes which it enumerates would be within the major clause were they not expressly excepted, and also that there was no purpose to except any others. Estate taxes were as well known at the time the provision was framed as the ones particularly excepted. Indeed, the same Act, by Section 400-410, expressly provides for their continued imposition and enforcement. Thus their omission from the excepting clause means that Congress did not intend to except them. The Act of 1916 calls the estate tax a 'tax' and particularly denominates it an 'estate tax'. This court recently has recognized that it is a duty or excise and is imposed in the exertion of the taxing power of the United States, New York Trust Co. vs. Eisner, ... U. S. .... * * * Here the estate tax not only accrued, which means became due, during the taxable year, 1918, but it was paid before the income for that year was r eturned or required to be returned. * * * We hold that under the terms of the Act of 1918 the deduction should have been allowed."

UNITED STATES GLUE CO. v. TOWN OF OAK CREEK
(Supreme Court of Wisconsin, June 16, 1915)
(161 Wis. 211; 153 N. W. 241)

Record: Income Tax Act of Wisconsin. Action to recover a portion of the tax paid. Judgment for plaintiff. Defendant appealed. Reversed and remanded with directions to dismiss the complaint. Case taken to U. S. Supreme Court on writ of error. Judgment affirmed. 247 U. S. 321.

Facts: Plaintiff was a corporation having its principal place of business in the defendant town. It had branch business places in several cities outside the state of Wisconsin. A part of the goods sold from the branches was shipped from the stocks on hand at the branches, and the rest was shipped from plaintiff's factory. The stock of goods at the branches was in part manufactured at the factory and sent to the branches, and the rest was purchased from manufacturers and dealers outside of Wisconsin and shipped from the places of purchase either directly or by way of plaintiff's factory to these branches. The statute under which the tax in question was collected provided that "any person engaged in business within and without the state shall, with respect to income other than that derived from rentals, stocks, bonds, securities or evidences of indebtedness, be taxed only upon that portion of such income as is derived from business transacted and property located within the state * * *."

Questions: (1) Was plaintiff taxable upon the income from the sale of goods delivered from its factory to customers outside the State of Wisconsin, either directly or through branch houses located outside of the state?

(2) Was plaintiff subject to tax upon income derived from the sale of goods purchased outside the state and shipped either directly or through plaintiff's factory to branches outside the state and thence sold to customers without the state?

(3) Was the tax upon all income other than that derived from sales of goods to customers within the state an interference with interstate commerce, and therefore unconstitutional?

Decision: (1) Income from the sale of manufactured articles to persons without the state, either directly or through branch houses located outside of the state and supplied from the home factory may be taxed by the state in which the home factory is situated. "The manufacture, the management and the conduct of the business at the home office are the controlling features in the process of disposing of the article produced by the factory and constitute the source out of which the income issues, and gives it a situs within the state under the income tax law."

(2) The income from sales made by a local manufacturing company of goods purchased outside the state and sold to buyers outside the state, either from its factory in the state or indirectly through branch houses out of the state is not income derived from "business transacted within the state" and therefore not taxable under the statute in question.

(3) A statute imposing an income tax on income from business transacted within the state, though such business involves trans-

actions in interstate commerce, does not violate the provisions of the Constitution giving Congress power to regulate interstate commerce, since the Constitution does not prevent the exercise of the state's taxing power so long as the tax does not impose a burden upon interstate commerce. The plaintiff cannot recover the tax paid on income from business transacted within the state, though the goods were shipped to buyers outside the state.

URQUHART v. MARION HOTEL CO.
(Supreme Court of Arkansas, April 2, 1917)
(128 Ark. 283; 194 S. W. 1)

Record: Act of Oct. 3, 1913. Action to recover interest due on bonds. Judgment for defendant in Circuit Court and plaintiff appealed. Affirmed.

Facts: Plaintiff brought her suit on bonds issued by defendant company, which contained the following clause: "The Marion Hotel Company, hereby promises to pay to the bearer, * * * without deduction from either such principal or interest, for any tax or taxes, which the Marion Hotel Company may be required to pay or retain therefrom, under any present or future law, the Marion Hotel Company agreeing to pay such tax or taxes."

Question: Was the plaintiff entitled to the full amount of interest due without deduction of the 1 per cent, which the company was required to withhold under the Federal income tax law?

Decision: The provision of the income tax law requiring withholding is intended only to facilitate the collection of the tax; the tax is not levied upon the bonds, nor primarily upon the interest thereon. The thing taxed is the income of the holder of the bond. The purpose and legal effect of the clause quoted from the bond was only to impose upon the company the duty of paying all taxes, of any character, imposed upon the property mortgaged, and to pay the tax upon the bonds and coupons as such. Since the tax was upon the income of the bondholder, the defendant did not promise to pay it, and the plaintiff cannot recover the interest free of the tax.

VAN DYKE v. CITY OF MILWAUKEE
(Supreme Court of Wisconsin, April 9, 1914)
(159 Wis. 460; 146 N. W. 812)

Record: Wisconsin Act of 1913. Action to recover part of an income tax paid to the city under protest. Demurrer to complaint overruled, and defendant appealed. Reversed and remanded. On a rehearing the court adhered to the conclusion in this opinion, 159 Wis. 460; 150 N. W. 510.

Facts: The plaintiff received dividends, declared and distributed by a going corporation out of a surplus on hand prior to the date when the income tax law went into effect. The complaint alleges that, if the reasonable value of the ore in the mine, together with the cost of mining and marketing, is deducted from the amount received for the ore, there remains no profit or income from the business. The complaint also alleges that there has been a depreciation in the value of the stock caused by the distribution of dividends. These deductions were not allowed by the assessor. Also prior to the effective date of the Act the plaintiff purchased certain bonds for which he paid a premium. He has been assessed a tax on the interest received on the bonds.

Questions: (1) In the case of a mining corporation, are ordinary dividends taxable as income without reference to how much of them is derived from capital, and how much from profit, that is, without reference to the value of the ore mined and the cost of mining it?

(2) Are dividends, declared and distributed by a going corporation out of surplus on hand before the law became effective, taxable as income for the year in which they are distributed?

(3) Can the stockholder deduct from the dividends, if taxable, the depreciation in the value of the stock caused by the distribution of dividends?

(4) Can a bondholder, who has purchased bonds at a premium, deduct annually a pro rata share of such premiums from the interest received?

Decision: (1) "Ordinary dividends declared by going corporations, including mining corporations, are and always have, in the common acceptance of the term, been regarded as income, spoken of and understood to be such by people generally. * * * . The task of tracing dividends declared by all sorts of corporations to their source to determine how much came from capital, and how much from income, strictly speaking, or how much from an enhancement of capital value, would be colossal in the amount of labor required, perplexing in character, and productive of almost endless litigation. * * * . It follows that ordinary dividends declared by a going corporation, including mining corporations, will be conclusively presumed as against stockholders to be from earnings or profits for purposes of taxation."

(2) "An affirmative answer must be given to this question * * * . As a stockholder he acquired no right to it until it was distributed in the form of a dividend. The profits of a corporation become income to stockholders when distributed as dividends, but not before."

(3) "The depreciation in the book value of its stock is in direct proportion to the distribution of surplus, and, if that were allowed to be deducted, there would be no income, for the book value of each share of stock before distribution exceeds its book value after distribution exactly by the amount distributed to it. No deductions can therefore be made."

(4) "If deductions were made when bought above par, additions should be made when purchased below par. Such a rule would be as burdensome in the administration of the law as tracing dividends to their source, and was plainly not contemplated by the statute which declares that all interest on bonds should be income." No deduction can therefore be made.

VAN RENSSELLAER v. DENNISON
(Supreme Court of N. Y., February Term, 1850)
(8 Barb. (N. Y.) 23)

Record: Action on covenant to recover rents and taxes paid on rents. Judgment for plaintiff for the rent, and for the defendant as to the taxes.

Facts: Plaintiff brought this suit under a lease by which the lessees covenanted to pay all taxes that might be thereafter taxed, charged or assessed to or upon the premises, or upon the lessors for and in respect of the said premises.   The plaintiff was assessed a tax upon the rents reserved in the lease as personal property.

Question: Is the defendant liable under the lease to reimburse the plaintiff for the payment of the tax in question?

Decision: The tax was not a tax charged or assessed upon the premises granted by the lease, nor upon the landlord for and in respect of such premises.   The tax was laid without reference to the premises, and in no sense "in respect of the premises," or their value. It was the income of the person which was taxed by the statute, and the defendant is not liable to the plaintiff for the taxes assessed upon such income.

VILLAGE OF WESTBY v. BEKKEDAL et. al.
(Supreme Court of Wisconsin, June 23, 1920)
(178 N. W. 451)

Record: Wisconsin Act of 1919.   Action by the Village of Westby against Bekkedal and others to recover taxes assessed. Judgment for plaintiff and defendants appealed.   Affirmed.

Facts: Bekkedal & Son were a partnership located in Wisconsin, engaged in the business of buying, storing, handling, and shipping of tobacco.   Rosenwald & Bro. were a partnership having its principal office and place of business in the city of New York and engaged in the selling, handling and merchandising of tobacco.   The two partnerships entered into a contract by the terms of which the Bekkedals were to buy tobacco of 1916 crop, raised in the State of Wisconsin, in joint account with the Rosenwalds, and attend to the packing and handling of the same.   The Rosenwalds agreed to attend to the marketing of the tobacco and apply all the net proceeds of any sales made to the credit of the joint account.   By the agreement the net profits or net lossess were to be shared, 60 per cent to the Rosenwalds and 40 per cent to the Bekkedals, according to the amount contributed by each.   The contract covered the 1916 crop but was to continue unless terminated by three months' notice. This contract was carried out by the parties for the year 1916, and all the proceeds of the sales were collected by the Rosenwalds at their office, and at the time the proceeds of such sales were received no part of the tobacco sold was located within the State of Wisconsin.

At the request of the income tax assessor, the Bekkedals without the knowledge or the authority of the Rosenwalds filed a joint return with the assessor. The Rosenwalds at no time, appeared before the board of review. There was also assessed against the defendants a tax on the personal property belonging to the two. The Rosenwalds claim that the net income from the transactions is not taxable to them, and that, if any part is taxable to them, they have the right to set off the amount of the personal property taxes. The Bekkedals also deny liability for the income tax.

Questions: (1) Does a contract between two parties, which provides that one is to do all the buying of a crop of tobacco for a certain year, and the other to do all the selling, create a partnership?

(2) If so, is all of the income of the partnership derived from business transacted without the state because the sales are made and the proceeds collected entirely without the state?

(3) If the partnership had income which was derived from property located or business transacted within the state, where and to whom was such income properly assessable?

(4) Are the Rosenwalds estopped to dispute the assessment by reason of their failure to appear before the board of review?

(5) Are the defendants entitled to set off personal property taxes in this suit?

Decision: (1) The contention of the defendants was that the agreement did not contemplate that each of the parties should be the agent of the other. "This agreement is based upon that provision of the contract which provides that the purchasing, storing, and handling, and shipping of the tobacco shall be exclusively within the control of the Bekkedals, and that the sale and disposition of the tobacco shall be exclusively in the hands of the Rosenwalds. It would seem to require no argument to show that considering the business as a whole, the Bekkedals were to act as agents for the Rosenwalds in the purchasing, handling, and shipping, because the Rosenwalds had a 60 per cent. interest in the tobacco purchased, and that as to the sales the Rosenwalds were to act as agents of the Bekkedals, the Bekkedals having a 40 per cent. interest in the proceeds of the sales when made. We think the contract in question created a partnership as defined by the Uniform Partnership Act."

(2) "Manifestly the total proceeds of the sales of the tobacco covered by the contract in question were not profits, hence not income. In order to determine what the profits transacted under the contract were, it was necessary to deduct from the gross proceeds of the sales made by the Rosenwalds their expenses, and cost of purchasing, storing, handling and shipping the tobacco incurred by the Bekkedals, and until that was done no determination could be made as to what was and what was not income, whether that be used in the statutory sense or in its ordinary business significance. The sales made by the Rosenwalds were one factor, and the purchasing, etc., by the Bekkedals were the other factor, the combination of which produced the profit. Hence to argue that, because the sales were entirely without the state, all of the income was derived from business without the state when it is conceded that a large part of the business was transacted within the state, is to argue from a false premise."

(3) "While the question has not been directly passed upon, the reasoning of many cases before this court is based upon the theory that a partnership has no entity distinct and apart from the persons who compose it. The partnership therefore, resided equally within the State of New York and the State of Wisconsin." Accordingly, it was held that that part of the income belonging to the Bekkedals was taxable within the State of Wisconsin, and that, as to the portion of the income belonging to the Rosenwalds, it was income derived partly from property and business within the State of Wisconsin and partly from business transacted without the state and should have been allocated.

(4) "As to the Rosenwalds, the return was made by their agent, who transacted the business for them within this state, and they therefore cannot complain that they were not notified of the return or that the assessment was made in accordance with it."

(5) "While under a strict construction of the statute it might be argued that the tax when paid in the form of a judgment is not paid to the city, town or village in the sense that payments are not made directly to them, we are of the opinion that the deduction of the amount to be paid to the village is authorized, inasmuch as it is the intent of the statute to give to the taxpayer this right."

VIOLETTE v. WALSH, COLLECTOR

(U. S. District Court, D. Montana, Feb. 11, 1921)

(272 Fed. 1014)

Record: National Prohibition Act and Rev. Stat. Secs. 3224 and 3251. In equity. Motion to dismiss granted.

Facts: Plaintiff seeks to enjoin collection by distraint of taxes and penalties assessed pursuant to Section 35, National Prohibition Act, upon him as a manufacturer of distilled spirits, intoxicating liquors. Among other things he alleges that he is not such manufacturer, and that the assessment and collection are illegal and a grievous hardship.

Questions: (1) Did the National Prohibition Act repeal the earlier law, i. e., Section 3251 Rev. Stat., imposing a tax on the manufacturer of distilled spirits, regardless of their purpose?

(2) If the earlier law is repealed, may the plaintiff have an injunction upon the theory that Section 35 of the National Prohibition Act does not provide for taxes, but for penalties as punishment?

Decision: (1) The National Prohibition Act only repealed inconsistent existing laws. The tax imposed by Rev. Stat., Section 3251, on the manufacturer of distilled spirits, not being inconsistent with the Act, is law today. A defendant will not be heard to say he is manufacturing for beverage purposes. That defendant is indicted for illicit manufacture and may be acquitted is immaterial; an acquittal would not relieve him of his obligation to pay, for the taxes are not penalties, fines, or forfeitures, in the sense understood in criminal law.

(2) But, even if the earlier law is repealed, since the collector holds otherwise and is pursuing his general jursidiction over the subject-matter, to determine occupation, taxable persons, character and amount of the tax, and since his assessment is of the color of a tax, and he claims it is valid. Section 3224 forbids that he be restrained, even as it does if the law be unconstitutional. Whether or not Section 3224 also applies to penalties illegally claimed, and whether or not in the instant case the penalties are part of the tax. is not for determination herein, but only in a case wherein the tax

has been at least tendered. See Kausch v. Moore, 268 Fed. 673. Accordingly, the bill to enjoin the collection of the taxes and penalties was dismissed.

VON BAUMBACH, COLLECTOR, v. SARGENT LAND CO.
(U. S. Supreme Court, January 15, 1917)
(242 U. S. 503)

Record: Act of August 5, 1909. Suits brought by the Sargent Land Co. and several other corporations to recover taxes, paid under protest, for the years 1909, 1910 and 1911. The judgments in the District Court were for the respondents (207 Fed. 423) which judgments were affirmed in the Circuit Court of Appeals for the Eighth Circuit (219 Fed. 31) and appeal was taken to this court on writs of certiorari. Judgments reversed.

Facts: Respondent corporations were organized in 1906, and the nature of their business was stated to be "the buying, owning, exploring and developing, leasing, improving, selling and dealing in lands, tenements and hereditaments, and the doing of all things incidental to the things above specified." In December, 1909, the articles of incorporation were amended to read as follows: "The general purpose of the corporation is to unite in one ownership the undivided fractional interests of its various stockholders in lands, tenements and hereditaments, and to own such property, and, for the convenience of its stockholders, to receive and distribute to them the proceeds of any disposition of such property at such times, in such amounts, and in such manner as the Board of Directors may determine." During the years 1909, 1910 and 1911 respondents received royalties under leases, all except one of which had been entered into prior to incorporation. Each of the leases provided that the owners of the property demised to the lessees, exclusively, all the land covered by the descriptions for the purpose of exploring for, mining and removing the merchantable iron ore which might be found therein for and during the period named. The lessees agreed to pay, in most cases, twenty-five cents per ton for all ore mined and removed. To insure the proper carrying on of the mining operations, respondents employed another corporation, engaged in engineering and inspection of ore properties, to provide supervision and inspection of the work upon respondents' properties, for which the inspecting company was paid from month to month, as statements were rendered. Since their organization the corporations disposed of certain lands, and also disposed of the stumpage on certain timber lands. Respondents were assessed upon their gross income, being the entire receipts from royalties and from sales of lots, land and stumpage, from which expenses and taxes were deducted, but no deduction was made on account of the depletion of the ore in the properties or on account of such sales.

Questions: (1) Were the respondent corporations organized for profit?

(2) Were the respondents carrying on or doing business during the years 1909, 1910 and 1911?

(3) Were moneys received by the respondents during those years in payment for iron ore under contracts covering their mineral lands, gross income or did they represent, in whole or in part, the conversion of the investment of the corporations from ore into money?

(4) If such moneys were gross income, are the respondents entitled to make any deductions therefrom on account of the depletion of their capital investment?

Decision: (1) The companies were organized for profit.

(2) They were carrying on or doing business within the meaning of the Act of 1909.

(3) The payments made by the lessees to the respondents were not in substance the proceeds of an outright sale of mining property, but, in view of the terms of the instruments, were in fact rents or royalties and must be held to come fairly within the term "income" as intended to be reached and taxed under the Corporation Tax Act.

(4) Under the Act of 1909, which permits as a deduction "a reasonable allowance for depreciation of property" the term "depreciation" is to be given its ordinary and usual significance, and does not include an allowance for the depletion of a mine.

WALKER, COLLECTOR v. GULF & I. RY. CO. OF TEXAS
(U. S. Circuit Court of Appeals, Fifth Cir., Jan. 12, 1921)
(269 Fed. 885)
Record: Act of August 5, 1909. Action to recover taxes paid under protest. Judgment for plaintiff. Defendant brought error. Modified as to amount and affirmed.

Facts: In 1910 the plaintiff was the owner of certain docks at Port Bolivar, Texas, which were necessary to handle its business, consisting largely of transportation of lumber for the export trade. The plaintiff was not authorized by the laws of Texas to own these docks, and, therefore, it organized a Terminal Company, to which it sold the docks in 1910 for shares of stock in that company and also for its note for $618,124.86 bearing 6 per cent interest. The Terminal Company's income was never sufficient to pay expenses, and so in 1911 and 1912 the plaintiff advanced it sums of money. The company was also unable to pay the plaintiff any interest on its note. Practically all of the company's business consisted of furnishing dock facilities for plaintiff's passengers and freight.

Questions: (1). Should the plaintiff have included in its returns for 1911 and 1912 interest due on notes due but not actually collected?

(2) Was plaintiff entitled to deduct in its returns money advanced to a subsidiary company to pay operating expenses?

Decision: (1) Interest accrued, but not actually collected, was not "income" under the aforesaid Act of Congress. This question was settled by the case of Maryland Casualty Co. v. United States, 251 U. S. 342.

(2) While the plaintiff was practically the sole stockholder and was the organizer of the Terminal Company, the operations of the latter were separately conducted, its books and accounts were kept separately, and it was managed by a separate set of offices. The two corporations were separate legal entities and the sum advanced by the plaintiff to the Terminal Company was not properly deductible as part of plaintiff's operating expense.

WALSH v. BREWSTER
(U. S. Supreme Court, March 28, 1921)
(Not reported)

Record: Revenue Act of 1916. Action at law to recover income taxes for year 1916, assessed in 1918, which were paid under protest. Case tried on agreed statement of facts. Judgment in favor of taxpayer. In error to Dist. Ct., D. Conn. (268 Fed. 208). Reversed in part, affirmed in part, and case remanded.

Facts: "The defendant in error was not a trader or dealer in stocks or bonds, but occasionally purchased and sold one or the other for the purpose of changing his investments.

"Three transactions are involved.

"The first relates to bonds of the Internal Navigation Company, purchased in 1909, for $191,000 and sold in 1916 for the same amount. The market value of these bonds on March 1, 1913, was $151,845, and the tax in dispute was assessed on the difference between this amount and the amount for which they were sold in 1916, viz. $39,155 * * *.

"The second transaction involved the purchase in 1902 and 1903 of bonds of the International Mercantile Marine Company for $231,300, which were sold in 1916 for $276,150. This purchase was made through an underwriting agreement such that the purchaser did not receive any interest upon the amount paid prior to the allotment to him of the bonds in 1906, and he claimed that interest upon the investment for the time which so elapsed should be added as part of the cost to him of the bonds.* * * It is stipulated that the market value of these bonds on March 1, 1913, was $164,480, and the Collector assessed the tax upon the difference between the selling price and this amount. * * *.

"The third transaction related to stock in the Standard Oil Company of California, received through the same stock dividend involved in Eisner v. Macomber, 252 U. S. 189."

Questions: (1) Is appreciation in value of capital assets realized by sale "income" within the scope of the Sixteenth Amendment?

(2) Where selling price is greater than March 1, 1913, value, but not greater than cost, is there any taxable gain?

(3) Can interest on an investment computed from date of payment to date of receipt of bonds, be added to the cash payment to determine real cost, no interest having been paid?

(4) Where March 1, 1913, value is less than cost and cost is less than selling price how is taxable gain determined?

Decision: (1) "The trial court held that this apparent gain (excess of selling price over value March 1, 1913) even though cost equalled selling price was capital assets and not taxable income under the Sixteenth Amendment to the Constitution of the United States, and rendered judgment in favor of the defendant in error for the amount of the tax which he had paid. The ground upon which this part of the judgment was justified below is held to be erroneous in No. 608, Merchants' Loan & Trust Company, as Trustee v. Julius F. Smietanka, Collector of Internal Revenue, this day decided."

(2) "Since the owner of the stock did not realize any gain on his original investment by the sale in 1916, the judgment was right in this respect, and under authority of the opinion and judgment in No. 663, Goodrich v. Edwards, Collector, also rendered this day, this part of the judgment is affirmed."

(3) The claim for including interest on investment as an addition to cost "was properly rejected by trial court under authority of Hay v. Gauley Mountain Coal Co., 247 U. S. 189."

(4) Where March 1st value is less than cost and cost is less than selling price, the taxable gain is "the difference between his investment of $231,300 and the amount realized by the sale, $276,150," or $44,850.

WARING v. SAVANNAH
(Supreme Court of Ga., January, 1878)
(60 Ga. 93)

Record: Act of December 30, 1874, of City of Savannah. Judgment for defendant and plaintiff brought error. Affirmed.

Facts: See questions.

Questions: (1) Is a city ordinance void under the Constitution of Georgia that exempts certain classes of property from taxation?

(2) Is a city ordinance void, under the Constitution of Georgia, that taxes real estate 2¼ per cent and interest on bonds, notes, judgments, etc., and the gross earnings of banks only one per cent?

(3) Is income property, as used in the Constitution of Georgia, and, therefore, taxed at the same rate as other property?

Decision: (1) This question is answered by the case of Mayer & Council of Athens v. Long, 54 Ga. 330. It was held in this case that the city could exempt certain classes of property from any tax whatsoever. The charters of Athens and Savannah are alike in this respect.

(2) The Constitution of Georgia at the date of this ordinance declared that "taxes shall be ad valorem only and uniform on all species of property taxed." "This clause admits of two constructions, one, that all property taxed must be taxed uniformly at the same rate; the other that each species must bear the same rate. All must be ad valorem; but one species may be at one rate, and another at a different rate." The latter view seems to have been in the minds of the framers of the constitution, and the courts have favored the same. "The true interpretation of the clause is doubtful, and in the case of doubt it is perhaps best, as the precise inequality in this case cannot be ascertained, to give the benefit of the doubt to the taxing power." If the city of Savannah could have exempted from tax altogether interest on bonds and gross earnings, the plaintiff cannot complain that it did tax these things even though it did not tax them as much as it did his real estate. The court has no power to equalize the tax on interest on bonds, etc., and real estate even if it were possible to do so. It was therefore held that this ordinance was not void.

(3) Income is not property and it has been held so in the State of Georgia since the case of Savannah v. Hartridge, 8. Ga. 23. "The fact is, property is a tree, income is the fruit. Labor is a tree, income the fruit; capital, the tree, income the fruit. The fruit, if not consumed as fast as it ripens, will germinate from the seed it encloses, and will produce other trees, and grow into more property; but so long as it is fruit merely, and plucked to eat, and consumed in eating, it is no tree, and will produce itself no fruit." Therefore, income is not property and is not to be taxed at the same rate as property.

WATERBURY GASLIGHT CO. v. WALSH, COLLECTOR
(U. S. District Court, Connecticut, October 3, 1915)
(228 Fed. 54)

Record: Corporation Excise Tax of August 5, 1909. Action by plaintiff against the Collector of Internal Revenue to recover back excise taxes for the years ending December 31, 1910, 1911 and 1912, respectively, under the provisions of Sec. 38 of the Act of August 5, 1909. Defendant collector filed an answer to which plaintiff interposed a demurrer. Demurrer sustained.

Facts: Plaintiff was a Connecticut corporation chartered for the purpose of manufacturing, selling and distributing gas, with all the necessary powers incidental and appertaining thereto. The complaint alleged that on March 30, 1894, plaintiff leased all of its property to the United Gas Improvement Co., a Pennsylvania corporation, for 20 years, in consideration for an annual rental; that the lease provided lessee should have the right to receive for its own use all benefits, income and profits from the use of the demised property; that lessee entered into possession and continued in such possession and occupation after date of the lease. Defendant's answer urged that plaintiff had no right under its charter to enter into this lease; that since April 1, 1894, the plaintiff applied for and obtained the passage of special acts by the General Assembly of the State of Connecticut, amending its charter, which acts explicitly recognized the lessor company rather than the lessee, as the active corporation engaged in the business; that by the terms of the lease the lessor bears the expense of alterations, improvements and additions to the plant, meters, etc., and continues actively in the management and maintenance of its property and the conduct of its business. Plaintiff's demurrer averred that if there is a lease de facto it cannot be attacked in a collateral proceeding of this nature; that the mere fact that charter amendments were applied for by plaintiff does not constitute carrying on or doing business that neither does the fact that the expense of additions or improvements are ultimately borne by plaintiff constitute the doing of business by it within the meaning of the Act.

Questions: (1) Is the lease in question ultra vires so as to be void?

(2) Was the plaintiff "carrying on business" within the meaning of the Corporation Tax of August 5, 1909?

Decision: (1) Lease was not ultra vires. The lease in question was not ultra vires in the absence of anything in the charter or the laws of the state prohibiting, although not expressly authorizing same to be done.

(2) Lessor corporation was not "carrying on or doing business" within meaning of Act of August 5, 1909. "As is pointed out in the Traction Companies case (223 Fed. 988) there is a

helpful analogy in observing an individual. It is not usually hard to decide, as the court there says, whether an individual is still in business or has retired, and if the latter, he does not lose that character because here and there in the receipt of his income, he does an item of business. I am convinced from a careful study of the lease and of the charter of plaintiff, and the various amendments referred to, that the plaintiff is within the criterion stated and that the demurrer should be sustained." Decree entered accordingly, allowing the plaintiff to recover the amount of taxes paid.

WEEKS v. SIBLEY
(U. S. District Court, N. D. Texas, October 22, 1920)
(269 Fed. 155)

Record: Revenue Act of 1918. Suit for injunction. Decree for complainant.

Facts: In 1918 an unincorporated joint-stock company, known as Thrift Oil & Gas Company No. 4, was organized to develop certain oil lands. Plaintiff acquired stock in this company in 1919. In that year the Company was dissolved and all its assets conveyed to the defendant, as trustee, with absolute control, under a trust deed which provided for periodical distribution of income. In the same year the trustee sold the trust property at a profit. The principal motive in dissolving the Company and in creating the trust was to lessen federal tax liability. The Bureau of Internal Revenue, however, ruled that the dissolution was a device to escape taxation, and ineffective as such, and that the tax should be paid in the same way as though the Company were still in existence. Complainant brought this suit to prevent the trustee from complying with the order of the Bureau. The Bureau and the U. S. District Attorney were notified of this suit but did not intervene.

Question: Was the dissolution of an association and the transfer of its property to a trustee, admittedly done for the purpose of lessening tax liability, valid?

Decision: Bearing in mind the accepted rule of construction that "the provisions of the taxing statutes are not to be extended by implication beyond the clear import of the language used, and that they are to be construed most strongly against the government and in favor of the taxpayer, it is the opinion of this court that the right to change the status of an organization, or to dissolve an organization in any legal manner, is not made ineffectual because the motive impelling the change is to reduce or avoid taxation in the future. The right to do so is an incidental right, inseparably connected with an individual's right to own and control his property. It is practically identical with the sale by a citizen of tax-burdened securities and the investment of the proceeds thereof in tax-exempt ones, for the purpose of reducing or avoiding taxation." Accordingly, the court enjoined the trustee from complying with the order of the Bureau of Internal Revenue.

WEISS, COLLECTOR v. MOHAWK MINING CO.
(U. S. Circuit Court of Appeals, Sixth Cir., March 2, 1920)
(264 Fed. 502, 505)

Record: Act of September 8, 1916. Action to recover taxes paid. Judgment for plaintiff below, and defendant brought error. Reversed. On petition for rehearing, June 15, 1920, petition denied. Petition for writ of certiorari denied by Supreme Court October 18, 1920 (41 Sup. Ct. 12).

Facts: The plaintiff on March 1, 1913, was lessee of certain mining property. Under the lease it was to pay the fee owners a royalty of 25 cents per ton, was to pay a certain minimum each year, and was given a term long enough to permit extraction of all the ore. The value of the ore on March 1, 1913, was stipulated to have been 50 cents per ton; that is to say, 25 cents per ton in addition to the royalty which must be paid when it was taken out. The plaintiff, in its return, claimed an allowance for depletion to the extent of this 25 cents excess per ton, being the value of its interest on March 1, 1913. The Commissioner declined to allow this deduction.

Question: Was a lessee of mining property entitled to a depletion allowance in computing net income under the 1916 Act?

Decision: The substantial principles established by the decisions are that both the royalty received by the fee owner and the sums received by the operating lessee above the cost of operation are income; that the statutory reduction for "depletion" cannot be twice credited, once to the fee owner and once to the lessee; and that the exemption belongs of right to the fee owner. The plaintiff is not entitled to a depletion allowance and cannot recover the taxes paid on the amount claimed for such a deduction. The case of U. S. v. Biwabik Co. (247 U. S. 116) was cited as controlling.

WELLS, COUNTY TREASURER, ads. ALDERMAN
(Supreme Court of South Carolina, April 12, 1910)
(85 S. C. 507; 67 S. E. 781)

Record: Act of South Carolina of March 5, 1897. Action at law to recover taxes paid under protest. Judgment for defendant, and plaintiff appealed. Affirmed.

Facts: The South Carolina act provided for a graduated tax on incomes to be collected in the same manner as other taxes. The law governing the levying and collecting of other taxes provided for notice to the taxpayer and a hearing before the county board of equalization, and a suit to recover. The plaintiff's income was derived from dividends received from corporations which paid a franchise and the usual taxes.

Questions: (1) Is a graduated tax on incomes unconstitutional under the Fourteenth Amendment of the Constitution of the United States as denying the plaintiff the equal protection of the laws?

(2) Is a tax on incomes which provides that notice be given the taxpayer, that he have a hearing before a board of equalization, and that he may recover of treasurer, a violation of the due process clause in Constitution of the United States?

(3) Does a tax upon the dividends received by a stockholder result in double taxation where the corporations had paid taxes on their property and on their franchises?

Decision: (1) "The right of the legislature of the state to make reasonable classifications of persons, and property for public purposes has been so often affirmed by the courts that it can be no longer questioned. If the classification is not arbitrary —that is, if it bears reasonable relation to the purposes to be effected—and if the constituents of each class are treated alike, under similar circumstances, and conditions, the rule of equality is satisfied."

(2) The court, quoting from 92 U. S. 575, said that "this board has its time of sitting fixed by law. Its sessions are not secret, no obstruction exists to the appearance of any one before it to assert a right or redress a wrong; and, in the business of assessing taxes, this is all that can be reasonably asked."

(3) "The rents and profits derived from real estate, and the products of the farm, may be taxed, though the land from which they are derived has also been taxed." This and the main case "may be instances of double taxation in one sense," but "there is no constitutional inhibition against such taxation."

WEST END ST. RY. CO. v. MALLEY, COLLECTOR

(U. S. Circuit Court of Appeals, First Cir., December 10, 1917)

(246 Fed. 625)

Record: Act of August 5, 1909, and Act of October 3, 1913. Action to recover back taxes assessed under the statutes above mentioned, which taxes were paid under protest. Judgment was rendered in the District Court of Massachusetts, in plaintiff's favor as to part of its claim in the sum of $2,608.17, under the first count of the declaration, but finding was had for defendant collector under the remaining second count. Both plaintiff and defendant sued out writs of error and the case was thereby brought to this court for review. Judgment affirmed. Judge Alrich filed a dissenting opinion. Petition for writ of certiorari denied by U. S. Supreme Court, April 15, 1918, 246 U. S. 271.

Facts: Plaintiff, a street railway corporation, having leased its lines and property to the Boston Elevated Ry. Co. in 1897, has not since operated them itself. They have been operated by the lessee which has regularly made rental payments called for by the lease. The taxes under the first count of the declaration were assessed against plaintiff, on the ruling that it was engaged in business within the meaning of the Act of August 5, 1909. The taxes under the second count were assessed under the provisions of the Act of October 3, 1913, on the ruling that payments made by the lessee corporation pursuant to the terms of the lease, to persons holding shares of plaintiff's stock and certified by it as then entitled to dividends, represented taxable income of the lessor corporation.

Questions: (1) Was the lessor corporation engaged in business within the meaning of the Act of August 5, 1909?

(2) Were the payments made as dividends to lessor's stockholders by lessee corporation pursuant to the terms of the consideration in the lease, taxable income of lessor?

Decision: (1) The plaintiff corporation was not "a corporation engaged in business," as contemplated by the statute in question, and therefore not subject to the tax imposed by it. The question thus presented we regard as controlled against the Government's view by the reasoning and result in New York Central, etc., Co. v. Gill, 219 Fed. 184; 134 C. C. A., 558, decided by this Court in 1915, the subsequent decisions cited by the District Court in its opinion in the present case, and the following still later decisions: McCoach v. Continental, etc., Co., 233 Fed. 976; 47 C. C. A., 650; Jasper, etc. Co. v. Walker, 238 Fed. 533; 151 C. C. A., 469. We find nothing in the agreed facts now before us which we can regard as sufficiently distinguishing this case from those dealt with in said decisions to warrant us in holding the District Court's conclusion erroneous."

(2) Dividend payments made by lessee corporation to stockholders of lessor company as consideration in the lease are taxable income of lessor company, having been made for the use of the corporation's property, not of the stockholders' property. Though they have each an interest in said property, they have no direct interest such as makes them its owners. "The agreement expressly refers to and treats these payments to stockholders as part of the agreed rent for the property and under it no stockholder could assert rights as lessor for want of any such interest in the leased property as would have enabled him to lease it or agree upon a rent for it." We agree with the opinion of the District Court that the total of these so-called dividends was within the meaning of the statute 'income arising or accruing' to the corporation. The District Court's conclusion is supported by a Court of Appeals decision. Anderson v. Morris, etc., Co., 261 Fed. 83, 90; 132 C. C. A. 327. Though it was the Corporation Tax Act of 1909 which was there under consideration, a question passed upon was whether or not such dividends paid to stockholders by the lessee were part of the lessors' entire net income * * * received by it from all sources during the year. So far as the difference in phraseology is of any significance, it favors

a more rather than a less, inclusive construction. This decision having been followed by Judge Ray in the same circuit, since the decision here appealed from, Rennsselaer, etc. Co. v. Irwin (D. C.) 239 Fed. 739, in a case arising like this under the Income Tax Statute of 1913, we are unable to find sufficient reason for a refusal to follow it in this circuit." The dividend payments by the lessee corporation to the stockholders of the lessor corporation constituted income taxable to the lessor corporation under Act of 1913.

WESTERN PAC. R. CO. v. SCOTT

(U. S. Circuit Court of Appeals, Ninth Cir., December 3, 1917)

(246 Fed. 545)

Record: Act of October 3, 1913. On petition by receivers, citation to collector to show cause why return should not be accepted as filed. Receiver was directed to make no returns or payment (236 Fed. 813), the citation was dismissed and collector appeals. Affirmed.

Facts: In accordance with the Income Tax Law of October 3, 1913, the receivers of the plaintiff corporation filed a return of net income of the road for 1915. The report showed no taxable income. The Treasury Department being of the opinion that certain deductions were not actual disbursements, disallowed certain interest deductions and ordered an assessment. After a hearing upon a petition filed by the receivers, the District Court ordered (1) the receivers to make no payment of income tax and (2) dismissed the order to show cause.

Questions: 1. Did the court exceed its jurisdiction in making the order complained of in view of Section 3224 Rev. Stat., which provides that no suit for the purpose of restraining the assessment or collection of a tax shall be maintained in any court?

(2) Does the Act of October 3, 1913, apply to the receivers of a corporation?

Decision: (1) Receivers are officers of the court, and by all authority may ask instructions from the court concerning the administration of property in their hands. That the questions presented to them involve taxes does not change the rule. Property in the hands of a receiver, is in the custody of the court, and while it is the duty of the receiver to pay lawfully imposed taxes without asking the sanction of the court, on the other hand, they are not bound to pay a tax which in their judgment is unlawful, without an order of the court, and it is their duty to apply to the court either for instruction or protection when they believe the legality of the tax is questionable.

(2) There are not clear and express words in the Income Tax Law of 1913 which provide for the imposition of the tax upon the business done and income received by receivers appointed by the court, and without certainty as to the meaning and scope of the language imposing the tax, doubt must be resolved in favor of the receivers. The court therefore directed the receiver to make no returns or payment.

WILKES-BARRE & W. VA. TRACTION CO. v. DAVIS, COLLECTOR

(U. S. District Court, M. D. Pennsylvania, June 3, 1914)

(214 Fed. 511)

Record: Act of August 5, 1909. Action at law to recover taxes paid under protest on net income under Section 38 of this Act. Judgment for plaintiff.

Facts: Plaintiff was incorporated under the Act of May 22, 1887, to operate a system of street railways in Laverne County, Pa. In 1910, by authority of the state law, it leased and transferred for a rental, to the Railway Co., for a term of 800 years, the system of street railways which it owned, operated and controlled. Thereafter, and since, it appears that plaintiff has engaged in no other business whatever than to maintain and preserve its corporate franchise, conserving the enjoyment of its corporate property to its lessee, receiving therefrom the rent reserved by the lease and distributing its income among its stockholders.

Question: Is plaintiff corporation subject to tax under Act of August 5, 1909?

Decision: The tax provided for by the Act of 1909 is not imposed on the franchise of the corporation, nor on its property but only on the "doing of business" in a corporate capacity as authorized. Plaintiff was not "doing business" as a traction company over the lines covered by the lease. The business of serving the public as a common carrier, which was the prime object of its incorporation was turned over to its lessee. For this purpose, the plaintiff must be regarded as out of business, and therefore not subject to taxation under Act of 1909.

WILCOX v. COUNTY COMMISSIONERS OF MIDDLESEX
(Supreme Court of Massachusetts, January Term, 1870)
(103 Mass. 544)

Record: Massachusetts Act. Petition for a writ of certiorari to reverse the refusal of the respondents to abate a tax assessed on petitioner's ·income. Petition dismissed.

Facts: The petitioner was a member of a firm dealing in leather, and was engaged in no other business. The firm was assessed and paid a tax on their stock in trade. The petitioner was later assessed on his income which was derived from this business. The statute provides that "no income shall be taxed which is derived from property subject to taxation."

Question: Is the income derived from a certain business so derived from the "stock in trade" that a tax upon the income is a tax upon the "stock in trade" which was taxed prior to the income tax?

Decision: "The income from a 'profession, trade or employment,' which is taxable under our system of laws, is an entirely different thing from the capital invested in the business, or the stock of goods in the purchase of which the whole or part of such capital may have been expended. The income meant by the statute is the income for the year, and is the result of the year's business * * *. It is the creation of capital, industry and skill. * * * The income to which the statute refers does not mean merely the profits derived from the sale of the goods that happened to be on hand at the date of the tax, but the profits derived from the dealings and business of the firm for the year. It would not relieve the petitioner from any part of his tax, though it should be found that the goods on hand at the date of the tax had yielded no profit whatever, and had contributed absolutely nothing towards making up the sum which he reported to the assessors as his income from that business * * * . The tax which has been assessed is not for an income derived from specific goods and merchandise" which in this case consisted of the stock in trade at a certain date, and was properly assessed.

In re WILDER'S STEAMSHIP CO.
(Supreme Court of Hawaii, March 27, 1905)
(16 Haw. 567)

Record: Hawaiian Act of 1901. Appeal by the tax assessor from the tax appeal court which sustained a claim of the taxpayer. Reversed.

Facts: The taxpayer built a steamer, which was kept in constant use for twenty-four years. The Federal inspectors notified the company that it would have to make extensive repairs before they would renew her certificate. The vessel was shortly afterwards broken up and sold for a small sum. The average life of a steamer is twenty years. The company returned the amount of the difference between the original cost and the price for which it was sold under the head "losses incurred in trade."

Question: Is the amount of the difference between the original cost of a steamer and the selling price of it, a "loss incurred in trade," during the last year in which the steamer is used?

Decision: "In the case the steamer. 'Moklin' was not lost, whether in consequence of the requirement of the Federal inspectors or because the steamer had become 'absolutely unsafe for use either as a freight vessel or as a passenger vessel.' The company could make no further use of its steamer and obtained by breaking it up and selling it its actual value * * * . This is not a loss which for the purpose of taxation is to be measured by its estimated earnings which the steamer might have made if it could have continued running; nor was it a loss, to be measured by the cost of replacing it with a new steamer."

WILDER v. HAWAIIAN TRUST CO.
(Supreme Court of Hawaii, July 17, 1911)
(20 Haw. 589)

Record: Hawaiian Act as amended by Acts of 1905 and 1909. Original submission on agreed facts, under the statute. Judgment for Hawaiian Trust Company.

Facts: The Hawaiian Trust Company was trustee under a will to pay from the income of the trust fund annuities to certain designated persons. The surplus income was to be distributed as part of the trust fund at the termination of the trust. The Trust Company has paid out the annuities for the year, and has a surplus. The statute levies a tax on incomes, and income is made to include "money and the value of all personal property acquired by gift or inheritance." It provides that trustees shall make a return to the assessor, and that all power, authorities and duties enacted in the chapter relating to personal and property taxes for levying, assessing, collecting, receiving and enforcing payments of tax shall be conferred for the same purposes in regard to this tax. The trustee is under a duty to pay the personal and property tax.

Questions: (1) Is the trustee required by the Act to make a return and be taxed on the net income received by it from the estate?

(2) Is the surplus income after the payment of the annuities exempt so that the trustees need pay no income tax on it?

Decisions: (1) "The Property Tax Act, looking at property as it exists on the annual assessment date, provides for the assessment of its value against the person who owns or holds the legal title. The Income Tax Act, on the other hand, looks to each individual, and provides that 'every person' shall be assessed with respect to the income 'derived' by him * * * . The trustee is not to be assessed upon the income which it has collected and paid over to the annuitants. The income, though collected by the trustee, was not, within the meaning of the statute, *derived* by the trustee, but by the annuitants." The trustee is, however, required to make a return.

(2) "As to the surplus income, we hold that it is not taxable during the period in which it is to accumulate. As above pointed out, the statute levies the tax upon incomes 'derived' by persons * * * . The surplus income of the Galbraith estate, which, pursuant to the terms of the will, is being received by and is accumulating in the hands of the trustee, is not, and, so long as it thus accumulates, will not, within the meaning of the income tax law, be 'derived' by any one. During the period of its accumulation no one will have the beneficial use of it or any part of it. It constitutes

a fund which, although it may steadily increase, is not taxable income. Pending its distribution it is beyond the purview of the Income Tax Act."

WILDER et al v. TREFRY
(Supreme Judicial Court of Mass., January 10, 1920)

(125 N. E. 689)

Record: Massachusetts Income Tax Law of 1916, section 2. Petition for abatement of tax. Denied.

Facts: Petitioners, domiciled in the State of Massachusetts, were the owners of the preferred stock of a New York corporation. The New York company was in arrears to the extent of $33\frac{1}{3}$ per cent in declaring the 6 per cent cumulative dividends to which owners of this stock were entitled in preference to the payment of any dividends upon the common stock. In full settlement of the $33\frac{1}{3}$ per cent unpaid dividends, the holders of the preferred stock accepted $7\frac{1}{2}$ per cent of the face value of their holdings in cash, 14 per cent in 6 per cent cumulative preferred stock, and 12 per cent in common stock.

Question: Do cash and shares of stock received by a shareholder in full settlement of dividends in arrears on cumulative preferred stock, constitute a "dividend" within the meaning of Section 2 of the Income Tax Law of 1916?

Decision: The provisions of the statute here applicable are as follows: "Section 2. Income of the following classes received by an inhabitant of this commonwealth during the calendar year prior to the assessment of the tax shall be taxed at the rate of 6 per cent per annum * * * . (b) Dividends on shares in all corporations and joint stock companies under the laws of any state or nation other than this commonwealth, except * * * . No distribution of capital whether in liquidation or otherwise shall be taxable as income under this section; but accumulated profits shall not be regarded as capital under this provision."

Money and stock were not received by the petitioners in payment of any debt due to them, as they were not creditors. They would have no enforceable claim against the corporation until a dividend should be declared. "The money they received was paid from accumulated earnings of the corporation, and the shares of stock were issued by a capitalization of and were accordingly based upon accumulated earnings of the corporation." The cash and stock accepted in payment of the unpaid dividends were declared expressly as a dividend and were accepted as such. "The word dividend 'carries no spell with it.' As ordinarily used, it is that portion of the profits which a corporation sets apart for distribution among its shareholders. While usually in cash, it is not necessarily so, but may be issued in the form of stock or notes. As used in the Income Tax Law of 1918 (Section 201) it is defined as 'any distribution made by a corporation * * * to its shareholders or members, whether in cash or in other property or in stock of the corporation, out of its earnings or profits * * * .'" Notwithstanding the attendant compromise of the stockholders' inchoate rights to a dividend wholly in cash, the income was received essentially as a dividend within the meaning of the Income Tax Law.

WILLINGHAM v. UNITED STATES
(U. S. Circuit Court of Appeals, Fifth Cir., October 13, 1913)
(208 Fed. 137)

Record: Rev. Stat., Sec. 3229. Defendant was convicted by the district court of selling whisky without paying the special government tax, and brings error. Reversed and remanded for a new trial.

Facts: A deputy internal revenue collector of the United States saw the defendant sell whisky and told him that if he would pay the tax for one year with 50 per cent penalty, he would not swear out a complaint, but if such payment was not made, a complaint would be sworn out. Relying upon the collector's statements, defendant made the payment, and the special stamp was issued to him. At the close of the evidence, defendant requested the court to give special instruction to the effect that if defendant was promised immunity if the tax was paid, he should be found not guilty. The District Court refused to give this instruction.

Question: Was the offer made by the deputy collector a compromise which would be binding upon the Government if accepted?

Decision: The Commissioner of Internal Revenue has the power under Rev. Stat., Sec. 3229, with the advice and consent of the Secretary of the Treasury, to compromise any civil or criminal case arising under the internal revenue laws. "The deputy collector undoubtedly had the authority to at least transmit the offer of compromise, and when he turned over the payment to his superior it was his duty to disclose to him that it was an offer in compromise. It is presumed that he did so, and the fact that the money was retained by the United States and the stamp issued to defendant would raise the presumption that the offer in compromise had been accepted. Under this statement of facts it was the duty of the District Court to submit the question to the jury and to grant the special instructions requested by the defendant or to substantially instruct the jury to the same effect in the general charge." The District Court refused to instruct the jury that if the defendant was promised immunity if the tax were paid he should be found not guilty and therefore this court remanded the case for a new trial.

WILLMANN et al. TRUSTEES IN LIQUIDATION
v. WALSH, COLLECTOR
(Conn. Sup. Court of Errors)
(T. D. 3166)

Record: Revenue Acts of 1916, 1917 and 1918, and Rev. Stat. Secs. 3224, 3226. Application for restraining order against collector denied. Appealed. Affirmed.

Facts: On February 27, 1919, Joseph Willmann et al., trustees in liquidation, petitioned the Superior Court for the issuance of an order limiting a period within which all claims against the Derby Manufacturing Co. should be presented and for such additional orders from time to time relative to the winding up of the affairs of the company as might be proper and necessary in accordance with the statutes of the State of Connecticut. On the same day the court issued an order providing that all claims against the company should be presented to said trustees within four months from February 27, 1919. Among the claims presented pursuant to this order was one of the United States, presented by James J. Walsh, Collector of Internal Revenue for the District of Connecticut, for additional income, excess profits and war profits taxes for the years 1916, 1917, and 1918; and also for taxes not then determined for that portion of 1919 up to the date of the cessation of business by such corporation.

On June 1, 1920, the trustees reported the claims of the United States wherein they disallowed the major portion thereof. The court entered an order approving the report and providing that written notice should be given to the United States, through the Commissioner of Internal Revenue, and to James J. Walsh, collector, that unless the disallowed portion of the claim was made the subject of application to the court for allowance within two weeks, the same should be barred. Thereafter, the United States attorney for the District of Connecticut filed a petition on behalf of the United States for the allowance of the entire claim. On June 29, 1920, the trustees in liquidation filed with the court an application for a restraining order against the collector, asking that the collector be restrained from interfering with their possession of the company's property, notwithstanding the fact that there was pending in the collector's office a claim in abatement covering the taxes in question, during the pendency of which no distraint proceedings would have been carried out by the collector. It was alleged that the trustees were officers of the court and that an interference by the collector with their possession would be a contempt of the court. Upon the hearing of this application, the Superior Court of New Haven County refused to grant the restraining order.

Question: Were the trustees in liquidation receivers of the court in relation to the property of the corporation, therefore bringing the property within the custody of the law and warranting the issuance of a restraining order against the collector?

Decision: The trustees in liquidation acting under the general statutes of the State of Connecticut are not receivers. Their possession of the assets of a corporation is not the custody of the law. The assets in their hands are therefore subject to such procedure for the collection of taxes of the United States as the laws of the United States permit. The court, therefore, correctly refused to issue the restraining order.

RE APPLICATION OF WILLMANN et al., TRUSTEES IN
LIQUIDATION

(Conn. Sup. Court of Errors)

(T. D. 3166)

Record: Revenue Acts of 1916, 1917, and 1918, and Rev. Stat.
Sec. 3224, 3226. Application for restraining order and for instructions from the court as to the duty of the trustees in relation to the
tax claims of United States, and for order by court to determine
what taxes, if any, were due the United States. Application denied
for want of jurisdiction. Appealed. Affirmed.

Facts: The facts are the same as those in the case of Willmann et al., Trustees in Liquidation, v. Walsh, Collector, supra,
except that this was an application made after relief prayed in that
case was denied.

Question: Did the State Court have jurisdiction to determine
the amount of taxes legally due the United States from a liquidating corporation?

Decision: "Under the record and facts found, it appears that
the collector of internal revenue presented claims of the United
States for taxes to the trustees. The trustees in a supplemental report to the Superior Court, filed June 1, 1920, reported these claims
and stated that there were five items of such claims and that the
trustees had paid two items and disallowed three items, and recommended the court to disallow the three items. The court on the
same day, obviously pro forma, disallowed the three items and ordered notice to be given to the United States and its collector of
internal revenue * * *. Upon notice to the collector of such
disallowance, he appeared in court and made application for an
order that the claim of the United States for taxes so disallowed be
paid. The collector, in his application, alleged that the three items
of Federal taxes in controversy were 'duly assessed by the proper
authority in behalf of the United States.' In the recommendation
of the trustees to the court for the disallowance of the three
items of Federal taxes there is no suggestion that such assessment
of Federal taxes as made against the corporation, whether legal or
not, was not made by the proper authority of the United States.

The trustees moved that the court proceed to a hearing and determination of the taxes legally due by the corporation to the United States. The court ruled that it then had no jurisdiction to hear and determine the amount of taxes legally due the United States from the corporation. This ruling of the court was correct.''

WOODS v. LEWELLYN

(U. S. Circuit Court of Appeals, Third Cir., June 18, 1918)

(252 Fed. 106)

Record: Act of October 3, 1913. Action at law to recover taxes paid under protest on net income under this Act. Judgment for defendant, plaintiff brought error. Affirmed.

Facts: Plaintiff was general agent of the Equitable Life Assurance Society, having a defined territory and empowered to appoint subordinates; he was obliged to pay part of the expenses, and his compensation was measured by fixed percentages of the premiums that were actually paid on policies obtained through him and accepted by the society. Some of these policies were renewed each year and thus it was that the agent's right to commissions on future renewals came then into being. The agent in making his return did not include the money received as commissions on renewals, but attached a statement to the return explaining that these were earned before the Income Tax Act of 1913 went into effect, and, claiming therefore, that they were not taxable.

Questions: (1) Are commissions derived from renewal premiums paid on policies that were obtained by plaintiff and accepted by the society in some earlier year taxable under Act of 1913 in the year received?

(2) Could the Act, although passed in October, 1913, tax plaintiff's income from March 1st, of that year?

(3) Was the plaintiff's return "false," so that the assessment, in May, 1915, of additional tax for 1913, was in time under paragraph E of the Act?

Decision: (1) Act of 1913 says: "Gains or profits and income derived from any source whatever is taxable under the Act." No doubt these commissions were earned by work done and money spent in the earlier years. Plaintiff had earned his pay, and had received part of it; to the rest, he then acquired a right, such as it was, but no determination could then be made how much the rest would be, and in no event could he receive it except in annual installments. The insured might die or policy might be allowed to apse. The commissions of a general life insurance agent derived from renewal premiums or policies obtained by him and accepted in some earlier year were subject to tax under Act of 1913 if such commissions were received any time subsequent to March 1, 1913.

(2) The Federal Income Tax Act, though passed October 3, 1913, could tax income received from March 1st of that year.

(3) A return which omits certain taxable income, even though explanatory note is attached thereto, containing complete information as to the omitted items, is "false," though not "fraudulent" under the 1913 Act.

WOOLNER v. THE UNITED STATES
(U. S. Court of Claims, December, 1877)
(13 Ct. Cls. 355)

Record: Rev. Stat., Sec. 3220. Action to recover tax paid. Judgment for claimant.

Facts: The claimants were distillers of spirits in possession of ten barrels of alcohol in the warehouse of their distillery, upon which there was a tax due of $801. This tax they paid to the collector in July, 1876, and again paid the same tax to the same collector in October of that year. Afterward, they made application to the Commissioner of Internal Revenue for refund and payment back of the amount thus paid in excess of what was legally and justly due. The Commissioner allowed the claim and certified the same to the accounting officers for payment where it met with the disapproval of the comptroller. Consequently, the amount claimed was not paid, and this action was commenced for its recovery.

Question: Did the court have authority to consider defendants' contention that the Commissioner did not have sufficient evidence upon which to found his decision?

Decision: Where the Commissioner of Internal Revenue in a case within the scope of his authority and jurisdiction has ordered a refund of an overpaid tax, a court cannot inquire into the sufficiency of the evidence before him. Claimant was, therefore, held entitled to recover the amount sued for.

WORTH BROS. CO. v. LEDERER, COLLECTOR
(U. S. Supreme Court, March 1, 1920)
(40 Sup. Ct. 282)

Record: Munitions Tax Act. Action to recover taxes paid. Judgment for defendant. Affirmed by Circuit Court of Appeals (258 Fed. 533) and plaintiff brought certiorari. Affirmed.

Facts: During the year 1916, plaintiff made the steel for and did the forging on certain shell bodies under an order from the Midvale Steel Company, to enable the latter company to carry out a contract with the French government for explosive shells. The plaintiff was taxed upon the profits realized from the sale of these forgings.

Question: Was a shell forging "any part of a shell" within the meaning of the Act imposing a tax upon persons manufacturing shells or any part thereof?

Decision: A shell is a definite article, and every element in the aggregation or composition or amalgamation of a shell is a part of it. Manifestly the shell body was not completely manufactured by either of the companies which were engaged in its production, but by the two acting together and each was liable for the profit made. Therefore, the plaintiff cannot recover the taxes imposed upon it as engaged in the manufacture of parts of shells.

WRIGHT v. BLAKESLEE
(U. S. Supreme Court, October, 1879)
(101 U. S. 174)

Record: Acts of June 30, 1864, and June 6, 1872. Action at law to recover succession tax paid under protest. Judgment for defendant and plaintiff brings error. Reversed.

Facts: "A, who died in October, 1846, devised his real estate to his daughter for life, with remainder in fee to her son B," plaintiff in this case, "should he survive her. She died in September, 1865. B was duly notified to make the return required by Section 14 of the Internal Revenue Act of June 30, 1864 * * * and on his refusal to do so was summoned in June, 1867, to appear before the assessor of the proper district. He appeared, and claimed 'that the estate was not liable to assessment for a succession tax.' Thereupon the assessor assessed a tax of one per cent upon the full value of the property, and added thereto a penalty of fifty per cent and costs—all of which B, July 20, 1867, paid under protest to the collector. The Commissioner of Internal Revenue, to whom B appealed, rendered a decision adverse to his claim, July 3, 1873. B brought this action, June 24, 1875, against the collector to recover the amount so paid."

Question: Was plaintiff's suit barred by the statute of limitations under the Act of June 6, 1872?

Decision: "On the 6th of June, 1872, by the fourth section of which it was provided, that all suits for the recovery of any internal tax alleged to have been erroneously assessed or collected, or any penalty claimed to have been collected without authority, should be brought within two years next after the cause of action accrued, and not after; and all claims for refunding any internal tax or penalty should be presented to the commissioner within two years next after the cause of action accrued, and not after; Provided, that actions for claims which had accrued prior to the passage of the Act should be commenced in the courts or presented to the Commissioner within one year from the date of such passage; And provided further, that where a claim should be pending before the Commissioner, the claimant might bring his suit within one year after such decision, and not after, 17 Stat. 257. When this Act was passed the claim in the present case had not been formally presented to the Commissioner, and so did not come within the last proviso, but, for the purpose of presentation to the Commissioner, it was embraced in the first proviso. The parties, therefore, had by the Act, one year to present their claim to the Commissioner; and it was thus presented on the third day of January, 1873, within the time allowed for that purpose. The Commissioner rendered his decision on the third day of July, 1873, and then for the first time, the parties had a right to bring suit against the collector. Then their cause of action first accrued against him. It is manifest, therefore, that the cause of action against the collector was not embraced within either the first or second proviso of the section just cited; and that it stood upon the primary enactment of that section, requiring that suit should be brought within two years next after the cause of action accrued. This would give the plaintiff until the 3rd of July, 1875, to bring this action."

ZONNE v. MINNEAPOLIS SYNDICATE

(U. S. Supreme Court, March 13, 1911)

(220 U. S. 187)

Record: Act of August 5, 1909. Appeal from U. S. Circuit Court of Appeals to review decree sustaining a demurrer to and dismissing a bill filed by a stockholder to restrain the corporation and its officers from complying with the Federal Corporation tax. Reversed.

Facts: The Minneapolis Syndicate was originally organized for and engaged in the business of letting stores and offices in a building owned by it, and collecting and receiving rents therefor. In 1906 the corporation demised and let all of the tracts, lots and parcels of land belonging to it to three men as trustees, for a term of 130 years from January 1, 1907, at an annual rental to be paid by said lessees to said corporation. At that time the corporation caused its articles of incorporation, which had theretofore been those of a corporation organized for profit, to be so amended as to read: "The sole purpose of the corporation shall be to hold the title' to the land in question "now vested in the corporation, subject to a lease thereof for a term of 130 years from January 1, 1907, and, for the convenience of its stockholders, to receive and to distribute among them, from time to time, the rentals that accrue under said lease, and the proceeds of any disposition of said land."

Question: Was the corporation "carrying on or doing business" within the meaning of the Act, thereby becoming liable for the special tax?

Decision: The Minneapolis Syndicate, after the demise of the property and reorganization of the corporation, was not engaged in doing business within the meaning of the Act. Court said, "It had wholly parted with control and management of the property; its sole authority was to hold the title subject to the lease for 130 years, to receive and distribute the rentals which might accrue under the terms of the lease, or the proceeds of any sale of the land if it should be sold. The corporation had practically gone out of business in connection with the property and had disqualified itself by the terms of reorganization from any activity in respect to it."

CADWALADER v. LEDERER, COLLECTOR
(District Court, E. D. Penn., January 24, 1921)
(273 Fed. 879) Affd. 274 Fed. 753

Record: Revenue Act of 1917, excess profits tax. At law. On motion for new trial after verdict for plaintiff, to recover tax. Motion denied.

Facts: "The plaintiff makes a profession of the practice of the law. Speaking in commercial terms, that is his business. * * * The plaintiff made return of the income derived from the practice of his profession, and based on this paid what we have called the excise tax. It happens that he is also executor and trustee of the estate of a deceased friend, and as such received a commission. Of this he also made a return, including it with other income received as income from other sources than his profession. Upon this he admits he should pay what we have called an income tax. The defendant, however, exacted payment, upon this part of his income, on the excise tax basis."

Questions: (1) Is the excess profits tax imposed by the 1917 Act an excise tax or an income tax?

(2) Is a lawyer, who happens to be an executor and trustee of a deceased friend, engaged in the business of acting as a fiduciary and thus liable to an excise tax measured by his income from this source?

(3) Who has the burden of making out the case in a suit to recover an exacted tax payment?

(4) Where the question raised is one of law and the case is to have an appellate experience should a new trial be granted?

Decision: (1) "It happens that the tax is measured by the income return. This is a mere coincidence, and this mere circumstance does not make an income tax of what is really an excise tax, which might be levied in the form of a flat sum. An excise tax is in a very real sense a charge made for the privilege enjoyed. Of course, in the sense of benefits received, this is also true of every tax."

(2) "As the case was tried, it now turns upon the question of law of whether liability to an excise tax depends upon the fact that

the taxpayer was doing what it is the recognized business of some people to do, or whether it depends upon the fact that the taxpayer made a business of doing what he did do. If the latter is the turning point of the case, we see no reason to disturb the verdict." Inasmuch as acting in a fiduciary relationship was out of the taxpayer's line even though it might result in his devoting practically the whole of his time to it, without involving the thought of making it his business, he was not taxed on the income derived therefrom on the excise tax basis.

(3) "The burden was, of course, upon the plaintiff to make out his case."

(4) "We find no trial errors, if the case was submitted upon the right theory, and, as already found, we see no reason to disturb the verdict. We are by no means so clear that the trial theory is the right theory upon which to enter judgment. If the case is to have an appellate experience, the only difference which the judgment entered makes is in the party appellant and appellee. There is no value in this difference which would justify a new trial."

Selected Rulings of
COMMITTEE ON APPEALS AND REVIEW,
Bureau of Internal Revenue
RULING 29-19-622
A. R. R. 7
(C. B. No. 1, p. 13)

Facts: Revenue Act of 1917. The M Company appealed from a ruling of the Income Tax Unit that its business did not fall within the scope of Sec. 209 of the Act. The corporation was engaged in freight forwarding business, having a home and branch offices. On January 1, 1917, its capital stock was 5x dollars and surplus x dollars. Taxable 1917 income was 3x dollars. Accounts receivable on December 31, 1916, were 5x and on December 31, 1917, 19x dollars; accounts payable at these dates were respectively 4x and 22x dollars. Invoices in the record showed that the income was obtained from other sources than commissions, and that the corporation customarily advanced the necessary transportation costs for individuals and concerns with whom it did business.

Decision: It seems that the income of this corporation is largely derived from the employment of capital. The advances made for transportation costs of customers appear to be a necessary part of the business and regularly made. A letter in the record shows that in 1917 the volume of its business was 244x dollars, from which it derived a reported income of 17x dollars. "These facts indicate that the use of capital in this business is not an incidental or minor factor but that the earnings may be attributed largely to the employment of capital." The ruling of the Income Tax Unit denying the company classification as a corporation with nominal capital within the provisions of Sec. 209 of the Revenue Act of 1917, was sustained.

RULING 1-20-665
A. R. R. 9
(C. B. No. 2, p. 293)

Facts: Revenue Act of 1918. The M Company paid on behalf of A and B, owners of most of its stock, the cost of obtaining certain patents on machinery which they invented. The company had the use of the patents as its own without compensation to the inventors. At the time patents were obtained, they being undeveloped were of problematical value, but in 1916 they were developed to prove of considerable value. It does not appear that any formal assignment of the patents had been made to the company. In 1916, in order to increase its capital, the company placed the patents on its books at a value of 2x dollars, and declared a stock dividend. The question was whether this amount could properly be included in invested capital.

Decision: The patents were not specifically paid for in cash, or by the issuance of any stock. They were apparently treated as belonging to the company, but it does not appear that anything was paid by the company other than cost, nor that at the time of supposed acquisition they had any value in excess of cost. Even assuming that they were not formally assigned to the company until 1916, it does not appear that any stock was issued in payment thereof. The stock dividend was no payment for the patent. It was distributed to others as well as to the patentees. Conclusion is that the value of the patents as carried on the books, 2x dollars, cannot be included in invested capital and that the decision of the Income Tax Unit must be affirmed.

RULING 1-20-664
A. R. R. 10
(C. B. No. 2, p. 279)

Facts: Revenue Act of 1918. At a meeting of stockholders of the M Company authorization was given to set aside a sufficient number of shares of its common stock for the benefit of such employees as desired to purchase under the prescribed conditions. A certain number of shares were accordingly set aside, part of which were taken by an officer of the company and the balance by other employees. The officer's stock was charged to his personal account which draws interest. The stock sold to the employees was subscribed for under an agreement which permitted payment in cash, part cash and part deferred payments, or all deferred, subject to conditions that payment of subscriptions should be in weekly installments; deferred payments to bear interest; agreement subject to cancellation, either on request of employee, failure to make payments, or by act of purchaser in attempting to sell his stock or agreement, or by dismissal or resignation of employee prior to the expiration of five years. Upon cancellation the employee was to receive from the company the full amount of all payments with interest and certain percentages of the difference between the subscription and market price of the stock, dependent upon the time held more than one year. Dividends on stock were to be credited to subscriber's account as additional payments, and in the event of cancellation not to be so credited, and subscriber not to be charged with interest on deferred payments. The question was whether the amount of the stock subscribed should be included in invested capital.

Decision: On these facts only so much of the subscription payments as have been actually received by the company may be recognized as invested capital from the date of such receipt. In the case of the officer's stock only so much as cancelled a credit balance in his personal account or was actually paid for by him can be recognized.

RULING 2-20-671

A. R. R. 13.

(C. B. No. 2, p. 78)

Facts: Revenue Act of 1918. An executory contract for purchase and sale of real estate was herein involved. The question was whether income was deemed to have arisen as of the year of the execution of the contract, or as of the subsequent year in which the real estate was conveyed and possession transferred. Section 213 (a) of the Revenue Act of 1918, was applied to the facts. In October, 1917, A entered into an agreement with B for the sale of real estate, to be conveyed March 1, 1918. A small part of the purchase price was paid when the contract was signed. A substantial part was paid at date of conveyance and the balance then secured by a mortgage.

Decision: The courts have held in numerous cases that from the execution of an executory contract of sale and purchase of real estate the vendee is regarded as the owner of the property and is clothed by the courts with the benefits and burdens of ownership and is entitled for most purposes to designate himself as owner. These cases, however, do not approach the question from a commercial standpoint but from the technical equitable doctrine of specific performance. To the question of the realization of gain or loss through the sale of real estate it is believed that different principles are applicable, and that the question should be decided from a commercial standpoint. During the period between October, 1917, and March 1, 1918, A, the vendor, had the legal title, the right of possession, and the right to the rents and profits which might arise out of this property. It is to be noted that an action for specific performance would not have put the vendee in possession during 1917, because he was not under the contract entitled to possession; nor was any negotiable instrument executed and delivered during 1917. Under these circumstances commercial usage does not sanction the conclusion that a substitution of assets had taken place prior to 1918, and the government is not warranted in treating the whole profit as realized. The committee, therefore, recommends that the income arising out of this transaction be taxable as for the year 1918 under the income tax and not for the year 1917 under the income and possibly the excess profits tax. The advance payment is to be regarded as the return of capital and assuming this to be less than the cost, no part of it is subject to income or profits tax for the year 1917. No opinion is expressed as to the result if the taxpayer receives negotiable instruments commercially equivalent to cash in a year prior to the year in which possession was to be delivered and deed was to pass.

RULING 3-20-680

A. R. R. 18

(C. B. No. 2, p. 50)

Facts: Revenue Act of 1918. Because of the following conditions peculiar to the tobacco industry, tobacco companies have made inventories on the average cash method, i. e., by a monthly averaging of the entire stock on hand.

(1) Method of purchasing in small lots of varying quantity and quality at widely fluctuating prices.

(2) Necessity of regrading and sorting purchases according to quality, color, texture, weight, crop, length and breadth of leaf, etc.

(3) Long period of time during which raw material must be held.

(4) Fact that crops of different years and from different localities vary in quality, and that crops of different years and different localities must be blended in varying proportions to get proper flavor and uniform product.

(5) Fact that oldest purchases are not and can not be used first because of this necessity for blending.

(6) Fact that product must be sold in containers, the size of which is regulated by statute, at a uniform price.

Decision: "These and other conditions make it impossible to apply ordinary methods of valuing the inventory of raw material. The widespread and long continued use of the average cost method is evidence that the industry has been unable to devise one which is better. In view of this peculiar combination of circumstances and in accordance with the principle of Art. 1583, which states, 'In any industry in which the usual rules for computation of cost of production are inapplicable, costs may be approximated upon such basis as may be reasonable and in conformity with established trade practice in the particular industry,' the method now used by the tobacco companies in question for inventorying raw materials, as represented to the Bureau, is approved for income tax purposes. The method followed, as understood by the committee, is an average cost method and not an average cost or market method. Accordingly, if the market should be below the average cost at the close of a given year, the average cost shall be the basis of valuation and not the lower market price. Companies adopting average cost methods of inventorying for income tax purposes should be required to adhere to that method in future years. For the reason, therefore, that in the case of the tobacco industry it has been demonstrated that no method more nearly approaching theoretical accuracy than the average cost method is practically possible, the committee recommends that this method of taking inventories of raw material in the tobacco industry should be recognized and permitted."

RULING 5-20-722
A. R. R. 19
(C. B. No. 2, p. 298)

Facts: Revenue Act of 1917. The firm of A was engaged in the produce commission business, but a proportion of its income was derived from buying produce outright and selling it for its own account. The firm wished to be assessed under Sec. 209 of the Act as a business having only a nominal capital. It appeared certain from its balance sheets that the income of the firm was derived about evenly from commissions on sales of produce belonging to others and from profits on sales of produce purchased for its own account. The firm enjoyed a substantial credit as well.

Decision: The facts, so far as disclosed, indicated that the firm employed a substantial amount of capital in its business, and, therefore, it was not entitled to consideration as a business employing only nominal capital.

RULING 7-20-736
A. R. R. 24
(C. B. No. 2, p. 16)

Facts: Revenue Acts of 1917 and 1918. The M Corporation conducted a commercial school with resident and home study instruction departments. The principal owners gave all of their time and attention to the preparation of courses, etc., and employed a number of teachers and clerks to assist them. Capital employed consists of furniture and fixtures and an amount of cash sufficient to provide for salaries of teachers and clerks, the amount of capital being nominal as compared to its gross income. The company appealed from the action of the Unit in holding it a non-personal service corporation.

Decision: It is expressly provided that business concerns which render professional or personal service shall not be taken out of the class of personal service corporations merely because of the size of their capital if the employment of such capital is necessitated by delay in the receipt of fees, etc., or if the fund is wholly or mainly used as a fund from which to advance salaries, etc., or to provide office furniture, accommodations and equipment. Therefore, the corporation was entitled to be classed as a personal service corporation.

RULING 9-20-773
A. R. R. 27
(C. B. No. 2, p. 139)

Facts: Revenue Act of 1918. Representatives of various steamship companies engaged in bulk transportation of ore, grain, coal and stone upon the Great Lakes, appealed from a decision of the Unit fixing 2 per cent as the rate of depreciation allowable upon steamships engaged in this practice. Disinterested parties entirely familiar with conditions concurred in the view that 33 years would probably be the life of such vessels without rebuilding. During the hearing it was urged that because of the history of lake transportation and the evidence that practically in cycles of 10 years a complete revolution in types of vessels utilized for this traffic has been brought about, additional allowance should be recognized in 1918 and subsequent years on account of presumed obsolescence.

Decision: 3 per cent is a reasonable allowance for depreciation of bulk freight steamships on the Great Lakes. Obsolescence should be limited to those cases where it can be shown that a type of vessel has been developed so much more economical than existing types, that no other than the new type will be built in future, and that a sufficient number of the new types to meet traffic requirements will be built within a certain definite period.

RULING 9-20-764
A. R. R. 33
(C. B. No. 2, p. 30)

Facts: Revenue Act of 1918. A appealed from the action of the Income Tax Unit in assessing a tax on the profit he made in 1916 of the sale of stock of the M Company. The profit was based on the market quotations on the stock as at March 1, 1913. The contention of A was that the book value of said stock on March 1, 1913, was much in excess of the market quotations and should be utilized as the basis for determining the profit.

Decision: The committee on appeal and review states that it is unable to agree with this contention. In sustaining the action of the Income Tax Unit the committee refers to T. D. 2979 amending Art. 102 of Regulations 50, relative to the method of computing the

fair average value of capital stock of insurance companies, wherein
it is stated that such fair average value for capital stock tax purposes
must not be confused with the market value of the shares where
it may be necessary to determine such value under other provisions
of the revenue laws. Ample authority, it is stated, can be found
to support the distinction between the value of capital stock or capital
assets of a company and the valuation of the shares owned by the
shareholders, quoting People v. Coleman, 27 N. E. 818. The question at issue, the committee states, is not the value of the capital
assets of the M Company, but the value of the shares held by A.
The following is the committee's conclusion: "The committee is
clearly of the opinion that, given a free and broad market, shares of
stock in a corporation were worth what they would bring, and that
the best evidence of what they would bring is the price they actually
did bring when offered for sale and sold upon the stock exchange.
M Company stock was freely dealt in before, on and after March
1, 1913, and the quotations as of that date are clearly the best evidence of the value of the shares on that date. The committee,
therefore, recommended that the action of the Unit in determining
profit on the basis of market quotations instead of book values be
sustained."

RULING 10-20-783

A. R. R. 36

(C. B. No. 2, p. 269)

Facts: Revenue Act of 1918. The question here under consideration was the determination of the war profits credit under Sec.
311 (c) (2) of the Act, where the company had no prewar period.
It is provided therein that the war profits credit, where the taxpayer was not in business during the whole of at least one calendar
year during the prewar period, should be $3,000 plus an amount
equal to the same percentage of the invested capital for the taxable
year as the average percentage of net income to invested capital
for the prewar period, of corporations engaged in a trade or business
of the same general class as the taxpayer; but such amount in no
case to be less than 10 per cent of the invested capital of the taxpayer for the taxable year. It there provided that "such average
percentage shall be determined by the commissioner on the basis
of data contained in returns made under Title II of the Revenue Act

of 1917, and the average known as the median shall be used." The M Company claimed that inequity and hardship was imposed on it through the application of the "median," and requested the Commissioner to determine its tax under the provisions of Sec. 328, because the median, as determined, allowed it a war profits credit of slightly in excess of 10 per cent. It was claimed this was not a representative percentage earned by corporations in the same general class of business during the prewar period. The committee states that the taxpayer had made an independent investigation, apparently taking into consideration only a few concerns similarly situated and claims these concerns earned over 20 per cent during the prewar period. It is said the bureau has computed the median by using the returns of all corporations in the same general class of business as that conducted by the M company.

Decision: Art. 783 of Regulations 45, interpreting Sec. 328 (supra) was quoted in part, and attention was called to the fact that Sec. 327 of the 1918 Act provides that in certain cases the tax shall be determined as provided in Sec. 328. It was pointed out, however, that in the instant case it could not be said that the Commissioner is unable to determine the invested capital, or that the taxpayer is a foreign corporation, or that a mixed aggregate of tangibles and intangibles has been paid in for stock, etc. Neither could it be said, the opinion holds, that the tax if determined without the benefit of this section would, owing to abnormal conditions affecting the capital or income of the corporation, work an exceptional hardship evidenced by a gross disproportion between the tax computed without the benefit of Sec. 327 and the tax computed by reference to representative corporations as provided in Sec. 328. Sec. 327, the committee says, does not apply to any case in which the tax is high merely because the corporation earned within the taxable year a high rate of profit upon a normal invested capital. The following is the committee's conclusion: "After analyzing the situation presented in the instant case the committee is of the opinion and recommends (1) that the median established as provided by law and published by the bureau be considered final and that the taxpayer is not entitled to consideration under the provisions of Sec. 328 of the state; (2) that there is no warrant in law or the regulations which authorizes the Commissioner to allow a larger percentage in this class of cases than that established by the median for the purposes of computing the war profits credit; and that (3) the instant case does not fall within any class of cases enumerated in Sec. 327, therefore, relief cannot be granted under Sec. 328."

Comment: The contents of the "median" above referred to, wherein average percentages of prewar income to prewar invested capital of general classes of corporations, grouped as to the trades or businesses, as provided for in Sec. 311 (c) (2) of the 1918 Revenue Act are given, was published in full in Commerce Clearing House Bulletin No. 17, dated December 4, 1919.

RULING 16-20-862
A. R. R. 45
(C. B. No. 2, p. 141)

Facts: Revenue Act of 1918, involving depreciation allowance under Sec. 214 (a) as interpreted by Art. 165 of Regulations 45. The facts are not stated in the ruling of the committee.

Decision: When delicate machinery designed for the manufacture of a certain product is used in manufacturing a product of much coarser materials for which use it is not fitted, and is operated at a heavy overload of its normal capacity, the owner is entitled to deduct from gross income an amount representing extraordinary depreciation.

RULING 13-20-802
A. R. R. 46
(C. B. No. 2, p. 17)

Facts: Revenue Act of 1918. The question involved was whether the corporation taxpayer was a personal service corporation, as defined in Sec. 200, of the 1918 Revenue Act, as interpreted by Art. 1523 of Regulation 45. The case comes to the Committee on Appeals and Reviews on an appeal of the M Corporation from a ruling of the Internal Revenue Bureau that the appellant is not a personal service corporation. This ruling was made upon a claim for abatement of capital stock tax for the taxable year ending June 30, 1919, in rejecting the claim. Among the corporations exempted by the statute from the capita lstock are personal service corporations.

The corporation in question is engaged in the business of insurance brokers and average adjusters dealing principally with questions relating to marine insurance. The corporation was formed by the consolidation of several firms of insurance brokers and adjusters. Each of the firms liquidated its prior business and contributed to the new corporation only the services of its partners and employees and the good will of its clients. Other than small amounts of office furniture none of these firms contributed any capital or tangible assets. To provide funds for expenses and advances to directors in anticipation of earnings preferred stock was issued and taken at par by the individual directors, the amount thereof being 2x dollars. In addition to this preferred stock there was outstanding on March 31, 1917, and March 31, 1918, approximately 3x dollars of common stock. This common stock was issued to members of the constituent firms and represented no tangible property and bore no relation whatever to any estimated value of good will, but was issued for an arbitrary amount as a basis for the apportionment of future earnings The articles of incorporation provide that no common stock shall be held by any one who is not an officer, director or employee of the corporation actively engaged in its services. As holders of common stock die or retire from active service their stock is turned back into the treasury, resulting in a decrease of outstanding common stock. As employees are promoted and made directors, shares of stock are allocated to them by the board of directors in recognition of services without other consideration which results in an increase in stock outstanding. Over 95 per cent of the gross income for each of the three fiscal years ended March 31, 1917, 1918 and 1919, was earned from commissions and adjustment fees On account of the fact that the principal business is marine insurance the company has on hand at all times large cash balances which actually belong to the insurance companies or clients for whom it acts. Its balance sheet of March 31, 1918, shows accounts receivable 6x dollars, cash 24x dollars, and accounts payable of 40x dollars. No substantial amount of capital is employed to lend to customers or to buy or carry goods on its own account, or to buy insurance for its clients, nor does it to any substantial extent finance or carry the accounts of its clients or customers. On the hearing of this case it was stated that all of the directors are daily actively engaged in the company's business.

Decision: It was stated in the opinion that the business being that of insurance brokerage and average adjustment, the latter a rather intricate branch of marine insurance, the corporation comes squarely within the definition of Art. 1523, Regulation 45, in that its income of 95 per cent thereof "is derived from a profession or business (a) which consists principally in rendering personal service (b) the earnings of which are to be ascribed primarily to the activities of the principal owners or stockholders, and (c) in which the employment of capital is not necessary or is only incidental." It appears, however, that some of the branches of the corporation engaged in the same character of business were separately incorporated, and the profits of these branches appear upon the parent corporation's return as "dividends received." Attention is called to Art. 1524 of Regulations 45 which provides that a corporation cannot be regarded as a personal service corporation if another corporation owns or controls substantially all of its stock. If literally construed this would prevent the subsidiary corporations from being classed as personal service corporations and would require their earnings to be taxed at the graduated excess profits tax rates, although the subsidiaries have little or no invested capital. Where the subsidiary is owned or controlled by a corporation subject to excess profits tax, the opinion states, then the reason for the rule laid down in Art. 1524 is obvious. No sound reason in fact appears where all of the group, parent as well as subsidiary, are engaged in the rendering of personal service, and the corporate entity is merely a legal fiction. The committee pointed out that Art. 1524 inferentially at least recognized in its phraseology that two personal service corporations may be owned by the same interests without taking either out of the classification of personal service corporations.

It was recommended that the next to the last sentence of Art. 1524 be amended to read as fol ows: "A corporation can not be considered a personal service corporation when another corporation (not itself a personal service corporation) owns or controls substantially all of its stock and of the stock of another corporation (not itself a personal service corporation) forming part of the same business enterprise is owned or controlled by the same interests—," and that the M corporation be classed as a personal service corporation under the Act of 1918, and that it be taxed at the 8 per cent rate for 1917.

Comment: Pursuant to this recommendation Art. 1524 was amended as suggested and the article as revised is contained in Regulations 45 (1920 Edition) promulgated on January 28, 1921.

RULING 17-20-879

A. R. R. 69

(C. B. No. 2, p. 28)

Facts: Revenue Act of 1918. The M Company was organized by A and B to take over certain investments owned by them, A holding about two-thirds and B one-third of the stock. Among the assets transferred to this company in exchange for its stock were certain shares in the N Company and the O Company. Subsequently the last named concerns were consolidated into a single corporation and the stock in these companies held by the M Company was exchanged for shares in the new corporation. Later A and B decided to liquidate the M Company and accordingly distributed to the stockholders the assets capable of segregation and distribution.

The sole question is whether or not the distribution so made is governed by the decision of the Supreme Court in Lynch v. Turrish (247 U. S. 221; T. D. 2729) or by the decision of the same court in Lynch v. Hornby (247 U. S. 339; T. D. 2731). In the former case the court held that a final liquidation dividend including no earnings accrued since March 1, 1913, was not subject to tax, while in the latter case it was held that a dividend distributed by a going concern was subject to tax irrespective of when the profits distributed were earned.

Decision: Even though the extreme view of the decision in the Turrish case be taken, that a liquidation dividend, whether final or not, was not taxable, it does not appear in the instant case that there was any formal vote of the stockholders declaring their intention to liquidate, and the balance sheets of the company from 1914 to 1918 show the original capital of the company to be unimpaired. The question as to which of the above court decisions governed the case under advisement had been submitted to the Solicitor;

he advised the Income Tax Unit that the only point definitely decided in the Turrish case was that a final liquidation dividend which included no earnings accrued since March 1, 1913, was not subject to income tax, and that under the circumstances the instant case is controlled by the Hornby case decision, since the dividend was not claimed to have been a final liquidating dividend and the balance sheets of the M Company from 1914 to 1918 showed the original capital assets unimpaired. "While the purpose of the stockholders may have been to liquidate, the committee is constrained to the view taken by the solicitor that the facts in the case do not meet the test laid down in the case of Lynch v. Turrish, and that the dividends distributed were subject to tax."

RULING 17-20-882
A. R. R. 70
(C. B. No. 2, p. 287)

Facts: Revenue Act of 1917. "The principal stockholder of a close corporation invented a certain article and turned over to the corporation his rights to the invention. After some litigation, a patent was granted to the inventor who turned it over to the corporation without consideration. The corporation was engaged in the manufacture and sale of the article both before and since the patent was issued." The question presented is whether the value of the patent may be included by the corporation in its invested capital for 1917.

Decision: "Sec. 207 of the Revenue Act of 1917, defining invested capital, provides for three classes of such capital, following the earlier Act of March 3, 1917." These three classes are (a) actual cash paid in, (b) tangible property paid in for stock or shares, (c) paid in or earned surplus. The committee reviews the earlier Act of March 3, 1917, and concludes therefrom that it was the intention of Congress to classify patents as tangible property. The Revenue Act of 1917 provides that tangible property under class (b) above may be included in invested capital when turned in for stock, "but this does not necessarily preclude the recognition of actual value of patents turned n as paid in surplus" as provided in class (c) above. The amount recognized as paid in surplus was the value of the invention at the time it was turned over to the company, and not its value when letters patent were issued. "The committee is, therefore, of the opinion that under the Revenue Act of 1917, the corporation would be entitled upon establishing the value of the patent turned over to the company without consideration, to include such value as invested capital."

RULING 18-20-906
A. R. R. 71
(C. B. No. 2, p. 290)

Facts: Revenue Act of 1918. The question arises under Sec. 326 of the 'Act whether appreciation can in any event be regarded as a part of earned surplus and therefore offset depreciation in the value of assets through wear, tear, and exhaustion. A corporation owns patents covering certain inventions made by its employees. The cost of securing the patents and the salaries of the employees whose inventions were patented were paid by the corporation and charged to expense account.

Decision: "Appreciation is in no event a part of earned surplus and cannot offset depreciation in the value of assets through wear, tear and exhaustion. Depreciation must first be figured in order to determine true earned surplus. In other words, earned surplus is believed to consist of realized gains or profits, and while such realized gains or profits must be reduced by any depreciation in value through use or exhaustion of the assets in which they are invested, any appreciation in value of those assets which is not yet realized can not be taken into consideration for the purpose of offsetting such decrease. The corporation may not include in its invested capital any amount representing either the cost of the patents or appreciation in their value."

RULING 19-20-919
A. R. R. 93
(C. B. No. 2, p. 142)

Facts: Revenue Act of 1917. M "corporation was compelled by operation of law to cease manufacturing operations in 1917. Under the ruling of the office, distilling propert'es which have not been sold and the value of which has been reduced by reason of the compulsory abandonment of their operations, take a reasonable allowance for exhaustion or obsolescence upon a proper showing of facts. The M Company, under this ruling, claimed a loss which after having been deducted left an apparent remaining value of 150x dollars." It was later found by the committee that sufficient depreciation had not been charged on certain items of the property in previous years, and upon a readjustment placed the depreciated value as of December 31, 1917, at 275x dollars. "Holding the company to the estimated residual value of 150x dollars, the Unit found that the loss was 125x dollars, leaving a part of the original claim to be disallowed. The plant was actually sold in 1918 for 25x dollars. The question before the committee was whether the company should be held to its estimate of 150x dollars on the value of the plant at the close of 1917.

Decision: The actual sale in 1918 for 25x dollars conclusively establishes that the estimate of 150x dollars was too high and the committee recommended that the loss as claimed be allowed in full.

RULING 19-20-918

A. R. R. 96

(C. B. No. 2, p. 129)

Facts: Revenue Act of 1917. A accepted a position in a different part of the country which made it necessary for him to sell his residence and move away. He suffered a loss from the sale and claimed it as a loss incurred in business under Sec. 5, par. (9) of the Act of 1917.

Decision: "Claim for this deduction is made on the ground that the loss 's a business loss and, therefore, not limited by the provisions of the Revenue Act of 1917 holding that losses not incurred in trade or business may be allowed only to the extent that there are incidental profits from which to deduct them." The loss resulting from sale of residence under the circumstances is not a loss "* * * actually sustained during the year incurred in business or trade," and the committee, "therefore, recommends that the action of the Unit in disallowing the loss be sustained."

RULING 19-20-920
A R. R. 97
(C. B. No. 2, p. 158)

Facts: Revenue Act of 1917. In 1915 the air shaft of M Company's mine caved in, causing the destruction of a fan, boiler, and drum. "The company did not charge off the loss in 1915 because it had no net income during that year, but in 1917 restored the equipment and claims the cost to be merely a replacement" under Sec. 215 of the Act of 1917.

Decision: "* * * The company clearly suffered a loss from casualty in 1915 which it doubtless would have charged off had it had income against which to charge it, and which it should now be required to charge off as of 1915. Therefore, the action of the Unit, in disallowing the amount of expenditures for replacement charged to expense in 1917, appears correct."

RULING 20-20-934
A. R. R. 98
(C. B. No. 2, p. 105)

Facts: Revenue Act of 1918, "* * * Sometime prior to November, 1915, B, a stockholder, director, and officer of the M Company, invented a certain device and * * * prepared drawings and working models and caused to be made payments covering government filing fees, attorneys' fees, traveling expenses to and from Washington, all of which was made in the interest of this corporation and leading up to his securing a patent on his invention, which was later transferred to the corporation for a nominal sum. The amounts expended by the corporation in securing this patent and deducted in its return for 1917, totaled 2x dollars * * *." This the company now concedes should be charged to capital account. An additional amount of x dollars was expended by the corporation in 1917, after it had acquired the patent, in defending its right, title and interest against infringement by other manufacturers. The question arises under Secs. 214 and 234 of the 1918 law, whether the last stated item should be allowed as a necessary operation expense of the corporation or should be capitalized.

Decision: "* * * The amounts expended by this corporation after it secured the patent are not a part of the cost of the prop-

erty for the reason that such amounts do not add to or prolong the
life of the property in question and cannot be considered as an
improvement or betterment.   The amount so expended having none
of the elements of improvement or betterment can not be returned
to the corporation through depreciation. * * * Only such
amounts as represent the actual cost of this patent can be deducted
by way of depreciation annually by this corporation.   The title
and ownership of the patent was in the corporation and the amounts
expended were not made in perfecting its title to the patent already
owned and used by the company.   The conclusion of the committee
is that the amounts expended by the corporation * * * after
the patent had been secured by B and had been transferred to the
corporation, constitute necessary operating expenses and should not
be capitalized.   In view of the foregoing the committee recommends
that the item of x dollars should be allowed as a necessary operating
expense."

RULING 21-20-963

A. R. R. 102

(C. B. No. 2, p. 277)

Facts: Revenue Act of 1917.   M Company is a corporation,
all of the stock of which was owned by three stockholders, A. B.
C.   During the lifetime of these stockholders no distribution of
profits was made and the earnings were allowed to accumulate from
year to year.   At the death of A, in 1907, the board of directors
passed a resolution ordering the reserve fund to be prorated and
credited to the deposit accounts of the three principal stockholders.
None of these profits was withdrawn; the business proceeded as
before and the profits were allowed again to accumulate until 1909,
when B died, and the same procedure was taken as in 1907; although
it does not appear in the record that there was any formal action on
the part of the directors, nor is the rate of the division nor the total
amount divided, shown.   From the inception of the business until
the present day, no dividend has been declared nor have any of the
profits been withdrawn from the business or segregated from the
surplus of the company except as hereinbefore stated; but against
the accounts credited as above, comparatively small charges have
been made from time to time to cover living expenses of two of
these stockholders.   No notes were issued for these credits or

interest charged thereon. Credit had been obtained from banks upon the strength of these credits. The question before the committee was whether the above described credits could be considered as invested capital under Sec. 207 of the Revenue Act of 1917, which provides:

"* * * As used in this title 'invested capital' does not include money or other property borrowed, and means, subject to the above limitations: (a) In the case of a corporation or partnership: (1) Actual cash paid in, * * * and (3) paid in or earned surplus and undivided profits used or employed in the business, * * *."

Decision: "Under Sec. 207, as above quoted, these credits are, in law, obviously either borrowed money or earned surplus and undivided profits. The very purpose for which and the circumstances under which they were created excludes them from consideration as 'surplus and undivided profits.' It was to determine exactly the equities of these stockholders in the profits or surplus, until that time undivided, that these credits were established." The claimant admitted that the rights of the three stockholders would be asserted as against the other stockholders but not against the general creditors. "That being true, they form no part at all of the 'surplus' of the corporation, and the alternative that they are borrowed money can not be escaped. These credits unquestionably rank, in law, with the claims of other general creditors; even though by the good faith and honor of these three stockholders, they would be voluntarily deferred until the claims of the other general creditors had been liquidated in full." These credits were a direct and fixed obligation of the corporation. They do not have the same status "among the corporation's liabilities as would have been the case had they, by formal action of the board been converted into capital stock and certificates issued therefor, or had the interested stockholders waived all proprietary rights to them and thus actually contributed them to surplus." The interpretation placed upon the above quoted section of the 1917 Act is in accordance with the interpretation given by Art. 813, Reg. 45. "Therefore, the committee is of the opinion that the Income Tax Unit was correct in disallowing as invested capital this amount."

RULING 20-20-945

A. R. R. 110

(C. B. No. 2, p. 303)

Facts: Revenue Act of 1917. N corporation was organized in 1909 with an authorized capital stock of 10x dollars fully paid in, of which 4x dollars is represented by cash and 6x dollars by working models, turned in by A, president of the corporation, for which he received stock in that amount. The corporation, since the date of its organization, has been engaged in the manufacture of machinery, and on January 1, 1917, it had an accumulated surplus of 85x dollars and capital stock of 10x dollars or a total capital as shown on the return for 1917 of 95x dollars. The patterns and patents turned over to N company by A were formerly owned by the M company and before its dissolution were carried on its books at valuation of 16x dollars and 45x dollars respectively. No part of the good will or patents of M company is represented in the capitalization of N company. The question is whether N company should be assessed under provisions of Secs. 201 and 207 of the Revenue Act of 1917 or should it be entitled to assessment under the provisions of Sec. 210.

Decision: N corporation has capital which is earning income but which cannot be used in the computation of its invested capital for 1917 under the statutory provisions of Sec. 207. Art. 52 of Reg. 41, provides among other things, that a claim for assessment under the provisions of Sec. 210 may arise in cases where "long established business concerns, which by reason of ultraconservative accounting or the form and manner of their organization would, through the operation of Sec. 207, be placed at a serious disadvantage in competing with representative concerns in a like or similar trade or business." In view of the foregoing it was held that N corporation should have been taxed under Sec. 210.

RULING 21-20-953

A. R. R. 113

(C. B. No. 2, p. 114)

Facts: Revenue Act of 1918. A, the administrator of an estate, had taken as a deduction from gross income of B's estate, interest which had accrued on notes of the decedent. Said accrued interest had been deducted from the decedent's estate in determining the amount of gross estate.· The question arose whether such accrued interest was an allowable deduction under Sec. 214 (a) of the Act of 1918.

Decision: "* * * If decedent did not keep his accounts upon some basis other than that of actual receipts and disbursements the amount of interest paid by the administrator of the estate of B was properly deductible from the income received by the administrator. Attention is called, however, to the fact that only the accrued interest on outstanding obligations may be deducted, and where interest upon an old note has been capitalized by giving a new note, representing the aggregate of the old note with interest accrued, only the amount of interest accrued upon the new note can be deducted, the new note representing payment of both principal and interest of the old. Upon the note originally for 5x dollars, covering which, with accrued interest of 2x dollars a new note for 7x dollars was given, only the interest accrued on the new note is an allowable deduction."

RULING 21-20-962

A. R. R. 116

(C. B. No. 2, p. 270)

Facts: Revenue Act of 1917. A "copartnership transferred its assets to the O Company and received in payment therefor debenture bonds in the amount of 10x dollars, payable in 30 years, bearing interest at the rate of 6 per cent per annum. The copartnership also received other good and valuable consideration in the form of common stock in the amount of 20x dollars, which was issued against good will, trade marks, etc. The debenture bonds issued in payment for the assets of the copartnership were delivered to the partners pro rata. The common stock issued was distributed to the partners in the same ratio as the bonds. The debenture bonds were issued in payment for the tangible assets of the copartnership * * * and the common stock was issued in payment for good will, trade mark, etc." The question arose whether the above described debenture bonds constituted borrowed money as used in Sec. 207 of the Revenue Act of 1917 and Art. 44 (b) of Reg. 41.

Decision: "In general, it might be said that it is always a question of fact whether a given amount paid or left in the business constitutes borrowed capital or paid in surplus. The general principle is that if interest is paid, or is to be paid, on any such amount, or if the stockholders or officers' right to repayment of any such amount ranks with or before that of general creditors, the amount so left with the corporation must be treated as borrowed capital. In the instant case, the bonds were issued in payment for property, interest has been regularly paid each year and has been deducted by the corporation in computing its net income for each year up to and including 1916, but no interest deduction on account of this indebtedness was claimed for 1917, even though the corporation actually paid 6 per cent on the outstanding debenture bonds. * * * The intent of the parties in this case was truly reflected in the form in which they organized their corporate business. They chose to organize and carry it on by creating a corporate debt to be repaid at a future date, plus a fixed rate of interest, evidenced by debenture bonds secured by a lien on corporate assets subordinate to claims of its general creditors. Bondholders have different rights or interests in corporate business and assets than would preferred stockholders. True, preferred stock might have been issued in lieu thereof,' as contended by the claimant, "but the parties elected otherwise, and they are bound by their act so long as the bonds in question are outstanding. The subordination of the lien of the bonds to claims of general creditors is not enough to render the bonds the equivalent of preferred stock. * * * The bonds in question are an obligation of the corporation to pay and in the judgment of the committee should be classed as 'borrowed capital'."

RULING 22-20-967
A. R. R. 126
(C. B. No. 2, p. 44)

Facts: Revenue Act of 1917. "The facts appear to be that the taxpayer individually built and owned a railroad which was constructed for the sole purpose of carrying the product of the taxpayer's mills to stations on other roads for distribution. The State Railroad Commission required the incorporation of this road, which was done in 1914. The appraised value of the property as of March

1, 1913, was 30x dollars, the cost of additions between that date and the date of incorporation being 12x dollars, making a total of 42x dollars. Against this amount bonds were issued to the amount of 20x dollars, the total proceeds being received by A, reducing his investment on the above basis to 22x dollars. Against this the commission permitted the issuance of stock in the amount of 30x dollars. The taxpayer now contends that at the time of incorporation the property was worth the 30x dollars for which it was incorporated, and that profit, if any, was made in 1914 at the time of incorporation and a loss suffered when the stock of the railroad was sold in 1917 for 27x dollars." The law involved in determining the question is Sec. 202 of the Revenue Act of 1917.

Decision: "The Unit has ignored the possibility of accretion in value of these assets between March 1, 1913, and the date of incorporation. Whatever accretion there may have been in these values would clearly, under the rulings of the office, be taxable profit when converted into stock of the corporation, since the stock would be deemed to be at least equal in value to the assets behind it. It is further contended by the taxpayer that under numerous decisions of the office where property is exchanged for stock the stock will be deemed to be worth its par value in the absence of evidence to the contrary. Had there been no appraisal of the property, the committee is of the opinion that this position would have been well taken and that the burden of proof would have been on the government to show that the stock was worth less than its par value, had the taxpayer claimed it to be of value equal to or greater than par. However, the appraisal about that time appears to establish that the property turned over to the corporation was worth less than the par value of the stock received. Undoubtedly that appraisal would have been recognized by the Unit in 1914 as establishing the fact that no profit was then realized by the taxpayer had he presented such claim during that year. The committee is therefore of the opinion that in the absence of evidence conclusively proving that at the time the property was turned over to the corporation in 1914 it was of greater value than indicated by the appraisal as of March 1, 1913, no profit can be deemed to have been made in 1914, and consequently that the difference between the value of the stock at that time so determined and the sale price of 1917 is taxable profit in the latter year."

RULING 23-20-982
A. R. R. 140
(C. B. No. 2, p. 55)

Facts: Revenue Act of 1918. A and Company, a partnership, was engaged in the wholesale liquor and cigar business. For inventory purposes, A and Company had marked up certain stocks on hand so as to include "carrying charges," and increased value due to ageing. These increases were not represented by actual disbursments nor had they ever been accrued and set up on the books of the company as a liability. In fact, the amounts had never been determined. The question before the committee is whether the valuation of the inventories by the above methods was allowable under Sec. 203 of the Revenue Act of 1918.

Decision: "If the actual accrued charges which must eventually be paid by the firm, either directly, or indirectly through credits to customers, can be accurately determined and applied to the liquor actually in stock at any specific date, such charges, if set up on the books as an existing liability, form proper additions to the cost price of the liquor then on hand; but this additional value must be determined by charges actually paid or to be paid and cannot be arrived at by the application of any empirical formula and cannot in any way include interest except on money actually borrowed for the purpose of carrying the liquor, nor any appreciation in value of the liquor through ageing."

RULING 26-20-1028
A. R. R. 155
(C. B. No. 2, p. 155)

Facts: Revenue Act of 1918. The O Company is a corporation manufacturing patent flours. It appears that in 1918 it sold large quantities of these flours, which, during war, were manufactured largely from substitutes. Upon the cessation of hostilities the Food Administration abolished the regulations covering the use of such substitutes, and as other products became available the public refused to purchase this flour. The taxpayer thereupon took back the stock which was in the hands of its jobbers. O Company claimed this loss against business of 1918.

Decision: Held that any loss sustained by it through the return of goods in 1919 which had been sold in 1918 is a loss of the year in which the goods were returned and not of the year in which the sales were made. The goods were actually sold and delivered to the consignees in 1918, and were retained by them throughout that year, so that there could have been no loss in that year "resulting from any material reduction of the value of the inventory" because such goods were not included in the inventory on December 31, 1918.

RULING 28-20-1064
A. R. R. 161
(C. B. No. 3, p. 345)

Facts: Revenue Act of 1917. M & Company, a corporation, claim 15x dollars as paid-in surplus in the determination of the corporation's invested capital for the purpose of adjusting excess profits tax. M & Company organized in 1911 as a consolidation of two pre-existing companies. Among other assets taken over were two improved pieces of real estate, the values of which are the basis of the present claim. At time of organization these assets were set up on the books at 3x dollars and 16x dollars. Of these amounts 1x dollars and 5x dollars represented the cost of the lots. A year later these lots, exclusive of improvement, were appraised and found to be 4x dollars and 17x dollars. The Unit rejected this claim on the theory that the appraisal, in order to be valid, must have been made on the exact date of conveyance.

Decision: In the opinion of the committee this is too narrow a construction. Evidence was produced to show that between January 1, 1911, date of transfer, and the date of this appraisal there was no appreciable increase in the value of real estate in the locality. The properties clearly had a value in excess of that at which they were taken on to the books of the corporation in consolidation, and it has been abundantly established to the satisfaction of the committee that the real estate had a value not less than 15x dollars in excess of the figure at which it was taken over. It

accordingly recommends that the claim of the corporation to an
addition of 15x dollars to its invested capital as paid in surplus be
allowed.

RULING 28-20-1063

A. R. R. 167

(C. B. No. 3, p. 333)

Facts: Revenue Act of 1918. The M Company contended
that a subscription agreement for the purchase of stock in a corporation by its officers and employees may be considered as tangible
property and included in invested capital, upon authority of Art.
833, Reg. 45, which holds that enforceable notes or other evidences
of indebtedness, either interest bearing or non-interest bearing, of
the subscriber for stock may be so considered.

Decision: So far as stock issued under subscription agreements
is concerned, the conclusion in A. R. R. 10 should stand, i. e., only
so much as an officer received credit for or so much as was actually
paid in by him will be recognized as invested capital, but a straight-
out unconditional subscription, charged to the account of the president, bearing interest and subsequently converted into a note, should
be recognized as invested capital under the provision of Art. 833.

RULING 28-20-1050

A. R. R. 173

(C. B. No. 3, p. 58)

Facts: Act of October 3, 1913, and Revenue Act of 1916.
A and others secured leases on land. Subsequently, and prior to
March 1, 1913, they entered into a contract with B under the conditions of which 3,000 acres of the land were to be assigned to B
under the so-called checkerboard plan and under which B obligated
himself in consideration of such assignment to define and develop
the field. If oil or gas was not found in the first well drilled to a
depth of 1,200 feet, B had the option of abandoning the contract.
The contention of the taxpayers is that since the defining and proving
of B's 3,000 acres, which would also define and prove the acreage
of A and his associates, would cost not less than 7x dollars; the leases
retained by A and others had an added value of at least 7x dollars
on March 1, 1913, by reason of this contract. B went upon the

land and drilled a well after March 1, 1913, and after the striking of oil, the A leases were transferred to a corporation formed to take over such leases in exchange for the stock of the corporation. This stock appears to have been sold by stockholders in 1916 for 15x dollars. The protest of the taxpayers appears to have grown out of the proposal to tax the stockholders at the 1916 rates on the difference between the cost to them of the leases and the consideration received for the stock.

Decision: In the opinion of the committee this is proceeding upon a manifestly erroneous theory. It has been the consistent position of the bureau that where property is exchanged for stock in a corporation formed to take over such property, the difference between the value of the stock received and the cost or value on March 1, 1913, of the property exchanged, is taxable gain or loss as the case may be. Consequently in the judgment of the committee, A and his associates were liable to tax in 1913 on the difference between the value as of March 1, 1913, of their leases and the value of the stock which they received in exchange in August, 1913. The Committee is, therefore, of the opinion that in determining the value as of March 1, 1913, x dollars the approximate cost of wells sufficient to determine whether or not oil was present, which cost to be defrayed by B, may be added to the original cost of securing the leases retained by A and associates, and that such figure should be accepted as the value on March 1, 1913. Therefore it is recommended that the original cost of the leases transferred to the corporation plus x dollars, the approximate cost of the wells sufficient to determine whether or not oil was present, be accepted as their value on March 1, 1913; that A and associates be allowed to file amended returns for 1913 reporting as taxable income the difference between such value and the value of the leases at the time they were turned over to the corporation; that the second value be treated as the cost to them of the stock sold in 1916 for 15x dollars and the profit or loss on the sale of the stock be computed on that basis.

RULING 31-20-1111
A. R. R. 209
(C. B. No. 3, p. 360)

Facts: Revenue Act of 1917. The M Company appealed against the constructive capital determined by the Income Tax Unit under the provisions of Sec. 210 of this Act, claiming that the constructive capital determined by reference to representative concerns was less than by the invested capital claimed and also less than the invested capital which can be definitely established to the satisfaction of the bureau.

Decision: The taxpayer shall have a deduction upon all the statutory invested capital which he can establish, and if in any case he is able to show to the satisfaction of the Unit that he has invested capital which can be recognized in excess of constructive capital found upon application of Sec. 210 the taxpayer should not be deprived of his right to have assessment based upon such statutory capital as he can show.

RULING 32-20-1115
A. R. R. 217
(C. B. No. 3, p. 76)

Facts: Revenue Acts of 1917 and 1918. The P Company appealed from the action of the Income Tax Unit denying it the right to file its returns for 1917 and 1918 on the basis of receipts and disbursements and requiring amended returns for those years on the accrual basis. The corporation contends that irrespective of the fact that its books have been kept on the accrual basis it has a right, under the law, to render returns on the basis of receipts and disbursements. An examination of the returns, and the accountant's report shows that the books have been kept on the accrual basis, that it has accounts receivable and that inventories have been taken, that the corporation did not use such inventories and accounts receivable in the computation of net income but filed its returns on the basis of actual receipts and disbursements.

Decisions: Any return which in the judgment of the Commissioner does not reflect the true income may be rejected by him and the corporation required to render a return on such basis and in such manner as he may prescribe. Both acts are specific on this point. In order to correctly reflect the true income of this corporation, both inventories and accounts receivable must enter into the computation of net incomes. "The action of the Unit in requiring this corporation to file an amended return for 1917 (on the accrual basis), and to take into consideration in the computation of its income both inventories and accounts receivable was proper and in accord with the law and regulations on this subject. With respect to the 1918 return, * * * in view of the specific wording of the law and regulations, there is but one conclusion which can be reached by the committee, and that is that the action of the Income Tax Unit in requiring an amended return for 1918, on the accrual basis was proper, and it is therefore recommended that this action of the Unit, as well as the action with respect to the 1917 return, be approved."

RULING 32-20-1124

A. R. R. 221

(C. B. No. 3, p. 320)

Facts: Revenue Act of 1917. The M Company was organized in July, 1915, and succeeded a corporation known as the N Company. It appears that prior to 1910, the corporation known as the N Company owned real estate and water power rights. In June, 1914, N Company became insolvent. Bankruptcy proceedings were instituted and in September, 1914, the corporation was declared by legal proceedings to be a bankrupt. In July, 1915, a new corporation was formed and came into existence as the M Company. It took over the rights of the old corporation from the trustee. The newly organized corporation made extensive changes; the only points of similarity between the M Company and the N Company are that the product manufactured is sold under the same trade name and is produced on the same location. The M Corporation contends that they should be allowed a deduction of 8% for the purpose of computing the excess profits tax, because they did not succeed to the trade or business of the N Company since it had become bankrupt and had not been in operation since the early part of 1914.

Decision: It appears that the M Corporation acquired the assets of the bankrupt corporation and that even though a consid-

crable amount was invested in new machinery, etc., the plant of the
new corporation is located in the same place and the product is
sold under the same trade name.   Therefore the committee is of
the opinion that the business now carried on by the M Company is
substantially a continuation of the trade or business carried on by
its predecessor, the N Company, and that this view is substantiated
by the fact that the product of the new corporation is sold under the
same trade name.   Committee, therefore, recommends fixing the
deduction for the purpose of computing the tax at 7 per cent, rather
than 8 per cent claimed by the corporation.

RULING 32-20-1119

A. R. R. 223

(C. B. No. 3, p. 140)

Facts: Act of October 3, 1913.   M Company is a corporation
doing business as wholesale distributors of merchandise.   For the
taxable year 1917, the volume of its business was 80x dollars, with
a net income of x dollars, after deducting officers' salaries amounting
to 7x dollars.   In the audit of this return the Unit allowed for salaries,
3x dollars, and disallowed 4x dollars, the additional tax assessed
being $1\frac{1}{2}$x dollars.   From this action the taxpayer appealed stating
that for the past thirteen years, or since 1906, the compensation
of the different officers and managers of the corporation has been
fixed with direct relation to the earnings of the company, i. e., all
of its profits above a 6% return on the preferred stock and 10%
return on the common stock have been given to its officers and managers.   The taxpayer then quoted from an office letter wherein it
is said that the department will not question compensation which is
paid as the result of open bargaining, or as the result of bona fide
contracts and arrangements entered into and followed prior to the
years in which the tax rates have been high, provided that such
payments are, in fact, purely for services.

Decision: The committee does not question the statement
of the taxpayer that the division of the profits has been a consistent
practice of the company since 1906; but such a consistent practice
is not sufficient to constitute an arm's length contract with the
officers and managers individually whereby each shall receive a
fixed and determined proportion of such excess profits, and that this

proportion was not fixed, but varied from year to year at the discretion of the directors of the business. It can not be said, therefore, that this distribution of profits occurred "as the result of open bargaining, or as the result of bona fide contracts and arrangements entered into and followed prior to" the year 1917, even though such payments were, in fact, purely for services, and in accordance with an established custom of the taxpayer. The committee therefore is of the opinion that where a distribution of this kind absorbs all the profits of the business, such a distribution cannot be regarded as an "ordinary and necessary" expense of the business, and that the excess over a reasonable amount for compensation should be disallowed. The Committee, therefore, recommends that the action of the Unit be sustained.

RULING 41-20-1239
A. R. R. 229
(C. B. No. 3, p. 354)

Facts: Revenue Act of 1917. The M Company contends that its invested capital as at December 31, 1916, should be increased by the cash surrender value of certain insurance policies carried on the life of its president. In this connection it appears that the corporation has regularly deducted as an operating expense for each year prior to 1917, the amount of premiums paid on such insurance policies and that on January 1, 1917, such policies had a cash surrender value of $1\frac{1}{2}x$ dollars which, it is urged, should be restored to the invested capital of the corporation.

Decision: As premiums paid by a corporation for insurance on the lives of its officers or employees payable to it cannot be deducted as expenses in computing taxable income, such insurance policies shall be considered tangible property under Art. 47 of Reg. 41 and may be included as invested capital of such corporation at their cash surrender value at the beginning of the taxable year. This ruling made by the Tax Reviewers has been carried forward and the same, in substance, is stated in Art. 846 of Reg. 45.

RULING 33-20-1130

A. R. R. 232

(C. B. No. 3, p. 142)

Facts: Revenue Acts of 1917 and 1918. The O Company, operated as a partnership, was in financial difficulties in 1905. At that time, by agreement with the principal creditor, a corporation was formed and two young men were induced to take charge of the business and operate it at a salary of 4x dollars a year, each, with the agreement that if they succeeded in making a success of the business they should be paid additional compensation. In 1917 and 1918 the additional compensation was paid. The corporation contends that it should be allowed to deduct the amounts so paid in its return for the year in which same was paid.

Decision: When additional compensation is agreed to be paid by a corporation to its officers at a future date, upon the happening of certain contingencies expected to result from the rendition of services, the amount of such compensation being left for future determination, the amount so paid is not to be treated as back salary and allocated to the years during which the services were rendered, but constitutes a business expense to the corporation for the taxable year in which the same was paid.

RULING 35-20-1168

A. R. R. 249

(C. B. No. 3, P. 145)

Facts: Revenue Acts of 1916, 1917 and 1918. This was an appeal of the executors of the estate of A against taxes assessed by the Income Tax Unit for the years 1916, 1917 and 1918. Questions of allowance of depreciation and net losses on operation of a farm, allowance of losses upon sale of A's residence and his private yacht, and the deductibility of losses sustained by A in the sale of certain securities were involved.

Decision: (1) Although the deceased operated the farm as a hobby and not as a commercial enterprise, and, therefore, losses incurred thereon during his lifetime, could not be properly deducted as necessary business expenses, losses incurred during the period of administration could be deducted by the executor in making the estate return, because, since the executor was compelled to carry on the farm until it could be disposed of, it could hardly be said that he carried it on as an enterprise conducted for pleasure.

(2) The loss upon the sale of an individual's residence is not deductible.

(3) In determining profit upon property which is not depreciable under income tax laws, in this case a pleasure yacht, the question of depreciation does not enter in, and the difference between the actual cost or the actual value on March, 1913, and the selling price is the profit or loss, without respect to any depreciation which may have been suffered in the meantime.

(4) A capitalist is not a dealer in stocks, if purchases are made with a view rather to the investment than to the trading profit, and is entitled to be classed as a dealer in securities only when the principal object of purchase or sale is the trading profit to be made. A, not being properly classifiable as a dealer in securities, was not entitled in 1917 to take his losses upon securities beyond his profits upon similar transactions.

RULING 34-20-1157
A. R. R. 250
(C. B. No. 3, p. 324)

Facts: Revenue Act of 1917. The capital stock of the M Company was controlled by two groups of stockholders. In 1906 A and B purchased from C and D the entire stock holdings of the latter, and agreed to pay par for the preferred, and book value for the common, and in addition the sum of x dollars. In the contract of sale the retiring stockholders agreed, as consideration for the purchase of the stock and payment of the price, not to engage in the business carried on by the corporation for twenty-five years. The sum of x dollars was represented by notes payable monthly. These notes were paid by the corporation in the following manner: Two or three days prior to the due date of each note the corporation's check for the amount would be given to A and deposited by him in his own bank. A would then pay C and D with his own check. Every three or six months a sufficient dividend was declared to take care of these monthly notes until the last one was paid. The amounts paid by the corporation to retire these notes were charged, not to capital expenditure, nor to business expenses, but to profit and loss. The company claimed the amount of x dollars should be admitted as good will in its invested capital.

Decision: The amount of x dollars paid to two retiring stockholders under a contract by which they agreed to refrain from entering into competition with the corporation for a period of years, was not a payment for good will, and not admissible as invested capital for the year 1917. The committee quoted from a solicitor's opinion in which two objections to the inclusion of such amount were made: (1) that there was doubt whether the agreement constituted "good will;" and, (2), granting that the agreement was intangible property within the meaning of the Act, the sum in question could not be included in invested capital since the facts do not show that the amount was paid by the corporation "therefor specifically as such in cash" as required by the Act, since a careful reading of the contract will show that nowhere is it stated that any specific amount of money was paid for the agreement in question.

RULING 40-20-1227

A. R. R. 233

(C. B. No. 3, p. 347)

Facts: Revenue Act of 1917. The Unit assessed additional tax based upon the disallowance of a portion of the M Company's claim for invested capital and the M Company appealed. The plant of the M Company is located some miles from a railroad or other transportation facilities, and is, therefore, dependent for its supply of raw material upon the product raised in the vicinity. The raw material is produced by plantation owners, and because of the transportation conditions, the plant can be operated successfully only if it obtains the entire output of the vicinity. The corporation which owned the plant prior to the M Company's acquiring it became involved in financial difficulties due to some differences which arose between the large plantation owners and the management of the corporation, which caused the plantation owners to make arrangements for a plant of their own, thus cutting off the source of raw material to this company. Thereafter the holder of a mortgage on the property of the company foreclosed it. Negotiations were then opened up between this creditor and the plantation owners for the sale of the plant to a new corporation to be formed by them. The plant was transferred to the new corporation, the M Company, in consideration of the company's notes secured by a mortgage upon the plant, and in consideration of the agreement that the plantation owners would each contract to sell to the new company all of their produce for a period of five years, the period during which the purchase money notes would mature. The M Company's claim is that by reason of the bringing together of the plant, which shortly before foreclosure was appraised at 200x dollars, and the contracts for raw material, that the plant was at once restored to its appraised value and that these contracts made with the company were so closely related to rights in the tangible property, to-wit, the plant, as to constitute contracts recognizable as tangible property within the meaning of Art. 811, justifying treatment of them as paid-in surplus.

Decision: Paid-in surplus, as its name implies, must be some tangible property transferred from the owners to a corporation, either as a gift or at a value less than the actual cash value of the property transferred, and in practically all cases where allowable, involves no substantial change in beneficial interest. In this case, the plant itself was not transferred to the company as a gift or for stock, but was bought by the company from an owner, not a stockholder in the company, for its notes, which notes have subsequently been paid off through earnings. Neither can contracts made with the company itself, and to which it is one of the parties, be held to be paid-in surplus. Contracts in any event, and where they may be regarded under the regulations as tangible assets, can only constitute paid-in surplus if the contracts were made between outside parties and the rights of either of those parties is then transferred to a corporation without adequate compensation. The committee is, therefore, compelled to recommend that the claim for paid-in surplus be rejected.

RULING 41-20-1230
A. R. R. 266
(C. B. No. 3, p. 131)

Facts: Revenue Acts of 1913, 1916 and 1917. A was an executive official of several corporations and a member of a partnership. These concerns were located at three different points, and it appeared that the taxpayer in his official capacity made daily trips between these various places by automobile, the ordinary train service being infrequent and inadequate; the entire expense thereof being directly paid by A. The automobile was used but a portion of the time for the purpose indicated, and one-half of the operating expense and depreciation was claimed by A personally as a business deduction.

Decision: Such portion of the upkeep and operating expenses of the taxpayer's automobile as was occasioned by its use in the taxpayer's business is a proper deduction as a business expense in the personal returns of the taxpayer.

RULING 41-20-1238
A. R. R. 268
(C. B. No. 3, p. 334)

Facts: In determining the invested capital of the M Company, a Georgia corporation, the field agent undertook to establish values as of 1898, on the theory that the company had been in continuous existence since that date. It appeared, however, that the charter of the original corporation expired in 190–, which fact was not called to the attention of the officers or stockholders until 190– at which time a new charter was secured. The question was whether the invested capital should be computed as of 1898 or as of 190–.

Decision: Under the laws of the State of Georgia, the corporation ceased to exist as a corporation when the charter expired in 190–. In the case of a reorganization prior to March 3, 1917, it was considered that the assets should be valued as of the date of transfer to the new corporation for determining the invested capital of such corporation for the taxable year, and consequently in this case that the invested capital should be determined as at the date of organization in 190–.

RULING 42-20-1245
A. R. R. 279
(C. B. No. 3, p. 168)

Decision: The subject of depreciation of steam schooners engaged in the coat-wise lumber trade has received the careful consideration of the Unit and at a conference between the President of the Ship Owners Association of the Pacific Coast, professional accountant representing that association and officials of the Income Tax Unit, it was agreed, after full discussion, that the proper annual rates of depreciation on vessels of this class engaged in this trade is 5%, based upon an expected life of twenty years.

RULING 42-20-1248
A. R. R. 284
(C. B. No. 3, p. 208)

Facts: Revenue Act of 1917. The executor and trustee of the estate of A, paid out during 1917, attorney's fees for services rendered in defending a suit brought to contest the will of the decedent and also in a suit to establish an equitable interest in certain lands, the legal title of which was in A during his lifetime. Under the will these lands were conveyed in trust to pay the income to certain beneficiaries. It further appears that the executor and trustee had no authority under the will to dispose of any part of these lands during the life af the widow and decedent's sister. The attorney for the taxpayer contended that, since under the terms of the will the executor and trustee were not authorized to sell any part of land, the will contemplated that all expenses, such as attorney's fees, should be paid from income and not from corpus, and, therefore, such fees were a proper deduction in the return filed for decedent's estate.

Decision: If, in the instant case, the suit in question had been filed and adjudicated during the lifetime of A, it could not be said that the attorney's fees in that case constituted an allowable deduction but must be considered as an addition to the cost of the property. The executor and trustee stand in A's place for the purpose of the settlement of the estate and the expenditure of x dollars as attorney's fees defending title to the property cannot be allowed **as** a deduction any more than it could have been allowed had A been living.

RULING 42-20-1252
A. R. R. 285
(C. B. No. 3, p. 367)

Facts: Revenue Acts of 1917 and 1918. In 1917 the M Company was organized under the laws of the State of Connecticut and took over the N Company, a Massachusetts corporation, organized in 1907, issuing its capital stock for the assets of the latter company, which was then dissolved. The charter of the reorganized corporation was drafted so that the corporation could engage in the collateral business of owning and renting real estate in addition to its regular business. This reorganization took place subsequent to March 3, 1917. After the aforesaid reorganization, A, principal stockholder of M Company, transferred certain real estate to the new corporation for stock. The Revenue Agent included in invested capital for both 1917 and 1918, the adjusted cost of such real estate to A. The question was also presented as to whether both corporations should file returns for 1917, or only the M Company.

Decision: (1) It will be noted that in Section 208 of the Revenue Act of 1917, the phrase "or change of ownership of property after March 3, 1917," does not appear, but Sec. 208 deals with reorganization, consolidation or change of ownership of the trade or business after March 3, 1917, where 50% of the control remains with the same person. Sec. 331 of the Revenue Act of 1918 goes a little further and takes in any change of ownership of property after March 3, 1917, where an interest or control in such trade or business or property of 50% or more remains in the same person or persons. Therefore, the adjustments made by the revenue agent for 1918 on account of the property acquired by the corporation from A after March 3, 1917, were proper, but were not proper for 1917 if the corporation can show that the real estate acquired had a value in excess of the cost as adjusted by the revenue agent.

(2) Where a distinctly new corporation comes into existence which takes over the property of an old corporation, both the old and new corporation will be required to file separate returns cover-

ing the periods of the year during which they were in active control of the business. Both the M and the N Company should file returns for the year 1917.

RULING 45-20-1294
A. R. R. 301
(C. B. No. 3, p. 188)

Facts: Revenue Act of 1918. An association erected a memorial building in a certain city which was utilized as a museum and depository for records, flags, trophies, etc., of the late war. The building was to contain a forum which was to be used solely for educational lectures and meetings, and not for any civic meetings in the ordinary sense. The charter of the association also authorized it "to construct, equip, operate and maintain other memorials, in the nature of statues, monuments, memorial assembly halls, memorial music halls, memorial art galleries, or any other building or thing to commemorate the memory of persons, causes, occasions, events or principles." The question arose whether contributions to the above described association were allowable deductions under Sec. 214 (a) 11 of the Revenue Act of 1918.

Decision: "A museum is clearly educational and has been so recognized in court decisions * * *." The association is not only operated exclusively for educational purposes but is organized for such in accordance with the statute authorizing the deductions in question. The other activities authorized in the charter, though they do not seem to be exclusively charitable or educational, "can be engaged in only with the view of teaching the public wholesome lessons, uplifting the public thought, improving the citizenship and administering to the people's need in the above respect. The Committee has, therefore, reached the conclusion that these purposes are, in the broad sense, also educational, and that under the circumstances the mere fact that they are authorized under the charter is not sufficient, in view of the fact that the operations will be clearly educational, to take the corporation out of the class contributions to which are deductible."

RULING 44-20-1282
A. R. R. 307
(C. B. No. 3, p. 344)

Facts: Revenue Act of 1918. The committee has had under consideration the appeal of the N Company against the ruling of the Income Tax Unit disallowing an item of 50x dollars claimed as good will in its invested capital for 1918. The facts appear to be that the N Company, a corporation succeeded N and Company, a partnership, in 1897. The partnership had been very profitable prior to incorporation, its average earnings for the five years just prior to 1897 being approximately 100x dollars. As its tangible assets presumably were substantially the same as when turned over to the corporation in 1897, 200x dollars, it is clear that its earnings indicated a good will worth at least as much as the tangible assets. The deed transferring assets to the corporation specifically recited that the 200x dollars in stock was paid for the trade name and good will of the business and the physical assets. The amount of the net tangible assets taken up on the books of the corporation was 200x dollars, the good will not being carried on the books as an asset at all.

Decision: "The denial of the item of 50x dollars claimed as invested capital appears to be based upon the assumption that if allowed at all it must be allowed as paid-in surplus, and the Unit has consistently and correctly, in the opinion of the committee, taken the attitude that no paid-in surplus is permissible directly or indirectly as to intangible assets conveyed. However, this amount may be allowed without its inclusion as paid-in surplus. The tangible assets taken over were raw materials and stock in trade which were sold prior to any income tax law. To distribute the purchase price of the tangibles and intangibles purchased as being 150x dollars for tangibles and 50x dollars for intangibles will have the effect of reducing the cost price of assets from 200x dollars to 150x dollars and consequently increasing the earned surplus by 50x dollars. It is clear that this is a case of acquisition for stock of a mixed aggregate of tangibles and intangibles such as would justify the application of Sec. 327 if satisfactory allocation of values can not be arrived at. In view of the history of the concern and the profits earned in excess of a return upon tangible assets, the committee is clearly of the opinion that the intangible assets were as readily worth 50x dollars as the tangibles were worth 150x dollars. However, as 50x dollars in 1918 is the maximum value which can be included in invested capital by reason of the purchase of intangible assets for stock, the committee recommends that the corporation be allowed to allocate the values at the time of purchase and to attribute to the tangibles a cost of 150x dollars and to the intangibles a cost of 50x dollars, and to adjust its books so as to increase its earned surplus by the sum of 50x dollars."

RULING 47-20-1318

A. R. R. 326

(C. B. No. 3, p. 361)

Decision: Revenue Act of 1917. If a corporation has paid no salaries to its officers during 1917, or has paid them salaries which were unusually low in comparison with the salaries paid to the officers of the competing concerns, and thereby created an abnormal condition which seriously affected its net income and tax liability, it may properly receive consideration with the view to determining its excess profits tax liability for 1917 in accordance with Sec. 210 of the Revenue Act of 1917. This section provides for an assessment on the basis of comparison with representative corporations.

RULING 48-20-1330

A. R. R. 327

(C. B. No. 3, p. 362)

Decision: Revenue Act of 1918. "Where a corporation operated its business with a large amount of borrowed capital during the year 1918, and thereby created an abnormal condition which rendered its invested capital disproportionate to its net income as evidenced by comparison with representative corporations engaged in a similar or like trade or business, and where it received insurance on the life of one of its officers which created an abnormal condition with respect to its net income, it may properly receive consideration with the view of determining its excess profits tax liability for 1918, in accordance with Secs. 327 and 328 of the Revenue Act of 1918."

RULING 50-20-1348
A. R. R. 332
(C. B. No. 3, p. 362)

Facts: Revenue Act of 1917. A, B and C acquired the business of the M Company and the N Company for cash. In each instance the business of the company was acquired and not capital stock. Each company so acquired was immediately incorporated with a capital stock of x dollars and A, B and C, the stockholders, turned over to D and E, without other consideration from these two gentlemen than their promise and agreement to conduct the business and do the advertising, one-half in the aggregate of the said stock. Subsequently D and E sold half of their interest to outside parties and received therefor in cash 64x dollars per share. Both companies were engaged in manufacturing. The question arose whether it was proper to assess M and N companies under the provisions of Sec. 210 of the Revenue Act of 1917.

Decision: "The business of each company is that of an ordinary commercial enterprise. The value of the capital stock of each is conclusively shown by the original purchases by A, B and C, and by cash sales between individuals in the year 191–, one year after incorporation. This value is not supported by personal services but by earning power (potential or otherwise) of certain property not reflected in the capitalization. This certain property is an intangible asset which was actually paid into the company at incorporation but at a nominal value. Had the certain property been a tangible asset, Art. 63, of Reg. 41, could be invoked for claiming a paid-in surplus. Art. 74 of Reg. 41 defines 'nominal capital' and prescribes certain tests, one of which is that corporations having a nominal capitalization but employing a substantial amount of capital in their business will not be construed as business having a nominal capital for purposes of excess profits tax. There is no provision in the law or regulations which gives effect to the inclusion of a substantial amount of capital of intangible nature when specifically paid in at nominal value. Manifestly, however, under such conditions the taxpayer is entitled to relief under the equitable provisions of the statute." It was accordingly recommended that the tax be assessed under Sec. 210, which provides for an assessment on the basis of comparison with representative corporations.

RULING 50-20-1345

A. R. R. 335

(C. B. No. 3, p. 244)

Facts: Revenue Act of 1918. A, now deceased, was the sole owner of the capital stock of the M Company, a holding company which was organized to hold title to certain property belonging to A, and that during his life time he took out a life insurance policy on his life and made it payable to the M Company upon his death, but reserved the right to change at any time the beneficiary named in the policy. He, as an individual, paid all the premiums on the policy, and upon his death the proceeds thereof were paid to the company. The question presented to the committee was as follows: "Do the proceeds of an insurance policy paid, under the circumstances stated above, upon the death of the insured to a corporate beneficiary, constitute taxable income to the recipient under Secs. 213 and 233 of the Revenue Act of 1918?"

Decision: "Sec. 213 (a) defines gross income as including certain specified items and the 'gains or profits and income derived from any source whatever.' It was then provided in Sec. 213 (b) (1) that the gross income should not include the proceeds of a life insurance policy paid to individual beneficiaries. * * * This provision of law shows by implication that Congress considered that 'gross income' would without the specific exclusion of the proceeds of life insurance policies paid to individual beneficiaries, or to the estate of the insured, comprehend the proceeds of all life insurance policies. * * *. From the foregoing it is reasonable to assume that Congress, by excluding from gross income the proceeds of life insurance policies payable to an individual beneficiary or the estate of the insured, intended that such proceeds should be included in gross income when received by beneficiaries other than individuals or the estate of the insured."

RULING 50-20-1349

A. R. R. 339

(C. B. No. 3, p. 169)

Facts: Revenue Act of 1918. A taxpayer's formula was depreciating in value. Question was raised as to whether depreciation might be claimed thereon and deducted.

Decision: Held that intangible assets, such as formulas, are not of a character of property subject to annual depreciation deductions. However, if after acquisition, a formula is found worthless, its cost may be charged off in toto in the taxpayer's return for the year in which its worthlessness was discovered.

RULING 55-20-1362

A. R. R. 352

(C. B. No. 3, p. 167)

Facts: Revenue Act of 1918. Taxpayer sustained a loss through bankruptcy of a debtor. Bankrupt estate was not closed at end of taxable year 1918. Receiver or trustee had made a report showing conditions and prospects of no dividends.

Decision: Held that a loss in bankruptcy may be established from estimate of the receiver or trustee, or by competent authority in approximate amount and so charged off in 1918, may be claimed as a deduction in return of that year, although such loss is not evidenced by a closed and completed transaction.

RULING 52-20-1366

A. R. R. 356

(C. B. No. 3, p. 330)

Facts: Revenue Act of 1917. The M Company was incorporated to take over the business of a partnership. Prior to incorporation the partners had allowed a portion of their earnings to remain in the business, such amounts being credited as "Special Accounts" of partners. Upon incorporation certain partners returned their pro rata share, received in distribution, and on the books of the corporation the amounts so paid were again credited to certain "Special Accounts." Since incorporation other amounts, acquired by declaration of dividend, were also credited to these accounts. These accounts were covered by notes which provided that demand for payment would not be made by the holder until all indebtedness of the company, which might be outstanding at the time notice that payment is desired was given, had been fully paid. The question presented was whether the corporation was entitled to include these special accounts in invested capital.

Decision: The liability was not to all of the stockholders pro rata according to the shareholdings. The obligations of the stockholders not to demand payment until the indebtedness was fully paid did not preclude the corporation from liquidating the liabilities at any time. The obligation of the notes to pay interest was not modified by the provision subrogating the principal to the general creditors and, accordingly, the notes could not be considered in the light of preferred stock. Manifestly, the "Special Accounts' do not represent either stock subscriptions or undivided increment of income. They represent, therefore, borrowed capital and hence are excluded from invested capital.

RULING 2-21-1393
A. R. R. 358

Facts: Revenue Act of 1917. At the time M Company was organized, in 1913, plant and equipment were turned in for capital stock at an arbitrary figure of 3x dollars. By an appraisal made in 1917 the plant was shown to have a value as of January 1, 1918, of 8x dollars, and was entered on the books at this amount. About a year later, for purposes of the tax return, the appraisal company established a value as of the date of incorporation in 1913, by deducting from the valuation as of January 1, 1917, the amount of acquisitions after 1913, and by allowing for depreciation and other adjustments. This computation showed a value of 7x dollars as of 1913. The corporation therefore claimed an addition of 4x dollars to invested capital, on account of a value of tangible property in excess of the par value of the stock issued therefor.

Decision: The committee referred to Com. Rec. 161, Ruling No. 28-20-1064, in which it was held that in order to establish such excess valuation, it was not necessary that the appraisal should have been made upon the exact date on which the tangible property had been conveyed to the corporation. However, the instant case does not fall within that ruling because here the appraisal was not made, as it was in the former case, as of the date of conveyance to the corporation, that is to say, in the light only of knowledge or facts ascertainable on that date and not in the light of subsequent happenings. Moreover in the former case the bureau was dealing only with real estate and buildings and the appraisal was made within two years of the date of valuation. The claim of the taxpayer was, therefore, denied in its entirety.

RULING 1-21-1377
A. R. R. 360

.   Facts: Revenue Act of 1918. The M Company included in its return contributions to the American Red Cross and United War Work Fund as a deduction under the head of general expenses. The company itemized the amount separately in a schedule filed with the return. The question was whether the company should be assessed a 5% penalty for negligence.

Decision: Inasmuch as there were no special instructions on the return form dealing with such contributions, and as many lawyers and accountants differed as to the deductibility thereof, and also in view of the fact that the bureau had not made up its mind at the time of the filing of the return, the committee is of the opinion that the error was due to an honest misunderstanding of the facts or the law of which an average reasonable man might be capable; and recommends that the penalty for negligence be not asserted in this or any other case where the amount of the contribution was specifically and separately listed in a schedule of general expenses supporting Item 12.

RULING 3-21-1394
A. R. R. 363

Facts: Revenue Act of 1917. The M Company took over the business of A, who was engaged in developing certain patents. The assets taken over consisted of x dollars, and liabilities aggregating $\frac{3}{4}x$ dollars were assumed; 2x dollars of capital stock was issued for the net assets; no additional funds were paid in. The patents did not prove a success but the corporation secured other patents for automobile bumpers, the use of which it sold to the N Company. The only income for 1917 consisted of royalties received from these patents and amounted to 4x dollars. The only disbursements were for salaries, attorney's fees, commissions and miscellaneous expenses. The principal stockholder, A, was obligated under the company's contracts, to devote his time to demonstrating, improving and developing the patents. The company claimed assessment under Sec. 209.

Decision: In the instant case capital (patents) is employed in the business. Royalties are the result of the employment of this capital. The company has paid-capital but its true invested capital can not be actually determined. Therefore, assessment under Sec. 209 was denied, but assessment under Sec. 210 by comparison was allowed.

RULING 3-21-1395
A. R. R. 364

Facts: Revenue Act of 1917. A partnership doing a brokerage business also engaged in certain purchases on its own account. Sales of such merchandise amounted to 22 per cent of sales on commission and yielded 30 per cent of the firm's net income. The firm stated that it had no branches, employed only one salesman, and was not responsible for losses in shipments, bad debts, etc. The partnership contended it should be assessed under Sec. 209 because its principal net income was due primarily to the personal activities of the two parties.

Decision: Because of the volume of business transacted by the partnership through direct buying and selling of merchandise, and the numerous accounts receivable and payable shown on the firm's balance sheets, assessment under Sec. 209 was denied. But, because the statutory invested capital was negligible in comparison with the volume of business transacted and seriously disproportionate to the invested capital of other taxpayers doing a similar business, assessment under Sec. 210 by comparison was approved.

RULING 4-21-1411
A. R. R. 373

Facts: Revenue Act of 1918. The M Company, incorporated in 1910, was a close family corporation, its entire capital stock being held by five individuals, all of whom were directors and three of whom were officers. The company contended that it was entitled to deduct contributions to Red Cross, Liberty Loan campaigns, and war worker's organizations as necessary expenses.

Decision: It has been consistently held that a corporation not entitled to classification as a personal service corporation, nor to exemption under the provisions of Sec. 231 of the Act, is entitled to only such deductions as are allowable under Sec. 234. The fact that a corporation is a "close" or "family" corporation does not change its taxable status, and the donations were, therefore, not deductible.

RULING 15-21-1560

A. R. R. 375

Facts: Act of October 3, 1913, and Revenue Act of 1916. In 1915 A received an item of 5x dollars as interest which had ac-erned and was due prior to March 1, 1913. The revenue agent included this item in computing his net income for 1915. The agent also included an item of 15x dollars as representing a profit received by A from the liquidation of a corporation in which A owned stock. It appeared that in December, 1915, the board of directors of this corporation adopted a resolution formally declaring a distribution of a portion of the assets of the corporation in the nature of a so-called liquidating dividend. This resolution recited that for the purpose of this distribution the transfer books of the company be closed December, 1915, and reopened January, 1916. At the same meeting another resolution was adopted providing for notice to each stockholder of the proposed distribution and request-ing him to elect whether he would receive stock of the M Company or cash, and notify the corporation not later than noon of January —, 1916. The assets of the corporation included stock of the M Com-pany and the stockholders were to be given the option of receiving the same in distribution or cash in lieu thereof. Pursuant to the resolution, a letter was sent to each stockholder in December, 1915, which stated:

"As soon after January —, 1916, as practicable, there will be sent by registered mail to each stockholder of record of this Company the certificates of stock (or, in the case of those electing to accept cash in lieu of shares of the M Company, the cash) to which the several stockholders of this company shall be entitled as their respective proportions of the distribution above mentioned."

The distribution was actually made after January .., 1916, and A received an amount in excess of the market value of his stock in the corporation, as of March 1, 1913.

As to the item of interest received in 1915 but which had accrued prior to March 1, 1913, A contended that the same was not taxable in 1915; and as to the distribution that this was constructively received in December, 1915, and hence was taxable at the 1915 rate.

Decision: (1) With respect to the item of 5x dollars, interest accrued prior to March 1, 1913, and received in 1915, it was recommended that the action of the Income Tax Unit holding this interest taxable in 1915, the year in which received, be reversed.

(2) As to the corporate distribution, the committee held that there can be no receipt, constructive or otherwise, when the thing to be received is not yet determined. Until exercise of the option by the stockholders, and communication to the corporation of the nature of the election, no payment could be made under the terms of the resolution declaring the distribution. Since election was a condition precedent to the right to demand payment, the case was deemed not to be within the provisions of Art. 53, of Reg. 45, and the income in question was held to be taxable at the 1916 rates.

RULING 5-21-1415
A. R. R. 377

Facts: Revenue Act of 1918. This was an appeal by a number of state and national banks from a ruling of the Income Tax Unit to the effect that depreciation deduction not charged off on the current books but represented by charges on ledger accounts in a controlling ledger could not be allowed. It appeared that the banks were required to submit periodical reports to governmental officials, which were made up from the current books and did not accurately show the investment in furniture and fixtures; neither did they show the correct undivided profits. The reports were made under oath, and the officials would not permit the banks to adjust on their books the investment amount even though the bank examiners had arbitrarily written down such assets upon the books of the bank.

Decision: Under the provisions of the Revenue Act of 1918 the Commissioner has power to compel a corporation to keep books which clearly reflect its net income and, therefore, he has power to reject a system of accounting which does not show the correct net income. It was, therefore, recommended that banks be permitted to keep such books and records as will enable them to file the correct returns, that such books or records may be made up from the current books and adjustments may be made thereon with respect to assets and depreciation, and that the books so kept for income tax purposes be accepted by the Income Tax Unit as an integral part of the accounting system of such bank.

RULING 9-21-1487
A. R. R. 390

Facts: Revenue Acts of 1917 and 1918. For three years prior to 1917, A and B, sole owners of the stock of M Company, and its principal officers, were each paid x dollars annual salary. In November, 1917, by resolution of the board of directors, this salary was increased to a total salaried expense of 5x dollars per annum. Of this aggregate amount for the two officers, the revenue agent disallowed 2x dollars prorated for 1917 and for the year 1918, making the salary of each $1\frac{1}{2}$x dollars per year as against $2\frac{1}{2}$x dollars. The Income Tax Unit reduced the disallowance from 2x dollars to x dollars, making the salaries of the officers 2x dollars each. The average yearly sales of the company from 1912 to 1916, inclusive, amounted to $45x. In the year 1916 the sales were $52x; in 1917, $72x; in 1918, $82x.

Decision: A salary deduction of 4x dollars for the taxable year is in fair comparison with that of similar industries; and, therefore, the action of the Income Tax Unit should be sustained.

RULING 10-21-1502
A. R. R. 413

Facts: Revenue Acts of 1917 and 1918. In order to carry on a business owned by a trust, a corporation with a nominal capital of 4x dollars was organized and the stock was issued in the name of the trustees. In 1911, the trust terminated and all of the capital stock of the corporation was sold by the trustees for 60x dollars. At that time the book value of the stock was 50x dollars, and in order to measure the value of the stock by the cash consideration that was paid to the trustees, there was set up an asset of good will in the amount of 10x dollars. The company contended that it was entitled to include in its invested capital the item of good will of 10x dollars. The following statements were contained in affidavits of the president of the corporation:

"As representative of the corporation, I had agreed to sell to myself and the other four individuals, the entire assets of the business of the M Company and the N Company. This was my intention; it was what we did.

"The matter of the transfer of this property to the new organization was never discussed, but what we were purchasing was minutely understood by all of us; that is to say that we were purchasing all of the assets of the business. No thought was given to the purchase of stock, and no thought was given as to the method of transfer."

Decision: The affidavit seems to have no material bearing on the case, since it is a matter of record that the corporation known as the M Company was never liquidated. A corporation cannot sell its assets and at the same time retain them. The M Company is doing business today under the charter issued at date of organization, and the same amount of capital stock is outstanding, namely 4x dollars. The transaction, accordingly, was between stockholders and individuals. It is admitted by the taxpayer that the 10x dollars in cash, in excess of the book value of the assets and forming a part of the cash consideration of 60x dollars, was never paid into the corporation, but went to the trustees and was distributed to the beneficiaries under the will. Hence, to include this 10x dollars in the assets of the N Company, through a credit of the surplus account of the company, would be the recognition of appreciation based on going concern value.

The earnings of the business of the M Company undoubtedly justify establishing good will, but good will can only be set up on the books of a corporation and considered as invested capital for tax purposes when acquired by direct purchase. The committee, therefore, found no basis on which to ignore the corporate entity and denied the claim of the taxpayer for including good will in the invested capital.

RULING 13-21-1528

A. R. R. 435

Facts; Revenue Act of 1917. The M Company, a corporation, during the taxable year 1917, paid its officers certain salaries and bonuses, the amount of which it deducted in its tax return. During that year the corporation declared a cash dividend and distributed in payment of such dividend certain securities held in its treasury, in which distribution it claimed a net loss of 11x dollars. The company also claimed a deduction arising from a loss resulting from the conversion of certain securities of the N Company into other securities of the O Company.

Decision: (1) That the full amount of salaries and bonuses actually earned by and paid to officers of the corporation in 1917 be allowed as a deduction.

(2) At the date of the dividend, the taxpayer unquestionably parted with title to the securities distributed in payment thereof and thus closed the transaction in them. Therefore, if the net value of the securities at that date was less than their net value on March 1, 1913, the taxpayer, as a matter of fact, sustained a loss in their distribution which should be allowed as a deduction.

(3) The difference between the market value of the securities of the M Company at March 1, 1913, and the latter market value of the new securities received in exchange therefor, should be allowed as a deduction.

RULING 13-21-1536

A. R. R. 436

Facts: Revenue Act of 1917. The M Company in 189– purchased with its stock the assets of five other companies. For these assets, consisting largely of patents, it issued 7y shares of preferred stock of the par value of 35x dollars, and 8y shares of common of the par value of 40x dollars. It claimed a value of 72x dollars, for these assets, representing the par value of the stock issued therefor. It appeared, however, that at the time of the reorganization the preferred shares of the company were subscribed for at par, and the shares of common stock were selling on the stock exchange at about one-third of par per share. Two questions were presented, (1) what was the value of the patents at the time of organization, and (2) whether or not the company was entitled to any invested capital by reason of the original issue of stock for patents which had long since expired.

Decision: (1) The committee rejected the appraisals of the patents which fixed the value thereof as equal to the par value of the stock issued therefor as being not so reliable as those made by the public at the time through the purchase and sale of the stock at or about the time of issuance. It was, therefore, recommended that the value of the assets acquired be fixed at 48x dollars, such valuation being based on the par value of the preferred stock, to-wit, 35x dollars, since shares of the preferred stock were sold for par, plus 13x dollars for the common stock, since such stock sold on the market for one-third of its par value.

(2) Invested capital originally paid in can be reduced only on one condition, that is, that it has been returned to the stockholders through liquidation. The loss of the original capital or its exhaustion in the business does not alter its recognizable status. The only thing which can be affected by the exhaustion of capital is the earned surplus, which may be adjusted, if necessary, to cover any loss or exhaustion of original values. Moreover, while patent values gradually merge into good will, the 20% limitation provided by Sec. 207 of the Revenue Act of 1917, does not apply to the good will so created, since under the express terms of the statute, it is applicable only where good will is acquired for stock.

RULING 17-21-1588
A. R. R. 464

Facts: Revenue Act of 1917. The M Company was engaged in the business of selling land on commission. Its four officers owned all of its stock and gave their entire attention to the business. The company had a paid-in capital of $2,000 and occasionally it had to borrow to meet payrolls and expenses. In taking over a subdivision for sale, the company obligated itself to bear all selling expenses in connection therewith. It also obligated itself to render various forms of service, such as planning and supervising the placing of properties on the market, making of sales and collections, and supervising the entire work of preparing the property for market. These duties were discharged in part by its four officers and in a large part by its superintendents, salesmen, and salaried office force. The company contended that it employed no more than a nominal capital in its business, that its income was derived solely from the activities of its officers, and hence that it should be assessed under Sec. 209.

It also appeared that, under its usual form of contract, the company was entitled to a commission of 10 to 30 per cent on the gross sales price of each property sold, that it usually received 5 per cent of such sales price from the initial payment, and a portion of each subsequent installment payment until its entire commission was satisfied. The collector refused to allow the company to make a return on the actual receipt and disbursement basis.

Decision: (1) It having been shown that the M company employed more than a nominal amount of capital in its business and derived a considerable part of its net income from services rendered by others than its four stockholders, assessment under Sec. 209 was denied.

(2) In view of the fact that the company was ultra conservative in its capitalization, and the further fact that the amount of capital it has invested in the business was insufficient at times to meet the needs of that business, and was less than normal as compared with the amount of business transacted and as compared with the amount of capital employed by other concerns doing a similar business, assessment under Sec. 210 by comparison was recommended.

(3) The action of the collector was not justified. The responsibilities and duties of the company under its contracts was not fully discharged until the last installment is received, and therefore, to report the full amount of commissions called for under sales contracts as income for the year when the contracts are entered into is to report as income for that year commissions which have not yet been fully earned and which in case of default, will never be received.

RULING 20-21-1635

A. R. R. 492

Facts: Revenue Act of 1918. Is income from an irrevocable trust taxable to the grantor, although the grantor is trustee? This question was involved from the following facts: A made an oral declaration of trust in specific personal property in favor of B, retaining in himself the legal title and possession, the agreement providing for the payment or crediting of the income to B subject to the demand of B.

Decision: Held that, since under the laws of Kentucky there was created an enforceable trust in the interest of B without the power of revocation on the part of the donor, the income therefrom is all taxable to the beneficiary.

RULING 21-21-1645

A. R. R. 500

Facts: Revenue Act of 1917. The M Company, engaging in a brokerage business in metals, had a paid-in capital stock of $\frac{1}{8}$x dollars, issued in three shares. Its only expenses were a salary of $\frac{5}{8}$x dollars to its president and $\frac{1}{4}$x dollars for incorporation and legal services. Ninety-nine per cent of its business consisted of brokerage collected on sales made to the N Company. The M Company made the contracts with the mills for such products as were desired by the N Company and received a certain brokerage over the mill-price. The M Company made the collections from the N Company and paid to the mills the price of the products purchased. No capital was necessary in these transactions, since the N Company was required to pay for the products prior to the date on which the M Company was required to pay the mills. No clerical work or other services were rendered except the placing of orders by the president. The M Company claimed it was entitled to be assessed under Sec. 209 as a personal service corporation.

Decision: It was only on the theory that the M Company could be held responsible under its contracts that assessment under Sec. 209 could be denied. The committee considered, however, that the nominal capital of the corporation clearly established the fact that it was not contemplated that it should be held responsible except by way of personal service to both the buyer and seller, and accordingly assessment as a personal service corporation under Sec. 209 was recommended.

RULING 22-21-1662

A. R. R. 519

Facts: Revenue Acts of 1917 and 1918. In May, 1917, A, the majority stockholder and president of the company, died. After his death the work of his office was conducted by B, the secretary and treasurer of the company. It was agreed by the principal stockholders and the beneficiaries of the estate of A that the additional duties entitled B to a salary of $3\frac{1}{3}x$ dollars for 1917 in place of x dollars which he had been receiving. However, the administrator of his estate, who held the majority of the stock, declined to ratify this arrangement. In 1919, the estate of A was settled, and in June of that year, by resolution of the board of directors, there was voted to B, $2\frac{1}{3}x$ dollars as additional salary for the year 1917, same to be paid from the individual profits of 1917. The company contended it was entitled to deduct from its gross income for 1917, such additional compensation.

Decision: The additional compensation of $2\frac{1}{3}x$ dollars was not paid or accrued in 1917; nor did there exist any legal liability for the payment of such additional compensation in that year. Therefore, it was recommended that the deduction be denied for 1917, but be allowed for 1919, in which year the payment was actually made.

RULING 26-21-1705

A. R. R. 542

Facts: Revenue Act of 1917. In 1917 the M Company suffered a loss through burglary of approximately 9x dollars, of which 5x dollars was made good by several stockholders. The company was insured against such a loss but the insurance companies contested liability. The taxpayer deducted no part of the loss in its 1917 return. In 1918 suit was instituted on the insurance policies and the lower court held that the companies were not liable. The taxpayer in that year deducted x dollars of the 4x dollars loss. The case was appealed and in 1919 the upper court affirmed the decision of the lower court. After this affirmation the taxpayer prepared amended returns for 1919, in which the remaining 3x dollars were deducted as a loss, and filed claims for refund and abatement.

Decision: The committee finds itself unable to sustain the argument advanced by the taxpayer that where under a contract of insurance a taxpayer is insured against loss of this character, such loss is not actually determined or sustained until compensation by the insurance companies pursuant to such contract, or, as is the instant case, until the question of liability has been determined in litigation. Viewed in the light of subsequent events and taking into consideration the decree of the lower and superior courts, it is manifest that no liability on the part of the insurance companies existed at any time, which undoubtedly establishes as a fact that the loss was sustained at the time the theft was committed in 1917. In view of the foregoing, the committee is of the opinion that in the instant case the amount of the determined loss is deductible in the taxpayer's return for the year 1917 only, and that the matter of litigation upon insurance policies and the resulting decrees handed down by the courts have no effect whatever upon the time when the loss was actually sustained.

RULING 27-21-1717

A. R. R. 545

Facts: Revenue Act of 1918. The M Company in 18—, issued and sold its own corporate obligations in the form of bonds, having a face value of $1,000 each. At maturity in 1918, the taxpayer issued a new set of bonds in exchange for the old bonds, thereby retiring the issue of 18—. All of the old issue, with the exception of y bonds, were in the hands of stockholders who agreed to the arrangement and accepted the new for the old bonds. However, the holder of y bonds refused to accept anything but cash, and accordingly the taxpayer purchased these bonds, having a face value of 5x dollars, for 4x dollars cash, or eighty cents on the dollar. On March 1, 1913, the bonds were worth less than eighty cents on the dollar. The question was whether the M Company was taxable upon the excess of the par value of the bonds over the price paid.

Decision: (1) The Supreme Court cases cited by the taxpayer as holding that the condition of the taxpayer as of March 1, 1913, is to be used as the basis of determining gain or loss in any transaction closed after that time, were cases in which the thing giving rise to the gain was an asset of the taxpayer, and in the opinion of the committee the principle relied upon applies only to such cases wherein the gains under consideration arise from the ownership of assets such as property of all considerations, property rights, rights in property, etc.

(2) In answer to the taxpayer's argument that he got the extra dollars when he started the transaction and that he got nothing at all in the later year, the committee held that: "Surely it cannot be said that the taxpayer in 18—, by borrowing money on its own obligation, to the extent of the face value of such obligations, acquired an asset of determinable value, thereby realizing income at that time."

It was, therefore, recommended that the assessment of additional tax for 1918 resulting from the addition to the company's gross income of the excess of the par value of the bonds over the price paid upon purchase thereof be sustained.

RULING 2-20-679
A. R. M. 12
(C. B. No. 2, p. 292)

Facts: At the request of the Commissioner this committee has given an oral hearing to representatives of the proprietary medicine manufacturers in general, and of the M Company in particular, upon the question of an addition to invested capital through the recognition of a portion of the amounts spent in prior years for advertising and developing trade-marks and trade brands. It was stated at the hearing that the methods pursued by the company named above are essentially similar to those followed by many other manufacturers engaged in the same industry, and that this case is a typical one. The asset of greatest value of the M Company is a formula and trade-mark. When this asset was acquired, the product had a certain sale in limited territory. Profits from the sale of the product were reinvested in development of new territory. For instance, if the company decided that it would undertake to develop any territory where it had previously sold no goods, it would institute an intensive advertising campaign in that territory by newspaper and other advertising agencies, distribution of samples, etc. The next year some other territory would be chosen. During this period of development it is claimed that the amount expended in advertising in a given territory was far in excess of the profits made from sales in such territory, and it is therefore claimed that a portion of all such expenditures is in reality a capital investment and not merely expense of selling, since it is an investment from which returns are to be expected in the future rather than in the immediate present.

Decision: It must be conceded that in theory some proportion of all advertising is in effect the building up of good will, but it is the judgment of the committee that it is impossible to allocate any definite percentages as between capital investment and selling costs.

It seems clear to the committee that no court would permit the disallowance of a proportion of reasonable advertising in a return of income on the ground that such advertising was a capital investment and not an actual necessary expense of business, and if that be true the converse must follow, namely: That the corporation can not claim that any proportion of such expense is capital investment and not business expense.

It was also brought out at the hearing that there have been a number of widely advertised trade-marks of this character sold within recent years and that such sales were usually made upon the basis of approximately a five-year return; that is to say, for a price five times the annual earning capacity. There are, therefore, satisfactory comparatives in the event that it is desired to treat other cases where there have been no sales as special cases under Secs. 327 and 328, since the cash paid for tangibles and intangibles affords a fair invested capital basis. It also seems reasonable to regard those cases where large sums have been spent in advertising, thereby invested capital, as being cases in which there are abnormal conditions affecting invested capital.

The committee, therefore, recommends that the percentage of tax to income in the cases of those corporation which have an adequate recognizable invested capital be determined, and that other cases which have no such invested capital be regarded as coming within the scope of Sec. 327 and the tax properly to be computed under Sec. 328.

RULING 2-20-674
A. R. M. 17
(C. B. No. 2, p. 144)

Facts: Revenue Act of 1917. The question raised was whether a lessor of mining property who received in a given year royalties that accrued over several years might, if he reports income on a cash receipt and payment basis, deduct from the royalties received such part of the depletion allowance as appertains to those royalties. A leased property to a coal mining company. Although coal was taken from the mines for several years, the company was sustaining losses. A agreed to waive his rights to the royalties until such time as the company was able to pay them. During the year 1917, A received royalties presumably including accruals of the preceding year, in whole or in part.

Decision: In each year profit or income from the property accrued as to the taxpayer. If his returns for these years had been made on an accrual basis, he would have been obligated to include the amount of this income, less the depletion accruing in each year, in his return for each year. Assuming he reported on a cash receipt and payment basis, as he did in the year 1917, for these several years, he was entitled, under the acts prevailing, to include only income actually received. Since the income thus reported included what would have been accrued income over a period of years, he is entitled to such deduction for depletion as accrued during such years. Accordingly the deductions for depletion are allowable, and if the amount of royalties received does not represent the full amount of the accrual, it is presumed that it represents the earliest accruals and is subject to such offsets for depletion as may be allocated to the earliest accruals.

RULING 2-20-676
A. R. M. 21
(C. B. No. 2, p. 211)

Decision: Revenue Act of 1918. If, upon the sale of the capital assets of a corporation to another corporation, shares of stock are surrendered by the old stockholders to the vendee corporation, the nature of the transaction is not changed from one of the sale by the corporation to one of sale of stock by the stockholders.

RULING 7-20-746

A. R. M. 23

(C. B. No. 2, p. 231)

Facts: The committee has considered the construction to be placed upon the words "negligence on the part of the taxpayer, but without intent to defraud," as used in Section 250 (b) of the Revenue Act of 1918. Article 1005, Regulations 45, states that "In general, negligence is attributable to the taxpayer if he computes the tax in disregard of the instructions on the return form or otherwise incorrectly, unless he can show that his error was due to an honest misunderstanding of the facts or the law of which an average reasonable man might be capable.

Decision: Negligence may consist in the failure to ascertain the specific provisions of the law and regulations appertaining to the return of income. In the average case, the instructions contained in the form cover the information to be submitted and refer the taxpayer to the provisions of the regulations that are to be followed. If the understatement positively conflicts with these instructions, or the references contained in the instructions, a presumption exists that the taxpayer has been negligent.

Further, if the taxpayer submits a return ignoring specific provisions of the law and regulations, he is presumed to have been negligent even though he is able to show that in doing so he relied upon some other person (not connected with the internal revenue service) who prepared the return or advised in its preparation. This section places upon the taxpayer the duty of knowing and understanding such parts of the regulations as are applicable to the submission of his return. This requirement should not be carried to the extent of expecting the judgment of the taxpayer on questions involving judgment to concur exactly with the judgment of representatives at the Bureau. If the understatement is due to writing off more depreciation than is proper, in the judgment of representatives of the Bureau, or the deductions of salaries which are excessive, or similar approximations, then negligence cannot be imputed to the taxpayer, unless the position taken is so unreasonable as to indicate bad faith.

It should be borne in mind that extraordinary cases may exist in which the facts may rebut the presumption of negligence. In these instances, the Committee is of the opinion that special appeals should be made by the taxpayer. It is believed that they will be so few that a ruling may be asserted if, in direct conflict with the specific provisions of the law and regulations, a return is understated.

RULING 3-20-692

A. R. M. 24

(C. B. No. 2, p. 231)

Facts: Advice has been requested as to whether or not penalty and interest should be asserted against taxpayers who violate the specific provisions of the regulations and of treasury decisions modifying or amending such regulations. The immediate cases under consideration arise specifically in connection with amortization deductions, it being stated that taxpayers have disregarded the instructions laid down in Treasury Decision 2859 and have taken preliminary deductions of more than 50 per cent of the cost of the property to be amortized. The regulations as amended by Treasury Decision 2859 provide that in certain cases "the basis for amortization calculation shall be the estimated value of the property to the taxpayer in terms of its actual use and employment in his going business, such value in no case to be less than the sale or salvage value of the property: Provided, however, that in no case shall the preliminary estimate (for purposes of returns to be made in 1919) of the amount of such amortization exceed 25 per cent of the cost of the property. In the final determination, the amount of the amortization allowance will be ascertained upon the basis of stable post war conditions under regulations to be promulgated when these conditions become apparent."

Decision: In any case where upon consideration it is held that a taxpayer was in fact entitled to more than 25 percent as amortization allowance, the 5 per cent and 1 per cent interest on account of negligence shall apply only to such amount of additional tax due on account of amortization claimed but disallowed in the return for 1918, and in the event that the case is reopened within a period of three years and an additional amount of amortization allowed, the penalty and interest will not attach to the amount of tax based upon the additional allowance granted. In other words, penalty and interest should attach only to such amount as upon final settlement is found to have been due to the Government and not paid at the time of filing returns by reason of the taxpayer ignoring the regulations.

RULING 9-20-767
A. R. M. 30
(C. B. No. 2, p. 109)

Facts: All the stock of a corporation was owned by four officers, who devoted all their time and attention to the business of the corporation, acting not only as officers but also as buyers, bookkeepers, etc. These officers drew only nominal salaries of $\frac{1}{16}$x dollars each for a number of years after organization. The gross sales increased from 11x dollars in the first year of the business to 64x dollars in 1916 and 90x dollars in 1917. Early in 1917, before the passage of any Excess Profits Tax Law, the Board of Directors fixed salaries of 2x dollars each for three of its officers and x dollars for the fourth. These salaries were paid in 1917 and deducted from gross income.

Decision: The amounts paid and deductible were reasonable and properly deductible from gross income.

RULING 9-20-765
A. R. M. 33
(C. B. No. 2, p. 52)

Facts: The committee was in receipt of a request for advice as to whether or not liquor dealers should be permitted to inventory floor stock and stock in bonded warehouses on December 31, 1919, at nothing for income tax purposes with the understanding that should the goods be later sold the full amount received therefrom must be returned as income.

Decision: While the committee recognizes the serious situation in which liquor dealers found themselves at the close of the year 1919

because of the effect of the prohibition law, it fails to find in the law
any warrant for eliminating from the inventory goods which have
not been destroyed or abandoned as worthless but which are recognized as having some value.   The prohibition law, as understood
by the committee, permits the use of distilled liquors and wine in the
manufacture of medicine and in the filling of prescriptions for medic-
inal use.   The provision for these legitimate demands therefore,
gives to the goods available to supply them some value, and it is
presumed that there can be readily established the market value for
the supplying of such demands.   It is true that the demand is not
sufficient to create a market for all of the goods held in stock, and that
an attempt to sell for this purpose at one time very considerable part
of the stock on hand would doubtless flood the market and bring
it down to a very low figure.   In a measure, however, this was true
before the enactment of prohibition laws, as the supply of liquor
on hand was always in excess of any convenient demand therefor.

The committee is therefore of the opinion that unless stocks of
liquor were on December 31, destroyed, given away to hospitals and
other charitable institutions, or abandoned to the proper authorities
as worthless, in which event they would not be included in the inventory on December 31, they must be taken into the inventory at cost,
or at cost or market, whichever is lower, and that there is no warrant
of law for ignoring stocks on hand in taking inventories at the close
of 1919 with the understanding that should they subsequently be
disposed of for value, the total value received would be reported as
income of the year in which disposed of.

RULING 10-20-777

A. R. M. 34

(C. B. No. 2, p. 31)

Facts: The committee has considered the question of providing
some practical formula for determining value as of March 1, 1913,
or of any other date, which might be considered as applying to tangible assets, but finds itself unable to lay down any specific rule of
guidance for determining the value of intangibles which would be
applicable in all cases and under all circumstances.   Where there is
no established market to serve as a guide the question of value,
even of tangible assets, is one largely of judgment and opinion, and

the same thing is even more true of intangible assets such as good will, trade-marks, trade brands, etc. However, there are several methods of reaching a conclusion as to the value of intangibles which the Committee suggests may be utilized broadly in passing upon questions of valuation, not to be regarded as controlling, however, if better evidence is presented in any specific case.

Decision: Where deduction is claimed for obsolescence or loss of good will or trade-marks, the burden of proof is primarily upon the taxpayer to show the value of such good will or trade-marks on March 1, 1913. Of course, if good will or trade-marks have been acquired for cash or other valuable considerations subsequent to March 1, 1913, the measure of loss will be determined by the amount of cash or value of other considerations paid therefor, and no deduction will be allowed for the value of good will or trade-marks built up by the taxpayer since March 1, 1913. The following suggestions are made, therefore, merely as suggestions for checks upon the soundness and validity of the taxpayers' claims. No obsolescence or loss with respect to good will should be allowed except in case of actual disposition of the asset or abandonment of the business.

In the first place, it is recognized that in numerous instances it has been the practice of distillers and wholesale liquor dealers to put out under well-known and popular brands only so much goods as could be marketed without affecting the established market price therefor and to sell other goods of the same identical manufacture, age, and character under other brands, or under no brand at all, at figures very much below those which the well-known brands commanded. In such case the difference between the price at which whisky was sold under a given brand name and also under another brand name, or under no brand, multiplied by the number of units sold during a given year gives an accurate determination of the amount of profit attributed to that brand during that year and where this practice is continued for a long enough period to show that this amount was fairly constant and regular and might be expected to yield annually that average profit, by capitalizing this earning at the rate, say, of 20 per cent, the value of the brand is fairly well established.

Another method is to compare the volume of business done under the trade-mark or brand under consideration and profits made, or by the business whose good will is under consideration, with the similar volume of business and profit made in other cases where good will or trade-marks have been actually sold for cash, recognizing as the value of the first the same proportion of the selling price of the second, as the profits of the first attributable to brands or good will, is of the similar profits of the second.

The third method and possibly the one which will most frequently have to be applied as a check in the absence of data necessary for the application of the preceding ones, is to allow out of average earnings over a period of years prior to March 1, 1913, preferably not less than five years, a return of 10 per cent upon the average tangible assets for the period. The surplus earnings will then be the average amount available for return upon the value of the intangible assets, and it is the opinion of the Committee that this return should be capitalized upon the basis of not more than five years' purchase—that is to say, five times the amount available as return from intangibles should be the value of the intangibles.

In view of the hazards of the business, the changes in popular tastes and the difficulties in preventing imitation or counterfeiting popular brands affecting the sales of the genuine goods, the committee is of the opinion that the figure given of 20 per cent return on intangibles is not unreasonable, and it recommends that no higher figure than that be attached in any case to intangibles without a very clear and adequate showing that the value of the intangibles was in fact greater than would be reached by applying this formula.

The foregoing is intended to apply particularly to businesses put out of existence by the prohibition law, but will be equally applicable so far as the third formula is concerned, to other businesses of a more or less hazardous nature. In the case, however, of valuation of good will of a business which consists of the manufacture or sale of standard articles of every-day necessity not subject to violent fluctuations and where the hazard is not so great, the committee is of the opinion that the figure for determination of the return on tangible assets might be reduced from 10 to 8 or 9 per cent, and that the percentage for capitalization of the return upon intangibles might be reduced from 20 to 15 per cent.

In any or all of the cases the effort should be to determine what net earnings a purchaser of a business on March 1, 1913, might reasonably have expected to receive from it, and therefore a representative period should be used for averaging actual earnings, eliminating any year in which there were extraordinary factors affecting earnings either way. Also, in the case of the sale of good will of a going business the percentage rate of capitalization of earnings applicable to good will shown by the amount actually paid for the business should be used as a check against the determination of good will value as of March 1, 1913, and if the good will is sold upon the basis of capitalization of earnings less than the figures above indicated as the ones ordinarily to be adopted, the same percentage should be used in figuring value as of March 1, 1913.

RULING 11-20-786
A. R. M. 36
(C. B. No. 2, p. 208)

Facts: Revenue Act of 1918. A corporation was organized for the purpose of acquiring and holding title to land and erecting thereon suitable buildings for conducting an assembly or a chautauqua, religious, educational and recreational in character. It derives income from ground rentals, sales of tickets, advertising space, hotel accommodations, etc. All expenditures made are in connection with hired talent or entertainment and the upkeep of buildings and grounds. It is stated that none of the income is paid to stockholders or individuals, but the articles of incorporation and by-laws do not prohibit the payment of dividends. Apparently, if the corporation goes out of existence, its stockholders would benefit directly through the distribution of the assets, as well as through the appreciation of such assets since their acquisition by the corporation.

Decision: Held, that the corporation does not come within the provisions of Section 231 (6) Revenue Act of 1918, and is required to file returns and pay any tax shown to be due.

RULING 13-20-810
A. R. M. 37
(C. B. No. 2, p. 172)

Facts: Revenue Act of 1918. The committee was requested to render a decision upon the following questions:

1. Whether the undistributable income of a trust or estate under the control of a citizen or resident fiduciary is taxed in the same manner as income accruing to an unmarried resident individual regardless of the citizenship or residence of the creator of the trust or estate and regardless of the citizenship or residence of persons for whom the income is accumulated for future distribution, under the terms of the will or trust.

2. Whether in such case the estate is entitled to a personal exemption of $1,000 regardless of the citizenship or residence of the creator of the trust or regardless of the ultimate beneficiaries or distributees.

3. Whether the income is taxable in such cases, where the fiduciary is a non-resident alien regardless of the residence or citizenship of the creator of the trust or estate, or regardless of the citizenship of the ultimate beneficiaries or distributees.

Decision: (1) That the undistributed net income of a trust estate under the control of a resident fiduciary and subject to the jurisdiction of a State or Territory of the United States, or to the District of Columbia, is taxable in the same manner as income accruing to an unmarried resident individual, irrespective of the fact that the creator of the trust may be a non-resident alien and irrespective of the fact that the ultimate beneficiaries may be non-resident aliens. The exemption to which a single person is entitled may properly be claimed regardless of the citizenship or residence of the creator of the trust or of the beneficiaries for whom the income is retained.

(2) That the income of an estate in process of administration in the courts of a state or territory of the United States or of the District of Columbia by a resident fiduciary is taxable as an entity, irrespective of the fact that the decedent may have been a non-resident individual and the beneficiaries or distributees may be non-resident aliens and the income may be, in whole or part, derived from foreign sources. The same specific exemption may properly be claimed as provided for (1) above. The income taxable to the estate is determined after applying the provisions of Section 219 (c).

(3) That non-resident alien fiduciaries of trusts subject to the jurisdiction of a foreign country are taxable on undistributed net

income from sources within the United States, irrespective of the fact that the creator of the trust or estate may be either a citizen or resident of the United States or a non-resident alien and the beneficiaries may be either citizens or residents of the United States or non-resident aliens. An exemption allowed a single person may properly be claimed, provided the fiduciary is a citizen or subject of a country which imposes an income tax and allows a similar credit to citizens of the United States not residing in such country.

(4) That the income of estates in process of administration in the courts of a foreign country by non-resident alien fiduciaries is taxable as an entity insofar as the income received is from sources within the United States, irrespective of the fact that the decedent may have been either non-resident alien or citizen of the United States and the beneficiaries in the distribution may be either non-resident aliens or citizens or residents of the United States. The same specific exemption as provided for in (3) above may be claimed under the same conditions and limitations.

RULING 13-20-804

A. R. M. 38

(C. B. No. 2, p. 54)

Facts: Revenue Act of 1918. Advice has been requested by the Income Tax Unit as to procedure when request is made by a taxpayer to change his basis of pricing inventory from cost, to cost or market, whichever is lower, or when it is discovered that inventories have been taken in the past on some basis not authorized by the Regulations.

Decision: It is the judgment of the committee that when request is made for permission to change from cost or market, whichever is lower, to cost for pricing inventories at the close of 1919, no objection is seen for granting the permission since it will have no effect on the tax if market was above cost at the close of 1918, and will increase the tax if market was lower than cost at that date; permission to be granted of course upon the condition that the new method will be followed consistently hereafter.

If inventories have been taken in the past on the basis of cost and request is now made to change to "cost or market, whichever is lower," the reasons for the request should be carefully scrutinized and the request refused if it appears that the principal reason therefor is to reduce the tax payable for 1919.

If the request is granted, however, in either of the above cases, it is unnecessary to require any amended return for prior years or any change in the opening inventory by reason of the same method of pricing.

Where change is necessitated because in the past a basis had been used not permitted by the regulations, now or then, amended returns, on one or the other of the two bases now authorized, from 1915 to date should be filed.

If the adjustments used in the amendment of returns as required above so affect the taxpayer as to occasion an inequality in the tax prior to the year 1915, such inequality may be remedied in the return for 1915 by the deduction from, or addition to, the tax accruing in that year of an amount equal to the net amount overpaid or underpaid in prior years; such amount to be determined by filing, with the return for 1915, a composite return for all prior years, accompanied by a statement showing the total adjustments for each of the years as for the entire period.

RULING 14-20-829
A. R. M. 39
(C. B. No. 2, p. 110)

Facts: Act of October 3, 1913, and Revenue Acts of 1916 and 1917. A, the president and treasurer of a close corporation, and B, its vice-president, each held 45 per cent of the outstanding capital stock. C, its secretary, held $3\frac{2}{3}$ per cent of the stock. Nominal salaries were paid to A and B. There was an agreement between A and B that A was to receive in addition to his share on his capital invested, direct compensation in proportion to the results he might achieve for the company. Accordingly A and C also, received in 1915, 1916 and 1917 as additional compensation 10 per cent and 1 per cent, respectively, of the profits.

Decision: That the amounts paid to A and C, although large, were not in proportion to stockholdings and having been paid according to agreements made in advance and for services rendered are held to be deductible as ordinary and necessary business expenses of the company.

RULING 17-20-881
A. R. M. 43
(C. B. No. 2, p. 281)

Facts: National banks at times declare dividends which instead of being paid to stockholders are carried with the consent of the stockholders to a stockholders' liability account in the name of a trustee, and the amount is vested in deals not countenanced by the Comptroller of the Currency. Such stockholders' trustee account, however, is a liability to the individual stockholders, and the assets in which the reserve is invested are the property of the trustee for the stockholders. The question is whether this reserve should be included in the invested capital of the bank, even though the bank includes the income from the reserve in its gross income.

Decision: It was admitted that from a technical viewpoint no part of this reserve should be included in the invested capital of the bank. Since, however, shares in the bank and in this reserve are on the same pro rata basis, and the stockholders are in fact an association, a consolidated return should be required of the bank and the association, the practical effect of which would be to include the amount of the reserve in the consolidated invested capital and the income from the reserve in the consolidated income. The committee therefore recommends that the returns as made, including the stockholder's reserve account in the capital of the bank, and the income therefrom in the income of the banks, be allowed to stand.

RULING 19-20-924
A. R. M. 46
(C. B. No. 2, p. 247)

Facts: Advice has been requested as to the course to be pursued in view of the apparent conflict between language used in Law Opinion 957 (p. 256, Cumulative Bulletin, December, 1919) and Articles 1034 and 1035 of Regulations 45 as to the proper construction of Section 252 of the Revenue Act of 1918 relating to credits for taxes overpaid for a previous year.

Decision: "The Committee is of the opinion that the conflict is more apparent than real and grows out of a confusion of ideas as to the legal and practical effect of a credit and claim for credit. Income taxes are assessed for specified periods and may be abated only if illegally or erroneously assessed; that is to say, in ordinary cases if the amount assessed is in excess of the correct amount due from the taxpayer. Manifestly the fact that the taxpayer has overpaid his taxes for a previous year can have no effect upon the amount of tax for which he is liable for a different year. Consequently, prior to the passage of the Act of 1918, when such conditions existed the only course which the office and the taxpayer could pursue was to collect the present amount in full and permit the taxpayer to file a claim for refund of any amount overpaid. Congress, recognizing the injustice and hardship frequently involved in such an awkward procedure, provided for crediting the amount of any previous over-payment against the taxes presently due. Such credit, when given, has the force and effect of an order of abatement and wipes out and cancels the assessment pro tanto. Clearly such a credit cannot be made until the facts have been carefully examined and the validity of the credit approved by the Commissioner. That is not to say, however, that a claim for credit has no effect until approved. The claim for credit may have precisely the same effect as a claim for abatement; that is, by forbearance of the collector it may suspend collection until it is acted upon by the Commissioner. If approved, credit is then given relieving both the collector and the taxpayer from any further liability. If rejected, interest is to be paid upon the amount suspended from the time it was due. This view of the law appears to be entirely consistent with its language and also with the purpose which it was believed Congress had in mind; that is to say, relief to the taxpayer from being required to pay into the Treasury amounts possibly large, at the same time that he is making a bona fide claim that other amounts are due him. As held in Law Opinion 957, it does not prevent the collector, if he so desires, from proceeding to collect at once just as he may do in the case of an abatement claim filed, but leaves it optional with him to suspend collection until such time as credit is given relieving both him and the taxpayer."

RULING 20-20-943

A. R. M. 51

(C. B. No. 2, p. 297)

Facts: Revenue Act of 1917. During the year 1917, and prior to August 6, 1917, the M Company paid a dividend, which was declared to have been paid out of earnings accumulated prior to March 1, 1913. At the date of the dividend payment, the excess of depletion allowable for 1917 on the basis of March 1, 1913, over the depletion actually sustained on the basis of cost, was an amount in excess of the dividend declared to have been paid out of earnings accumulated prior to March 1, 1913. The M Company therefore contends that before any impairment of invested capital as of December 31, 1916, is determined because of the dividend payment, there should be taken into consideration the realization of the appreciation in values as of March 1, 1913, which has been converted into cash and reflected on its books during the current year.

Decision: "The M Company having by appropriate action declared the dividend out of earnings accumulated prior to March 1, 1913, and so advised its stockholders, will not now be heard to say that the dividend was actually paid out of earnings of the current year." Following the decision in the case of Baldwin Locomotive Works v. McCoach, 221 Fed. 59 and the decisions of the Supreme Court as to the taxation of appreciation to March 1, 1913, it is clear that the realization of such appreciation is an earning of the year in which such appreciation is realized, although under the latter decisions it is not a taxable earning. "Since the excess profits tax law definitely holds that earnings of the taxable year are not to be included in earned surplus or undivided profits, realization of appreciation in values to March 1, 1913, is not a proper addition to invested capital as the realization takes place, as contended for by the company. It is therefore held that the dividend payment of the M Company must be deemed to have been paid from earnings or profits realized prior to March 1, 1913, and therefore that the invested capital of the company must be reduced by that amount, and secondly, that realization during the taxable year of appreciation in value to March 1, 1913, cannot be included in the invested capital of the taxable year."

RULING No. 26-20-1023

A. R. M. 59

(C. B. No. 2, p. 20)

Facts: Revenue Act of 1918. M Company desires to be classed as a personal service corporation. The stock of the corporation is all held by three principal stockholders who devote their entire time and attention to the business. The company has built up a staff of agents and employees in all parts of the world, most of whom are experts in their own line and many of them are skilled engineers of long experience.

Decision: It can hardly be said that the income of the M Company can be ascribed primarily to the activities of its principal owners and stockholders, but is rather a combination of the activities of the managers of the various foreign agencies who are not stockholders. While it is true that neither the law nor the regulations require that the income of the corporation shall be derived solely from the activities of the principal stockholders, the law and regulations do provide certain tests which a corporation must meet before it can be given personal service corporation classifications. This corporation apparently deals largely in the services of others who are not connected with the corporation through stock ownerships but merely as employees. In view of this the company does not meet with the requirements of Article 1523, Regulations 45, and may not be classed as a personal service corporation.

RULING 25-20-1022

A. R. M. 60

(C. B. 2, p. 313)

Revenue Act of 1917. The question is submitted whether or not where there was a change of corporate entity prior to March 3, 1917, without change of officers or directors, or proportions of stockholdings, the new corporation is limited in its invested capital to that which might be claimed by the old corporation, or whether in such case the new corporation is entitled to recognize the cash value of assets for which its stock was issued, not in excess of the par value thereof. The uniform practice has been to treat every corporate entity as the creation of a new organization. The only exception to this has been the case of a mere change of domicile; that is to say, surrender of charter in one state and taking out of a new charter in a different state without change in the amount of stock, or the identity of the stockholders or capital and surplus as it appears on the books of the corporation. Both corporations in question are entitled to the actual cash value of the properties paid-in in 1916.

RULING 28-20-1049
A. R. M. 67
(C. B. No. 3, p. 54)

Facts: Act of 1916. Claim of A for the refunding of 5x dollars, individual income tax for 1916. The amount in question was assessed against the taxpayer upon a liquidating dividend of the M Company received by him. The M. Company's operations had been very profitable and in 1916 it was reorganized, two new corporations being formed. The assets of the M Company were transferred to these two new corporations for the issuance of stock and of debenture bonds. The M Company thereby came into possession of stocks and bonds and thereupon distributed the stocks and bonds so received to its stockholders and liquidated. The question raised is whether the exchange or surrender of the stock of the M Company for stock in another company, the beneficial interest remaining the same, involved taxable profit to the stockholders.

Decision: It has been the uniform practice of the departmet in dealing with exchanges of stock in one corporation for stock in another corporation, to recognize the different entities and regard the exchange of the stock as an exchange of property for other property within the meaning of Section 202 of the Act of 1918 and the similar provisions of prior laws. Claim rejected.

RULING 29-20-1081
A. R. M. 71
(C. B. No. 3, p. 348)

Facts: Revenue Act of 1918. The M Company had made no formal declaration of dividends but a book entry had been made noting and crediting to each stockholder the share of each year's earnings to which he would be entitled under a dividend declaration, the individual shareholders having returned their shares of such earnings in their personal returns and paid the income tax thereon. Now the question is whether the balances to the credit of individual stockholders are invested capital.

Decision: It appears in the present case that each stockholder has been credited with the amount of the earnings attributable to his stock and that no interest has been or is to be paid upon the amounts standing to the credit of these stockholders, no formal declaration of a dividend has been made by the board of directors, and it appears that under the state law the stockholders do not rank with general creditors with respect to such credits. Under these circumstances the amounts so credited should be regarded as being a part of the earned surplus of the corporation to be included in invested capital.

RULING 45-20-1288

A. R. M. 89

(C. B. No. 3, p. 361)

Revenue Act of 1918. "The provision of Section 327 of the Revenue Act of 1918, denying the benefits of that Section to corporations 50 per cent or more of the gross income of which consists of income derived from Government contracts on a cost-plus basis was, in the opinion of the Committee, designed to cover cases in which the contractor was assured of a profit irrespective of cost, and in which the Government rather than the contractor assumed the risk of loss. Where the unfinished work of a contractor was commandeered by the Government and it was agreed that he should receive the same compensation as he would have received under the private contract, the fact that he was subsequently compensated on a cost-plus basis after the work was completed does not, in the opinion of the committee, operate to change the legal situation in this respect."

RULING 47-20-1309

A. R. M. 93

(C. B. No. 3, p. 40)

Facts: Revenue Act of 1918. During 1914, 1915, 1916, and the first four months of 1917 this company was actively engaged in the purchase of live stock at various points in the West and South and the sale of it to the European countries then engaged in the war with Germany. It was necessary to use very considerable sums of money in the business, which grew rapidly, consequently no dividends were declared during those years and the large surplus accumulated was left intact. When the United States entered the war the European countries discontinued their purchases, and as the United States Government had other plans, it declined the offer of the company to avail itself of the facilities of this company for the purchase of live stock. The active business of the corporation therefore practically came to an end in May, 1917. At a meeting of the directors held in May, 1917, the surplus net profits earned during the years 1914 and 1915 were found to be the sum of 800x dollars and the surplus profits earned during the year 1916 were found to be 600x dollars. The directors thereupon passed a resolution which reads, in part, as follows:

"Resolved, That a dividend be, and hereby is, declared out of surplus profits earned during the years 1914 and 1915 in the amount of 800x dollars; and that a dividend be, and hereby is, declared out of surplus profits earned during the year 1916 in the amount of 600x dollars."

In July, 1917, a meeting of the board of directors was held at which the sale of the various pieces of real estate owned by the company for specific sums offered was authorized, and in February, 1918, a stockholders' meeting was held at which it was unanimously agreed that the capital stock should be returned to the stockholders according to the number of shares held by them on that date, and that all other assets of said corporation should be distributed and paid as dividends to the stockholders after reserving a sum estimated to be sufficient to pay income and war taxes and any other taxes, debts or claims valid against the company. The same day a directors' meeting was held and the surplus available for distribution was reported as 220x dollars in excess of the capital of the company aggregating 150x dollars. The resolution was thereupon passed declaring a dividend out of the surplus fund and providing for a distribution of the capital of the company. The question before the committee was whether the above described dividends should be treated as distributions of profit by the corporation subject only to surtax in the hands of the recipients, or as liquidating dividends subject to both normal and surtax upon the profits made above the cost of the stock under Section 201 of the Revenue Act of 1918.

Decision: The committee recommended that "The dividends received in 1917, by the stockholders of the M Company be treated as what they were, a distribution of earnings or profits accumulated subsequent to March 1, 1913, and subject to tax in the hands of the stockholders as provided by Section 31 of the Revenue Act of 1917, but that the entire amounts distributed as a single and final dividend in 1918, including both the capital of the company and the remaining surplus be treated as proceeds from the sale of stock subject to tax according to the rule laid down in Law Opinion 557."
* * * "Where a corporation distributes a dividend consisting only of earnings or profits prior to any vote or resolution providing for liquidation of the company such dividends cannot be regarded as l'quidating dividends notwithstanding the stockholders of the corporation subsequently voted to go into liquidation and to distribute its remaining capital." Therefore, the distribution in the first year was a dividend, subject only to surtax, but the entire distribution in the second year was a liquidation dividend, subject to both normal tax and surtax to the extent that it exceeded cost of the stock.

RULING 47-20-1312
A. R. M. 95
(C. B. No. 3, p. 172)

Facts: Revenue Act of 1917. In January, 1902, the M Company, then a newly organized corporation, acquired ownership of eight patents issuing therefor to A, the patentee, 900x dollars of stock of the corporation. This amount was subsequently increased 2x dollars by expenses of acquisition. The patents so acquired, except one, issued in 1900, had expired prior to January 1, 1917, but as of March 1, 1913, all but one were in effect. Fifteen new patents had, however, been added to the company's patents between date of incorporation and March 1, 1913. These additional patents were not capitalized. No depreciation was taken by the taxpayer on the patents which were capitalized, until the year 1917, when 1-17 of the book value was charged to expenses notwithstanding the fact that all except one of them had expired prior to January 1, 1917.

Decision: "The case then comes clearly under the provisions of Article 174, Paragraph 552, and Article 167, Paragraph 494, Regulations 33, revised, governing the collection of the income tax imposed by the Revenue Act of 1917. The basis for deduction authorized under the provisions of Article 174 is the return of capital on an asset, the use of which in the trade or business is definitely limited in duration. The taxpayer did not elect, during the life of the patents acquired in 1902, to provide for this return of capital. Had he made this provision his surplus for invested capital purposes under the Revenue Act, would have been correspondingly reduced. He, therefore, cannot now claim in a high taxable year, after the expiration of the life of the patents, an amount equivalent to 1-17 of the cost, thereby securing the benefit not only of a reduction in his taxable income for the year 1917, but the advantage of the investment which in value is subject only to the definite limitations prescribed by the Act and the regulations."

RULING 49-20-1331

A. R. M. 100

(C. B. No. 3, p. 66)

Facts: Revenue Act of 1918. The following modifications of existing regulations prescribing methods of valuing inventories was contended for by cotton merchants, grain merchants and others seeking special rulings for that purpose:

(1) To *add* to the value of the physical inventory: (a) The value, at "cost" or "cost or market whichever is lower," of all commodities purchased to be received at some future date, the title to which does not pass to the taxpayer until the commodities have been reduced to physical possession; (b) Potential losses, not realized within the taxable year, on transactions in futures.

(2) To *deduct* from the value of the physical inventory: (c) The value at "cost" or "cost or market whichever is lower," of all commodities sold to be delivered at some future date, the title to which does not pass to the purchaser until the date of delivery, irrespective of whether or not such commodities are in the possession of the taxpayer at the date of the contract for sale; (d) Potential gains, not realized within the taxable year, on transactions in futures.

Decision:　Case (a) is specially covered by Article 1581, which provides that "title to the merchandise included in the inventory should be vested in the taxpayer and goods merely ordered for future delivery and for which no transfer of title has been affected should be excluded," and by the opinion of the Attorney General of the United States as expressed in T. D. 3044 (Cumulative Bulletin No. 3, page 83), wherein the Attorney General, in discussing the legality of including in an inventory a certain commodity which the taxpayer was under a binding contract to receive and pay for after the close of his fiscal year, says: "The company did not own it (the commodity in question), but only had a contract for its purchase. It could not, therefore, have properly been included in an inventory of the company's property as of that date.

"The committee is of the opinion that from the facts as stated the opinion of the Attorney General of the United States could not have been different, and that the regulation above quoted is sound and should stand as written.　There is no essential difference between goods ordered or goods "purchased" for future delivery, so long as there is no transfer of title until the goods are actually received. Case (a) is therefore disposed of and, per contra, by analogy; case (c) also, for if commodities purchased but not received cannot be included in an inventory where title has not passed, it is clear that under the same circumstances and conditions, commodities sold but not delivered cannot be deducted therefrom.　In the consideration of cases (b) and (d) the question arises whether potential gains or losses on transactions in "futures" can be held to form an integral part of the cost of the commodity or commodities in which the taxpayer deals.　The fact that these transactions may be simultaneous is no argument for regarding them as identical, for it is obvious that the commodity may be retained and the "future" contract "covered" or closed out, or that the commodity may be disposed of and the "future" contract still remain open, without any effect whatever upon the other transaction of each pair.　This being so, it is unavailing to say that each pair of transactions, even though conducted simultaneously, should be regarded as one transaction, a fluctuation in the market price of either element of which affects the cost to the taxpayer of the other.　There is in fact no profit or loss in the purchase of a commodity until the transaction has been completed by the sale of that particular commodity, nor is there any profit or loss in a transaction in 'futures' until the transaction has actually been closed. To hold otherwise would be contrary to the plain and obvious facts; and it can hardly be seriously contended, and it is certain that it cannot be successfully maintained, that a potential gain or loss in 'futures' can operate to affect an inventory, when an actual realized gain or loss would admittedly have no such effect. The Committee is of the opinion (1) that transactions in "futures," unclosed at the end of the taxable year, form no integral part of the cost of the commodity included in the taxpayer's physical inventory, and (2) that the basis of (a) cost, or (b) cost or market whichever is lower, is the only admissible basis for the valuation of a physical inventory in the computation of statutory net income for income tax purposes."

RULING 2-21-1392
A. R. M. 105

Facts: Revenue Act of 1918. The following case was submitted as typical of other similar cases pending. When the Excess Profits Tax Act of 1917 was passed the lumber interests were strongly of the opinion that under the Act they were entitled to include in invested capital the increase in value of their properties through growth of timber. They, accordingly, filed returns for 1917 in which they included in invested capital such appreciation in value. These returns were not audited prior to the time for filing 1918 returns, so that at such time no additional tax had been assessed. Many of the lumbermen in their 1918 returns computed invested capital as they had done in their 1917 returns. No question of penalty for negligence arose as to the 1917 returns, since that provision was not enacted until the Act of 1918 was passed, and the question was whether the 5 per cent penalty should attach to the returns filed for 1918.

Decision: (1) Penalty should not attach to those returns where the amount of the appreciation which had been included in invested capital was specifically shown.

(2) Where the amount of the invested capital not computed in accordance with the regulations was not specifically shown the penalty should attach.

(3) In general penalties for negligence should not attach in any case where full disclosure, permitting the Department to make assessment of additional taxes if it desires to do so, is made on the return.

RULING 18-21-1614
A. R. M. 106

Facts: The committee was in receipt of a memorandum from the Income Tax Unit requesting advice relative to the practice of field agents in reducing earned surplus by deductions for depreciation where none had been claimed in the past, or where a lower rate had been claimed than is ordinarily allowable with respect to the depreciable assets in question.

Decision: It is the judgment of the committee that there is no warrant for reducing earned surplus because of alleged failure to charge off sufficient depreciation in the past, unless the depreciable assets of the corporation are valued on its books at the beginning of the taxable year at an amount in excess of their actual value at that time. This is particularly true where the corporation in prior years earned positive income from which larger deductions for depreciation might have been taken, if in the opinion of the officers and directors of the corporation such larger charges had been justified. Nothing herein is to be construed as precluding the income tax unit from adjusting depreciation, either by way of increase or decrease, where there is at hand affirmative evidence that as at the beginning of the taxable year the amount of depreciation written off in prior years was insufficient or excessive. The correct attitude of the Bureau and the proper conduct of its field agents, in particular, are plainly set forth in that part of Art. 839 of Reg. 45, which reads:

"Adjustments in respect of depreciation or depletion in prior years will be made or permitted only upon the basis of affirmative evidence that as at the beginning of the taxable year the amount of depreciation or depletion written off in prior years was sufficient or excessive as the case may be."

RULING 30-21-1748
A. R. M. 106 Explained

In answer to a specific inquiry, the Committee on Appeals and Review issued a memorandum stating that the words "actual value" as used in Comm. Mem. 106 means "sound value," which is "original cost" (or value as of March 1, 1913, if applicable) including additions and betterments charged to capital accounts less depreciation sustained. The use of an appraisal as the basis for a claim for addition to invested capital is apparently recognized by a statement to the effect that one method of varying such claim is by determining the plant efficiency and the other is by determining the value of the capital assets remaining, the latter method being probably more practical, even though the former may be more accurate.

The Committee further stated: "Many cases have been brought to the attention of the Committee where corporations have been in existence for a long period of years, some of which corporations have been in existence several times the ordinary estimated life of the depreciable assets and yet those assets are today in first-class condition and worth the figure at which they are carried on the books, although no depreciation has been charged as such and no additions to capital accounts have been made. In such cases it is obvious that depreciation has been adequately cared for by charges to expense, although it frequently happens that it is impossible at this late date to segregate and specify such charges and there is no warrant in the law or the regulations for requiring the depreciable assets in such cases to be written down below the figure at which they are carried on the books, since to do so is to reduce earned surplus twice, once through the original charge to expense (whether proper or improper) and again through an arbitrary depreciation charge required by the Bureau to be set up against earned surplus for the purpose of computing invested capital.

"The controlling rule in this matter is found in that part of Art. 389 of Reg. 45, which reads:

" 'Adjustments with respect to depreciation or depletion in prior years will be made or permitted only upon the basis of affirmative evidence that as at the beginning of the taxable year the amount of depreciation or depletion written off in prior years was insufficient or excessive, as the case may be.'

"Mere failure in prior years to have written off on the books the maximum or ordinary rate of depreciation is not in itself 'affirmative evidence.' There is no warrant for reducing earned surplus because of alleged failure to charge off sufficient depreciation in the past, unless the depreciable assets of the corporation was valued on its books at the beginning of the taxable year at an amount in excess of their sound value as of that time."

RULING 10-21-1497
A. R. M. 112

Facts: Revenue Act of 1917. M Company paid out as dividends all of its earnings for 1917 so that at the end of the year sufficient earnings were not available against which to charge depreciation due to actual wear and tear of the physical property used in its business. The question presented was whether the company could claim on its return for the year 1917 a deduction for depreciation.

Decision: In computing the taxable net income of a corporation, it cannot be denied a deduction on account of depreciation actually sustained and charged off, even though after paying dividends there remains an amount of surplus and earnings insufficient to cover depreciation; and in such case the book value of the assets must be reduced by an amount equal to the difference between the amount of the depreciation actually sustained and charged off and the amount of the earnings and surplus available for depreciation at the end of the taxable period.

RULING 16-21-1574
A. R. M. 121

Facts: Revenue Act of 1918. The question involved was whether a taxpayer was bound by the option he exercised in prior years of including excise taxes in the cost of merchandise in calculating his inventories, rather than to charge them to business expense.

Decision: Held that the wholesale liquor dealer in question, who for years prior to 1918 exercised the option of including excise taxes in cost of merchandise in calculating inventory, may not amend such inventory and treat such taxes as business expenses for 1918.

RULING 22-21-1659
A. R. M. 128

Facts: Revenue Act of 1917. A owned a number of shares of stock in the M Company, which in 1916 increased its capital stock and gave to each shareholder a right to purchase new shares in proportion to the number of old shares owned by him, at one-half of the par value thereof. The corporation transferred from surplus to capital an amount equal to one-half the par value of the new shares issued under this arrangement. A purchased a certain number of these shares; and in 1917 he sold part of his stock holdings. The question was whether the profit or loss from this sale should be computed in accordance with the provisions of Art. 1547 of Reg. 45.

Decision: Whether the difference between the cash paid for the stock and its par value be considered a true stock dividend or not, the effect on the taxpayer in relation to the determination of the cost of the new stock is similar to a stock dividend, and the same principles are applicable in determining the cost of such stock. Therefore, the profit or loss from the sale of the new stock in 1917 should be determined by prorating the entire cost of the old and new stock in accordance with Art. 1547 of Reg. 45.

RULING 24-21-1683
A. R. M. 129

Facts: Revenue Act of 1918. The M Company sold canned goods to the Government in 1918, conditioned upon guaranteed quality in July, 1919. In May, 1919, on inspection it was found that a certain portion of the goods were spoiled. It was agreed in a bill for resale executed by the representatives of the Government and the taxpayer that the latter should take the goods back and pay to the United States the provisional price less deductions for recanning, relabeling, etc. The company, therefore, contended that the apparent profit, which had been reported for 1918, should be cancelled, and that the goods should be added at cost to the inventory at the close of 1918.

Decision: It is evident that resale to the taxpayer at original purchase prices less certain definite concessions was, in substance, a compromise sale and was a new transaction. As of December 31, 1918, the goods in question were not the property of the taxpayer. The committee, therefore, was of the opinion that two transactions were involved and that the M Company could not take into its 1918 inventory the goods in question.

RULING 27-21-1719
A. R. M. 134

Facts: Revenue Act of 1917. The M Company was incorporated in 189... It acquired for stock and cash various trademarks, formulae, etc., between 189.. and 1916. During these years it spent various sums of money in advertising and developing these intangible assets. In 1905 and 1906, by action of its board of directors, these sums of money were capitalized by being charged to trademarks, formulae, etc. In some instances the sums so capitalized had been expended during the same year and in other instances during prior years. The company claimed allowances of these sums as invested capital for the taxable year 1917.

Decision: The committee followed a prior unpublished ruling under the 1918 Act. In this ruling it was held that Article 841 of Regulation 45 was drawn for the purpose of preventing the inclusion in surplus or invested capital, for the taxable year 1918, of amounts charged to expenses prior thereto, when the intent was to evade taxation. No fraud could be inferred where the restoration to invested capital occurred before March, 1909, thus conclusively demonstrating the intention of the directors in regard to such expenditures many years before the Income and Excess-Profits Tax law was passed. The same principles were held applicable to 1917, and the expenditures were held a part of the invested capital.

RULING 31-21-1750
A. R. M. 135

Facts: The leading grain and cotton exchanges of the country and some of the leading individual dealers in those commodities appeared by counsel or in person before the Committee to urge that "hedge" transactions in "futures" should be accorded recognition in the taxpayers' balance sheet at the close of each taxable year and should be thus taken into consideration in computing taxable income. Such consideration had been denied by the Income Tax Unit to taxpayers engaged in these lines of business for the reason that transactions in "futures" have been held not to be "closed transactions" within the meaning of the Regulations where such transactions, entered into in one taxable year, had been carried forward into the year following. In such holdings, the Unit appears to have relied very largely upon Committee Memorandum, No. 100 (C. B. 3, p. 66.)

Decision: The Committee explained that the Comm. Mem. 100, upon which the Unit evidently based its decision, dealt only with the inclusion in *inventories* of purchases to be received in the future and sales for future deliveries and was not to be extended further. The evidence presented in this case showed that it had been the universal practice for 50 years for dealers in the commodities above mentioned to base their profit or loss for a specified accounting period upon firm contracts such as those below described and that no other method truly reflected net income in the lines of business in question. The Committee accordingly held that:

"Dealers in cotton and grain, and in such other commodities as are dealt in in a similar manner, may, for the purposes of determining taxable income, incorporate in their balance sheets at the close of any taxable year, such open "future" contracts to which they are parties as are "hedges" against actual "stock" or cash transactions; provided, that no purely speculative transactions in "futures" not offset by actual "stocks" are cash transactions, may be so included or taken into the taxpayers' account in any manner until such transactions are actually closed by liquidation; and provided further, that the value of the commodity covered by such open "future" contracts shall not be added to nor deducted from the inventory of the taxpayer."

Pages 707 to 752 have been omitted in this edition printed January, 1924, because they have been superseded by a *Revised Table of Cases* and *Revised Index* printed in the Supplement at pages 1013 to 1087.